Fodor's 07

HAWAI'I

Where to Stay and Eat
for All Budgets

Must-See Sights
and Local Secrets

Ratings You Can Trust

Fodor's Travel Publications   New York, Toronto, London, Sydney, Auckland
www.fodors.com

FODOR'S HAWAI'I 2007

Editors: Mary Beth Bohman and Ruth Craig

Editorial Production: David Neal Downing and Bethany Cassin Beckerlegge

Editorial Contributors: Wanda Adams, Don Chapman, Andy Collins, Elaine Gast, Jack Jeffrey, Katherine Nichols, Chad Pata, Kim Steutermann Rogers, Cathy Sharpe, Mark Sullivan, Amanda Theunissen, Cheryl Tsutsumi, Joana Varawa, Amy Westervelt, Shannon Wianecki, Maggie Wunsch, Katie Young

Maps & Illustrations: David Lindroth, *cartographer* William Wu, with additional cartography provided by Henry Columb, Mark Stroud, and Ali Baird, Moon Street Cartography; Rebecca Baer and Bob Blake, *map editors*

Design: Fabrizio La Rocca, *creative director;* Siobhan O'Hare, Chie Ushio, Tim Malaney, Brian Panto, Moon Sun Kim

Photography: Melanie Marin, *senior picture editor*; Cover Photo (waterfall, Maui): Thinkstock/ Creatas

Production/Manufacturing: Angela L. McLean

ISBN-10: 1–4000–1676–2

ISBN-13: 978–1–4000–1676–1

ISSN: 0071–6421

SPECIAL SALES

This book is available for special discounts for bulk purchases for sales promotions or premiums. Special editions, including personalized covers, excerpts of existing books, and corporate imprints, can be created in large quantities for special needs. For more information, write to Special Markets/ Premium Sales, 1745 Broadway, MD 6-2, New York, New York 10019, or e-mail specialmarkets@ randomhouse.com.

AN IMPORTANT TIP & AN INVITATION

Although all prices, opening times, and other details in this book are based on information supplied to us at press time, changes occur all the time in the travel world, and Fodor's cannot accept responsibility for facts that become outdated or for inadvertent errors or omissions. So **always confirm information when it matters,** especially if you're making a detour to visit a specific place. Your experiences—positive and negative—matter to us. If we have missed or misstated something, **please write to us.** We follow up on all suggestions. Contact the Hawai'i editor at editors@fodors. com or c/o Fodor's at 1745 Broadway, New York, NY 10019.

PRINTED IN THE UNITED STATES OF AMERICA

10 9 8 7 6 5 4 3 2 1

Be a Fodor's Correspondent

Your opinion matters. It matters to us. It matters to your fellow Fodor's travelers, too. And we'd like to hear it. In fact, we *need* to hear it.

When you share your experiences and opinions, you become an active member of the Fodor's community. That means we'll not only use your feedback to make our books better, but we'll publish your names and comments whenever possible. Throughout our guides, look for "Word of Mouth," excerpts of your unvarnished feedback.

Here's how you can help improve Fodor's for all of us.

Tell us when we're right. We rely on local writers to give you an insider's perspective. But our writers and staff editors—who are the best in the business—depend on you. Your positive feedback is a vote to renew our recommendations for the next edition.

Tell us when we're wrong. We're proud that we update most of our guides every year. But we're not perfect. Things change. Hotels cut services. Museums change hours. Charming cafés lose charm. If our writer didn't quite capture the essence of a place, tell us how you'd do it differently. If any of our descriptions are inaccurate or inadequate, we'll incorporate your changes in the next edition and will correct factual errors at fodors.com *immediately.*

Tell us what to include. You probably have had fantastic travel experiences that aren't yet in Fodor's. Why not share them with a community of like-minded travelers? Maybe you chanced upon a beach or bistro or B&B that you don't want to keep to yourself. Tell us why we should include it. And share your discoveries and experiences with everyone directly at fodors.com. Your input may lead us to add a new listing or highlight a place we cover with a "Highly Recommended" star or with our highest rating, "Fodor's Choice."

Give us your opinion instantly at our feedback center at www.fodors.com/feedback. You may also e-mail editors@fodors.com with the subject line "Hawai'i Editor." Or send your nominations, comments, and complaints by mail to Hawai'i Editor, Fodor's, 1745 Broadway, New York, NY 10019.

You and travelers like you are the heart of the Fodor's community. Make our community richer by sharing your experiences. Be a Fodor's correspondent.

Aloha!

Tim Jarrel, Publisher

CONTENTS

UNDERSTANDING HAWAI'I

HAWAI'I IN FOCUS

CLOSE UPS

MAPS & CHARTS

ABOUT THIS BOOK

Our Ratings

Sometimes you find terrific travel experiences and sometimes they just find you. But usually the burden is on you to select the right combination of experiences. That's where our ratings come in.

As travelers we've all discovered a place so wonderful that its worthiness is obvious. And sometimes that place is so unique that superlatives don't do it justice: you just have to be there to know. These sights, properties, and experiences get our highest rating, **Fodor's Choice,** indicated by orange stars throughout this book.

Black stars highlight sights and properties we deem **Highly Recommended,** places that our writers, editors, and readers praise again and again for consistency and excellence.

By default, there's another category: any place we include in this book is by definition worth your time, unless we say otherwise. And we will.

Disagree with any of our choices? Care to nominate a place or suggest that we rate one more highly? Visit our feedback center at www. fodors.com/feedback.

Budget Well

Hotel and restaurant price categories from ¢ to $$$$ are defined in the Where to Stay and Where to Eat sections of each chapter. Real prices are listed at the end of each hotel and restaurant review. For attractions, we always give standard adult admission fees; reductions are usually available for children, students, and senior citizens. Want to pay with plastic? **AE, D, DC, MC, V** following restaurant and hotel listings indicate if American Express, Discover, DinersClub, MasterCard, and Visa are accepted.

Restaurants

Unless we state otherwise, restaurants are open for lunch and dinner daily. We mention dress only when there's a specific requirement and reservations only when they're essential or not accepted—it's always best to book ahead.

Hotels

Assume that hotels have private bath, phone, and TV unless we state otherwise. We always list facilities but not whether you'll be charged an extra fee to use them, so when pricing accommodations, find out what's included.

Many Listings
- ★ Fodor's Choice
- ★ Highly recommended
- ⊠ Physical address
- ✛ Directions
- ⌖ Mailing address
- ☎ Telephone
- 🖷 Fax
- ⊕ On the Web
- ✉ E-mail
- ⌲ Admission fee
- ☉ Open/closed times
- ☰ Credit cards

Hotels & Restaurants
- ⬚ Hotel
- ⇋ Number of rooms
- ☖ Facilities
- ✕ Restaurant
- ⬗ Reservations
- 🏛 Dress code
- ↘ Smoking
- ◊♀ BYOB
- ✕⬚ Hotel with restaurant that warrants a visit

Outdoors
- ⚐ Golf
- ⛺ Camping

Other
- ☾ Family-friendly
- 🏿 Contact information
- ⇨ See also
- ⊠ Branch address
- ☞ Take note

WHAT'S WHERE

O'AHU 	O'ahu—where Honolulu and Waikīkī are—is a great big lū'au. If this is your first trip, O'ahu should definitely serve as your jumping-off point. Here, on the third-largest island, you'll find 75% of the state's population. Waikīkī beach offers a gentle introduction to water-related pursuits, while the North Shore's monster winter surf challenges the nerves of professional surfers. The island's museums and historic and cultural sites will ground you, at least a bit, in Hawai'i history. The widest range of restaurants as well as the best nightlife scene are here, too. And the island, with its knife-edged mountain ranges, verdant green valleys, territorial-era architecture, and ring of white-sand beaches, is just the Hawai'i you came to see.
MAUI 	*Maui nō ka 'oi*—Maui is the best, the most, the top of the heap. To those who know the island well, there's good reason for the superlatives. The second-largest in the Hawaiian chain, the Valley Isle has made a name for itself with its tropical allure, arts and cultural activities, and miles of perfect-tan beaches. Popularity and success have led to some modern-day problems: too many cars, for example. Still, from the chilly heights of Haleakalā to the below-sea-level taro beds of Ke'anae Peninsula, Maui continues to weave a spell over the more than 2 million people who visit its shores each year. Pursuits range from hiking in a crater to swimming under a waterfall to diving with sea turtles.This is without question the most diversified island, recommended for a family or group with divergent interests.
THE BIG ISLAND 	Hawai'i, the Big Island, is a land with two faces, watched over by snowcapped Mauna Kea and steaming Mauna Loa. On the west, the sunny Kona side of the island has parched, lava-strewn lowlands and uplands blessed with misty mornings and sunny afternoons. Upscale resorts line the coast, with the touristy, heavily trafficked town of Kailua-Kona serving as social and economic center. The uplands vary from the cowboy country of the northern ranches to southern hillsides planted in coffee, vanilla orchids, macadamia nuts, and tropical fruits. To the east, the rain- and mist-shrouded Hilo side is characterized by flower farms, a fishing fleet, waterfalls, and rainbows. Southwest of Hilo looms one of the world's most active volcanoes. Here, in Volcanoes National Park, lava has been flowing for more than a decade. The sheer size of the Big Island, larger than all of the other islands combined, can be its main draw-

	back for the explorer—you can drive and drive and drive and drive between attractions. So plan your time accordingly.
KAUA'I	The oldest inhabited island in the chain, Kaua'i has always been one-of-a-kind. These days, the counterculture is of the artsy and alternative sort with a dash of surfer insouciance. The island's geography contributes to its individuality: the remote, northwestern shore known as Nā Pali (The Cliffs) Coast boasts folding sea cliffs thousands of feet high; the island's center is occupied by impossibly wet and jagged mountains; and the shores feature more sandy beaches per mile of coastline than any other Hawaiian island. Driving the single highway that circles the island is a bit of an adventure, especially given the hordes of chickens who all seem to have heard the joke about crossing the road. Kayaking, hiking, and birding are world-class, and the first sight of Waimea Canyon will stop your heart.
MOLOKA'I	Moloka'i is the least changed, most laid-back of the Islands. To Hawaiians, she is *Moloka'i-nui-a-Hina,* the great child of the moon goddess; some believe hula was born here. Today, Moloka'i offers only two struggling resorts and one tiny town. Its charms include the unforgettable mule ride down a cliff trail to Kalaupapa Peninsula; the rich Kamakou Preserve, a 2,774-acre wildlife refuge; world-class deep-sea fishing; and plenty of peace and quiet. The Visitors' Bureau dubs it "The Friendly Isle," but development-resistant residents would prefer it to be the forgotten isle. This is a place where you should expect to conform to the lifestyle, not the other way around.
LĀNA'I	Even many locals have never been to Lāna'i because, for years, there was nothing to see but mile upon mile of pineapple and red-dirt roads. Two upscale resorts offer the usual island mix of sun and sand, plus archery and shooting, four-wheel-drive excursions, and superb scuba diving. Both attract the well-heeled in search of privacy, but the luxe shine has worn a bit. Do stroll Dole Park, the town square; if there's a local event on, you'll meet the bulk of the population in minutes.

ISLAND FINDER

Not sure which Hawaiian island is your kind of paradise? Any island would make a memorable vacation, but not every one has that particular mix of attributes that makes it perfect for you. Use this chart to compare how each island measures up to your vacation dreams. Looking for great nightlife and world-class surfing? O'ahu would fit the bill. Hate crowds but love scuba? Lāna'i is your place. You can also consult What's Where to learn more about the specific attractions of each island.

	O'AHU	MAUI	BIG ISLAND	KAUA'I	MOLOKA'I	LĀNA'I
Beaches						
Activities & Sports	●	●	●	◐	◐	◐
Deserted	◐	◐	◐	●	●	◐
Party Scene	●	●	◐	○	○	○
City Life						
Crowds	●	◐	◐	◐	○	○
Urban Development	●	◐	◐	◐	○	○
Entertainment						
Hawaiian Cultural Events	◐	◐	●	◐	●	◐
Museums	●	◐	◐	◐	○	○
Nightlife	●	◐	○	○	○	○
Performing Arts	●	◐	○	○	○	○
Shopping	●	◐	◐	○	○	○
Lodging						
B&Bs	◐	●	●	●	○	○
Condos	●	●	●	●	○	○
Hotels & Resorts	●	●	●	◐	○	●
Vacation Rentals	◐	◐	◐	●	◐	○
Nature						
Rainforest Sights	◐	◐	◐	●	◐	○
Volcanic Sights	○	◐	●	○	○	○
Wildlife	○	◐	●	●	◐	◐
Sports						
Golf	◐	●	●	◐	○	●
Hiking	◐	◐	●	●	◐	◐
Scuba	◐	●	●	◐	◐	●
Snorkeling	◐	●	●	◐	◐	◐
Surfing	●	◐	◐	◐	◐	○
Windsurfing	◐	●	◐	◐	◐	○

KEY: ● Noteworthy ◐ Some ○ Little or None

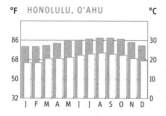

°F HONOLULU, O'AHU °C

WHEN TO GO

Long days of sunshine and fairly mild year-round temperatures make Hawai'i an all-season destination. Most resort areas are at sea level, with average afternoon temperatures of 75°F–80°F during the coldest months of December and January; during the hottest months of August and September the temperature often reaches 90°F. Only at high elevations does the temperature drop into the colder realms, and only at mountain summits does it reach freezing.

Most travelers head to the Islands in winter. From mid-December through mid-April, visitors from the mainland and other areas covered with snow find Hawai'i's sun-splashed beaches and balmy trade winds appealing. This high season means that fewer travel bargains are available; room rates average 10%–15% higher during this season than the rest of the year.

Rainfall can be high in winter, particularly on the north and east shores of each island. Generally speaking, you're guaranteed sun and warm temperatures on the west and south shores no matter what time of year. Kaua'i's and the Big Island's northern sections get more annual rainfall than the rest of Hawai'i, and so much rain falls on Kaua'i's Mount Wai'ale'ale (approximately 472 inches of rain, or 39 feet), that it's considered the wettest place on earth.

Climate

Moist trade winds drop their precipitation on the north and east sides of the islands, creating tropical climates, while the south and west sides remain hot and dry with desertlike conditions. Higher "Upcountry" elevations typically have cooler, and often misty conditions.

Average maximum and minimum temperatures for Honolulu are listed at left; the temperatures throughout the Hawaiian Islands are similar.

🔳 **Forecasts Weather Channel Connection** ⊕ www.weather.com.

ONLY IN HAWAI'I HOLIDAYS

If you happen to be in the Islands on March 26 or June 11, you'll notice light traffic and busy beaches—these are state holidays not celebrated anywhere else. March 26 recognizes the birthday of Prince Jonah Kūhio Kalaniana'ole, a member of the royal line who served as a delegate to Congress and spearheaded the effort to set aside homelands for Hawaiian people. June 11 honors the first island-wide monarch, Kamehameha I; locals drape his statues with lei and stage elaborate parades. May 1 isn't an official holiday, but it's the day when schools and civic groups celebrate the quintessential Island gift, the flower lei, with lei-making contests and pageants. Statehood Day is celebrated on the third Friday in August (Admission Day was August 21, 1959). Another holiday much celebrated is Chinese New Year, in part because many Hawaiians married Chinese immigrants. Homes and businesses sprout bright-red good-luck mottoes, lions dance in the streets, and everybody eats *gau* (steamed pudding) and *jai* (vegetarian stew). The state also celebrates Good Friday as a spring holiday, a favorite for family picnics.

QUINTESSENTIAL HAWAI'I

Traveling to Hawai'i is as close as an American can get to visiting another country while staying within the United States. There's much to learn and understand about the state's indigenous culture, the hundred years of immigration that resulted in today's blended society, and the tradition of aloha that has welcomed millions of visitors over the years.

Polynesian Paralysis

You may find that you suffer from "Polynesian paralysis" when you arrive—a pleasurable enervation, an uncontrollable desire to lie down and sleeeeeeeep. Go with it. Besides the fact that it's an actual physical condition caused by abrupt changes in temperature, humidity, and time zones, it'll give you a feel of the old days in Hawai'i, when a nap under a tree wasn't the rarity it is today.

Native Knowledge

An Iowan is from Iowa and a Californian is from California, but Hawaiians are members of an ethnic group. Use Hawaiian only when speaking of someone who *get koko* (has Hawaiian blood); otherwise, say Islanders or Hawai'i people. *Kama'āina* (child of the land) are people who are born here, whatever their ethnicity. "Local" is the catch-all term for the mélange of customs, foodways, beliefs, and cultural "secret handshakes" that define those who are deeply entrenched in the Island way of life.

When a visitor says "back in the states" or "stateside," it sets Islanders' teeth on edge—Hawai'i has been the 50th state for almost 50 years.

Learn How to Holoholo

That's not a hula. Holoholo means to go out for the fun of it—an aimless stroll,

ride, or drive. "Wheah you goin', braddah?" "Oh, holoholo." It's local-speak for Sunday drive, no plan, it's not the destination but the journey. Try setting out without an itinerary.

Act Like a Local

You might never truly pass; Islanders can spot a fresh sunburn or tender feet at 1,000 paces. But adopting local customs is a firsthand introduction to the Islands' unique culture. So live in T-shirts and shorts. Wear cheap rubber flip-flops, but call them slippers. Wave people into your lane on the highway, and, when someone lets you in, give them a wave of thanks in return. Never, ever blow your horn, even when the pickup truck in front of you is stopped for a long session of "talk story" right in the middle of the road. Learn to shaka: pinky and thumb extended, middle fingers curled in, waggle sideways. Eat white rice with every-thing. When someone says "Aloha!," answer "Aloha no!" ("and a real big aloha back to you"). And—as the locals say—"no make big body" (try not to act like you own the place).

Have a Hula

"Hula is the language of the heart, therefore the heartbeat of the Hawaiian people." Thousands—from tots to seniors—devote hours each week to hula classes. All these dancers need some place to show off their stuff. The result is a network of hula competitions (generally free or very inexpensive) and free performances in malls and other public spaces. Many resorts offer hula instruction or "hula-cise." To watch hula, especially in the ancient style, is to understand that this was a sophisticated culture—skilled in many arts, including not only poetry, chant, and dance but also in constructing instruments and fashioning adornments.

IF YOU LIKE

Full Body Adventures

Ready for a workout with just enough risk to make things interesting? The Islands are your destination for adventures—paddling, hiking, biking, and surfing among them. One thing you can't do is rock-climb; formations are too crumbly and unstable. Get ready to earn that umbrella drink at sunset.

- **Kayaking Nā Pali Coast, Kaua'i.** Experience the majesty of this stunning shoreline of sheer cliffs and deep-cut valleys from the water. This once-in-a-lifetime adventure is a summer-only jaunt.

- **Haleakalā Downhill, Maui.** Tour operators drive you and your rented bike literally into the clouds, then let you loose to pedal and coast, pedal and coast, down the long looping Haleakalā Highway. Don't let them talk you into this unless you've ridden a bike in traffic recently.

- **Surfing.** You can't learn to surf in a day, but with the proper instruction, you'll probably manage at least a ride or two—and the thrill is unforgettable. Upper body strength is a must. Beach boys offer quickie lessons; if you're serious, look for a reputable surfing school with multiday training sessions.

The Underwater World

Hawai'i is heaven for snorkelers and divers. Nearly 600 species of tropical fish inhabit the colorful coral reefs and lava tubes. Incredible spots are easy to reach; picking which ones to try is a matter of time, expense, and personal preference. Snorkeling is easy. Equipment rentals and excursions are inexpensive, and even fraidy-cats, first-timers, and people with claustrophobia can handle the relatively simple skill set required.

- **Molokini, Maui.** The tiny quarter-moon of Molokini, a half-sunken crater that forms a naturally sheltered bay, is a snorkeler's dream. Sometimes too many snorkelers have the same dream—go in the early morning for the least human company.

- **Tables & Shark's Cove, O'ahu.** Snorkelers *and* divers in your group? Tables, a series of onshore reefs, offers safe paddling, while neighboring Shark's Cove is the most popular cavern dive on the island. These are summer-only spots, however, as winter storms kick up that legendary North Shore surf.

- **Kealakekua Bay, the Big Island.** Dramatic cliffs shelter this marine reserve, where spinner dolphins and tropical fish greet snorkelers and kayakers.

- **Cathedrals & Sergeant Major Reef, Lāna'i.** If you want to avoid crowds, we've got one word for you: Lāna'i. Hulopo'e Beach has safe and interesting snorkeling, while Cathedrals and Sergeant Major Reef are legendary for diving.

Complete Indulgence

Hawai'i's resort hotels know how to pamper you. Their goal is to fulfill your every desire so completely that you never feel the need, or indeed the energy, to go off property.

- **Halekūlani Hotel, O'ahu.** What Waikīkī's venerable Halekūlani lacks in size, it more than makes up for in service. There is quite simply nothing that is too much to ask. Expect the exceptional in the signature restaurant, La Mer.

- **Spa Grande at the Grand Wailea Hotel, Maui.** Dissolve your stress in the *termé,* a hydrotherapy circuit including baths from Roman to Japanese furo and Swiss-jet showers.

- **The Lodge at Moloka'i Ranch, Moloka'i.** This Old West–style lodge offers rustic luxury on an intimate scale (there are 22 suites). You can do anything from boating to mountain biking, but nothing beats curling up in front of the large stone fireplace.

- **Mauna Lani Bay Hotel & Bungalows, Big Island.** If you really want to indulge yourself, rent a lagoon-side bungalow the size of a small house, complete with butler service.

- **Hyatt Regency Kaua'i, Kaua'i.** This is another got-everything resort: it's family- and honeymooner-friendly with large rooms and beautiful views (whale-watching from the balcony, no less). Its best feature, however, is the Anara Spa, where treatment rooms open onto private gardens.

Lying Back at the Beach

No one ever gets as much beach time in Hawai'i as they planned to, it seems, but it's a problem of time, not beaches. Beaches of every size, color (even green), and description line the state's many shorelines. They have different strengths: some are great for sitting but not so great for swimming; some offer beach-park amenities like lifeguards and showers, whereas others are more private and isolated. Read up before you head out.

- **Kailua & Lanikai Beaches, O'ahu.** Popular see-and-be-seen spots, these slim, white-sand beaches draw sunbathers, walkers, swimmers, and kayakers to O'ahu's Windward shores.

- **Mākena (Big & Little) Beach, Maui.** Big Beach is just that—its wide expanse and impressive length can swallow up a lot of folks, so it never feels crowded. Little Beach, over the hill, is where the nude sunbathers hang out.

- **Hāpuna Beach, Big Island.** This wide white-sand beach has it all: space, parking, and, in summer when waters are calm, swimming, snorkeling, and bodysurfing.

- **Po'ipū Beach Park, Kaua'i.** Kaua'i has more beautiful and more isolated beaches, but, if you're looking to sunbathe, swim, picnic, and people-watch, this one is right up there.

- **Hulopo'e Beach, Lāna'i.** The protected half-circle of white sand fronting the Mānele Resort offers grassy areas for picnicking, clear waters for snorkeling and swimming, and tide pools for exploring.

CRUISING THE HAWAIIAN ISLANDS

Cruising has become extremely popular in Hawai'i. For first-time visitors, it's an excellent way to get a taste of all the islands; and if you fall in love with one or even two, you know how to plan your next trip. It's also a comparatively inexpensive way to see Hawai'i. The limited amount of time in each port can be an argument against cruising—there's enough to do on any island to keep you busy for a week, so some folks feel shortchanged by cruise itineraries.

Cruising to Hawai'i

Until 2001 it was illegal for any cruise ships to stop in Hawai'i unless they originated from a foreign port, or were including a foreign port in their itinerary. The law has changed, but most cruises still include a stop in the Fanning Islands, Ensenada, or Vancouver. Gambling is legal on the open seas, and your winnings are tax-free; most cruise ships offer designated smoking areas and now enforce the U.S. legal drinking age (21) on Hawai'i itineraries.

Carnival Cruises. They call them "fun ships" for a reason—Carnival is all about keeping you busy and showing you a good time, both on board and on shore. Great for families, Carnival always plans plenty of kid-friendly activities, and their children's program rates high with the little critics. Carnival offers itineraries starting in Ensenada, Vancouver, and Honolulu. Their ships stop on Maui (Kahului and Lahaina), the Big Island (Kailua-Kona and Hilo), O'ahu, and Kaua'i. ☎ 888/227-6482 ⊕ www.carnival.com.

Celebrity Cruises. Celebrity's focus is on service, and it shows. From their waitstaff to their activity directors to their fantastic Hawaiian cultural experts, every aspect of your trip has been well thought out. They cater more to adults than children, so this may not be the best line for families. Celebrity's Hawai'i cruises depart from Los Angeles and stop in Maui (Lahaina), O'ahu, the Big Island (Hilo and Kailua-Kona), and Kaua'i. ☎ 800/647-2251 ⊕ www.celebrity.com.

Holland America. The grande dame of cruise lines, Holland America has a reputation for service and elegance. Holland America's Hawai'i cruises leave and return to San Diego, CA, and stop on Maui (Lahaina), the Big Island (Kailua-Kona and Hilo), O'ahu, and for half a day on Kaua'i. ☎ 877/724-5425 ⊕ www.hollandamerica.com.

Norwegian Cruise Lines. Norwegian has traditionally been one of the more casual cruise lines and offers a variety of service, activity, and excursion options. The latest addition to their fleet, *Pride of Hawai'i*, has expensive suites; but all the boats maintain a family-friendly focus (there are no casinos). The only line with ships not required to stop in foreign ports, NCL Pride itineraries originate either in San Francisco, Kahului (Maui), or Honolulu and include stops on Maui (Kahului), O'ahu, the Big Island (Hilo and Kona), and Kaua'i (Nāwiliwili). ☎ 800/327-7030 ⊕ www.ncl.com.

Princess Cruises. Princess strives to offer affordable luxury. Their prices start out a little higher, but you get more bells and whistles (more affordable balcony rooms, nice decor, more restaurants to choose from, personalized service). They're not fantastic for kids, but they do a great job of keeping teenagers occupied. Princess' Hawaiian cruise is 15 days, round-trip from Los Angeles, with a service call in Ensenada. The *Island Princess* stops in Maui (Lahaina), the Big Island (Hilo and Kailua-Kona), O'ahu, and Kaua'i. ☎*800/774–6237* ⊕ *www.princess.com.*

Royal Caribbean. Royal Caribbean's cruises originate in Los Angeles only, and stop in Maui (Lahaina), Kaua'i, O'ahu, and the Big Island (both Hilo and Kailua-Kona). In keeping with its reputation for being all things to all people, Royal Caribbean offers a huge variety of activities and services on board and more excursions on land than any other cruise line. ☎*800/521–8611* ⊕ *www.royalcaribbean.com.*

Cruising within Hawai'i

If you'd like to cruise from island to island, Norwegian is the only major cruise line option. For a different experience, Hawai'i Nautical offers cruises on smaller boats.

Norwegian Cruise Lines. Norwegian is the only major operator to offer interisland cruises in Hawai'i. Three of their ships cruise the islands—*Pride of Aloha* (older, Hawaiian-themed, priced lowest), *Pride of Hawai'i* (brand new, the most chic of the three, suites available, Hawaiian themed, slightly pricier), and *Pride of America* (Vintage Americana theme, very new, big family focus with lots of connecting staterooms and suites). All three offer 7-day itineraries within the islands, stopping on Maui, *O'ahu*, the Big Island, and overnighting in Kaua'i; the *Pride of America* offers guests two additional itineraries, one includes more time on Maui and the other more time at sea. ☎ *800/327–7030* ⊕ *www.ncl.com.*

Hawai'i Nautical. Offering a completely different sort of experience, Hawai'i Nautical provides private multiple day interisland cruises on their catamarans, yachts, and sailboats. Prices are higher, but service is completely personal, right down to the itinerary. ☎ *808/234-7245* ⊕ *www.hawaiinautical.com.*

TIPS

❶ On all but the *Pride of America, Pride of Hawai'i,* and *Pride of Aloha* cruises (operated by Norwegian Cruise Lines), you must bring a passport as you will be entering foreign ports of call.

❷ Think about booking your own excursions directly. You'll often pay less for greater value. For example, if you want to take a surfing lesson on O'ahu, visit one of the beachside shacks to find excellent instructors who offer better deals to individuals than they do to the cruise lines.

❸ Tendering in Maui can be a tedious process—if you want to avoid a little bit of the headache (and hours waiting in the sun), be sure to book an excursion there through the ship and you'll have smooth sailing.

❹ Most Mainland cell phones will work without a hitch on board between the islands and at all Hawaiian ports of call.

WEDDINGS & HONEYMOONS

With everything from turquoise bays surrounded by perfect white crescents to hidden waterfalls tucked into tropical rain forests, it's easy to see why Hawai'i is such a popular destination for all things romantic—weddings, honeymoons, anniversaries, you name it. The weather is perfect; the people are warm; the scenery is beautiful; there's an easy, laid-back feel to everything; and, let's face it, everyone looks fantastic after a few days lounging on a beach.

Wedding Planning

The logistics. You must apply in person for a wedding license in Hawai'i, but you can download, fill in, and print the application from the State government's Web site: www. hawaii.gov/health/vital-records/vital-records/marriage/index.html. There's no waiting period and no blood test required. The cost is $60, which must be paid in cash. The license is valid for 30 days. Your certificate of marriage will be mailed to you after the wedding; for $10 you can put a rush on the certificate, which can be very useful for brides intending to change their last names.

The ceremony. The idea of planning a wedding in a strange place, thousands of miles away, may be enough to cause night sweats for some, but fear not. Hawai'i is home to some of the world's best wedding planners, many of whom are employed by—go figure—the more popular destination wedding resorts. The first decision is to pick an island—Maui or O'ahu for the sandy beach wedding, Kaua'i for the rain-forest tropical wedding, the Big Island for the unique–adventure wedding, Lāna'i for the upscale elegant gathering, Moloka'i for the über-traditional Hawaiian wedding. Narrow your locations down and contact a few planners for quotes. Many planners work with caterers and florists and offer packages; the resort-based planners have a variety of packages on offer. They're all used to people shopping around, so don't be afraid to bargain.

Those wishing to steer clear of the resort wedding and tap into old Hawai'i may also want the help of a local planner, unless they have personal knowledge of their chosen destination or trustworthy friends or family in the area who can help taste food, scout locations, and meet potential officiants. There are certain things that are just too difficult to research from a distance, and having a wedding planner doesn't mean that your wedding will be expensive, nor does it mean that you'll end up with a Mainland wedding in Hawai'i or some sort of Hawaiian kitsch wedding (unless of course that's what you want!). These are people who know Hawai'i well and can help you find the perfect secluded beach, the local florist with the most beautiful orchids, a house on the water for you and your inner circle, and the best caterer to roast your pig in the backyard.

The traditions. Most people who wed on Hawai'i incorporate local traditions to some extent. These can include Hawaiian music, ancient Hawaiian chants and blessings, and traditional Hawaiian food at the reception. A simple lei exchange is customary for most couples—some include only the bride and groom, others splurge and get leis for everyone. Typically green maile garlands are for grooms, and strands of pink and white pīkake flowers are for brides. In a traditional Hawaiian wedding ceremony, the officiant, called the *kahuna pule* in Hawaiian, binds the couple's hands together with a maile lei.

Honeymoon Planning

Hawai'i is a popular destination not only for everything it's got going for it, but for everything it's not as well—it's not all that far away; it's not outside the United States yet seems like another country; and it's not outrageously expensive if you plan well.

As for romance, yes, Hawai'i's romantic clichés–sunsets, beach strolls, moonlight walks–still work their magic, but there are also plenty of more unique ways to experience the romance of Hawai'i, whether you're looking to explore or just veg out together for awhile. Each of the islands has its own claims to fame—O'ahu has the nightlife and the amazing North Shore surf; Maui is known as the romantic island; the Big Island is known as the adventure island; and Kaua'i is much loved for its solitude and wild beauty. But all offer a mix of attractions, and don't forget that it's easy and relatively inexpensive to island hop.

Almost as important as your choice of island is your accommodation choice. Although Hawai'i is home to dozens of world-class resorts all waiting to anticipate your every need, there are also several secluded B&Bs that are the perfect blend of luxury and total privacy. Most B&Bs have a honeymoon room or suite, and many of them offer stand-alone cottages. For even more privacy, there are several homes for rent throughout the islands, many of which are in stunning locations and often rent for less per night than rooms at the big resorts. Each island has its own B&B association, which inspects properties and lists the best of them.

O'ahu

WORD OF MOUTH

"Why I love O'ahu? . . . The trade winds breezing through and just the electric energy that IS O'ahu. And of course all the rest— the magic I feel when my toes first sink into the warm sand as I head off on my maiden walk on Waikīkī beach, looking toward Diamond Head and heading straight for the Banyan Bar at the Moana!"

—bashfulL

WELCOME TO O'AHU

Getting Oriented

O'ahu, the third largest of the Hawaiian Islands, is not just Honolulu and Waikīkī. It is looping mountain trails on the western Wai'anae and eastern Ko'olau ranges. It is monster waves breaking on the golden beaches of the North Shore. It is country stores and beaches where turtles are your swimming companions.

TOP 5
Reasons to Go

1 **Waves:** Boogie board or surf some of the best breaks on the planet.

2 **Pearl Harbor:** Remember Pearl Harbor with a visit to the *Arizona* Memorial.

3 **Diamond Head:** Scale the crater whose iconic profile looms over Waikīkī.

4 **Nightlife:** Raise your glass to the best party scene in Hawai'i.

5 **The North Shore:** See O'ahu's country side—check out the famous beaches from Sunset to Waimea Bay and hike to the remote tip of the island.

West O'ahu—which includes Central O'ahu highlands, the leeward coast and the Hawaiian communities of Nānākuli and Wai'anae—is finding a new identity as a "second city" of suburban homes and tech firms, coexisting with agriculture and traditional lifestyles.

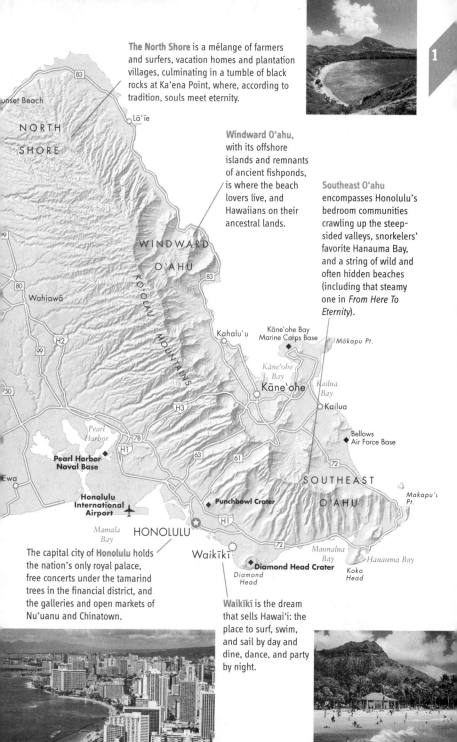

The North Shore is a mélange of farmers and surfers, vacation homes and plantation villages, culminating in a tumble of black rocks at Ka'ena Point, where, according to tradition, souls meet eternity.

Windward O'ahu, with its offshore islands and remnants of ancient fishponds, is where the beach lovers live, and Hawaiians on their ancestral lands.

Southeast O'ahu encompasses Honolulu's bedroom communities crawling up the steep-sided valleys, snorkelers' favorite Hanauma Bay, and a string of wild and often hidden beaches (including that steamy one in *From Here To Eternity*).

The capital city of **Honolulu** holds the nation's only royal palace, free concerts under the tamarind trees in the financial district, and the galleries and open markets of Nu'uanu and Chinatown.

Waikiki is the dream that sells Hawai'i: the place to surf, swim, and sail by day and dine, dance, and party by night.

unset Beach

Lā'ie

NORTH SHORE

83

WINDWARD

O'AHU

83

Wahiawā

80

99

H2

750

H3

KO'OLAU MOUNTAINS

Kahalu'u

Kāne'ohe Bay Marine Corps Base

Mōkapu Pt.

Kāne'ohe Bay

Kāne'ohe

Kailua Bay

Kailua

Bellows Air Force Base

Pearl Harbor

78

H1

Pearl Harbor Naval Base

Ewa

Honolulu International Airport

63

61

72

SOUTHEAST

O'AHU

Makapu'u Pt.

Mamala Bay

HONOLULU

Punchbowl Crater

H1

72

Waikīkī

Diamond Head Crater

Diamond Head

Maunalua Bay

Hanauma Bay

Koko Head

9

99

O'AHU PLANNER

When You Arrive

Honolulu International Airport is 20 minutes from Waikīkī (40 during rush hour). Car rental is across the street from baggage claim. A cumbersome and inefficient airport taxi system requires you to line up to a taxi wrangler who radios for cars (about $25 to Waikīkī). Other options: TheBus ($2, one lap-size bag allowed) or public airport shuttle ($8).

■ TIP→ Ask the driver to take H1, not Nimitz Highway, at least as far as downtown, or your introduction to paradise will be Honolulu's industrial back side.

Set the Stage

Head to Longs or Wal-Mart on your first day and buy a cheap Styrofoam cooler, grass beach mats, beach towels, floats for the kids, sun protection, and bottled water. What to do with all this stuff when you head for home? Leave it in the hotel room (you'll have gotten your money's worth). Better yet—look for a group that's just checking in and make a welcome gift of your survival kit.

What's New in 2007

O'ahu is under much-needed renovation with Waikīkī hotels and streets, the H–1 freeway, the Bishop Museum, and Pearl Harbor all affected. Enquire closely about renovation near the hotel you choose. And anytime you visit an attraction, call ahead to be sure hours haven't changed, and the particular things you want to see aren't closed.

Get Out of Town

They'll tell you, wrongly, that O'ahu means "the gathering place." But scholars agree that no one knows what this ancient word really means. In any case, the island is a literal gathering place—for 800,000-plus residents and several thousand more visitors every day. If noise, traffic, and crowding in Waikīkī and Honolulu get to you, head in any direction—you'll soon see that O'ahu has a rural side of exceptional beauty and even tranquility.

Car Rentals

Waikīkī and Honolulu can realistically be done without a car. Public buses and free shuttles reach most important sites. If you want to see the North Shore or the Windward beaches, you'll need to rent a car.

TIPS→

■ If you are staying in Waikīkī, rent a car only on the days when you wish to go farther afield. You don't need a car in Waikīkī itself, and inconveniently located hotel parking garages charge everyone (even hotel guests) close to $20 a day, plus tips.

■ Renting a Mustang convertible is a sure sign that you're a tourist and practically begs "come burglarize me." A good rule of thumb: When the car is out of your sight even for a moment, it should be empty of anything you care about.

To Island-Hop or Stop?

Should you try to fit another island into your trip or stay put in O'ahu? Tough call. Although none of the islands is more than 30 minutes away from another by air, security hassles, transport and check-in all swallow up precious vacation hours. If you've got less than a week, do O'ahu well and leave the rest for the next trip. With a week, you can give three good tour days to O'ahu (Pearl Harbor, Honolulu, and one rural venture), then head to a Neighbor Island for some serious beach time and maybe an adventure or two. If you do decide to island-hop, book in advance; you'll get a better fare by packaging your travel.

■ TIP→ **If you want to get along on the Neighbor Islands, don't compare them to Honolulu and never call them "the outer islands"—that's insultingly O'ahu-centric.**

Will It Rain?

There's a reason why Hawai'i's most-watched TV news show doesn't have a weather forecaster. Weather here is blissfully predictable: mid-to low 80s, morning showers at high elevations and in misty valleys, trade winds 5 to 15 miles per hour. The only reason anyone listens to the weather is to find out if the surf is up (especially in winter) and when low tide will be (for fishing).

Timing Is Everything

When to visit? Winter is whales (November through March) and waves (surf competitions December through February). In fall, the Aloha Festivals celebrate island culture in September. In summer, the Islands honor the king who made them a nation, Kamehameha I, on June 11, with parades and events on all islands. O'ahu's one-of-a-kind Pan-Pacific Festival backs up to Kamehameha Day, bringing together hundreds of performers from Japan's seasonal celebrations.

Guided Activities

When it comes to surfing, you come to O'ahu. For a much less exhausting trip beyond the breaks, try a short sail on a beach catamaran from Waikīkī. This chart lists average prices per person for O'ahu's most popular guided activities.

ACTIVITY	COST
Aerial Tours (1/2 hr.)	$100–$140
Beach Catamaran Sails	$12–$20
Deep-Sea Fishing (1/2 day)	$120–$150
Golf (green fee)	$40–$165
Kayak Tours	$75–$100
Lū'au	$56–$195
Shark Encounters	$120
Snorkel Cruises (2–3 hrs.)	$50–$100
Surfing Lessons (1–2 hrs.)	$50–$100
Whale-Watching (2–3 hrs.)	$100–$120

1-Day Itineraries

To experience even a fraction of O'ahu's charms, you need a minimum of four days and a bus pass. Five days and a car is better: Waikīkī is at least a day, Honolulu and Chinatown another, Pearl Harbor the better part of another. Each of the rural sections can swallow a day each, just for driving, sightseeing and stopping to eat. And that's before you've taken a surf lesson, hung from a parasail, hiked a loop trail, or visited a botanical garden. The following itineraries will take you to our favorite spots on the island.

First day in Waikīkī:
You'll be up at dawn due to the time change and dead on your feet by afternoon due to jet lag. Have a dawn swim, change into walking gear, and head east along Kalākaua Avenue to Monsarrat Avenue, and climb Diamond Head. After lunch, nap in the shade, do some shopping, or visit the nearby East Honolulu neighborhoods of Mō'ili'ili and Kaimukī, rife with small shops and good, little restaurants. End the day with an early, interesting, and inexpensive dinner at one of these neighborhood spots.

Windward Exploring:
For sand, sun, and surf, follow H-1 east to keyhole-shaped Hanauma Bay for picture-perfect snorkeling, then round the southeast tip of the island with its windswept cliffs and the famous Hālona Blowhole. Fly a kite or watch body surfers at Sandy Beach. Take in Sea Life Park. In Waimānalo, stop for local-style plate lunch, or punch on through to Kailua, where there's intriguing shopping and good eating.

The North Shore:
Hit H1 westbound and then H2 to get to the North Shore. You'll pass through pineapple country, then drop down a scenic winding road to Waialua and Hale'iwa. Stop in Hale'iwa town to shop, to experience shave ice, and to pick up a guided dive or snorkel trip. On winding Kamehameha Highway, stop at famous big-wave beaches, take a dip in a cove with a turtle, and buy fresh island fruit at roadside stands.

Pearl Harbor: Pearl Harbor is an almost all-day investment. Be on the grounds by 7:30 AM to line up for *Arizona* Memorial tickets. Clamber all over the USS *Bowfin* submarine. Finally, take the free trolley to see the Mighty Mo battleship. If it's Wednesday or Saturday, make the 5-minute drive *mauka* (toward the mountains) for bargain-basement shopping at the sprawling Aloha Stadium Swap Meet.

Town time: If you are interested in history, devote a day to Honolulu's historic sites. Downtown, see 'Iolani Palace, the Kamehameha Statue, and Kawaiaha'o Church. A few blocks east, explore Chinatown, gilded Kuan Yin Temple, and artsy Nu'uanu with its galleries. On the water is the informative Hawai'i Maritime Center. Hop west on H-1 to the Bishop Museum, the state's anthropological and archeological center. And a mile up Pali Highway is Queen Emma Summer Palace, whose shady grounds were a royal retreat.

■ For more details, *see* Exploring *and* Beaches on O'ahu in this chapter.

OFFERING BOTH THE BUZZ of modern living in jam-packed Honolulu (the state's capital), and the allure of slow-paced island life on its northern and eastern shores, O'ahu is, in many ways, the center of the Hawaiian universe. O'ahu is home to Waikīkī, the most famous Hawaiian beach with some of the world's most famous surf on the North Shore; and the Islands' best known historical site—Pearl Harbor. If it's isolation, peace, and quiet you want, O'ahu is probably not for you, but if you'd like a bit of spice with your piece of paradise, this island provides it.

By far the state's most populous island, more than 875,000 people (over 75% of Hawai'i's total population) call O'ahu home. Traveling by plane and on cruise ships, an average of nearly 84,000 people visit O'ahu a day, making it a very busy place and one of the most popular tourist destinations in the United States.

Geology

Encompassing 597 square mi, O'ahu is the third-largest island in the Hawaiian chain. Scientists believe the island was formed about 4 million years ago by two volcanoes: Wai'anae and Ko'olau. Wai'anae, the older of the two, makes up the western side of the island, while Ko'olau shapes the eastern side. Central O'ahu is an elevated plateau bordered by the two mountain ranges, with Pearl Harbor to the south. Several of O'ahu's most famous natural landmarks, including Diamond Head and Hanauma Bay, are tuff rings and cinder cones formed during a renewed volcanic stage (roughly 1 million years ago).

Flora & Fauna

Due to its elevation, the eastern (Ko'olau) side of O'ahu is much cooler and wetter than the western side of the island, which tends to be dry and arid. The island's official flower, the little orange *ilima,* grows predominantly in the east, but leis throughout the island incorporate *ilima.* Numerous tropical fish call the reef at Hanauma Bay home, migrating humpback whales can be spotted off the coast past Waikīkī and Diamond Head from December through April, spinner dolphins pop in and out of the island's bays, and dozens of islets off O'ahu's eastern coast provide refuge for endangered seabirds.

History

O'ahu is the most populated island because early tourism to Hawai'i started here. Although Kīlauea volcano on Hawai'i was a tourist attraction in the late 1800s, it was the building of the Moana Hotel on Waikīkī Beach in 1901 and subsequent advertising of Hawai'i to wealthy San Franciscans that really fueled tourism in the islands. O'ahu was drawing tens of thousands of guests yearly when, on December 7, 1941, Japanese Zeros appeared at dawn to bomb Pearl Harbor. Though tourism understandably dipped during the war (Waikīkī Beach was fenced with barbed wire), the subsequent memorial only seemed to attract more visitors, and O'ahu remains hugely popular with tourists to this day.

On O'ahu Today

Even more so than the rest of the islands, O'ahu feels the need to diversify its economy in an effort to weaken its dependence on the tourism industry. To that end, the government has spent the last decade wooing big business. New tech jobs and businesses have brought new money, and many youngsters who left the island when they came of age have returned to open up stores, galleries, and theaters. The city has put some money into renovating run-down neighborhoods, particularly downtown's Chinatown, which has been spruced up with new boutiques, restaurants, and modern-art galleries.

EXPLORING OʻAHU

Diamond Head & Kapiʻolani Park

By Wanda Adams

Diamond Head Crater is perhaps Hawaiʻi's most recognizable natural landmark. It got its name from sailors who thought they had found precious gems on its slopes; these later proved to be calcite crystals, fool's gold. Hawaiians saw a resemblance in the sharp angle of the crater's seaward slope to the oddly shaped head of the ʻahi fish and so called the it Lēʻahi, though later they Hawaiianized the English name to Kaimana Hila. It is commemorated in a widely-known hula—"*A ʻike i ka nani o Kaimana Hila, Kaimana Hila, kai mai iluna*/We saw the beauty of Diamond Head, Diamond Head set high above."

Kapiʻolani Park lies in the shadow of the crater. King David Kalākaua established the park in 1887, named it after his queen, and dedicated it "to the use and enjoyment of the people." Kapiʻolani Park is a 500-acre expanse where you can play all sorts of field sports, enjoy a picnic, see wild animals at the Honolulu Zoo, or hear live music at the Waikīkī Shell or the Kapiʻolani Bandstand. It's also the start and finish point for many weekend walks; check local newspapers or gohawaii.com.

> ### UNDER THE STARS
>
> Waikīkī's entertainment scene isn't just dinner shows and lounge acts. There are plenty of free or nearly free offerings right on the beach and at Kapiʻolani Park. Queen's Surf Beach hosts the popular Sunset on the Beach, which brings big-screen showings of recent Hollywood blockbusters to the great outdoors. Also, during the summer months, the Honolulu Zoo has weekly concerts, and admission is just $1. (⇨ *See* Entertainment & Nightlife)

❶ **Diamond Head State Monument and Park.** Panoramas from this 760-foot
Fodor'sChoice extinct volcanic peak, once used as a military fortification, extend
★ from Waikīkī and Honolulu in one direction and out to Koko Head in the other, with surfers and windsurfers scattered like confetti on the cresting waves below. This 360-degree perspective is a great orientation for first-time visitors. On a clear day, look to your left past Koko Head to glimpse the outlines of the islands of Maui and Molokaʻi. To enter the park from Waikīkī, take Kalākaua Avenue east, turn left at Monsarrat Avenue, head a mile up the hill, and look for a sign on the right. Drive through the tunnel to the inside of the crater. The ¾-mi trail to the top begins at the parking lot. New lighting inside the summit tunnel and a spiral staircase eases the way, but be aware that the hike to the crater is a strenuous upward climb; if you aren't in the habit

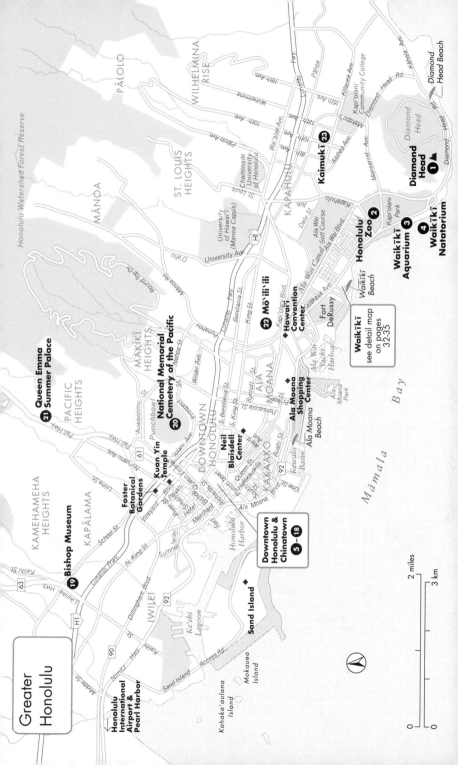

Greater Honolulu

PÁLOLO

WILHELMINA RISE

Honolulu Watershed Forest Reserve

MÁNOA

ST. LOUIS HEIGHTS

Diamond Head Beach

Kaimukī 23

Kapi'olani Community College

Diamond Head Rd.

Diamond Head 1

University of Hawai'i (Manoa Capus)

University Ave.

Ala Wai Canal Golf Course

Honolulu Zoo 2

Kapi'olani Park

Waikīkī Aquarium 3

Waikīkī Natatorium 4

MAKIKI HEIGHTS

National Memorial Cemetery of the Pacific 20

Hawai'i Convention Center

Mō'ili'ili 22

Waikīkī Beach

Fort DeRussy

Waikīkī see detail map on pages 32–35

Mámala Bay

PACIFIC HEIGHTS

Queen Emma Summer Palace 21

Kuan Yin Temple

DOWNTOWN HONOLULU

ALA MOANA

Ala Wai Yacht Harbor

Foster Botanical Gardens

Neil Blaisdell Center

KAKA'AKO

Ala Moana Shopping Center

Ala Moana Beach

Ala Moana Park

KAMEHAMEHA HEIGHTS

Pali Hwy.

Bishop Museum 19

KAPĀLAMA

Honolulu Harbor

Downtown Honolulu & Chinatown 5 – 18

IWILEI

Sand Island

Honolulu International Airport & Pearl Harbor

Ke'ehi Lagoon

Mokuea Island

Kahaka'aulana Island

Sand Island Access Rd.

0   2 miles

0   3 km

of getting much exercise, this might not be for you. Take bottled water with you to ensure that you stay hydrated under the tropical sun. ■ TIP➡ **To beat the heat and the crowds, rise early and make the hike before 8 AM.** As you walk, note the color of the vegetation; if the mountain is brown, Honolulu has been without significant rain for a while; but if the trees and undergrowth glow green, it's the wet season when rare Hawaiian marsh plants revive on the floor of the crater. Keep an eye on your watch if you're there at day's end, because the gates close promptly at 6. ⊠ *Diamond Head Rd. at 18th Ave., Waikīkī* ☎ *808/ 587–0285* ⊕ *www.state.hi.us/dlnr/dsp/oahu.html* ⟹ *$1 per person, $5 per vehicle.* ☉ *Daily 6–6.*

☾ ❷ **Honolulu Zoo.** To get a glimpse of the endangered *nēnē*, the Hawai'i state bird, check out the Kipuka Nēnē Sanctuary. Though many animals seem to prefer to remain invisible, the monkeys appear to enjoy being seen and are a hoot to watch. It's best to get to the zoo right when it opens, since the animals are livelier in the cool of the morning. There are bigger and better zoos, but this one, though showing signs of neglect due to budget constraints, is a lush garden and has some great programs. On Wednesday evenings in summer, there's The Wildest Show in Town, a series of concerts ($1 admission). On weekends look for the Zoo Fence Art Mart, on Monsarrat Avenue on the Diamond Head side outside the zoo, for affordable artwork by contemporary artists. The offerings for families are also appealing. Consider a family sleepover inside the zoo during Snooze in the Zoo events, which take place on a Friday or Saturday night every month. Or just head for the petting zoo, where kids can make friends with a llama and meet Abbey, the zoo's resident monitor lizard. There's also an exceptionally good gift shop. Metered parking is available all along the *makai* (ocean) side of the park and in the lot next to the zoo. TheBus (routes 22 and 58) makes stops here along the way to and from Ala Moana Center and Sea Life Park. ⊠ *151 Kapahulu Ave., Waikīkī* ☎ *808/971–7171* ⊕ *www.honoluluzoo. org* ⟹ *$6* ☉ *Daily 9–4:30.*

Ins & Outs of Waikīkī   See Page 31

☾ ❸ **Waikīkī Aquarium.** This amazing little attraction harbors more than 2,500 organisms and 420 species of Hawaiian and South Pacific marine life, endangered Hawaiian monk seals, sharks, and the only chambered nautilus living in captivity. The Edge of the Reef exhibit showcases five different types of reef environments found along Hawai'i's shorelines. Check out the Sea Visions Theater, the biodiversity exhibit, and the self-guided audio tour, which is included with admission. Programs include Exploring the Reef at Night, Shark Nites, Stingray Tracking, and Aquarium After Dark activities. Give the aquarium an hour, including 10 minutes for a film in its Sea Visions Theater. ⊠ *2777*

Continued on page 37

INS & OUTS OF WAIKĪKĪ

Waikīkī is all that is wonderful about a resort area, and all that is regrettable. On the wonderful side: swimming, surfing, parasailing, and catamaran-riding steps from the street; the best nightlife in Hawai'i;

shopping from designer to dime store; and experiences to remember: the heart-lifting rush the first time you stand up on a surfboard, watching the old men play cutthroat checkers in the beach pavilions, eating fresh grilled snapper as the sun slips into the sea. As to the regrettable: clogged streets, body-lined beaches, $5 cups of coffee, tacky T-shirts, $20 parking stalls, schlocky artwork, the same street performers you saw in Atlantic City, drunks, ceaseless construction—all rather brush the bloom from the plumeria.

Modern Waikīkī is nothing like its original self, a network of streams, marshes, and islands that drained the inland valleys. The Ala Wai Canal took care of that in the 1920s. More recently, new landscaping, walkways, and a general attention to infrastructure have brightened a façade that had begun distinctly to fade.

But throughout its history, Waikīkī has retained its essential character: an enchantment that cannot be fully explained and one that, though diminished by high-rises, traffic, and noise, has not yet disappeared. Hawaiian royalty came here, and visitors continue to follow, falling in love with sharp-prowed Diamond Head, the sensuous curve of shoreline with its baby-safe waves, and the strong-footed surfers like moving statues in the golden light.

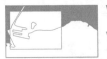

WAIKĪKĪ WEST

TOP 5 THINGS TO DO IN WAIKĪKĪ

1. Hike the Diamond Head trail.
2. Take a surfing lesson.
3. Shop.
4. Go on a catamaran cruise.
5. Lie on the beach.

Source: Hotel concierges

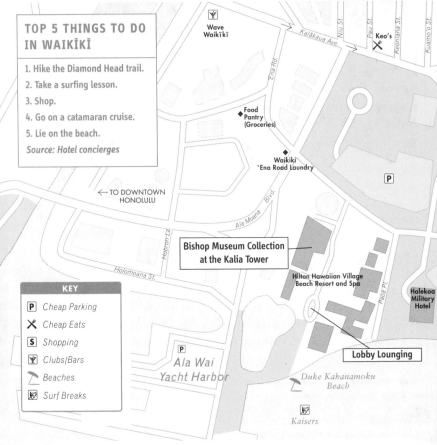

Wave Waikīkī

Kalākaua Ave.

Niu St.

Pau St.

Keoniana St.

Kuamo'o St.

Keo's

Ena Rd.

Food Pantry (Groceries)

Waikīkī 'Ena Road Laundry

P

← TO DOWNTOWN HONOLULU

Ala Moana Blvd.

Hobron Ln.

Bishop Museum Collection at the Kalia Tower

Holomoana St.

Hilton Hawaiian Village Beach Resort and Spa

Paoa Pl.

Halekoa Military Hotel

KEY

P	Cheap Parking
✕	Cheap Eats
S	Shopping
☼	Clubs/Bars
⌐	Beaches
▨	Surf Breaks

P

Ala Wai Yacht Harbor

Lobby Lounging

Duke Kahanamoku Beach

▨ *Kaisers*

CHEAP EATS

Keo's, 2028 Kūhiō: Breakfast.

Malia Cafe, 2211 Kūhiō: American/local diner.

Pho Old Saigon, 2270 Kūhiō: Vietnamese.

Japanese noodle shops: Try Menchanko-Tei, Waikīkī Trade Center; Ezogiku, 2164 Kalākaua.

■ **TIP →** Thanks to the many Japanese nationals who stay here, Waikīkī is blessed with lots of cheap, authentic Japanese food, particularly noodles. Plastic representations of food in the window are an indicator of authenticity and a help in ordering.

SHOP, SHOP, SHOP/PARTY, PARTY, PARTY

2100 Kalākaua: Select high-end European boutiques (Chanel, Gucci, Yves Saint Laurent).

Island Treasures Antique Mall: Hawaiian collectibles from precious to priceless. 2145 Kūhiō Ave. 808/922-8223.

Wave Waikīkī: This multistory madhouse of sound and writhing bodies is a bit rough around the edges but hugely popular with locals. 1877 Kalākaua Ave. 808/941-0424.

Zanzabar: Upscale Zanzabar is a different club every night—Latin, global, over 30, under 18.

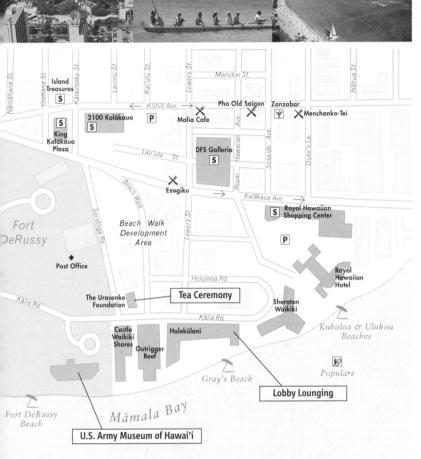

Waikīkī Trade Center, 2255 Kūhiō Ave. 808/924-3939.

RAINY-DAY IDEAS

Lobby lounging: Among Waikīkī's great gathering spots are Halekūlani's tranquil courtyards with gorgeous flower arrangements and glimpses of the famous, and the Hilton Hawaiian Village's flagged pathways with koi ponds, squawking parrots, and great shops.

Bishop Museum Collection at the Kalia Tower, Hilton Hawaiian Village: This 8,000-square-foot branch of Hawai'i's premier cultural archive illuminates life in Waikīkī through the years and the history of the Hawaiian people. 2005 Kalia Rd. 808/947-2458. $7. Daily 10-5.

Tea Ceremony, Urasenke Foundation: Japan's mysterious tea ceremony demonstrated. 245 Saratoga Rd. 808/923-3059. $3 donation. Wed., Fri. 10-noon.

U.S. Army Museum of Hawai'i: Exhibits, including photographs and military equipment, trace the history of Army in the Islands. Battery Randolph, Kalia Rd., Fort DeRussy. 808/438-2821. Free. Tues.-Sun. 10-4:15.

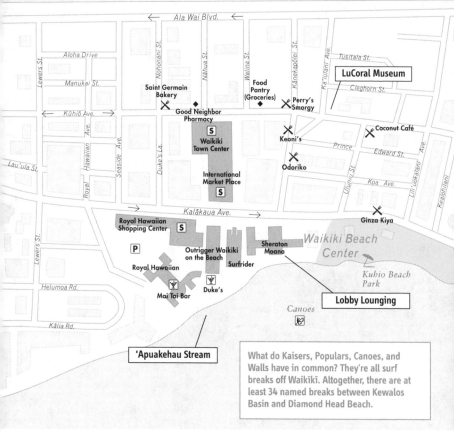

Ala Wai Blvd.

Aloha Drive

Manukai St.

Saint Germain Bakery

Kūhiō Ave.

Food Pantry (Groceries)

Perry's Smorgy

LuCoral Museum

Cleghorn St.

Good Neighbor Pharmacy

S Waikiki Town Center

Keoni's

Coconut Café

Prince

Edward St.

Odoriko

International Market Place **S**

Koa Ave.

Kalākaua Ave.

Ginza Kiya

Royal Hawaiian Shopping Center **S**

P

Outrigger Waikiki on the Beach

Sheraton Moana

Waikiki Beach Center

Royal Hawaiian

Surfrider

Kuhio Beach Park

Helumoa Rd.

Mai Tai Bar

Duke's

Lobby Lounging

Kālia Rd.

Canoes

'Apuakehau Stream

Lewers St., Nohonani St., Nāhua St., Walina St., Kānekapōlei St., Kāʻiulani Ave., Tusitala St., Duke's La., Seaside Ave., Royal Hawaiian Ave., Lau'ula St., Uluniu St., Lili'uokalani Ave., Kealohilani Ave.

What do Kaisers, Populars, Canoes, and Walls have in common? They're all surf breaks off Waikīkī. Altogether, there are at least 34 named breaks between Kewalos Basin and Diamond Head Beach.

CHEAP EATS

Coconut Cafe, 2441 Kūhiō: Burgers, sandwiches under $5; fresh fruit smoothies.

Ginza Kiya, 2464 Kalākaua: Japanese noodle shop.

Keoni's, Outrigger East Hotel, 150 Kāiulani Ave.: Breakfasts at rock-bottom prices.

Odoriko, King's Village, 131 Kāiulani Ave.: Japanese noodle shop.

Perry's Smorgy Restaurant, 2380 Kūhiō: family-friendly American food; brunch under $10.

■ TIP → **To save money, go inland. Kūhiō, one block toward the mountains from the main drag** of Kalākaua, is lined with less expensive restaurants, hotels, and shops.

SHOP, SHOP, SHOP/PARTY, PARTY, PARTY

Sheraton Moana Surfrider: Pick up a present at Noeha Gallery or Sand People. Then relax with a drink at the venerable Banyan Veranda. The radio program *Hawai'i Calls* first broadcast to a mainland audience from here in 1935.

Duke's Canoe Club, Outrigger Waikīkī: Beach party central.

Mai Tai Bar at the Royal Hawaiian: Birthplace of the mai tai.

KEY

P	Cheap Parking
✕	Cheap Eats
S	Shopping
🍸	Clubs/Bars
⌐	Beaches
🏄	Surf Breaks
ℹ	Tourist Information

Liliuokalani Garden

Pualani Wy.

Waimanu Wy.

Kaneloa

Ave.

Ave.

ʻŌhua

Paoakalani

← Kūhiō Ave. →

Kapahulu Ave.

Cartwright Rd.

Lemon Rd.

Honolulu Zoo

TO DIAMOND → HEAD
ℹ

Walls
🏄

Queen's Surf

Sans Souci

RAINY-DAY IDEAS

Lobby lounging: Check out the century-old, period-furnished lobby and veranda of the Sheraton Moana Surfrider Hotel on Kalākaua.

LuCoral Museum: Exhibit and shop explores the world of coral and semiprecious stones; wander about or take $2 guided tour and participate in jewelry-making activity. 2414 Kūhiō.

WHAT THE LOCALS LOVE

Paid-parking–phobic Islanders usually avoid Waikīkī, but these attractions are juicy enough to lure locals:

■ **Auntie Genoa Keawe**, old-style lūʻau music Thursday at the Waikīkī Beach Marriott Resort and Spa.

■ **Pan-Pacific Festival-Matsuri in Hawaii**, a summer cultural festival that's as good as a trip to Japan.

■ **Aloha Festivals in September**, the legendary floral parade and evening show of contemporary Hawaiian music.

■ **The Wildest Show in Town**, summer concerts at the Honolulu Zoo.

■ **Sunset on the Beach**, free films projected on an outdoor screen at Queen's Beach, with food and entertainment.

ʻAPUAKEHAU STREAM

Wade out just in front of the Outrigger Waikīkī on the Beach and feel a current of chilly water curling around your ankles. This is the last remnant of three streams that once drained the inland valleys behind you, making of Waikīkī a place of swamps, marshes, taro and rice paddies, and giving it the name "spouting water." High-ranking chiefs surfed in a legendary break gouged out by the draining freshwater and rinsed off afterward in the stream whose name means "basket of dew." The Ala Wai Canal, completed in the late 1920s, drained the land, reducing proud ʻApuakehau Stream to a determined phantom passing beneath Waikīkī's streets.

WHAT'S NEW & CHANGING

Waikīkī, which was looking a bit shopworn, is in the midst of many makeovers. Ask about noise, disruption, and construction when booking. In addition to fresh landscaping and period light fixtures along Kalākaua and a pathway that encircles Ala Wai Canal, expect:

1. BEACH WALK: Virtually every structure in the area bounded by Beach Walk, Lewers Street, and Kalia and Saratoga roads is coming down or dressing up in a $460 million, 7.9-acre project masterminded by an arm of the local Outrigger Hotel chain. Two older hotels will emerge as newly branded Embassy Suites and Fairfield properties, along with a dynamic and diverse retail complex of local and name-brand shops and restaurants (completion late 2006).

2. ROYAL HAWAIIAN SHOPPING CENTER AND INTERNATIONAL MARKETPLACE: The fortress-like Royal Hawaiian Shopping Center in the center of Kalākaua Avenue will become an open, inviting space with a palm grove and a new mix of shops and restaurants (completion 2006). And tacky International Marketplace shops will give way to a low-rise compound of entertainment spaces, kiosks, and water features, with many historic trees preserved (completion 2007).

3. CIRQUE HAWAI'I: This acrobatic show with an international cast is so new at this writing that there's no way to predict its staying power, though local reviews have been good. ⊠ *325 Seaside Ave.,* ☎ *808/922-0017,* ⊡ *$55-$95.*

GETTING THERE

It can seem impossible to figure out how to get to Waikīkī from H–1. The exit is far inland, and even when you follow the signs, the route jigs and jogs; it sometimes seems a wonder that more tourists aren't found starving in Kaimukī.

FROM EASTBOUND H-1 (COMING FROM THE AIRPORT):
1. To western Waikīkī (Fort DeRussy and most hotels): Take the Punahou exit from H–1, turn right on Punahou and get in the center lane. Go right on Beretania and almost immediately left onto Kalākaua, which takes you into Waikīkī.

2. To eastern Waikīkī (Kapi'olani Park): Take the King Street exit, and stay on King for two blocks. Go right on Kapahulu, which takes you to Kalākaua.

FROM WESTBOUND H-1:
Take the Kapi'olani Boulevard exit. Follow Kapi'olani to McCully, and go left on McCully. Follow McCully to Kalākaua, and you're in Waikīkī.

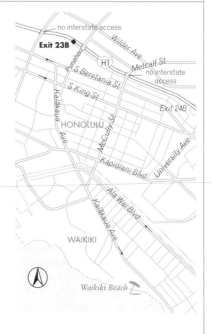

Kalākaua Ave., Waikīkī ☎ *808/923–9741* ⊕ *www.waquarium.org* ⊠ *$9* ⊙ *Daily 9–4:30.*

❹ Waikīkī War Memorial Natatorium. This 1927 World War I monument, dedicated to the 102 Hawaiian servicemen who lost their lives in battle, stands proudly—its 20-foot archway, which was completely restored in 2002, is floodlighted at night. The 100-meter saltwater swimming pool, the training spot for Olympians Johnny Weissmuller and Buster Crabbe and the U.S. Army during World War II, is closed as the facility has fallen into disrepair while a debate rages within city government about whether to refurbish the pool or leave only the archway monument. ⊠ *2777 Kalākaua Ave., Waikīkī.*

NEED A BREAK? According to legend, Robert Louis Stevenson once sat beneath the eponymous *hau* tree in the courtyard of the **Hau Tree Lānai** (⊠ 2863 Kalākaua Ave. ☎ 808/ 921-7066). You can enjoy the same shade, plus breakfast, lunch, or dinner, at this find in the New Otani Kaimana Beach Hotel, next to the Natatorium.

Chinatown

The name Chinatown has always been a misnomer. Though three-quarters of O'ahu's Chinese lived closely packed in these 25 acres in the late 1800s, even then the neighborhood was half Japanese. Today, you hear Vietnamese and Tagalog as often as Mandarin and Cantonese, and there are touches of Japan, Singapore, Malaysia, Korea, Thailand, Samoa, and the Marshall Islands.

Perhaps a more accurate name is the one used by early Chinese: Wah Fau, "Chinese port," signifying a landing and jumping-off place. Chinese laborers, as soon as they completed their plantation contracts, hurried into the city to start businesses here. It's a launching point for today's immigrants, too: Southeast Asian shops almost outnumber Chinese; stalls carry Filipino specialities like winged beans and goat meat; and in one tiny space, knife-wielding Samoans skin coconuts to order.

TIMING Chinatown is immediately north of downtown Honolulu—it's flat, compact, and easily explored in half a day. ■ TIP➔ **The best time to visit Chinatown is morning, when the *popos* (grandmas) shop–it's cool, and you can enjoy a cheap dim sum breakfast.** Chinatown is a seven-day-a-week oper-

SHOPS

You'll find ridiculously inexpensive gifts throughout Chinatown: folding fans for $1 and coconut purses for $5 at **Maunakea Marketplace,** for example. Curio shops sell porcelain statues and woks, ginseng and Mao shoes. If you sew, or have a yen for a brocade *cheong sam*, visit **Imperial Tailors and Gifts and 1010 Fabrics** (North King Street and Maunakea). Narrow, dim and dusty **Bo Wah Trading Co.** (1037 Maunakea), is full of inexpensive cooking utensils. **Chinatown Cultural Plaza** offers fine-quality jade.

Chinatown is Honolulu's lei center, with shops strung along Beretania and Maunakea. In spring, look for gardenia nosegays wrapped in ti leaves.

ation. Sundays are especially busy with families sharing dim sum in rau-
cous dining hall–size restaurants.

A caution: Hotel Street was Honolulu's red-light district and A'ala Park,
just across the Nu'uanu stream, shelters many homeless people and
more than a few drug users. A police station in the heart of the district
has tamped down crime, and the area is perfectly safe by day—even pan-
handling is rare. But at night, park in a well-lighted place, travel with
the crowds, and be alert. ■ TIP→ Look for well-marked municipal parking
lots on Smith, Bethel, Nu'uanu, and Beretania; these charge a third of what
the private lots demand.

Weekly tours of Chinatown are offered on Tuesday by the Chinese
Chamber of Commerce (⇨ See O'ahu Sightseeing Tours). If you're here
between January 20 and February 20, check local newspapers or go-
hawaii.com for Chinese New Year activities.

⑤ Chinatown Cultural Plaza. This sprawling multistory shopping square surrounds a courtyard with an incense-wreathed shrine and Moongate stage
for holiday performances. The Chee Kung Tong Society has a beautifully
decorated meeting hall here; a number of such *tongs* (meeting places) are
hidden on upper floors in Chinatown. ⊠ *100 N. Beretania, Chinatown.*

⑥ Izumo Taisha Shrine. From Chinatown Cultural Plaza, cross a stone
bridge to visit Okuninushi No Mikoto, a *kami* (god) who is believed in
Shinto tradition to bring good fortune if properly courted (and thanked
afterward). ⊠ *N. Kukui and Canal, Chinatown* 🕾 *No phone.*

Kuan Yin Temple. A couple of blocks *mauka* (toward the mountains) from
Chinatown is the oldest Buddhist temple in the Islands. Mistakenly
called a goddess by man, Kuan Yin, also known as Kannon, is a bod-
dhisatva—one who chose to remain on earth doing good even after achieving enlightenment. Transformed from a male into a female figure
centuries ago, she is credited with a particular sympathy for women.
You will see representations of her all over the Islands: with a lotus flower
(beauty from the mud of human frailty) as at the temple; pouring out
a pitcher of oil (like mercy flowing); or as a sort of Madonna with a
child. Visitors are permitted but be aware this is a practicing place of
worship. ⊠ *170 N. Vineyard, Downtown* 🕾 *808/533–6371.*

⑦ Maunakea Marketplace. On the corner of Maunakea and Hotel streets
is this plaza surrounded by shops, an indoor market and a food court.
Within the Marketplace, the **Hawaiian Chinese Cultural Museum and
Archives** (🖅 $2 ☉ Mon.–Sat. 10–2) displays historic photographs and
artifacts. ■ TIP→ If you appreciate fine tea, visit the Tea Hut, an unpretentious counter inside a curio shop. ⊠ *1120 Maunakea St., Chinatown*
🕾 *808/524–3409.*

⑨ Nu'uanu Avenue. Nu'uanu Avenue forms Chinatown's southern border.
There and on Bethel Street are clustered art galleries, restaurants, a
wineshop, an antiques auctioneer, a dress shop or two, one tiny theater
space (The Arts at Mark's Garage), and one historic stage (the Hawai'i
Theatre). **First Friday** art nights, when galleries stay open in the evening,
draw crowds. ⊠ *Nu'uanu Ave., Chinatown.*

Downtown Honolulu & Chinatown

Kuan Yin Temple

◆ Foster Botanical Gardens

PUNCH-BOWL CRATER

CHINATOWN

The Bus & police vehicles only

Tamarind Park ◆

Honolulu Harbor

Sand Island

Kewalo Basin

0 — 550 yards
0 — 500 meters

Street labels: 'A'ala St., Maunakea, Nu'uanu, Kukui St., Vineyard Blvd., Lunalilo Hwy., 'Iolani Ave., Pali Hwy., N. Beretania, River St., Pauahi, Kekaulike, Maunakea, Smith, King St., N. Hotel St., Bethel St., Fort St. (pedestrians only), Nu'uanu, Bishop St., S. Hotel St., Alakea, Queen Emma, Miller St., Punchbowl St., S. Beretania St., Merchant St., Richards St., Mililani, S. King St., Kapi'olani Blvd., Fort St., Queen St., Punchbowl St., South St., Ala Moana Blvd., Pohukaina, Keawe, Keaubou, Cooke, Kawaiaha'o, Queen St., Waimanu, Iliniwai, Auahi St., Coral, Cooke, 'Ohe, Halekauwila, Kamani, Ward Ave., Auahi St., 'Āhui

★ **❽ O'ahu Marketplace.** Here is a taste of old-style Chinatown, where you're likely to be hustled aside as a whole pig (dead, of course) is wrestled through the crowd and where glassy-eyed fish of every size and hue lie stacked forlornly on ice. Try the bubble tea (juices and flavored teas with tapioca bubbles inside) or pick up a bizarre magenta dragonfruit for breakfast. ⊠ *N. King St., at Kekaulike, Chinatown.*

Downtown Honolulu

Honolulu's past and present play a delightful counterpoint throughout the downtown sector. Postmodern glass-and-steel office buildings look down on the Aloha Tower, built in 1926 and, until the early 1960s, the tallest structure in Honolulu. Hawai'i's history is told in the architecture of these few blocks: the cut-stone turn-of-the-20th-century storefronts of Merchant Street, the gracious white-columned American-Georgian manor that was the home of the Islands' last queen, the jewel-box palace occupied by the monarchy before it was overthrown, the Spanish-inspired stucco and tile-roofed Territorial-era government buildings, and the 21st-century glass pyramid of the First Hawaiian Bank Building.

> ### WHERE DO I PARK?
>
> The best parking downtown is street parking along Punchbowl Street—when you can find it. There are also public parking lots (75¢ per half hour for the first two hours) in buildings along Alakea, Smith, Beretania, and Bethel streets (Gateway Plaza on Bethel Street is a good choice).

TIMING Plan a couple of hours for exploring downtown's historic buildings, more if you're taking a guided tour or walk. The best time to visit is in the cool and relative quiet of the morning or on weekends when downtown is all but deserted except for the historic sites. To reach Downtown Honolulu from Waikīkī by car, take Ala Moana Boulevard to Alakea Street and turn right; three blocks up on the right, between South King and Hotel, there's a municipal parking lot in Ali'i Place on the right. You can also take Route 19 or 20 of TheBus to the Aloha Tower Marketplace or take a trolley from Waikīkī.

Main Attractions

❿ **'Iolani Palace.** America's only royal residence was built in 1882 on the FodorśChoice site of an earlier palace, and it contains the thrones of King Kalākaua ★ and his successor (and sister) Queen Lili'uokalani. Bucking the stereotype of the primitive islander, the palace had electricity and telephone lines installed even before the White House did. Downstairs galleries showcase the royal jewelry, and kitchen and offices of the monarchy. The palace is open for guided tours only, and reservations are essential. ■ TIP→ **If you're set on taking a tour, it might be worthwhile to call for reservations a few weeks in advance.** Take a look at the gift shop, formerly the 'Iolani Barracks, built to house the Royal Guard. ⊠ *King and Richards Sts., Downtown Honolulu* ☎ *808/522–0832* ⊕ *www. iolanipalace.org* 🎫 *Grand Tour $20, downstairs galleries only $6* ☉ *Grand Tour Tues.–Sat. 9–2, with tours beginning on ½ hr; galleries tour, Tues.–Sat. 9–4.*

①① **Kamehameha I Statue.** This downtown landmark pays tribute to the Big Island chieftain who united all the warring Hawaiian Islands into one kingdom at the turn of the 18th century. The statue, which stands with one arm outstretched in welcome, is one of three originally cast in Paris, France, by American sculptor T. R. Gould; the original—which was lost at sea for a time and had to be replaced by this one—was salvaged and now is in Kapa'au, on the Big Island, near the king's birthplace. Each year on the king's birthday, June 11, the statue is draped in fresh lei that reach lengths of 18 feet and longer. There's a parade that processes past the statue, and Hawaiian civic clubs, the women in hats and impressive long *holokū* dresses and the men in sashes and cummerbunds, pay honor to the leader whose name means "The Lonely One." ⊠ *417 S. King St., outside Ali'iōlani Hale, Downtown Honolulu.*

①② **Kawaiaha'o Church.** Fancifully called Hawai'i's Westminster Abbey, this 14,000-coral-block house of worship witnessed the coronations, weddings, and funerals of generations of Hawaiian royalty. Each of the building's coral blocks was quarried from reefs offshore at depths of more than 20 feet and transported to this site. Interior woodwork was created from the forests of the Ko'olau Mountains. The upper gallery has an exhibit of paintings of the royal families. The graves of missionaries and of King Lunalilo are adjacent. Services in English and Hawaiian are held each Sunday, and the church members are exceptionally welcoming, greeting newcomers with lei; their affiliation is United Church of Christ. Although there are no guided tours, you can look around the church at no cost. ⊠ *957 Punchbowl St., at King St., Downtown Honolulu* ☎ *808/522–1333* 🎫 *Free* ☉ *English service Sun. at 8 AM and Wed. at 6 PM, Hawaiian service Sun. at 10:30 AM.*

> ### A HAWAIIAN SERVICE
>
> Native Hawaiians who adopted Christianity brought with them a keen appreciation of protocol and a love of the poetic turn of phrase. Sunday worship at Kawaiaha'o Church affirms this with its greeters in white holokū, lei for visitors, and blessings and songs given in Hawaiian. In this cradle of Protestant Christianity in the Islands, a prerequisite for the pastor is fluency in both languages. Don't worry; sermons are in English.

Also Worth Seeing

☺ ①④ **Aloha Tower Marketplace.** Two stories of shops and kiosks sell island-inspired clothing, jewelry, art, and home furnishings. The Marketplace, also has restaurants, and live entertainment. For a bird's-eye view of this working harbor, take a free ride up to the observation deck of Aloha Tower. Cruise ships dock at Piers 9 and 10 alongside the Marketplace and are often greeted and sent out to sea with music and hula dancing at the piers' end. ⊠ *1 Aloha Tower Dr., at Piers 8, 9, and 10, Downtown Honolulu* ☎ *808/528–5700, 808/566–2337 for entertainment info* ⊕ *www.alohatower.com* ☉ *Mon.–Sat. 9–9, Sun. 9–6.*

☺ ①③ **Hawai'i Maritime Center.** The story of the Islands begins on the seas. The **Kalākaua Boat House** has interactive exhibits where you can learn about Hawai'i's whaling days, the history of Honolulu Harbor, the

Clipper seaplane, and surfing and windsurfing in Hawai'i. Moored next to the Boat House is the *Falls of Clyde.* Built in 1778, this four-masted, square-rigged ship once brought tea from China to the U.S. West Coast and is now used as a museum. Self-guided audio tours are available in English, Japanese, and Korean. When it's not sailing, the voyaging canoe *Hokule'a* is docked at the end of the pier. The building of this vessel, which helped spark the Hawaiian cultural renaissance, proved that Hawaiians were masters of craftmanship and navigation. It has made numerous traditional-style voyages between islands and even to the Marquesas and Rapa Nui (Easter Island). ⊠ *Ala Moana Blvd. at Pier 7, Downtown Honolulu* ☎ *808/536–6373* ⊕ *www. bishopmuseum.org/exhibits/hmc/hmc.html* ⊡ *$7.50* ☉ *Daily 8:30–5.*

⑮ Hawai'i State Art Museum. Hawai'i was one of the first states in the nation to legislate that a portion of the taxes paid on commercial building projects be set aside for the purchase of artwork. A few years ago, the state purchased an ornate period-style building (built to house the headquarters of a prominent developer) and dedicated 12,000 feet on the second floor to the art of Hawai'i in all its ethnic diversity. The **Diamond Head Gallery** features new acquisitions and thematic shows from the State Art Collection and the State Foundation on Culture and the Arts. The **'Ewa Gallery** houses more than 150 works documenting Hawai'i's visual-arts history since becoming a state in 1959. Also included are a sculpture gallery as well as a café, a gift shop, and educational meeting rooms. ⊠ *250 S. Hotel St., 2nd fl., Downtown Honolulu* ☎ *808/586–0300* ⊕ *www.hawaii.gov/sfca* ⊡ *Free* ☉ *Tues.–Sat. 10–4.*

⑯ Hawai'i State Capitol. The capitol's architecture is richly symbolic: the columns resemble palm trees, the legislative chambers are shaped like volcanic cinder cones, and the central court is open to the sky, representing Hawai'i's open society. Replicas of the Hawai'i state seal, each weighing 7,500 pounds, hang above both its entrances. The building, which in 1969 replaced 'Iolani Palace as the seat of government, is surrounded by reflecting pools, just as the Islands are embraced by water. A pair of statues, often draped in lei, flank the building: one of the beloved queen Lili'uokalani and the other of the sainted Fr. Damien de Veuster. ⊠ *215 S. Beretania St., Downtown Honolulu* ☎ *808/586–0146* ⊡ *Free* ☉ *Guided tours on request weekday afternoons.*

⑱ Honolulu Academy of Arts. Originally built around the collection of a Honolulu matron who donated much of her estate to the museum, the academy and is housed in a maze of courtyards, cloistered walkways, and quiet low-ceilinged spaces. The Academy has an impressive permanent collection that includes Hiroshige's *ukiyo-e* Japanese prints, donated by James Michener; Italian Renaissance paintings; and American and European art. The newer Luce Pavilion complex, nicely incorporated into the more traditional architecture of the place, has a traveling-exhibit gallery, a Hawaiian gallery, an excellent café, and a gift shop. The Academy Theatre screens art films. This is also the jumping-off place for tours of Doris Duke's estate, Shangri-La (⇨ Shangri La CloseUp). Call about special exhibits, concerts, and films. ⊠ *900 S. Beretania St., Downtown*

Honolulu ☎ 808/532–8700 ⊕ www.honoluluacademy.org ✉ $7 Academy, free 1st Wed. of month ☉ Tues.–Sat. 10–4:30, Sun. 1–5.

⑰ Mission Houses Museum. The determined Hawaiʻi missionaries arrived in 1820, gaining royal favor and influencing every aspect of island life. Their descendants became leaders in government and business. You can walk through their original dwellings, including a white-frame house that was prefabricated in New England and shipped around the Horn— it's Hawaiʻi's oldest wooden structure. Certain areas of the museum may be seen only on a one-hour guided tour. Costumed docents give an excellent picture of what mission life was like. Rotating displays showcase such arts as Hawaiian quilting. ⊠ *553 S. King St., Downtown Honolulu ☎ 808/531–0481 ⊕ www.lava.net/~mhm ✉ $10 ☉ Tues.–Sat. 10–6; guided tours at 11, 1, 2:45, and 4:30.*

Around Honolulu

Downtown Honolulu and Chinatown can easily swallow up a day's walking, sightseeing, and shopping. Surrounding the city's core are another day's worth of attractions. One reason to venture farther afield is the chance to glimpse Honolulu neighborhoods. Note the several species of classic Hawaiʻi homes including the tiny green-and-white plantation-era house with its corrugated tin roof, two windows flanking a central door and small porch; and the breezy bungalow with its swooping Thai-style roofline and two wings flanking screened French doors through which breezes blow into the living room. Note the tangled "Grandma-style" gardens and many *ohana* houses—small homes in the backyard or perched over the garage, allowing extended families to live together. Carports, which rarely house cars, are the island version of rec rooms, where parties are held and neighbors sit to "talk story." Sometimes you'll see gallon jars on the flat roofs of garages or carports: these are pickled lemons fermenting in the sun. Also in the neighborhoods, you'll find the folksy restaurants and takeout spots favored by Islanders.

■ TIP→ **If you have a Costco card, you'll find the cheapest gas on the island at the Costco station on Arakawa Street between Dillingham Boulevard and Nimitz Highway. Gas gets more expensive the farther you are from town.**

⑲ Bishop Museum. Founded in 1889 by Charles R. Bishop as a memorial to his wife, Princess Bernice Pauahi Bishop, the museum began as a repository for the royal possessions of this last direct descendant of King Kamehameha the Great. Today it's

---

WHAT DOES IT MEAN?

T-shirts and bumper stickers common in Oʻahu may stump you. Here's a guide:

■ Eddie Would Go: Inspirational reference to big-wave surfer Eddie Aikau, who lost his life attempting to save those aboard a swamped voyaging canoe.

■ Walaʻau: Gossip. The name of a popular Kauaʻi radio show.

■ Kau Inoa: Put or place your name. Urges Hawaiians to sign up to help organize a Native Hawaiian governing entity.

■ If can, can; if no can, no can: Pidgin for "whatever."

■ Got koko?: Got blood, meaning, are you Hawaiian?

the Hawai'i State Museum of Natural and Cultural History and houses more than 24.7 million items that tell the history of the Hawaiian Islands and their Pacific neighbors. The latest addition to the complex is a natural-science wing with state-of-the-art interactive exhibits. Venerable but sadly aging Hawaiian Hall, which is slated for a multimillion-dollar renovation, houses Polynesian artifacts: lustrous feather capes, the skeleton of a giant sperm whale, photography and crafts displays, and an authentic, well-preserved grass house inside a two-story 19th-century Victorian-style gallery. Also check out the planetarium, daily hula and Hawaiian crafts demonstrations, special exhibits, and the Shop Pacifica. The building alone, with its huge Victorian turrets and immense stone walls, is worth seeing. ⊠ *1525 Bernice St., Kalihi* ☎ *808/847-3511* ⊕ *www.bishopmuseum.org* ⊠ *$14.95* ☉ *Daily 9–5.*

㉓ Kaimukī. This is one of the few real pedestrian neighborhoods on O'ahu, with several blocks of intriguing stores and restaurants plus the quirky Movie Museum (a 17-seat theater equipped with easy chairs and playing only vintage and art films). A couple of shops offer original, handmade fashion designs: Double Paws Wear and Montsuki. Harry's Music is an exceptional source of vintage Hawaiian recordings, sheet music, songs books, and instruments. During the holidays, Kaimukī hosts some great weekend craft fairs. Park on the street or in lots behind Wai'lae shops between 11th and 12th or 12th and Kokohead. ⊠ *West of Diamond Head.*

㉒ Mō'ili'ili. Don't be befuddled by the name with all its diacritical marks, just enjoy the flower and lei shops (especially Le Fleur), restaurants (Spices, Fukuya Delicatessen), and little stores such as Kuni Island Fabrics, a great source for Hawaiian quilting and other crafting materials; Siam Imports for goodies from Thailand; and Revolution Books, Honolulu's only leftist book shop. ⊠ *South King Street between Hausten and Wai'alae Ave.*

| Pearl Harbor | See Page 45 |

㉓ National Memorial Cemetery of the Pacific (in Punchbowl Crater). Nestled in the bowl of Puowaina, or Punchbowl Crater, this 112-acre cemetery is the final resting place for more than 44,000 U.S. war veterans and family members. Among those buried here is Ernie Pyle, the famed World War II correspondent who was killed by a Japanese sniper off the northern coast of Okinawa. Puowaina, formed 75,000–100,000 years ago during a period of secondary volcanic activity, translates to "Hill of Sacrifice." Historians believe this site once served as an altar where ancient Hawaiians offered sacrifices to their gods. ■ TIP→ **The cemetery has unfettered views of Waikīkī and Honolulu—perhaps the finest on O'ahu.** ⊠ *2177 Puowaina Dr., Nu'uanu* ☎ *808/532-3720* ⊕ *www.cem.*

Continued on page 51

USS *West Virginia* (BB48), 7 December 1941

PEARL HARBOR

December 7, 1941. Every American then alive recalls exactly what he or she was doing when the news broke that the Japanese had bombed Pearl Harbor, the catalyst that brought the United States into World War II.

Although it was clear by late 1941 that war with Japan was inevitable, no one in authority seems to have expected the attack to come in just this way, at just this time. So when the Japanese bombers swept through a gap in Oʻahu's Koʻolau Mountains in the hazy light of morning, they found the bulk of America's Pacific fleet right where they hoped it would be: docked like giant stepping stones across the calm waters of the bay named for the pearl oysters that once prospered there. More than 2,000 people died that day, including 49 civilians. A dozen ships were sunk. And on the nearby air bases, virtually every American military aircraft was destroyed or damaged. The attack was a stunning success, but it lit a fire under America, which went to war with "Remember Pearl Harbor" as its battle cry. Here, in what is still a key Pacific naval base, the attack is remembered every day by thousands of visitors, including many curious Japanese, who for years heard little World War II history in their own country. In recent years, the memorial has been the site of reconciliation ceremonies involving Pearl Harbor veterans from both sides.

GETTING AROUND

Pearl Harbor is both a working military base and the most-visited O'ahu attraction. Three distinct destinations share a parking lot and are linked by footpath, shuttle, and ferry.

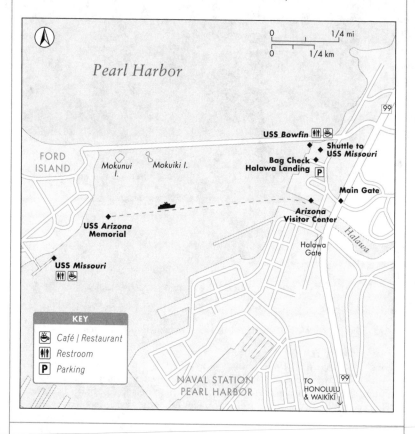

The USS *Arizona* visitor center is accessible from the parking lot. The *Arizona* Memorial itself is in the middle of the harbor; get tickets for the ferry ride at the visitor center. The USS *Bowfin* is also reachable from the parking lot. The USS *Missouri* is docked at Ford Island, a restricted area of the naval base. Vehicular access is prohibited. To get there, take a shuttle bus from the station near the *Bowfin*.

ARIZONA MEMORIAL

Snugged up tight in a row of seven battleships off Ford Island, the USS *Arizona* took a direct hit that December morning, exploded, and rests still on the shallow bottom where she settled.

A visit to the *Arizona* Memorial begins prosaically—a line, a ticket that assigns you to a group and tour time, a wait filled with shopping, visiting the museum, and strolling the grounds. When your number is called, you watch a 23-minute documentary film then board the ferry to the memorial. The swooping, stark-white memorial, which straddles the wreck of the USS *Arizona,* was designed by Honolulu architect Alfred Preis to represent both the depths of the low-spirited, early days of the war, and the uplift of victory. After the carnival-like courtyard, a somber, contemplative mood descends upon visitors during the ferry ride; this is a place where 1,777 people died. Gaze at the names of the dead carved into the wall of white marble. Scatter flowers (but no lei—the string is bad for the fish). Salute the flag. Remember Pearl Harbor.

808/422–0561
www.nps.gov/usar

USS *MISSOURI* (BB63)

Together with the *Arizona* Memorial, the *Missouri's* presence in Pearl Harbor perfectly bookends America's WWII experience that began December 7, 1941, and ended on the "Mighty Mo's" starboard deck with the signing of the Terms of Surrender.

Surrender of Japan, USS *Missouri*, 2 September 1945

In the parking area behind the USS *Bowfin* Museum, board a jitney for a breezy, eight-minute ride to Ford Island and the teak decks and towering superstructure of the *Missouri,* docked for good in the very harbor from which she first went to war on January 2, 1945. The last battleship ever built, the *Missouri* famously hosted the final act of WWII, the signing of the Terms of Surrender. The commission that governs this floating museum has surrounded her with buildings tricked out in WWII style—a canteen that serves as an orientation space for tours, a WACs and WAVEs lounge with a flight simulator the kids will love ($5 for one person, $18 for four), Truman's Line restaurant serving Navy-style meals, and a Victory Store housing a souvenir shop and covered with period mottos ("Don't be a blabateur").

■ TIP→ Definitely hook up with a tour guide (additional charge) or purchase an audio tour ($2)—these add a great deal to the experience.

The *Missouri* is all about numbers: 209 feet tall, six 239,000-pound guns, capable of firing up to 23 mi away. Absorb these during the tour, then stop to take advantage of the view from the decks. The Mo is a work in progress, with only a handful of her hundreds of spaces open to view.

808/423–2263 or 888/877–6477
www.ussmissouri.com

USS *BOWFIN* (SS287)

SUBMARINE MUSEUM & PARK

Launched one year to the day after the Pearl Harbor attack, the USS *Bowfin* sank 44 enemy ships during WWII and now serves as the centerpiece of a museum honoring all submariners.

Although the *Bowfin* no less than the *Arizona* Memorial commemorates the lost, the mood here is lighter. Perhaps it's the childlike scale of the boat, a metal tube just 16 feet in diameter, packed with ladders, hatches, and other obstacles, like the naval version of a jungle gym. Perhaps it's the World War II-era music that plays in the covered patio. Or it might be the museum's touching displays—the penciled sailor's journal, the Vargas girlie posters. Aboard the boat nicknamed Pearl Harbor Avenger, compartments are fitted out as though "Sparky" was away from the radio room just for a moment, and "Cooky" might be right back to his pots and pans. The museum includes many artifacts to spark family conversations, among them a vintage dive suit that looks too big for

Shaquille O'Neal. A caution: The *Bowfin* could be hazardous for very young children; no one under four allowed.

808/423–1341
www.bowfin.org

CALL FOR ACTION

Pearl Harbor attractions operate with the aid of nonprofit organizations; the *Missouri* and *Bowfin* receive no government funds at all. A $34 million campaign has begun to rebuild the inadequate and aging *Arizona* Memorial visitor center and create a series of mini-museums that do justice to the events that took place at Pearl Harbor. If fund-raising goes as planned, the center likely will close in 2007 during renovations.

Want to help?

Arizona Memorial
www.pearlharbormemorial.com, raising funds for a new visitor center

USS *Missouri* Memorial Association
www.ussmissouri.com, membership program supports ongoing restoration

Bowfin
www.bowfin.org; no online giving, send check to USS *Bowfin*, 11 Arizona Memorial Dr., Honolulu, HI 96818

PLAN YOUR PEARL HARBOR DAY LIKE A MILITARY CAMPAIGN

DIRECTIONS

Take H–1 west from Waikīkī to Exit 15A and follow signs. Or take TheBus route 20 or 47 from Waikīkī. Beware high-priced private shuttles. It's a 30-minute drive from Waikīkī.

WHAT TO BRING

Picture ID is required during periods of high alert; bring it just in case.

You'll be standing, walking, and climbing all day. Wear something with lots of pockets and a pair of good walking shoes. Carry a light jacket, sunglasses, hat, and sunscreen.

No purses, packs, or bags are allowed. Take only what fits in your pockets. Cameras are okay but without bulky bags. A private bag storage booth is near the *Arizona* Memorial parking lot. Leave nothing in your car; theft is a problem despite bicycle security patrols.

HOURS

Hours are 8 AM to 5 PM for all attractions. However, the *Arizona* Memorial starts giving out tickets on a first-come, first-served basis at 7:30 AM; the last tickets are given out at 3 PM. Spring break, summer, and holidays are busiest, and tickets sometimes run out.

TICKETS

Arizona: Free. Add $5 for museum audio tours.

Missouri: $16 adults, $8 children. Add $6 for chief's guided tour or audio tour; add $33 for in-depth, behind-the-scenes tours.

Bowfin: $10 adults, $3 children. Add $2 for audio tours. Children under 4 may go into the museum but not aboard the *Bowfin*.

KIDS

This might be the day to enroll younger kids in the hotel children's program. Preschoolers chafe at long waits, and attractions involve some hazards for toddlers. Older kids enjoy the *Bowfin* and *Missouri*, especially.

MAKING THE MOST OF YOUR TIME

Expect to spend three hours minimum—that's if you hustle and skip audio tours. The better part of a day is better.

At the *Arizona* Memorial, you'll get a ticket, be given a tour time, and then have to wait — anywhere from 15 minutes to 3 hours. Everyone has to pick up their own ticket so you can't hold places. If you've got an hour or more, skip over to the *Bowfin* to fill the time.

SUGGESTED READING

Pearl Harbor and the USS Arizona Memorial, by Richard Wisniewski. $5.95. 64-page magazine-size quick history.

Bowfin, by Edwin P. Hoyt. $14.95. Dramatic story of undersea adventure.

The Last Battleship, by Scott C. S. Stone. $11.95. Story of the Mighty Mo.

va.gov/nchp/nmcp.htm 🎟 *Free* ☉ *Mar.–Sept. daily 8–6:30, Oct.–Feb. daily 8–5:30.*

★ ㉑ **Queen Emma Summer Palace.** Queen Emma and her family used this stately white home, built in 1848, as a retreat from the rigors of court life in hot and dusty Honolulu during the mid-1800s. It has an eclectic mix of European, Victorian, and Hawaiian furnishings and has excellent examples of Hawaiian quilts and koa-wood furniture as well as the queen's wedding dress and other memorabilia. ⊠ *2913 Pali Hwy.* 🕾 *808/595–3167* ⊕ *www.daughtersofhawaii.org* 🎟 *$5* ☉ *Self-guided or guided tours daily 9–4.*

Southeast Oʻahu

Driving southeast from Waikīkī on busy four-lane Kalanianaʻole Highway, you'll pass a dozen bedroom communities tucked into the valleys at the foot of the Koʻolau Range, with just fleeting glimpses of the ocean from a couple of pocket parks. Suddenly, civilization falls away, the road narrows to two lanes, and you enter the rugged coastline of Kokohead and Ka Iwi.

This is a cruel coastline: dry, windswept, and rocky shores, with untamed waves that are notoriously treacherous. While walking its beaches, do not turn your back on the ocean, don't venture close to wet areas where high waves occasionally reach, and heed warning signs.

At this point, you're passing through Koko Head Regional Park. On your right is the bulging remnant of a pair of volcanic craters that the Hawaiians called Kawaihoa, known today as Kokohead. To the left is Koko Crater and the area of the park that includes a a hiking trail, a dryland botanical garden, a firing range, and a riding stable. Ahead is a sinuous shoreline with scenic pull-outs and beaches to explore. Named the Ka Iwi Coast (*iwi*, "ee-vee," are bones—sacred to Hawaiians and full of symbolism) for the channel just offshore, this area was once home to a ranch and small fishing enclave that were destroyed by a tidal wave in the 1940s.

TIMING Driving straight from Waikīkī to Makapuʻu Point takes from a half to a full hour, depending on traffic. There aren't a huge number of sights per se in this corner of Oʻahu, so a couple of hours should be plenty of exploring time, unless you really stop and spend time at a particular point.

What to See

❷❻ **Hālona Blowhole.** Below a scenic turnout along the Koko Head shoreline, this oft-photographed lava tube sucks the ocean in and spits it out. Don't get too close, as conditions can get dangerous. ■ **TIP→ Look to your right to see the tiny beach below that was used to film the wave-washed love scene in From Here to Eternity.** In winter this is a good spot to watch whales at play. Offshore, the islands of Molokaʻi and Lānaʻi call like distant sirens, and every once in a while Maui is visible in blue silhouette. Take your valuables with you and lock your car, because this scenic location is a hot spot for petty thieves. ⊠ *Kalanianaʻole Hwy., 1 mi east of Hanauma Bay.*

Shangri La

HEIRESS DORIS DUKE'S MARRIAGE AT AGE 23 to a man much older than herself didn't last. But their around-the-world honeymoon tour did leave the "Poor Little Rich Girl" with two lasting loves: Islamic art and architecture, which she first encountered on that journey; and Hawai'i, where the honeymooners made an extended stay while Doris learned to surf and made friends with Islanders who were unimpressed by her wealth.

Now visitors to her beloved Islands—where she spent most winters—can share both loves by touring her home. The sought-after tours, which are coordinated by and begin at the downtown Honolulu Academy of Arts, start with a visit to the Arts of the Islamic World Gallery. A short van ride then takes small groups on to the house itself, just on the far side of Diamond Head.

In 1936 Duke bought 5 acres at Black Point, down the coast from Waikīkī, and began to build and furnish the first home that would be all her own. She called it Shangri La. For more than 50 years, the home was a work always in progress as Duke traveled the world, buying furnishings and artifacts, picking up ideas for her Mughul garden, for the Playhouse in the style of an Irani pavilion, and for the water terraces and tropical gardens. When she died in 1993, Duke left instructions that her home was to become a center for the study of Islamic art, open to the public for tours.

To walk through the house and its gardens—which have remained much as Duke left them with only some minor conservation-oriented changes—is to experience the personal style of someone who saw everything as raw material for her art.

With her trusted houseman, Jin de Silva, she literally built the elaborate Turkish (or Damascus) Room, trimming tiles and painted panels to fit the walls and building a fountain of her own design.

One aspect of the home that clearly takes its inspiration from the Muslim tradition is the entry: an anonymous gate, a blank white wall, and a wooden door which bids you "Enter herein in peace and security" in Arabic characters. Inside, tiles glow, fountains tinkle, shafts of light illuminate artworks through arches and high windows. This was her private world, entered only by trusted friends.

Tickets are $25; children under 12 are not admitted. Tours are available Wednesday through Saturday by reservation only. First tour is 8:30 AM, last tour 1:30 PM; tours take 2½ hours. All tours begin at the Academy of Arts, 900 S. Beretania. To arrange for tickets, go to www.honoluluacademy. org or call 808/532-3853.

★ ☾ ㉕ **Hanauma Bay Nature Preserve.** The exterior wall of a volcanic crater collapsed, opening it to the sea and thereby giving birth to O'ahu's most famous snorkeling destination. Even from the overlook, the horseshoe-shape bay is a beauty, and you can easily see the reefs through the clear aqua waters. The wide beach is a great place for sunbathing and picnics. This is a marine conservation district, and regulations prohibit feeding the fish. Visitors are required to go through the Education Center before trekking down to the bay. The center provides a cultural history of the area and exhibits about the importance of protecting its marine life. Check out the "Today at the Bay" exhibit for up-to-date information on daily tides, ocean safety warnings, and activities. Food concessions and equipment rentals are also onsite. ■ TIP→ **Come early to get parking, as the number of visitors allowed per day is limited.** Also note that the bay is best in the early hours before the waters are churned up. Call for current conditions. Weather permitting, Hanauma Bay by Starlight events are held on the second Saturday of every month, extending the opening hours to 10 PM. ⊠ *7455 Kalaniana'ole Hwy.* ☎ *808/396–4229* ☞ *Donation $5; parking $1; mask, snorkel, and fins rental $8; tram from parking lot to beach $1.50 round-trip* ☉ *Wed.–Mon. 6–6.*

㉗ **Makapu'u Point.** This spot has breathtaking views of the ocean, mountains, and the windward islands. The point of land jutting out in the distance is **Mōkapu Peninsula,** site of a U.S. Marine base. The spired mountain peak is **Mt. Olomana.** In front of you on the long pier is part of the **Makai Undersea Test Range,** a research facility that's closed to the public. Offshore is **Manana Island (Rabbit Island),** a picturesque cay said to resemble a swimming bunny with its ears pulled back. Ironically enough, Manana Island was once overrun with rabbits, thanks to a rancher who let a few hares run wild on the land. They were eradicated in 1994 by biologists who grew concerned that the rabbits were destroying the island's native plants.

Nestled in the cliff face is the **Makapu'u Lighthouse,** which became operational in 1909 and has the largest lighthouse lens in America. The lighthouse is closed to the public, but near the Makapu'u Point turnout you can find the start of a mile-long paved road (closed to traffic). Hike up to the top of the 647-foot bluff for a closer view of the lighthouse and, in winter, a great whale-watching vantage point. ⊠ *Kalaniana'ole Hwy., turnout above Makapu'u Beach.*

㉔ **Paikō Peninsula.** This slim spit is reached by a narrow residential road that dead-ends at the Paikō Lagoon State Reserve, which is off-limits to the public. However, in Hawai'i, all beaches are public to the highwater line, and there's a beach access pathway just a few houses before the road's end. Turn left when you get to the beach and find your spot near where the houses end. Secluded within the confines of the bay, private and quiet, this is a lovely place to spend a morning or afternoon swimming, snorkeling, reading, and dozing. ⊠ *Kalaniana'ole Hwy., just past Niu Valley, on the right, on Paikō Dr.*

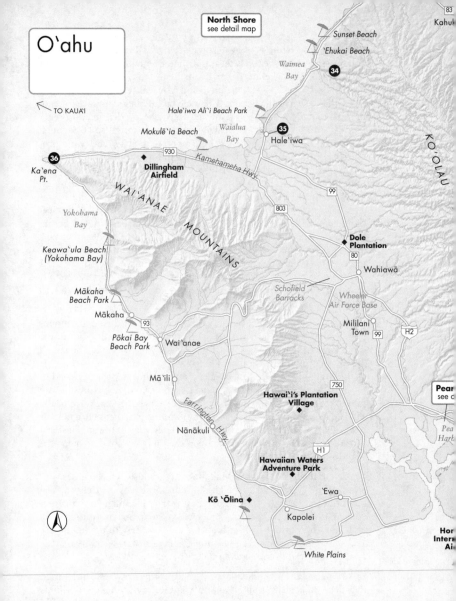

O'ahu

TO KAUA'I

North Shore
see detail map

Sunset Beach

'Ehukai Beach

Waimea
Bay

34

Hale'iwa Ali'i Beach Park

Waialua
Bay

35

Hale'iwa

Mokulē'ia Beach

930

Kamehameha Hwy.

36

Ka'ena
Pt.

**Dillingham
Airfield**

99

Yokohama
Bay

803

Keawa'ula Beach
(Yokohama Bay)

**Dole
Plantation**

80

Wahiawā

W A I 'A N A E

M O U N T A I N S

KO'OLAU

Kahuku

83

Mākaha
Beach Park

Schofield
Barracks

Wheeler
Air Force Base

Mililani
Town

99 **H2**

Mākaha

93

Pōkai Bay
Beach Park

Wai'anae

Mā'ili

750

**Hawai'i's Plantation
Village**

Pearl
see d

Farrington Hwy.

Pea
Harb

Nānākuli

H1

**Hawaiian Waters
Adventure Park**

Kō 'Ōlina

'Ewa

Kapolei

Hon
Inter
Ai

White Plains

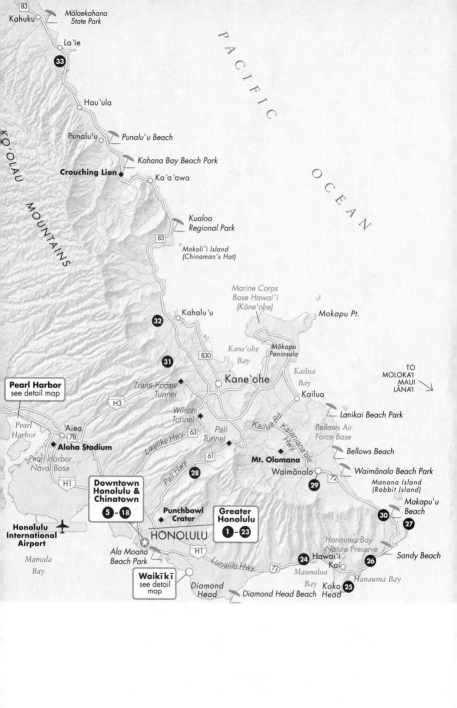

Windward O'ahu

To look at Honolulu's topsy-turvy urban sprawl, you would never suspect the Windward side existed. It's a secret Oahuans like to keep, so they can watch the look of awe on the faces of their guests when the car emerges from the tunnels through the mountains and they gaze for the first time on the panorama of turquoise bays and emerald valleys watched over by the knife-edged Ko'olau ridges. Jaws literally drop. Every time. And this just a 15-minute drive from downtown.

It is on this side of the island that many Native Hawaiians live. Evidence of traditional lifestyles is abundant in crumbling fish ponds, rock platforms that once were altars, taro patches still being worked, and throw-net fishermen posed stock-still above the water (though today, they're invariably wearing polarized sunglasses, the better to spot the fish).

Here, the pace is slower, more oriented toward nature. Beach-going, hiking, diving, surfing, and boating are the draw, along with a visit to the Polynesian Cultural Center, poking through little shops and wayside stores.

TIMING You can easily spend an entire day exploring Windward O'ahu, or you can just breeze on through, nodding at the sights on your way to the North Shore. Waikīkī to Windward is a drive of less than half an hour; to the North Shore via Kamehameha Highway along the Windward Coast is one hour minimum.

Main Attractions

31 **Byodo-In Temple.** Tucked away in the back of the Valley of the Temples cemetery is a replica of the 11th-century Temple at Uji in Japan. A 2-ton carved wooden statue of the Buddha presides inside the main temple building. Next to the temple building are a meditation house and gardens set dramatically against the sheer, green cliffs of the Ko'olau Mountains. You can ring the 5-foot, 3-ton brass bell for good luck and feed some 10,000 carp that inhabit the garden's 2-acre pond. ⊠ *47-200 Kahekili Hwy., Kāne'ohe* ☎ *808/239–8811* ⊟ *$2* ☼ *Daily 8:30–4:30.*

NEED A BREAK?   Generations of children have purchased their beach snacks and sodas at **Kalapawai Market** (⊠ 306 S. Kalāheo Ave.), near Kailua Beach. A windward landmark since 1932, the green-and-white market has distinctive charm. It's a good source for your carryout lunch, since there's no concession stand at the beach.

28 **Nu'uanu Pali Lookout.** This panoramic perch looks out to windward O'ahu. It was in this region that King Kamehameha I drove defending forces over the edges of the 1,000-foot-high cliffs, thus winning the decisive battle for control of O'ahu. ■ TIP→ From here you can see views that stretch from Kāne'ohe Bay to Mokoli'i (Chinaman's Hat), a small island off the coast, and beyond. Temperatures at the summit are several degrees cooler than in warm Waikīkī, so bring a jacket along. And hang on tight to any loose possessions; it gets extremely windy at the lookout. Lock your car; break-ins have occurred here. ⊠ *Top of Pali Hwy.* ☼ *Daily 9–4.*

Offshore Islands and Rocks. As you drive the Windward and North Shores along Kamehameha Highway, you'll note a number of interesting geological features. At Kualoa look to the ocean and gaze at the uniquely shaped little island of **Mokoliʻi** (little lizard), a 206-foot-high sea stack also known as Chinaman's Hat. According to Hawaiian legend, the goddess Hiʻiaka, sister of Pele, slew the dragon Mokoliʻi and flung its tail into the sea, forming the distinct islet. Other dragon body parts—in the form of rocks, of course—were scattered along the base of nearby Kualoa Ridge. TIP➔ In Lāʻie, if you turn right on Anemoku Street, and right again on Naupaka, you come to a scenic lookout where you can see a group of islets, dramatically washed by the waves.

🐚 ㉝ **Polynesian Cultural Center.** Re-created, individual villages showcase the lifestyles and traditions of Hawaiʻi, Tahiti, Samoa, Fiji, the Marquesas Islands, New Zealand, and Tonga. This 45-acre center, 35 mi from Waikīkī, was founded in 1963 by the Church of Jesus Christ of Latter-day Saints. It houses restaurants, hosts lūʻaus, and demonstrates cultural traditions such as tribal tattooing, fire dancing, and ancient customs and ceremonies. The expansive open-air shopping village carries Polynesian handicrafts. ■ TIP➔ If you're staying in Honolulu, see the center as part of a van tour so you won't have to drive home late at night after the two-hour evening show. Various packages are available, from basic admission to an all-inclusive deal. Every May, the PCC hosts the World Fire Knife Dance Competition, an event that draws the top fire knife dance performers from around the world. ⊠ *55-370 Kamehameha Hwy., Lāʻie* ☎ *808/293–3333 or 800/367–7060* ⊕ *www.polynesia.com* ⊠ *$50–$218* ⊙ *Mon.–Sat. 12:30–9:30. Islands close at 6:30.*

㉜ **Senator Fong's Plantation and Gardens.** The one-time estate of the late Hiram Fong, the first Asian-American to be elected to Congress, this 700-acre garden is now open for tours. Twice-daily one-mile (10:30 AM and 1 PM), one-hour walking tours explore the park's five lush valleys, each named for a U.S. president that Fong served under during his 17-year tenure in the Senate. The visitor center has a snack bar and gift shop. ⊠ *47-285 Pūlama Rd., off Kahekili Hwy., 2 mi north of Byodo-In Temple, Kahaluʻu* ☎ *808/239–6775* ⊕ *www.fonggarden.net* ⊠ *$14.50* ⊙ *Daily 10 AM–2 PM.*

Also Worth Seeing

🐚 ㉚ **Sea Life Park.** Dolphins leap and spin, penguins frolic, and a killer whale performs impressive tricks at this marine-life attraction 15 mi from Waikīkī at scenic Makapuʻu Point. In addition to a 300,000-gallon Hawaiian reef aquarium, there are the Pacific Whaling Museum, the Hawaiian Monk Seal Care Center, and a breeding sanctuary for Hawaiʻi's endangered *Honu* sea turtle. There are several interactive activities such as a stingray encounter, an underwater photo safari, and a "Splash University" dolphin-training session (⇨ *See* Water Activities & Tours *later in this chapter*). Inquire about the park's behind-the-scenes tour for a glimpse of dolphin-training areas and the seabird rehabilitation center. ⊠ *41-202 Kalanianaʻole Hwy., Waimānalo* ☎ *808/259–7933 or 886/365–7446* ⊕ *www.sealifepark.com* ⊠ *$26* ⊙ *Daily 9:30–5.*

㉙ **Waimānalo.** This modest little seaside town flanked by chiseled cliffs is worth a visit. Its biggest draw are its beautiful beaches, offering glorious views to the windward side. **Bellows Beach** is great for swimming and bodysurfing, and **Waimānalo Beach Park** also safe for swimming. Down the side roads, as you head *mauka,* (toward the mountains) are little farms that grow a variety of fruits and flowers. Toward the back of the valley are small ranches with grazing horses. ■ TIP→ **If you see any trucks selling corn and you're staying at a place where you can cook it, be sure to get some in Waimānalo. It may be the sweetest you'll ever eat, and the price is the lowest on O'ahu.** ⊠ *Kalaniana'ole Hwy.*

The North Shore

An hour from town and a world away in atmosphere, O'ahu's North Shore, roughly from Kahuku Point to Ka'ena Point, is about small farms and big waves, tourist traps and other-worldly landscapes. Parks and beaches, roadside fruit stands and shrimp shacks, a bird sanctuary and a valley preserve offer a dozen reasons to stop between the one-time plantation town of Kahuku and the surf mecca of Hale'iwa.

Hale'iwa has had many lives, from resort getaway in the 1900s to plantation town through the 20th century to its life today as a surf and tourist magnet. Beyond Hale'iwa is the tiny village of Waialua, a string of beach parks, an airfield where gliders, hang-gliders, and parachutists play, and, at the end of the road, Ka'ena Point State Recreation Area, which offers a brisk hike, striking views and whale-watching in season.

TIMING Pack wisely for a day's North Shore excursion: swim and snorkel gear, light jacket and hat (the weather is mercurial, especially in winter), sunscreen and sunglasses, bottled water and snacks, towels and a picnic blanket, and both sandals and close-toed shoes for hiking. A small cooler is nice; you may want to pick up some fruit or fresh corn. As always, leave valuables in the hotel safe and lock the car whenever you leave it.

> **WAVING IN THE WIND**
>
> The North Shore is sarong territory. As you drive along Kamehameha Highway, you'll see squares of colorful fabric flapping in the breeze, drawing your attention to roadside shops. You can pay anything from $5 to $25 for a sarong (*pa'u* in Hawaiian, *pareu* in Tahitian), but the best prices are here, far from town. Sarongs come in handy as beach cover-ups, bathrobes, evening shawls, skirts, scarves, and even picnic blankets. Along with a bikini and some rubber slippers, they are standard beach-girl wear.

From Waikīkī, the quickest route to the North Shore is H–1 east to H–2 north and then the Kamehameha Highway past Wahiawā; you'll hit Hale'iwa in just less than an hour. The Windward route (H–1 east, H–3 through the mountains, and Kamehameha Highway north) takes at least 90 minutes to Hale'iwa.

What to See

㉟ Hale'iwa. During the 1920s this seaside hamlet boasted a posh seaside hotel at the end of a railroad line (both long gone). During the 1960s, hippies gathered here, followed by surfers from around the world.

Continued on page 63

Imagine picking your seat for free at the Super Bowl or wandering the grounds of Augusta National at no cost during The Masters, and you glimpse the opportunity you have when attending the Vans Triple Crown of Surfing on the North Shore.

NORTH SHORE SURFING & THE TRIPLE CROWN

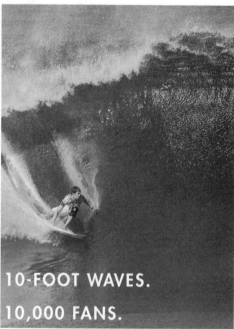

10-FOOT WAVES.
10,000 FANS.
TOP 50 SURFERS.

Long considered the best stretch of surf breaks on Earth, the North Shore surf area encompasses 6 mi of coastline on the northwestern tip of O'ahu from Hale'iwa to Sunset Beach. There are over 20 major breaks within these 6 mi. Winter storms in the North Pacific send huge swells southward which don't break for thousands of miles until they hit the shallow reef of O'ahu's remote North Shore. This creates optimum surfing all winter long and was the inspiration for having surf competitions here each holiday season.

Every November and December the top 50 surfers in world rankings descend on "The Country" (as Oahuans call the North Shore) to decide who is the best all-around surfer in the world. Each of the three invitation-only contests that make up the Triple Crown has its own winner; competitors also win points based on the final stand-

ings. The surfer who racks up the most points overall, wins the Vans Triple Crown title. The first contest is held at **Hale'iwa Beach,** the second at **Sunset Beach.** The season reaches its crescendo at the most famous surf break in the world, the **Banzai Pipeline.**

The best part is the cost to attend the events—nothing; your seat for the show—wherever you set down your beach towel. Just park your car, grab your stuff, and watch the best surfers in the world tame the best waves in the world.

The only surfing I understand involves a mouse.

The contests were created not only to fashion an overall champion but also to attract the casual fan to the sport. Announcers explain each ride over the loudspeakers, discussing the nuances and values being weighed by the judges. A scoreboard displays points and standings during the four days of each event.

If this still seems incomprehensible to you, the action on the beach can also be exciting as some of the most beautiful people in the world are attracted to these contests.

For more information, see www.triplecrownofsurfing.com.

What should I bring?

Pack for a day at the Triple Crown the way you would for any day at the beach—sunblock, beach towel, bottled water, and, if you want something other than snacks, food.

These contests are held in rural neighborhoods (read: few stores), so pack anything you might need during the day. Also, binoculars are suggested, especially for the contest at Sunset. The pros will be riding huge outside ocean swells, and it can be hard to follow from the beach without binoculars. Hale'iwa's breaks and Pipeline are considerably closer to shore, but binoculars will let you see the intensity on the contestants' faces.

Hale'iwa Ali'i Beach Park
Vans Triple Crown Contest #1: OP Pro Hawaii

The Triple Crown gets underway with high-performance waves (and the know-how to ride them) at Hale'iwa. Though lesser known than the other two breaks of the Triple Crown, it is the perfect wave for showing off: the contest here is full of sharp cutbacks (twisting the board dramatically off the top or bottom of the wave), occasional barrel rides, and a crescendo of floaters (balancing the board on the top of the cresting wave) before the wave is destroyed on the shallow tabletop reef called the Toilet Bowl. The rider who can pull off the most tricks will win this leg. Also, the beach park is walking distance from historic Hale'iwa town, a mecca to surfers worldwide who make their pilgrimage here every winter to ride the waves. Even if you are not a fan, immersing yourself in their culture will make you one by nightfall.

Sunset Beach
Vans Triple Crown Contest #2: O'Neill World Cup of Surfing

At Sunset, the most guts and bravado win the day. The competition is held when the swell is at 8 to 12 feet and from the northwest. Sunset gets the heaviest surf because it is the exposed point on the northern tip of O'ahu. Surfers describe the waves here as "moving mountains." The choice of waves is the key to this contest as only the perfect one will give the competitor a ride through the jigsaw-puzzle outer reef, which can kill a perfect wave instantly, all the way into the inner reef. Big-bottom turns (riding all the way down the face of the wave before turning dramatically back onto the wave) and slipping into a super-thick tube (slowing down to let the wave catch you and riding inside its vortex) are considered necessary to carry the day.

Banzai Pipeline
Vans Triple Crown Contest #3: Rip Curl Pipeline Masters

It is breathtaking to watch the best surfers in the world disappear into a gaping maw of whitewash for a few seconds only to emerge from the other side unscathed. Surfing the Pipeline showcases their ability to specialize in surfing, to withstand the power and fury of a 10-foot wave from within its hollow tube.

How does the wave become hollow in the first place? When the deep ocean floor ascends steeply to the shore, the waves that meet it will pitch over themselves sharply, rather than rolling. This pitching causes a tube to form, and in most places in the world that tube is a mere couple of feet in diameter. In the case of Pipeline, however, its unique, extremely shallow reef causes the swells to open into 10-foot-high moving hallways that surfers can pass through. Only problem: a single slip puts them right into the raggedly sharp coral heads that caused the wave to pitch in the first place. Broken arms and boards are the rule rather than the exception for those who dare to ride and fail.

■ TIP➔ **The Banzai Pipeline is a surf break, not a beach. The best place to catch a glimpse of the break is from 'Ehukai Beach.**

When Are the Contests?

The first contests at Hale'iwa begin the second week of November, and the Triple Crown finishes up right before Christmas.

Surfing, more so than any other sport, relies on Mother Nature to allow competition. Each contest in the Triple Crown requires only four days of competition, but each is given a window of twelve days. Contest officials decide by 7 AM of each day whether the contest will be held or not, and they release the information to radio stations and via a hotline (whose number changes each year, unfortunately). By 7:15, you will know if it is on or not. Consult the local paper's sports section for the hotline number or listen to the radio announcement. The contests run from 8:30 to 4:30, featuring half-hour heats with four to six surfers each.

If big crowds bother you, go early on in the contests, within the first two days of each one. While the finale of the Pipeline Masters may draw about 10,000 fans, the earlier days have the same world-class surfers with fewer than a thousand fans.

Sunset Beach
Banzai Pipeline
83 Waiale'e
Waimea Bay Waimea
Hale'iwa Beach Waimea Bay Beach Co. Park
Kaunala Ridge
Waimea Valley
Audubon Society
83
Hale'iwa Beach Co. Park Kawailoa Beach Waihe'e (Waimea) Falls 80 Pupukea
Kawailoa
Hale'iwa

How Do I Get There?

If you hate dealing with parking and traffic, take TheBus. It will transport you from Waikīkī to the contest sites in an hour for $2 and no hassle.

If you must drive, watch the news the night before. If they are expecting big waves that night, there is a very good chance the contest will be on in the morning. Leave by 6 AM to beat the crowd. When everybody else gets the news at 7:15 AM that the show is on, you will be parking your car and taking a snooze on the beach waiting for the surfing to commence.

Parking is limited so be prepared to park alongside Kamehameha Highway and trek it in.

But I'm not coming until Valentine's Day.

There doesn't need to be a contest underway for you to enjoy these spots from a spectator's perspective. The North Shore surf season begins in October and concludes at the end of March. Only the best can survive the wave at Pipeline. You may not be watching Kelly Slater or Andy Irons ripping, but if the waves are up, you will still see surfing that will blow your mind. Also, there are surf contests year-round on all shores of O'ahu, so check the papers to see what's going on during your stay. A few other events to be on the lookout for:

Buffalo's Annual Big Board Surfing Classic
Generally held in March at legendary waterman "Buf-

falo" Keaulana's home beach of Mākaha, this is the Harlem Globetrotters of surfing contests. You'll see tandem riding, headstands, and outrigger canoe surfing. The contest is more about making the crowds cheer than beating your competitors, which makes it very accessible for the casual fan.

Converse Hawaiian Open
During the summer months, the waves switch to the south shore, where there are surf contests of one type or another each week. The Open is one of the biggest and is a part of the US Professional Longboard Surfing Championships. The best shoot it out every August on the waves Duke Kahanamoku made famous at Queen's Beach in Waikīkī.

Quiksilver in Memory of Eddie Aikau Big Wave Invitational
The granddaddy of them all is a one-day, winner-take-all contest in 25-foot surf at Waimea Bay. Because of the need for huge waves, it can be held only when there's a perfect storm. That could be at any time in the winter months, and there have even been a few years when it didn't happen at all. When Mother Nature does comply, however, it is not to be missed. You can hear the waves from the road, even before you can see the beach or the break.

SHAVE ICE

Island-style shave ice (never shaved ice—it's a pidgin thing) is said to have been born when neighborhood kids hung around the icehouse, waiting to pounce on the shavings from large blocks of ice, carved with ultrasharp Japanese planes that created an exceptionally fine-textured granita.

In the 1920s, according to the historian for syrup manufacturer Malolo Beverages Co., Chinese vendors developed sweet fruit concentrates to pour over the ice.

The evolution continued with mom-and-pop shops adding their own touches, such as secreting a nugget of Japanese-style sweet bean paste in the center, or a small scoop of ice cream, adding *li hing* powder (a sweet spice), or deftly pouring multitoned cones.

There's nothing better on a sticky, hot day. Try Waiola on Kapahulu or, in Hale'iwa, Aoki's or Matsumoto's.

Today Hale'iwa is a fun mix, with old general stores and contemporary boutiques, galleries, and eateries. Be sure to stop in at **Lili'uokalani Protestant Church,** founded by missionaries in the 1830s. It's fronted by a large, stone archway built in 1910 and covered with night-blooming cereus. ⊠ *Follow H–1 west from Honolulu to H–2 north, exit at Wahiawā, follow Kamehameha Hwy. 6 mi, turn left at signaled intersection, then right into Hale'iwa* ⊕ *www.haleiwamainstreet.com.*

NEED A BREAK? For a real slice of Hale'iwa life, stop at **Matsumoto's** (⊠ 66-087 Kamehameha Hwy. ⊕ www.matsumotoshaveice.com), a family-run business in a building dating from 1910, for shave ice in every flavor imaginable. For something different, order a shave ice with *adzuki* beans—the red beans are boiled until soft, mixed with sugar, and then placed in the cone with the ice on top.

36 Ka'ena Point State Recreation Area. The name means "the heat" and, indeed, this windy, barren coast lacks both shade and fresh water (or any man-made amenities). Pack water, wear sturdy close-toed shoes, don sunscreen and a hat, and lock the car. The hike is along a rutted dirt road, mostly flat and 3 mi long, ending in a rocky, sandy headland. It is here that Hawaiians believed the souls of the dead met with their family gods, and, if judged worthy to enter the afterlife, leapt off into eternal darkness at Leinaaka'uane, just south of the point. In summer and at low tide, the small coves offer bountiful shelling; in winter, don't venture near the water. Rare native plants dot the landscape. November through March, watch for humpbacks, spouting and breaching. Binoculars and a camera are highly recommended. ⊠ *North end of Kamehameha Hwy.*

★ ☺ **34 Waimea Valley Audubon Center.** Waimea may get lots of press for the giant winter waves in the bay, but the valley itself is a newsmaker and an ecological treasure in its own right. The National Audubon Society is working to conserve and restore the natural habitat. Follow the Kamananui Stream up the valley through the 1,800 acres of gardens. The botanical

O'AHU SIGHTSEEING TOURS

Guided tours are convenient; you don't have to worry about finding a parking spot or getting admission tickets. You'll likely gain insights that you wouldn't get on your own. Most of the tour guides have taken special Hawaiiana classes in history and lore, and many are certified by the state of Hawai'i. On the other hand, you won't have the freedom to proceed at your own pace, nor will you have the ability to take a detour trip if something else catches your attention.

BUS & VAN TOURS

Ask exactly what the tour includes in the way of actual get-off-the-bus stops and window sights.

Polynesian Adventure Tours. ☎ 808/833–3000 ⊕ www.polyad. com.

Polynesian Hospitality. ☎ 808/ 526–3565 ⊕ www.kobay.com.

Roberts Hawai'i. ☎ 808/539–9400 ⊕ www.robertshawaii.com.

THEME TOURS

Culinary Tour of Chinatown. Anthony Chang of the Chinese Chamber of Commerce leads tours of noodle shops, dim sum parlors, food courts, bakers, and other food vendors. ☎ 808/533–3181.

E Noa Tours. Certified tour guides conduct Circle Island, Pearl Harbor, and shopping tours. ☎ 808/591–2561 ⊕ www.enoa.com.

Hawaiian Islands Eco-tours, Ltd. Experienced guides take nature lovers and hikers on limited-access trails for tours. ☎ 808/236–7766.

Home of the Brave and Top Gun Tours. Perfect for military-history buffs. Narrated tours visit O'ahu's military bases and the National Memorial Cemetery of the Pacific. ☎ 808/396–8112 ⊕ www.pearlharborhq.com.

Matthew Gray's Hawaii Food Tours. Three different restaurant tour itineraries include samplings, meals, and discussion of Hawai'i foodways. ☎ 808/926–3663 ⊕ www.hawaiifoodtours.com.

Polynesian Cultural Center. An advantage of this tour is that you don't have to drive yourself back to Waikīkī after dark if you take in the evening show. ☎ 808/293–3333 or 808/923–1861 ⊕ www.polynesia. com.

WALKING TOURS

American Institute of Architects (AIA) Downtown Walking Tour. See Downtown Honolulu from an architectural perspective. ✉ American Institute of Architects, ☎ 808/545–4242.

Chinatown Walking Tour. Meet at the Chinese Chamber of Commerce for a fascinating peek into herbal shops, an acupuncturist's office, open-air markets, and specialty stores. ✉ Chinese Chamber of Commerce. ☎ 808/533–3181.

Hawai'i Geographic Society. A number of unique Downtown Honolulu historic temple and archaeology walking tours are available. ☎ 808/538–3952.

Honolulu Time Walks. Costumed narrators explore the mysteries of Honolulu, its haunts, and historic neighborhoods. ✉ 2634 S. King St., Suite 3, Downtown Honolulu ☎ 808/943–0371.

Waikīkī Beach, O'ahu.

(*top*) Catching a wave. (*bottom*) Garden of the Gods, Lānaʻi. (*opposite page, top*) Fire eater. (*opposite page, bottom*) Children with haku (head) lei.

(*top*) Waikīkī, O'ahu. (*bottom left*) Hula dancers. (*bottom right*) Hawai'i Volcanoes National Park, Big Island. (*opposite page*) Wai'anapanapa State Park, Maui.

(*top*) Surfers, North Shore, O'ahu. (*bottom*) Lava flow, Hawai'i Volcanoes National Park, Big Island.

(*top left*) Golf Course at Mauna Lani Resort, Big Island. (*top right*) Haleakalā National Park, Maui. (*bottom*) Nā Pali Coast, Kaua'i.

(*top left*) Coffee picking contest, Kona, Big Island. (*top right*) Cyclists, North Shore sea cliffs overlooking Kalau-papa peninsula, Moloka'i. (*bottom*) Green Sea Turtles.

collections here include over 5,000 species of tropical flora, including a superb gathering of Polynesian plants. It's the best place on the island to see native species, such as the endangered Hawaiian moorhen. You can also see the remains of the Hale O Lono *heiau* along with other ancient archaeological sites; evidence suggests that the area was an important spiritual center. At the back of the valley, **Waihī Falls** plunges 45 feet into a swimming pond. ■ TIP→ **Bring your suit–a swim is the perfect way to end your hike. There's a lifeguard and changing room. Be sure to bring mosquito repellent, too; it gets buggy.** ✉ *59-864 Kamehameha Hwy., Haleʻiwa* ☎ *808/638–9199* ⊕ *www.audubon.org* ✉ *$8, parking $2* ☉ *Daily 9:30–5.*

■ NEED A BREAK?	The chocolate *haupia* pie at **Ted's Bakery** (✉ 59-024 Kamehameha Hwy., near Sunset Beach ☎ 808/638–8207) is legendary. Stop in for a take-out pie or for a quick plate lunch or sandwich.

West (Leeward) & Central Oʻahu

If you've got to leave one part of this island for the next trip, this is the part to skip. It's a longish drive to West Oʻahu by island standards–45 minutes to Kapolei from Waikīkī and 90 minutes to Waiʻanae–and the central area has little to offer. The attraction most worth the trek to West Oʻahu is Hawaiʻi's Plantation Village in Waipahu, about a half hour out of town; it's a living-history museum built from actual homes of turn-of-the-century plantation workers. In Central Oʻahu, check out the Dole Plantation for all things pineapple.

BEACHES

By Chad Pata

Tropical sun mixed with cooling trade winds and pristine waters make Oʻahu's shores a literal heaven on Earth. But contrary to many assumptions, the island is not one big beach. There are miles and miles of coastline without a grain of sand, so you need to know where you are going to fully enjoy the Hawaiian experience.

Much of the island's southern and eastern coast is protected by inner reefs. The reefs provide still coastline water but not much as far as sand is concerned. However, where there are beaches on the south and east shores, they are mind-blowing. In West Oʻahu and on the North Shore you can find the wide expanses of sand you would expect for enjoying the sunset. Sandy bottoms and outside reefs make the water an adventure in the winter months. Most visitors assume the seasons don't change a thing in the Islands, and they would be right—except for the waves, which are big on the south shore in summer and placid in winter. It's exactly the opposite on the north side where winter storms bring in huge waves, but the ocean turns to glass come May and June.

Waikīkī

The 2½-mi strand called Waikīkī Beach extends from Hilton Hawaiian Village on one end to Kapiʻolani Park and Diamond Head on the other. Although it's one continuous piece of beach, it's as varied as the people that inhabit the Islands. Whether you're an old-timer looking to enjoy

BEACH SAFETY

Yes, the beaches are beautiful, but always be cognizant of the fact you are on a little rock in the middle of the Pacific Ocean. The current and waves will be stronger and bigger than any you may have experienced. Riptides can take you on a ride they call the "Moloka'i Express"—only problem is that it doesn't take you to the island of Moloka'i but rather out into the South Pacific.

Never swim alone. It is hard for even the most attentive lifeguards to keep their eyes on everyone at once, but a partner can gain their attention if you should run into trouble. There are many safe spots, but always pay attention to the posted signs. The lifeguards change the signs daily, so the warnings are always applicable to the day's conditions. If you have any doubts, ask a lifeguard for an assessment. They're professionals and can give you competent advice.

Use sunblock early and often. The SPF you choose is your own, but we suggest nothing lower than 30 if you plan to spend more than an hour in the sun.

the action from the shade or a sports nut wanting to do it all, you can find every beach activity here without ever jumping in the rental car.

■ TIP→ **If you're staying outside the area, our best advice is to park at either end of the beach and walk in.** Plentiful parking exists on the west end at the Ala Wai Marina, where there are myriad free spots on the beach as well as metered stalls around the harbor. For parking on the east end, Kapi'olani Park and the Honolulu Zoo both have metered parking for $1 an hour—more afford-able than the $10 per hour the resorts want. We highlight the differences in this famous beach from west to east, letting you know not only where you may want to sunbathe but why.

BEACHES KEY

🚻	Restroom
🚿	Showers
🏄	Surfing
🤿	Snorkel/Scuba
🚻	Good for kids
P	Parking

🐚 **Duke Kahanamoku Beach.** Named for Hawai'i's fa-mous Olympic swimming champion, Duke Ka-hanamoku, this is a hard-packed beach with the only shade trees on the sand in Waikīkī. It's great

Waikīkī O'ahu

Sans Souci Beach 🚻 🚿 🚻

Queen's Surf Beach 🚻 🚿 🚻 🤿 🏄

Kūhiō Beach Park 🚻 🚿 🚻 🏄

Kahaloa and Ulukou Beaches 🚻 🚿 🏄

Ft. DeRussy Beach Park 🚻 🚿 🚻

Duke Kahanamoku Beach 🚻 🚿 🚻

Kapi'olani Park

Kalākaua Ave.

0 — 10 miles
0 — 15 km

for families with young children because of the shade and the calmest waters in Waikīkī, thanks to a rock wall that creates a semiprotected cove. The ocean clarity here is not as brilliant as most of Waikīkī because of the stillness of the surf, but it's a small price to pay for peace of mind about youngsters. ⊠ *In front of Hilton Hawaiian Village Beach Resort and Spa ⚬ Toilets, showers, food concession.*

Fort DeRussy Beach Park. Even before you take the two newly refurbished beach parks into account, this is one of the finest beaches on the south side of Oʻahu. Wide, soft, ultrawhite beaches with gently lapping waves make it a family favorite for running/jumping/frolicking fun (this also happens to be where the NFL holds their rookie sand football game every year). Add to that the new, heavily-shaded grass grilling area, sand volleyball courts, and aquatic rentals, making this a must for the active visitor. ⊠ *In front of Fort DeRussy and Hale Koa Hotel ⚬ Lifeguard, toilets, showers, food concession, picnic tables, grills, playground.*

Kahaloa and Ulukou Beaches. The beach widens back out here, creating the "it" spot for the bikini crowd. Beautiful bodies abound, as do activities. This is where you find most of the sailing catamaran charters for a spectacular sail out to Diamond Head or surfboard and outrigger canoe rentals for a ride on "Hawaiʻi's Malibu" at **Canoe's** surf break. Great music and outdoor dancing beckon the sand-bound visitor to Duke's Bar and Grill, where shirt and shoes not only aren't required, they're discouraged. ⊠ *In front of Royal Hawaiian Hotel and Sheraton Moana Surfrider ⚬ Lifeguard, toilets, showers, food concession.*

Kūhiō Beach Park. Due to recent renovations, this beach has seen a renaissance. Now bordered by a landscaped boardwalk, it's great for romantic walks any time of day. Check out the Kūhiō Beach hula mound nightly at 6:30 for free hula and Hawaiian-music performances; weekends there's a torch-lighting ceremony at sunset. Surf lessons for beginners are available from the beach center here every half hour. ⊠ *Past Sheraton Moana Surfrider Hotel to Kapahulu Ave. pier ⚬ Lifeguard, toilets, showers, food concession.*

Queen's Surf. So named as it was once the site of Queen Liliʻuokalani's beach house. A mix of families and gay couples gathers here, and it seems as if someone is always playing a steel drum. Every weekend movie screens are set up on the sand, and major motion pictures are shown after the sun sets. In the daytime, there are banyan trees for shade and volleyball nets for pros and amateurs alike (this is where Misty May and Kerri Walsh play while in town). The water fronting Queen's Surf is an aquatic preserve, providing the best snorkeling in Waikīkī. ⊠ *Across from entrance to Honolulu Zoo ⚬ Lifeguard, toilets, showers, picnic tables, grills.*

Sans Souci. Nicknamed Dig-Me Beach because of its outlandish display of skimpy bathing suits, this small rectangle of sand is nonetheless a good sunning spot for all ages. Children enjoy its shallow, safe waters that are protected by the walls of the historic Natatorium, an Olympic-size saltwater swimming arena. Serious swimmers and triathletes also swim in the channel here, beyond the reef. Sans Souci is favored by locals wanting to avoid the crowds while still enjoying the convenience of Waikīkī. ⊠ *Across from Kapiʻolani Park, between New Otani Kaimana Beach Hotel and Waikīkī War Memorial Natatorium ⚬ Lifeguard, toilets, showers, picnic tables.*

Honolulu

The city of Honolulu only has one beach, the monstrous Ala Moana. It hosts everything from Dragon Boat competitions to the Aloha State Games.

Ⓒ **Ala Moana Beach Park.** Ala Moana has a protective reef, which makes it ostensibly a ½-mi wide saltwater swimming pool. After Waikīkī, this is the most popular beach among visitors. To the Waikīkī side is a peninsula called Magic Island, with shady trees and paved sidewalks ideal for jogging. Ala Moana also has playing fields, tennis courts, and a couple of small ponds for sailing toy boats. This beach is for everyone, but only in the daytime. It's a high-crime area after dark. ⊠ *Honolulu, near Ala Moana Shopping Center and Ala Moana Blvd. From Waikīkī take Bus 8 to shopping center and cross Ala Moana Blvd.* ⚴ *Lifeguard, toilets, showers, food concession, picnic tables, grills, parking lot.*

Southeast O'ahu

Much of Southeast O'ahu is surrounded by reef, making most of the coast uninviting to swimmers, but the spots where the reef opens up are true gems. The drive along this side of the island is amazing with its sheer lava-rock walls on one side and deep-blue ocean on the other. There are plenty of restaurants in the suburb of Hawai'i Kai, so you can make a day of it, knowing that food isn't far away. Beaches are listed from south to north.

Ⓒ **Hanauma Bay Nature Preserve.** Picture this as the world's biggest open-air aquarium. You go here to see fish, and fish you'll see. Due to their exposure to thousands of visitors every week, these fish are more like family pets than the skittish marine life you might expect. An old volcanic crater has created a haven from the waves where the coral has thrived. There's an educational center where you must watch a nine-minute video about the nature preserve before being allowed down to the bay. ■ TIP→ **The bay is best early in the morning (around 7), before the crowds arrive; it can be difficult to park later in the day.** No smoking is allowed, and the beach is closed on Tuesday. **Hanauma Bay Dive Tours** (☎ 808/256–8956) runs snorkeling, snuba, and scuba tours to Hanauma Bay with transportation from Waikīkī hotels. ⊠ *7455 Kalaniana'ole Hwy.* ☎ *808/396–4229* ⚴ *Lifeguard, toilets, showers, food concession, picnic tables, parking lot* 🎫 *Donation $5; parking $1; mask, snorkel, and fins rental $8; tram from parking lot to beach $1.50* ☉ *Wed.–Mon. 6–7.*

Sandy Beach. Probably the most popular beach with locals on this side of O'ahu, the broad, sloping beach is covered with sunbathers there to watch **the Show** and soak up rays. The Show is a shore break that's like no other in the Islands. Monster ocean swells rolling into the beach combined with the sudden rise in the ocean floor causes waves to jack up and crash magnificently on the shore. Young and old brave this danger to get some of the biggest barrels you can find for bodysurfing, but always keeping in mind the beach's other nickname, "Break Neck Beach." Use extreme caution when swimming here, but feel free to kick back and watch the drama unfold from the comfort of your beach chair. ⊠ *Makai of Kalaniana'ole Hwy., 2 mi east of Hanauma Bay* ⚴ *Lifeguard, toilets, showers, picnic tables.*

1

Windward O'ahu

The Windward side lives up to its name with ideal spots for windsurfing and kiteboarding, or for the more intrepid, hang gliding. For the most part the waves are mellow, and the bottoms are all sand—making for nice spots to visit with younger kids. The only drawback is that this side does tend to get more rain. But, as beautiful as the vistas are, a little sprinkling of "pineapple juice" shouldn't dampen your experience; plus it turns on the waterfalls that cascade down the Ko'olaus. Beaches are listed from north to south.

Makapu'u Beach. A magnificent beach protected by Makapu'u Point welcomes you to the Windward side. Hang gliders circle above the beach, and the water is filled with body boarders. Just off the coast you can see Bird Island, a sanctuary for aquatic fowl, jutting out of the blue. The currents can be heavy, so check with a lifeguard if you're unsure of safety. Before you leave, take the prettiest (and coldest) outdoor shower available on the island. Being surrounded by tropical flowers and foliage while you rinse off that sand will be a memory you will cherish from this side of the rock. ⊠ *Across from Sea Life Park on Kalaniana'ole Hwy., 2 mi south of Waimānalo* ⚓ *Lifeguard, toilets, showers, picnic tables, grills.*

ⓒ **Waimānalo Beach Park.** This is a "local" beach, busy with picnicking families and active sports fields. Treat the beach with respect (read: don't litter) and lock your car. This beach is one of the island's most beautiful. Expect a wide stretch of sand; turquoise, emerald, and deep-blue seas; and gentle shore-breaking waves that are fun for all ages to play in. ⊠ *South of Waimānalo town, look for signs on Kalaniana'ole Hwy.* ⚓ *Lifeguard, toilets, showers, picnic tables.*

Bellows Beach. Bellows is the same exact beach as Waimānalo, but it's under the auspices of the military, making it more friendly for visitors. The park area is excellent for camping, and ironwood trees provide plenty of shade. There's no food

GOT A GOZA?

For sun bathing, buy a *goza*, a Japanese beach mat. Everyone knows the frustration of getting out of the ocean and lying down on your beach towel, only to have it quickly become a 20-pound, sand-caked nuisance. The straw gozas keep the sand off your bum without absorbing all the water a towel would, giving you a cool, comfortable place to recline on the beach. Weighing just ounces and costing just pennies, it will be the best thing you buy on your trip.

concession, but McDonald's and other take-out fare is right outside the entrance gate. ⊠ *Entrance on Kalanianaʻole Hwy., near Waimānalo town center* ⟨ *Lifeguard, toilets, showers, picnic tables, grills.*

★ **Lanikai Beach Park.** Think of the beaches you see in commercials: peaceful blue waters, perfectly soft sand, families and dogs frolicking mindlessly. It's an ideal spot for camping out with a book. Plenty of action from wind- and kite surfers will keep nonreaders occupied. ⊠ *Past Kailua Beach Park; street parking on Mokulua Dr. for various public–access points to beach* ⟨ *Lifeguard, showers.*

FodorsChoice **Kailua Beach Park.** This is like a big Lanikai Beach, but a little windier ★ and a little wider. It's a better spot for a full day at the beach, though. A line of palms provides shade on the sand, and a huge park has picnic pavilions where you can escape the heat or feed the hordes. This is the "it" spot if you're looking to try your hand at windsurfing. ⊠ *Near Kailua town, turn right on Kailua Rd. at market, cross bridge, then turn left into beach parking lot* ⟨ *Lifeguard, toilets, showers, picnic tables, grills, playground, parking lot.*

Kualoa Regional Park. Grassy expanses border a long, narrow stretch of beach with spectacular views of Kāneʻohe Bay and the Koʻolau Mountains, making Kualoa one of the island's most beautiful picnic, camping, and beach areas. Dominating the view is an islet called Mokoliʻi, better known as Chinaman's Hat, which rises 206 feet above the water. You can swim in the shallow areas year-round. The one drawback is that it's usually windy, but the wide-open spaces are ideal for kite flying. ⊠ *North of Waiāhole, on Kamehameha Hwy.* ⟨ *Lifeguard, toilets, showers, picnic tables, grills.*

☾ **Kahana Bay Beach Park.** Local parents often bring their children here to wade in safety in the very shallow, protected waters. This pretty beach cove has a long sand strip that is great for walking and a cool, shady grove of tall ironwood and pandanus trees that is ideal for a picnic. An ancient Hawaiian fishpond, which was in use until the '20s, is visible nearby. The water here is not generally a clear blue due to the run-off from the heavy rains in the valley. ⊠ *North of Kualoa Park on Kamehameha Hwy.* ⟨ *Lifeguard, toilets, showers, picnic tables.*

North Shore

"North Shore, where the waves are mean, just like a washing machine" sing the Kaʻau Crater Boys about this legendary side of the island. And in winter they are absolutely right. At times the waves overtake the road, stranding tourists and locals alike. When the surf is up, there will even be

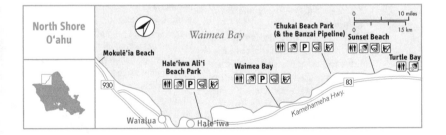

signs on the beach telling you how far to stay back so that you aren't swept out to sea. The most prestigious big-wave contest in the world, "The Eddie Aikau," is held at Waimea Bay on waves the size of a six-story building. The Triple Crown of Surfing (⇨ *See* North Shore Surfing and the Triple Crown) roams across three beaches in the winter months.

All this changes come summer when this tiger turns into a kitty with water smooth enough to water ski on and ideal for snorkeling. The fierce Banzai Pipeline surf break becomes a great dive area, allowing you to explore the deadly coral heads that have claimed so many on the ultra-hollow tubes that are created here in winter. But even with the monster surf subsided, this is still a time for caution. Lifeguards become more scarce, and currents don't go away just because the waves do.

This all being said, it's a place like no other on earth and must be explored. From the turtles at Mokulē'ia to the tunnels at Shark's Cove, you could spend your whole trip on this side and not be disappointed. Beaches are listed from east to west.

Turtle Bay. Now known more for its resort than its magnificent beach, Turtle Bay is mostly passed over on the way to the more known beaches of Sunset and Waimea. But for the average visitor with the average swimming capabilities, this is the place to be on the North Shore. The crescent-shape beach is protected by a huge sea wall. You can see and hear the fury of the northern swell, while blissfully floating in cool, calm waters. The convenience of this spot is also hard to pass up—there is a concession selling sandwiches and sunblock right on the beach. ⊠ *4 mi north of Kahuku on Kamehameha Hwy. Turn into the resort and let the guard know where you are going; they offer free parking to beach guests.* ♿ *Toilets, showers, concessions, picnic tables.*

★ **Sunset Beach.** The beach is broad, the sand is soft, the summer waves are gentle, and the winter surf is crashing. Many love searching this shore for the puka shells that adorn the necklaces you see everywhere. ■ TIP→ Use caution in the water; at times the current can come ripping around the point. Carryout truck stands selling shave ice, plate lunches, and sodas usually line the adjacent highway. ⊠ *1 mi north of 'Ehukai Beach Park on Kamehameha Hwy.* ♿ *Lifeguard, toilets, showers, picnic tables.*

'Ehukai Beach Park & the Banzai Pipeline. What sets 'Ehukai apart is the view of the famous **Banzai Pipeline**, where the winter waves curl into magnificent tubes, making it an experienced wave-rider's dream. It's also an inexperienced swimmer's nightmare, though spring and summer waves are more accommodating to the average swimmer. Except when the surf contests are going on, there's no reason to stay on the central strip. Travel either way on the beach, and the conditions remain the same. But the population thins out, leaving you with a magnificent stretch of sand all to yourself. ⊠ *Small parking lot borders Kamehameha Hwy. 1 mi north of Foodland at Pūpūkea* ♿ *Lifeguard, toilets, showers, parking lot.*

Fodor'sChoice **Waimea Bay.** Made popular in that old Beach Boys song "Surfin' U.S.A.," ★ Waimea Bay is a slice of big-wave heaven, home to king-size 25- to 30-foot winter waves. Summer is the time to swim and snorkel in the calm waters. The shore break is great for novice bodysurfers. Due to its pop-

SHRIMP SHACKS

NO DRIVE TO THE NORTH SHORE is complete without a shrimp stop. Shrimp stands dot Kamehameha Highway from Kahaluʻu to Kahuku. For under $10, you can get a shrimp plate lunch or a snack of chilled shrimp with cocktail sauce, served from a rough hut or converted vehicle (many permanently immobile), with picnic table seating.

The shrimp shack phenomenon began with a lost lease and a determined restaurateur. In 1994, when Giovanni and Connie Aragona couldn't renew the lease on their Haleʻiwa deli, they began hawking their best-selling dish—an Italian-style scampi preparation involving lemon, butter, and lots of garlic—from a truck alongside the road. About the same time, aquaculture was gaining a foothold in nearby Kahuku, with farmers raising sweet, white shrimp and huge, orange-whiskered prawns in shallow freshwater ponds. The ready supply and the success of the first shrimp truck led to many imitators.

Though it's changed hands, that first business lives on as Giovanni's Original Shrimp Truck, parked in Kahuku town. Signature dishes include the garlic shrimp and a spicy shrimp sautée, both worth a stop.

But there's plenty of competition—at least seven stands, trucks, or stalls are operating at any given time, with varying menus (and quality).

Don't be fooled that all that shrimp comes fresh from the ponds; much of it is imported. The only way you can be sure you're buying local farm-raised shrimp is if the shrimp is still kicking. Romy's Kahuku Prawns and Shrimp Hut is an arm of one of the longest-running aquaculture farms in the area; they sell live shrimp and prawns along with excellent plate lunches. The panfried shrimp and buttery, locally-raised corn from the bright yellow Shrimp Shack, parked at Kaya Store in Punaluʻu, is first-rate, too.

ularity, the postage-stamp parking lot is quickly filled, but everyone parks along the side of the road and walks in. ■ TIP→ **Use some caution as currents can get out of hand.** ⊠ *Across from Waimea Valley, 3 mi north of Haleʻiwa on Kamehameha Hwy.* ⟁ *Lifeguard, toilets, showers, picnic tables, parking lot.*

Haleʻiwa Aliʻi Beach Park. The winter waves are impressive here, but in summer the ocean is like a lake, ideal for family swimming. The beach itself is big and often full of locals. Its broad lawn off the highway invites volleyball and Frisbee games and groups of barbecuers. This is also the opening break for the Triple Crown of Surfing, and the grass is often filled with art festivals or carnivals. ⊠ *North of Haleʻiwa town center and past harbor on Kamehameha Hwy.* ⟁ *Lifeguard, toilets, showers, picnic tables.*

Mokuleʻia Beach Park. There is a reason why the producers of the TV show *Lost* chose this beach for their set. On the remote northwest point of the island, it is about 10 mi from the closest store or public restroom; you could spend a day here and not see another living soul. And that is precisely its beauty—all the joy of being stranded on a deserted island without the trauma of the plane crash. The beach is wide and white, the waters bright blue (but a little choppy) and full of sea turtles and other marine life. Mokulēʻia is a great secret find, just remember to pack supplies and use caution as there are no lifeguards. ⊠ *East of Haleʻiwa town center, across from Dillingham Airfield.* ♿ *No facilities.*

West (Leeward) Oʻahu

The North Shore may be known as "Country," but the West side is truly the rural area on Oʻahu. There are commuters from this side to Honolulu, but many are born, live, and die on this side with scarcely a trip to town. For the most part, there's less hostility and more curiosity toward outsiders. Occasional problems have flared up, mostly due to drug abuse that has ravaged the fringes of the island. But the problems have generally been car break-ins, not violence. So, in short, lock your car, don't bring valuables, and enjoy the amazing beaches.

The beaches on the west side are expansive and empty. Most Oʻahu residents and tourists don't make it to this side simply because of the drive; in traffic it can take almost 90 minutes to make it to Kaʻena Point from Downtown Honolulu. But you'll be hard-pressed to find a better sunset anywhere. Beaches are listed here in a south to north direction, starting from just west of Honolulu.

White Plains. Concealed from the public eye for many years as part of the Barbers Point Naval Air Station, this beach is reminiscent of Waikīkī but without the condos and the crowds. It is a long, sloping beach with numerous surf breaks, but it is also mild enough at shore for older children to play freely. It has views of Pearl Harbor and, over that, Diamond Head. Although the sand lives up to its name, the real joy of this beach comes from its history as part of a military property for the better part of a century. Expansive parking, great restroom facilities, and numerous tree-covered barbecue areas make it a great day-trip spot. As a bonus, a Hawaiian monk seal takes up residence here several months out of the year (seals are rarely seen anywhere in the Islands). ⊠ *Take the Makakilo exit off H–1 West, turn left. Follow it into the base gates, make a left. Follow the blue signs to the beach.* ♿ *Lifeguard, toilets, showers, picnic tables.*

★ ☺ **Kō ʻOlina.** This is the best spot on the island if you have small kids. The resort commissioned a series of four man-made lagoons, but, as they have to provide public beach access, you are the winner. Huge rock walls protect the lagoons, making them into perfect spots for the kids to get their first taste of the ocean without getting bowled over. The large expanses of seashore grass and hala trees that surround the semicircle beaches are made-to-order for naptime. And, if walks are in order, there is a 1½-mi jogging track connecting the lagoons. Keep in mind that, due to its perfection for *keikis*, Kō ʻOlina is popular. The parking lot fills up quickly when school is out and on weekends, so try to get there before 10 AM. The biggest parking lot is at the farthest lagoon from the entrance. ⊠ *23 mi west of Honolulu. Take Kō 'Olina exit off H–1 West and proceed to guard shack.* ♿ *Toilets, showers, concessions.*

Mākaha Beach Park. This beach provides a slice of local life most visitors don't see. Families string up tarps for the day, fire up hibachis, set up lawn chairs, get out the fishing gear, and strum 'ukuleles while they "talk story" (chat). Legendary waterman Buffalo Kaeulana can be found in the shade of the palms playing with his grandkids and spinning yarns of yesteryear. In these waters Buffalo not only invented some of the most outrageous methods of surfing, but also raised his world-champion son Rusty. He also made Mākaha the home of the world's first international surf meet in 1954 and still hosts his Big Board Surfing Classic. The swimming is generally decent in summer, but avoid the big winter waves. With its long, slow-building waves, it's a great spot to try out long boarding. ⊠ *1½ hrs west of Honolulu on H–1 Hwy. then Farrington Hwy.* ♿ *Lifeguards, toilets, showers, picnic tables, grills.*

WATER ACTIVITIES & TOURS

By Chad Pata   There's more to the beach than just lying on it. O'ahu is rife with every type of activity you can imagine. Most are offered in Waikīkī, right off the beach. Rainbow-colored parachutes dot the horizon as parasailers improve their vantage point on paradise. The blowing of conch shells announces the arrival of the beach catamarans that sail around Diamond Head Crater. Meanwhile, the whitecaps of Waikīkī are sliced by all manner of craft, from brilliant red outrigger canoes to darting white surfboards.

A rule of thumb is that the ocean is much more wily and unpredictable on O'ahu's north- and west-facing shores, but that's also why those sides have the most famous waves on Earth. So pick your activity side according to your skill level.

Boat Tours & Charters

Hawai'i Nautical. It's a little out of the way, but the experiences with this local company are worth the drive. Catamaran cruises lead to snorkeling with dolphins, gourmet dinner cruises head out of beautiful Kō 'Olina harbor, and sailing lessons are available on a 20-foot sailboat and a 50-foot cat. If you're driving out from Waikīkī, you may want to make a day of it, with sailing in the morning then 18 holes on the gorgeous resort course in the afternoon. Two-hour cruise rates with snacks and two drinks begin at $65 per person. ⊠ *Kō 'Olina Harbor, Kō 'Olina Marriot Resort, Kapolei* ☎ *808/234–7245.*

Hawai'i Sailing Adventures. Looking to escape the "cattle-maran" experience? Then this charter, with its goal of exclusivity and the largest private sailing yacht in the Islands, is for you. They have capacity for up to 50 guests but prefer smaller crowds, and they specialize in dinners catered to your specs. When you want a sail for a romantic occasion or a family reunion unfettered by crowds of people you don't know, try their yacht *Emeraude* and ask for Captain Roger. Two-hour dinner-cruise rates with unlimited super well drinks (drinks made with premium liquors like Tanqueray No. Ten or Grey Goose) begin at $119 per person. ✉ *Kewalo Basin, Slip S, Honolulu* ☎ *808/596–9696.*

Sashimi Fun Fishing. A combination trip suits those who aren't quite ready to troll for big game in the open–ocean swells. Sashimi Fun Fishing runs a dinner cruise with fishing and music. They keep close enough to shore that you can still see Oʻahu and jig for a variety of reef fish. The cruise includes a local barbecue dinner, and you can also cook what you catch. The four-hour dinner-cruise rates with hotel transportation begin at $63 per person. ☎ *808/955–3474.*

> ### LOOK FIRST
>
> With all water activities, check out your environment: are there rocks in the surf zone? Which way is the current pulling? Where are the closest lifeguard stands? It's always a good idea to spend at least 15 minutes on the beach watching the break you intend to surf. This allows you not only to check for dangerous areas and the size of the surf but also to see what spot is breaking cleanest and will therefore be the most fun.

Boogie Boarding & Bodysurfing

Boogie boarding (or sponging) has become a popular alternative to surfing for a couple of reasons. First, the start-up cost is much less—a usable board can be purchased for $30 to $40 or can be rented on the beach for $5 an hour. Second, it's a whole lot easier to ride a boogie board than to tame a surfboard.

Most grocery and convenience stores sell boogie boards. Though the boards do not rival what the pros use, you won't notice a difference in their handling on smaller waves. ■ TIP➔ **Another small investment you'll want to make is surf fins.** These smaller, sturdier versions of dive fins sell for $25–$35 at surf and dive stores, sporting-goods stores, or even Wal-Mart. Most beach stands do not rent fins with the boards. Though they are not necessary for boogie boarding, fins do give you a tremendous advantage when you are paddling into waves. If you plan to go out in bigger surf, we would also advise you to get fin leashes to prevent loss. For bodysurfing, you definitely want to invest in fins.

If the direction of the current or dangers of the break are not readily apparent to you, don't hesitate to ask a lifeguard for advice.

Best Spots

Boogie boarding and bodysurfing can be done anywhere there are waves, but, due to a paddling advantage surfers have over spongers, it's usually more fun to go to exclusively boogie-boarding spots.

Kūhiō Beach Park (✉ Waikīkī, past Sheraton Moana Surfrider Hotel to Kapahulu Ave. pier) is an easy spot for the first timer to check out the action. Try **The Wall,** a break so named for the break wall in front of the beach. It's a little crowded with kids, but it's close enough to shore to keep you at ease. There are dozens of breaks in Waikīkī, but the Wall is the only one solely occupied by spongers. Start out here to get the hang of it before venturing out to **Canoes** or **Kaiser Bowl's.**

The best spot on the island for advanced boogie boarding is **Sandy Beach** (⌖ 2 mi east of Hanauma Bay on Kalaniana'ole Hwy.) on the Windward side. It's a short wave that goes right and left, but the barrels here are unparalleled for pure sponging. The ride is intense and breaks so sharply that you actually see the wave suck the bottom dry before it crashes on to it. That's the reason it's also called "Break Neck Beach." It's awesome for the advanced, but know its danger before enjoying the ride.

Equipment Rentals

There are more than 30 rental spots on Waikīkī Beach, all offering basically the same prices. But if you plan to do it for more than just an hour, we would suggest buying a board for $20 to $30 at an ABC convenience store and giving it to a kid when you're preparing to end your vacation. It will be more cost-effective for you and will imbue you with the Aloha spirit while making a kid's day.

Deep-Sea Fishing

The joy of fishing in Hawai'i is that there isn't really a season; it's good year-round. Sure, the bigger yellowfin tuna ('ahi) are generally caught in summer, and the coveted spearfish are more frequent in winter, but you can still catch them any day of the year. You can also find dolphin fish (mahimahi), wahoo (ono), skip jacks, and the king—Pacific blue marlin—ripe for the picking on any given day.

When choosing a fishing boat in the Islands, look for the older, grizzled captains who have been trolling these waters for half a century. All the fancy gizmos in the world can't match an old tar's knowledge of the waters.

The general rule for the catch is an even split with the crew. Unfortunately, there are no freeze-and-ship providers in the state, so unless you plan to eat the fish while you're here, you'll probably want to leave it with the boat. Most boats do offer mounting services for trophy fish; ask your captain. Besides the gift of fish, a gratuity of 10% to 20% is standard. It's up to the fisherman; use your own discretion depending on how you felt about the overall experience.

■ TIP➔ Trying to get out on the cheap with half-day excursions can be a way to cut costs, but we suggest the full charter. It dramatically improves your odds of catching something, and that after all is why you're out there.

Boats & Charters

Inter-Island Sportfishing. The oldest-running sportfishing company on O'ahu also boasts the largest landed blue marlin—more than 1,200 pounds. With two smaller boats and the 53-foot *Maggie Joe* (which can hold up to 25), they can manage any small party with air-conditioned cabins and cutting-edge fishing equipment. They also work with Grey's Taxidermy, the world's largest marine taxidermist, to mount the monster you reel in. Half-day exclusive charter rates for groups of six begin at $700. ☎ 808/591–8888 ⊕ www.fish-hawaii.com.

Magic Sportfishing. The awards Magic has garnered are too many to mention here, but we can tell you their magnificent 50-foot *Pacifica* fishing yacht is built for comfort, fishing or otherwise. Unfortunately, Magic can accommodate only up to six. Full-day exclusive charter rates for groups of six begin at $950. ☎ *808/596–2998.*

Dolphin Encounters

Pods of dolphins surround the Islands, and spotting them can be as easy as just getting yourself out in the ocean. They are wild animals and do not follow a schedule, but a catamaran sail off Waikīkī will usually net you a spotting. Dolphins also generally make appearances shortly after sunrise on the West Shore and can be clearly observed from beaches like Makua and Mākaha. And while they won't have the peppy music of Sea World in the background, their jumping and spinning is even more awe-inspiring when you realize they are just doing it for fun rather than for a reward.

Sea Life Park. Dolphins are just one of the attractions at this outdoor marine-life park. Seals, sting rays, and Hawaiian sea turtles are also in residence. Rates for the 45-minute interaction sessions with their Atlantic bottlenose dolphins in the saltwater lagoon begin at $140. The in-the-water action includes belly rides along the surface as you hold onto a dolphin's pectoral fin. ✉ *41-202 Kalaniana'ole Hwy., Waimānalo* ☎ *808/259–7933 or 886/365–7446.*

★ **Wild Side Speciality Tours.** This west-side charter follows the wild spinner dolphins that make their home off of Makua Beach. The marine biologists who conduct the tours evaluate the dolphins' mood; when the animals are playful and open to interaction, you are allowed to jump in and snorkel with them. If the dolphins seem strained or agitated, then you watch from the boat. There are no guarantees as these are wild animals. Rates for the four-hour sail begin at $95 per person. ✉ *Wai'anae Boat Harbor, Slip A-11* ☎ *808/306–7273* ⊕ *www.sailhawaii.com.*

Jet Skiing, Wakeboarding & Waterskiing

Aloha Parasail/Jet Ski. Jet ski in the immense Ke'ehi Lagoon as planes from Honolulu International take off and land right above you. After an instructional safety course, you can try your hand at navigating their buoyed course. They provide free pickup and drop-off from Waikīkī. The Waverunners run about $40 per person for 45 minutes of riding time. ☎ *808/521–2446.*

Hawai'i Sports Wakeboard and Water Ski Center. Hawai'i Sports turns Maunalua Bay into an action water park with activities for all ages. While dad's learning to wakeboard, the kids can hang on for dear life on bumper tubes, and mom can finally get some peace parasailing over the bay with views going to Diamond Head and beyond. There are also banana boats that will ride six, Jet Skis for two, and scuba missions. Half-hour Jet Ski rental rates begin at $49 per person, and package deals are available. ✉ *Koko Marina Shopping Center, 7192 Kalaniana'ole Hwy., Hawai'i Kai* ☎ *808/395–3773* ⊕ *www. hawaiiwatersportscenter.com.*

Kayaking

Kayaking is quickly becoming a top choice for visitors to the Islands. Kayaking alone or with a partner on the open ocean provides a vantage point not afforded by swimming and surfing. Even amateurs can travel long distances and keep a lookout on what's going on around them.

This ability to travel long distances can also get you into trouble. ■ TIP→ **Experts agree that rookies should stay on the Windward side.** Their reasoning is simple: if you tire, break or lose an oar, or just plain pass out, the onshore winds will eventually blow you back to the beach. The same cannot be said for the offshore breezes of the North Shore and West O'ahu.

Kayaks are specialized: some are better suited for riding waves while others are designed for traveling long distances. Your outfitter can address your needs depending on your activities.

Best Spots

★ The hands-down winner for kayaking is **Lanikai Beach** (⊠ Past Kailua Beach Park; street parking on Mokulua Drive for various public-access points to beach) on the Windward side. This is perfect amateur territory with its still waters and onshore winds. If you're feeling more adventurous, it's a short paddle out to the Mokes. This pair of islands off the coast has beaches, surf breaks on the reef, and great picnicking areas. Due to the distance from shore (about a mile), the Mokes usually afford privacy from all but the intrepid kayakers. Lanikai is great year-round, and most kayak-rental companies have a store right up the street in Kailua.

For something a little different try **Kahana River** (⊠ Empties into Kahana Bay, 8 mi east of Kāne'ohe), also on the Windward side. The river may not have the blue water of the ocean, but the Ko'olau Mountains, with waterfalls aplenty when it's raining, are magnificent in the background. It's a short jaunt, about 2 mi round-trip, but it is packed with rain-forest foliage and the other rain-forest denizen, mosquitos. Bring some repellent and enjoy this light workout.

Equipment Rentals & Tours

Go Bananas. Staffers make sure that you rent the appropriate kayak for your abilities, and they also outfit the rental car with soft racks to transport the boat to the beach. The store also carries clothing and kayaking accessories. Full-day rates begin at $30 for single kayaks, and $42 for doubles. ⊠ 799 Kapahulu Ave., Honolulu ☎ 808/737–9514.

Twogood Kayaks Hawai'i. The one-stop shopping outfitter for kayaks on the Windward side offers rentals, lessons, guided kayak tours, and even weeklong camps if you want to immerse yourself in the sport. Guides are trained in history, geology, and birdlife of the area. Kayak a full day with a guide for $89; this includes lunch, snorkeling gear, and transportation from Waikīkī. Although their rental prices are about $10 more than average, they do deliver the boats to the water for you and give you a crash course in ocean safety. Full-day rates begin at $49 for single kayaks, and $59 for doubles. ⊠ 345 Hahani St., Kailua ☎ 808/262–5656 ⊕ www.twogoodkayaks.com.

SURF WITH THE WHOLE FAMILY

For simple, cheap fun in Waikīkī, outrigger canoes are often overlooked. Everyone is clamoring to learn to surf or to go for a sail, but no one notices the long, funny-looking boats in front of Duke's that allow you to do both for much cheaper. At $10 for three rides, the price hasn't changed in a decade, and the thrill hasn't changed in centuries. You can get a paddle, but no one expects you to use it—the beach boys negotiate you in and out of the break as they have been doing all their lives. If you think taking off on a wave on a 10-foot board is a rush, wait until your whole family takes off on one in a 30-foot boat!

Kiteboarding

⇨ *See* Windsurfing & Kiteboarding.

Sailing

For a sailing experience in O'ahu, you need go no farther than the beach in front of your hotel in Waikīkī. Strung along the sand are seven beach catamarans that will provide you with one-hour rides during the day and 90-minute sunset sails. Look for $12 to $15 for day sails and $15 to $20 for sunset rides. ■ TIP➡ **They all have their little perks and they're known for bargaining so feel free to haggle, especially with the smaller boats.** Some provide drinks for free, some charge for them, and some let you pack your own, so keep that in mind when pricing the ride.

If you would like a fancier ride, ⇨ *see* Boat Tours & Charters.

Mai'Tai Catamaran. Taking off from in front of the Sheraton Hotel, this cat is the fastest and sleekest on the beach. If you have a need for speed and enjoy a little more upscale experience, this is the boat for you. ☎ *808/ 922–5665.*

Na Hoku II Catamaran. The diametric opposite of Mai'Tai, this is the Animal House of catamarans with reggae music and cheap booze. Their motto is "Cheap drinks, Easy Crew." They're beached right out in front of Duke's Barefoot Bar at the Outrigger Waikīkī Hotel and sail five times daily. ☎ *808/239–3900* ⊕ *www.nahokuii.com.*

Scuba Diving

All the great stuff to do atop the water sometimes leads us to forget the real beauty beneath the surface. Although snorkeling and snuba (more on that later) do give you access to this world, nothing gives you the freedom of scuba.

The diving on O'ahu is comparable with any you might do in the tropics, but its uniqueness comes from the isolated environment of the Islands. There are literally hundreds of species of fish and marine life that you can only find in this chain. Adding to the singularity of diving here is the human history of the region. Military activities and tragedies of the 20th century filled the waters surrounding O'ahu with wreckage that the ocean creatures have since turned into their homes.

Although instructors certified to license you in scuba are plentiful in the Islands, we suggest that you get your PADI certification before coming as a week of classes may be a bit of a commitment on a short vacation. You can go on introductory dives without the certification, but the best dives require it.

Best Spots

Hanauma Bay (✉ 7455 Kalaniana'ole Hwy.) is an underwater state park and a popular dive site in Southeast O'ahu. The shallow inner reef of this volcanic crater bay is filled with snorkelers, but its floor gradually drops from 10 to 70 feet at the outer reef where the big fish prefer the lighter traffic. It's quite a trek down into the crater and out to the water so you may want to consider a dive-tour company to do your heavy lifting. Expect to see butterfly fish, goatfish, parrot fish, surgeonfish, and sea turtles.

★ The best shore dive on O'ahu is **Shark's Cove** (✉ Across from Foodland in Pūpūkea) on the North Shore, but it's only accessible during the summer months. Novices can drift along the outer wall, watching everything from turtles to eels. Veterans can explore the numerous lava tubes and tunnels where diffused sunlight from above creates a dreamlike effect in spacious caverns. It's 10- to 45-feet deep, ready-made for shore diving with a parking lot right next to the dive spot. Three Tables, just west, is an alternative for the more timid snorkeler or diver. Be cautious the later in the year you go to either of these sights; the waves pick up strength in fall, and the reef can be turned into a washboard for you and your gear. Both are null and void during the winter surf sessions.

Charters, Lessons & Equipment

Reeftrekkers. The owners of the slickest dive Web site in Hawai'i are also the *Scuba Diving* Reader's Choice winners for the past four years. Using the dive descriptions and price quotes on their Web site, you can plan your excursions before ever setting foot on the island. Two-tank boat dive rates begin at $95 per person. ☎ 808/943–0588 ⊕ *www.reeftrekkers.com.*

Surf-N-Sea. The North Shore headquarters for all things water-related is great for diving that side as well. There is one interesting perk—the cameraman can shoot a video of you diving. It's hard to see facial expressions under the water, but it still might be fun for those that need documentation of all they do. Two-tank boat dive rates begin at $110 per person. ☎ 808/637–3337 ⊕ *www.surfnsea.com.*

Snorkeling

One advantage that snorkeling has over scuba is that you never run out of air. That and the fact that anyone who can swim can also snorkel without any formal training. A favorite pastime in Hawai'i, snorkeling can be done anywhere there's enough water to stick your face in it. Each spot will have its great days depending on the weather and time of year, so consult with the purveyor of your gear for tips on where the best viewing is that day. Keep in mind that the North Shore should only be attempted when the waves are calm, namely in the summertime.

■ TIP➔ **Think of buying a mask and snorkel as a prerequisite for your trip—they make any beach experience better.** Just make sure you put plenty of sunblock on your back because once you start gazing below, your head may not come back up for hours.

Best Spots

As Waimea Bay is to surfing, **Hanauma Bay** (✉ 7455 Kalaniana'ole Hwy.) in Southeast O'ahu is to snorkeling. By midday it can look like the mall at Christmas with all the bodies, but with over a half-million fish to observe, there's plenty to go around. Due to the protection of the narrow mouth of the cove and the prodigious reef, you will be hard-pressed to find a place you will feel safer while snorkeling.

Directly across from the electric plant outside of Kō 'Olina resort, **Electric Beach** (✉ 1 mi west of Kō 'Olina) in West O'ahu has become a haven for tropical fish. The expulsion of hot water from the plant warms the ocean water, attracting all kinds of wildlife. Although the visibility is not always the best, the crowds are thin, and the fish are guaranteed. Just park next to the old train tracks and enjoy this secret spot.

Equipment Rental

Snorkel Bob's. We suggest buying your gear, unless it's going to be a one-day affair. Either way, Snorkel Bob's has all the stuff you'll need (and a bunch of stuff you don't) to make your water adventures enjoyable. Also feel free to ask the staff about the good spots at the moment, as the best spots can vary with weather and seasons. ✉ *700 Kapahulu Ave.* ☎ *808/735–7944.*

Snorkel Sails

Kahala Kai. The *Kahala Kai* sails out of Kewalo Basin in Honolulu—very convenient if you have other plans in town. Take a two-hour sail out to sea turtle breeding grounds where 50-foot-plus visibility makes for great snorkeling with loads of sea life from turtles and reef fish to dolphins, and, in the wintertime, whales. Rates for a two-hour sail, all equipment included, begin at $45 per person; ask for Captain Roger. ☎ *808/227–3556.*

> ### SHARK!
>
> "You go in the cage, cage goes in the water, you go in the water, shark's in the water . . ." You remember this line from *Jaws,* and now you get to play the role of Richard Dreyfus, as **North Shore Shark Adventures** provides you with an interactive experience out of your worst nightmare. The tour allows you to swim and snorkel in a cage as dozens of sharks lurk just feet from you in the open ocean off the North Shore, and all for just $120. ☎ *808/228-5900* ⊕ *sharktourshawaii.com.*

Kō 'Olina Kat. The dock in Kō 'Olina harbor is a little more out of the way, but this is a much more luxurious option than the town snorkel cruises. Three-hour tours of the west side of O'ahu are punctuated with stops for observing dolphins from the boat and a snorkel spot well populated with fish. All gear, snacks, sandwiches, and two alcoholic beverages make for a more complete experience, but also a pricier one (starting at $99.50 per person). ☎ *808/234–7145.*

Snuba

Snuba, the marriage of scuba and snorkeling, gives the nondiving set their first glimpse of the freedom of scuba. Snuba utilizes a raft with a standard air tank on it and a 20-foot air hose that hooks up to a regulator. Once attached to the hose, you can swim, unfettered by heavy tanks and weights, up to 15 feet down to chase fish and examine reef for as long as you fancy. If you ever get scared or need a rest, the raft is right there, ready to support you. Kids eight years and older can use the equipment. It can be pricey, but then again, how much is it worth to be able to sit face-to-face with a 6-foot-long sea turtle and not have to rush to the surface to get another breath? At **Hanauma Bay Snuba Dive** (☎ 808/256–8956), a three-hour outing (with 45 minutes in the water) costs $87.

Submarine Tours

***Atlantis* Submarines.** This is the underwater venture for the unadventurous. Not fond of swimming but want to see what you have been missing? Board this 64-passenger vessel for a ride down past shipwrecks, turtle breeding grounds, and coral reefs galore. Unlike a trip to the aquarium, this gives you a chance to see nature at work without the limitations of mankind. The tours, which leave from the pier at the Hilton Hawaiian Village, are available in several languages and run from $69 to $115. ⊠ *Hilton Hawaiian Village Beach Resort and Spa, 2005 Kālia Rd., Waikīkī, Honolulu 96815* ☎ *808/973–1296.*

Surfing

Perhaps no word is more associated with Hawai'i than surfing. Every year the best of the best gather here to have their Super Bowl: the Triple Crown of Surfing. The pros dominate the waves for a month, but the rest of the year belongs to people like us, just trying to have fun and get a little exercise.

O'ahu is unique because it has so many famous spots: Banzai Pipeline, Waimea Bay, Kaiser Bowls, and Sunset Beach resonate in young surfers' hearts the world over. The renown of these spots comes with a price: competition for those wave. The aloha spirit lives in many places but not on premium waves. If you're coming to visit and want to surf these world-famous breaks, you need to go out with a healthy dose of respect and patience. As long as you follow the rules of the road and concede waves to local riders, you should not have problems. Just remember that locals view these waves as their property, and everything should be all right.

If you're nervous and don't want to run the risk of a confrontation, try some of the alternate spots listed below. They may not have the name recognition, but the waves can be just as great.

Best Spots

In Waikīkī, try getting out to **Populars**, a break at **Ulukou Beach** (⊠ Waikīkī, in front of Royal Hawaiian Hotel). Nice and easy, Popu-

SURF SMART

A few things to remember when surfing in O'ahu:

• The waves switch with the seasons—they're big in the south in summer, and they loom large in the north in winter. If you're not experienced, it's best to go where the waves are small. There will be fewer crowds, and your chances of injury dramatically decrease.

• Always wear a leash. It may not look the coolest, but when your board gets swept away from you and you're swimming a half mile after it, you'll remember this advice.

• Watch where you're going. Take a few minutes and watch the surf from the shore. Observe how big it is, where it's breaking, and how quickly the sets are coming. This knowledge will allow you to get in and out more easily and to spend more time riding waves and less time paddling.

lars never breaks too hard and is friendly to both the rookie and the veteran. The only downside here is the half-mile paddle out to the break, but no one ever said it was going to be easy. Plus the long pull keeps it from getting overcrowded.

White Plains Beach (⊠ In former Kalaeloa Military Installation) is a spot where trouble will not find you. Known among locals as "mini-Waikīkī," it breaks in numerous spots, preventing the logjam that happens with many of O'ahu's more popular breaks. As part of a military base in West O'ahu, the beach was closed to the public until a couple of years ago. It's now occupied by mostly novice to intermediate surfers, so egos are at a minimum, though you do have to keep a lookout for loose boards.

Surf Shops

C&K Beach Service. To rent a board in Waikīkī, visit the beach fronting the Hilton Hawaiian Village. Rentals cost $10 to $15 per hour, depending on the size of the board, and $18 for two hours. Small group lessons are $50 per hour with board, and trainers promise to have you riding the waves by lesson's end. ☎ *No phone.*

Surf 'N Sea. This is the Wal-Mart of water for the North Shore. Rent a short board for $5 an hour or a long board for $7 an hour ($24 and $30 for full-day rentals). Lessons cost $69 for two hours. Depending on how you want to attack your waves, you can also rent boogie boards or kayaks. ⊠ *62-595 Kamehameha Hwy.* ☎ *808/637–9887* ⊕ *www.surfnsea.com.*

Surfing Lessons

🌀 **Hawaiian Fire, Inc.** Off-duty Honolulu firefighters—and some of Hawai'i's
FodorsChoice most knowledgeable water-safety experts—man the boards at one of
★ Hawai'i's hottest new surfing schools. Lessons include equipment, safety and surfing instruction, and two hours of surfing time (with lunch break) at a secluded beach near Barbers Point. Transportation is avail-

able from Waikīkī. Two-hour group-lesson rates begin at $97 per person, $139 per person for a private lesson. ☎ 808/737–3473 or 888/955–7873 ⊕ *www.hawaiianfire.com.*

North Shore Eco-Surf Tours. The only prerequisites here are "the ability to swim and the desire to surf." North Shore Eco-Surf has a more relaxed view of lessons, saying that the instruction will last somewhere between 90 minutes and four hours. The group rate begins at $65 per person, $120 for a private lesson. ☎ 808/638–9503 ⊕ *www.ecosurf-hawaii.com.*

Whale-Watching

November is marked by the arrival of snow in most of America, but in Hawai'i it marks the return of the humpback whale. These migrating behemoths move south from their North Pacific homes during the winter months for courtship and childbirth and what a display they conduct. Watching males and females alike throwing themselves out of the ocean and into the sunset awes even the saltiest of sailors. Newborn calves riding gently next to their two-ton mothers will stir you to your core. These gentle giants can be seen from the shore as they make quite a splash, but there is nothing like having your boat rocking beneath you in the wake of a whale's breach.

At Hawai'i Sailing Adventures (⇨ *See* Boat Tours & Charters), two-hour whale-watching cruise rates with dinner start at $119.

★ **Wild Side Specialty Tours.** Boasting a marine biologist crew, this west-side tour boat takes you to undisturbed snorkeling areas. Along the way you can view dolphins, turtles, and, in winter, whales. The tours leave early (7 AM) to catch the wildlife still active, so it's important to plan ahead as they're an hour outside Honolulu. Four-hour whale-watching cruise rates with Continental breakfast start at $95. ⊠ *Wai'anae Boat Harbor, Slip A11* ☎ 808/306–7273.

Windsurfing & Kiteboarding

Those who call windsurfing and kiteboarding cheating because they require no paddling have never tried hanging on to a sail or kite. It will turn your arms to spaghetti quicker than paddling ever could, and the speeds you generate . . . well, there's a reason why these are considered extreme sports.

Windsurfing was born here in the Islands. For amateurs, the Windward side is best because the onshore breezes will bring you back to land even if you don't know what you're doing. The new sport of kite surfing is tougher but more exhilarating as the kite will sometimes take you in the air for hundreds of feet. We suggest only those in top shape try the kites, but windsurfing is fun for all ages.

> **ON THE SIDELINES**
>
> Watch the pros jump and spin on the waves during July's **Pan Am Hawaiian Windsurfing World Cup** (☎ 808/734–6999) off Kailua Beach. August's **Wahine Classic** (☎ 808/521–4322), held off Diamond Head point, features the world's best female boardsailors.

Equipment Rentals & Lessons

Kailua Sailboard and Kayaks Company. The appeal here is that they offer both beginner and high-performance gear. They also give lessons, either at $69 for a three-hour group lesson or $35 for a one-hour individual lesson (you must rent a board half-day at $39). Since both options are around the same price, we suggest the one-hour individual lesson; then you have the rest of the day to practice what they preach. ✉ *130 Kailua Rd., Kailua* ☎ *808/262–2555.*

Naish Hawai'i. If you like to learn from the best, try out world-champion Robby Naish and his family services. Not only do they build and sell boards, rent equipment, provide accommodation referrals, but they also offer their windsurfing and kiteboarding expertise. A four-hour package, including 90 minutes of instruction and a four-hour board rental, costs $55. ✉ *155A Hamakua Dr., Kailua* ☎ *808/261–6067* ⊕ *www. naish.com.*

GOLF, HIKING & OUTDOOR ACTIVITIES

Aerial Tours

By Chad Pata

★ **Island Seaplane Service.** Harking back to the days of the earliest air visitors to Hawai'i, the seaplane has always had a special spot in island lore. The only seaplane service still operating in Hawai'i takes off from Ke'ehi Lagoon. Flight options are either a half-hour south and eastern O'ahu shoreline tour or an hour island circle tour. The *Pan Am Clipper* may be gone, but you can revisit the experience for $99 to $179. ✉ *85 Lagoon Dr., Honolulu* ☎ *808/836–6273.*

Makani Kai Helicopters. This may be the best way to now see the infamous and now closed Sacred Falls park, where a rock slide killed 20 people and injured dozens more; Makani Kai dips their helicopter down to show you one of Hawai'i's former favorite hikes. There's also a Waikīkī by Night excursion that soars by the breathtaking Honolulu city lights. Half-hour tour rates begin at $109 per person, and customized charters are available starting at $550 per hour. ✉ *110 Kapalulu Pl., Honolulu* ☎ *808/834–5813* ⊕ *www.makanikai.com.*

The Original Glider Rides. "Mr. Bill" has been offering piloted glider (sailplane) rides over the northwest end of O'ahu's North Shore since 1970. These are piloted scenic rides for one or two passengers in sleek, bubble-top, motorless aircraft. You'll get aerial views of mountains, shoreline, coral pools, windsurfing sails, and, in winter, humpback whales. Reservations are recommended; 10-, 15-, 20-, and 30-minute flights leave every 20 minutes daily 10–5. The charge for one passenger is $59–$139, depending on the length of the the flight; two people fly for $138–$238. ✉ *Dillingham Airfield, Mokulē'ia* ☎ *808/677–3404.*

Biking

O'ahu's coastal roads are flat and well paved. On the downside, roads are also awash in vehicular traffic. Frankly, biking is no fun in either Waikīkī or Honolulu, but things are a bit better outside the city. Be sure to take along a nylon jacket for the frequent showers on the Windward side and remember that Hawai'i is paradise after the fall: lock up your bike.

Honolulu City and County Bike Coordinator (☎ 808/527–5044) can answer all your biking questions concerning trails, permits, and state laws.

Best Spots

Biking the North Shore may sound like a great idea, but the two-lane road is narrow and traffic-heavy. We suggest you try the **West Kaunala Trail** (⊠ End of Pūpūkea Rd. This road is next to Foodland, the only grocery store on North Shore). It's a little tricky at times, but with the rain forest surroundings and beautiful ocean vistas you'll hardly notice your legs burning on the steep ascent at the end. It's about 5½ mi round-trip. Bring water because there's none on the trail unless it comes from the sky.

Our favorite ride is in central O'ahu on the **'Aiea Loop Trail** (⊠ Central O'ahu, just past Kea'iwa Heiau State Park, at end of 'Aiea Heights Dr.). There's a little bit of everything you expect to find in Hawai'i—wild pigs crossing your path, an ancient Hawaiian *heiau* (holy ground), and the remains of a World War II crashed airplane. Campsites and picnic tables are available along the way and, if you need a snack, strawberry guava trees abound. Enjoy the foliage change from bamboo to Norfolk pine in your climb along this 4½-mi track.

Bike Shops & Clubs

Blue Sky Rentals & Sports Center. Known more for motorcycles than for man-powered bikes, Blue Sky does have bicycles for $18 per day (from 8 to 6), $26 for 24 hours, and $75 per week—a $100 deposit is required for weekly rentals. The prices include a bike, a helmet, a lock, and a water bottle. ⊠ *1920 Ala Moana Blvd., across from Hilton Hawaiian Village, Waikīkī, Honolulu* ☎ *808/947–0101.*

Boca Hawai'i LLC. This is your first stop if you want to do intense riding. The triathlon shop, owned and operated by top athletes, has full-suspension Trek 4500s for $35 a day with a two-day minimum ($25 for each additional day). Call ahead and reserve a bike as supplies are limited. ⊠ *330 Cooke St., next to Bike Factory, Kaka'ako, Honolulu* ☎ *808/591–9839.*

Golf

Unlike those of the Neighbor Islands, the majority of O'ahu's golf courses are not associated with hotels and resorts. In fact, of the island's three-dozen-plus courses, only five are tied to lodging and none of them are in the tourist hub of Waikīkī.

Green Fees: Green fees listed here are the highest course rates per round on weekdays/weekends for U.S. residents. (Some courses charge non-U.S. residents higher prices.)

> **CARTS**
>
> Unless you play a muni or certain daily fee courses, plan on taking a cart. Riding carts are mandatory at most courses and are included in the green fees.

Discounts are often available for resort guests and for those who book tee times on the Web. Twilight fees are usually offered, call individual courses for information.

Honolulu

Ala Wai Municipal Golf Course. Just across the Ala Wai Canal from Waikīkī, Ala Wai is said to host more rounds than any other U.S. course. Not that it's a great course, just really convenient, being Honolulu's only public city course. Although residents can obtain a city golf card that allows automated tee times over the phone, the best bet for a visitor is to show up and expect a minimum hour's wait. The course itself is flat. Robin Nelson did some redesign work in the 1990s, adding mounding, trees, and a lake. The Ala Wai Canal comes into play on several holes on the back nine, including the treacherous 18th. ⊠ *404 Kapahulu Ave., Waikīkī* ☎ *808/733–7387, 808/739–1900 golf shop* ⚑ *18 holes. 5861 yds. Par 70. Green Fee: $42* ☞ *Facilities: Driving range, putting green, golf carts, pull carts, rental clubs, pro shop, lessons, restaurant, bar.*

Southeast Oʻahu

Hawaiʻi Kai Golf Course. The **Championship Golf Course** (William F. Bell, 1973) winds through a Honolulu suburb at the foot of Koko Crater. Homes (and the liability of a broken window) come into play on many holes, but that is offset by views of the nearby Pacific and a crafty routing of holes. With several lakes, lots of trees, and bunkers in all the wrong places, Hawaiʻi Kai really is a championship golf course, especially when the trade winds howl. The **Executive Course** (1962), a par-55 track, is the first of only three courses in Hawaiʻi built by Robert Trent Jones Sr. Although a few changes have been made to his original design, you can find the usual Jones attributes, including raised greens and lots of risk-reward options. ⊠ *8902 Kalanianaʻole Hwy., Hawaiʻi Kai* ☎ *808/ 395–2358* ⊕ *www.hawaiikaigolf.com* ⚑ *Championship Course: 18 holes. 6222 yds. Par 72. Green Fee: $80/$90. Executive Course: 18 holes. 2223 yds. Par 55. Green Fee: $37/$42* ☞ *Facilities: Driving range, putting green, golf carts, pull carts, rental clubs, pro shop, lessons, restaurant, bar.*

Windward Oʻahu

Koʻolau Golf Club. Koʻolau Golf Club is marketed as the toughest golf course in Hawaiʻi and one of the most challenging in the country. Dick Nugent and Jack Tuthill (1992) routed 10 holes over jungle ravines that require at least a 110-yard carry. The par-4 18th may be the most difficult closing hole in golf. The tee shot from the regular tees must carry 200 yards of ravine, 250 from the blue tees. The approach shot is back across the ravine, 200 yards to a well-bunkered green. Set at the windward base of the Koʻolau Mountains, the course is as much beauty as beast. Kāneʻohe Bay is visible from most holes, orchids and yellow ginger bloom, the shama thrush (Hawaiʻi's best singer since Don Ho) chirrups, and waterfalls flute down the sheer, green mountains above. ⊠ *45-550 Kionaole Rd., Kāneʻohe* ☎ *808/236–4653* ⊕ *www. koolaugolfclub.com* ⚑ *18 holes. 7310 yds. Par 72. Green Fee: $135* ☞ *Facilities: Driving range, putting green, golf carts, rental clubs, pro shop, golf academy, restaurant, bar.*

Fodor'sChoice **Luana Hills Country Club.** In the cool, lush Maunawili Valley, Pete and
★ Perry Dye created what can only be called target jungle golf. In other
words, the rough is usually dense jungle, and you may not hit driver on
three of the four par-5s, or several par-4s, including the perilous 18th
that plays off a cliff to a narrow green protected by a creek. Mt. Olomana's twin peaks tower over Luana Hills. The back nine wanders deep
into the valley, and includes an island green (par-3 11th) and perhaps
the loveliest inland hole in Hawai'i (par-4 12th). ⊠ *770 Auloa Rd., Kailua*
☎ *808/262–2139* ⊕ *www.luanahills.com* ⅂. *18 holes. 6164 yds. Par
72. Green Fee: $125* ☞ *Facilities: Driving range, putting green, golf carts,
rental clubs, pro shop, restaurant, bar.*

Olomana Golf Links. Bob and Robert L. Baldock are the architects of record
for this layout, but so much has changed since it opened in 1969 that
they would recognize little of it. A turf specialist was brought in to improve fairways and greens, tees were rebuilt, new bunkers added, and
mangroves cut back to make better use of natural wetlands. ■ TIP→ **But
what really puts Olomana on the map is that this is where wunderkind Michelle
Wie learned the game.** ⊠ *41-1801 Kalaniana'ole Hwy., Waimānalo*
☎ *808/259–7926* ⊕ *www.olomanagolflinks.com* ⅂. *18 holes. 6326
yds. Par 72. Green Fee: $80* ☞ *Facilities: Driving range, putting green,
golf carts, pull carts, rental clubs, pro shop, lessons, restaurant, bar.*

North Shore

Turtle Bay Resort & Spa. When the Lazarus of golf courses, the **Fazio Course**
at Turtle Bay (George Fazio, 1971), rose from the dead in 2002, Turtle
Bay on O'ahu's rugged North Shore became a premier golf destination.
Two holes had been plowed under when the Palmer Course at Turtle
Bay (Arnold Palmer and Ed Seay, 1992) was built, while the other seven
lay fallow, and the front nine remained open. Then new owners came
along and re-created holes 13 and 14 using Fazio's original plans, and
the Fazio became whole again. It's a terrific track with 90 bunkers. The
gem at Turtle Bay, though, is the **Palmer Course**. The front nine is
mostly open as it skirts Punaho'olapa Marsh, a nature sanctuary, while
the back nine plunges into the wetlands and winds along the coast. The
short par-4 17th runs along the rocky shore, with a diabolical string of
bunkers cutting diagonally across the fairway from tee to green. ⊠ *57-
049 Kuilima Dr., Kahuku* ☎ *808/293–8574* ⊕ *www.turtlebayresort.com*
⅂. *Fazio Course: 18 holes. 6535 yds. Par 72. Green Fee: $155. Palmer
Course: 18 holes. 7199 yds. Par 72. Green Fee: $165* ☞ *Facilities: Dri-
ving range, putting green, golf carts, rental clubs, pro shop, lessons, restaurant, bar.*

West (Leeward) & Central O'ahu

★ **Coral Creek Golf Course.** On the 'Ewa Plain, 4 mi inland, Coral Creek is
cut from ancient coral—left from when this area was still under water.
Robin Nelson (1999) does some of his best work in making use of the
coral, and of some dynamite, blasting out portions to create dramatic
lakes and tee and green sites. They could just as easily call it Coral Cliffs,
because of the 30- to 40-foot cliffs Nelson created. They include the par-
3 10th green's grotto and waterfall, and the vertical drop-off on the right
side of the par-4 18th green. An ancient creek meanders across the

course, but there's not much water, just enough to be a babbling nuisance. ✉ *91-1111 Geiger Rd., 'Ewa Beach* ☎ *808/441–4653* ⊕ *www. coralcreekgolfhawaii.com* ⅋ *18 holes. 6818 yds. Par 72. Green Fee: $130* ☞ *Facilities: Driving range, putting green, golf carts, rental clubs, pro shop, lessons, restaurant, bar.*

Kō 'Olina Golf Club. Hawai'i's golden age of golf-course architecture came to O'ahu when Kō 'Olina Golf Club opened in 1989. Ted Robinson, king of the water features, went splash-happy here, creating nine lakes that come into play on eight holes, including the par-3 12th, where you reach the tee by driving behind a Disney-like waterfall. Tactically, though, the most dramatic is the par-4 18th, where the approach is a minimum 120 yards across a lake to a two-tiered green guarded on the left by a cascading waterfall. Today, Kō 'Olina, affiliated with the adjacent 'Ihilani Resort and Spa (guests receive discounted rates), has matured into one of Hawai'i's top courses. You can niggle about routing issues—the first three holes play into the trade winds (and the morning sun), and two consecutive par-5s on the back nine play into the trades—but Robinson does enough solid design to make those of passing concern. ✉ *92-1220 Ali'inui Dr., Kapolei* ☎ *808/676–5300* ⊕ *www.koolinagolf.com* ⅋ *18 holes. 6867 yds. Par 72. Green Fee: $160* ☞ *Facilities: Driving range, putting green, golf carts, rental clubs, pro shop, golf academy, restaurant, bar.*

Royal Kunia Country Club. At one time the PGA Tour considered buying Royal Kunia Country Club and hosting the Sony Open there. It's that good. ■ TIP➔ **Every hole offers fabulous views from Diamond Head to Pearl Harbor to the nearby Wai'anae Mountains, and Robin Nelson's eye for natural sight lines and dexterity with water features adds to the visual pleasure.** ✉ *94-1509 Anonui St., Waipahu* ☎ *808/688–9222* ⊕ *www. royalkuniacc.com* ⅋ *18 holes. 7007 yds. Par 72. Green Fee: $110/$120* ☞ *Facilities: Driving range, putting green, golf carts, rental clubs, pro shop, restaurant.*

Waikele Golf Course. Outlet stores are not the only bargain at Waikele. The adjacent golf course is a daily fee course that offers a private club-like atmosphere and a terrific Ted Robinson (1992) layout. The target off the tee is Diamond Head, with Pearl Harbor to the right. Robinson's water features are less distinctive here, but define the short par-4 fourth hole, with a lake running down the left side of the fairway and guarding the green; and the par-3 17th, which plays across a lake. The par-4 18th is a terrific closing hole, with a lake lurking on the right side of the green. At this writing, the course was closed for renovations but scheduled to be open by early 2007. ✉ *94-200 Paioa Pl., Waipahu* ☎ *808/ 676–9000* ⊕ *www.golfwaikele.com* ⅋ *18 holes. 6261 yds. Par 72. Green Fee: $125* ☞ *Facilities: Driving range, putting green, golf carts, rental clubs, pro shop, lessons, restaurant, bar.*

Hiking

The trails of O'ahu cover a full spectrum of environments: desert walks through cactus, slippery paths through bamboo-filled rain forest, and scrambling rock climbs up ancient volcanic calderas. The only thing you won't find is an overnighter as even the longest of hikes won't take you more than half a day. In addition to being short in length, many of the prime hikes are located within ten minutes of downtown Waikīkī, meaning that you won't have to spend your whole day getting back to nature.

Best Spots

Every vacation has requirements that must be fulfilled so that when your neighbors ask, you can say, "Yeah, did it." **Diamond Head Crater** is high on that list of things to do on O'ahu. It's a hike easy enough that even grandma can do it, as long as she takes a water bottle because it's hot and dry. Only a mile up, a clearly marked trail with handrails scales the inside of this extinct volcano. At the top, the fabled 99 steps take you up to the pill box overlooking the Pacific Ocean and Honolulu. It's a breathtaking view and a lot cheaper than taking a helicopter ride for the same photo op. ✛ *Diamond Head Rd. at 18th Ave. Enter on east of crater; there's limited parking inside, most park on street and walk in.*

> ## ON THE TRAIL
>
> There are a couple things to remember when hiking on O'ahu:
>
> - When hiking the waterfall and rain-forest trails, use insect repellant. The dampness draws huge swarms of bloodsuckers that can ruin a walk in the woods very quickly.
>
> - Volcanic rock is very porous and therefore likely to be loose. Rock climbing is strongly discouraged as you never know which little ledge is going to go.
>
> - Always let someone know where you are going and never hike alone. As little as the island is, many hikers have gotten lost for a week or longer.

Fodor'sChoice ★ Travel up into the valley beyond Honolulu to make the **Mānoa Falls** hike. Though only a mile long, this path passes through so many different ecosystems that you feel as if you're in an arboretum. Walk among the elephant ear ape plants, ruddy fir trees, and a bamboo forest straight out of China. At the top is a 150-foot falls with a small pool not quite suited for swimming but good for wading. This hike is more about the journey than the destination; make sure you bring some mosquito repellent because they grow 'em big up here. ✛ *Behind Mānoa Valley in Paradise Park. Take West Mānoa Rd. to end, park on side of road, and follow trail signs in.*

For the less adventurous hiker and anyone looking for a great view, there is the **Makapu'u Lighthouse Trail.** The paved trail runs up the side of Makapu'u Point in southeast O'ahu. Early on the trail is surrounded by lava rock, but, as you ascend, foliage begins taking over the barren rock with the tiny white koa haole flower and the cream-tinged spikes of the kiawe. Once atop the point, you begin to understand how alone these Islands are in the Pacific. The easternmost tip of O'ahu, this is where the island divides the sea, giving you a spectacular view of the cobalt ocean meeting the land in a cacophony of white caps. To the south are several tide pools and the lighthouse, while the eastern view looks down upon Rabbit and Kāohikaipu Islands, two bird sanctuaries just off the coast. The 2-mi round-trip hike is a great break on a circle-island trip.

✛ *Take Kalaniana'ole Hwy to the base of Makapu'u Point. Look for the asphalt strip snaking up the mountain.*

Guided Hikes

Hawai'i Nature Center. A good choice for families, the center in upper Makīkī Valley conducts a number of programs for both adults and children. There are guided hikes into tropical settings that reveal hidden waterfalls and protected forest reserves. ⊠ *2131 Makīkī Heights Dr., Makīkī Heights 96822* ☎ *808/955–0100.*

O'ahu Nature Tours. Guides explain the native flora and fauna that is your companion on glorious sunrise, hidden waterfall, mountain forest, rain forest, and volcanic walking tours. ☎ *808/924–2473* ⊕ *www. oahunaturetours.com.*

Horseback Riding

Kualoa Ranch. This ranch across from Kualoa Beach Park on the Windward side leads trail rides in the Ka'a'awa Valley. Rates for a one-hour trail ride begin at $47. Kualoa has other activities such as windsurfing, jet skiing, all-terrain-vehicle trail rides, and children's activities, which may be combined for half- or full-day package rates. ⊠ *49-560 Kamehameha Hwy., Ka'a'awa* ☎ *808/237–8515* ⊕ *www.kualoa.com.*

Turtle Bay Stables. This is the only spot on the island where you can take the horses on the beach. The stables here are part of the North Shore resort, but can be utilized by nonguests. The sunset ride is a definite must if you are a friend of our four-legged friends. Rates for a 45-minute trail ride begin at $45. ⊠ *4 mi north of Kahuku in the Turtle Bay Resort* ☎ *808/293–8811.*

Tennis

O'ahu has 181 public tennis courts that are free and open for play on a first-come, first-served basis; you're limited to 45 minutes of court time if others are waiting to play. A complete listing is free of charge from the **Department of Parks and Recreation** (⊠ Tennis Unit, 650 S. King St., Honolulu 96813 ☎ 808/971–7150 ⊕ www.co.honolulu.hi.us).

Kapi'olani Park, on the Diamond Head end of Waikīkī, has two tennis locations. The **Diamond Head Tennis Center** (⊠ 3908 Pākī Ave. ☎ 808/ 971–7150), near Kapi'olani Park, has nine courts open to the public. There are more than a dozen courts for play at **Kapi'olani Tennis Courts** (⊠ 2748 Kalākaua Ave. ☎ 808/971–2510). The closest public courts to the 'ewa end of Waikīkī are in **Ala Moana Park** (⊠ Ala Moana Blvd. ☎ 808/592–7031).

The **Pacific Beach Hotel** (⊠ 2490 Kalākaua Ave., Waikīkī ☎ 808/922–1233) has rooftop tennis courts that are open to nonguests for a fee.

Forty-five minutes from Waikīkī, on O'ahu's 'Ewa Plain, are two championship tennis courts at the **Hawai'i Prince Golf Club** (⊠ 91-1200 Ft. Weaver Rd., 'Ewa Beach ☎ 808/944–4567); shuttle service is available from the Hawai'i Prince Hotel Waikīkī for hotel guests.

Volleyball

There are sand volleyball courts in Waikīkī near Fort DeRussy. They are open to the public, so talent levels vary. However, with a winner-plays-on policy, you won't be disappointed with the level as the day progresses. For more advanced play, there is an area at Queen's Beach, but you have to bring your own nets, which leads to a little more court possessiveness. But this is the area where you will find the college kids and pros hitting it while they are in town.

SHOPPING

By Katherine Nichols

Eastern and Western traditions meet on O'ahu, where savvy shoppers find luxury goods at high-end malls and scout tiny boutiques and galleries filled with pottery, blown glass, woodwork, and Hawaiian print clothing by local artists. ■ TIP→ **Exploring downtown Honolulu, Kailua on the Windward side, and the North Shore often yields the most original merchandise.** Some of these small stores also carry a myriad of imported clothes and gifts from around the world—a reminder that, on this island half-way between Asia and the United States, shopping is a multicultural experience.

Waikīkī

Shopping Centers

DFS Galleria Waikīkī. Hermès, Cartier, and Calvin Klein are among the shops at this enclosed mall, as well as Hawai'i's largest beauty and cosmetic store. An exclusive boutique floor caters to duty-free shoppers only. Amusing and authentic Hawaiian-style shell necklaces, soaps, and printed wraps are rewards for anyone willing to wade through the pervasive tourist schlock along the Waikīkī Walk, an area of fashions, arts and crafts, and gifts. The Kālia Grill and Starbucks offer a respite for weary shoppers. ✉ *Kalākaua and Royal Hawaiian Aves., Waikīkī* ☎ *808/931–2655.*

King Kalākaua Plaza. Banana Republic and Niketown—both two stories high and stocked with the latest fashions—anchor the King Kalākaua Plaza. ✉ *2080 Kalākaua Ave., Waikīkī* ☎ *808/955–2878.*

Royal Hawaiian Shopping Center. Completely renovated in 2006 to create a more open and inviting façade, this three-block-long center may still be in flux in 2007. The final tenant mix includes more than 100 stores including Hawaiian Heirloom Jewelry Collection by Philip Rickard, which also has a museum with Victorian jewelry pieces. Bike buffs can check out the Harley-Davidson Motor Clothes and Collectibles Boutique, and the Ukulele House may inspire musicians to learn a new instrument. There are restaurants and even a post office. ✉ *2201 Kalākaua Ave., Waikīkī* ☎ *808/922–0588* ⊕ *www.shopwaikiki.com.*

2100 Kalākaua. Tenants of this elegant, town house–style center include Chanel, Coach, Tiffany & Co., Yves Saint Laurent, Gucci, and Tod's. ✉ *2100 Kalākaua Ave., Waikīkī* ☎ *808/550–4449* ⊕ *www.2100kalakaua.com.*

Books

Bestsellers. This shop in the Hilton's Rainbow Bazaar is a branch of the local independent bookstore chain. They stock novelty Hawai'i memorabilia as well as books on Hawaiian history, local maps and travel guides, and Hawaiian music. ⊠ *Hilton Hawaiian Village Beach Resort and Spa, 2005 Kālia Rd. Waikīkī* ☎ *808/953–2378.*

Boutiques

Vera Wang Boutique at Halekulani. A broad range of luxury goods, from ready-to-wear and accessories to china and crystal, reflects Vera Wang's design and style sensibilities. This lifestyle-themed shop also stocks Wang's new jewelry line, stylish eyewear, fragrances, lingerie, and tableware. ⊠ *Halekūlani, 2199 Kālia Rd.* ☎ *808/923–2311* ⊕ *www. halekulani.com.*

Clothing

Cinnamon Girl. Adorable matching mother/daughter dresses in subtle tropical prints, flower-adorned rubber slippers, and fun accessories. Shops also located in Ala Moana Center and Ward Warehouse. ⊠ *Sheraton Moana Surfrider, 2365 Kalākaua Ave.* ☎ *808/922–5536* ⊕ *www. cinnamongirl.com.*

Moonbow Tropics. An elegant selection of silk Tommy Bahama Aloha shirts, as well as tropical styles for women. ⊠ *Sheraton Moana Surfrider, 2365 Kalākaua Ave., Waikīkī* ☎ *808/924–1496* ⊕ *www. moonbowtropics.com.*

Reyn's. Reyn's is a good place to buy the aloha-print fashions residents wear. This company manufacturers its own label in the islands, has 13 locations statewide, and offers styles for men, women, and children. ⊠ *Sheraton Waikīkī, 2255 Kalākaua Ave., Waikīkī* ☎ *808/923–0331.*

Gifts

Gallery Tokusa. *Netsuke* is a toggle used to fasten small containers to obi belts on a kimono. Gallery Tokusa specializes in intricately carved netsuke, both antique and contemporary, and one-of-a-kind necklaces. ⊠ *Halekulani, 2199 Kālia Rd., Waikīkī* ☎ *808/923–2311.*

Norma Kress Gallery. Emerging native Hawaiian and Pacific Island artists show their work at this hotel gallery, highlighted with pottery, sculpture, paintings, drawings, and photography. ⊠ *Hawai'i Prince Hotel, 100 Holomana St., Waikīkī* ☎ *808/952–4761.*

★ **Sand People.** This little shop stocks easy-to-carry gifts, such as fish-shaped Christmas ornaments, Hawaiian-style notepads, charms in the shape of flip-flops (known locally as slippers), soaps, and ceramic clocks. Also located in Kailua. ⊠ *Sheraton Moana Surfrider, 2369 Kalākaua, Waikīkī* ☎ *808/924–6773* ⊕ *www.sandpeople.com.*

Honolulu: Downtown & Chinatown

Shopping Centers

Getting to the Ala Moana and Downtown Honolulu shopping centers from Waikīkī is quick and inexpensive thanks to **TheBus** and the **Waikīkī Trolley.**

Ala Moana Shopping Center. One of the nation's largest open-air malls is five minutes from Waikīkī by bus. Designer shops in residence include Gucci, Louis Vuitton, Gianni Versace, and Emporio Armani. All of Hawai'i's major department stores are here, including Neiman Marcus, Sears, and Macy's. More than 240 stores and 60 restaurants make up this 50-acre complex. One of the most interesting shops is Shanghai Tang. First opened in Hong Kong, the store imports silks and other fine fabrics, and upholds the tradition of old-style Shanghai tailoring. To get to the mall from Waikīkī, catch TheBus lines 8, 19, or 20 or hop aboard the Waikīkī Trolley's pink line, which comes through the area every half-hour. A one-way ride is $2. ⊠ *1450 Ala Moana Blvd., Ala Moana* ☎ *808/955–9517 special events and shuttle service.*

Aloha Tower Marketplace. Billing itself as a festival marketplace, Aloha Tower cozies up to Honolulu Harbor. Along with restaurants and entertainment venues, it has 80 shops and kiosks selling mostly visitor-oriented merchandise, from expensive sunglasses to exceptional local artwork to souvenir refrigerator magnets. Don't miss the aloha shirts and fancy hats for dogs at Pet Gear, and the curious mix of furniture, stationery, and clothing in Urban Rejuvenation. To get there from Waikīkī take the E-Transit Bus, which goes along TheBus routes every 15 minutes. ⊠ *1 Aloha Tower Dr., at Piers 8, 9, and 10, Downtown Honolulu* ☎ *808/566–2337* ⊕ *www.alohatower.com.*

Ward Centers. Heading west from Waikīkī toward Downtown Honolulu, you'll run into a section of town with five distinct shopping-complex areas; there are more than 120 specialty shops and 20 restaurants here. The Entertainment Complex features 16 movie theaters. A "shopping concierge" can assist you in navigating your way through the center, which spans four city blocks. For distinctive Hawaiian gift stores, visit Nohea Gallery and Native Books/Na Mea Hawaii, carrying quality work from Hawai'i artists, including mu'umu'u, lauhala products, and unparalleled Niihau shell necklaces. Island Soap and Candle Works (808/591–0533) makes all of its candles and soaps on-site with Hawaiian flower scents. Take TheBus routes 19 or 20; Fare is $2 one way. Follow The Waikīkī Trolley yellow line, which comes through the area every 45 minutes. ⊠ *1050–1200 Ala Moana Blvd., Ala Moana.*

Books

Bestsellers. Hawai'i's largest independent bookstore has its flagship shop in Downtown Honolulu on Bishop Square. They carry books by both local and national authors. There are also locations of Bestsellers at the Honolulu International Airport and in Waikīkī at the Hilton Hawaiian Village. ⊠ *1001 Bishop St., Downtown Honolulu* ☎ *808/528–2378.*

★ **Native Books/Na Mea Hawai'i.** In addition to clothing for adults and children and unusual artwork such as Niihau shell necklaces, this boutique's book selection covers Hawaiian history and language, and offers children's books set in the Islands. ⊠ *Ward Warehouse, 1050 Ala Moana Blvd.* ☎ *808/596–8885.*

Clothing

Anne Namba Designs. Anne Namba brings the beauty of classic kimonos to contemporary fashions. In addition to women's apparel, she's also

TROPICAL FLOWERS & FRUIT

Bring home fresh pineapple, papaya, or coconut to share with friends and family. Orchids also will brighten your home and remind you of your trip to the Islands. By law, all fresh-fruit and plant products must be inspected by the Department of Agriculture before export. Be sure to inquire at the shop about the Department of Agriculture rules so a surprise confiscation doesn't spoil your departure. In most cases, shipping to your home is best.

Kawamoto Nursery. Kawamoto grows all flowers on its three-acre orchid farm near Downtown Honolulu. Their specialty is the Cattleylea, a favorite for Mother's Day, and they have decades of experience shipping temperamental orchids to the Mainland. ☒ *2630 Waiomao Rd.* ☎ *808/732–5808* ⊕ *www.kawamotoorchids.com.*

Tropical Fruits Distributors of Hawai'i. Avoid the hassle of airport inspections. This company specializes in packing inspected pineapple and papaya; they will deliver to your hotel and to the airport check-in counter, or ship to the mainland United States and Canada. Think about ordering on the Web, unless you are planning a trip to the North Shore. ⌂ *64-1551 Kamehameha Hwy. 808/847–3234* ☒ *Ilalo St., Wahiawa* ☎ *800/697–9100* ⊕ *www.dolefruithawaii.com.*

designed a men's line and a wedding couture line. ☒ *324 Kamani St., Downtown Honolulu* ☎ *808/589–1135.*

Hilo Hattie. Busloads of visitors pour in through the front doors of the world's largest manufacturer of Hawaiian and tropical aloha wear. Once shunned by Honolulu residents for its three-shades-too-bright tourist wear, it has become a favorite source for island gifts, macadamia nut and chocolate packages, and clothing. Free shuttle service is available from Waikīkī. ☒ *700 N. Nimitz Hwy., Iwilei* ☎ *808/535–6500.*

★ **Shanghai Tang.** First opened in Hong Kong, Shanghai Tang now has its 11th branch at Ala Moana. An emphasis on workmanship and the luxury of fine fabrics upholds the tradition of old-Shanghai tailoring. They do custom work for men, women, and children. ☒ *Ala Moana Shopping Center, Ala Moana* ☎ *808/942–9800.*

Food

Honolulu Chocolate Company. To really impress those back home, pick up a box of gourmet chocolates here. They dip the flavors of Hawai'i, from Kona coffee to macadamia nuts, in fine chocolate. ☒ *Ward Centre, 1200 Ala Moana Blvd., Ala Moana* ☎ *808/591–2997.*

Longs Drugs. For gift items in bulk, try one of the many outposts of Longs, the perfect place to stock up on chocolate-covered macadamia nuts—at reasonable prices—to carry home. ☒ *Ala Moana Shopping Center, 1450 Ala Moana Blvd., 2nd level, Ala Moana* ☎ *808/941–4433* ☒ *Kāhala Mall, 4211 Wai'alae Ave., Kāhala* ☎ *808/732–0784.*

Gifts

Robyn Buntin Galleries. Chinese nephrite-jade carvings, Japanese lacquer and screens, and Buddhist sculptures are among the international pieces displayed here. ⊠ *820 S. Beretania St., Downtown Honolulu* ☎ *808/545-5572.*

Hawaiian Arts & Crafts

Hawaiian Quilt Collection. Traditional island comforters, wall hangings, pillows, and other Hawaiian-print quilt items are the specialty here. ⊠ *Ala Moana Center, 1450 Ala Moana Blvd., Ala Moana* ☎ *808/946-2233.*

Louis Pohl Gallery. Modern works from some of Hawai'i's finest artists. ⊠ *1111 Nu'uanu Ave., Downtown Honolulu* ☎ *808/521-1812* ⊕ *www.louispohlgallery.com.*

My Little Secret. The word is out that this is a wonderful selection of Hawaiian arts, crafts, and children's toys. ⊠ *Ward Warehouse, 1050 Ala Moana Blvd., Ala Moana* ☎ *808/596-2990.*

Na Hoku. If you look at the wrists of *kama'āina* women, you are apt to see Hawaiian heirloom bracelets fashioned in either gold or silver in a number of island-inspired designs. Na Hoku sells jewelry in designs, such as that on these bracelets, that captures the heart of the Hawaiian lifestyle in all its elegant diversity. ⊠ *Ala Moana Center, 1450 Ala Moana Blvd., Ala Moana* ☎ *808/946-2100.*

Nohea Gallery. These shops are really galleries representing over 450 artists who specialize in koa furniture, bowls, and boxes, as well as art glass and ceramics. Original paintings and prints—all with an island theme—add to the selection. They also carry unique handmade Hawaiian jewelry with ti leaf, maile, and coconut-weave designs. ■ TIP➔ **The koa photo albums in these stores are easy to carry home and make wonderful gifts.** ⊠ *Ward Warehouse, 1050 Ala Moana Blvd., Ala Moana* ☎ *808/596-0074* ⊠ *Ward Center, 1200 Ala Moana Blvd., Ala Moana* ☎ *808/591-9001.*

Leis

■ TIP➔ **Airport lei are highly overpriced, so head to Chinatown as the locals do for the best deals.**
Maunakea Street is lined with shop after shop displaying hanging lei. Most of these are family-run businesses that have been around for decades. Prices range from $3 to $30. With most of the shops on this street, you can pull up right outside the front door, jump out of the car, and buy a beautiful, fragrant memento of your vacation.

> **BUYING LEIS**
>
> For the best-smelling flowers, try pīkake, ginger, or pua kenikeni. The green pakalana flower and bright orange 'ilima blossom are beautiful but shrink quickly in the heat. If you want a lei that will last you a few days, try crown flower or a woven Thailand jumbo orchid lei. For something really special, get a colorful *haku* (head) lei, which is made from flowers, ferns, and native foliage—they're available year-round.

Honolulu: East

Kapahulu

Kapahulu begins at the Diamond Head end of Waikīkī and continues up to the H-1 freeway. Shops and restaurants are located primarily on Kapahulu Avenue, which like many older neighborhoods, should not be judged at first glance. It is full of variety.

Bailey's Antiques & Aloha Shirts. Vintage aloha shirts are the specialty at this kitschy store. Prices start at $3.99 for the 10,000 shirts in stock, and the tight space and musty smell are part of the thrift-shop atmosphere. Antiques hunters can also buy old-fashioned postcards, authentic military clothing, funky hats, and denim jeans from the 1950s. ⊠ *517 Kapahulu Ave., Kapahulu* ☎ *808/734–7628.*

Kāhala & Hawai'i Kai

Kāhala Mall. The upscale residential neighborhood of Kāhala, near the slopes of Diamond Head, is 10 minutes by car from Waikīkī. The only shopping of note in the area is located at the indoor mall, which has 90 stores, including Macy's, Gap, Reyn's Aloha Wear, and Barnes & Noble. Don't miss fashionable boutiques such as **Ohelo Road** (☎ 808/735–5525), where contemporary clothing for all occasions fills the racks. Eight **movie theaters** (☎ 808/733–6233) provide post-shopping entertainment. ⊠ *4211 Wai'alae Ave., Kāhala* ☎ *808/732–7736.*

Island Treasures. Local residents come here to shop for gifts that are both unique and within reach of almost every budget, ranging in price from $1 to $5,000. Located next to Zippy's and overlooking the ocean, the store has handbags, toys, jewelry, home accessories, soaps and lotions, and locally-made original artwork. Certainly the most interesting shop in Hawai'i Kai's suburban-mall atmosphere, this store is also a good place to purchase CDs of some of the best Hawaiian music. ⊠ *Koko Marina Center, 7192 Kalaniana'ole Hwy. Hawai'i Kai* ☎ *808/396–8827.*

Windward O'ahu

The Balcony Gallery. Known almost exclusively to Kailua residents, this small, out-of-the-way gallery features contemporary paintings, photographs, glass, woodwork, ceramics, and jewelry from artists in the Islands. Join them from 2 to 5 PM on the second Sunday of every month for a tour of 15 art venues in the area. Gallery hours are limited; call before you go. ⊠ *442A Uluniu St., Kailua* ☎ *808/263–4434* ☉ *Closed Sun. and Mon.*

Bookends. The perfect place to shop for gifts, or just take a break with the family, this bookstore feels more like a small-town library, welcoming browsers to linger for hours. The large children's section is filled with toys and books to read. ⊠ *600 Kailua Rd., Kailua* ☎ *808/261–1996.*

★ **Global Village.** Tucked into a tiny strip mall near Maui Tacos, this boutique features contemporary apparel for women, Hawai'ian-style children's clothing, and unusual jewelry and gifts from all over the world. Look for Kula Cushions eye pillows (made with lavender grown on Maui), coasters in the shape of flip-flops, a wooden key holder shaped like a surfboard, and placemats made from lauhala and other natural fibers, plus accessories you won't find anywhere else. ⊠ *Kailua Village Shops, 539 Kailua Rd., Kailua* ☎ *808/262–8183* ⊕ *www.globalvillagehawaii.com.*

Fodor'sChoice ★ **Jeff Chang Pottery & Fine Crafts.** With store locations downtown and in Waikīkī, Jeff Chang has become synonymous with excellent craftsmanship and originality in raku pottery, blown glass, and koa wood. Gift ideas include petroglyph stoneware coasters, photo albums covered in Hawaiian print fabric, blown-glass penholders and business card holders, and Japanese Aeto chimes. The owners choose work from 300 different local and national artists. ⊠ *Kailua Village Shops, 539 Kailua Rd., Kailua* ☎ *808/262–4060.*

Under a Hula Moon. Exclusive tabletop items and Pacific home decor, such as shell wreaths, shell night lights, Hawaiian-print kitchen towels, and Asian silk clothing, define this eclectic shop. ⊠ *Kailua Shopping Center, 600 Kailua Rd., Kailua* ☎ *808/261–4252* ⊕ *www. underahulamoon.com.*

North Shore

The Growing Keiki. Frequent visitors return to this store year after year. They know they'll find a fresh supply of original, hand-picked, Hawaiian-style clothing for youngsters. ⊠ *66-051 Kamehameha Hwy., Hale'iwa* ☎ *808/637–4544* ⊕ *www.thegrowingkeiki.com.*

Outrigger Trading Company. Though this shop has been in business since 1982, its upstairs location in the North Shore Marketplace often gets bypassed when it shouldn't. Look for Jam's World patchwork tablecloths with an aloha flair, shell boxes, mobiles made of ceramic fish and driftwood, stained-glass ornaments, and beach-glass wind chimes. Other novelties include hula girl and bamboo lamps and silk-screened table runners. ⊠ *North Shore Marketplace, 66-250 Kamehameha Hwy., Hale'iwa.*

Fodor'sChoice ★ **Silver Moon Emporium.** This small boutique carries everything from Brighton accessories and fashionable T-shirts to Betsy Johnson formal wear, and provides attentive yet casual personalized service. Their stock changes frequently, and there's always something wonderful on sale. No matter what your taste, you'll find something for everyday wear or special occasions. ⊠ *North Shore Marketplace, 66-250 Kamehameha Hwy., Hale'iwa* ☎ *808/637–7710.*

Surf Town Coffee Roasters. Luscious chocolate is made right there in the store, and owners Dave and JulieAnn Hoselton buy coffee beans from Kaua'i, Moloka'i, and the Big Island. Look for their own secret blend called "Dawn Patrol," with a picture of their dog on the package. The Hoseltons are also artists. She creates decorative feather *kahili* (a Hawaiian ceremonial staff), and he makes Hawaiian wooden bowls. Enjoy sipping coffee while shopping for art. ⊠ *66-470 Kamehameha Hwy., Hale'iwa* ☎ *808/637–3000.*

West Oʻahu Bargains

Aloha Stadium Swap Meet. This thrice-weekly outdoor bazaar attracts hundreds of vendors and even more bargain hunters. Every Hawaiian souvenir imaginable can be found here, from coral shell necklaces to bikinis, as well as a variety of ethnic wares, from Chinese brocade dresses to Japanese pottery. There are also ethnic foods, silk flowers, and luggage in aloha floral prints. Shoppers must wade through the typical sprinkling of used and stolen goods to find value. ■ TIP→ Wear comfortable shoes, use sunscreen, and bring bottled water. The flea market takes place in the Aloha Stadium parking lot Wednesday and weekends from 6 to 3. Admission is 50 cents. Several shuttle companies serve Aloha Stadium for the swap meet, including VIP Shuttle 808/839–0911; Rabbi Shuttle 808/922–4900; Reliable Shuttle 808/924–9292; and Hawaii Supertransit 808/841–2928. The average cost is $9 per person, round-trip. For a cheaper but slower ride, take TheBus. Check routes at www.thebus.org. ⊠ *99-500 Salt Lake Blvd., ʻAiea* ☎ *808/486–6704.*

Waikele Premium Outlets. Anne Klein Factory, Donna Karan Company Store, Kenneth Cole, and Saks Fifth Avenue Outlet anchor this discount destination. You can take a shuttle to the outlets, but the companies do change over frequently. One to try: Moha Shuttle 808/216–8006; $15 round trip. ✛ *H–1 Hwy., 30 min. west of Downtown Honolulu* ⊠ *Waikele* ☎ *808/676–5656.*

> ### CALABASH
>
> A calabash is a wooden bowl used in ancient Polynesia for food and water. Hawaiians elevated it from a necessity to a work of art. Carved from one log and hand turned on a lathe in a labor-intensive process, Hawaiian calabash is distinct from other bowls—wider at the sides and narrower at the top. Woods used include koa, kou, mango, milo, kamani, macadamia nut, and pine. The word calabash is derived from the French and Spanish words that mean gourd, or pumpkin—a reference to shape only. Available at Surf Town Coffee Roasters in Haleʻiwa, Nohea Gallery at Ward Warehouse, Jeff Chang in Kailua, and other galleries.

SPAS

J. W. Marriott ʻIhilani Resort & Spa. Soak in warm seawater among velvety orchid blossoms at this unique Hawaiian hydrotherapy spa. Thalassotherapy treatments combine underwater jet massage with color therapy and essential oils. Specially designed treatment rooms have a hydrotherapy tub, a Vichy-style shower, and a needle shower with 12 heads. The spa's Pua Kai line of natural aromatherapy products includes massage and body oil, bath crystals and body butter, which combine ingredients such as ginger, jasmine, rose petals, coconut and grape seed oil. ⊠ *J. W. Marriott ʻIhilani Resort & Spa, 92-1001 ʻŌlani St., Kapolei* ☎ *808/679–0079* ⊕ *www.ihilani.com* ✂ *$115, 50-min lomi lomi massage* ᾿ *Hair salon, hot tubs (indoor and outdoor), sauna, steam room. Gym with: cardiovascular machines, free weights, weight-training equipment. Services: aromatherapy, body wraps and scrubs, facials, mas-*

sage, thalassotherapy. Classes and programs: aerobics, body sculpting, dance classes, fitness analysis, guided walks, personal training, Pilates, tai chi, yoga.

Mandara Spa at the Hilton Hawaiian Village Beach Resort & Spa. From its perch in the Kālia Tower, Mandara Spa, an outpost of the chain that originated in Bali, overlooks the mountains, ocean, and Downtown Honolulu. Fresh Hawaiian ingredients and traditional techniques headline an array of treatments. Try an exotic upgrade, such as reflexology or an eye treatment using Asian silk protein. The delicately scented, candlelit foyer can fill up quickly with robe-clad conventioneers, so be sure to make a reservation. There are spa suites for couples, a private infinity pool, and a cafe. ⊠ *Hilton Hawaiian Village Beach Resort and Spa, 2005 Kālia Rd., Waikīkī* ☎ *808/949–4321* ⊕ *www.hiltonhawaiianvillage. com* ☞ *$115, 50-min lomi lomi massage* ⚲ *Hair salon, hot tubs (indoor and outdoor), sauna, steam room. Gym with: cardiovascular machines, free weights, weight-training equipment. Services: aromatherapy, body wraps and scrubs, facials, massages.*

Nā Hō'ola at the Hyatt Regency Waikīkī Resort & Spa. Nā Hō'ola is the largest spa in Waikīkī, sprawling across the fifth and sixth floors of the Hyatt, with 19 treatment rooms, jet baths, and Vichy showers. Arrive early for your treatment to enjoy the postcard views of Waikīkī Beach. Four packages identified by Hawai'i's native healing plants—noni, kukui, awa, and kalo—combine various body, face, and hair treatments and span 2½–4 hours. The Champagne of the Sea body treatment employs a self-heating mud wrap to release tension and stress. The small exercise room is for use by hotel guests only. ⊠ *Hyatt Regency Waikīkī Resort and Spa, 2424 Kalākaua Ave., Waikīkī* ☎ *808/921–6097* ⊕ *www. hyattwaikiki.com* ☞ *$110, 50-min lomi lomi massage* ⚲ *Sauna. Gym with: cardiovascular machines. Services: aromatherapy, body scrubs and wraps, facials, hydrotherapy, massage.*

Serenity Spa Hawai'i. Want to jump start your "just back from Hawai'i" tan without burning to a crisp? Consider the Golden Touch tanning massage, which combines a massage with tan accelerators, sunscreen, and scented oils. Only steps off the beach, this day spa provides aromatherapy treatments, massages, and facials. You can mix and match treatments from the menu to create a specialized package. ⊠ *Outrigger Reef on the Beach, 2169 Kālia Rd., Waikīkī* ☎ *808/926–2882* ⊕ *www. serenityspahawaii.com* ☞ *$95, 50-min lomi lomi massage* ⚲ *Showers, hair salon. Services: massage, facials, body treatments, waxing, makeup.*

SpaHalekulani. SpaHalekulani mines the traditions and cultures of the Pacific Islands with massages, body, and facial therapies. Try the Polynesian Nonu, which uses warm stones and healing nonu gel. The invigorating Japanese Ton Ton Amma massage is another popular choice. The exclusive line of bath and body products is scented by maile, lavender orchid, hibiscus, coconut passion, or Manoa mint. ⊠ *Halekūlani Hotel, 2199 Kālia Rd., Waikīkī* ☎ *808/931–5322* ⊕ *www.halekulani.com* ☞ *$180, 75-min lomi lomi massage* ⚲ *Use of facilities is specific to treatment but may include Japanese furo bath, steam shower or whirlpool tub. Services: hair salon, nail care, massage, facials, body treatments.*

The Spa Luana at Turtle Bay Resort. Luxuriate at the ocean's edge in this serene spa. Don't miss the tropical Pineapple Pedicure ($65), administered outdoors overlooking the North Shore. Tired feet soak in a bamboo bowl filled with coconut milk before the pampering really begins with Hawaiian algae salt, island bee honey, kukui nut oil, and crushed pineapple. There are private spa suites, an outdoor treatment cabana that overlooks the surf, an outdoor exercise studio, and a lounge area and juice bar. ⊠ *Turtle Bay Resort, 57-091 Kamehameha Hwy., North Shore* ☏ *808/447–6868* ⊕ *www.turtlebayresort.com* ☞ *$105, 50-min lomi lomi massage* ⚬ *Hair salon, steam room, outdoor hot tub. Gym with: free weights, cardiovascular machines, weight-training equipment. Services: facials, massages, body treatments, waxing. Classes and programs: aerobics, Pilates, yoga.*

ENTERTAINMENT & NIGHTLIFE

By Katie Young

Many first-time visitors arrive in the Islands expecting to see scenic beauty and sandy beaches but not much at night. That might be true on some of the other Islands, but not in Oʻahu. Honolulu sunsets herald the onset of the best nightlife scene in the Islands.

Local artists perform every night of the week along Waikīkī's Kalākaua and Kūhiō avenues and in Downtown Honolulu; the clubs dance to every beat from Top 40 to alternative to '80s.

The arts also thrive alongside the tourist industry. Oʻahu has an established symphony, a thriving opera company, chamber music groups, and community theaters. Major Broadway shows, dance companies, and rock stars also make their way to Honolulu. Check the local newspapers— *MidWeek,* the *Honolulu Advertiser,* the *Honolulu Star-Bulletin,* or the *Honolulu Weekly*—for the latest events.

Whether you make it an early night or stay up to watch that spectacular tropical sunrise, there's lots to do in paradise.

Entertainment

Lūʻau

The lūʻau is an experience that everyone, both local and tourist, should have. Today's lūʻau still adhere to traditional foods and entertainment, but there's also a fun, contemporary flair. With most, you can even watch the roasted pig being carried out of its *ʻimu,* a hole in the ground used for cooking meat with heated stones.

Lūʻau cost anywhere from $56 to $195. Most that are held outside of Waikīkī offer shuttle service so you don't have to drive. Reservations are essential.

Germaine's Lūʻau. Widely regarded as the most folksy and local, this lūʻau is held in Kalaeloa in Leeward Oʻahu. The food is the usual multi-course, all-you-can-eat buffet, but it's very tasty. It's a good lūʻau for first-timers and it's reasonably priced. Expect a lively crowd on the 35-minute bus ride from Waikīkī. Admission includes buffet, Polynesian show, and shuttle transport from Waikīkī. ☎ 808/949–6626 *or* 800/367–5655 ⊕ *www.germainesluau.com* ✉ *$56* ☉ *Daily at 6. Closed Mon. in winter.*

Paradise Cove Lū'au. The scenery is the best here—the sunsets are unbelievable. Watch Mother Nature's special-effects show in Kapolei/Kō 'Olina Resort in leeward O'ahu, a good 27 mi from the bustle of Waikīkī. The party-hearty atmosphere is kid-friendly with Hawaiian games, canoe rides in the cove, and lots of predinner activities. The stage show includes a fire-knife dancer, singing emcee, and both traditional and contemporary hula. Basic admission includes buffet, activities and the show, and shuttle transport from Waikīkī. You pay extra for table service and box seating. ☎ 808/842–5911 ⊕ *www.paradisecovehawaii.com* ✉ *$65–$110* ☉ *Daily at 5:30, doors open at 5.*

FodorśChoice **Polynesian Cultural Center Ali'i Lū'au.** This elaborate lū'au has the sharpest
★ production values but no booze (it's a Mormon-owned facility). It's held amid the seven re-created villages at the Polynesian Cultural Center in the North Shore town of Lā'ie, about an hour's drive from Honolulu. The lū'au includes tours of the park with shows and activities. Package rates vary depending on activities and amenities (personalized tours, reserved seats, buffet vs. dinner service, backstage tour, etc.). Waikīkī transport included. ☎ 808/293–3333 *or* 800/367–7060 ⊕ *www. polynesia.com* ✉ *$80–$195* ☉ *Mon.–Sat. center opens at noon; lū'au starts at 5.*

Cocktail & Dinner Cruises

Dinner cruises depart either from the piers adjacent to the Aloha Tower Marketplace in Downtown Honolulu or from Kewalo Basin, near Ala Moana Beach Park, and head along the coast toward Diamond Head. There's usually dinner, dancing, drinks, and a sensational sunset.

■ **TIP→ Get a good spot on deck early to enjoy the sunset, however, because everyone tends to pile outside at once.** Except as noted, dinner cruises cost approximately $40–$110, cocktail cruises $25–$40. Most major credit cards are accepted.

Ali'i Kai **Catamaran.** Patterned after an ancient Polynesian vessel, this huge catamaran casts off from Aloha Tower with 1,000 passengers. The deluxe dinner cruise has two bars, a huge dinner, and an authentic Polynesian show with colorful hula music. The food is good, the after-dinner show loud and fun, and everyone dances on the way back to shore. Rates begin at $66 and include round-trip transportation, the dinner buffet, and one drink. ✉ *Pier 5, street level, Honolulu* ☎ *808/539–9400 Ext. 5.*

Paradise Cruises. Prices vary depending on which deck you choose on the 1,600-passenger, four-deck *Star of Honolulu.* For instance, a seven-course French-style dinner and live jazz on the top deck starts at $165. A steak-and-crab feast on level two starts at $78. This ship also features daily Hawaiiana Lunch cruises that offer lei-making and 'ukulele and hula lessons starting at $45. Evening excursions also take place on the 340-passenger *Starlet I* and 230-passenger *Starlet II,* which offer three-course dinners beginning at $43. Also bring your bathing suit for a morning cruise for $63 complete with ocean fun on a water trampoline and slide, and feast on a barbecue lunch before heading back to shore. ✉ *1540 S. King St., Honolulu* ☎ *808/983–7827* ⊕ *www.paradisecruises.com.*

ISLAND SOUNDS

Hawai'i has a vigorous music scene largely invisible outside the state but central to its cultural identity. The Grammy Awards only got around to recognizing Hawaiian music with an award in 2005, but local artists sell thousands of albums and regularly tour island conclaves on the mainland, even playing Carnegie Hall. Like country, Hawaiian music has several subcategories: indigenous chant; early Western-style choral music; "traditional" songs that span the 20th century; contemporary Hawaiian, which melds all of the above with rock, pop, and even folk; instrumental slack key guitar and 'ukulele music; reggae and rap mixes. Most islands boast at least one Hawaiian music station—often two; one for classic Hawaiian, one for more contemporary stuff. Performers to listen for include the Cazimero Brothers, Keali'i Reichel, and Israel Kamakawiwo'ole (just say "Iz"). Or you might get a kick out of Don Tiki's revival of the '60s-era xylophone-and-bird-call school of island music.

Cocktail & Dinner Shows

Cocktail shows run $30 to $43, and the price usually includes one cocktail, tax, and tip. Dinner-show food is usually buffet-style with a definite local accent. Dinner shows are all in the $55 to $99 range. In all cases, reservations are essential. ■ TIP→ **Artists tend to switch venues, so call in advance to check the evening's lineup.**

Creation: A Polynesian Odyssey. A daring Samoan fire-knife dancer is the highlight of this show that traces Hawai'i's culture and history, from its origins to statehood. ✉ *'Āinahau Showroom, Sheraton Princess Ka'iulani Hotel, 120 Ka'iulani Ave., Waikīkī* ☎ *808/931–4660* ☼ *Dinner shows Tues.–Sun. at 6.*

Don Ho. Four decades ago, Don Ho put Waikīkī entertainment on the map, and his song "Tiny Bubbles" became a trademark. His show, a Polynesian revue (with a cast of young and attractive Hawaiian performers), has found the perfect home in this intimate club inside the Waikīkī Beachcomber Hotel. ✉ *Waikīkī Beachcomber Hotel, 2300 Kalākaua Ave., Waikīkī* ☎ *808/923–3981* ☼ *Shows Sun., Tues., Thurs. at 8, with cocktail and dinner seatings.*

★ **Magic of Polynesia.** Hawai'i's top illusionist, John Hirokawa, displays mystifying sleight of hand in this highly entertaining show, which incorporates contemporary hula and island music into its acts. ✉ *Waikīkī Beachcomber Hotel, 2300 Kalākaua Ave., Waikīkī* ☎ *808/971–4321* ☼ *Nightly at 8.*

(ᐠ **Polynesian Cultural Center.** Easily one of the best on the Islands, this show has soaring moments and an "erupting volcano." The performers are students from Brigham Young University's Hawai'i campus. ✉ *55-370 Kamehameha Hwy., Lā'ie* ☎ *808/293–3333 or 800/367–7060* ⊕ *www.polynesia.com* ☼ *Mon.–Sat. 12:30–9:30.*

Film

Sunset on the Beach. It's like watching a movie at the drive-in, minus the car and the impossible speaker box. Think romantic and cozy; bring a blanket and find a spot on the sand to enjoy live entertainment, food from top local restaurants, and a movie feature on a 40-foot screen. Held twice a month on Waikīkī's Queens Surf Beach across from the Honolulu Zoo, Sunset on the Beach is a favorite event for both locals and tourists. If the weather is blustery, beware of flying sand. ☎ 808/923–1094 ⊕ www.waikikiimprovement.com.

Music

Hawai'i Opera Theater. Better known as "HOT," the Hawai'i Theater has been known to turn the opera-challenged into opera lovers. All operas are sung in their original language with projected English translation. Tickets range from $29 to $100. ⊠ *Neil Blaisdell Center Concert Hall, Ward Ave. and King St., Downtown Honolulu* ☎ *808/ 596–7858* ⊕ *www.hawaiiopera.org.*

Honolulu Symphony Orchestra. In recent years, the Honolulu Symphony has worked hard to increase its appeal to all ages. The orchestra performs at the Neil Blaisdell Concert Hall under the direction of the young, dynamic Samuel Wong. The Honolulu Pops series, with performances under the summer stars at the Waikīkī Shell, features top local and national artists under the direction of talented conductor-composer Matt Cattingub. Tickets are $17–$59. ⊠ *Dole Cannery, 650 Iwilei Rd., Suite 202, Iwilei* ☎ *808/ 792–2000* ⊕ *www.honolulusymphony.com.*

> ### MAI TAIS
>
> The cocktail known around the world as the mai tai recently celebrated its 50th birthday. While the recipe has changed slightly over the years, the original formula, created by bar owner Victor J. "Trader Vic" Bergeron, included two ounces of 17-year-old J. Wray & Nephew rum over shaved ice, ½ ounce Holland Dekuyper orange curacao, ¼ ounce Trader Vic's rock candy syrup, ½ ounce French Garier orgeat syrup, and the juice of one fresh lime. Done the right way, this tropical drink still lives up to the name "mai tai!" meaning, "out of this world!"

Honolulu Zoo Concerts. For almost two decades, the Honolulu Zoo Society has sponsored Wednesday evening concerts from June to August on the zoo's stage lawn. Listen to local legends play everything from Hawaiian to jazz to Latin music. ■ TIP➔ **At just $1 admission, this is one of the best deals in town.** Take a brisk walk through the zoo exhibits before they close at 5:30 PM or join in the family activities; bring your own picnic for the concert, which starts at 6 PM. It's an alcohol-free event, and there's a food concession for those who come unprepared. ⊠ *151 Kapahulu Ave., Waikīkī* ☎ *808/926–3191* ⊕ *www.honoluluzoo.org* 🔁 *$1* ⊙ *Gates open at 4:30.*

Bars & Clubs

O'ahu is the best of all the islands for nightlife. The locals call it *pau hana* but you might call it "off the clock and ready for a cocktail." The literal translation of the Hawaiian phrase means "done with work."

You can find a bar in just about any area on Oʻahu. Most of the clubs, however, are centralized to Waikīkī, Ala Moana, and Downtown Honolulu. The drinking age is 21 on Oʻahu and throughout Hawaiʻi. Many bars will admit younger people but will not serve them alcohol. By law, all establishments that serve alcoholic beverages must close by 2 AM. The only exceptions are those with a cabaret license, which have a 4 AM curfew. ■ TIP➔ **Most clubs have a cover charge of $5 to $10, but with some establishments, getting there early means you don't have to pay.**

Bars

WAIKĪKĪ **Banyan Veranda.** The Banyan Veranda is steeped in history. From this location the radio program *Hawaiʻi Calls* first broadcast the sounds of Hawaiian music and the rolling surf to a U.S. mainland audience in 1935. Today, a variety of Hawaiian entertainment continues to provide the perfect accompaniment to the sounds of the waves. ⊠ *Sheraton Moana Surfrider, 2365 Kalākaua Ave., Waikīkī* ☎ *808/922–3111.*

Cobalt Lounge. Take the glass elevator up 30 stories to enjoy the sunset. Floor-to-ceiling windows offer breathtaking views of Diamond Head and the Waikīkī shoreline. Leather sofas and cobalt-blue lighting set the "blue" Hawaiʻi mood. After darkness falls, you can find soft lights, starlight, and dancing in this lounge in the center of the Hanohano Room. ⊠ *Sheraton Waikīkī, 2255 Kalākaua Ave., Waikīkī* ☎ *808/922–4422* ☽ *1st and 3rd Sat. of month.*

★ **Duke's Canoe Club.** Making the most of its oceanfront spot on Waikīkī Beach, Duke's presents "Concerts on the Beach" every Friday, Saturday, and Sunday with contemporary Hawaiian musicians like Henry Kapono. National musicians like Jimmy Buffett have also performed here. At Duke's Barefoot Bar, solo Hawaiian musicians take the stage nightly, and it's not unusual for surfers to leave their boards outside to step in for a casual drink after a long day on the waves. ⊠ *Outrigger Waikīkī, 2335 Kalākaua Ave., Waikīkī* ☎ *808/922–2268.*

Mai Tai Bar at the Royal Hawaiian. The bartenders sure know how to make one killer mai tai—just one could do the trick. This is, after all, the establishment that came up with the famous drink in the first place. The pink, umbrella-covered tables at the outdoor bar are front-row seating for Waikīkī sunsets and an unobstructed view of Diamond Head. Contemporary Hawaiian music is usually on stage, and the staff is extremely friendly. ⊠ *Royal Hawaiian Hotel, 2259 Kalākaua Ave., Waikīkī* ☎ *808/923–7311.*

Moana Terrace. Three floors up from Waikīkī Beach, this open-air terrace is the home of Aunty Genoa Keawe, the "First Lady of Hawaiian Music." Her falsetto sessions include jams with the finest of Hawaiʻi's musicians. ⊠ *Waikīkī Beach Marriott Resort, 2552 Kalākaua Ave., Waikīkī* ☎ *808/922–6611.*

Shore Bird Oceanside Bar and Grill. This Waikīkī beachfront bar spills right out onto the sand. Local bands play nightly until 1 AM. ⊠ *Outrigger Reef on the Beach hotel, 2169 Kālia Rd., Waikīkī* ☎ *808/922–2887.*

Tiki's Grill and Bar. Get in touch with your primal side at this restaurant–bar overlooking Kuhio Beach. Tiki torches, tiki statues, and other South Pacific art set the mood. A twenty-something mix of locals and tourists comes on the weekends to get their fill of kitschy-cool. There's nightly

Izakaya

JAPANESE PUB-RESTAURANTS, called *izakaya* (ee-ZAH-ka-ya), are sprouting in the Islands like *matsutake* mushrooms in a pine forest. They began as oases for homesick Japanese nationals but were soon discovered by adventurous locals, who appreciated the welcoming atmosphere, sprawling menus, and later dining hours.

Expect to be greeted by a merry, full-staff cry of "Irrashaimase!", offered an *oshibori* (hot towel) and a drink, and handed a menu of dozens (sometimes many dozens) of small-plate, made-to-order dishes.

You can find *yakitori* (grilled dishes), tempura (deep-fried dishes), *donburi* (rice bowls), sushi and sashimi, *nabemono* and *shabu-shabu* (hot pots), noodles (both soup and fried), okonomiyaki (chop suey-type omelets), and a bizarre assortment of *yoshoku* dishes (Western foods prepared in Japanese style, such as hamburgers in soy-accented gravy, fried chicken with a mirin glaze, odd gratins, and even pizza).

Full bars are usual; a wide choice of lager-type beers and good-to-great sakes are universal. Many specialize in single-malt scotch, but wine lists are generally short.

Izakaya menus are often confusing, many staff speak marginal English, and outings can get expensive fast (liquor plus small-plate prices equals eyes bigger than stomach). Prices range from $5 for a basket of edamame (steamed, salted soybeans) to $20 or more for *wafu* (seasoned, grilled steak, sliced for sharing). Start by ordering drinks and edamame or silky-textured braised *kabocha*

pumpkin. This will keep the waiter happy. Then give yourself a quarter of an hour to examine the menu, ogle other people's plates, and seek recommendations. Start with one dish per person and one for the table; you can always call for more. Here are a few spots to try:

Imanas Tei. Go early to this cosy, out-of-the-way restaurant for its tasteful, simple decor and equally tasteful and simply perfect sushi, sashimi, *nabe* (hot pots prepared at the table), and grilled dishes; reservations taken from 5 to 7 PM; after that, there's always a line. ⊠ 2626 S. King, Mō'ili'ili ☎ 808/941-2626 or 808/934-2727 ⊟ AE, DC, MC, V ☞ $8-$25.

Izakaya Nonbei. Teruaki Mori designed this pub to put you in mind of a northern inn in winter in his native Japan; dishes not to miss—*karei kara-age* (delicate deep-fried flounder) and *dobinmushi* (mushroom consomme presented in a teapot). ⊠ 3108 Olu St., Kapahulu ☎ 808/734-5573 ⊟ AE, D, DC, MC, V ☞ $7-$20.

Tokkuri-Tei. This is a favorite of locals for the playful atmosphere that belies the excellence of the food created by chef Hideaki "Santa" Miyoshi, famous for his quirky menu names (Nick Jagger, Spider Poke); just say "Moriwase, kudasai" ("chef's choice, please"), and he'll order for you. ⊠ 611 Kapahulu Ave., Kapahulu ☎ 808/739-2800 ⊟ AE, D, DC, MC, V ☞ $13-$25.

Also worth a visit: **Mr. Oji-san** (⊠ 1018 Kapahulu Ave., Kapahulu ☎ 808/735-4455) for family-style izakaya specialties; and **Kai Okonomi Cuisine** (⊠ 1427 Makaloa, Ala Moana ☎ 808/944-1555) for Osaka-style omlelets.

— By Wanda Adams

entertainment featuring contemporary Hawaiian musicians. Don't leave without sipping on a "lava flow." It's served in a whole coconut, which is yours to keep at the end of the night. ✉ *ResortQuest Waikīkī Beach Hotel, 2570 Kalākaua Ave., Waikīkī* ☎ *808/923–8454.*

ELSEWHERE IN
HONOLULU

Anna Bannana's. Generations of Hawai'i college students have spent more than an evening or two at this legendary two-story, smoky dive near the University of Hawai'i campus. A living-room atmosphere makes it a comfortable place to hang out. Here, the music is fresh, loud, and sometimes experimental. Live music happens Friday and Saturday, starting at 9 PM. There's also open mike night for amateurs on Monday. ✉ *2440 S. Beretania St., Mō'ili'ili* ☎ *808/946–5190.*

Don Ho's Grill. This popular waterfront restaurant in the Aloha Tower Marketplace houses the Tiny Bubbles Bar, famous for its "suck 'em up" mai tai, a Don Ho classic. The dinner hour features Hawaiian musicians like Jerry Santos and Robert Cazimero. If you're lucky, you might catch a glimpse of the famous Ho, who frequents the restaurant. On the weekend, live bands play reggae music from 10 PM to 2 AM. ✉ *Aloha Tower Marketplace, 1 Aloha Tower Dr., Downtown Honolulu* ☎ *808/ 528–0807.*

Little Vino. Step inside this small wine bar, and you'd think you have just arrived in Italy. The walls are painted to look like a rustic countryside with beautiful vineyards. Relax on one of the leather couches or at a table and enjoy wines hand-selected by the restaurant's master sommelier and Italian tapas (small plates) if you're hungry. ✉ *Restaurant Row, 500 Ala Moana Blvd., Kaka'ako* ☎ *808/524–8466* ☻ *Wed. and Thurs. 5:30–9:30 PM, Fri. and Sat. 5:30–10:30 PM.*

★ **Mai Tai Bar at Ala Moana Center.** After a long day of shopping, the Mai Tai Bar on the third floor of Ala Moana Center is a perfect spot to relax. There's live entertainment and two nightly happy hours: one for food items and another strictly for specialty drinks. There's never a cover charge and no dress code, but to avoid waiting in line, get there before 9 PM. ✉ *1450 Ala Moana Blvd., Ala Moana* ☎ *808/947–2900.*

Opium Den & Champagne Bar at Indigo's. This bar at the edge of Chinatown resembles a joint right out of a film noir. Jazz plays early in the evening on Tuesday; late-night DJs spin trance, Top 40, funk, disco, and rock on weekends. In addition to champagne, happy hour features sake martinis and complimentary pūpū buffet. ✉ *Indigo Euroasian Cuisine, 1121 Nu'uanu Ave., Downtown Honolulu* ☎ *808/521–2900.*

Spice Lounge. One of the newest night events to hit O'ahu is the Spice Lounge at E&O Trading Company restaurant. The lounge takes on the Far East Asian marketplace feel of the restaurant in a two-phase Friday-night party. In the early evening, a DJ on the outside patio plays '70s and '80s retro music to a crowd of young professionals. After 10 PM, the Spice Lounge takes over the inside restaurant as well, where a DJ spins a mix of R&B and house music. One night a month, the promoter also throws a special themed event, such as the recent Miss Hawaiian Tropic state contest. There are pūpū specials until 11:30 PM, bottle service, and reserved VIP tables. It's a comfortable place to hang. ✉ *E&O Trading Company at Ward Centre, 3rd fl., 1200 Ala Moana Blvd., Kaka'ako* ☎ *808/957–0303.*

Boardrider's Bar & Grill. Recently renamed Boardriders, this spot tucked away in Kailua Town has long been the venue for local bands to strut their stuff. Renovations have spruced up the space, which now includes pool tables, dart boards, foosball, and eight TVs for sports viewing with the local and military crowd. Look for live entertainment—reggae to alternative rock to good old-fashioned rock-n-roll—Wednesday through Saturday from 10:30 PM to 1:30 AM. Cover ranges from $3 to $10. ☒ 201-A Hamakua Dr., Kailua ☎ 808/261–4600.

Breaker's Restaurant. Just about every surf contest post-party is celebrated at this family-owned establishment, as the owner's son, Benji Weatherly, is a pro surfer himself. Surfing memorabilia, including surfboards hanging from ceiling, fills the space. The restaurant/bar is open from 11 AM to 9:30 PM with a late-night menu until midnight. But things start to happen around 9 PM on Thursday for the 18-and-over crowd, who cruise while the DJ spins, and there's live music on Saturdays. The party goes until 2 AM. ☒ Marketplace Shopping Center, 66-250 Kamehameha Hwy., Hale'iwa ☎ 808/637–9898.

The Shack. This sports bar and restaurant is about the only late-night spot you can find in Southeast O'ahu. After a day of snorkling at Hanauma Bay, stop by to kick back, have a beer, eat a burger, watch some sports or play a game of pool. It's open until 2 AM nightly. ☒ Hawai'i Kai Shopping Center, 377 Keahole St., Hawai'i Kai ☎ 808/396–1919.

Dance Clubs

Feng Shui Ultralounge. This once-a-week club event is the creation of party-master Justin Yoshino. After the dinner rush leaves Ciao Mein restaurant, the spacious venue is transformed into the only indoor–outdoor nightlife experience in Honolulu. There are complimentary appetizers and two dance floors featuring everything from deep house to hip-hop. With five bars, it's easy to get a drink; there's also ample space to get away from the booming music and lounge on a poolside chair. Dress code—no slippers, shorts, head wear, jerseys, or T-shirts—is strictly enforced. ☒ Hyatt Regency Waikīkī Resort and Spa, 2424 Kalākaua Ave., Waikīkī ☎ 808/957–0303 ⊙ Sat. at 9:30 PM.

Hula's Bar and Lei Stand. Hawai'i's oldest and best-known gay-friendly nightspot offers calming panoramic outdoor views of Diamond Head and the Pacific Ocean by day and a high-energy club scene by night. Check out the soundproof, glassed-in dance floor. ☒ Waikīkī Grand Hotel, 134 Kapahulu Ave., 2nd fl., Waikīkī ☎ 808/923–0669.

Nashville Waikīkī. Country music in the tropics? You bet! Put on your paniolo (Hawaiian cowboy) duds and mosey on out to the giant dance floor. There are pool tables, dartboards, line dancing, and free dance lessons (Wednesday at 6:30 PM) to boot. Look for wall-to-wall crowds on the weekend. ☒ Ohana Waikīkī West Hotel, 2330 Kūhiō Ave., Waikīkī ☎ 808/926–7911.

Wave Waikīkī. This venue has stood the test of time, anchoring the Waikīkī entertainment scene for more than two decades. Dance to live rock and roll until 1:30 AM and recorded music after that. It can be a rough scene (the place has seen more than its fair share of drunken fisticuffs), but the bands are tops. Late nights, the music here definitely goes "underground." ✉ *1877 Kalākaua Ave., Waikīkī* ☎ *808/941–0424.*

Wonder Lounge at the W Diamond Head. The hotel's Diamond Head Grill restaurant is also an after-hours nightclub, full of hip, young professionals who enjoy martinis and the chance to do some not-so-serious networking. Look for a younger group on Saturday. Enjoy some fantastic (though pricey) eats until midnight, and keep dancing until 2 AM. ✉ *W Honolulu—Diamond Head, 2885 Kalākaua Ave., Waikīkī* ☎ *808/922–1700* ⊙ *Fri. and Sat. at 9 PM.*

> ### PŪPŪ
>
> Entertaining Hawaiian style means having a lot of pūpū–the local term for appetizers or hors d'oeuvres. Locals eat these small portions of food mostly as they wind down from their work day, relax, and enjoy a couple of beers. Popular pūpū include sushi, tempura, teriyaki chicken skewers, barbecue meat, and our favorite: poke (pronounced "po-keh"), or raw fish, seasoned with seaweed, shoyu, and other flavorings. We call them "local kine grinds."

Zanzabar. Traverse a winding staircase and make an entrance at Zanzabar where DJs spin top hits, from hip-hop to soul and techno to trance. It's easy to find a drink at this high-energy nightspot with its three bars. Not exactly sure how to get your groove on? Zanzabar offers free Latin dance lessons every Tuesday at 8 PM. Most nights are 21 and over, Sunday, Tuesday, Wednesday, and Thursday allow 18 and over in for $15. ✉ *Waikīkī Trade Center, 2255 Kūhiō Ave., Waikīkī* ☎ *808/924–3939.*

ELSEWHERE IN HONOLULU

★

The Ocean Club. The Ocean Club has withstood the test of time while other local nightclubs have failed. The indoor venue plays mostly Top 40 and hip-hop music. Tuesday is Ladies' Night featuring $2 drinks. Thursday is Paddler's Night so wear aloha-print attire and avoid the cover charge. The last Saturday of every month is the Piranha Room, where the club is decorated according to various themes, go-go dancers mesmerize, and the place is packed. There's half-price *pūpū* until 8 PM. All nights are 23 and over except Thursday; dress code—no beach or athletic wear—is strictly enforced. ✉ *Restaurant Row, 500 Ala Moana Blvd., Kaka'ako* ☎ *808/531–8444* ⊙ *Tues., Thurs., Fri. at 4:30 PM, Sat. at 7 PM.*

WHERE TO EAT

By Wanda Adams

O'ahu, where the majority of the Islands' 2,000-plus restaurants are located, offers the best of all worlds: it's got the foreignness and excitement of Asia and Polynesia, but when the kids need McDonald's, or when you just have to have a Starbucks latte, they're here, too.

Budget for a $$$$ dining experience at the very top of the restaurant food chain, where chefs Alan Wong, Roy Yamaguchi, George Mavrothalassitis, and others you've read about in *Gourmet* put a sophisticated and unforgettable spin on local foods and flavors. Savor seared 'ahi tuna in sea urchin beurre blanc or steak marinated in Korean kim chee sauce.

Spend the rest of your food dollars where budget-conscious locals do: in plate-lunch places and small ethnic eateries, at roadside stands and lunch wagons, or at window-in-the-wall delis. Munch a musubi rice cake, slurp shave ice with red bean paste, order up Filipino pork adobo with two scoops of rice and macaroni salad.

In Waikīkī, where most visitors stay, you can find choices from gracious rooms with a view to surprisingly authentic Japanese noodle shops. But hop in the car, or on the trolley or bus, and travel just a few miles in any direction, and you can save your money and get in touch with the real food of Hawai'i.

Kaimukī's Wai'alae Avenue, for example, offers one of the city's best espresso bars, a hugely popular Chinese bakery, a highly recommended patisserie, an exceptional Italian bistro, a dim sum restaurant, Mexican food (rare here), and a Hawai'i regional cuisine standout, 3660 on the Rise—all in three blocks and 10 minutes from Waikīkī. Chinatown, 10 minutes in the other direction and easily reached by the Waikiki Trolley, is another dining (and shopping) treasure, not only for Chinese but also Vietnamese, Filipino, Malaysian, Indian, and Eurasian food, and even a chic little tea shop.

WHAT IT COSTS				
$$$$	$$$	$$	$	¢
RESTAURANTS over $35	$27–$35	$18–$26	$10–$17	under $10

Restaurant prices are for one main course at dinner.

Waikīkī

American–Casual

¢–$ ✕ **Eggs 'n Things.** A favorite of Waikīkī hotel workers for its late hours (11 PM to 2 PM daily), this restaurant on the first floor of an obscure budget hotel has a hearty, country-style menu with a few island touches (tropical pancake syrups, fresh grilled fish) and a permanent line out front. ⊠ *Hawaiian Monarch Hotel, 1911–B Kalākaua Ave., Waikīkī* ☎ *808/949–0820* ▭ *No credit cards* ☉ *No dinner. $7–$14.*

¢–$ ✕ **Wailana Coffee House.** Budget-conscious snowbirds, night owls with a yen for karaoke, all-day drinkers of both coffee and the stronger stuff, hearty eaters and lovers of local-style plate lunches contentedly rub shoulders at this venerable diner and cocktail lounge at the edge of Waikīkī. Most checks are under $9; $1.95 children's menu. Open 24 hours a day, 7 days a week, 365 days a year. ⊠ *Wailana Condominium, ground floor, 1860 Ala Moana Blvd. (corner of 'Ena Rd. and Ala Moana), Waikīkī* ☎ *808/955–1674* ⌲ *Reservations not accepted* ▭ *AE, D, DC, MC, V. $5–$15.*

¢   ✕ **Teddy's Bigger Burgers.** They do but three things at Teddy's—burgers, fries, shakes—but they do them very, very well. The burgers are beefy, the fries crisply perfect, the shakes rich and sweet. The original location

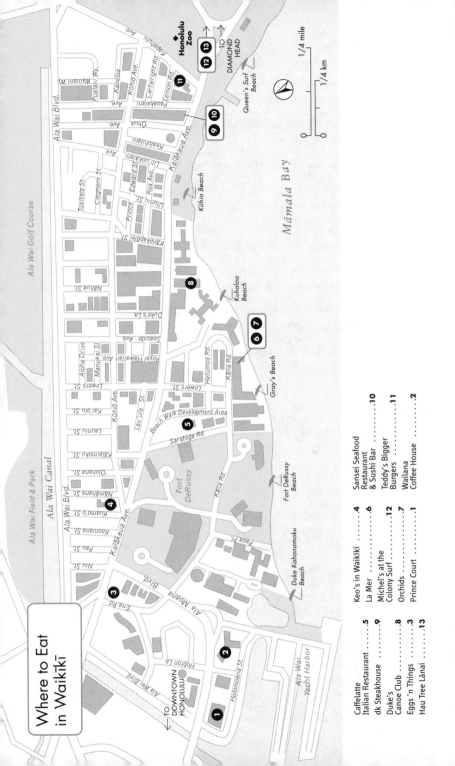

Where to Eat in Waikīkī

Ala Wai Golf Course

Ala Wai Field & Park

Ala Wai Canal

Māmala Bay

Honolulu Zoo

TO DIAMOND HEAD

Queen's Surf Beach

Kūhio Beach

Kuhaloa Beach

Gray's Beach

Fort DeRussy Beach

Duke Kahanamoku Beach

Ala Wai Yacht Harbor

TO DOWNTOWN HONOLULU

Fort DeRussy

Beach Walk Development Area

1/4 mile
1/4 km

Streets: Kalākaua Ave., Ala Wai Blvd., Ala Moana Blvd., Kūhio Ave., Kalaimoku St., Kuamoʻo St., Kanekapolu St., Seaside Ave., Royal Hawaiian Ave., Lewers St., Kaiulu St., Laʻau ʻula St., Launiu St., Kalaimoku St., ʻOlohana St., Namahana St., Pau St., Niu St., Ena Rd., Hobron La., Holomoana St., Helumoa Rd., Kalia Rd., Duke's La., Nahua St., Kānekapōlei St., Prince Edward St., Uluniu Ave., Koa Ave., Liliʻuokalani Ave., Kealohilani Ave., ʻOhua Ave., Paokalani Ave., Lemon Rd., Cartwright Rd., Kanekapolu Ave., Kūhio Ave., Kaneloa, Puatani Wy., Wainani Wy., Kapahulu Ave., Saratoga Rd., Kaiulani Ave., Tusitala St., Cleghorn St., Paoa Pl.

Caffelatte
Italian Restaurant **5**
dk Steakhouse **9**
Duke's
Canoe Club **8**
Eggs 'n Things **3**
Hau Tree Lānai **13**

Keo's in Waikīkī **4**
La Mer **6**
Michel's at the
Colony Surf **12**
Orchids **7**
Prince Court **1**

Sansei Seafood
Restaurant
& Sushi Bar **10**
Teddy's Bigger
Burgers **11**
Wailana
Coffee House **2**

in Waikīkī has given birth two others in Kailua and Hawai'i Kai. ⊠ *134 Kapahulu Ave. Waikīkī* ☎ *808/926-3444* ▤ *No credit cards. $6–$8.*

Contemporary

$$–$$$$ ✕ **Prince Court.** Though little heralded, this restaurant overlooking Ala Wai Yacht Harbor is a multifaceted success, offering exceptional high-end lunches and dinners, daily one-price buffets at every meal, and sold-out weekend brunches. The style is contemporary island cuisine (portobello mushroom and crab hash napoleon, Pacific snapper with wild mushroom ragout) but with many Eastern touches, as this hotel is popular with Japanese nationals. ⊠ *Hawai'i Prince Hotel, 100 Holomoana St., Waikīkī* ☎ *808/ 944–4494* ᕔ *Reservations essential* ▤ *AE, D, DC, MC, V. $25–$42.*

$–$$$ ✕ **Hau Tree Lānai.** The many-branched, vinelike hau tree is ideal for sitting under, and it's said that the one that spreads itself over this beachside courtyard is the very one that shaded Robert Louis Stevenson as he mused and wrote about Hawai'i. In any case, diners are still enjoying the shade, though the view has changed—the gay-friendly beach over the low wall is paved with hunky sunbathers. The food is unremarkable island casual, but we like the place for late-afternoon or early-evening drinks, pūpū, and people-watching. ⊠ *New Otani Kaimana Beach Hotel, 2863 Kalākaua Ave., Waikīkī* ☎ *808/921–7066* ⊕ *www.kaimana. com* ᕔ *Reservations essential* ▤ *AE, D, DC, MC, V. $15–$32.*

$–$$ ✕ **Duke's Canoe Club.** Notorious as the spot where Jimmy Buffett did a free, impromptu concert that had people standing six-deep on the beach outside, Duke's is both an open-air bar and a very popular steak-and-seafood grill. It's known for its Big Island pork ribs, huli-huli (rotisserie) chicken, and grilled catch of the day, as well as for a simple and economical Sunday brunch. A drawback is that it's often loud and crowded, and the live contemporary Hawaiian music often stymies conversation. ⊠ *Outrigger Waikīkī on the Beach, 2335 Kalākaua Ave., Waikīkī* ☎ *808/922–2268* ᕔ *Reservations essential* ▤ *AE, DC, MC, V. $12–$25.*

French

★ $$$$ ✕ **La Mer.** La Mer, like the hotel in which it's housed (Halekūlani, "House Befitting Heaven"), is pretty much heavenly. The softly lighted, low-ceiling room has its windows open to the breeze, the perfectly framed vista of Diamond Head, and the faint sound of music from a courtyard below. The food captures the rich and yet sunny flavors of the south of France in one tiny, exquisite course after another. We recommend the degustation menu; place yourself in the sommelier's hands for wine choices from the hotel's exceptional cellar. ⊠ *Halekūlani, 2199 Kālia Rd., Waikīkī* ☎ *808/923–2311* ᕔ *Reservations essential* ⌂ *Jacket required* ▤ *AE, DC, MC, V* ⊗ *No lunch. $38–$48.*

$$$–$$$$ ✕ **Michel's at the Colony Surf.** With its wide-open windows so close to the water that you literally feel the soft mist at high tide, this is arguably the most romantic spot in Waikīkī for a sunset dinner for two. Venerable Michel's is synonymous with fine dining in the minds of Oahuans who have been coming here for 20 years. The menu is tres, tres French with both classic choices (escargot, foie gras) and more contemporary dishes (potato-crusted onaga fish). There's dinner nightly, and Sunday brunch. ⊠ *Colony Surf, 2895 Kalākaua Ave., Waikīkī* ☎ *808/923–6552* ᕔ *Reservations essential* ▤ *AE, D, DC, MC, V* ⊗ *No lunch. $28–$40.*

Italian

$$$ ✕ **Caffelatte Italian Restaurant.** Every dish at this tiny trattoria run by a Milanese family is worth ordering, from the gnocchi in a thick, rich sauce of Gorgonzola to spinach ravioli served with butter and basil. The tiramisu is the best in town, and the sugared orange slices in Russian vodka are a perfect ending to a meal. Each person must order three courses (appetizer, main course, and dessert). There's no parking, so walk here if you can. One drawback: no air-conditioning, so it can be warm and noisy due to open windows. ✉ *339 Saratoga Rd., 2nd level, Waikīkī* ☎ *808/924–1414* ▤ *AE, DC, MC, V* ⊗ *Closed Tues. $35.*

> **BEST BREAKFAST**
>
> **Big City Diner** (Ala Moana & Kailua). Start the day like a local: rice instead of toast, fish or Portuguese sauce instead of bacon, even noodles.
>
> **Cinnamon's Restaurant** (Kailua). Voted best for breakfast in a local newspaper poll, Cinnamon's does all the breakfast standards.
>
> **Duke's Canoe Club** (Waikīkī). Duke's has an $11.95 buffet at breakfast.
>
> **Eggs 'n Things** (Waikīkī). This is a longtime favorite for late hours and country-style food with island touches.

Japanese

★ **$–$$$** ✕ **Sansei Seafood Restaurant & Sushi Bar.** D. K. Kodama's Japanese-based Pacific Rim cuisine is an experience not to be missed, from early-bird dinners (from 5:30 PM) to late-night appetizers and sushi (until 2 AM Thursday–Saturday, with karaoke). The specialty sushi here—mango-crab roll, foie gras nigiri with eel sauce, and more—leaves California rolls far behind. We fantasize about the signature calamari salad with spicy Korean sauce and crisp-tender calamari. Cleverly named and beautifully prepared dishes come in big and small plates or in a $35 six-course tasting menu. Finish with tempura-fried ice cream or Mama Kodama's brownies. ✉ *Waikīkī Beach Marriott Resort and Spa, 2552 Kalākaua Ave., Waikīkī* ☎ *808/931–6286* ▤ *AE, D, MC, V. $16–$30.*

Seafood

$$–$$$$ ✕ **Orchids.** Perched along the seawall at historic Gray's Beach, Orchids is beloved of power breakfasters, ladies who lunch, and family groups celebrating at the elaborate Sunday brunch. La Mer, upstairs, is better known for evening, but we have found dinner at Orchids equally enjoyable. The fold-back walls open to the breezes, the orchids add splashes of color, the seafood is perfectly prepared, and the wine list is intriguing. Plus, it is more casual and a bit less expensive than La Mer. Whatever meal you have here, finish with the hotel's signature coconut layer cake. ✉ *Halekūlani, 2199 Kālia Rd., Waikīkī* ☎ *808/923–2311* ⌕ *Reservations essential* ▤ *AE, D, DC, MC, V. $22–$40.*

Steak

$$–$$$$ ✕ **dk Steakhouse.** Around the country, the steak house has returned to prominence as chefs rediscover the art of dry-aging beef and of preparing the perfect béarnaise sauce. D. K. Kodama's chic second-floor restaurant characterizes this trend with such presentations as the sybaritic 22-ounce bone-in rib eye aged 15 days in-house and Oscar of filet mignon with blue crab. The restaurant shares space, but not a menu, with Kodama's Sansei Seafood Restaurant & Sushi Bar; sit at the bar perched between the two and you can order from either menu. ☒ *Waikīkī Beach Marriott Resort and Spa, 2552 Kalākaua Ave., Waikīkī* ☏ *808/ 931–6280* ☐ *AE, D, MC, V* ☉ *No lunch. $19–$55.*

Thai

$–$$ ✕ **Keo's in Waikīkī.** Many Islanders—and many Hollywood stars—got their first taste of pad thai noodles, lemongrass, and coconut milk curry at one of Keo Sananikone's restaurants. This one, perched right at the entrance to Waikīkī, characterizes his formula: a bright, clean space awash in flowers with intriguing menu titles and reasonable prices. Evil Jungle Prince, a stir-fry redolent of Thai basil, flecked with chilies and rich with coconut milk, is a classic. Also try the apple bananas in coconut milk. ☒ *2028 Kūhiō Ave., Waikīkī* ☏ *808/951–9355* ☐ *AE, D, DC, MC, V. $10–$18.*

Honolulu: Ala Moana, Downtown & Chinatown

American–Casual

¢–$ ✕ **Contemporary Cafe.** Little known but much appreciated by those who have discovered it, this tasteful lunch spot offers toothsome but light and healthful food of a kind that's woefully rare in Honolulu. The short but well-selected menu runs to housemade soups, crostini of the day, innovative sandwiches garnished with fruit, and a hummus plate with fresh pita. Located in the exclusive Makīkī Heights neighborhood above the city, the restaurant spills out of the ground floor of The Contemporary Museum onto the lawn. ☒ *The Contemporary Museum, 2411 Makīkī Heights Dr., Makīkī* ☏ *808/523–3362* ⚑ *Reservations not accepted* ☐ *AE, D, DC, MC, V* ☉ *No dinner. $7–$10.*

¢–$ ✕ **Pavilion Cafe.** The cool courtyards and varied galleries of the Honolulu Academy of Arts are well worth a visit and, afterward, so is Mike Nevin's popular lunch restaurant. The café overflows onto a lānai from which you can ponder Asian statuary and a burbling water feature while you wait for your salade niçoise or signature Piadina Sandwich (fresh-baked flatbread rounds stuffed with arugula, tomatoes, basil, and cheese). Reservations recommended. ☒ *Honolulu Academy of Arts, 900 S. Beretania St., Downtown Honolulu* ☏ *808/532–8734* ☐ *AE, D, DC, MC, V* ☉ *No dinner. Closed Sun. and Mon. $8–$12.*

★ ¢–$ ✕ **Side Street Inn.** Famous as the place where celebrity chefs gather after hours, local boy Colin Nishida's pub is on an obscure side street near Ala Moana Shopping Center. It is worth searching for, despite annoying smoke and sometimes surly staff, because Nishida makes the best darned pork chops and fried rice in the world. Local-style bar food comes in huge, share-plate portions. This is a place to dress any way you like, nosh all night, watch sports on TV, and sing karaoke until they boot you out. Pūpū (in portions so large as to be dinner) is from 4 PM to 12:30 AM daily. Reservations for large parties only. ☒ *1225 Hopaka St., Ala Moana* ☏ *808/591–0253* ☐ *AE, D, DC, MC, V* ☉ *No lunch weekends. $8–$15.*

¢ ✕ **Big City Diner.** These unfussy retro diners offer a short course in local-style breakfasts—rice instead of potatoes, fish or Portuguese sausage instead of bacon, steaming bowls of noodles—with generous portions, low prices, and pronounced flavors. Breakfast is served all day. ⊠ *Ward Entertainment Center, 1060 'Auahi St., Ala Moana* ☎ *808/591–8891* ⊟ *AE, D, MC, V. $5–$9.*

Barbecue

¢–$$ ✕ **Dixie Grill.** Southern food is hard to come by in Hawai'i, so this eatery and its Pearl City cousin are always crowded with military families and other expats from below the Mason-Dixon line hungry for hush puppies, grits, barbecue (pulled or on the bone, in different styles), and Dixie beer. The odd custom of yelling out the names of certain specials, and clanging a bell to herald their arrival, means the place is loud. But it's also family-friendly with a sand box for the kids. ⊠ *404 Ward Ave., Kaka'ako* ☎ *808/596–8359* ⊟ *AE, D, DC, MC, V. $5–$21.*

Chinese

¢–$ ✕ **Legend Seafood Restaurant.** Do as the locals do: start your visit to Chinatown with breakfast dim sum at Legend. If you want to be able to hear yourself think, get there before 9 AM, especially on weekends. And don't be shy: Use your best cab-hailing technique and sign language to make the cart ladies stop at your table and show you their wares. The pork-filled steamed buns, hearty spare ribs, prawn dumplings, and still-warm custard tarts will fortify you for shopping. ⊠ *Chinese Cultural Plaza, 100 N. Beretania St., Chinatown* ☎ *808/532–1868* ⊟ *AE, D, DC, MC, V. $5–$15.*

¢–$ ✕ **Little Village Noodle House.** Unassuming and budget-friendly, Little Vil-
Fodor$Choice lage sets a standard of friendly and attentive service to which every Chi-
★ nese restaurant should aspire. We have roamed the large, pan-China menu and found a new favorite in everything we've tried: shredded beef, spinach with garlic, Shanghai noodles, honey-walnut shrimp, orange chicken, dried green beans. Two words: go there. ⊠ *1113 Smith St., Chinatown* ☎ *808/545–3008* ⊟ *AE, D, MC, V. $7–$15.*

¢–$ ✕ **Mei Sum Chinese Dim Sum Restaurant.** In contrast to the sprawling and noisy halls in which dim sum is generally served, Mei Sum is compact and shiny bright. It's open daily, serving nothing but small plates from 7:45 AM to 8:45 PM. Be ready to guess and point at the color photos of dim sum favorites as not much English is spoken, but the delicate buns and tasty bits are exceptionally well prepared. ⊠ *65 N. Pauahi St., Chinatown* ☎ *808/531–3268* ⊟ *No credit cards. $3–$10.*

Contemporary

$$–$$$$ ✕ **Chai's Island Bistro.** Chai Chaowasaree's stylish, light-bathed and orchid-draped lunch and dinner restaurant expresses the sophisticated side of this Thai-born immigrant. He plays East against West on the plate in signature dishes such as *kataifi* (baked and shredded phyllo), macadamia-crusted prawns, 'ahi *katsu* (tuna steaks dredged crisp Japanese breadcrumbs and quickly deep-fried), crispy duck confetti spring rolls, and seafood risotto. Some of Hawai'i's best-known contemporary Hawaiian musicians play brief dinner shows here Wednesday through Sunday. ⊠ *Aloha Tower Marketplace, 1 Aloha Tower Dr., Downtown Honolulu* ☎ *808/585–0012* ⊟ *AE, D, DC, MC, V* ⊗ *No lunch Sat.–Mon. $18–$36.*

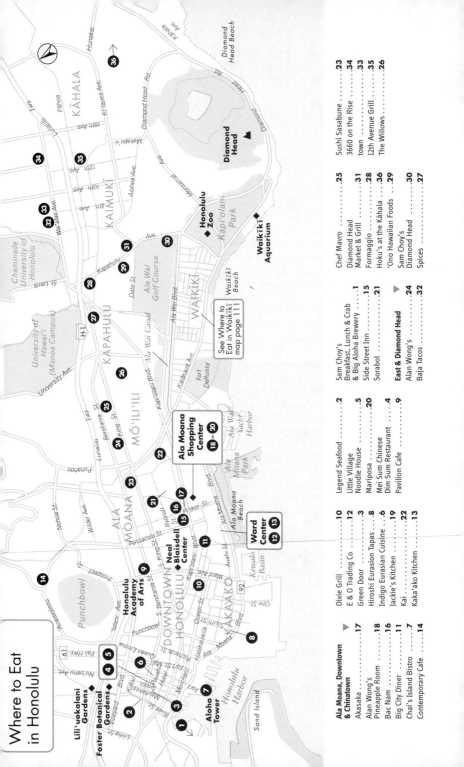

Where to Eat in Honolulu

Lili'uokalani Gardens ◆

Foster Botanical Gardens ◆

KĀHALA

KĀHALA

Diamond Head Beach

Diamond Head

KAIMUKI

Honolulu Zoo ◆

Kapi'olani Park

Waikīkī Aquarium ◆

Chaminade University of Honolulu

University of Hawai'i (Manoa Campus)

KAPAHULU

MŌ'ILI'ILI

Ala Wai Golf Course

WAIKĪKĪ

Waikīkī Beach

Ala Moana Shopping Center **18 – 20**

See Where to Eat in Waikīkī map page 111

Ala Moana Park

Ala Wai Yacht Harbor

ALA MOANA

Neal Blaisdell Center ◆

Ala Moana Beach

Punchbowl

Honolulu Academy of Arts ◆

DOWNTOWN HONOLULU

KAKA'AKO

Ward Center **12 13**

Keuhole Basin

Aloha Tower ◆

Honolulu Harbor

Sand Island

1

$–$$$$ ✕ **Alan Wong's Pineapple Room.** This is not your grandmother's department store restaurant. It's über-chef Alan Wong's more casual second spot, where chef de cuisine Neil Nakasone plays intriguing riffs on local food themes. We are frankly addicted to the spicy chili-fried soybeans and the Pineapple Room Baby Back Ribs. Pleasant surroundings and very professional service. Reservations recommended. ⊠ *Macy's, Ala Moana Center, 1450 Ala Moana Blvd., Ala Moana* ☎ *808/945–6573* ▤ *AE, D, DC, MC, V. $10–$36.*

$$–$$$ ✕ **Indigo Eurasian Cuisine.** Owner Glenn Chu sets the mood for an evening out on the town: the walls are redbrick, the ceilings are high, and from the restaurant's lounge next door comes the sultry sound of late-night jazz. Take a bite of goat cheese won tons with four-fruit sauce followed by rich Mongolian lamb chops. After dinner, duck into the hip Green Room lounge or Opium Den & Champagne Bar for a nightcap. If you're touring downtown at lunchtime, the Eurasian buffet is an especially good deal at $15.95 per person. ⊠ *1121 Nu'uanu Ave., Downtown Honolulu* ☎ *808/521–2900* ▤ *AE, D, DC, MC, V. $19–$30.*

$–$$$ ✕ **Mariposa.** Yes, the wee little cups of bouillion are there at lunch, and the popovers, but in every other regard, chef Douglas Lum's menu departs from the Nieman Marcus model, incorporating a clear sense of Pacific place. The veranda, open to the breezes and view of Ala Moana Park, twirling ceiling fans, and life-size hula-girl murals say Hawai'i. The popovers come with jam made from native poha berries—a relative of the gooseberry—and local fish are featured nightly in luxuriant specials. ⊠ *Nieman Marcus, Ala Moana Center, 1450 Ala Moana, Ala Moana* ☎ *808/951–3420* ⌕ *Reservations essential* ▤ *AE, D, DC, MC, V. $10–$30.*

$–$$ ✕ **La Mariana Restaurant & Sailing Club.** Just past downtown Honolulu, tucked away in the industrial area of Sand Island, is this friendly South Seas–style restaurant. Over the past 50 years, nonagenarian owner Annette Nahinu has bought up kitsch from other restaurants, even importing the piano (and piano player) from the beloved Tahitian Lānai, so it's tikis to the max here. The food—grilled seafood, steaks—is just okay; but go for the sing-along fun and the feeling that Don the Beachcomber might walk in any minute. ⊠ *50 Sand Island Rd., Iwilei* ☎ *808/848–2800* ▤ *AE, D, DC, MC, V. $11–$20.*

¢–$$ ✕ **E & O Trading Co.** Named for the colonial-era Eastern & Orient Trading Co., this restaurant's decor recalls a bustling mercantile district in some Asian port. Like a merchant ship, the Southeast Asian grill menu hops from Singapore to Korea, Japan to India. The Indonesian corn fritters are a must, as are the Burmese ginger salad and the silky-textured, smoky-flavored marinated portobello satay. To match the unusual menu, the bar creates some unusual mixtures with infusions and fresh juices. ⊠ *Ward Centre, 1200 Ala Moana Blvd., Kaka'ko* ☎ *808/591–9555* ▤ *AE, D, DC, MC, V. $7–$22.*

¢–$$ ✕ **Hiroshi Eurasion Tapas.** Built around chef Hiroshi Fukui's signature style of "West & Japan" cuisine, this sleek dinner house focuses on small plates to share (enough for two servings each if you're friendly with your dining partner), with an exceptional choice of hard-to-find wines by the glass and in flights. Do not miss Hiroshi's braised veal cheeks (he was doing them before everyone else), the locally raised kampachi fish carpaccio, or the best *misoyaki* (marinated in a rich miso-soy blend, then grilled) butterfish ever. ✉ *1341 Kapi'olani Blvd., Ala Moana* ☎ *808/955-0552* ▭ *AE, D, MC, V* ✆ *No lunch. $7–$22.*

¢–$ ✕ **Jackie's Kitchen.** The first U.S. outlet of a chain owned by international film star Jackie Chan is a lot like the martial-arts movie king's films: surprisingly charming. We didn't expect much but found ourselves enjoying the food, the bartenders flipping bottles about, the silly souvenir glasses, the movies playing on flat screens all over the place. Kids love it, and their parents will find much to enjoy, too. Caution: With all the keepsakes for sale, this could get expensive. ✉ *Ala Moana Shopping Center, third level, 1450 Ala Moana Blvd., Ala Moana* ☎ *808/943-2426* ⌨ *Reservations not accepted* ▭ *AE, D, DC, MC, V. $8–$17.*

¢–$ ✕ **Kaka'ako Kitchen.** Russell Siu was the first of the local-boy fine dining chefs to open a place of the sort he enjoys when he's off-duty, serving high-quality plate lunches (housemade sauce instead of from-a-mix brown gravy, for example). Here you can get your two scoops of rice, either white or brown, and green salad instead of the usual macaroni salad, grilled fresh fish specials, and vegetarian options. Breakfast is especially good with combos like corned-beef hash and eggs and exceptional baked goods such as *poi* bread. ✉ *Ward Centre, 1200 Ala Moana Blvd., Kaka'ako* ☎ *808/596-7488* ⌨ *Reservations not accepted* ▭ *No credit cards. $7–$15.*

Japanese

¢–$$ ✕ **Akasaka.** Step inside this tiny sushi bar tucked behind the Ala Moana Hotel, and you'll swear you're in some out-of-the-way Edo neighborhood in some indeterminate time. Greeted with a cheerful "Iraishaimasu!" (Welcome!), you sink down at a diminutive table or perch at the handful of seats at the sushi bar. It's safe to let the sushi chefs here decide (omakase-style) or you can go for the delicious grilled specialties, such as scallop *battayaki* (grilled in butter). Award-winning and deservedly so. Reservations accepted for groups only. ✉ *1646 B Kona St., Ala Moana* ☎ *808/942-4466* ▭ *AE, D, DC, MC, V* ✆ *No lunch Sun. $9–$25.*

¢–$ ✕ **Kai.** This chic little spot opened in 2005 and introduced Honolulu to *okonomiyaki,* the famous savory pancakes that are a specialty of Osaka, with mix-and-match ingredients scrambled together on a griddle then drizzled with various piquant sauces. The combinations may at times strike you as bizarre, but you can always order simpler grilled dishes. Reservations recommended. ✉ *1427 Makaloa St., Ala Moana* ☎ *808/944-1555* ▭ *AE, D, DC, MC, V* ✆ *No lunch. Closed Mon. $8–$17.*

Korean

¢–$$ ✕ **Sorabol.** The largest Korean restaurant in the city, this 24-hour eatery, with its impossibly tiny parking lot and maze of booths and private rooms, offers a vast menu encompassing the entirety of day-to-day Korean cuisine, plus sushi. English menu translations are cryptic at best. Still, we love it for wee hour "grinds": *bi bim bap* (veggies, meats, and eggs on steamed rice), *kal bi* and *bulgogi* (barbecued meats), and meat or fish *jun* (thin fillets fried in batter). ✉ *805 Ke'eaumoku St., Ala Moana* ☎ *808/947-3113* ▭ *AE, DC, MC, V. $6–$20.*

Seafood

$$–$$$$ ✕ **Sam Choy's Breakfast, Lunch and Crab & Big Aloha Brewery.** In this casual setting, great for families, diners can down crab and lobster—but since these come from elsewhere, we recommend the catch of the day, the *char siu* (Chinese barbecue), baby back ribs, or Sam's special fried *poke* (flash-fried tuna). This eatery's warehouse size sets the tone for its *bambucha* (huge) portions. An on-site microbrewery brews five varieties of Big Aloha beer. Sam Choy's is in Iwilei past Downtown Honolulu on the highway heading to Honolulu International Airport. ✉ *580 Nimitz Hwy., Iwilei* ☎ *808/ 545–7979* 🖃 *AE, D, DC, MC, V. $19–$40.*

> ### MALASSADAS
>
> Donuts without a hole, malassadas are a contribution of the Portuguese, who came to the Islands to work on the plantations. Roughly translated, the name means half-cooked, which refers to the origin of these deep-fried, heavily sugared treats: they are said to have been created as a way to use up scraps of rich, buttery egg dough. A handful of bakeries specialize in malassadas (Leonard's on Kapahulu, Agnes in Kailua, Champion on Beretania); restaurants sometimes serve an uscpale version stuffed with fruit puree; they're inevitable at fairs and carnivals. Eat them hot or not at all.

Southeast Asian

¢–$ ✕ **Bac Nam.** Tam and Kimmy Huynh's menu is much more extensive than most, ranging far beyond the usual *pho* (beef noodle soup) and *bun* (cold noodle dishes). Coconut milk curries, an extraordinary crab noodle soup, and other dishes hail from both from North and South Vietnam. The atmosphere is welcoming and relaxed, and they'll work with you to make choices. Reservations accepted for groups of six or more. ✉ *1117 S. King St., Downtown* ☎ *808/597–8201* 🖃 *MC, V. $6–$12.*

¢–$ ✕ **Green Door.** Closet-sized and fronted by a green door and a row of welcoming Chinese lanterns, this 12-seat café in Chinatown has introduced Honolulu to budget- and tastebud-friendly Malaysian and Singaporean foods, redolent of spices and crunchy with fresh vegetables. ✉ *1145 Maunakea St., Chinatown* ☎ *808/533–0606* 🖃 *No credit cards* 🖃 *Reservations not accepted* ⊘ *Closed Mon. $5–$12.*

Honolulu: East & Diamond Head

Contemporary

$$$–$$$$ ✕ **Alan Wong's.** This worthy restaurant is like that very rare shell you
Fodor'sChoice stumble upon on a perfect day at the beach—well polished and with-
★ out a flaw. We've never had a bad experience here, and we've never heard of anyone else doing so, either. The "Wong Way," as it's not-so-jokingly called by his staff, includes an ingrained understanding of the aloha spirit, evident in the skilled but unstarched service, and creative and playful interpretations of island cuisine. Try Da Bag (seafood steamed in a Mylar pouch), Chinatown Roast Duck Nachos, and Poki Pines (rice-studded seafood wonton appetizers). With a view of the Ko'olau Mountains, warm tones of koa wood and lauhala grass weaving, you forget you're on the third floor of an office building. Not to be missed. ✉ *Mc-*

Cully Court, 1857 S. King St., 3rd fl., Mō'ili'ili ☎ *808/949–2526* ▭ *AE, MC, V* ☉ *No lunch. $25–$38.*

$$$–$$$$ ✕ **Chef Mavro.** George Mavrothalassitis, who took two hotel restaurants
Fodor'sChoice   to the top of the ranks before founding this James Beard Award-win-
★   ning dinner house, admits he's crazy. Crazy because of the care he takes
to draw out the truest and most concentrated flavors, to track down
the freshest fish, to create one-of-a-kind wine pairings that might strike
others as mad. But for this passionate Provençal transplant, there's no
other way. The menu changes quarterly, every dish (including dessert)
matched with a select wine. We recommend the multicourse tasting menus
(beginning at $66 for four courses without wine, up to $137 for six courses
with wine). Etched-glass windows screen the busy street-corner scene
and all within is mellow and serene with starched white tablecloths, fresh
flowers, wood floors, contemporary island art. ✉ *1969 S. King St.,
Mō'ili'ili* ☎ *808/944–4714* ⌔ *Reservations essential* ▭ *AE, DC, MC,
V* ☉ *No lunch. $32–$42.*

★ **$$–$$$$** ✕ **Hoku's at the Kāhala.** Everything about this room speaks of quality
and sophistication: the wall of windows with their beach views, the avant-
garde cutlery and dinnerware, the solicitous staff and border-busting Pacific Rim cuisine. They do tend to get a bit architectural (lots of edible
stacks and towers), but the food invariably tastes every bit as good as
it looks. The international breads and the dessert sampler in particular
are noteworthy. ✉ *The Kāhala, 5000 Kāhala Ave., Kāhala* ☎ *808/
739–8780* ▭ *AE, D, MC, V* ☉ *No lunch Sat. $22–$39.*

$–$$$ ✕ **Sam Choy's Diamond Head.** Sam Choy has been called the Paul Prud-
homme of Hawai'i and aptly so: both are big, welcoming men with magic
in their hands and a folksy background in small, rural towns. Choy grew
up cooking for his parents' lū'au business and now has an empire:
restaurants, TV show, cookbooks, commercial products, and his two
best chef-friends are Prudhomme and Emeril Lagasse. Here, Choy and
staff interpret local favorites in sophisticated ways, and the fresh fish is
the best. The portions, like Sam's smile, are huge. ✉ *449 Kapahulu Ave.,
Kapahulu* ☎ *808/732–8645* ▭ *AE, D, MC, DC, V. $15–$35.*

★ **$–$$$** ✕ **3660 on the Rise.** This casually stylish eatery is a 10-minute drive from
Waikīkī in the up-and-coming culinary mecca of Kaimukī. Sample Chef
Russell Siu's New York Steak Alae'a Alae'a (steak grilled with Hawaiian clay salt), the crab cakes, or the signature 'ahi katsu wrapped in nori
and deep-fried with a wasabi-ginger butter sauce. Siu combines a deep
understanding of local flavors with a sophisticated palate, making this
place especially popular with homegrown gourmands. The dining room
can feel a bit snug when it's full (as it usually is); go early or later. ✉ *3660
Wai'alae Ave., Kaimukī* ☎ *808/737–1177* ▭ *AE, DC, MC, V. $10–$30.*

¢–$$$ ✕ **12th Avenue Grill.** We love this clean, well-lighted place on a back street
where chef Kevin Hanney dishes up diner chic, including macaroni and
cheese glazed with house-smoked Parmesan and topped with savory bread-
crumbs. The kim chee steak, a sort of teriyaki with kick, is a winner.
Go early (5) or late (8:30). Enjoy wonderful, homey desserts. There's a
small, reasonably priced wine list. Reservations recommended. ✉ *1145C
12th Ave., Kaimukī* ☎ *808/732–9469* ⌕ *BYOB* ▭ *MC, V* ☉ *No
lunch. Closed Sun. $8–$27.*

MUSUBI

MUSUBI NEEDS TRANSLATION.
Here are cakes of steamed rice like thick decks of cards, topped with something that resembles spoiled luncheon meat, and bound in a strip of black like a paper band around a stack of new bills. Swathed in plastic, they sit on the counter of every mom-and-pop store and plate-lunch place in Hawai'i, selling for $1.50, $1.95. And T-shirted surfers with sandy feet, girls in *pareus*, and *tutus* (grandmas) in *mu'umu'u* are munching these oddities with apparent delight.

"Huh?," says the visitor.

So, a quick dictionary moment: *musubi* (*moo*-sue-bee), a cake of steamed Japanese-style rice topped with some sweet-salty morsel and held together with *nori* (seaweed). Most common form: Spam musubi, popularized in the early 1980s by vendor Mitsuko Kaneshiro.

Kaneshiro turned her children's favorite snack into a classic—Spam slices simmered in a sugar-soy mixture atop rectangular rice cakes, with nori for crisp contrast. The flavor is surprisingly pleasant and satisfying, like a portable rice bowl.

Musubi has its roots in Japan, where rice cakes are standard festival, funeral, and family fare. But Islanders carried the tradition far afield, topping rice with slices of teriyaki chicken, sandwiching tuna salad between two cakes, dressing the rice in piquant slivers of scarlet pickled plum, toasted sesame, and strips of seaweed.

These ubiquitous tidbits are Hawai'i's go-food, like hot dogs or pretzels on a New York street. Quality varies, but if you visit a craft fair or stumble on a school sale and see homemade musubi—grab one and snack like a local.

¢-$$ ✕**town.** Tell us how old you are, and we'll tell you whether you're likely to enjoy town (yes, the "t" is lower case). The motto here is "local first, organic whenever possible, with aloha always." Pretty much everyone agrees that chef-owner Ed Kenney's vaguely Mediterranean menu ranges from just fine (pastas and salads) to just fabulous (buttermilk panna cotta). But if you're over 40, you'll probably be put off by the minimalist decor, the shrieking-level acoustics, and the heedlessly careless waitstaff, who have a tendency to get lost. Young people don't seem bothered by either circumstance. The restaurant serves an inexpensive Continental breakfast, as well as lunch and dinner. ✉ *3435 Wai'alae Ave., Kaimukī* ☎ *808/735–5900* ⬧ *Reservations essential* 🍴 *BYOB* 🖃 *MC, V* 🕑 *Closed Sun. $4–$20.*

Delicatessens

¢-$ ✕**Diamond Head Market & Grill.** Kelvin Ro's one-stop spot is a plate-lunch place, a gourmet market, a deli and bakery and espresso bar, too—and it's a five-minute hop from Waikīkī hotels. A take-out window offers grilled sandwiches or plates ranging from teriyaki beef to portobello mushrooms. The market's deli case is stocked with a range of heat-and-eat entrées from risotto cakes to lamb stew; specials change daily. There are packaged Japanese bento lunchboxes, giant scones, enticing desserts, even a small wine selection. ✉ *3158 Monsarrat Ave., Diamond Head* ☎ *808/ 732–0077* ⌂ *Reservations not accepted* ▭ *AE, D, MC, V. $5–$15.*

Hawaiian

$$–$$$ ✕ **The Willows.** An island dream, this restaurant is made up of pavilions overlooking a network of ponds (once natural streams flowing from mountain to sea). The island-style comfort food, served buffet-style, includes the trademark Willows curry along with Hawaiian dishes such as *laulau* (a steamed bundle of ti leaves containing pork, butterfish, and taro tops) and local favorites such as Korean barbecue ribs. In 2005 Chef Jay Matsukawa added a new sit-down restaurant-within-a-restaurant serving rustic French food. ✉ *901 Hausten St., Mōʻiliʻili* ☎ *808/952–9200* ⌂ *Reservations essential* ▭ *AE, D, MC, V. $19–$28.*

¢–$ ✕ **ʻOno Hawaiian Foods.** The adventurous in search of a real local food experience should head to this no-frills hangout. You know it has to be good if residents are waiting in line to get in. Here you can sample *poi*, *lomi lomi* salmon (salmon massaged until tender and served with minced onions and tomatoes), laulau, *kālua* pork (roasted in an underground oven), and *haupia* (a light, gelatin-like dessert made from coconut milk). Appropriately enough, the Hawaiian word *ʻono* means delicious. ✉ *726 Kapahulu Ave., Kapahulu* ☎ *808/737–2275* ⌂ *Reservations not accepted* ▭ *No credit cards* ☉ *Closed Sun. $6–$14.*

Japanese

¢–$$ ✕ **Sushi Sasabune.** You may find this restaurant's approach exasperating and a little condescending. Although it's possible to order from the menu, you're strongly encouraged to order omakase-style (oh-*mah*-ka-say, roughly, "trust me"), letting the chef send out his choices for the night. The waiters keep up a steady mantra: "Please, no shoyu on this one." "One piece, one bite." But then you take the first bite of California baby squid stuffed with Louisiana crab or unctuous *toro* (ʻahi belly) smeared with a light soy reduction, and any trace of annoyance will vanish. Caution: the courses come very rapidly; ask to be served every other time. Even bigger caution: the courses, generally two pieces of sushi or six to eight slices of sashimi, add up fast. It's easy to spend more than $100 in a half hour, not counting drinks. Still, the meal will be as unforgettable as the tab. ✉ *1419 S. King St., Mōʻiliʻili* ☎ *808/947–3800* ⌂ *Reservations essential* ▭ *AE, D, DC, MC, V* ☉ *Closed Sun. No lunch Sat. and Mon. $8–$20.*

Mexican

¢   ✕ **Baja Tacos.** One of the first California-style taquerias in the Islands, Baja Tacos offers authentic flavors, house-made salsas, Mexican-style small plates, enchiladas, pork carnitas, and *adobada* (marinated pork) and, of course, tacos—to take out or eat in. Perfect for post-beach. ✉ *3040 Waiʻalae Ave., Kaimuki* ☎ *808/737–5893* ⌂ *Reservations not accepted* ▭ *No credit cards. $4–$8.*

Southeast Asian

¢–$ ✕ **Spices.** The creation of a well-traveled trio of friends who enjoy the foods of Southeast Asia, Spices is alluringly decorated in spice-like oranges and reds and offers a menu far from the beaten path, even in a city rich in restaurants of this region. They claim inspiration but not au-

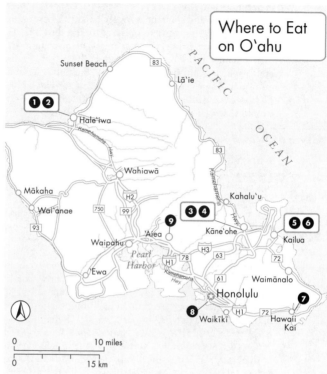

Where to Eat on O'ahu

thenticity and use island ingredients to advantage. Vegetarian-friendly. ⊠ *2671 S. King St., Mō'ili'ili* ☎ *808/949–2679* ⌧ *Reservations essential* ▤ *MC, V* ⊗ *Closed Mon. $8–$12.*

Wine Bars

¢–$ ✕ **Formaggio.** All but invisible on the back side of a strip mall, Formaggio seeks to communicate the feel of a catacomb in Italy, and largely succeeds with dim lighting and soft, warm tones. Choose a small sip or an entire bottle from the 40 or so they offer, enjoy the guitar music, then ponder the small-dish menu of pizzas, panini, and hot and cold specialties such as eggplant Napoleon and melting short ribs in red wine. ⊠ *Market City Shopping Center, rear, lower level, 2919 Kapi'olani Blvd., Kaimukī* ☎ *808/739–7719* ⌧ *Reservations not accepted* ▤ *AE, MC, V* ⊗ *No lunch. Closed Sun. $8–$14.*

Southeast O'ahu: Hawai'i Kai

Contemporary

★ $$–$$$$ ✕ **Roy's.** Roy Yamaguchi's flagship restaurant across the highway from Maunalua Bay attracts food-savvy visitors like the North Shore attracts surfers. But it has a strong following among well-heeled Oahuans from surrounding neighborhoods who consider the place as an extension of their homes and Roy's team their personal chefs. For this reason, Roy's is always busy and sometimes overly noisy. It's best to visit later in the evening if you're sensitive to pressure to turn the table. The wide-ranging and ever-interesting Hawaiian fusion menu changes daily except for such signature dishes as szechuan spiced BBQ baby back ribs, Roy's Original blackened 'ahi with soy mustard butter sauce, and a legendary meat loaf. There's an exceptional wine list. ⊠ *Hawai'i Kai Corporate Plaza, 6600 Kalaniana'ole Hwy., Hawai'i Kai* ☎ *808/396–7697* ⌲ *Reservations essential* ═ *AE, D, DC, MC, V. $17–$30.*

Windward O'ahu: Kailua & Kāne'ohe

American–Casual

$–$$ ✕**Buzz's Original Steakhouse.** Virtually unchanged since it opened in 1967, this cozy maze of rooms opposite Kailua Beach Park is filled with the enticing aroma of grilling steaks. It doesn't matter if you're a bit sandy (but no bare feet). Stop at the salad bar, order up a steak, a burger, teri chicken, or the fresh fish special. If you sit at the bar, expect to make friends. ⊠ *413 Kawailoa Rd., Kailua* ☎ *808/261–4661* ═ *No credit cards. $13–$23.*

¢–$ ✕**Cinnamon's Restaurant.** Known for uncommon variations on common breakfast themes (pancakes, eggs Benedict, French toast, home fries and eggs), this neighborhood favorite is tucked into a hard-to-find Kailua office park; call for directions. Lunch and dinner feature local-style plate lunch and a diner-style menu. ⊠ *315 Uluniu, Kailua* ☎ *808/261–8724* ═ *D, DC, MC, V* ☉ *No dinner Sun.–Wed. $3–$10.*

¢ ✕**Boots & Kimo's Homestyle Kitchen.** If you're wondering what aloha spirit is all about, check out this family-owned, local-style restaurant in the industrial backwaters of Kāne'ohe where brothers Ricky and Jesse Kiakona treat their guests like family. At breakfast, the signature dish is macadamia nut pancakes; at lunch, *pulehu* (grilled) ribs. Generous portions at family-friendly prices. ⊠ *1321 Heikili St., Suite 102, Kāne'ohe* ☎ *808/263–7929* ⌲ *Reservations not accepted* ═ *No credit cards. $5–$7.*

Chinese

$–$$ ✕**Pah Ke's Chinese Restaurant.** Chinese restaurants tend to be interchangeable but this one—named for the local pidgin term for Chinese—is worth the drive over from Honolulu for its focus on healthier cooking techniques, its seasonal specials such as cold soups and salads made from locally raised produce, and its exceptional East–West desserts. The menu offers all the usual suspects, but ask host Raymond Siu, a former hotel pastry chef, if he's got anything different and interesting in the kitchen, or call ahead to ask for a special menu. ⊠ *46-018 Kamehameha Hwy., Kāne'ohe* ☎ *808/235–4505* ═ *AE, MC, V. $13–$23.*

The North Shore: Hale'iwa

American/Casual

¢ ✕**Kua 'Aina Sandwich.** A must-stop spot during a drive around the island, this North Shore eatery specializes in large, hand-formed burgers heaped with bacon, cheese, salsa, and pineapple. The crispy shoestring fries alone are worth the trip. You can also check out Kua ʻAina's south-shore location across from the Ward Centre in Honolulu. ⊠ *66-160 Kamehameha Hwy., Haleʻiwa* ☎ *808/637–6067* ✉ *1116 Auahi St., Ala Moana* ☎ *808/591–9133* ⌦ *Reservations not accepted* ⊟ *No credit cards. $4–$7.*

¢ ✕ **Ted's Pies.** It's a bakery, yes, famous for its chocolate *haupia* pie (layered coconut custard and chocolate pudding topped with whipped cream). But it's also favored by surfers and area residents for quick breakfasts, sandwiches, or plate lunches, to go or eaten on a handful of umbrella shaded tables outside. ⊠ *59-024 Kamehameha Hwy., Haleʻiwa* ☎ *808/638–8207* ⌦ *Reservations not accepted* ⊟ *DC, MC, V. $4–$7.*

WHERE TO STAY

By Maggie
Wunsch

Waikīkī has a lot to offer—namely, the beach, shopping, restaurants, and nightlife, all within walking distance of your hotel. Business travelers stay on the western edge, near the Hawaiʻi Convention Center, Ala Moana, and downtown Honolulu. As you head east, Ala Moana Boulevard turns into Kalākaua Avenue, Waikīkī's main drag. This is hotel row (mid-Waikīkī), complete with historic boutique hotels, newer high-rises, and megaresorts. Bigger chains like Sheraton, Outrigger, ResortQuest, and Ohana have multiple properties along the strip, so it can get a little confusing. Surrounding the hotels and filling their lower levels is a flurry of shopping centers, restaurants, bars, and clubs. As you get closer to Diamond Head Crater, the strip opens up again, with the Honolulu Zoo and Kapiʻolani Park providing green spaces. There's a handful of smaller hotels and condos at this end for those who like their Waikīkī with a side of quiet.

Waikīkī is still the resort capital of this island and the lodging landscape is constantly changing. As of this writing, by October 2006 the Waikīkī Beach Walk will have opened on 8 acres within the confines of Beach Walk, Lewers and Saratoga streets, and Kālia Road. It comprises a multitiered entertainment complex, cultural center, hotels, and vacation ownership properties. Also, Kō ʻOlina Resort and Marina, about 15 minutes from the airport in West Oʻahu, looms large on the horizon—this ongoing development already contains the J. W. Marriott ʻIhilani Resort, Marriott Kō ʻOlina Beach Vacation Club, and some outstanding golf courses but is slated, over the coming decade, to see the construction of an extensive planned resort community and marina, an aquarium, dozens of restaurants and shops, more hotels, and extensive vacation-ownership rentals.

UNDER CONSTRUCTION

At this writing, areas of Waikīkī were under much-needed renovation. The Beach Walk development near Fort DeRussy and the revitalization of the Royal Hawaiian Shopping Center and the International Marketplace—both on Kalākaua Avenue in central Waikīkī—in particular are noteworthy. Enquire closely about noise, disruption, and construction when choosing a hotel.

Casual Windward and North Shore digs are shorter on amenities but have laid-back charms all their own. O'ahu offers a more limited list of B&Bs than other islands because the state stopped licensing them here in the 1980s; many of those operating here now do so under the radar. If you can't find your match below, contact a reservation service to make reservations at one of O'ahu's reputable B&Bs. The good news is, legislators on O'ahu are taking another look at this industry, and it's possible that B&Bs will flourish here again in the next decade.

For a complete list of every hotel and condominium on the island, write or call the Hawai'i Visitors & Convention Bureau for a free *Accommodation Guide.*

WHAT IT COSTS				
$$$$	**$$$**	**$$**	**$**	**¢**
over $340	$261–$340	$181–$260	$100–$180	under $100

Hotel prices are for two people in a standard double room in high season. Condo price categories reflect studio and one-bedroom rates.

Waikīkī

Hotels & Resorts

$$$$ ⊡ **Halekūlani.** Honeymooners and others seeking seclusion amidst the
Fodor'sChoice   frenetic activity of the Waikīkī scene find it here. Halekūlani exempli-
★   fies the translation of its name—the "house befitting heaven." From the moment you step inside the lobby, the attention to detail and service wraps you in luxury. It begins with private registration in your guest room and extends to the tiniest of details, such as complimentary tickets to the Honolulu Symphony, Contemporary Art Museum, and Honolulu Academy of Arts. Spacious guest rooms, artfully appointed in marble and wood, have ocean views and extra large lānai. If you want to honeymoon in the ultimate style, we recommend the 2,125-square-foot Vera Wang Suite, created by the noted wedding-dress designer herself. It's entirely Vera, right down to the signature soft-lavender color scheme. Outside, the resort's freshwater pool has an orchid design created from more than 1½ million glass mosaic tiles. Gray's Beach, which fronts the hotel just beyond the pool, is small and has been known to disappear at high tide. ⊠ *2199 Kālia Rd., Waikīkī 96815* ☏ *808/923–2311 or 800/ 367–2343* ☒ *808/926–8004* ⊕ *www.halekulani.com* ⬎ *412 rooms, 44 suites* ♤ *3 restaurants, room service, in-room data ports, Wi-Fi, in-room safes, cable TV, in-room DVD players, pool, health club, hair salon, spa, beach, 3 bars, shops, dry cleaning, Internet room, business services, parking (fee), no-smoking rooms* ▤ *AE, DC, MC, V. $385–$660.*

$$$$ ⊡ **Outrigger Waikīkī on the Beach.** This star jewel of Outrigger Hotels & Resorts sits on one of the finest strands of Waikīkī beach, where throughout the year, the hotel plays host to canoe regattas, the World Ocean Games lifeguard competition, and the Honolulu Marathon. The 16-story resort's guest rooms have rich dark-wood furnishings, Hawaiian art, and lānai that offer either ocean or Waikīkī skyline views. The popular Duke's Canoe Club has beachfront concerts under the stars.

The resort's new Plantation Spa was slated to open in mid 2006. ✉ *2335 Kalākaua Ave., Waikīkī 96815* ☎ *808/923–0711 or 800/688–7444* 🖷 *808/921–9798* 🌐 *www.outrigger.com* ☞ *500 rooms, 30 suites* ⚒ *3 restaurants, room service, A/C, in-room broadband, in-room data ports, in-room safes, some kitchenettes, refrigerators, cable TV with movies and video games, pool, gym, hot tub, beach, 6 bars, theater, shops, children's programs (ages 5–13), dry cleaning, laundry facilities, business services, parking (fee), no-smoking rooms* ▭ *AE, D, DC, MC, V. $349–$739.*

$$$$ 🏨 **Royal Hawaiian Hotel.** The high octane mai tais at this resort's outdoor Mai Tai Bar made the drink famous. But the drinks aren't the only thing that's legendary at the Pink Palace of the Pacific, so nicknamed for its cotton-candy color. The Royal was built in 1927 by Matson Navigation Company for its luxury-cruise passengers. A modern tower has since been added, but we're partial to the romance and architectural detailing of the Royal's historic wing with its canopy beds, Queen Anne–style desks, and color motifs that range from soft mauve to soothing sea foam. If you want a lānai for sunset viewing, rooms in the oceanfront tower are your best bet. The Royal's weekly lū'au—the only oceanfront lū'au in Waikīkī—is held Monday evenings underneath the stars on the Ocean Lawn. ✉ *2259 Kalākaua Ave., Waikīkī 96815* ☎ *888/488–3535, 808/923–7311, or 866/500–8313* 🖷 *808/924–7098* 🌐 *www.royal-hawaiian. com* ☞ *472 rooms, 53 suites* ⚒ *2 restaurants, room service, A/C, in-room broadband, Web TV, minibars, cable TV, pool, hair salon, spa, beach, bar, shops, children's programs (ages 5–12), Internet, business services, car rental, parking (fee), no-smoking rooms* ▭ *AE, DC, MC, V. $395–$680.*

$$$$ 🏨 **Waikīkī Beach Marriott Resort.** On the eastern edge of Waikīkī, this
★ flagship Marriott sits across from Kūhiō Beach. Deep Hawaiian woods and bold tropical colors fill the hotel's two towers, which have ample courtyards and public areas open to ocean breezes and sunlight. Rooms in the Kealohilani Tower are some of the largest in Waikīkī, and the Paokalani Tower's Diamond Head–side rooms offer breathtaking views of the crater and Kapi'olani Park. All rooms have private lānai. If you want to keep that laid-back vacation spirit to the very end, use Baggage Direct's mobile skycap service in the main lobby. This TSA-certified agency will take your bags and check them through to your final destination right from the hotel. No more schlep-
ping. ✉ *2552 Kalākaua Ave., Waikīkī 96815* ☎ *808/922–6611 or 800/367–5370* 🖷 *808/921–5222* 🌐 *www. marriottwaikiki.com* ☞ *1,310 rooms, 13 suites* ⚒ *6 restaurants, room service, A/C, in-room broadband, in-room data ports, Web TV, Wi-Fi, in-room safes, refrigerators, cable TV with movies, 2 pools, gym, spa, 2 bars, business services, parking (fee), no-smoking rooms* ▭ *AE, D, MC, V. $375–$585.*

> **PRIVATE BEACHES IN HAWAI'I?**
>
> The Royal Hawaiian Hotel and the Sheraton Moana Surfrider are the only hotels in Waikīkī with property lines that extend out into the sand. They have created private roped-off beach areas that can only be accessed by hotel guests. The areas are adjacent to the hotel properties at the top of the beach.

WHERE TO STAY IN WAIKĪKĪ & OʻAHU

Hotels & Resorts

★ HOTEL NAME	Worth Noting	Cost $	Pools	Beach	Golf Course	Tennis Courts	Gym	Spa	Children's Programs	Rooms	Restaurants	Other	Location
28 Ala Moana Hotel	Near Ala Moana Shopping	175–570	1				yes			1,217	4		Ala Moana
3 Doubletree Alana Waikīkī	Near Convention Center	140–220	1				yes	yes		313	1		Waikīkī
★ 9 Halekūlani	Great restaurants	385–660	1	yes			yes	yes		456	3	shops	Waikīkī
1 Hawaiʻi Prince Hotel	Near Convention Center	325–465	1		yes		yes	yes		578	3	shops	Waikīkī
★ 4 Hilton Hawaiian Village	Fabulous views, fireworks	239–535	5	yes			yes	yes	5–12	4,061	20	shops	Waikīkī
19 Hyatt Regency Waikīkī	Beach across the street	210–530	1				yes	yes	5–12	1,230	5	shops	Waikīkī
33 J. W. Marriott ʻIhilani	Ko ʻOlina Resort, spa	370–600	2	yes	yes	6	yes	yes	5–12	423	4	shops	West Oʻahu
29 The Kāhala	Dolphin Quest	345–735	1	yes			yes	yes		364	5	shops	Kāhala
2 Marc Hawaiʻi Polo	Near Ala Moana shopping	99–135	1							106		kitchens	Waikīkī
18 Ohana East	2 blocks to beach	199–209	1				yes			440	3	kitchens	Waikīkī
16 Ohana Waikīkī Beachcomber	1 block to beach, 3 shows	245–295	1						5–12	507	1		Waikīkī
8 Outrigger Reef	Good value	269–599	1	yes			yes		5–12	885	3		Waikīkī
13 Outrigger Waikīkī	Duke's Canoe Club	349–739	1	yes			yes		5–13	530	3	kitchens	Waikīkī
22 Radisson Waikīkī Prince K.	2 blocks to beach	199–239	1				yes			620	1		Waikīkī
26 ResortQuest Waikīkī Beach	Beach across the street	255–450	1							728	3	shops	Waikīkī
21 Royal Grove Hotel	Good value	45–75	1							85		no A/C	Waikīkī
12 Royal Hawaiian Hotel	Mai Tai Bar	395–680	1	yes				yes	5–12	525	2	shops	Waikīkī
14 Sheraton Moana Surfrider	Landmark historic wing	310–625	1	yes					5–12	839	2	shops	Waikīkī
17 Sheraton Princess Kaiulani	1 block to beach	185–380	1				yes		5–12	1,166	3		Waikīkī
11 Sheraton Waikīkī	30th Floor Cobalt Lounge	300–620	2	yes			yes		5–12	1,823	3	shops	Waikīkī
★ 31 Turtle Bay Resort	Beach cottages, trails	350–780	2	yes	yes	10	yes	yes	5–12	511	4	shops	North Shore
★ 24 Waikīkī Beach Marriott	Great sushi, spa	375–585	2	yes			yes	yes		1,323	6		Waikīkī

10 Waikīkī Parc	1 block to beach	160–333	1		yes			298	2		*Waikīkī*
20 Waikīkī Sand Villa	3 blocks to beach	109–190	1					214	1		*Waikīkī*
Condos											
6 The Breakers	1 block to beach	130	1					64		kitchens	*Waikīkī*
★ 7 Castle Waikīkī Shores	Great value	265–340		yes				168	1	kitchens	*Waikīkī*
15 Ilima Hotel	3 blocks to beach	214–249	1		yes			99		kitchens	*Waikīkī*
34 Marriott Kō 'Olina Beach Club	Kō 'Olina Resort, spa	319–609	2	yes	yes	6	5–12	200	2	kitchens	*West O'ahu*
5 Outrigger Luana	2 blocks to beach	210–375	1		yes			217		kitchens	*Waikīkī*
25 ResortQuest Waikīkī Banyan	1 block to beach	200–275	1			1		310		kitchens	*Waikīkī*
23 ResortQuest Waikīkī Beach Tower	1 block to beach	505–585	1			1		140		kitchens	*Waikīkī*
B&Bs & Vacation Rentals											
32 Backpackers Vacation Inn	Near Waimea Bay	22–250						25		no A/C	*North Shore*
27 Diamond Head B&B	Near Diamond Head Crater	130						3		no A/C	*Waikīkī*
30 Ingrid's	Kailua, Japanese garden	150						2		kitchens	*Windward O'ahu*

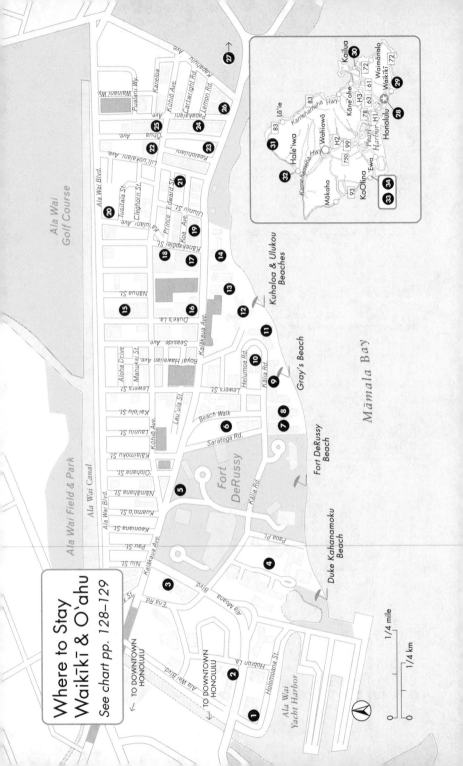

Where to Stay
Waikīkī & Oʻahu

See chart pp. 128–129

Ala Wai Golf Course

Ala Wai Field & Park

Māmala Bay

Fort DeRussy

Ala Wai Yacht Harbor

Ala Wai Canal

Kuhaloa & Ulukou Beaches

Gray's Beach

Fort DeRussy Beach

Duke Kahanamoku Beach

← TO DOWNTOWN HONOLULU

← TO DOWNTOWN HONOLULU

1/4 mile

1/4 km

$$$–$$$$ ⊞ **Hawai'i Prince Hotel Waikīkī.** This slim high-rise fronts Ala Wai Yacht Harbor at the *'ewa* edge of Waikīkī, close to Honolulu's downtown business districts, the convention center, and Ala Moana's outdoor mall. There's no beach here, but Ala Moana Beach Park is a 10-minute stroll away along the Harbor, and the hotel also offers complimentary shuttle service around Waikīkī and its surrounding beaches. It's the only resort in Waikīkī with a golf course—the 27-hole Arnold Palmer–designed golf course is in 'Ewa Beach, about a 45-minute ride from the hotel. The sleek, modern Prince looks to Asia both in its high-style decor and such pampering touches as the traditional *oshiburi* (chilled hand towel) for refreshment upon check-in. Floor-to-ceiling windows overlooking the harbor sunsets make up for the lack of lānai. ⊠ *100 Holomoana St., Waikīkī 96815* ☏ *808/956–1111 or 866/774–6236* 🖷 *808/944–4491* ⊕ *www.hawaiiprincehotel.com* ↻ *521 rooms, 57 suites* ⌕ *3 restaurants, room service, A/C, in-room data ports, in-room safes, minibars, cable TV, 27-hole golf course, pool, gym, hair salon, spa, hot tub, bar, shops, babysitting, business services, parking (fee), no-smoking rooms* ▭ *AE, DC, MC, V. $325–$465.*

$$$–$$$$ ⊞ **Outrigger Reef on the Beach.** Value and a location right on the beach near to Fort DeRussy are the draw here. Beginning in late 2006 or early 2007, this hotel will serve as the beachfront anchor for the new Waikīkī Beach Walk complex. Plans are underway to enhance this resort's interiors to complement the Waikīkī Beach Walk. Try to get an ocean view or oceanfront accommodation; the other rooms have less enchanting views of the walls of the Waikīkī Shores condominium next door. Most rooms have only showers, and all except those in the standard category have lānai. Kids who sign up for the Reef's Island Explorer program get their own backpack and binoculars at check-in. ⊠ *2169 Kālia Rd., Waikīkī 96815* ☏ *808/923–3111 or 800/688–7444* 🖷 *808/924–4957* ⊕ *www. outrigger.com* ↻ *846 rooms, 39 suites* ⌕ *3 restaurants, room service, A/C, in-room data ports, refrigerators, cable TV with movies and video games, pool, gym, beach, 4 bars, nightclub, laundry facilities, children's programs (ages 5–12), business services, parking (fee), no-smoking rooms* ▭ *AE, D, DC, MC, V. $269–$599.*

$$$–$$$$ ⊞ **Sheraton Moana Surfrider.** Outrageous rates of $1.50 per night were the talk of the town when the "First Lady of Waikīkī" opened her doors in 1901. The *Hawai'i Calls* radio program was broadcast from the veranda during the 1940s and '50s. Today the Moana is still a wedding and honeymoon favorite with its sweeping main staircase and period furnishings in its historic main wing, the Moana. You can even renew your wedding vows during the Moana's weekly Promise Me Again ceremony held Saturday evenings underneath the stars of the Banyan Courtyard. In the late 1950s, the Diamond Head Tower was built. In the '70s, the Surfrider hotel went up next door—all three merged into one hotel in the 1980s. The newly refurbished Surfrider has oceanfront suites with two separate lānai, one for sunrise and one for sunset viewing. Relax on the private beach or in a cabana by the pool. ⊠ *2365 Kalākaua Ave., Waikīkī 96815* ☎ *808/922–3111, 888/488–3535, or 866/ 500–8313* 🖷 *808/923–0308* ⊕ *www.moana-surfrider.com* 📱 *793 rooms, 46 suites* ⚏ *2 restaurants, snack bar, room service, A/C, in-room data ports, in-room safes, cable TV, pool, hair salon, beach, 3 bars, shops, children's programs (ages 5–12), dry cleaning, laundry service, parking (fee), no-smoking rooms* ⊟ *AE, DC, MC, V. $310–$625.*

$$$–$$$$ 🏨 **Sheraton Waikīkī.** Towering over its neighbors on the prow of Waikīkī's famous sands, the Sheraton is center stage on Waikīkī Beach. Designed for the convention crowd, it's big and busy; the ballroom, one of O'ahu's largest, hosts convention expos, concerts, and boxing matches. A glass-wall elevator, with magnificent views of Waikīkī, ascends 30 stories to the Hano Hano Room's skyline Cobalt lounge and restaurant in the sky. The resort's best beach is on its Diamond Head side, fronting the Royal Hawaiian Hotel. Lānai afford views of the ocean, Waikīkī, or mountains. If you don't shy away from crowds, this could be the place. The advantage here is that you have at your vacation fingertips a variety of amenities, venues, and programs, as well as a location smack dab in the middle of Waikīkī. Don't forget, we're talking living large here, so even the walk to your room could hike off a few of those calories consumed in mai tais. ⊠ *2255 Kalākaua Ave., Waikīkī 96815* ☎ *888/ 488–3535, 808/922–4422, or 866/500–8313* 🖷 *808/923–8785* ⊕ *www. sheratonwaikiki.com* 📱 *1,695 rooms, 128 suites* ⚏ *3 restaurants, room service, A/C, in-room broadband, Web TV, refrigerators, cable TV, 2 pools, health club, hair salon, beach, 4 bars, dance club, babysitting, shops, children's programs (ages 5–12), dry cleaning, laundry service, business services, parking (fee), no-smoking rooms* ⊟ *AE, DC, MC, V. $300–$620.*

★ $$–$$$$ 🏨 **Hilton Hawaiian Village Beach Resort and Spa.** Location, location, location. The HHV sprawls over 22 acres on Waikīkī's widest stretch of beach. It has the perfect neighbor in Fort DeRussy, whose green lawns create a buffer zone to the high-rise lineup of central Waikīkī. The Hilton makes the most of its prime real estate—surrounding the five hotel towers with lavish gardens, an aquatic playground of pools, a lagoon, cascading waterfalls, koi ponds, penguins, and pink flamingos. Rainbow Tower, with its landmark 31-story mural, has knockout views of Diamond Head. Rooms in all towers have lānai offering ocean, city, or Waikīkī beach views. More of a city than a village, the HHV has an ABC sundries store, a bookstore, Louis Vuitton, and a post office. Culture comes in the form of an outpost of the Bishop Museum and the contemporary Hawaiian art gracing the public spaces. It even has its own pier, docking point for the Atlantis Submarine. The sheer volume of options, including free stuff (lei making, poolside hula shows, and fireworks), make the HHV a good choice for families. This is a megaresort and a convention destination. On the positive side, that means unusual perks, like check-in kiosks (complete with room keys) in the baggage-claim area at the airport. On the negative side, it means that there's usually big doings afoot on-site. ✉ *2005 Kālia Rd., Waikīkī 96815* ☎ *808/949–4321 or 800/221–2424* 🖷 *808/951–5458* ⊕ *www.hiltonhawaiianvillage.com* ⇨ *3,432 rooms, 365 suites, 264 condominiums* ♨ *20 restaurants, room service, A/C, in-room broadband, in-room safes, minibars, cable TV with movies, 5 pools, gym, spa, beach, snorkeling, 5 bars, shops, babysitting, children's programs (ages 5–12), dry cleaning, laundry service, Internet room, business services, car rental, parking (fee), no-smoking rooms* ☰ *AE, D, DC, MC, V. $239–$535.*

$$–$$$$ 🖬 **Hyatt Regency Waikīkī Resort and Spa.** Across the street from the Kūhiō Beach section of Waikīkī, the Hyatt is actually oceanfront, as there's no resort between it and the Pacific Ocean. A pool-deck staircase leads directly to street level, for easy beach access. An open-air atrium with three levels of shopping, a two-story waterfall, and free nightly live entertainment make this one of the liveliest lobbies anywhere. An activity center offers kids' programs, including lei-making lessons, 'ukulele lessons, and field trips to the aquarium and zoo. ✉ *2424 Kalākaua Ave., Waikīkī 96815* ☎ *808/923–1234 or 800/633–7313* 🖷 *808/923–7839* ⊕ *www. hyattwaikiki.com* ⇨ *1,212 rooms, 18 suites* ♨ *5 restaurants, room service, A/C, in-room data ports, in-room safes, minibars, cable TV with movies, pool, gym, spa, 3 bars, shops, children's programs (ages 5–12), business services, parking (fee), no-smoking rooms* ☰ *AE, D, DC, MC, V. $210–$530.*

$$–$$$$ 🖬 **ResortQuest Waikīkī Beach Hotel.** A three-story volcano, backlighted in a faux eruption, crawls up the side of this hotel opposite Kūhiō Beach and near Kapi'olani Park. Rooms are hip Hawaiiana, in colors ranging from neon pineapple yellow to hot lava tropical print red. The retro version of '60s island life continues with little touches like hand-painted bamboo curtains on the closets and surfboards used as entry signs. The Tiki Bar and Grill completes the retro experience. The third-floor pool deck is where all the action takes place. In the early mornings, there's an international food court where guests can choose complimentary breakfast munchies to pack in a takeout cooler bag and head to the beach across the street to catch some early morning wave action. In the evenings, the poolside bar breaks out with Hawaiian music that ranges from traditional to Jawaiian (Hawaiian sound with a reggae beat). There's also a Cold Stone Creamery and a Wolfgang Puck's Express, both on the street level. ✉ *2570 Kalākaua Ave., Waikīkī 96815* ☎ *808/922–2511 or 877/997– 6667* 🖷 *808/923–3656* ⊕ *www.rqwaikikibeachhotel.com* ⇨ *716 rooms, 12 suites* ♨ *3 restaurants, A/C, in-room safes, refrigerators, cable TV, in-room data ports, pool, shops, laundry facilities, parking (fee), no-smoking rooms* ☰ *AE, D, DC, MC, V. $255–$450.*

$$–$$$$ 🖬 **Sheraton Princess Kaiulani.** This hotel sits across the street from its sister property, the Sheraton Moana Surfrider. You can sleep here, taking advantage of lower rates, overseeing the bustle of Waikīkī from your private lānai, and dining at any of the oceanfront Sheratons, while charging everything back to your room at the Princess Kaiulani. Kids here can participate in the Keiki Aloha activity program, which is headquartered two blocks down the street at the Sheraton Waikīkī. Rooms are in two towers—some peer over the Moana's low-rise historic wing at the ocean. It's a two-minute stroll to the beach. The hotel's pool is streetside facing Kalākaua Avenue. ⊠ *120 Kaiulani Ave., Waikīkī 96815* ☎ *808/922–5811, 888/488–3535, or 866/500–8313* 📠 *808/931–4577* ⊕ *www.princesskaiulani.com* 🛏 *1,152 rooms, 14 suites* ♢ *3 restaurants, room service, A/C, in-room data ports, cable TV, pool, gym, bar, children's programs (ages 5–12), business services, no-smoking rooms* ▤ *AE, D, DC, MC, V. $185–$380.*

> ### HOSPITALITY SUITES
>
> Many hotels and resorts offer hospitality suites–large lounges with comfortable furnishings, luggage lockers, and shower facilities–for your use before you check in or after you check out. You can set up your laptop or take a quick nap until your hotel room is ready, or you can freshen up there if you choose to spend your last hours on the beach before leaving for the airport. This can save on early check-in and late check-out fees.

$$–$$$ 🏨 **Ohana Waikīkī Beachcomber Hotel.** This newest addition to the Ohana hotels family is pretty much entertainment central, featuring the legendary Don Ho as well as the popular Blue Hawai'i and Magic of Polynesia revues. Set almost directly across from the Royal Hawaiian Shopping Center and adjacent to the International Marketplace, the hotel has a third-floor pool deck that offers the perk of front-row seating for any of Waikīkī's parades or Hoolaulea street party festivals that happen year-round. It's a family-friendly place, with cultural activities that include 'ukulele and hula lessons as well as arts and crafts. Rooms have private lānai and Polynesian motifs. On the hotel's ground level is an entrance to Macy's department store, and across the street is a public accessway that opens up to the beach fronting the Royal Hawaiian hotel. ⊠ *2300 Kalākaua Ave., Waikīkī 96815* ☎ *808/922–4646 or 800/462-6262* 📠 *808/923–4889* ⊕ *www.waikikibeachcomber.com* 🛏 *500 rooms, 7 suites* ♢ *Restaurant, snack bar, room service, A/C, minibars, refrigerators, cable TV, in-room data ports, pool, outdoor hot tub, bar, children's programs (ages 5–12), laundry facilities, Internet room, parking (fee), no-smoking rooms* ▤ *AE, DC, MC, V. $245–$295.*

$–$$$ 🏨 **Waikīkī Parc.** One of the best-kept secrets in Waikīkī is this boutique hotel owned by the same group that manages the Halekūlani across the street. The Waikīkī Parc offers the same attention to detail in service and architectural design as the larger hotel but lacks the beachfront location and higher prices. The guest rooms in this high-rise complex have plantation-style shutters that open out to the lānai. Rooms have sitting areas, writing desks, flat-screen TVs. The hotel's heated pool and sundeck are eight floors up, affording a bit more privacy and peace for sunbathers. ⊠ *2233 Helumoa Rd., Waikīkī 96815* ☎ *808/921–7272 or 800/422–0450* 🖷 *808/923–1336* ⊕ *www.waikikiparc.com* ⤶ *298 rooms* ⌂ *Restaurant, room service, A/C, in-room data ports, in-room safes, cable TV, in-room broadband, pool, gym, business services, parking (fee); no-smoking* ▭ *AE, D, DC, MC, V. $160–$333.*

> **LĀNAI**
>
> Islanders love their porches, balconies, and verandas—all wrapped up in the single Hawaiian word, "lānai." When booking, ask about the lānai and be sure to specify the view (understanding that top views command top dollars). Also, check that the lānai is not merely a step-out or Juliet balcony, with just enough room to lean against a railing—you want a lānai that is big enough for patio seating.

$$ 🏨 **Ohana East.** The flagship property for Ohana Hotels in Waikīkī is next to the Sheraton Princess Kaiulani on the corner of Kaiulani and Kūhiō avenues; it's only two blocks from the beach. If you want to be in central Waikīkī and don't want to pay beachfront lodging prices, the Ohana East offers decent rates and is within walking distance of the beach, shopping, restaurants, and nightclubs. It tends to pull in plenty of group travelers. Don't expect any fancy lobbies or outdoor gardens here. Accommodations range from hotel rooms to suites with kitchenettes. Certain rooms on lower floors have no lānai, and some rooms have showers only. Ohana East also offers 14 floors of no-smoking rooms as well as a fitness center and privileges at Outrigger's Serenity Spa in the Outrigger Reef on the Beach. ⊠ *150 Kaiulani Ave., Waikīkī 96815* ☎ *808/ 922–5353 or 800/462–6262* 🖷 *808/926–4334* ⊕ *www.ohanahotels.com* ⤶ *420 rooms, 20 suites* ⌂ *3 restaurants, room service, A/C, in-room broadband, in-room safes, some kitchenettes, refrigerators, cable TV with video games, pool, gym, hair salon, bar, laundry facilities, parking (fee), no-smoking floors* ▭ *AE, D, DC, MC, V. $199–$209.*

$$ 🏨 **Radisson Waikīkī Prince Kūhiō.** You enter the Radisson through a lobby of rich wood detailing, contemporary fabrics, and magnificent tropical floral displays. Two blocks from Kūhiō Beach and across the street from the Marriott Waikīkī, this 37-story high-rise is on the Diamond Head end of Waikīkī. The Lobby Bar mixes up tropical cocktails, an island-style pūpū menu, wireless access, and a wide-screen plasma TV for sports fans and news junkies. If marriage is on your mind, note the wedding gazebo anchoring the hotel gardens. Book on an upper floor if you want to see the ocean from your lānai. ⊠ *2500 Kūhiō Ave., Waikīkī 96815* ☎ *808/922–8811 or 800/333–3333* 🖷 *808/921–5507* ⊕ *www. radisson.com/waikikihi* ⤶ *620 rooms* ⌂ *Restaurant, room service, A/C, cable TV, in-room broadband, in-room data ports, in-room safes, pool, gym, hot tub, bar, laundry facilities, business services, parking (fee), no-smoking rooms* ▭ *AE, D, DC, MC, V. $199–$239.*

$–$$ 🏨 **Doubletree Alana Waikīkī.** The location (a 10-minute walk from the Hawai'i Convention Center), three phones in each room, and the 24-hour business center and gym meet the requirements of the Doubletree's global business clientele, but the smallness of the property, the staff's attention to detail, the signature Doubletree chocolate chip cookies upon arrival, and the Japanese-style *furo* deep-soaking tubs resonate with vacationers. All rooms in the 19 story high rise have lānai, but they overlook the city and busy Ala Moana Boulevard across from Fort DeRussy. To get to the beach, you either cross Fort DeRussy or head through the Hilton Hawaiian Village. ⊠ *1956 Ala Moana Blvd., Waikīkī 96815* ☎ *808/941–7275 or 800/222–8733* 🖷 *808/949–0996* ⊕ *www.alana-doubletree.com* ⌑ *268 rooms, 45 suites* ⚐ *Restaurant, room service, A/C, in-room data ports, in-room safes, cable TV, pool, gym, bar, business services, car rental, parking (fee), no-smoking rooms* ▤ *AE, D, MC, V. $140–$220.*

$–$$ ⊞ **Waikīkī Sand Villa.** Families and others looking for an economical rate return to the Waikīkī Sand Villa year after year. It's on the corner of Kaiulani Avenue and Ala Wai Boulevard, a three-block walk to restaurants and the beach. There's a high-rise tower and a three-story walkup building of studio accommodations with kitchenettes. Rooms are small but well-planned. Corner deluxe units with lānai overlook Ala Wai Canal and the golf course. There's a fitness center with 24-hour access. Complimentary Continental breakfast is served poolside beneath shady coconut trees, and the hotel's Sand Bar comes alive at happy hour with a great mix of hotel guests and locals who like to hang out and "talk story." The Sand Bar also has computers and Web cams. ⊠ *2375 Ala Wai Blvd., Waikīkī 96815* ☎ *808/922–4744 or 800/247–1903* 🖷 *808/923–2541* ⊕ *www.sandvillahotel.com* ⌑ *214 rooms* ⚐ *Restaurant, in-room broadband, in-room safes, refrigerators, pool, hot tub, bar, shop, parking (fee), no-smoking rooms* ▤ *AE, D, DC, MC, V. $109–$190.*

¢–$ ⊞ **Marc Hawai'i Polo Inn and Tower.** This small hotel fronts busy Ala Moana Boulevard on the *'ewa* end of Waikīkī. Although it doesn't offer much in the way of lobby space, ocean views, or room amenities, it is one block from both Ala Moana Shopping Center and Ala Moana Beach Park. Here you have the option of standard hotel rooms or studios with kitchenettes. If you're not about to spend your vacation slaving away in the kitchen but like the thought of having access to a microwave or want a private lānai, reserve a room in the Bamboo category or a minisuite. Room interior decor pays tribute to Hawai'i polo enthusiasts, and front desk staff are happy to assist with driving directions to the playing fields at Mokuleia and Waimānalo—pack a picnic if you go. ⊠ *1696 Ala Moana Blvd., Waikīkī 96815* ☎ *808/949–0061 or 800/535–0085* 🖷 *808/949–4906* ⊕ *www.marcresorts.com* ⌑ *106 rooms* ⚐ *A/C, in-room safes, some kitchenettes, some microwaves, cable TV, pool, shop, laundry facilities, parking (fee), no-smoking rooms* ▤ *AE, DC, MC, V. $99–$135.*

¢ ⊞ **Royal Grove Hotel.** Two generations of the Fong family have put their heart and soul into the operation of this tiny (by Waikīkī standards), six-story hotel that feels like a throwback to the days of boarding houses, where rooms were outfitted for function, not style, and served up with a wealth of home-style hospitality at a price that didn't break the bank. During the hot summer months, seriously consider splurging on the highest-end accommodations, which feature air-conditioning, lānai, and small kitchens. The hotel's pool is its social center in the evenings, where you can usually find at least one or more members of the Fong

1

family strumming a 'ukulele, dancing hula, and singing songs in the old Hawaiian style. On special occasions, the Fongs host a potluck dinner by the pool. Little touches that mean a lot include free use of boogie boards, surfboards, beach mats, and beach towels. The hotel is two blocks from Waikīkī's Kūhiō Beach. On property are a tiny sushi bar, a natural foods deli, and an authentic Korean barbecue plate-lunch place. For extra value, inquire about the Grove's weekly and monthly rates. ⊠ *151 Uluniu Ave., Waikīkī 96815* ☎ *808/923–7691* 🖷 *808/922–7508* ⊕ *www. royalgrovehotel.com* ⟿ *78 rooms, 7 suites* ⚭ *kitchenettes, pool* ⊟ *AE, D, DC, MC, V. $45–$75.*

Condos

★ **$$$$** 🏨 **ResortQuest Waikīkī Beach Tower.** You'll find the elegance of a luxury all-suite condominium combined with the intimacy and service of a boutique hotel at this Kalākaua Avenue address. Facing Kuhio Beach, this 40-story resort offers spacious (1,100–1,400 square feet) one- and two-bedroom suites with gourmet kitchens and windows that open to views of Waikīkī and the Pacific Ocean. Amenities include twice-daily maid service, washer-dryers, and spacious private lānai. Valet parking is included. ⊠ *2470 Kalākaua Ave., Waikīkī 96815* ☎ *808/926–6400 or 866/774–2924* 🖷 *808/926–7380* ⊕ *www.rqwaikikibeachtower.com* ⟿ *140 units* ⚭ *Room service, A/C, in-room data ports, in-room safes, kitchens, cable TV, in-room DVD players, tennis court, pool, outdoor hot tub, sauna, billiards, paddle tennis, laundry facilities, parking, no-smoking rooms,* ⊟ *AE, D, DC, MC, V. 1-bedroom $540–$585, 2-bedroom $640–$705.*

★ **$$–$$$$** 🏨 **Outrigger Luana.** At the entrance to Waikīkī near Fort DeRussy Park this condo-hotel's two-story lobby is appointed in rich, Hawaiian-wood furnishings with island-inspired fabrics, along with a mezzanine lounge as comfortable as any living room back home. Units are furnished with the same mix of rich woods with etched accents of pineapples and palm trees. At bedside, hula-dancer and beach-boy lamps add another Hawaiian residential touch. The recreational deck features a fitness center, pool, and barbecue area with tables that can be enclosed cabana-style for privacy when dining outdoors. One-bedroom suites each have two lānai. ⊠ *2045 Kalākaua Ave., Waikīkī 96815* ☎ *808/955–6000 or 800/688–7444* 🖷 *808/943–8555* ⊕ *www.outrigger.com* ⟿ *218 units* ⚭ *BBQs, A/C, in-room data ports, in-room safes, some kitchens, some kitchenettes,*

CONDO COMFORTS

Foodland The local chain has two locations near Waikīkī: **Market City** (⊠ 2839 Harding Ave., near intersection with Kapahulu Ave. and highway overpass, Kaimukī ☎ 808/734–6303) and **Ala Moana Center** (⊠ 1450 Ala Moana Blvd., ground level, Ala Moana ☎ 808/949–5044).

Food Pantry A smaller version of Foodland, Food Pantry also has apparel, beach stuff, and tourist-oriented items. ⊠ 2370 Kuhio Ave., across from Miramar hotel, Waikīkī ☎ 808/923–9831.

Blockbuster Video (⊠ Ala Moana Shopping Center, 451 Piikoi St., Ala Moana ☎ 808/593–2595).

Pizza Hut (☎ 808/643–1111 for delivery statewide).

---

cable TV *with movies, pool, gym, laundry facilities, parking (fee), business services* = *AE, D, DC, MC, V. Studios $210–$265, 1-bedroom $325–$375, 2-bedroom $600.*

$$$ ▦ **Castle Waikīkī Shores.** Nestled between Fort DeRussy Beach Park and
★   the Outrigger Reef on the Beach, this is the only condo right on Waikīkī Beach. Units include studios and one- and two-bedroom suites, each with private lānai and panoramic views of the Pacific Ocean. The beach directly fronting the building is nothing to write home about, but it's only a few steps to the large expanse of beach at Fort DeRussy. Many of these units have full kitchens, but some only have kitchenettes so be sure you inquire when booking. Families love this place for its spaciousness, while others love it for its quiet location on the 'ewa end of Waikīkī. ✉ *2161 Kālia Rd., Waikīkī 96815* ☎ *808/952–4500 or 800/367–2353* 🖷 *808/952–4580* ⊕ *www.castleresorts.com* ➷ *168 units* ⟨₺⟩ *A/C, in-room data ports, in-room safes, some kitchens, some kitchenettes, cable TV, beach, laundry facilities, parking (fee), no-smoking rooms* = *AE, D, DC, MC, V. 1-bedroom $265–$340, 2-bedroom $425–$595.*

$$–$$$ ▦ **ResortQuest Waikīkī Banyan.** The recreation deck, here has outdoor grills, a heated swimming pool, two hot tubs, a children's playground, a mini-putting green, and volleyball, basketball, and tennis courts. The welcoming lobby is decorated in warm tropical woods with plenty of seating to enjoy the trade winds. One-bedroom suites contain island-inspired decor and have complete kitchens and lānai that offer Diamond Head or ocean views. ✉ *201 Ohua Ave., Waikīkī 96815* ☎ *808/922–0555 or 866/774–2924* 🖷 *808/922–0906* ⊕ *www.rqwaikikibanyan.com* ➷ *310 units* ⟨₺⟩ *BBQs, A/C, in-room broadband, in-room data ports, kitchens, cable TV, tennis court, pool, outdoor hot tub, sauna, basketball, volleyball, shop, playground, parking (fee), laundry facilities, no-smoking rooms* = *AE, D, DC, MC, V. 1-bedroom $200–$275.*

$$ ▦ **Ilima Hotel.** Tucked away on a residential side street near Waikīki's Ala Wai Canal, this locally owned 17-story condominium-style hotel is a gem. The glass-wall lobby with koa-wood furnishings, original Hawaiian artwork, and friendly staff create a Hawaiian home-away-from-home. One of the selling points of this place is the decent rate for its spacious studios with kitchenettes, as well as its one- and two-bedroom suites with full kitchens, Jacuzzi baths, cable TV with free HBO and Disney channels, multiple phones, and spacious lānai. It's a two-block walk to Waikīkī Beach, shopping and Kalākala Avenue restaurants. The parking is free but limited. When the spots are full, you park on the street. ✉ *445 Nohonani St., Waikīkī 96815* ☎ *808/923–1877 or 800/801–9366* 🖷 *808/924–2617* ⊕ *www.ilima.com* ➷ *99 units* ⟨₺⟩ *A/C, in-room data ports, in-room safes, kitchens, cable TV, some in-room broadband, pool, gym, sauna, laundry facilities, parking, no-smoking rooms* = *AE, DC, MC, V. 1-bedroom $214–$249, 2-bedroom $302–$325.*

$ ▦ **The Breakers.** For a taste of Hawai'i in the '60s, right after statehood, go retro at this low-rise hotel a mere half block from Waikīkī Beach. The Breakers' six two-story buildings surround its pool and overlook gardens filled with tropical flowers. Guest rooms have Japanese-style shoji doors that open to the lānai, kitchenettes, and bathrooms with showers only. Units 130, 132, and 134 have views of the Urasenke Teahouse. This tiny haven is in the shadow of the ongoing construction, expected to last through 2006, of the Waikīkī Beach Walk and all the sounds that go with it. Once Beach Walk is finished, however, The Breakers will enjoy enviable proximity to this new entertainment and retail complex. The resort is very popular thanks to its reasonable prices and great location. Parking is limited, but it's free. ⊠ *250 Beach Walk, Waikīkī 96815* ☎ *808/ 923–3181 or 800/426–0494* 🖷 *808/923–7174* ⊕ *www.breakers-hawaii. com* 🛏 *64 units* ⚴ *Restaurant, A/C, kitchenettes, pool, bar, parking* 🖃 *AE, DC, MC, V. 1-bedroom $130, 2-bedroom $145.*

B&Bs & Vacation Rentals

$ 🏠 **Diamond Head Bed and Breakfast.** Many a traveler and resident would love to own a home like this art-filled B&B at the base of Waikīkī's famous Diamond Head crater, one of the city's most exclusive neighborhoods. Each of the three guest rooms feature koa-wood furnishings and private bath, and they open to a lānai and a big backyard filled with the sounds of birds and rustling trees. For a bit more privacy, book the ground-floor suite, which offers a separate living room and a bedroom with a queen bed. If you want to experience a bit of Hawaiian history, request the room that includes the extra-large hand-carved koa bed that once belonged to a Hawaiian princess. The closest beach is the intimate Sans Souci near the Natatorium; it's hard to imagine that busy Waikīkī is a short stroll from the house. Reservations should be made three to four months in advance. ⊠ *3240 Noela Dr., Waikīkī 96815* 🕭 *Reservations: Hawai'i's Best Bed and Breakfasts, Box 485, Laupahoehoe, 96767* ☎ *808/962–0100, 800/262–9912 reservations* 🖷 *808/962–6360* ⊕ *www.bestbnb.com* 🛏 *2 rooms, 1 suite* ⚴ *No A/C, no room phones, no smoking* 🖃 *No credit cards. $130, 2-night minimum.*

Honolulu Beyond Waikīkī

$$$$ 🏠 **The Kāhala.** Hidden away in the wealthy residential neighborhood of Kāhala (on the other side of Diamond Head from Waikīkī), this elegant oceanfront hotel has played host to both presidents and princesses as one of Hawai'i's very first luxury resorts. The Kāhala is flanked by the exclusive Waialae Golf Links and the Pacific Ocean—surrounding it in a natural tranquility. Pathways meander out along a walkway with benches tucked into oceanfront nooks for lazy viewing. The oceanfront Chi Fitness Center offers outdoor yoga and Pilates. The reef not far from shore makes the waters here calm enough for young swimmers to try their water wings. You can also sign up for dolphin interactions in the 26,000-square-foot-lagoon. Rooms combine touches of

---

CHOOSING A VACATION RENTAL

Hawai'i's Best Bed and Breakfasts (☎ 808/962-0100 or 800/262-9912 ⊕ www.bestbnb.com) inspects and selects the top B&B's island-wide for its booking service. They also have vacation rentals and condos on all of the other major islands.
Pat's Kailua Beach Properties (☎ 808/261-1653 or 808/262-4128 🖷 808/261-0893 ⊕ www. patskailua.com) books beachfront accommodations in the windward community of Kailua.
Team Real Estate (☎ 808/637-3507 or 800/982-8602 🖷 808/637-8881 ⊕ www.teamrealestate.com) manages cottages, oceanfront homes, and condos on the North Shore.

Asia and old Hawai'i, with mahogany furniture, teak parquet floors, hand-loomed area rugs, local art, and grass-cloth wall coverings. Culinary buffs should inquire if the Kāhala Culinary Academy is in session. Teens 16 and up are welcome to don an apron and pick up tips alongside the adults. If you plan to visit the second week of January and love golf, ask for a view of the course so you can have a bird's eye view of the PGA Sony Open from your lānai. ⊠ *5000 Kāhala Ave., Kāhala 96816* ☎ *808/739–8888 or 800/367–2525* 🖷 *808/739–8000* ⊕ *www.kahalaresort.com* 🛏 *331 rooms, 33 suites* ⌂ *5 restaurants, room service, A/C, in-room broadband, in-room data ports, in-room safes, minibars, cable TV with movies, pool, gym, hair salon, spa, beach, bike rentals, 2 bars, shops, babysitting, children's program (ages 5–12) business services, parking (fee), no-smoking rooms* ➡ *AE, D, DC, MC, V. $345–$735.*

RESERVATIONS

After your online research but before you book a room, try calling the hotels directly. Sometimes on-property reservationists can hook you up with the best deals, and they usually have the most accurate 411 not only about rooms but also about hotel amenities and local happenings. If you use a toll-free number, ask for the location of the calling center you've reached. If it's not O'ahu, double-check information and rates by calling the hotel's local number to guarantee your best accommodations.

$–$$$$ 🖫 **Ala Moana Hotel.** Shoppers might wear out their Manolos here; the hotel is connected to O'ahu's biggest mall, the Ala Moana Shopping Center, by a pedestrian ramp, and it's a four-block stroll away from the Victoria Ward Centers. Business travelers can walk one block in the opposite direction to the Hawai'i Convention Center. Swimmers, surfers, and beachgoers make the two-minute walk to Ala Moana Beach Park across the street. In 2005 this hotel converted into a hotel condominium. What does this mean for guests? The place has been newly renovated. Gone are the '70s-style hotel rooms, which have been transformed into 21st-century custom-designed studio accommodations with cherrywood furnishings, kitchenettes, flat-screen wall-mounted TVs, and lānai with glass railings and outdoor seating. The recreation deck features a pool, cabanas, a poolside bar, yoga and Pilates outdoor studios, and a fitness center. ⊠ *410 Atkinson Dr., Ala Moana 96814* ☎ *808/955–4811 or 888/367–4811* 🖷 *808/944–6839* ⊕ *www.alamoanahotel.com* 🛏 *1,150 studios, 67 suites* ⌂ *4 restaurants, A/C, room service, in-room safes, in-room broadband, minibars, cable TV, pool, gym, 2 bars, dance club, nightclub, parking (fee), no-smoking rooms* ➡ *AE, DC, MC, V. $175–$570.*

Windward O'ahu

$ 🖫 **Ingrid's.** This B&B in the Windward bedroom community of Kailua features a one-bedroom upstairs studio with decor that mimics those found in traditional Japanese inns, with shoji screen doors and black-tile counters. Ingrid is one of the island's most popular hosts, and she has created a little Zen of tranquillity in this unit that also features a kitchenette, deep soaking tub, and has its own private entrance. Guests have access to the pool, and Kailua Beach is less than 1 mi away. Three- to four-month advance reservations are advised. ✉ *Pauku St., Kailua 96734* ➲ *Reservations: Hawai'i's Best Bed and Breakfasts, Box 485, Laupahoehoe, 96767* ☎ *808/962–0100, 800/262–9912 reservations* 🖷 *808/962–6360* ⊕ *www.bestbnb.com* ⤴ *2 rooms* ♴ *A/C, kitchenettes; no room phones* ⊟ *No credit cards. $150, 4-night minimum.*

North Shore

$$$$ 🔲 **Turtle Bay Resort.** Some 880 acres of raw natural Hawai'i landscape
Fodor$Choice is your playground at this glamorous resort on O'ahu's scenic North Shore.
★ Set out on the edge of Kuilima Point, Turtle Bay has spacious guest rooms averaging nearly 500 square feet, with lānai that showcase stunning peninsula views. In winter, when the big waves roll ashore, you get a front-row seat for watching the powerful surf. The sumptuous oceanfront beach cottages come complete with Brazilian walnut floors, teak rockers on the lānai, and beds you can sink right into while listening to the sounds of the ocean. Turtle Bay has a Hans Heidemann Surf School, horse stables, a spa, and the only 36-hole golf facility on O'ahu to keep you busy. There are two swimming pools, one with an 80-foot waterslide. While out exploring Turtle Bay's 12 mi of nature trails, don't be surprised if you suddenly find yourself *Lost.* The hit television series has been known to frequent the resort's beaches, coves, and natural forests for location filming. ✉ *57-091 Kamehameha Hwy., Box 187, Kahuku 96731* ☎ *808/293–8811 or 800/203–3650* 🖷 *808/293–9147* ⊕ *www. turtlebayresort.com* ⤴ *373 rooms, 40 suites, 42 beach cottages, 56 ocean villas* ♴ *4 restaurants, room service, A/C, refrigerators, cable TV, 2 18-hole golf courses, 10 tennis courts, 2 pools, gym, spa, beach, horseback riding, 2 bars, shops, children's programs (ages 5–12), no-smoking rooms* ⊟ *AE, D, DC, MC, V. $350–$780.*

¢–$$ 🔲 **Backpackers Vacation Inn and Plantation Village.** Here's laid-back Hale'iwa surfer chic at its best. Spartan in furnishings, rustic in amenities, and definitely very casual in spirit, Backpackers is at Pūpūkea Beach Marine Sanctuary, otherwise known as Three Tables Beach. It's a short stroll to Waimea Bay. This is the place to catch z's between wave sets. Accommodations include hostel-type dorm rooms, double rooms (some with a double bed, others with two single beds), studios, and cabins. Some have kitchenettes; it's a three-minute walk to the supermarket. ✉ *59-788 Kamehameha Hwy., Hale'iwa 96712* ☎ *808/638–7838* ⊕ *www.backpackers-hawaii.com* 🖷 *808/638–7515* ⤴ *25 rooms* ♴ *BBQs, some kitchenettes, laundry facilities; no A/C, no phones in some rooms, no TV in some rooms* ⊟ *MC, V. $22–$250.*

West (Leeward) O'ahu

$$$$ 🔲 **J. W. Marriott 'Ihilani Resort & Spa.** Forty-five minutes and a world away from the bustle of Waikīkī, this sleek, 17-story resort anchors the still-developing Kō 'Olina Resort and Marina on O'ahu's leeward coastline. Honeymooners, NFL Pro Bowlers, and even local residents looking for a Neighbor Island experience without the hassle of catching a flight come to 'Ihilani for first-class R&R. The resort sits on one of Kō 'Olina's seven lagoons and features a lū'au cove, tennis garden, wedding chapel, yacht marina, and a Ted Robinson–designed 18-hole championship golf facility. Rooms here are spacious with 650 square feet; color schemes of sea foam, fresh peach, or sandy cream; marble bathrooms with deep soaking tubs; spacious private lānai with teak furnishings; in-room CD players; and high-tech control systems (lights, temperature controls). Most have ocean views. A rental car is pretty much a necessity here. ⊠ *92-1001 ʻŌlani St., Kapolei 96707* ☎ *808/679–0079 or 800/626–4446* 🖷 *808/679–0080* ⊕ *www.ihilani.com* 🖘 *387 rooms, 36 suites* ♂ *4 restaurants, room service, A/C, minibars, cable TV, 18-hole golf course, 6 tennis courts, 2 pools, health club, spa, beach, shops, babysitting, children's programs (ages 5–12), business services, no-smoking rooms* ☰ *AE, DC, MC, V. $370–$600.*

$$$–$$$$ 🖭 **Marriott Kō ʻOlina Beach Vacation Club.** If you have your heart set on getting away to Oʻahu's western shores, check out the Marriott, which is primarily a vacation-ownership property. This property does offer nightly rental rates for its rooms, which range from hotel-style standard guest rooms to expansive and elegantly appointed one- or two-bedroom guest villa apartments. Interior decor soothes in rich reds, greens, and creamy soft yellows with furnishings made of rare Hawaiian koa wood. The larger villas (1,240 square feet) have three TVs, full kitchens, and separate living and dining areas. Situated on 30 acres of Kō ʻOlina, fronting a lagoon, this resort has two pools (one with sandy-beach bottom), a fitness center, and four outdoor hot tubs (including one overlooking the ocean that's ideal for sunset soaks). ⊠ *92-161 Waipahe Pl., Kapolei 96707* ☎ *808/679–4900 or 877/229–4484* 🖷 *808/679–4910* ⊕ *www.marriottvacationclub.com* 🖘 *200 units* ♂ *2 restaurants, A/C, Wi-Fi, in-room safes, kitchens, cable TV, in room DVD players, 18-hole golf course, 6 tennis courts, 2 pools, outdoor hot tubs, gym, beach, marina, bar, shops, children's programs (ages 5–12), parking (fee)* ☰ *AE, DC, MC, V. $319–$609.*

OʻAHU ESSENTIALS

Transportation

BY AIR

Most nonstop flights to Honolulu International originate in Los Angeles or San Francisco. Flying time from the West Coast is 4½ to 5 hours.

CARRIERS: Carriers flying into Honolulu from the mainland United States include Aloha, ATA, America West, American, Continental, Delta, Hawaiian, Northwest, and United.

Charter flights are the least expensive and the least reliable—with chronically late departures and occasional cancellations. They also tend to depart less frequently (usually once a week) than do regularly scheduled flights. The savings may be worth the potential annoyance, however. ⇨ *See* Smart Travel Tips A to Z.

AIRPORTS: More direct flights, by more domestic and international air carriers, arrive at and depart from Honolulu International Airport (HNL) than at any other airport in Hawaiʻi. If you find yourself waiting at the airport with extra time on your hands, kill some time at the Pacific Aerospace Museum, open daily, in the main terminal. It includes a 1,700-square-foot, three-dimensional, multimedia theater presenting the history of flight in Hawai'i, and a full-scale space-shuttle flight deck. Hands-on exhibits include a mission-control computer program tracing flights in the Pacific.

🛈 **Honolulu International Airport (HNL)** ☎ 808/836-6411 ⊕ www.ehawaiigov.org.

TO & FROM THE AIRPORT: Some hotels have their own pickup service. Check when you book.

There are taxis right at the airport baggage-claim exit. At $2.50 start-up plus $2.30 for each mile, the fare to Waikīkī will run approximately $25–$35, plus tip. If your baggage is oversized, there is an additional charge of $3.50.

Roberts Hawai'i runs an airport shuttle service to and from Waikīkī. The fare is $8 one way, $14 round-trip. Look for a representative at the baggage claim. Call for return reservations only. TheBus, the municipal bus, will take you into Waikīkī for only $2, but you are allowed only one bag, which must fit on your lap.

🛈 **Roberts Hawai'i** ☎ 808/539-9400. **TheBus** ☎ 808/848-5555 ⊕ www.thebus.org.

BY BUS
In Waikīkī, in addition to TheBus and the Waikīkī Trolley, there are also a number of brightly painted private buses, many free, that will take you to such commercial attractions as dinner cruises, garment factories, and the like.

THEBUS: You can go all around the island or just down Kalākaua Avenue for $2 on Honolulu's municipal transportation system, affectionately known as TheBus. You're entitled to one free transfer per fare if you ask for it when boarding. Exact change is required, and dollar bills are accepted. A four-day pass for visitors costs $20 and is available at ABC convenience stores in Waikīkī. Monthly passes cost $40.

There are no official bus-route maps, but you can find privately published booklets at most drugstores and other convenience outlets. The important route numbers for Waikīkī are 2, 4, 8, 19, 20, and 58. If you venture afield, you can always get back on one of these.

🛈 **TheBus** ☎ 808/848-5555 ⊕ www.thebus.org.

WAIKĪKĪ TROLLEY: The Waikīkī Trolley has three lines and dozens of stops that allow you to design your own itinerary while riding on brass-trimmed, open-air trolleys. The Honolulu City Line (Red Line) travels between Waikīkī and the bishop Museum and includes stops at Aloha Tower, Ala Moana, and downtown Honolulu, among others. The Ocean Coast Line (Blue Line) provides a tour of O'ahu's southeastern coastline, including Diamond Head Crater, Hanauma Bay and Sea Life Park. The Ala Moana Shuttle Line (Pink Line) stops at Ward Center and Ala Moana Shopping Center. The trolleys depart from the DFS Galleria Waikīkī. A one-day, three-line ticket costs $25. Four-day tickets, also good for any ofht the three lines, are $45.

🛈 **Waikīkī Trolley** ☎ 808/591-2561 or 800/824-8804 ⊕ www.waikikitrolley.com.

BY CAR

Waikīkī is only 2½-mi long and ½-mi wide, which means you can usually walk to where you are going. However, if you plan to venture outside of Waikīkī, a car is essential.

Roads and streets, although perhaps unpronounceable to visitors, are at least well marked. Bear in mind that many streets in Honolulu are one way. Major attractions and scenic spots are marked by the distinctive HVCB sign with its red-caped warrior.

Driving in rush-hour traffic (6:30–8:30 AM and 3:30–5:30 PM) in Honolulu can be exasperating, because left turns are prohibited at many intersections and many roads turn into contra-flow lanes. Parking along many streets is curtailed during these hours, and towing is strictly enforced. Read the curbside parking signs before leaving your vehicle, even at a meter. Remember not to leave valuables in your car. Rental cars are often targets for thieves.

O'ahu's drivers are generally courteous, and you rarely hear a horn. People will slow down and let you into traffic with a wave of the hand. A friendly wave back is customary. If a driver sticks a hand out the window in a fist with the thumb and pinky sticking straight out, this is a good thing: it's the *shaka*, the Hawaiian symbol for "hang loose," and is often used to say "thanks," as well.

Hawai'i has a seat-belt law for front-seat passengers and those under the age of 18 in the back seats. Children under 40 pounds must be in a car seat, available from your car-rental agency.

CAR RENTAL: During peak seasons—summer, Christmas vacations, and February—reservations are necessary. Rental agencies abound in and around the Honolulu International Airport and in Waikīkī. Alamo, Avis, Budget, Hertz, and National rent in O'ahu. ⇨ *See* Smart Travel Tips A to Z.

🚗 Local Agencies: **JN Car and Truck Rentals** ☎ 808/831-2724 ⊕ www.jnautomotive.com **VIP** ☎ 808/922-4605.

BY TAXI

You can usually get a taxi right outside your hotel. Most restaurants will call a taxi for you. Rates are $2.50 at the drop of the flag, plus $2.30 per mile. Flat fees can also be negotiated for many destinations—just ask your driver. Drivers are generally courteous, and the cars are in good condition, many of them air-conditioned.

Contacts & Resources

EMERGENCIES

To reach the police, fire department, or an ambulance in an emergency, dial **911**.

A doctor, laboratory-radiology technician, and nurses are always on duty at Doctors on Call. Appointments are recommended but not necessary. Dozens of kinds of medical insurance are accepted, including Medicare, Medicaid, and most kinds of travel insurance.

Kūhiō Pharmacy is Waikīkī's only pharmacy and handles prescription requests only until 4:30 PM. Longs Drugs is open evenings at its Ala Moana location and 24 hours at its South King Street location (15 minutes from Waikīkī by car). Pillbox Pharmacy, located in Kaimukī, will deliver prescription medications for a small fee.

🖪 Doctors & Dentists **Doctors on Call** ✉ Sheraton Princess Kaiulani Hotel, 120 Kaiulani Ave., Waikīkī ☎ 808/971-6000.

🖪 Emergency Services **Coast Guard Rescue Center** ☎ 808/541-2450.

🖪 Hospitals **Castle Medical Center** ✉ 640 Ulukahiki, Kailua ☎ 808/263-5500. **Kapiolani Medical Center for Women and Children** ✉ 1319 Punahou St., Makiki Heights, Honolulu ☎ 808/983-6000. **Queen's Medical Center** ✉ 1301 Punchbowl St., Downtown Honolulu, Honolulu ☎ 808/538-9011. **Saint Francis Medical Center-West** ✉ 91-2141 Ft. Weaver Rd., 'Ewa Beach ☎ 808/678-7000. **Straub Clinic** ✉ 888 S. King St., Downtown Honolulu, Honolulu ☎ 808/522-4000.

🖪 Pharmacies **Kūhiō Pharmacy** ✉ Outrigger West Hotel, 2330 Kūhiō Ave., Waikīkī ☎ 808/923-4466. **Longs Drugs** ✉ Ala Moana Shopping Center, 1450 Ala Moana Blvd., 2nd level, Ala Moana ☎ 808/949-4010 ✉ 2220 S. King St., Mō'ili'ili ☎ 808/947-2651. **Pillbox Pharmacy** ✉ 1133 11th Ave., Kaimukī ☎ 808/737-1777.

VISITOR INFORMATION

🖪 **Hawai'i Visitors & Convention Bureau** ✉ Waikīkī Business Plaza, 2270 Kalākaua Ave., Suite 801, Honolulu 96815 ☎ 808/923-1811 or 800/464-2924 ⊕ www.gohawaii. com. **O'ahu Visitor Bureau** ☎ 877/525-6248 ⊕ www.visit-oahu.com. **Surf Report** ☎ 808/973-4383. **Weather** ☎ 808/973-4381.

Maui

Adult Green Sea Turtle (Chelonia mydas).

WORD OF MOUTH

"There is no question in my mind—the Road to Hāna is a fantastic trip. We have taken the trip four times and loved it every time. Our best two trips were the ones where we spent the night. That way we could take our time and enjoy all the sights and activities." –LGay

"Mākena State Park's cliffs were nice to photograph, and if you're looking for rainbows, seems there is always one behind Lahaina in a light rain. (Just like in the postcards.)"

–Peterman

WELCOME TO MAUI

TOP 5
Reasons to Go

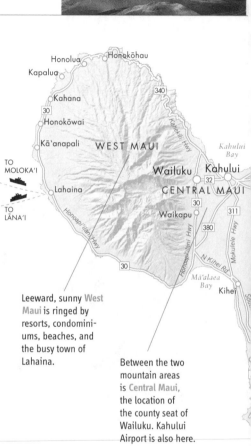

1 **The Road to Hāna:** Each curve of this legendary cliff-side road pulls you deeper into the lush green rain forest of Maui's eastern shore.

2 **Haleakalā National Park:** Explore the lava bombs, cinder cones, and silverswords at the gasp-inducing, volcanic summit of Haleakalā, the House of the Sun.

3 **Ho'okipa Beach:** The world's top windsurfers will dazzle you as they maneuver above the waves like butterflies shot from cannons.

4 **Wai'ānapanapa State Park:** Take a dip at the stunning black-sand beach or in the cave pool where an ancient princess once hid.

5 **Resorts, Resorts, Resorts:** Opulent gardens, pools, restaurants, and golf courses make Maui's resorts some of the best in the Islands.

Leeward, sunny West Maui is ringed by resorts, condominiums, beaches, and the busy town of Lahaina.

Between the two mountain areas is Central Maui, the location of the county seat of Wailuku. Kahului Airport is also here.

Getting Oriented

Maui, the second largest island in the Hawaiian chain, is made up of two distinct circular landmasses. The smaller landmass, on the western part of the island, consists of 5,788-foot Pu'u Kukui and the rain-chiseled West Maui Mountains. The large landmass composing the eastern half of Maui is Haleakalā, with its cloud-wreathed volcanic peak.

The island's northeastern, windward side is largely one great rain forest, traversed by the Road to Hāna.

Island residents affectionately call the regions climbing up the slope of Haleakalā crater Upcountry.

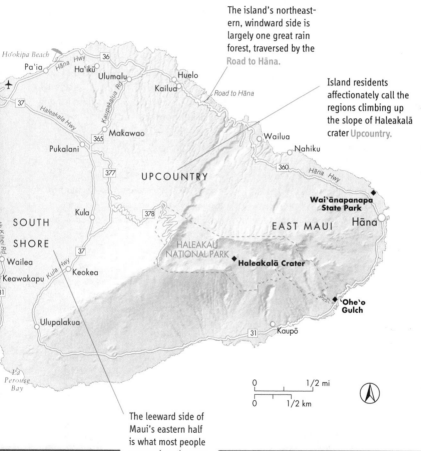

Ho'okipa Beach
Pa'ia · Ha'ikū
Ulumalu
Huelo
Kailua
Road to Hāna
Wailua
Nahiku
Makawao
Pukalani
UPCOUNTRY
360 · Hāna Hwy
Kula
Wai'ānapanapa State Park
SOUTH
SHORE
EAST MAUI
Hāna
Wailea
Keawakapu · Keokea
HALEAKALĀ NATIONAL PARK
Haleakalā Crater
Ulupalakua
'Ohe'o Gulch
31 · Kaupō
La Perouse Bay

0   1/2 mi
0   1/2 km

The leeward side of Maui's eastern half is what most people mean when they say South Shore. This popular area is sunny and warm year-round and is home to the beautiful resort area, Wailea.

MAUI PLANNER

When You Arrive

Most visitors arrive at Kahului Airport. The best way to get from the airport to your destination is in your own rental car. The major car-rental companies have desks at the airport and can provide a map and directions to your hotel. ■ TIP→ **Arriving flights in Maui tend to land around the same time. This can lead to extremely long lines at the car-rental windows. If possible, send one member of your group to pick up the car while the others wait for the baggage.**

Getting Around

If you need to ask for directions, try your best to pronounce the multi-vowel road names. Locals don't use (or know) highway route numbers and will respond with looks as lost as yours.

Tips for High-Season Travelers

If you're coming during the peak season, be sure to book hotels and car rentals ahead of time. Advance booking of activities is also a good idea. This will ensure you get to do the activity you want and can often save you 10% or more if you book on individual outfitters' Web sites.

Traffic tends to overwhelm the island's simple infrastructure during these busy times. Try to avoid driving during typical commuter hours, and always allow extra travel time to reach your destination.

Where to Stay

Deciding where to stay is difficult, especially if you're a first-time visitor. To help narrow your choices, consider what type of property you'd like to stay at (big, flashy resort or private vacation rental) and what type of island climate you're looking for (beachfront strand or remote rain forest). If you're staying for more than a week, we recommend breaking your trip into two or even three parts. Moving around may sound daunting, and will rule out longer-stay discounts, but remember: each area of the island offers tons to do. If you stay in one spot, chances are you'll spend a lot of time driving to the sites and activities elsewhere.

Car Rentals

A rental car is a must on Maui. It's also one of the biggest expenses of your trip, especially when you add in the price of gasoline—higher on Maui than on O'ahu or the mainland.

TIPS→

■ Soft-top jeeps are a popular option, but they don't have much space for baggage and it's impossible to lock anything into them. Four-wheel-drive vehicles are the most expensive options and not really necessary.

■ Don't be surprised if there is an additional fee for parking at your hotel or resort. Parking is not always included in your room rate or resort fee. Booking a car-hotel or airfare package can save you money. Even some B&Bs offer packages—it never hurts to ask.

Island-Hopping

If you have a week or more on Maui you may want to set aside a day or two for a trip to Moloka'i or Lāna'i. Tour operators such as Trilogy offer day-trip packages to Lāna'i which include snorkeling and a van tour of the island. Ferries are available to both islands. (The Moloka'i channel can be rough, so avoid ferry travel on a blustery day.)

Now that airport security checks and high prices have made island-hopping more of a challenge, your best bet for quick, scenic travel is a small air taxi. If you're not averse to flying on four- to 12-seaters, book with Pacific Wings or Hawai'i Air Taxi (see Maui Essentials at the end of this chapter). Pacific Wings flies to several small airports—Hāna, Maui, and Kalaupapa, Moloka'i, for instance—in addition to the main airports. Hawai'i Air Taxi provides service only between Maui and Kailua-Kona on the Big Island.

■ TIP➜ **Most interisland flights on Hawaiian or Aloha are routed through O'ahu, even when it's out of the way.**

Will it Rain?

Typically the weather on Maui is drier in summer (more guaranteed beach days) and rainier in winter (greener foliage, better waterfalls). Throughout the year, West Maui and the South Shore (the leeward areas) are the driest, sunniest areas on the island—hence all the resorts here. East Maui and Hāna (the windward areas) get the most rain, are densely forested, and abound with waterfalls and rainbows.

Timing is Everything

Each season brings its own highlights to Maui. The humpback whales start arriving in November, are in full force by February, and are gone by April. The biggest North Shore waves also show up in winter, whereas kiteboarders and windsurfers enjoy the windy, late summer months. Jacarandas shower Upcountry roads in lilac-color blossoms in spring, and the truly astounding silverswords burst forth their blooms in summer. Fall is the quietest time on the island, a good time for a getaway. And, of course, there's what's known as high season—June through August, Christmas, and spring break—when the island is jam-packed with visitors.

Guided Activities

In winter, Maui is *the* spot for whale-watching. Sure, you can see whales on other islands, but they're just passing through to get to their real hang-out. The same could be said for windsurfers and kiteboarders, Maui's North Shore is their mecca. This chart lists rough prices for Maui's most popular guided activities.

ACTIVITY	COST
Deep-Sea Fishing	$80–$180
Golf	$60–$300
Helicopter Tours	$125–$370
Lū'au	$65–$100
Kayaking Tours	$65–$140
Parasailing	$48–$55
Snorkel Cruises	$80–$180
Surfing Lessons	$55–$325
Whale-Watching	$20–$55
Windsurfing	$80–$120

1-Day Itineraries

Maui's landscape is incredibly diverse, offering everything from underwater encounters with eagle rays to treks across moonlike terrain. Although daydreaming at the pool or on the beach may fulfill your initial island fantasy, Maui has much more to offer. The following one-day itineraries will take you to our favorite spots on the island.

A Day at the Beach in West Maui.

West Maui has some of the island's most beautiful beaches, though many of them are hidden by megaresorts. If you get an early start, you can begin your day snorkeling at Slaughterhouse Beach (in winter, D. T. Fleming Beach is a better option as it's less rough). Then spend the day beach-hopping through Kapalua, Nāpili, and Kāʻanapali as you make your way south. You'll want to get to Lahaina before dark so you can spend some time exploring the historic whaling town before choosing a restaurant for a sunset dinner.

Focus on Marine Life on the South Shore.

Start your South Shore trip early in the morning, and head out past Mākena into the rough lava fields of rugged La Pérouse Bay. At the road's end, the ʻĀhihi-Kīnaʻu Marine Preserve has no beach, but it's a rich spot for snorkeling and getting to know Maui's spectacular underwater world. Head to Kīhei for lunch then enjoy the afternoon learning more about Maui's marine life at the Maui Ocean Center at Māʻalaea.

The Road to Hāna.

This cliff-side driving tour through rain-forest canopy reveals Maui's lushest and most tropical terrain. It will take a full day, especially if you plan to make it all the way to ʻOheʻo Gulch. You'll pass through communities where old Hawaiʻi still thrives, and where the forest runs unchecked from the sea to the summit. You'll want to make frequent exploratory stops. To really soak in the magic of this place, consider staying overnight in Hāna town. That way you can spend a full day winding toward Hāna, hiking and exploring along the way, and the next day traveling leisurely back to civilization.

Haleakalā National Park, Upcountry & the North Shore.

If you don't plan to spend an entire day hiking in Haleakalā National Park, this itinerary will at least allow you to take a peek at it. Get up early and head straight for the summit of Haleakalā (if you're jet-lagged and waking up in the middle of the night, you may want to get there in time for sunrise). Plan to spend a couple of hours exploring the various look-out points in the park. On your way down the mountain, turn right on Makawao Avenue and head into the little town of Makawao. You can have lunch here, or make a left on Baldwin Avenue and head downhill to the town of Pāʻia, where there are a number of great lunch spots and shops to explore. Spend the rest of your afternoon at Pāʻia's main strip of sand, Hoʻokipa Beach.

■ *For more details see* Exploring; Beaches; Water Activities & Tours; and Golf, Hiking & Other Adventures *on Maui in this chapter.*

"MAUI NŌ KA ʻOI" is what locals say—it's the best, the most, the top of the heap. To those who know Maui well, there's good reason for the superlatives. Combining the best of both old and new Hawaiʻi, Maui's miles of perfect-tan beaches, lush green valleys, historic villages, top-notch windsurfing and diving, stellar restaurants and high-end hotels, and variety of art and cultural activities have made it an international favorite. Maui weaves a spell over the more than 2 million people who visit its shores each year, and many decide to return for good.

At 729 square miles, Maui is the second-largest Hawaiian island, but offers more miles of swimmable beaches than any of the other islands. Despite growth over the past few decades, the local population is still fairly small, totaling only 117,644.

Geology

Maui is made up of two volcanoes, one now extinct and the other dormant, that erupted long ago and joined into one island. The resulting depression between the two is what gives the island its nickname, the Valley Isle. West Maui's 5,788-foot Puʻu Kukui was the first volcano to form, a distinction that gives that area's mountainous topography a more weathered look. Rainbows seem to grow wild over this terrain as gentle mists fill the deeply eroded canyons. The Valley Isle's second volcano is the 10,023-foot Haleakalā, where desert-like terrain butts up against tropical forests.

Flora & Fauna

Haleakalā crater is one of few homes to the rare silversword plant. Part of the sunflower family, the silversword is not particularly stunning most of the year, but from July to September when the silversword blooms Haleakalā is awash in beautiful little red flowers and their older, faded silver cousins. Also calling Haleakalā home are a few hundred nēnē—the Hawaiian state bird (related to the Canadian duck), currently fighting its way back from extinction. Maui is one of the better islands for whale-watching, and migrating humpbacks can be seen off the island's coast from December to April, and sometimes into May.

History

Maui's history is full of firsts—Lahaina was the first capital of Hawaiʻi and the first destination of the whaling industry (early 1800s), which explains why the town still has that fishing-village vibe; Lahaina was also the first stop for missionaries (1823). Although they tried to squash aspects of Hawaiian culture, the missionaries also invented the Hawaiian alphabet, taught natives to read and write, and built a printing press in Lahaina, accomplishments that are largely responsible for the existence of written Hawaiian history today. Maui also boasts the first sugar plantation in Hawaii (1849) and the first Hawaiian luxury resort (Hotel Hāna-Maui, 1946).

On Maui Today

In the mid-1970s, savvy marketers saw a way to improve Maui's economy by promoting the Valley Isle to golfers and luxury travelers. The ploy worked all too well; Maui's visitor count continues to swell far ahead of that of its neighbor islands. Impatient traffic now threatens to overtake the ubiquitous aloha spirit, development encroaches on agricultural lands, and county planners struggle to meet the needs of a burgeoning population. But Maui is still carpeted with an eyeful of green, and for every tailgater, there's a carefree local on "Maui time" who stops for each pedestrian, whale spout, and sunset.

Legends & Mythology

The Valley Isle's namesake, the demigod Maui, is a well-known Polynesian trickster. When his mother Hina complained of too few hours in the day to dry her *tapa* cloth (traditional Hawaiian bark cloth, used for decoration and clothing for special occasions), Maui promised to slow the sun. Hearing this Moemoe teased Maui for boasting, but undeterred, the demigod wove a strong cord and lassoed the sun. Angry, the sun scorched the fields until an agreement was reached: during summer, the sun would travel more slowly. In winter, it would return to its quick pace. For ridiculing Maui, Moemoe was turned into a large rock that still juts from the water near Kahakualoa.

EXPLORING MAUI

Updated by
Shannon
Wianecki

Maui is more than a sandy beach with palm trees. The natural bounty of this place is impressive. Pu'u Kukui, the 5,788-foot interior of the West Maui Mountains, is one of the earth's wettest spots—annual rainfall of 400 inches has sculpted the land into impassable gorges and razor-sharp ridges. On the opposite side of the island, the blistering lava fields at 'Āhihi-Kīn'au receive scant rain. And just above this desert, *paniolo,* Hawaiian cowboys, herd cattle on rolling, fertile ranchlands reminiscent of Northern California.

But nature isn't all Maui has to offer—it's also home to a rich and vivid culture. In small towns like Pā'ia and Hāna you can see remnants of the past mingling with modern-day life. Ancient *heiau* (Hawaiian stone platforms once used as places of worship) line busy roadways. Old coral and brick missionary homes now house broadcasting networks. The antique smokestacks of sugar mills tower above communities where the children blend English, Hawaiian, Japanese, Chinese, Portuguese, Filipino, and more into one colorful language. Hawai'i is a melting pot like no other. Visiting an eclectic mom-and-pop shop (like Komoda's Bakery) can feel like stepping into another country, or back in time. The more you look here, the more you will find.

West Maui

Separated from the remainder of the island by steep *pali* (cliffs), West Maui has a reputation for attitude and action. Once upon a time, this was the haunt of whalers, missionaries, and the kings and queens of Hawai'i. Anchored by the amusing old whaling town of Lahaina, West Maui was the focus of development when Maui set out to become a premier tourist destination in the 1960s. Today, crowds stroll Front Street in Lahaina, beating the heat with ice cream or shave ice, while pleasure-seekers indulge in golf, shopping, and white-sand beaches in the Kā'anapali and Kapalua resort areas.

Main Attractions

9 Baldwin Home. In 1836, missionary and doctor Dwight Baldwin moved his family into this attractive house of coral and stone. The home has been carefully restored to reflect the period; many of the original furnishings remain. You can view the family's grand piano, the carved four-poster bed, and most interestingly, Dr. Baldwin's dispensary. During a brief tour conducted by Lahaina Restoration Foundation volunteers, you'll be shown the "thunderpot" and told how the doctor single-handedly inoculated 10,000 Maui residents for smallpox. ⊠ *696 Front St., Lahaina* ☎ *808/661–3262* ⊕ *www. lahainarestoration.org* 🎫 *$3* ☉ *Daily 10–4.*

> **WALKING TOURS**
>
> Lahaina's fascinating side streets are best explored on foot. Both the Baldwin Home and the Lahaina Court House offer free self-guided walking-tour brochures and maps. The Court House booklet is often recommended and includes more than 50 sites. The Baldwin Home brochure is less well known but, in our opinion, easier to follow. It details a short but enjoyable loop tour of the town.

11 Banyan Tree. This massive tree was planted in 1873. It's the largest of its kind in the state and provides a welcome retreat for the weary who come to sit under its awesome branches. The Banyan Tree is a terrific spot to be when the sun sets—mynah birds settle in here for a screeching symphony, which can be an event in itself. ■ TIP→ **The Banyan Tree is a popular and hard-to-miss meeting place if your party splits up for independent exploring.** ⊠ *Front St., between Hotel and Canal Sts., Lahaina.*

12 Hale Paʻahao (Old Prison). Lahaina's jailhouse dates to rowdy whaling days. Its name literally means "stuck-in-irons house," referring to the wall shackles and ball-and-chain restraints. The compound was built in the 1850s by convict laborers out of blocks of coral that had been salvaged from the demolished waterfront fort. Most prisoners were sent here for desertion, drunkenness, or reckless horse riding. Today, a wax figure representing an imprisoned old sailor tells his recorded tale of woe. ⊠ *Waineʻe and Prison Sts., Lahaina* 🎫 *Free* ☉ *Daily 8–5.*

3 Kāʻanapali. In ancient times, this area was known for its bountiful fishing and its seaside cliffs. Puʻu Kekaʻa, known today as "Black Rock" was the site of many a heroic warrior's leap. But times change, the sleepy fishing village was washed away by the wave of Hawaiʻi's new economy: tourism. Clever marketers built this sunny shoreline into a playground for the world's vacationers. The theatrical look of Hawaiʻi tourism—planned resort communities where luxury homes mix with high-rise hotels, fantasy swimming pools, and a theme-park landscape—all began right here in the 1960s. Three miles of uninterrupted white beach and placid water form the front yard for this artificial utopia, with its 40 tennis courts and two championship golf courses. The six major hotels here are all worth visiting just for a look around, especially the Hyatt Regency Maui, which has a multimillion-dollar art collection and South African penguins in the lobby. ⊠ *2435 Kāʻanapali Pkwy., Kāʻanapali.*

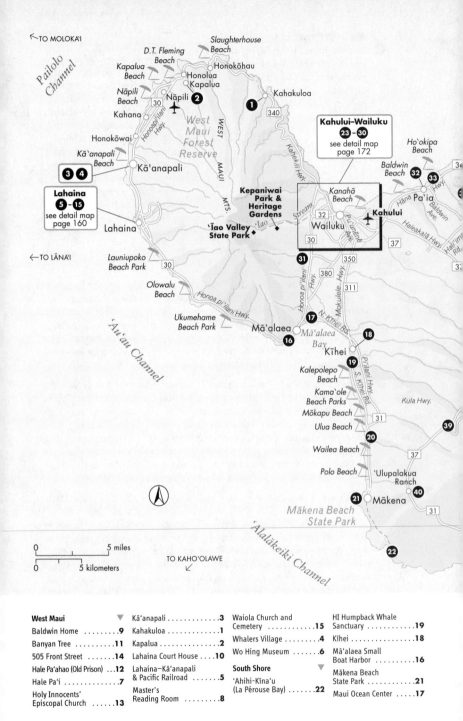

TO MOLOKA'I

Pailolo Channel

Slaughterhouse Beach

D.T. Fleming Beach

Honokōhau

Kapalua Beach

Honolua

Napili Beach

Kapalua **2**

Kahakuloa

Nāpili

30

1

340

Kahana

Honokōwai

Kā'anapali Beach

3 **4**

Kā'anapali

West Maui Forest Reserve

WEST MAUI MTS.

Honoapi'ilani Hwy.

Kahekili Hwy.

Kahului–Wailuku
23–**30**
see detail map
page 172

Ho'okipa Beach

Baldwin Beach

32

33

3

Hāna Pa'ia

Baldwin Ave.

Lahaina
5–**15**
see detail map
page 160

Lahaina

Kepaniwai Park & Heritage Gardens

'Īao Valley State Park

'Īao

Stream

Kanahā Beach

Kahului

Wailuku

32

Pu'unēnē Ave.

30

37

Haleakalā Hwy.

Hāli'i...

Hāli'ima Rd.

3

TO LĀNA'I

Launiupoko Beach Park

30

31

350

380

311

Honoapi'ilani Hwy.

Olowalu Beach

Honoa pi'ilani Hwy.

Ukumehame Beach Park

Mā'alaea

16

17

Mā'alaea Bay

N. Kīhei Rd.

Mokulele Hwy.

Kīhei

'Au'au Channel

Kalepolepo Beach

Kama'ole Beach Parks

Mōkapu Beach

Ulua Beach

18

19

Pi'ilani Hwy.

S. Kīhei Rd.

Kula Hwy.

39

Wailea Beach

20

37

Polo Beach

'Ulupalakua Ranch

40

Mākena Beach State Park

21

Mākena

31

'Alalākeiki Channel

22

0   5 miles

0   5 kilometers

TO KAHO'OLAWE

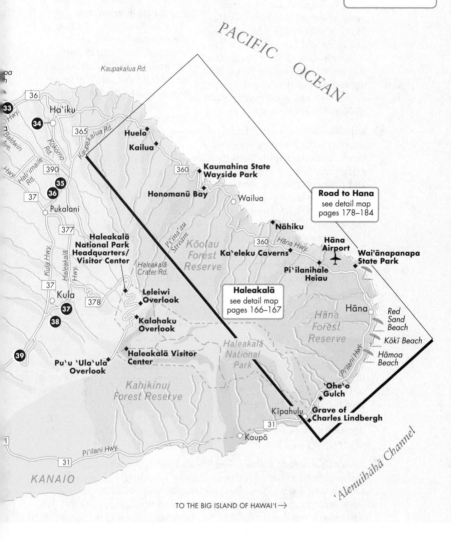

Maui

PACIFIC OCEAN

Kaupakalua Rd.

Ha'iku

36

34

33

Kokomo Rd.

365

Kaupakalua Rd.

Huelo

Kailua

360

Kaumahina State
Wayside Park

Honomanū Bay

Wailua

390

35

36

37

Pukalani

377

Haleakalā
National Park
Headquarters/
Visitor Center

Pi'ina'au Stream

Kōolau
Forest
Reserve

Nāhiku

360

Hāna Hwy.

Ka'eleku Caverns

Road to Hana
see detail map
pages 178–184

Hāna
Airport

Wai'ānapanapa
State Park

Kula Hwy.

37

Haleakalā Hwy.

Kula

378

37

38

39

Pu'u 'Ula'ula
Overlook

Haleakalā
Crater Rd.

Leleiwi
Overlook

Kalahaku
Overlook

Haleakalā Visitor
Center

Pi'ilanihale
Heiau

Haleakalā
see detail map
pages 166–167

Hāna
Forest
Reserve

Hāna

Red
Sand
Beach

Kōkī Beach

Hāmoa
Beach

Haleakalā
National
Park

Pi'ilani Hwy.

Kahikinui
Forest Reserve

'Ohe'o
Gulch

Kīpahulu

**Grave of
Charles Lindbergh**

31

Kaupō

1

31

Pi'ilani Hwy.

KANAIO

'Alenuihāhā Channel

TO THE BIG ISLAND OF HAWAI'I →

❶ Kahakuloa. Untouched by progress, this tiny village is a relic of pre–jet travel Maui. Remote villages similar to Kahakuloa used to be tucked away in several valleys of this area. Many residents still grow taro and live in the old Hawaiian way. This is the wild side of West Maui. True adventurers will find terrific snorkeling and swimming along this coast, as well as some good hiking trails. ⊠ *North end of Honoapi'ilani Hwy.*

> **CHEAP EATS**
>
> In contrast to Kapalua's high-end glitz, the old **Honolua Store,** just above the Ritz-Carlton, still plies the groceries, fish nets, and household wares it did in planta-tion times. Hefty plate lunches, served at the deli until 2:30 PM, are popular with locals. ⊠ *504 Office Rd., Kapalua* ☎ *808/669–6128* ⏲ *Daily 6 AM–8 PM.*

❷ Kapalua. Beautiful and secluded, Kapalua is the West Side's northern-most resort community. Mists regularly envelop Kapalua, which is cooler and quieter than its southern neighbors. The landscape of tall Cook pines and rolling fairways is reminiscent of Lāna'i, and the beaches and din-ing—among Maui's finest—appeal to dedicated golfers and celebrities who want to be left alone. The Maui Land & Pineapple Company owns the sprawling area known as Kapalua Resort, which includes the Ritz-Carlton, three golf courses, several freestanding restaurants, and the sur-rounding fields of Maui Gold pineapple. Kapalua's plantation history survives at the old **Honolua Store,** just above the Ritz-Carlton, where steam-ing plate lunches are still popular with locals. ⊠ *Bay Dr., Kapalua.*

★ **❿ Lahaina Court House.** The Lahaina Restoration Foundation occupies this charming old government building in the center of town. Pump the knowl-edgeable staff for interesting trivia and ask for their walking-tour brochure, a comprehensive map to historic Lahaina sites. Erected in 1859 and restored in 1999, the building has served as a customs and court house, governor's office, post office, vault and collector's office, and po-lice court. On August 12, 1898, its postmaster witnessed the lowering of the Hawaiian flag when Hawai'i became a U.S. territory. The flag now hangs above the stairway. You'll also find terrific museum displays, the active Lahaina Arts Society, an art gallery, and, perhaps in greatest demand, a public restroom. ⊠ *649 Wharf St., Lahaina* ☎ *808/661–0111* ⊠ *Free* ⏲ *Daily 9–5.*

⓯ Waiola Church and Cemetery. The Waiola Cemetery is actually older than the neighboring church; it dates back to the death of Kamehameha the Great's sacred wife, Queen Keōpūolani. She was one of the first Hawai-ian monarchs to convert to Christianity and was buried here in 1823. The church was erected in 1832 by Hawaiian chiefs and was originally named Ebenezer by the queen's second husband and widower, Gover-nor Hoapili. Aptly immortalized in James Michener's *Hawai'i* as the church that wouldn't stand, it was burned down twice and demolished in two windstorms. The present structure was put up in 1953 and named Waiola (water of life). ⊠ *535 Waine'e St., Lahaina* ☎ *808/661–4349.*

☾ **❹ Whalers Village.** A giant bony whale greets shoppers to Whalers Village. While the kids hit Honolua Surf shop, mom can peruse Versace, Prada,

Coach, and several fine jewelry stores at this casual, classy mall fronting Kā'anapali Beach. At the beach entrance, you'll find several good restaurants, including Leilani's and Hula Grill. On the third floor, visit the **Whalers Village Museum,** to hear stories of the 19th-century *Moby-Dick* era. Baleen, ambergris, and other mysterious artifacts are on display. A short film features Hawaiian turtles and the folklore surrounding them. ⊠ *2435 Kā'anapali Pkwy., Kā'anapali.* ☎ *808/661–4567* ⊕ *www. whalersvillage.com* ☒ *Free.*

★ **⑥ Wo Hing Museum.** Smack-dab in the center of Front Street, this eye-catching Chinese temple reflects the importance of early Chinese immigrants to Lahaina. Built by the Wo Hing Society in 1912, the museum now contains beautiful artifacts, historic photos of old Lahaina, and a Taoist altar. Bon dances and moon festivals are held annually on the grounds. Don't miss the films playing in the rustic theater next door—some of Thomas Edison's first films, shot in Hawai'i circa 1898, show Hawaiian wranglers herding steer onto ships. Ask the docent for some starfruit from the tree outside, for the altar or for yourself. ⊠ *858 Front St., Lahaina* ☎ *808/661–5553* ☒ *$1* ☉ *Daily 10–4.*

Also Worth Seeing

⑭ 505 Front Street. The quaint, New England–style mall on this quiet stretch of Front Street has many treasures, notably a resident endangered sea turtle. Year after year, turtle 5690 awes researchers and tourists alike by laying a record eight nests in the sand just steps from the mall. Catching sight of a nestling is rare, but 505's superb restaurants, galleries, surf shack, day spa, and local designer's boutique are accessible any day of the week. ⊠ *South end of Front St. near Shaw St., Lahaina.*

⑦ Hale Pa'i. Protestant missionaries established Lahainaluna Seminary as a center of learning and enlightenment in 1831. Six years later, they built this printing shop. Here at the press, they and their young Hawaiian scholars created a written Hawaiian language and used it to produce a Bible, history texts, and a newspaper. An exhibit displays a replica of the original Rampage press and facsimiles of early printing. The oldest U.S. educational institution west of the Rockies, the seminary now serves as Lahaina's public high school. ⊠ *980 Lahainaluna Rd., Lahaina* ☎ *808/661–3262* ☒ *Donations accepted* ☉ *Weekdays 10–3.*

⑬ Holy Innocents' Episcopal Church. Built in 1908, this beautiful open-air church is decorated with paintings depicting Hawaiian versions of Christian symbols, including a Hawaiian Madonna and child, rare or extinct birds, and native plants. The congregation is beautiful also, typically dressed in traditional clothing from Samoa and Tonga. Anyone is welcome to slip into one of the pews, carved from native woods. Queen Liliuokalani, Hawai'i's last reigning monarch, lived in a large grass house on this site as a child. ⊠ *South end of Front St. near Mokuhina St., Lahaina.*

🐾 **⑤ Lahaina–Kā'anapali & Pacific Railroad.** Affectionately called the Sugarcane Train, this is Maui's only passenger train. It's an 1890s-vintage railway that once shuttled sugar but now moves sightseers between Kā'anapali and Lahaina. This quaint little attraction with its singing

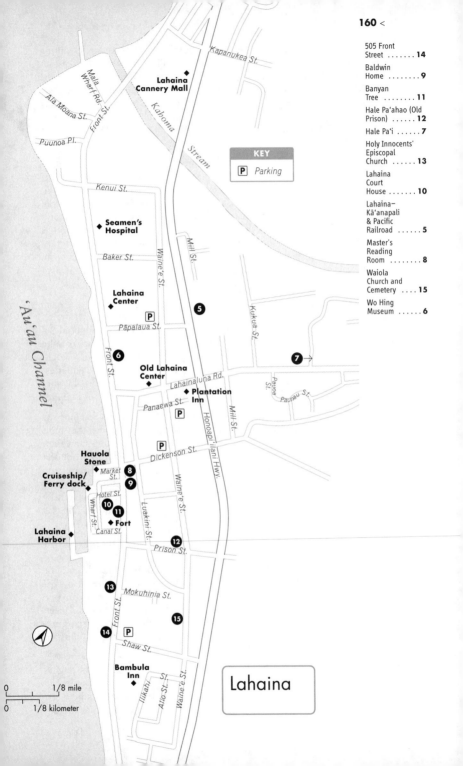

KEY

P Parking

Kapanukea St.

Mala Wharf Rd.

Ala Moana St.

Front St.

Lahaina
Cannery Mall

Kahoma

Stream

Puunoa Pl.

Kenui St.

'Au'au Channel

Seamen's
Hospital

Baker St.

Waine'e St.

Mill St.

Lahaina
Center

P

Pāpalaua St.

5

6

Front St.

Old Lahaina
Center

Kukua St.

Lahainaluna Rd.

7

Payoe St.

Paunau St.

Plantation
Inn

Panaewa St.

P

Mill St.

Honoapi'ilani Hwy.

P

Dickenson St.

Hauola
Stone

Market St.

8

Cruiseship/
Ferry dock

9

Hotel St.

Waine'e St.

10

Wharf St.

11

Fort

Luakini St.

Lahaina
Harbor

Canal St.

12

Prison St.

13

Mokuhinia St.

15

Front St.

14

P

Shaw St.

Bambula
Inn

Ilikahi St.

Atio St.

Waine'e St.

Lahaina

0   1/8 mile

0   1/8 kilometer

conductor is a big deal for Hawai'i but probably not much of a thrill for those more accustomed to trains (though children like it no matter where they grew up). A barbecue dinner with entertainment is offered on Thursday at 5 PM. ⊠ *1½ blocks north of Lahainaluna Rd. stoplight, at Hinau St., on Honoapi'ilani Hwy., Lahaina* ☎ *808/661– 0080* 🖼 *Round-trip $15.75, one-way $11.50, dinner train $65* ☉ *Daily 10:15–4.*

8 **Master's Reading Room.** This could be Maui's oldest residential building, constructed in 1834. In those days the ground floor was a mission's storeroom, and the reading room upstairs was for sailors. Today it houses local art and crafts for sale. ⊠ *Front and Dickenson Sts., Lahaina* ☎ *808/661–3262.*

The South Shore

Blessed by more than its fair share of sun, the southern shore of Haleakalā was an undeveloped wilderness until the 1970s. Then the sun-worshippers found it; now restaurants, condos, and luxury resorts line the coast from the world-class aquarium at Mā'alaea Harbor, through working class Kīhei, to lovely Wailea, a resort community rivaling those on West Maui. Farther south, the road disappears and unspoiled wilderness still has its way.

Because the South Shore includes so many fine beach choices, a trip here (if you're staying elsewhere on the island) is an all-day excursion—especially if you include a visit to the aquarium. Get active in the morning with exploring and snorkeling, then shower in a beach park, dress up a little, and enjoy the cool luxury of the Wailea resorts. At sunset, settle in for dinner at one of the area's many fine restaurants.

Main Attractions

18 **Kīhei.** Twenty-five years ago a scant few adventurers lived in Kīhei. Now about one-third of the Maui population lives here in one of the fastest-growing towns in America. Traffic lights and minimalls may not fit your notion of paradise, but Kīhei offers dependably warm sun, excellent beaches, and a front-row seat to marine life of all sorts. The county beach parks such as Kama'ole I, II, and III have lawns, showers, and picnic tables. Besides all the sun and sand, the town's relatively inexpensive condos and excellent restaurants make this a home base for many Maui visitors.

21 **Mākena Beach State Park.** "Big Beach" they call it—a huge stretch of heavenly golden sand without a house or hotel in sight. More than a decade ago, Maui citizens campaigned successfully to preserve this beloved beach from development. It's still wild, lacking in modern amenities (such as plumbing) but frequented by dolphins, turtles, and glorious sunsets. At the far left end of the beach, skim boarders catch air. On the right rises the beautiful hill called Pu'u Ōla'i, a perfect cinder cone. A climb over the steep rocks at this end leads to "Little Beach," where the (technically illegal) clothing-optional attitude prevails. On Sunday, Little Beach is a mecca for drummers and island gypsies. On any day of the week watch out for the mean shore break—those crisp, aquamarine waves are responsible for more than one broken arm.

★ ⓱ **Maui Ocean Center.** You'll feel as though you're walking from the seashore down to the bottom of the reef, and then through an acrylic tunnel in the middle of the sea at this aquarium, which focuses on Hawai'i and the Pacific. Special tanks get you close up with turtles, rays, sharks, and the unusual creatures of the tide pools. The center is part of a growing complex of retail shops and restaurants overlooking the harbor. ☒ *Enter from Honoapi'ilani Hwy., Rte. 30, as it curves past Mā'alaea Harbor, Mā'alaea* ☎ *808/270–7000* ⊕ *www.mauioceancenter.com* ▱ *$20* ☾ *Daily 9–5.*

⓴ **Wailea.** Wailea, the South Shore's resort community, is slightly quieter and drier than its West Side sister, Kā'anapali. The first two resorts were built here in the late 1970s. Soon a cluster of upscale properties sprung up, including the Four Seasons and the Fairmont Kea Lani. The luxury of the resorts (edging on overindulgence) and the simple grandeur of the coastal views make the otherwise stark coast an outstanding destination. A handful of perfect little beaches all have public access, and a paved beach walk allows you to stroll among all the properties, restaurants, and sandy coves.

Also Worth Seeing

⓶ **'Āhihi-Kīna'u (La Pérouse Bay).** Beyond Mākena Beach, the road fades away into a vast territory of black-lava flows, the result of Haleakalā's last eruption some 200 years ago. Also known as La Pérouse Bay, this is where Maui received its first official visit by a European explorer— the French admiral Jean-François de Galaup, Comte de La Pérouse, in 1786. Before it ends, the road passes through the 'Āhihi-Kīna'u Marine Preserve, an excellent place for morning snorkel adventures. This is also the start of the Hoapili Trail, or "the King's Trail," where you can hike through the remains of one of Maui's ancient villages.

★ **Coastal Nature Trail.** A paved beach walk allows you to stroll among Wailea's prettiest properties, restaurants, and rocky coves. The trail teems with joggers in the morning hours. The *makai,* or ocean, side is landscaped with exceptionally rare native plants. Look for the silvery *hinahina,* named after the Hawaiian moon goddess because of its color. In winter this is a great place to watch whales. ☒ *Accessible from Polo or Wailea Beach parks.*

☾ ⓳ **HI Humpback Whale Sanctuary.** The Sanctuary Education Center is beside a restored ancient Hawaiian fishpond, in prime humpback-viewing territory. Whether the whales are here or not, the center is a great stop for youngsters curious to know how things work underwater. Interactive displays and informative naturalists will explain it all. Throughout the year, the center hosts intriguing activities, ranging from moonlight tidal pool explorations to "Two-ton talks." ☒ *726 S. Kīhei Rd., Kīhei* ☎ *808/879– 2818 or 800/831–4888* ⊕ *www.hawaiihumpbackwhale.noaa.gov* ▱ *Free* ☾ *Daily 10–3.*

Kealia Pond National Wildlife Reserve. Long-legged stilts casually dip their beaks in the shallow waters of this wildlife reserve as traffic shuttles by. If you take time to read the interpretive signs on the new board-walk, you'll learn that endangered hawksbill turtles return to the sandy dunes here year after year. Sharp-eyed birders may catch sight of oc-casional migratory visitors, such as a falcon or osprey. ⊠ *N. Kīhei Rd., Kīhei* ⌖ *Free.*

⑯ Māʻalaea Small Boat Harbor. With only 89 slips and so many good rea-sons to take people out on the water, this active little harbor needs to be expanded. Below the mall's snazzy aquarium stands a small Shinto shrine, dedicated to the fishing god Ebisu Sama. Across the street, a giant hook often swings heavy with the sea's bounty, proving the worth of the shrine. Surfers fantasize about the famed surf break to the left of the harbor. The elusive spot, called "freight train" rarely breaks, but when it does, it's said to be the fastest in the world. Plans for inter-island ferry service and new public restrooms are in the works; until then, you can find restrooms in the adjoining shopping mall. ⊠ *Off Honoapiʻilani Hwy., Rte. 30.*

Shops at Wailea. Louis Vuitton, Tiffany, and the sumptuous Cos Bar lure shoppers to this elegant mall. Honolulu Coffee brews perfect shots of espresso to fuel those shop 'til you drop types. The kids can buy logo shirts in Pacific Sun while mom and dad ponder vacation ownership up-stairs. Tommy Bahama's, Ruth's Chris, and Longhi's are all good din-ing options. ⊠ *3750 Wailea Alanui, Wailea* ☏ *808/891–6770* ⊕ *www. shopsatwailea.com.*

Central Maui

Kahului, where you most likely landed when you arrived on Maui, is the industrial and commercial center of the island. The area was devel-oped in the early '50s to meet the housing needs of the large sugarcane interests here, specifically those of Alexander & Baldwin. The company was tired of playing landlord to its many plantation workers and sold land to a developer who promised to create affordable housing. The scheme worked, and "Dream City," the first planned city in Hawaiʻi, was born.

West of Kahului, Wailuku, the county seat since 1950, is the most charming town in Central Maui—though it wasn't always so. Its name means "Water of Destruction," after the fateful battle in ʻĪao Valley that

> **TIMING**
>
> You can explore Central Maui com-fortably in little more than a half day. These are good sights to squeeze in on the way to the air-port, or if you want to combine sightseeing with shopping. Hikers may want to expand their outing to a full day to explore ʻĪao Valley State Park.

pitted King Kamehameha I against Maui warriors. Wailuku was a po-litically important town until the sugar industry began to decline in the 1960s and tourism took hold. Businesses left the cradle of the West Maui Mountains and followed the new market to the shore, where tourists arrived by the boatload. Wailuku still houses the county government, but has the feel of a town that's been asleep for several decades. The interesting shops and offices now inhabiting Main Street's plantation-style buildings serve as reminders of a bygone era.

Main Attractions

25 Bailey House. This was the home of Edward and Caroline Bailey, two prominent missionaries who came to Wailuku to run the first Hawaiian girls' school on the island, the Wailuku Female Seminary. The school's main function was to train girls in the "feminine arts." It once stood next door to the Baileys' home, which they called Halehōʻikeʻike (House of Display), but locals always called it the Bailey House, and the sign painters eventually gave in. The Maui Historical Society runs a museum in the plastered stone house, with a small collection of artifacts from before and after the missionaries' arrival and with Mr. Bailey's paintings of Wailuku. The Hawaiian Room has exhibits on the making of tapa cloth, as well as samples of pre-Captain Cook weaponry. ⊠ *2375A Main St., Wailuku* ☎ *808/244–3326* ⊕ *www.mauimuseum. org* ⊡ *$5* ⊙ *Mon.–Sat. 10–4.*

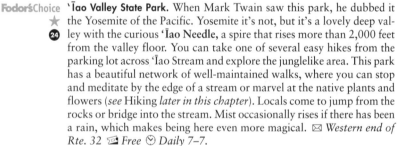

| Haleakalā National Park | See Page 165 |

FodorsChoice ★ **'Iao Valley State Park.** When Mark Twain saw this park, he dubbed it the Yosemite of the Pacific. Yosemite it's not, but it's a lovely deep valley with the curious 'Iao Needle, a spire that rises more than 2,000 feet from the valley floor. You can take one of several easy hikes from the parking lot across 'Iao Stream and explore the junglelike area. This park has a beautiful network of well-maintained walks, where you can stop and meditate by the edge of a stream or marvel at the native plants and flowers (*see* Hiking *later in this chapter*). Locals come to jump from the rocks or bridge into the stream. Mist occasionally rises if there has been a rain, which makes being here even more magical. ⊠ *Western end of Rte. 32* ⊡ *Free* ⊙ *Daily 7–7.*

© 23 Kepaniwai Park & Heritage Gardens. This county park is a memorial to Maui's cultural roots, with picnic facilities and ethnic displays dotting the landscape. Among the displays are an early-Hawaiian shack, a New England–style saltbox, a Portuguese-style villa with gardens, and dwellings from such other cultures as China and the Philippines. Next door, the Hawaiʻi Nature Center has an interactive exhibit and hikes good for children.

The peacefulness here belies the history of the area. During his quest for domination, King Kamehameha I brought his troops from the Big Island of Hawaiʻi to the Valley Isle in 1790 and waged a successful and particularly bloody battle against the son of Maui's chief, Kahekili, near Kepaniwai Park. An earlier battle at the site had pitted Kahekili himself against an older Big Island chief, Kalaniʻōpuʻu. Kahekili prevailed, but the carnage was so great that the nearby stream became known as

Continued on page 171

HALEAKALĀ NATIONAL PARK

HALEAKALA CRATER

From Tropics to the Moon! Two hours, 38 mi, 10,023 feet—those are the unlikely numbers involved in reaching Maui's highest point, the summit of Haleakalā. Nowhere else on earth can you drive from sea level (Kahului) to 10,023 feet (the summit) in only 38 mi. And what's more shocking—in that short vertical ascent, you'll journey from lush, tropical-island landscape to the stark, moonlike basin of the volcano's enormous, otherworldly crater.

Established in 1916, Haleakalā National Park covers an astonishing 27,284 acres. Haleakalā Crater is the centerpiece of the park though it's not actually a crater. Technically, it's an erosional valley, flushed out by water pouring from the summit through two enormous gaps. The mountain has terrific camping and hiking, including a trail that loops through the crater, but the chance to witness this unearthly landscape is reason enough for a visit.

THE CLIMB TO THE SUMMIT

To reach Haleakalā National Park and the mountain's breathtaking summit, take Route 36 east of Kahului to the Haleakalā Highway (Route 37). Head east, up the mountain to the unlikely intersection of Haleakalā Highway and Haleakalā Highway. If you continue straight the road's name changes to Kula Highway (still Route 37). Instead, turn left onto Haleakalā Highway—this is now Route 377. After about 6 mi, make a left onto

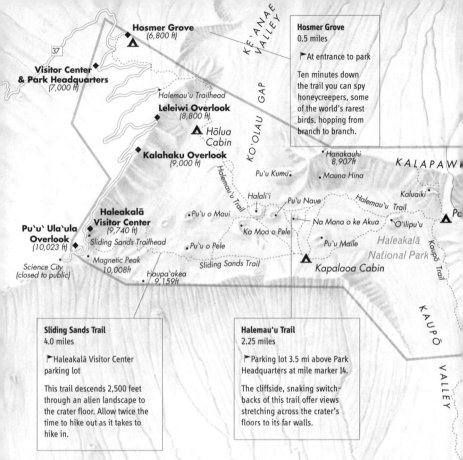

Hosmer Grove
(6,800 ft)

37

Visitor Center & Park Headquarters
(7,000 ft)

Halemau'u Trailhead

Leleiwi Overlook
(8,800 ft)

▲ *Hōlua Cabin*

Kalahaku Overlook
(9,000 ft)

Haleakalā Visitor Center
(9,740 ft)

Pu'u' Ula'ula Overlook
(10,023 ft)

Sliding Sands Trailhead

Science City (closed to public)

Magnetic Peak 10,008 ft

Haupa'akea • 9,159 ft

Halemau'u Trail

KE'ANAE VALLEY

KO'OLAU GAP

Hosmer Grove
0.5 miles

▶At entrance to park

Ten minutes down the trail you can spy honeycreepers, some of the world's rarest birds, hopping from branch to branch.

Hanakauhi 8,907 ft

KALAPAW

Pu'u Kumu • *Mauna Hina*

Halali'i *Pu'u Naue* *Halemau'u Trail* *Kaluaiki*

Pu'u o Maui *Na Mana o ke Akua* *O'ilipu'u*

Ka Moa o Pele *Pu'u Maíle*

Pu'u o Pele *Haleakalā National Park*

Sliding Sands Trail ▲ *Kapalaoa Cabin*

Pc ▲

Kaupō Trail

KAUPŌ VALLEY

Sliding Sands Trail
4.0 miles

▶Haleakalā Visitor Center parking lot

This trail descends 2,500 feet through an alien landscape to the crater floor. Allow twice the time to hike out as it takes to hike in.

Halemau'u Trail
2.25 miles

▶Parking lot 3.5 mi above Park Headquarters at mile marker 14.

The cliffside, snaking switchbacks of this trail offer views stretching across the crater's floors to its far walls.

Crater Road (Route 378). After several long switchbacks (look out for downhill bikers!) you'll come to the park entrance.

■ TIP➔ Before you head up Haleakalā, call for the latest park weather conditions (☏ 808/877–5111). Extreme gusty winds, heavy rain, and even snow in winter are not uncommon. Because of the high altitude, the mountaintop temperature is often as much as 30 degrees cooler than that at sea level. Be sure to bring a jacket. Also make sure you have a full tank of gas. No service stations exist beyond Kula.

There's a $10 parking fee to enter the park; but it's good for one week and can

be used at 'Ohe'o Gulch (Seven Sacred Pools), so save your receipt.

6,800 feet, Hosmer Grove. Just as you enter the park, Hosmer Grove has campsites and interpretive trails (*see* Hiking & Camping *on page 169*). Park rangers maintain a changing schedule of talks and hikes both here and at the top of the mountain. Call the park for current schedules.

7,000 feet, Park Headquarters/Visitor Center. Not far from Hosmer Grove, the Park Headquarters/Visitor Center (open daily from 8 to 4) has trail maps

P̣AWILI   RIDGE

▲ Palikū Cabin

Kipahulu Valley
Biological Reserve
No public access

Kīpahulu   VALLEY

ṇaupō Trail

PŌ   VALLEY

Waimoku
Falls

31

Makahiku
Falls

Kuloa Point

Okina

Pacific Ocean

0   ½ mi

0   ½ km

SUNRISE AT THE SUMMIT

Sunrise at the summit has become the thing to do. You need an hour and a half from the bottom of **Haleakalā Highway** (Route 37) to Pu'u 'Ula'ula Overlook. Add to that the time of travel to the highway—at least 45 minutes from Lahaina or Kīhei. *The Maui News* posts the hour of sunrise every day. Remember the Alpine-Aeolian summit is *freezing* at dawn (Alpine indicates cold, Aeolian indicates windy). Bring hotel towels, blankets—anything you can find to stay warm. Also keep in mind, the highly touted colors of sunrise are weather-dependent. Sometimes they're spectacular and sometimes the sun just comes up without the fanfare.

and displays about the volcano's origins and eruption history. Hikers and campers should check-in here before heading up the mountain. Maps, posters, and other memorabilia are available at the gift shop.

8,800 feet, Leleiwi Overlook. Continuing up the mountain, you come to Leleiwi Overlook. A short walk to the end of the parking lot reveals your first awe-inspiring view of the crater. The small hills in the basin are volcanic cinder cones (called *pu'u* in Hawaiian), each with a small crater at its top, and each the site of a former eruption.

WHERE TO EAT

KULA LODGE (✉ Haleakalā Hwy., Kula ☎ 808/878-2517) serves hearty breakfasts from 7 to 11 AM, a favorite with hikers coming down from a sunrise visit to Haleakalā's summit, as well as those on their way up for a late-morning tramp in the crater. Spectacular ocean views fill the windows of this mountainside lodge.

If you're here in the late afternoon, it's possible you'll experience a phenomenon called the Brocken Specter. Named after a similar occurrence in East Germany's

Silversword

Harz Mountains, the specter allows you to see yourself reflected on the clouds and encircled by a rainbow. Don't wait all day for this because it's not a daily occurrence.

9,000 feet, Kalahaku Overlook. The next stopping point is Kalahaku Overlook. The view here offers a different perspective of the crater and at this elevation, the famous silversword plant grows amid the cinders. This odd, endangered beauty grows only here, and at the same elevation on the Big Island's two peaks. It begins life as a silver, spiny-leaf rosette and is the sole home of a variety of native insects (it's the only shelter around). The silversword reaches maturity between 7 and 17 years, when it sends forth a 3- to 8-foot-tall stalk with several hundred tiny sunflowers. It blooms once, then dies.

9,740 feet, Haleakalā Visitor Center. Another mile up is the Haleakalā Visitor Center (open daily from sunrise to 3 PM). There are exhibits inside, and a trail from here leads to White Hill—a short, easy walk that will give you an even better view of the valley.

10,023 feet, Puʻu ʻUlaʻula Overlook. The highest point on Maui is the Puʻu ʻUlaʻula Overlook, at the 10,023-foot summit. Here you find a glass-enclosed lookout with a 360-degree view. The building is open 24 hours a day, and this is where visitors gather for the best sunrise view. Dawn begins between 5:45 and 7, depending on the time of year. On a clear day you can see the islands of Molokaʻi, Lānaʻi, Kahoʻolawe, and Hawaiʻi (the Big Island). On a *really* clear day you can even spot Oʻahu glimmering in the distance.

■ TIP→ The air is very thin at 10,000 feet. Don't be surprised if you feel a little breathless while walking around the summit. Take it easy and drink lots of water. Anyone who has been scuba diving within the last 24 hours should not make the trip up Haleakalā.

On a small hill nearby, you can see **Science City**, an off-limits research and communications center straight out of an espionage thriller. The University of Hawaiʻi maintains an observatory here, and the Department of Defense tracks satellites.

For more information about Haleakalā National Park, contact the **National Park Service** (☎ 808/572–4400 ⊕ www.nps.gov/hale).

HIKING & CAMPING

Exploring Haleakalā Crater is one of the best hiking experiences on Maui. The volcanic terrain offers an impressive diversity of colors, textures, and shapes—almost as if the lava has been artfully sculpted. The barren landscape is home to many plants, insects, and birds that exist nowhere else on earth and have developed intriguing survival mechanisms, such as the sun-reflecting, hairy leaves of the silversword, which allow it to survive the intense climate.

Stop at park headquarters to register and pick up trail maps on your way into the park.

1-Hour Hike. Just as you enter Haleakalā National Park, **Hosmer Grove** offers a short 10-minute hike, and an hour-long, ½-mi loop trail into the Waikamoi Cloud Forest that will give you insight into Hawai'i's fragile ecology. Anyone can go on the short hike, whereas the longer trail through the cloud forest is accessible only with park ranger-guided hikes. Call park headquarters for the schedule. Facilities here include six campsites (no permit needed, available on a first-come first-served basis), pit toilets, drinking water, and cooking shelters.

4 Hour Hikes. Two half-day hikes involve descending into the crater and returning the way you came. The first, **Halemau'u Trail** (trailhead is between mile markers 14 and 15), is 2 mi round-trip. The cliffside, snaking switchbacks of this trail offer views stretching across the crater's pu'u-speckled floor to its far walls. On clear days you can peer through the Ko'olau Gap to Hāna. Native flowers and shrubs grow along the trail, which is typically misty and cool (though still exposed to the sun). When you reach the gate at the bottom, head back up.

The other hike, which is 5 mi round-trip, descends down **Sliding Sands Trail** (trailhead is at the Haleakalā Visitor Center) into an alien landscape of reddish black cinders, lava bombs, and silverswords. It's easy to imagine life before humans in the solitude and silence of this place. Turn back when you hit the crater floor.

■ TIP→ Bring water, sunscreen, and a reliable jacket. These can be demanding hikes if you're unused to the altitude. Take it slowly to acclimate, and give yourself additional time for the uphill return trip.

8-Hour Hike. The recommended way to explore the crater in a single, but full day is to go in two cars and ferry yourselves back and forth between the head of **Halemau'u Trail** and the summit. This way, you can hike from the summit down **Sliding Sands Trail**, cross the crater's floor, investigate the **Bottomless Pit** and **Pele's Paint Pot**, then climb out on the switchback trail (**Halemau'u**). When you emerge, the shelter of your waiting car will be very welcome (this is an 11.2-mi hike). If you don't have two cars, hitching a ride from Halemau'u back to the summit should be relatively safe and easy.

■ TIP➜ Take a backpack with lunch, water, sunscreen, and a reliable jacket for the beginning and end of the 8-hour hike. This is a demanding trip, but you will never regret or forget it.

Overnight Hike. Staying overnight in one of Haleakalā's three cabins or two wilderness campgrounds is an experience like no other. You'll feel like the only person on earth when you wake up inside this enchanted, strange landscape. Nēnē and 'u'au (endangered storm petrels) make charming neighbors. The cabins, each tucked in a different corner of the crater's floor, are equipped with 12 bunk beds, wood-burning stoves, fake logs, and kitchen gear.

Hōlua cabin is the shortest hike, less than 4 hours (3.7 mi) from Halemau'u Trail. **Kapala'oa** is about 5 hours (5.5 mi) down Sliding Sands Trail. The most cherished cabin is **Palikū**, a solid eight-hour (9.3-mi) hike starting from either trail. It's nestled against the rain-forested cliffs above the Kaupō Gap. To reserve a cabin you have to apply to the National Park Service at least 90 days in advance and hope the lottery system is kind to you. Tent campsites at Hōlua and Palikū are free and easy to reserve on a first-come, first-served basis.

■ TIP➜ Toilets and nonpotable water are available—bring iodine tablets to purify the water. Open fires are not allowed and packing out your trash is mandatory.

For more information on hiking or camping, or to reserve a cabin, contact the National Park Service (✉ Box 369, Makawao 96768 ☎ 808/572-9306 ⊕ www.nps.gov/hale).

OPTIONS FOR EXPLORING

If you're short on time you can drive to the summit, take a peek inside, and drive back down. But the "House of the Sun" is really worth a day of your vacation time. There are lots of ways to experience the crater: by foot, bicycle, horseback, or helicopter.

BIKING

You cannot bike within the crater, but you can cruise the 38 mi from the summit down the outside of the mountain all the way to Pā'ia at sea level. The views along the way are exquisite, but dodging traffic can be a headache. If you rent bikes on your own, you'll need someone to ferry you up. Tours provide shuttle service and equipment.

HELICOPTER TOURS

Viewing Haleakalā from above can be a mind-altering experience, if you don't mind dropping $200 per person for a few blissful moments above the crater. Most tours buzz Haleakalā, where airspace is regulated, then head over to Hanā in search of waterfalls.

HORSEBACK RIDING

Several companies offer half-day, full-day, and even overnight rides into the crater. Advanced or at least confident riders can travel up the stunning Kaupō Gap with Charley's Trail Rides and stay overnight at Palikū.

For complete information on any of these activities, see Golf, Hiking & Other Adventures *later in this chapter*

Wailuku (water of destruction) and the place where fallen warriors choked the stream's flow was called Kepaniwai (the water dam). ⊠ '*Iao Valley Rd., Wailuku* 🖾 *Free* ⊙ *Daily 7–7.*

26 Market Street. An idiosyncratic assortment of shops makes Wailuku's Market Street a delightful place for a stroll. The Good Fortune Trading Company and Brown-Kobayashi carry interesting antiques and furnishings, while Gallerie Ha and the Sig Zane are sophisticated studio gift shops. Café Marc Aurel brews excellent espresso, which you can enjoy while sampling the selection of new and used CDs at the corner music shop. ⊠ *Wailuku.*

Also Worth Seeing

30 Alexander & Baldwin Sugar Museum. "A&B," Maui's largest landowner, was one of the "Big Five" companies that spearheaded the planting, harvesting, and processing of sugarcane. Although Hawaiian cane sugar is now being supplanted by cheaper foreign versions—as well as by sugar derived from inexpensive sugar beets—the crop was for many years the mainstay of the Hawaiian economy. The museum is in the old plantation manager's house across from the post office and the still-operating sugar refinery (black smoke billows up when cane is burning). Historic photos and artifacts explain how sugar is harvested and how the industry dramatically transformed Maui's natural and cultural landscape. ⊠ *3957 Hansen Rd., Pu'unēnē* ☎ *808/871–8058* 🖾 *$5* ⊙ *Mon.–Sat. 9:30–4:30; last admission at 4.*

27 Haleki'i-Pihana Heiau State Monument. Stand here at either of the two *heiau* (ancient Hawaiian stone platforms once used as places of worship) and imagine the king of Maui surveying his domain. That's what Kahekili, Maui's last fierce king, did, and so did Kamehameha the Great after he defeated Kahekili's soldiers. Today the view is most instructive. Below, the once-powerful 'Iao Stream has been sucked dry and boxed in by concrete. Before you is the urban heart of the island. The suburban community behind you is all Hawaiian Homelands—property owned solely by native Hawaiians. ⊠ *End of Hea Pl., off Kuhio Pl. from Waiehu Beach Rd., Rte. 340, Kahului* 🖾 *Free* ⊙ *Daily 7–7.*

29 Maui Arts & Cultural Center. An epic fund drive by the citizens of Maui led to the creation of this $32 million facility. The top-of-the-line Castle Theater seats 1,200 people on orchestra, mezzanine, and balcony levels; rock stars play the A&B Amphitheater. The MACC (as it's called) also includes a small black-box theater, an art gallery with interesting exhibits, and classrooms. The building itself is worth a visit: it incorporates work by Maui artists, and its signature lava-rock wall pays tribute to the skills of the Hawaiians. But the real draw is the Schaeffer International Gallery, which houses superb rotating exhibits. ⊠ *One Cameron Way, Kahului* ☎ *808/242–2787, 808/242–7469 box office* ⊕ *www.mauiarts.org* ⊙ *Weekdays 9–5.*

28 Maui Nui Botanical Gardens. The fascinating plants grown here are representative of pre-contact Hawai'i. Both native and Polynesian-introduced species are cultivated—including ice-cream bananas, varieties of sweet potatoes and sugarcane, native poppies, hibiscus, and *anapanapa,*

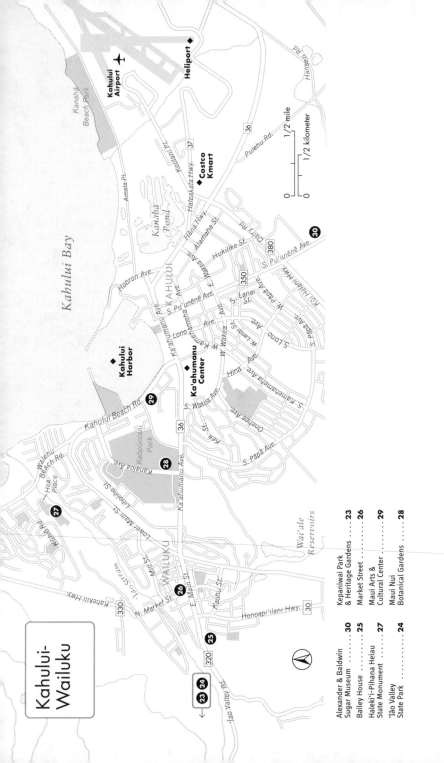

Kahului-Wailuku

Kahului Bay

Kahului Airport

Heliport ◆

Kanahā Beach Park

Kanahā Pond

Kahului Harbor ◆

Kaʻahumanu Center

Costco Kmart ◆

Waiʻale Reservoirs

WAILUKU

KAHULUI

Hansen Rd

Pulehu Rd.

Puʻunēnē Ave.

Hāna Hwy

Haleakala Hwy

Keolani Pl.

Amala Pl.

Hobron Ave.

Kaʻahumanu Ave.

Lono Ave.

W. Kamehameha Ave.

S. Puʻunēnē Ave.

Alamaha St.

Hukilike St.

Dairy Rd

E. Wakea Ave.

S. Lanai St.

W. Papa Ave.

S. Papa Ave.

Koʻi Helani Hwy

S. Lono Ave.

W. Lanai St.

W. Wakea Ave.

Hina Ave.

S. Kamehameha Ave.

Onehee Ave.

S. Wakea Ave.

Eha St.

Kanaloa Ave.

Kahului Beach Rd.

Keōpūolani Park

Lower Main St.

Limahana St.

N. Market St.

Mill St.

E. Main St.

S. High St.

Kaohu St.

ʻĪao Stream

ʻĪao Valley Rd.

Kahekili Hwy

Wailuku Beach Rd.

Kuihelani Rd.

Hea Place

Honoapiʻilani Hwy

320

330

30

36

36

37

350

380

1/2 mile

1/2 kilometer

0

N

Alexander & Baldwin
Sugar Museum **30**
Bailey House **25**
Halekiʻi-Pihana Heiau
State Monument **27**
ʻĪao Valley
State Park **24**

Kepaniwai Park
& Heritage Gardens **23**
Market Street **26**
Maui Arts &
Cultural Center **29**
Maui Nui
Botanical Gardens **28**

CLOSE UP

The Boy Who Raised an Island

ACCORDING TO LEGEND, the island of Maui was named after a demigod whose father, Akalana, kept the heavens aloft and whose mother, Hina, guarded the path to the netherworld. Of their children, Maui was the only one who possessed magic powers, though he wasn't a good fisherman and was teased mercilessly by his brothers for it. Eventually, the cunning young Maui devised a way to catch his own fish: he distracted his brothers and pulled his line across theirs, switching the hooks and stealing the fish they had caught.

When Maui's brothers caught on to his deception, they refused to take him fishing. To console Maui, his father gave him a magic hook, the Manaiakalani. Akalana said that the hook was fastened to the heavens and

when it caught land a new continent would be born. Maui was able to convince his brothers to take him out one more time. As they paddled deep into the ocean, he chanted a powerful spell, commanding the hook to catch "the Great Fish." The hook caught more than a fish—as they paddled along, mountain peaks were lifted out of the water's depths.

As the mountains began to rise, Maui told his brothers to paddle quickly without looking back. They did so for two days, at which point their curiosity proved too much. One of the brothers looked back, and as he stopped paddling, Maui's magic line snapped. Maui had intended to raise an entire continent, but had only an island to show for his efforts.

2

a plant that makes a natural shampoo when rubbed between your hands. Ethnobotany tours and presentations are offered on occasion. ⊠ *150 Kanaloa Ave.* ☎ *808/249–2798* ☺ *Mon.–Sat. 8–4.*

☺ ③ **Maui Tropical Plantation & Country Store.** When Maui's once-paramount crop declined in importance, a group of visionaries decided to open an agricultural theme park on the site of this former sugarcane field. The 60-acre preserve, on Route 30 just outside Wailuku, offers a 30-minute tram ride through its fields with an informative narration covering growing processes and plant types. Children will probably enjoy the historical-characters exhibit as well as fruit tasting, coconut husking, and lei-making demonstrations, not to mention some entertaining spider monkeys. There's a restaurant on the property and a country store specializing in made in Maui products. ⊠ *Honoapi'ilani Hwy., Rte. 30, Waikapu* ☎ *808/244–7643* ☺ *Free; tram ride with narrated tour $9.50* ☺ *Daily 9–5.*

Upcountry Maui & the North Shore

North Shore action centers around the colorful town of Pā'ia and the windsurfing mecca, Ho'okipa Beach. Blasted by winter swells and wind, Maui's north shore draws water-sports thrill-seekers from around the world. But there's much more to this area of Maui than coastline. Inland, a lush, waterfall-fed Garden of Eden beckons. In forested pockets, wealthy hermits have carved out a little piece of paradise for themselves. A few of them are even willing to invite you in, as guests at their vacation rentals.

As you venture up the mountain, you find yourself "Upcountry"—the name locals have given to the west-facing slope of Haleakalā. This idyllic region is responsible for much of Hawai'i's produce—lettuce, tomatoes, strawberries, and sweet Maui onions for starters. As you drive along you'll notice cactus thickets mingled with purple jacaranda, wild hibiscus, and towering eucalyptus trees. Upcountry is also fertile ranch land; cowboys still work the fields of the historic 20,000-acre 'Ulupalakua Ranch and the 32,000-acre Haleakalā Ranch. Keep an eye out for *pueo*, Hawai'i's native owl, which hunts these fields during daylight hours.

Main Attractions

③③ Ho'okipa Beach. There's no better place on this or any other island to watch the world's finest windsurfers in action. The surfers know five different surf breaks here by name. Unless it's a rare day without wind or waves, you're sure to get a show. ■ TIP→ **It's not safe to park on the shoulder. Use the ample parking lot at the county park entrance.** ⊠ *2 mi past Pā'ia on Rte. 36.*

FodorsChoice
★

③⑥ Makawao. This once-tiny town has managed to hang on to its country charm (and eccentricity) as it has grown in popularity. The district was originally settled by Portuguese and Japanese immigrants who came to Maui to work the sugar plantations and then moved Upcountry to establish small farms, ranches, and stores. Descendants now work the neighboring Haleakalā and 'Ulupalakua ranches. Every July 4 the *paniolo* (Hawaiian cowboy) set comes out in force for the Makawao Rodeo. The crossroads of town—lined with chic shops and down-home eateries—reflects a growing population of people who came here just because they liked it. For those seeking lush greenery rather than beachside accommodations, there are great, secluded little B&Bs in and around the town. ⊠ *Intersection of Baldwin and Makawao Aves.*

★ **③②** **Pā'ia.** This little town was once a sugarcane enclave, with a mill and plantation camps. The town boomed during World War II when the marines set up camp in nearby Ha'ikū. The old HC&S sugar mill finally closed and no sign of the military remains, but the town continues to thrive. In the '70s Pā'ia became a hippie town as dropouts headed for Maui to open boutiques,

TIMING

Most travelers cruise through the North Shore on their way to Hāna. The small town of Pā'ia takes little more than an hour to explore fully. If you'd like to poke around the area's beaches and restaurants, you could easily turn it into a day's outing, especially if you head up Upcountry. From Kīhei or Kā'anapali it takes between 45 minutes and an hour to get to either Pā'ia or Makawao–depending on traffic. Tedeschi Winery and other Upcountry destinations are further, at least another half hour along Kula Highway. Its a good idea to combine a Haleakalā crater expedition with a tour of Upcountry and a meal on the North Shore.

MAUI SIGHTSEEING TOURS

This is a big island to see in one day, so tour companies tend to offer specialized tours, visiting either Haleakalā or Hāna and its environs. A tour of Haleakalā and Upcountry is usually a half-day excursion and is offered in several versions by different companies for about $60 and up. The trip often includes stops at a protea farm and at Tedeschi Vineyards, Maui's only winery. A Haleakalā sunrise tour starts before dawn so that you can get to the top of the dormant volcano before the sun peeks over the horizon. Because they offer island-wide hotel pickup, many sunrise trips leave around 2:30 AM.

A tour of Hāna is almost always done in a van, since the winding road to Hāna just isn't built for bigger buses. Of late, Hāna has so many of these one-day tours that it seems as if there are more vans than cars on the road. Still, to many it's a more relaxing way to do the drive than behind the wheel of a car. Guides decide where you stop for photos. Tours run from $80 to $120.

When booking a tour, remember that some tour companies use air-conditioned buses, whereas others prefer small vans. Then you've got your minivans, your microbuses, and your minicoaches. The key is to ask how many stops you get and how many other passengers will be onboard—otherwise you could end up on a packed bus, sightseeing through a window.

Most of the tour guides have been in the business for years. Some were born in the Islands and have taken special classes to learn more about their culture and lore. They expect a tip ($1 per person at least), but they're just as cordial without one.

Maui Pineapple Plantation Tour. Explore one of Maui's pineapple plantations on this tour that takes you right into the fields in a company van. The 2½-hour, $26 trip gives you first-hand experience of the operation and its history, some incredible views of the island, and the chance to pick a fresh pineapple for yourself. Tours depart weekday mornings and afternoons from the Kapalua Logo Shop. ✉ *Kapalua Resort Activity Desk, 500 Office Rd., Kapalua* ☎ *808/669-8088.*

Polynesian Adventure Tours. This company uses large buses with floor-to-ceiling windows. The drivers are fun and really know the island. ☎ *808/877-4242 or 800/622-3011* ⊕ *www.polyad.com.*

Roberts Hawai'i Tours. This is one of the state's largest tour companies, and its staff can arrange tours with bilingual guides if asked ahead of time. Eleven-hour trips venture out to Kaupo, the wild area past Hāna. ☎ *808/871-6226 or 800/767-7551* ⊕ *www.roberts-hawaii.com.*

Temptation Tours. Temptation Tours has targeted members of the affluent older crowd (though almost anyone would enjoy these tours) who don't want to be herded onto a crowded bus. Tours in plush six-passenger limovans explore Haleakalā and Hāna, and range from $110 to $249 per person. The "Hāna Sky-Trek" includes a return trip via helicopter—perfect for those leery of spending the entire day in a van. ☎ *808/877-8888* ⊕ *www.mauitours.us.*

galleries, and unusual eateries. In the '80s windsurfers discovered nearby Hoʻokipa Beach and brought an international flavor to Pāʻia. At the intersection of Hāna Highway and Baldwin Avenue, eclectic boutiques supply everything from high fashion to hemp oil candles. The restaurants provide excellent people-watching and an array of dining options. Pāʻia is the last place to snack before the pilgrimage to Hāna. ⊠ *Intersection of Hāna Hwy. (Hwy. 36) and Baldwin Ave.*

HAWAIIAN CREAM PUFFS, YUM!

One of Makawao's most famous landmarks is **Komoda Store & Bakery** (3674 Baldwin Ave.; 808/572–7261)—a classic mom-and-pop store that has changed little in three-quarters of a century—where you can get a delicious cream puff if you arrive early enough. They make hundreds but sell out each day.

The Road to Hāna — See Page 177

Also Worth Seeing

38 Aliʻi Kula Lavender. Reserve a spot for tea or lunch at this lavender farm with a falcon's view. It's *the* relaxing remedy for those suffering from too much sun, shopping, or golf. Owners Aliʻi and Lani lead tours through winding paths of therapeutic lavender varieties, proteas, succulents, and rare Maui wormwood. Their logo, a larger-than-life dragonfly, darts above chefs who are cooking up lavender-infused shrimp appetizers out on the lānai. The gift shop abounds with the farm's own innovative lavender products. ⊠ *1100 Waipoli Rd., Kula* ☎ *808/878–3004* ⊕ *www.mauikulalavender.com* ⊡ *$25* ⚓ *Reservations essential* ⏱ *Daily 9–4, tours at 11 AM.*

34 Haʻikū. At one time this area vibrated around a couple of enormous pineapple canneries. Both have been transformed into rustic warehouse malls. At Haʻikū cannery you can snack on pizza at Colleen's or get massaged by the students at Spa Luna. Up Kokomo Road is a large puʻu capped with a grove of columnar pines, and the **4th Marine Division Memorial Park.** During World War II American GIs trained here for battles on Iwo Jima and Saipan. Locals nicknamed the cinder cone Giggle Hill because it was a popular hangout for Maui women and their favorite servicemen. ⊠ *Intersection of Haʻikū and Kokomo Rds.*

35 Hui Noʻeau Visual Arts Center. The main house of this nonprofit cultural center on the old Baldwin estate, just outside the town of Makawao, is an elegant two-story Mediterranean-style villa designed in the 1920s by the defining Hawaiʻi architect C. W. Dickey. "The Hui" is the grande dame of Maui's well-known arts scene. The exhibits are always satisfying, and the grounds might as well be a botanical garden. The Hui also offers classes and maintains working artists' studios. ⊠ *2841 Baldwin Ave., Makawao* ☎ *808/572–6560* ⊡ *Free* ⏱ *Daily 10–4.*

Continued on page 186

ROAD TO HĀNA

As you round the impossibly tight turn, a one-lane bridge comes into view. Beneath its worn surface, a lush forested gulch plummets toward the coast. The sound of rushing water fills the air, compelling you to search the overgrown hillside for waterfalls. This is the Road to Hāna, a 55-mi journey into the unspoiled heart of Maui. Tracing a centuries-old path, the road begins as a well-paved highway in Kahului and ends in the tiny town of Hāna on the islands' rain-gouged windward side.

Despite the twists and turns, the road to Hāna is not as frightening as it may sound. You're bound to be a little nervous approaching it the first time; but afterwards you'll wonder if somebody out there is making it sound tough just to keep out the hordes. The challenging part of the road takes only an hour and a half, but you'll want to stop often and let the driver enjoy the view, too. Don't expect a booming city when you get to Hāna. Its lure is its quiet timelessness. Like the adage says, the journey *is* the destination.

During high season, the road to Hāna tends to clog—well, not clog exactly, but develop little choo-choo trains of cars, with everyone in a line of six or a dozen driving as slowly as the first car. The solution: leave early (dawn) and return late (dusk). And if you find yourself playing the role of locomotive, pull over and let the other drivers pass. You can also let someone else take the turns for you—several companies offer van tours, which make stops all along the way (*see* Maui Sightseeing Tours *earlier in this chapter*).

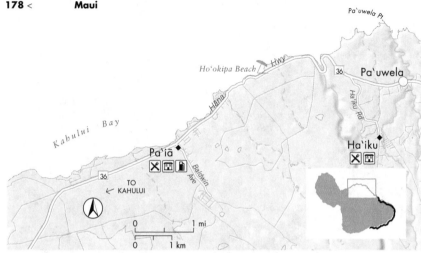

DRIVING THE ROAD TO HĀNA

Begin your journey in Pā'ia, the little town on Maui's North Shore. Be sure to fill up your gas tank here. There are no gas stations along Hāna Highway, and the station in Hāna closes by 6 PM. You should also pick up a picnic lunch. Lunch and snack choices along the way are limited to rustic fruit stands.

About 10 mi past Pā'ia, at the bottom of Kaupakalua Road, the roadside mileposts begin measuring the 36 mi to Hāna town. The road's trademark noodling starts about 3 mi after that. Once the road gets twisty, remember that many residents make this trip frequently. You'll recognize them because they're the ones zipping around every curve. They've seen this so many times before they don't care to linger. Pull over to let them pass.

All along this stretch of road, waterfalls are abundant. Roll down your windows. Breathe in the scent of guava and ginger. You can almost hear the bamboo growing. There are plenty of places to pull completely off the road and park safely. Do this often, since the road's curves make driving without a break difficult.

❶ Twin Falls. Keep an eye out for the fruit stand just after mile marker 2. Stop here

and treat yourself to some fresh sugarcane juice. If you're feeling adventurous, follow the path beyond the stand to the paradisiacal waterfalls known as Twin Falls. Once a rough trail plastered with NO TRESPASSING signs, this treasured spot is now easily accessible. In fact, there's usually a mass of cars surrounding the fruit stand at the trailhead. Several deep, emerald pools sparkle beneath waterfalls and offer excellent swimming and photo opportunities.

While it's still private property, the NO TRESPASSING signs have been replaced by colorfully painted arrows pointing away from residences and toward the falls. ■ TIP→ **Bring water shoes for crossing streams along the way. Swim at your own risk and beware: flash floods here and in all East Maui stream areas can be sudden and deadly. Check the weather before you go.**

❷ Huelo & Kailua. Dry off and drive on past the sleepy country villages of Huelo (near mile marker 5) and Kailua (near mile marker 6). The little farm town of Huelo has two quaint churches and several lovely B&Bs. It's a good place to stay if you value privacy, but it also provides an opportunity to meet local residents and learn about a rural lifestyle you might not expect to find on the Islands. The same can

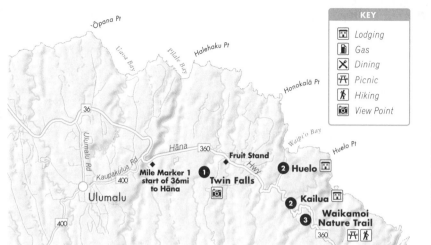

be said for nearby Kailua, home to Alexander & Baldwin's irrigation employees.

❸ **Waikamoi Nature Trail.** Between mile markers 9 and 10, the Waikamoi Nature Trail sign beckons you to stretch your car-weary limbs. A short (if muddy) trail leads through tall eucalyptus trees to a coastal vantage point with a picnic table and barbecue. Signage reminds visitors QUIET, TREES AT WORK and BAMBOO PICKING PERMIT REQUIRED. Awapuhi, or Hawaiian shampoo ginger, sends up fragrant shoots along the trail.

❹ **Puahokamoa Stream.** About a mile farther, near mile marker 11, you can stop at the bridge over Puahokamoa Stream. This is one of many bridges you cross en route from Pā'ia to Hāna. It spans pools and waterfalls. Picnic tables are available, but there are no restrooms.

❺ **Kaumahina State Wayside Park.** If you'd rather stretch your legs and use a flush toilet, continue another mile to Kaumahina State Wayside Park (at mile marker 12). The park has a picnic area, restrooms, and a lovely overlook to the Ke'anae Peninsula. Hardier souls can camp here, with a permit. The park is open from 8 AM to 4 PM and admission is free. ☎ 808/984–8109.

⏲ | **TIMING TIPS**

With short stops, the drive from Pā'ia to Hāna should take you between two and three hours one way. Lunching in Hāna, hiking, and swimming can easily turn the round-trip into a full-day outing. Since there's so much scenery to take in, we recommend staying overnight in Hāna. It's worth taking time to enjoy the waterfalls and beaches without being in a hurry. Try to plan your trip for a day that promises fair, sunny weather—though the drive can be even more beautiful when it's raining. ■ TIP→ If you decide to spend a night or two in Hāna, you may want to check any valuable luggage with the valet at your previous hotel. That way, you won't have to leave it in your car unattended when you stop to see the sights on your way to Hāna.

Ke'anae Peninsula

Near mile marker 14, before Ke'anae, you find yourself driving along a cliff side down into deep, lush Honomanū Bay, an enormous valley, with a rocky black-sand beach.

The Honomanū Valley was carved by erosion during Haleakalā's first dormant period. At the canyon's head there are 3,000-foot cliffs and a 1,000-foot waterfall, but don't try to reach them. There's not much of a trail, and what does exist is practically impassable.

6 Ke'anae Arboretum. Another 4 mi brings you to mile marker 17 and the Ke'anae Arboretum where you can add to your botanical education or enjoy a challenging hike into a forest. Signs help you learn the names of the many plants and trees now considered native to Hawai'i. The meandering Pi'ina'au Stream adds a graceful touch to the arboretum and provides a swimming pond.

You can take a fairly rigorous hike from the arboretum if you can find the trail at one side of the large taro patch. Be careful not to lose the trail once you're on it. A lovely forest waits at the end of the 25-minute hike. Access to the arboretum is free.

7 Ke'anae Overlook. A half mile farther down Hāna Highway you can stop at the Ke'anae Overlook. From this obser-

vation point, you can take in the patchwork-quilt effect the taro farms create below. The people of Ke'anae are working hard to revive this Hawaiian agricultural art and the traditional cultural values that the crop represents. The ocean provides a dramatic backdrop for the farms. In the other direction there are awesome views of Haleakalā through the foliage. This is a great spot for photos.

■ TIP→ Coming up is the halfway mark to Hāna. If you've had enough scenery, this is as good a time as any to turn around and head back to civilization.

8 Wailua Overlook. Between mile markers 20 and 21 you find Wailua Overlook. From the parking lot you can see Wailua Canyon, but you have to walk up steps to get a view

Taro Farm viewed from Hāna Highway

of Wailua Village. The landmark in Wailua Village is a church made of coral, built in 1860. Once called St. Gabriel's Catholic Church, the current Our Lady of Fatima Shrine has an interesting legend surrounding it. As the story goes, a storm washed enough coral up onto shore to build the church and then took any extra coral back to sea.

9 Waikāni Falls. After another ½ mi, past mile marker 21, you hit the best falls on the entire drive to Hāna, Waikāni Falls. Though not necessarily bigger or taller than the other falls, these are the most dramatic falls you'll find in East Maui. That's partly because the water is not diverted for sugar irrigation; the taro farmers in Wailua need all the runoff. This is a particularly good spot for photos.

10 Nahiku. At about mile marker 25 you see a road that heads down toward the ocean and the village of Nahiku. In ancient times this was a busy settlement with hundreds of residents. Now only about 80 people live in Nahiku, mostly native Hawaiians and some back-to-the-land types. A rubber grower planted trees here in the early 1900s, but the experiment didn't work out, and Nahiku was essentially abandoned. The road ends at the sea in a pretty landing. This is the rainiest, densest part of the East Maui rain forest.

Coffee Break. Back on the Hāna Highway, about 10 minutes before Hāna town, you can stop for—of all things—espresso. The tiny, colorful **Nahiku Ti Gallery and Coffee Shop** (between mile markers 27 and 28) sells local coffee, dried fruits and candies, and delicious (if pricey) banana bread. Sometimes the barbecue is fired up and you can try fish skewers or baked breadfruit (an island favorite nearly impossible to find elsewhere). The Ti Gallery sells Hawaiian crafts.

11 Ka'eleku Caverns. If you're interested in exploring underground turn left onto 'Ula'ino Road, just after mile marker 31, and follow the signs to Ka'eleku Caverns. **Maui Cave Adventures** leads amateur spelunkers into a system of gigantic lava tubes, accentuated by colorful underworld formations.

Monday through Thursday, from 10:30 to 3:30, you can take a self-guided, 30- to 45-minute tour for $11.95 per person. Friday and Saturday, choose either the 75-minute walking tour (at 11:15 AM; $29 per person) or the 2½-hour adventure tour (at 1:15 PM; $79 per person). Gear—gloves, flashlight, and hard hat—is provided, and visitors must be at least six years of age (15 years of age for the adventure tour). Call ahead to reserve a spot on the guided tours. ☎ 808/248–7308 ⊕ www.mauicave.com.

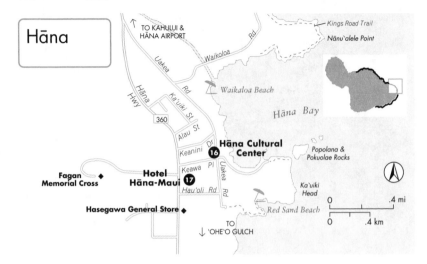

Hāna

TO KAHULUI &
HĀNA AIRPORT

Kings Road Trail

Nānu`alele Point

Waikoloa Rd

Uakea Rd

Waikaloa Beach

Hāna Hwy

Ka`uiki St

360

Hāna Bay

Alau St

Keanini Dr

Hāna Cultural
Center

16

Popolana &
Pokuolae Rocks

Keawa Pl

17

Uakea Rd

Fagan
Memorial Cross

Hotel
Hāna-Maui

Hau'oli Rd

Ka`uiki
Head

Hasegawa General Store

Red Sand Beach

TO
↓ 'OHE'O GULCH

0   .4 mi

0   .4 km

★ **⑫ Piʻilanihale Heiau.** Continue on ʻUlaʻino Road, which doubles back for a mile, loses its pavement, and even crosses a stream before reaching Kahanu Garden and Piʻilanihale Heiau, the largest prehistoric monument in Hawaiʻi. This temple platform was built for a great 16th-century Maui king named Piʻilani and his heirs. This king also supervised the construction of a 10-foot-wide road that completely encircled the island. (That's why his name is part of most of Maui's highway titles.)

Hawaiian families continue to maintain and protect this sacred site as they have for centuries, and they have not been eager to turn it into a tourist attraction. However, they now offer a brochure so you can tour the property yourself for $5 per person. Parties of four or more can reserve a guided tour, for $10 per person, by calling 48 hours in advance. Tours include the 122-acre **Kahanu Garden**, a federally funded research center focusing on the ethnobotany of the Pacific. The *heiau* and garden are open weekdays from 10 AM to 2 PM. ☎ 808/248–8912.

⑬ Hāna Airport. Back on the Hāna Highway, and less than ½ mi farther, is the turnoff for the Hāna Airport. Think of Amelia Earhart. Think of Waldo Pepper. If these picket-fence runways don't turn your thoughts to the derring-do of barnstorming pilots, you haven't seen enough old movies. Only the smallest planes can land and depart here, and when none of them happens to be around, the lonely wind sock is the only evidence that this is a working airfield. ☎ 808/248–8208.

★ **⑭ Waiʻanapanapa State Park.** Just beyond mile marker 32 you reach Waiʻanapanapa State Park, home to one of Maui's only volcanic-sand beaches and some freshwater caves for adventurous swimmers to explore. The park is right on the ocean, and it's a lovely spot to picnic, camp, hike, or swim. To the left you'll find the black-sand beach, picnic tables, and cave pools. To the right you'll find cabins and an ancient trail which snakes along the ocean past blowholes, sea arches, and archaeological sites.

The tide pools here turn red several times a year. Scientists say it's explained by the arrival of small shrimp, but legend claims the color represents the blood of Popoalaea, a princess said to have been murdered in one of the caves by her husband, Chief Kaakea. Whichever you choose to believe, the drama of the landscape itself—black sand, green beach vines, azure water—is bound to leave a lasting impression.

With a permit you can stay in state-run cabins here for less than $45 a night—the price varies depending on the number of people—but reserve early. They often book up a year in advance. ☎ 808/984–8109.

⓯ **Hāna.** By now the relaxed pace of life that Hāna residents enjoy should have you in its grasp, so you won't be discouraged to learn that town is little more than a gas station, a post office, and a ramshackle grocery.

Hāna, in many ways, is the heart of Maui. It's one of the few places where the slow pulse of island life is still strong. The town centers on its lovely circular bay, dominated on the right-hand shore by a pu'u called Ka'uiki. A short trail here leads to a cave, the birthplace of Queen Kā'ahumanu. This area is rich in Hawaiian history and legend. Two miles beyond town another pu'u presides over a loop road that passes two of Hāna's best beaches—Koki and Hāmoa. The hill is called Ka Iwi O Pele (Pele's Bone). Offshore here, at tiny 'Ālau Island, the demigod Maui supposedly fished up the Hawaiian islands.

Sugar was once the mainstay of Hāna's economy; the last plantation shut down in the '40s. In 1946 rancher Paul Fagan built the **Hotel Hāna-Maui** and stocked the surrounding pastureland with cattle. The cross you see on the hill above the hotel was put

there in memory of Fagan. Now it's the ranch and hotel that put food on most tables, though many families still farm, fish, and hunt as in the old days. Houses around town are decorated with glass balls and nets, which indicate a fisherman's lodging.

⓰ **Hāna Cultural Center Museum.** If you're determined to spend some time and money in Hāna after the long drive, a single turn off the highway onto Ukea Street, in the center of town, will take you to the Hāna Cultural Center Museum. Besides operating a well-stocked gift shop, it displays artifacts, quilts, a replica of an authentic *kauhale* (an ancient Hawaiian living complex, with thatch huts and food gardens), and other Hawaiiana. The knowledgeable staff can explain it all to you. ☎ 808/248–8622.

⓱ **Hotel Hāna-Maui.** With its surrounding ranch, the upscale hotel is the mainstay of Hāna's economy. It's pleasant to stroll around this beautifully rustic property. The library houses interesting, authentic Hawaiian artifacts. In the evening, while local musicians play in the casual lobby bar, their friends jump up to dance hula. The Sea Ranch cottages across the road, built to look like authentic plantation housing from the outside, are also part of the hotel. *See* Where to Stay *later in this chapter for more information.*

Hala Trees, Wai'anapanapa State Park

Hāna

Don't be suprised if the mile markers suddenly start descending as you head past Hāna. Technically, Hāna Highway (Route 360) ends at the Hāna Bay. The road that continues south is Pi'ilani Highway (Route 31)—though everyone still refers to it as the Hāna Highway.

⑱ Hāmoa Beach. Just outside Hāna, take a left on Haneo'o Loop to explore lovely Hāmoa. Indulge in swimming or bodysurfing at this beautiful salt-and-pepper beach. Picnic tables, restrooms, and showers beneath the idyllic shade of coconut trees offer a more than comfortable rest stop.

The road leading to Hāmoa also takes you to **Kōkī Beach**, where you can watch the Hāna surfers mastering the swells and strong currents, and the seabirds darting over **Ālau,** the palm-fringed islet off the coast. The swimming is safer at Hāmoa.

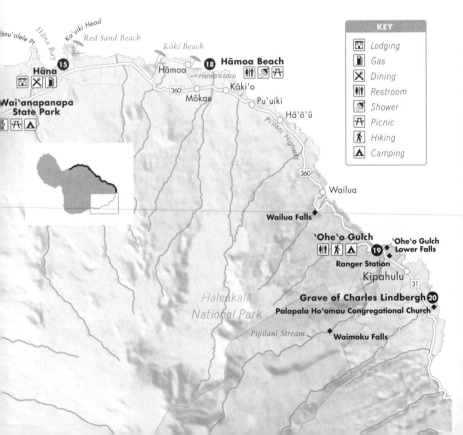

★ ⑲ **'Ohe'o Gulch.** Ten miles past town, at mile marker 42, you'll find the pools at 'Ohe'o Gulch. One branch of Haleakalā National Park runs down the mountain from the crater and reaches the sea here, where a basalt-lined stream cascades from one pool to the next. Some tour guides still call this area Seven Sacred Pools, but in truth there are more than seven, and they've never been considered sacred. You can park here—for a $10 fee—and walk to the lowest pools for a cool swim. The place gets crowded, since most people who drive the Hāna Highway make this their last stop.

If you enjoy hiking, go up the stream on the 2-mi hike to **Waimoku Falls.** The trail crosses a spectacular gorge, then turns into a boardwalk that takes you through an amazing bamboo forest. You can pitch a tent in the grassy campground down by the sea. *See* Hiking *later in this chapter for more information.*

⑳ **Grave of Charles Lindbergh.** Many people travel the mile past 'Ohe'o Gulch to see the Grave of Charles Lindbergh. You see a ruined sugar mill with a big chimney on the right side of the road and then, on the left, a rutted track leading to Pala-pala Ho'omau Congregational Church. The simple one-room church sits on a bluff over the sea, with the small graveyard on the ocean side. The world-renowned aviator chose to be buried here because he and his wife, writer Anne Morrow Lindbergh, spent a lot of time living in the area. He was buried here in 1974. Since this is a churchyard, be considerate and leave everything exactly as you found it. Next to the churchyard on the ocean side is a small county park, a good place for a peaceful picnic.

Kaupō Road. The road to Hāna continues all the way around Haleakalā's back side through 'Ulupalakua Ranch and into Kula. The desertlike area, with its grand vistas, is unlike anything else on the island, but the road itself is bad, some-

TROPICAL DELIGHTS

The drive to Hāna wouldn't be as enchanting without a stop or two at one of the countless fruit and flower stands alongside the highway. Every ½ mi or so a thatched hut tempts passersby with apple bananas, liliko'i (passion fruit), avocados, or starfruit just plucked from the tree. Leave 50¢ or $1 in the can for the folks who live off the land. Huge bouquets of tropical flowers are available for a handful of change, and some farms will ship.

times impassable in winter. Car-rental agencies call it off-limits to their passenger cars and there is no emergency assistance available. The danger and dust from increasing numbers of speeding jeep drivers are making life tough for the residents, especially in Kaupō, with its 4 mi of unpaved road. The small communities around East Maui cling tenuously to the old ways. Please keep them in mind if you do pass this way. If you can't resist the adventure, try to make the drive just before sunset. The light slanting across the mountain is incredible. At night, giant potholes, owls, and loose cattle can make for some difficult driving.

③⁹ Keōkea. More of a friendly gesture than a town, this tiny outpost is the last bit of civilization before Kula Highway becomes the winding backside road, heading east around to Hāna. A coffee tree pushes through the sunny deck at Grandma's Coffee Shop, the morning watering hole for Maui's cowboys who work at 'Ulupalakua or Kaupō ranch. Keōkea Gallery next door sells some of the most original artwork on the island. ■ TIP➔ The only restroom for miles is across the street at the public park, and the view makes stretching your legs worth it.

③⁷ Kula Botanical Gardens. This well-kept garden has assimilated itself naturally into its craggy 6-acre habitat. There are beautiful trees here, including native koa (prized by woodworkers)and *kukui* (the state tree, a symbol of enlightenment). There's also a good selection of proteas, the flowering shrubs that have become a signature flower crop of Upcountry Maui. A natural stream feeds into a koi pond, which is also home to a pair of African cranes. ✉ *638 Kekaulike Hwy., Kula* ☎ *808/878–1715* ✉ *$5* ☉ *Daily 9–4.*

④⁰ Tedeschi Vineyards and Winery. You can tour the winery and its historic grounds, the former Rose Ranch, and sample the island's only wines: a pleasant Maui Blush, Maui Champagne, and Tedeschi's annual Maui Nouveau. The top-seller, naturally, is the pineapple wine. The tasting room is a cottage built in the late 1800s for the frequent visits of King Kalākaua. The cottage also contains the **'Ulupalakua Ranch History Room,** which tells colorful stories of the ranch's owners, the *paniolo* tradition that developed here, and Maui's polo teams. The old General Store may look like a museum, but in fact it's an excellent pit stop. ✉ *Kula Hwy., 'Ulupalakua Ranch* ☎ *808/878–6058* ⊕ *www.mauiwine.com* ✉ *Free* ☉ *Daily 9–5, tours at 10:30 and 1:30.*

BEACHES

Updated by
Elaine Gast

Of all the Hawaiian islands, Maui's beaches are some of the most diverse. You'll find the pristine, palm-lined shores you expect with waters as clear and inviting as sea-green glass, but you'll also discover rich red- and black-sand beaches, craggy cliffs with surging whitecaps, and year-round sunsets that quiet the soul. As on the other isles, all Maui's beaches are public—but that doesn't mean it's not possible to find a secluded cove where you can truly get away from the world.

The island's leeward shores (the South Shore and West Side) have the calmest, sunniest beaches. Hit the beach early, when the aquamarine waters are as accommodating as bathwater. In summer, afternoon winds can be a sandblasting force, which can chase even the most dedicated sun worshippers away. From November through March, the South and West beaches are also great spots to watch the parade of whales that spend the winter in Maui's waters.

Windward shores (the North Shore and East Maui) offer more adventurous beachgoing. Beaches face the open ocean (rather than other islands) and tend to be rockier and more prone to powerful swells. This is particularly true in winter, when the legendary North Shore becomes a playground for experienced big-wave riders. Don't let this keep you

BEACH SAFETY

The ocean is an amazing but formidable playground. Conditions can change quickly throughout the day. Pay attention to any signs or flags warning of high surf, rough currents, or jellyfish. It's best to watch the surf for a while before entering. Notice where other people are swimming and how often swells come in. Swells arrive in sets of five or six. If you should get caught in a largish swell, don't panic. Take a deep breath and dive beneath each oncoming wave. When you feel comfortable, you can swim back to shore with the swell.

Remember the ocean is also home to an array of fragile marine life. Never stand on or touch coral reefs. Hefty fines apply to anyone who chases or grabs at turtles, dolphins, and other federally protected animals. It's wise to avoid swimming at dawn, dusk, or in murky waters.

away completely—some of the island's best beaches are those remote slivers of volcanic sand found on the wild windward shore.

West Maui

West Maui beaches are legendary for their glittering aquamarine waters banked by long stretches of golden sand. Reef fronts much of the western shore, making the underwater panorama something to behold. The beaches listed here start in the north at Kapalua and head south past Kāʻanapali and Lahaina. Note that there are a dozen roadside

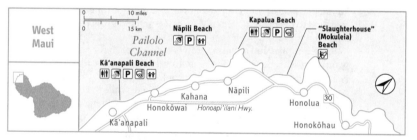

beaches to choose from on Route 30; those listed here are the ones we like best.

"Slaughterhouse" (Mokuleia) Beach. The island's northernmost beach is part of the Honolua-Mokuleia Marine Life Conservation District. "Slaughterhouse" is the surfers' nickname for what is officially Mokuleia. When the weather permits, this is a great place for bodysurfing and sunbathing. Concrete steps and a green railing help you get down the sheer cliff to the sand. The next bay over, Honolua, has no beach but offers one of the best surf breaks in Hawaiʻi. Often you can see competitions happening there; look for cars pulled

BEACHES KEY

🚻	*Restroom*
🚿	*Showers*
🏄	*Surfing*
🤿	*Snorkel/Scuba*
👫	*Good for kids*
🅿️	*Parking*

off the road and parked in the pineapple field. ⊠ *Mile marker 32 on Rte. 30 past Kapalua* ♿ *No facilities.*

Kapalua Beach. Kapalua was once named the world's nicest beach. Walk through the tunnel at the end of Kapalua Place and you'll see why—the beach fronts a pristine bay good for snorkeling, swimming, and general lazing. Located just north of Nāpili Bay, this lovely, sheltered shore often remains calm late into the afternoon, although there may be strong currents offshore. This area is quite popular and is bordered by the Kapalua Resort so don't expect to have the beach to yourself. ⊠ *From Rte. 30, turn onto Kapalua Pl., walk through tunnel* ♿ *Toilets, showers, parking lot.*

> ## THE SUN
>
> By far the biggest danger on the island is sunburn. The tropical sun is strong. Even at 9 AM, high SPF sunscreen—30 SPF or higher—is a must. Rash guards, those clingy-looking lycra swim shirts, offer the best protection. Before seeking shade under a coconut palm, be aware that winds can be strong enough to knock fruit off the trees and onto your head (go ahead and giggle but this really can and does happen).

★ ☺ **Nāpili Beach.** Surrounded by sleepy condos, this round bay is a turtle-filled pool lined with a sparkling white crescent of sand. Sunbathers love this beach. The shore break is steep but gentle and it's easy to keep an eye on kids here as the entire bay is visible from any point in the water. The beach is right outside the Nāpili Kai Beach Club, a popular little resort for honeymooners, only a few miles south of Kapalua. It's also a terrific sunset spot. ⊠ *5900 Lower Honoapi'ilani Hwy., look for Nāpili Pl. or Hui Dr.* ♿ *Showers, parking lot.*

☺ **Kā'anapali Beach.** Stretching from the Sheraton Maui at its northernmost point to the Hyatt Regency Maui at its southern tip, Kā'anapali Beach is lined with resorts, condominiums, restaurants, and shops. If you're looking for quiet and seclusion, this is not the beach for you. But if you want lots of action, lay out your towel here. Also called "Dig Me Beach," this is one of Maui's best people-watching spots: catamarans, windsurfers, and parasailers head out from here while the beautiful people take in the scenery. A cement pathway weaves along the length of this 3-mi-long beach, leading from one astounding resort to the next.

The drop-off from Kā'anapali's soft, sugary sand is steep, but waves hit the shore with barely a rippling slap. The area at the northernmost end (in front of the Sheraton Maui), known as Black Rock, has prime snorkeling. The fish and eels here are tame from hand-feeding, but be aware—they can still bite! ⊠ *Follow any of 3 Kā'anapali exits from Honoapi'ilani Hwy. and park at any hotel* ♿ *Toilets, showers, parking lot.*

Launiupoko State Wayside Park. Launiupoko is the beach park of all beach parks. Both a surf break and a beach, it offers a little something for everyone with its inviting stretch of lawn, soft white sand, and gentle waves. The shoreline reef creates a protected wading pool, perfect for small children. Outside the reef, beginner surfers will find good longboard rides. From the long sliver of beach (good for walking), you'll enjoy superb views of Neighbor Islands, and land side, of deep valleys jetting through the West Maui mountains. Because of its endless sunshine and serenity—not to mention its many amenities—Launiupoko draws a crowd on the weekends, but there's space for everyone (and overflow parking across the street). ⊠ *On Rte. 30, just south of Lahaina at mile marker 18* ♿ *Toilets, showers, picnic tables, grills/firepits.*

The South Shore

Sandy beach fronts nearly the entire southern coastline of Maui, from Kīhei at the northern end to Mākena at the southern tip. The farther south you go, the better the beaches get. Kīhei has excellent beach parks right in town, with white sand, showers, restrooms, picnic tables, and barbecues. Good snorkeling can be found along the beaches' rocky borders. As good as Kīhei is, Wailea is even better. Wailea's beaches are cleaner, facilities tidier, and views even more impressive. ■ TIP→ **Note that break-ins have been reported at many of these beach parking lots.** As you head out to Mākena, the terrain gets wilder. Bring lunch, water, and sunscreen with you. The following South Shore beaches are listed from north Kīhei southeast to Mākena.

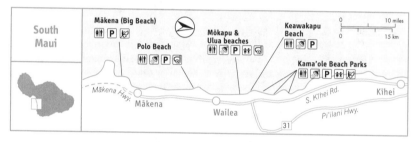

Kama'ole I, II, and III. Three steps from South Kīhei Road, you can find three golden stretches of sand separated by outcroppings of dark, jagged lava rocks. You can walk the length of all three beaches if you're willing to get your feet wet. The northernmost of the trio, Kama'ole I (across from the ABC Store, in case you forgot your sunscreen), offers perfect swimming with a sandy bottom a long way out and an active volleyball court. If you're one of those people who likes your beach sans the sand, there's also a great lawn for you to spread out on at the south end of the beach. Kama'ole II is nearly identical minus the lawn. The last beach, the one with all the people on it, is Kama'ole III, perfect for throwing disk or throwing down a blanket. This is a great family beach, complete with a playground, volleyball net, barbecues, kite flying, and frequently, rented inflatable castles—a birthday-party must for every cool kid living on the island.

Locally known as "Kam" I, II, and III, all three beaches have great swimming and lifeguards. In the morning the water can be as still as a lap pool. Kam III offers terrific breaks for beginning bodysurfers. ■ TIP→ **The public restrooms have seen better days; decent facilities are found at convenience stores and eateries across the street.** ⊠ *S. Kīhei Rd., between Ke Ali'i Alanui Rd. and Keonekai Rd.* ♿ *Lifeguard, toilets, showers, picnic tables, grills/firepits, playground, parking lot.*

Keawakapu Beach. Who wouldn't love Keawakapu with its long stretch of golden sand, near-perfect swimming, and stunning views of the crater? It's great fun to walk or jog this beach south into Wailea (you can go all the way to the Renaissance), as the path is lined with remarkable residences—can you guess which one belongs to Stephen King? The winds pick up in the afternoon, so beware of irritating sand storms. Keawakapu has two entrances: one at the Mana Kai Maui Resort (look for the blue "shoreline access" sign and the parking at Kilohana Street), and the second at the dead end of Kīhei Road. Toilets are portable. ⊠ *S. Kīhei Rd., at Kilohana St.* ⚒ *Toilets, showers, parking lot.*

Mōkapu & Ulua. Look for a little road and public parking lot wedged between the first two big Wailea resorts—the Renaissance and the Marriott. This gets you to Mōkapu and Ulua beaches. Though there are no lifeguards, families love this place. Reef formations create tons of tide pools for kids to explore and the beaches are protected from major swells. Snorkeling is excellent at Ulua, the beach to the left of the entrance. Mōkapu, to the right, tends to be less crowded. ⊠ *Wailea Alanui Dr., south of Renaissance resort entrance* ⚒ *Toilets, showers, parking lot.*

Polo Beach. From Wailea Beach you can walk to this small, uncrowded crescent fronting the Fairmont Kea Lani resort. Swimming and snorkeling are great here and it's a good place to whale-watch. As at Wailea Beach, private cabanas occupy prime sandy real estate, but there's plenty of room for you and your towel, and even a nice grass picnic area. The pathway connecting the two beaches is a great spot to jog or leisurely take in awesome views of nearby Molokini and Kahoʻolawe. Rare native plants grow along the ocean, or *makai*, side of the path; the honey-sweet smelling one is *naio*, or false sandalwood. ⊠ *Wailea Alanui Dr., south of Fairmont Kea Lani resort entrance* ⚒ *Toilets, showers, picnic tables, grills/firepits, parking lot.*

Fodor'sChoice
★

Mākena (Big Beach). Locals successfully fought to give Mākena—one of Hawaiʻi's most breathtaking beaches—state park protection. Also known as "Big Beach," this stretch of deep-golden sand abutting sparkling aqua water is 3,000 feet-long and 100-feet wide. It's never crowded, no matter how many cars cram into the lots. The water is fine for swimming, but use caution. ■ TIP➡ **The shore dropoff is steep and swells can get deceptively big.** Despite the infamous "Mākena cloud," a blanket that rolls in during the early afternoon and obscures the sun, it rarely rains here. For a dramatic view of Big Beach, climb Puʻu Ōlaʻi, the steep cinder cone near the first entrance. Continue over the cinder cone's side to discover "Little Beach"—clothing-optional by popular practice. (Officially, nude sunbathing is illegal in Hawaiʻi.) On Sunday, free spirits of all kinds crowd Little Beach's tiny shoreline for a drumming circle and bonfire. Little Beach has the island's best bodysurfing (no pun intended). Skim boarders catch air at Big Beach's third entrance. Each of the three paved entrances has portable toilets. ⊠ *Off Wailea Alanui Dr.* ⚒ *Toilets, parking lot.*

The North Shore

Many of the folks you see jaywalking in Pāʻia sold everything they owned to come to Maui and live a beach bum's life. Beach culture abounds on the North Shore. But these folks aren't sunbathers, they're big-wave riders, windsurfers, or kiteboarders. The North Shore is their challenging sports arena. Beaches here face the open ocean and tend to be rougher and windier than beaches elsewhere on Maui—but don't let that scare you off. On calm days, the reef-speckled waters are truly beautiful and offer a quieter and less commercial beach-going experience than the leeward shore. Beaches below are listed from Kahului (near the airport) eastward to Ho'okipa.

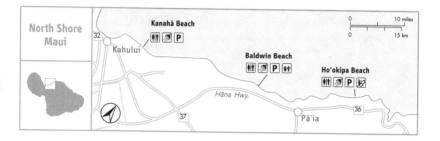

Kanahā Beach. Windsurfers, kiteboarders, joggers, and picnicking families like this long, golden strip of sand bordered by a wide grassy area with lots of shade. The winds pick up in the early afternoon, making for the best kiteboarding and windsurfing conditions—if you know what you're doing, that is. The best spot for watching kiteboarders is at the far left end of the beach. ⊠ *Drive through airport and make right onto car-rental road (Koeheke); turn right onto Amala Pl. and take any left (there are 3 entrances) into Kanahā* ⚲ *Toilets, showers, picnic tables, grills/firepits, parking lot.*

Baldwin Beach. A local favorite, just west of Pā'ia town, Baldwin Beach is a big body of comfortable white sand. This is a good place to stretch out, jog, or swim, though the waves can sometimes be choppy and the undertow strong. Don't be afraid of those big brown blobs floating beneath the surface, they're just pieces of alien seaweed awash in the surf. You can find shade along the beach beneath the ironwood trees, or in the large pavilion, a spot regularly overtaken by local parties and community events.

The long, shallow pool at the Kahului end of the beach is known as "Baby Beach." Separated from the surf by a flat reef wall, this is where ocean-loving families bring their kids (and sometimes puppies) to practice a few laps. The view of the West Maui Mountains is hauntingly beautiful from here. ⊠ *Hāna Hwy., 1 mi west of Baldwin Ave.* ⚲ *Lifeguard, toilets, showers, picnic tables, grills/firepits, parking lot.*

Ho'okipa Beach. If you want to see some of the world's finest windsurfers in action, hit this beach along Hāna Highway. The sport was largely developed right at Ho'okipa and has become an art and a career to some. This beach is also one of Maui's hottest surfing spots, with waves as high as 20 feet. This is not a good swimming beach, nor the place to go windsurfing unless you're an expert, but plenty of picnic tables and barbecues are available for hanging out and watching the pros. Bust out your telephoto lens at the cliff-side lookout. ⊠ *2 mi past Pāʻia on Rte. 36* ♿ *Toilets, showers, picnic tables, grills/firepits, parking lot.*

East Maui

Hāna's beaches will literally stop you in your tracks, they're that beautiful. Black-and-red sands stand out against pewter skies and lush tropical foliage creates picture-perfect scenes, which seem too breathtaking to be real. Rough conditions often preclude swimming, but that doesn't mean you can't explore the shoreline. Beaches below are listed in order from the west end of Hāna town eastward.

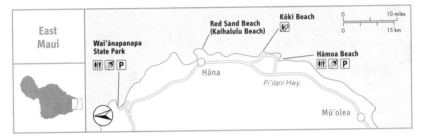

★ **Waiʻānapanapa State Park.** Small but rarely crowded, this beach will remain in your memory long after visiting. Fingers of white foam rush onto a black volcanic pebble beach fringed with green beach vines and palms. Swimming here is both relaxing and invigorating: strong currents bump smooth stones up against your ankles while seabirds flit above a black, jagged sea arch draped with vines. At the edge of the parking lot, a sign tells you the sad story of a doomed Hawaiian princess. Stairs lead through a tunnel of interlocking Polynesian *hau* branches to an icy cave pool—the secret hiding place of the ancient princess. ■ TIP➔ **You can swim in this pool, but be wary of mosquitoes!** In the other direction, a 3-mi, dramatic coastal path continues beyond the campground, past sea arches, blowholes, and cultural sites all the way to Hāna town. ⊠ *Hāna Hwy. near mile marker 32* ♿ *Toilets, showers, picnic tables, grills/ firepits, parking lot.*

Red Sand Beach (Kaihalulu Beach). Kaihalulu Beach, better known as Red Sand Beach, is unmatched in its raw and remote beauty. It's not simple to find but when you round the last corner of the trail and are confronted with the sight of it, your jaw is bound to drop. Earthy red cliffs tower above the deep-maroon sand beach and swimmers bob about in a turquoise blue lagoon formed by volcanic boulders just offshore (it's like floating around in a giant natural bathtub). It's worth spending a night in Hāna just to make sure you can get here early and have some time to enjoy it before anyone else shows up. ■ TIP➔ **Getting here is not easy and you have to pass through private property along the way–do so at your own risk.** You need to tread carefully up and around Kaʻuiki (the red cinder hill); the cliff-side cinder path is slippery and constantly eroding. Hiking is not recommended in shoes without traction, or in bad weather. By popular practice, clothing on the beach is optional.

> ✉ *At end of Uákea Rd. past baseball field. Park near community center, walk through grass lot to trail below cemetery* ⛭ *No facilities.*

Kōkī Beach. You can tell from the trucks parked every which way alongside the road that this is a favorite local surf spot. ■ TIP→ **Watch conditions before swimming or bodysurfing, because the riptides here can be mean.** Look for awesome views of the rugged coastline and a sea arch on the left end. *Iwa,* or white-throated frigate birds, dart like pterodactyls over Alau islet offshore. ✉ *Haneoʻo Loop Rd., 2 mi east of Hāna town* ⛭ *No facilities.*

Hāmoa Beach. Why did James Michener describe this stretch of salt-and-pepper sand as the most "South Pacific" beach he'd come across, even though it's located in the North Pacific? Maybe it was the perfect half-moon shape, speckled with the shade of palm trees. Perhaps he was intrigued by the jutting black coastline, often outlined by rain showers out at sea, or the pervasive lack of hurry he felt once settled in here. Whatever it was, many still feel the lure. The beach can be crowded but nonetheless relaxing. Expect to see a few chaise lounges and a guest-only picnic area set up by the Hotel Hāna-Maui. At times, the churning surf might intimidate beginning swimmers, but bodysurfing can be great here. ✉ *½ mi past Kōki Beach on Haneoʻo Loop Rd., 2 mi east of Hāna town* ⛭ *Toilets, showers, picnic tables, parking lot.*

WATER ACTIVITIES & TOURS

Updated by
Elaine Gast

Getting into (or onto) the water will be the highlight of your Maui trip. At Lahaina and Māʻalaea harbors you can board boats for snorkeling, scuba diving, deep-sea fishing, whale-watching, parasailing, and sunset cocktail adventures. You can learn to surf, catch a ferry to Lānaʻi, or grab a seat on a fast inflatable. Along the leeward coastline, from Kāʻanapali on the West Shore all the way down to the tip of ʻĀhihi-Kīnaʻu on the South Shore, you can discover great snorkeling and swimming. If you're a thrill-seeker, head out to the North Shore and Hoʻokipa, where surfers, kiteboarders, and windsurfers catch big waves and big air.

Boogie Boarding & Bodysurfing

Bodysurfing and "sponging" (as boogie boarding is called by the regulars) are great ways to catch some waves without having to master surfing—and there's no balance or coordination required. A boogie board (or "sponge") is softer than a hard, fiberglass surfboard, which means you can ride safely in the rough-and-tumble surf zone. If you get tossed around (which is half the fun), you don't have a heavy surfboard nearby to bang your head on, but you do have something to hang onto. Serious spongers invest in a single short-clipped fin to help propel them into the wave.

How to Catch a Wave

The technique for catching waves is the same with or without a board. Swim out to where the swell is just beginning to break, and position yourself toward shore. When the next wave comes, lie on your board (if you have one), kick like crazy, and catch it! You'll feel the push of the wave as you glide in front of the gurgling, foamy surf. When bodysurfing, put your arms over your head, bring your index fingers together (so you look like the letter 'A'), and stiffen your body like a board to achieve the same effect. If you don't like to swim too far out, stick with boogie boarding and bodysurfing close to shore. Shore break (if it isn't too steep) can be exhilarating to ride. You'll know it's too steep if you hear the sound of slapping when the waves hit the sand. You're looking for waves that curl over and break farther out, then roll, not slap onto the sand. Always watch first to make sure the conditions aren't too strong.

Best Spots

If you don't mind nudity (officially illegal, but practiced nonetheless), **Little Beach** (⊠ On Mākena Rd., first entrance to Mākena State Beach Park; climb rock wall at north end of beach) is the best break on the island for boogie boarding and bodysurfing. The shape of the sandy shoreline creates waves that break a ways out and tumble on into shore. Because it's sandy, you only risk stubbing a toe on the few submerged rocks, not a reef floor. Don't even think about boogie boarding at neighboring Big Beach—you'll be slapped like a flapjack onto the steep shore.

Kama'ole III (⊠ S. Kīhei Rd.) is another good spot for bodysurfing and boogie boarding. It has a sandy floor, with 1- to 3-foot waves breaking not too far out. It's often crowded late into the day, especially on weekends when local kids are out of school. Don't let that chase you away, the waves are wide enough for everyone.

On the North Shore, **Pāia Bay** (⊠ Just before Pāia town, beyond large community building and grass field) has waves suitable for spongers and bodysurfers. ■ TIP➜ **Park in the public lot across the street and leave your valuables at home, as this beach is known for break-ins.**

Equipment Rentals

Most condos and hotels have boogie boards available to guests—some in better condition than others (but beat-up boogies work just as well for beginners). You can also pick up a boogie board from any discount shop, such as Kmart or Long's Drugs, for upward of $30.

Auntie Snorkel. You can rent decent boogie boards here for $5 a day, or $15 a week. ⊠ 2439 S. Kīhei Rd., Kīhei ☎ 808/879–6263.

Honolua Surf. "Waverider" boogie boards with smooth undersides (better than the bumpy kind) can be rented from this surf shop for $8 a day, or $35 a week (with a $100 deposit). ⊠ 2411 S. Kīhei Rd., Kīhei ☎ 808/874–0999 ⊠ 845 Front St., Lahaina ☎ 808/661–8848.

Deep-Sea Fishing

If fishing is your sport, Maui is your island. In these waters you'll find 'ahi, *aku* (skipjack tuna), barracuda, bonefish, *kawakawa* (bonito), mahimahi, Pacific blue marlin, ono, and *ulua* (jack crevalle). You can fish year-round and you don't need a license. ■ TIP➜ **Because boats fill up fast during busy seasons (Christmas, spring break, tournament weeks), consider booking reservations before coming to Maui.**

Plenty of fishing boats run out of Lahaina and Māʻalaea harbors. If you charter a private boat, expect to spend in the neighborhood of $600 to $800 for a thrilling half day in the swivel seat. You can share a boat for much less if you don't mind close quarters with a stranger who may get seasick, drunk, or worse . . . lucky! Before you sign up, you should know that some boats keep the catch. They will, however, fillet a nice piece for you to take home. And if you catch a real beauty, you might even be able to have it professionally mounted.

■ TIP→ **Don't go out with a boater who charges for the fish you catch—that's harbor robbery.** You're expected to bring your own lunch and nonglass beverages. (Shop the night before, it's hard to find snacks at 6 AM.) Boats supply coolers, ice, and bait. 10%–20% tips are suggested.

Boats & Charters

★ **Finest Kind Inc.** A record 1,118-pound blue marlin was reeled in by the crew aboard *Finest Kind,* a lovely 37-foot Merritt kept so clean you'd never guess the action it's seen. Ask Captain Dave about his pet frigate bird—he's been around these waters long enough to befriend other expert fishers. This family-run company operates four boats and specializes in live bait. ✉ *Lahaina Harbor, Slip 7* ☎ *808/661–0338* ⊕ *www.finestkindsportfishing.com.*

Iwa Lele Extreme Sportfishing. If you're serious about catching fish, and don't mind the 4:30 AM check-in time, this trip's for you. On a 39-foot custom Force, Captain Fuzzy will get you to the best fishing spots before the masses. You'll troll with lures and live bait—and hopefully, catch the big one. Check out their Web site for good fishing FAQs. ✉ *Lahaina Harbor* ☎ *808/661–1118* ⊕ *www.fishmaui.com.*

Strikezone. This is the only charter that offers morning bottom-fishing trips (for smaller fish such as snapper), as well as deep-sea trips (for the big ones—ono, āhi, mahimahi, and marlin). Strikezone is a 43-foot Delta that offers plenty of room (16-person max). Lunch and soft drinks are included, and on bottom-fishing trips you can keep your catch. The cost is $150 per person for a pole; spectators can ride for $75. The six-hour bottom-fishing trip runs Monday, Wednesday, Friday, and Saturday; the six-hour deep-sea trips run Tuesday, Thursday, and Sunday. All trips leave at 6:30 AM. ✉ *Māʻalaea Harbor, Slip 64, Māʻalaea* ☎ *808/ 879–4485.*

Kayaking

Kayaking is a fantastic way to experience Maui's coast up close. Floating aboard a plastic popsicle stick is easier than you might think, and allows you to cruise out to vibrant, living coral reefs and waters where dolphins and even whales roam. Kayaking can be a leisurely paddle or a challenge of heroic proportion, depending on your ability, the location, and the weather. ■ TIP→ **You can rent kayaks independently, but we recommend taking a guide.** An apparently calm surface can hide extremely strong ocean currents—and you don't *really* want to take an unplanned trip to Tahiti! Most guides are naturalists who will steer you away from surging surf, lead you to pristine reefs, and point out camouflaged fish, like the stalking hawkfish. Not having to schlep your gear on top of your rental car is a bonus. A half-day tour runs around $75. Custom tours can be arranged.

If you decide to strike out on your own, tour companies will rent kayaks for the day with paddles, life vests, and roof racks, and many will meet you near your chosen location. Ask for a map of good entries and plan to avoid paddling back to shore against the wind (schedule extra time for the return trip regardless). When you're ready to snorkel, secure your belongings in a dry pack onboard and drag your boat by its bowline behind you. (This isn't as bad as it sounds).

Best Spots

On the West Side, past the steep cliffs on the Honoapiilani Highway and before you hit Lahaina, there's a long stretch of inviting coastline, including **Ukumehame** and **Olowalu** beaches (⊠ Between mile markers 12 and 14 on Rte. 30). This is a good spot for beginners; entry is easy and there's much to see in every direction. If you want to snorkel, the best visibility is farther out at Olowalu, at about 25 feet depth. ■ TIP→ Watch for sharp *kiawe* thorns buried in the sand on the way into the water.

Mākena Landing (⊠ Off Mākena Rd.) is an excellent taking-off point for a South Maui adventure. Enter from the paved parking lot or the small sandy beach a little south. The bay itself is virtually empty, but the right edge is flanked with brilliant coral heads and juvenile turtles. If you round the point on the right, you come across **Five Caves**, a system of enticing underwater arches. In the morning you may see dolphins, and the arches are havens for lobsters, eels, and spectacularly hued butterfly fish. Check out the million-dollar mansions lining the shoreline and guess which celebrity lives where.

Equipment Rentals & Tours

Maui Sea Kayaking. Since 1988, this company has been guiding small groups (four-person trips) to secret spots along Maui's coast. They take great care in customizing their outings. For example, the guides accommodate kayakers with disabilities as well as senior kayakers, and they also offer kid-size gear. Among their more unusual programs are kayak surfing and wedding-vow renewal. Trips leave from various locations, depending upon the weather. ☎ 808/572–6299 ⊕ *www.maui.net/~kayaking.*

OUTRIGGER-CANOE RACES

Polynesians first traveled to Hawai'i by outrigger canoe, and racing the traditional craft is favorite pastime on the Islands. Canoes were revered in old Hawai'i, and no voyage could begin without a blessing, ceremonial chanting, and a hula performance to ensure a safe journey. In Lahaina in mid-May, the two-week **Festival of Canoes** (☎ 808/667–9193 ⊕ www.visitlahaina.com) includes a torch-lighting and awa-drinking ceremony, arts-and-crafts demonstrations, a chance for international canoe enthusiasts to mingle and observe how Polynesian vessels are rigged, and the launching of a "Parade of Canoes."

FodorsChoice **South Pacific Kayaks.** These guys pi-
★ oneered recreational kayaking on
Maui—they know their stuff. Guides
are friendly, informative, and eager
to help you get the most out of your
experience; we're talking true, fun-
loving, kayak geeks. Some activity
companies show a strange lack of
care for the marine environment;
South Pacific stands out as adventurous *and* responsible. They offer a
variety of trips leaving from both West Side and South Shore locations,
including an advanced four-hour "Molokini Challenge." ☎ 800/776–
2326 or 808/875–4848 ⊕ *www.southpacifickayaks.com.*

> **TAKE NOTE**
>
> The ʻĀhihi-Kīnaʻu Natural Area Reserve at the southernmost point of
> South Maui is closed to commercial
> traffic and you may not take rented
> kayaks into the reserve.

Kiteboarding

Catapulting up to 40 feet in the air above the breaking surf, kiteboarders hardly seem of this world. Silken kites hold the athletes aloft for precious seconds—long enough for the execution of mind-boggling
tricks—then deposit them back in the sea. This new sport is not for the
weak-kneed. No matter what people might tell you, it's harder to learn
than windsurfing. The unskilled (or unlucky) can be caught in an up-
wind and carried far out in the ocean, or worse—dropped smack on the
shore. Because of insurance (or the lack thereof), companies are not allowed to rent equipment. Beginners must take lessons, and then purchase their own gear. Devotees swear after your first few lessons,
committing to buying your kite is easy.

Aqua Sports Maui. "To air is human," or so they say at Aqua Sports, which
calls itself the local favorite of kiteboarding schools. They've got a great
location right near Kite Beach, at the west (left) end of Kanaha Beach,
and offer basic through advanced kiteboarding lessons. Rates start at
$210 for a three-hour basics course taught by certified instructors.
⊠ *90 Amala Pl., near Kite Beach, Kahului* ☎ *808/242–8015* ⊕ *www.
mauikiteboardinglessons.com.*

Hawaiian Sailboarding Techniques. Pro kiteboarder Alan Cadiz will have
you safely ripping in no time over at Naish Beach, (¼ mi past the bridge
on Amala Place, just past Kaʻa Point). A "Learn to Kitesurf" package
starts at $225 for a three-hour private lesson, all equipment included.
HST is in the highly regarded Hi Tech Surf & Sports store, located in
the Triangle Square shopping center. ⊠ *425 Koloa St., Kahului* ☎ *808/
871–5423* ⊕ *www.hstwindsurfing.com.*

Parasailing

Parasailing is an easy, exhilarating way to earn your wings: just strap
on a harness attached to a parachute, and a powerboat pulls you up and
over the ocean from a launching dock or a boat's platform. ■ TIP➔ **Keep
in mind, parasailing is limited to Maui's West Side, and "thrill craft"—including parasails—are prohibited in Maui waters during humpback whale calving
season, December 15 to April 15.**

West Maui Parasail. Launch 400 feet above the ocean for a bird's eye view of Lahaina, or be daring at 800 feet for smoother rides and better views. The captain will be glad to let you experience a "toe dip" or "freefall" if you request it. For safety reasons, passengers weighing less than 100 pounds must be strapped together in tandem. Hour-long trips departing from Lahaina Harbor, Slip #15, include 10-minute flights and run from $53 to $60. Early-bird (8–9 AM) flights are cheapest. ☎ 808/661–4060 ⊕ www.maui.net/~parasail.

Rafting

The high-speed, inflatable rafts you find on Maui are nothing like the raft that Huck Finn used to drift down the Mississippi. While passengers grip straps, these rafts fly, skimming and bouncing across the sea. Because they're so maneuverable, they go where the big boats can't— secret coves, sea caves, and remote beaches. Two-hour trips run around $50, half-day trips upward of $100. ■ TIP→ **Although safe, these trips are not for the faint of heart. If you have back or neck problems or are pregnant, you should reconsider this activity.**

Blue Water Rafting. One of the only ways to get to the stunning Kenaio coast (the roadless southern coastline beyond ʻĀhihi-Kīnaʻu), this rafting tour begins trips conveniently at the Kīhei Boat ramp. Dolphins, turtles, and other marine life are the highlight of this adventure, along with sea caves, lava arches, and views of Haleakalā. Two-hour trips start at $45; longer trips cost $90 to $115 and include a deli lunch. ✉ 7777 South Kīhei Rd., Kīhei ☎ 808/879–7238 ⊕ www.bluewaterrafting.com.

Ocean Riders. This West Side tour crosses the ʻAuʻAu channel to Lānaʻi's Shipwreck Beach, then circles the island for 70 minutes of remote coast. For snorkeling, the "back side" of Lānaʻi is one of Hawaiʻi's unsung marvels. Tours depart from Mala Wharf, at the northern end of Front Street and include snorkle gear, a fruit breakfast, and a deli lunch. ✉ Lahaina ☎ 808/661–3586 ⊕ www.mauioceanriders.com.

Sailing

With the islands of Molokaʻi, Lānaʻi, Kahoʻolawe, and Molokini a stone's throw away, Maui waters offer visually arresting backdrops for sailing adventures. Sailing conditions can be fickle, so some operations throw in snorkeling or whale-watching, and others offer sunset cruises. Winds are consistent in summer, but variable in winter, and afternoons are generally windier all throughout the year. Prices range from around $35 for two-hour trips to $75 for half-day excursions. ■ TIP→ **You won't be sheltered from the elements on the trim racing boats, so be sure to bring a hat (one that won't blow away), a light jacket or cover-up, sunglasses and extra sunscreen.**

Boats & Charters

America II. This one-time America's Cup contender offers an exciting, intimate alternative to crowded catamarans. For fast action, try a tradewind sail. Sunset sails are generally calmer—a good choice if you don't want to spend two hours fully exposed to the sun. Plan to bring a change of clothes, because you will get wet. ⊠ *Harbor Slip #5, Lahaina* ☎ *808/667–2195.*

Paragon. If you want to snorkel and sail, this is your boat. Many snorkel cruises claim to sail but actually motor most of the way; Paragon is an exception. Both Paragon vessels (one catamaran in Lahaina, the other in Māʻalaea) are ship-shape, and crews are competent and friendly. Their mooring in Molokini Crater is particularly good, and they often stay after the masses have left. The Lānaʻi trip includes a picnic lunch on the beach, snorkeling, and an afternoon blue water swim. Extras on their trips to Lānaʻi include mai tais and sodas, hot and cold pūpūs, champagne. ⊠ *Lahaina and Māʻalaea Harbors* ☎ *808/244–2087* ⊕ *www. sailmaui.com.*

Scotch Mist Charters. Follow the wind aboard this 50-foot Santa Cruz sailing yacht. Two-hour snorkeling, sunset, or whale-watching trips focus on the sail, and usually carry less than 25 passengers. ⊠ *Lahaina Harbor Slip #2* ☎ *877/464–6284 or 808/661–0386* ⊕ *www. scotchmistsailingcharters.com.*

Scuba Diving

Maui is just as scenic underwater as it is on dry land. It's common to see huge sea turtles, eagle rays, and small reef sharks, not to mention many varieties of angelfish, parrotfish, eels, and octopi. Unlike other popular dive destinations, most of the species are unique to this area. For example, of Maui's 450 species of reef fish, 25% are endemic to the island. Dives are best in the morning, when visibility can hold a steady 100 feet. If you're a certified diver, you can rent gear at any Maui dive shop simply by showing your PADI or NAUI card. If you're not certified, hook up with a dive shop for an introductory underwater tour ($100–$160). Tours include tanks and weights. ■ TIP➜ Before signing on with any of these outfitters, it's a good idea to ask a few pointed questions about your guide's experience, the weather outlook, and the condition of the equipment.

Best Spots

Honolua Bay (⊠ Between mile markers 32 and 33 on Rte. 30, look for narrow dirt road to left) has beach entry. This West Maui marine preserve is alive with many varieties of coral and tame tropical fish, including large *ulua, kāhala,* barracuda, and manta rays. With depths of 20 to 50 feet, this is a popular summer dive spot, good for all levels. ■ TIP➜ High surf often prohibits winter dives.

Only 3 mi offshore, **Molokini Crater** is world renowned for its deep, crystal-clear, fish-filled waters. A crescent-shape islet formed by the eroding top of a volcano, the crater is a marine preserve ranging 10 to 80 feet in depth. The numerous tame fish and brilliant coral dwelling within the crater make it a popular introductory dive site. On calm days, exploring the back side of Molokini (called Back Wall) can be a dramatic sight for advanced divers—giving them visibility of up to 150 feet. The enormous dropoff into the ʻAlalākeiki Channel (to 350 feet) offers

Diving 101

IF YOU'VE ALWAYS WANTED GILLS, Hawai'i is a good place to get them. Although the bulky, heavy equipment seems freakish on shore, underwater it allows you to move about freely, almost weightlessly. As you descend into another world, you slowly grow used to the sound of your own breathing and the strangeness of being able to do so 30-plus feet down.

Most resorts offer introductory dive lessons in their pools, which allow you to acclimate to the awkward breathing apparatus before venturing out into the great blue. If you aren't starting from a resort pool, no worries. Most intro dives take off from calm, sandy beaches, such as Ulua or Kā'anapali. If you're bitten by the deep-sea bug and want to continue diving, you should get certified. Only certified divers can rent equipment or go on more adventurous dives, such as night dives, open-ocean dives, and cave dives.

There are several certification companies, including PADI, NAUI, and SSI. PADI, the largest, is the most comprehensive. Once you begin your certification process, stick with the same company. The dives you log will not apply to another company's certification. (Dives with a PADI instructor, for instance, will not count toward SSI certification). Remember that you will not be able to fly or go to the airy summit of Haleakalā within 24 hours of diving. Open Water certification will take three to four days and cost around $300. From that point on, the sky . . . or rather, the sea's the limit!

---

awesome seascapes, black coral, and chance sightings of larger pelagic fish and sharks.

On the South side, a popular dive spot is **Mākena Landing,** also called **Five Graves** or **Five Caves.** About 7/10 mi down Mākena Road, you'll feast on underwater delights—caves, ledges, coral heads, and an outer reef home to a large green sea turtle colony (called "Turtle Town"). ■ TIP➔ Entry is rocky lava, so be careful where you step. This area is for the more experienced diver. Rookies can enter farther down Mākena Road at Mākena Landing, and dive to the right.

Equipment Rental & Dive Tours

★ **Ed Robinson's Diving Adventures.** Ed wrote the book, literally, on Molokini. Because he knows so much, he includes a "Biology 101" talk with every dive. An expert marine photographer, he offers diving instruction and boat charters to South Maui, the back side of Molokini, and Lāna'i. Weekly night dives are available, and there's a 10% discount if you book three or more days. Check out the Web site for good info and links on scuba sites, weather, and sea conditions. ⊠ *50 Koki St., Kīhei* ☎ *808/879–3584 or 800/635–1273* ⊕ *www.mauiscuba.com.*

Maui Dive Shop. With six locations island-wide, Maui Dive Shop offers scuba charters, diving instruction, and equipment rental. Excursions, offering awe-inspiring beach and boat dives, go to Molokini Back Wall (most advanced dive), Shipwreck Beach on Lāna'i, and more. Night dives and customized trips are available, as are full SSI and PADI certificate programs. ✉ *1455 S. Kīhei Rd., Kīhei* ☎ *808/879–3388 or 800/542–3483* ⊕ *www.mauidiveshop.com.*

Shaka Divers. Shaka provides personalized dives including a great four-hour intro dive ($79), a refresher course ($79), scuba certification ($350), and shore dives ($49) to Mākena, Ulua, Five Graves (at Mākena Landing), Turtle Town, Bubble Cave, Black Sand Beach, and more. Typical dives last about an hour, with 30 to 45 feet visibility. Dives can be booked on short notice, with afternoon tours available (hard to find on Maui). Shaka also offers night dives, torpedo scooter dives, and "bug hunt" expeditions (lobster hunts). Look for the Scuba Bus, blowing bubbles as it drives down the road. ✉ *24 Hakoi Pl., Kīhei* ☎ *808/250–1234* ⊕ *www.shakadivers.com.*

> **OCEAN ETIQUETTE**
>
> "Look, don't touch," is a good motto in the ocean where many creatures don't mind company, but may reveal hidden stingers if threatened. One more warning: never stand or bump against coral. Touching it—even briefly—can kill the delicate creatures residing within the hard shell.

Snorkeling

No one should leave Maui without ducking underwater to meet a sea turtle, moray eel, or Humuhumunukunukuāpuáa—the state fish. Visibility is best in the morning, before the wind picks up.

There are two ways to approach snorkeling—by land or by sea. Daily around 7 AM, a parade of boats heads out to Lāna'i or Molokini Crater, that ancient cone of volanic cinder off the coast of Wailea. Boat trips offer some advantages—deeper water, seasonal whale-watching, crew assistance, lunch, and gear. But you don't need a boat; much of Maui's best snorkeling is found just steps from the road. Nearly the entire leeward coastline from Kapalua south to 'Āhihi-Kīna'u offers prime opportunities to ogle fish and turtles. If you're patient and sharp-eyed, you may glimpse eels, octopi, lobsters, eagle rays, and even a rare shark or monk seal.

Best Spots

Snorkel sites here are listed from north to south, starting at the northwest corner of the island.

On the west side of the island, just past Kapalua, **Honolua Bay** Marine Life Conservation District (✉ Between mile markers 32 and 33 on Rte. 30, dirt road to left), has a superb reef for snorkeling. When conditions are calm, it's one of the island's best spots with tons of fish and colorful corals to observe. ■ TIP➔ **Make sure to bring a fish key with you here, as you're sure to see many species of triggerfish, filefish, and wrasses.** The coral formations on the right side of the bay are particularly dramatic and feature pink, aqua, and orange varieties. Take care entering the water, there's no beach here and the rocks and concrete ramp can be slippery.

The northeast corner of this windward-facing bay periodically gets hammered by big waves in winter and high-profile surf contests are held here. Avoid the bay then, and after a heavy rain (you'll know because Honolua stream will be running across the access path).

Just minutes south of Honolua, dependable **Kapalua Bay** (⊠ From Rte. 30, turn onto Kapalua Pl., and walk through tunnel) beckons. As beautiful above the water as it is below, Kapalua is exceptionally calm, even when other spots get testy. Needle and butterfly fish dart just past the sandy beach, which is why it's sometimes crowded. ■ TIP→ **Sand can be particularly hot here, watch your toes!**

Fodor's Choice We think **Black Rock** (⊠ In front of Kāʻanapali Sheraton Maui, Kāʻana-
★ pali Pkwy.), at the northernmost tip of Kāʻanapali Beach, is tops for snorkelers of any skill. The entry couldn't be easier—dump your towel on the sand in front of the Sheraton Maui resort and in you go. Beginners can stick close to shore and still see lots of action. Advanced snorkelers can swim beyond the sand to the tip of Black Rock, or Kekaʻa Point, to see larger fish and eagle rays. One of the underwater residents, a turtle named "Volkswagen" for its hefty size, can be found here. He sits very still; you must look closely. Equipment can be rented on-site. Parking, in a small lot adjoining the hotel, is the only hassle.

Along Honoapiʻilani Highway (Route 30) there are several favorite snorkel sites including the area just out from the cemetery at **Hanakaoʻo Beach Park** (⊠ Near mile marker 23 on Rte. 30). At depths of 5 and 10 feet, you can see a variety of corals, especially as you head south toward **Waihikuli Wayside Park.** Farther down the highway, the shallow coral reef at **Olowalu** (⊠ South of Olowalu General Store on Rte. 30, at mile marker 14) is good for a quick underwater tour, though the best spot is a ways out, at depths of 25 feet or more. Closer to shore, the visibility can be hit or miss, but if you're willing to venture out about 50 yards, you'll have easy access to an expansive coral reef with abundant fish life—no boat required. Swim offshore toward the pole sticking out of the reef. Except for during a South swell, this area is calm and good for families with small children; turtles are plentiful.

Excellent snorkeling is found down the coastline between Kīhei and Mākena. The best spots are along the rocky fringes of Wailea's **Mōkapu, Ulua, Wailea,** and **Polo** beaches (⊠ Off Wailea Alanui Rd.). Find one of the public parking lots sandwiched between Wailea's luxury resorts, and enjoy these beaches' sandy entries, calm waters with relatively good visibility, and variety of fish species. Of the four beaches, Ulua has the best reef. You can glimpse a box-shape pufferfish here, and listen to snapping shrimp and parrot fish nibbling on coral.

At the very southernmost tip of paved road in South Maui lies **ʻĀhihi-Kīnaʻu** Natural Area Reserve (⊠ Just before end of Mākena Alanui Rd., follow marked trails through trees), also referred to as La Pérouse Bay. Despite its barren, lava-scorched landscape, the area recently gained such popularity with adventurers and activity purveyors that it had to be closed to commercial traffic. A ranger is stationed at the parking lot to assist visitors. It's difficult terrain and sometimes crowded, but if you make use of the rangers' suggestions (stay on marked paths, wear sturdy shoes to hike in and out), you can experience some of the reserve's out-

standing treasures, such as the sheltered cove known as the "fishpond."
■ TIP➔ Be sure to bring water, this is a hot and unforgiving wilderness.

Snorkel Cruises

Molokini Crater, a moon-shape crescent about 3 mi off the shore of Wailea, is the most popular snorkel cruise destination. You can spend half a day floating above the fish-filled crater for about $80. Some say it's not as good as it's made out to be, and that it's too crowded, but others consider it to be one of the best spots in Hawai'i. Visibility is generally outstanding and fish are incredibly tame. Snorkeling excurions usually include visits to two locales, lunch, gear, instruction, and possible whale or dolphin sightings. Your second stop will be somewhere along the leeward coast, either "Turtle Town" near Mākena or "Coral Gardens" toward Lahaina. ■ TIP➔ Be aware that on blustery mornings, there's a good chance the waters will be too rough to moor in Molokini and you'll end up snorkeling some place off the shore, which you could have driven to for free. For the safety of everyone on the boat, it's the captain's prerogative to choose the best spot for the day.

Snorkel cruises vary slightly—some serve mai tais and steaks; others offer beer and cold cuts. You might prefer a large ferry boat to a small sailboat, or vice versa. Some captains troll for fish along the way, and, if they're lucky, will occasionally catch big game fish such as a marlin or mahimahi. If you've tried snorkeling and are tentatively thinking about scuba, you may want to try snuba, a cross between the two. With snuba, you dive down 20 feet below the surface, only you're attached to an air hose from the boat. Many of the boats now offer snuba as well as snorkeling; expect to pay between $45 and $65.

Whatever trip you choose, be sure you know where to go to board your vessel; getting lost in the harbor at 6 AM is a lousy start to a good day. ■ TIP➔ Bring sunscreen, an underwater camera (they're double the price onboard), a towel, and a cover-up for the windy return trip.

★ **Ann Fielding's Snorkel Maui.** For a personal introduction to Maui's undersea universe, this guided tour is the indisputable authority. A marine biologist, Fielding—formerly with the University of Hawai'i, Waikīkī Aquarium, and the Bishop Museum, and the author of several guides to island sea life—is the Carl Sagan of Hawai'i's reef cosmos. She'll not only show you fish, but she'll also introduce you to *individual* fish. This is a good first experience for dry-behind-the-ears types. Snorkel trips include lunch and equipment. ☎ 808/572–8437 ⊕ *www. maui.net/~annf*.

Maui Classic Charters. This company offers two top-rate snorkel trips at a good value. Hop aboard the *Four Winds II*, a 55-foot, glass-bottom catamaran, for one of the most dependable snorkel trips around. You'll spend more time than the other charter boats do at Molokini and enjoy turtle-watching on the way home. The trip includes optional snuba ($45 extra), and a deluxe barbecue lunch, beer, wine, and soda. For a faster ride, try the *Maui Magic*, Mā'alaea's fastest power cat. This boat takes fewer people (45 max) than some of the larger vessels, and as an added bonus, they offer snuba and play Hawaiian music on the ride.

This one's good for kids. ✉ *Māʻalaea Harbor Slips #55 and #80* ☎ *808/879–8188 or 800/736–5740* ⊕ *www.mauicharters.com.*

★ ☺ **Pacific Whale Foundation.** The knowledgeable folks here will treat you to a Molokini adventure like the others, only with a more ecological bent. Accordingly, they serve gardenburgers alongside the requisite barbecue chicken and their fleet runs on bona-fide biodiesel fuel. This is an A-plus trip for kids, the crew assists with an on-board junior naturalist program and throws in a free wildlife guide and poster. The multihulled boats are smooth and some have swim on–off platforms. Best of all, a portion of the profits go to protecting the very treasures you're paying to enjoy. ✉ *Māʻalaea Harbor Slip* ☎ *800/942–5311 or 808/249–8811* ⊕ *www.pacificwhale.org.*

Paragon. With this company, you get to snorkel and sail—they have some of the fastest vessels in the state. As long as conditions are good, you'll hit prime snorkel spots in Molokini, Lānaʻi and occasionally, Coral Gardens. The Lānaʻi trip includes a Continental breakfast, a picnic lunch on the beach, snacks, open bar, a snorkel lesson, and plenty of time in the water. The friendly crew takes good care of you, making sure you get the most value and enjoyment from your trip. ✉ *Lahaina and Māʻalaea Harbors* ☎ *808/244–2087* ⊕ *www.sailmaui.com.*

Trilogy Excursions. The longest-running operation on Maui is the Coon family's Trilogy Excursions. They have six beautiful multihulled sailing vessels (though they usually only sail for a brief portion of the trip) at three departure sites. All excursions are manned by energetic crews who will keep you entertained with stories of the islands and plenty of corny jokes. A full-day catamaran cruise to Lānaʻi includes Continental breakfast and a deli lunch onboard; a guided van tour of the island; a "Snorkeling 101" class; and time to snorkel in the waters of Lānaʻi's Hulopoʻe Marine Preserve (Trilogy has exclusive commercial access). There's a barbecue dinner on Lānaʻi, and an optional dolphin safari. The company also offers a Molokini and Honolua Bay snorkel cruise. Many people consider a Trilogy excursion the highlight of their trip—but if you're not a good group-activity person, or if you are looking to really sail, there may be better options for you. ✉ *Māʻalaea Harbor Slip #99, or Lahaina Harbor* ☎ *808/661–4743 or 800/874–2666* ⊕ *www.sailtrilogy.com.*

Snorkel Equipment Rental

Most hotels and vacation rentals offer free use of snorkel gear. Beachside stands fronting the major resort areas rent equipment by the hour or day. ■ TIP➔ **Don't shy away from asking for instructions, a snug fit makes all the difference in the world. A mask fits if it sticks to your face when you inhale deeply through your nose. Fins should cover your entire foot (unlike diving fins, which strap around your heel).** If you're squeamish about using someone else's gear, (or need a prescription lens) pick up your own at any discount shop. Costco and Longs have better prices than ABC stores; dive shops have superior equipment.

Maui Dive Shop. You can rent pro gear (including optical masks, boogie boards, and wet suits) from six locations island-wide. Pump these guys for weather info before heading out, they'll know better than last night's news forecaster, and they'll give you the real deal on conditions. ✉ *1455 S. Kīhei Rd., Kīhei* ☎ *808/873–3388* ⊕ *www.mauidiveshop.com.*

Snorkel Bob's. If you need gear, Snorkel Bob's will rent you a mask, fins, and a snorkel, and throw in a carrying bag, map, and snorkel tips for as little as $9 per week. Avoid the circle masks and go for the split-level, it's worth the extra cash. ✉ *Nāpili Village Hotel, 5425 Lower Honoapiʻilani Hwy., Nāpili* ☎ *808/669–9603* ✉ *1217 Front St., Lahaina* ☎ *808/661–4421* ✉ *1279 S. Kīhei Rd., Kīhei* ☎ *808/875–6188* ✉ *2411 S. Kīhei Rd., Kīhei* ☎ *808/879–7449* ⊕ *www.snorkelbob.com.*

Surfing

Maui's diverse coastline has surf for every level of waterman or woman. Waves on leeward-facing shores (West and South Maui) tend to break in gentle sets all summer long. Surf instructors in Kīhei and Lahaina can rent you boards, give you onshore instruction, and then lead you out through the channel, where it's safe to enter the surf. They'll shout encouragement while you paddle like mad for the thrill of standing on water—some will even give you a helpful shove. These areas are great for beginners, the only danger is whacking a stranger with your board or stubbing your toe against the reef.

The North Shore is another story. Winter waves pound the windward coast, attracting water champions from every corner of the world. Adrenaline addicts are towed in by Jet Ski to a legendary, deep-sea break called *Jaws*. Waves here periodically tower upward of 40 feet, dwarfing the helicopters seeking to capture unbelievable photos. The only spot for viewing this phenomenon (which happens just a few times a year) is on private property. So, if you hear the surfers next to you crowing about Jaws "going off," cozy up and get them to take you with them.

Whatever your skill, there's a board, a break, and even a surf guru to accommodate you. A two-hour lesson is a good intro to surf culture. Surf camps are becoming increasingly popular, especially with women. One- or two-week camps offer a terrific way to build muscle and self-esteem simultaneously. **Maui Surfer Girls** (⊕ www.mauisurfergirls.com) immerses adventurous young ladies in wave-riding wisdom during two-week camps. Coed camps are sponsored by **Action Sports Maui** (⊕ www.actionsportsmaui.com).

Best Spots

Beginners can hang 10 at Kīhei's **Cove Park** (✉ S. Kīhei Rd., Kīhei), a sometimes crowded but reliable 1- to 2-foot break. Boards can easily be rented across the street, or in neighboring Kalama Park parking lot. The only bummer is having to balance the 9-plus-foot board on your head while crossing busy South Kīhei Road. But hey, that wouldn't stop world-famous longboarder Eddie Aikau, now would it?

Long- or shortboarders can paddle out anywhere along Lahaina's coastline. One option is at **Launiupoko State Wayside** (✉ Honoapiʻilani Hwy. near mile marker 18). The east end of the park has an easy break, good for beginners. Even better is **Ukumehame** (⊠ Honoapiʻilani Hwy. near mile marker 12), also called "Thousand Peaks." You'll soon see how the spot got it's name, the waves here break again and again in wide and consistent rows, giving lots of room for beginning and intermediate surfers.

For advanced wave riders, **Hoʻokipa Beach Park** (⊠ 2 mi past Pāʻia on Hāna Hwy.) boasts several well-loved breaks, including "Pavilions," "Lanes," "the Point," and "Middles." Surfers have priority until 11 AM, when windsurfers move in on the action. ■ TIP→ **Competition is stiff here, and the attitudes can be "aggro." If you don't know what you're doing, consider watching from the shore.**

You can find out the wave report each day by checking page 2 of the *Maui News,* logging onto the Glen James weather site at ⊕ www. hawaiiweathertoday.com, or calling ☎ 808/871–5054 (for the weather forecast) or ☎ 808/877–3611 (for the surf report).

Surf Shops & Lessons

Big Kahuna. Rent surfboards (soft-top longboards) here for $15 for two hours, or $20 for the day. The shop also offers surf lessons, and rents kayaks and snorkel gear. Located across from Cove Park. ⊠ *Island Surf Bldg., 1993 S. Kīhei Rd. #2, Kīhei* ☎ *808/875–6395.*

★ **Goofy Foot.** Surfing "goofy foot" means putting your right foot forward. They might be goofy, but we like the right-footed gurus here. Their safari shop is just plain cool and only steps away from "Breakwall," a great beginner's spot in Lahaina. Two-hour classes with five or fewer students are $55, and six-hour classes with lunch and an ocean-safety course are $250. They promise you'll be standing within a two-hour lesson—or it's free. ⊠ *505 Front St., Lahaina* ☎ *808/244–9283* ⊕ *www. goofyfootsurfschool.com.*

Hi Tech Surf & Sports. Locals hold Hi Tech with the utmost respect. They have some of the best boards, advice, and attitudes around. Rent surf boards for $20 per day (or soft boards for $14); $112 for the week. They rent even their best models—choose from longboards, shortboards, and hybrids. All rentals come with board bags, roof rags, and oh yeah, wax. ⊠ *425 Koloa St., Kahului* ☎ *808/877–2111* ⊕ *www.htmaui.com.*

Nancy Emerson School of Surfing. Nancy's motto is "If my dog can surf, so can you." Instructors here will get even the most shaky novice riding with their "Learn to Surf in One Lesson" program. A private lesson with Nancy herself—a pro surf champion and occasional Hollywood stunt double—costs $215 for one hour or $325 for two; lessons with her equally qualified instructors are $100 for one hour and $165 for two. They provide the boards and rash guards. ⊠ *505 Front St., Lahaina* ☎ *808/244–7873* ⊕ *www.mauisurfclinics.com.*

Windsurfing

Something about Maui's wind and water stirs the spirit of innovation. Windsurfing, invented in the 1950s, found its true home at Hoʻokipa in 1980. Seemingly overnight, windsurfing pros from around the world flooded

Maui's north shore. Equipment evolved, amazing film footage was captured, and a new sport was born.

If you're new to the action, you can get lessons from the experts island-wide. For a beginner, the best thing about windsurfing is (unlike surfing) you don't have to paddle. Instead, you have to hold on like heck to a flapping sail, as it whisks you into the wind. Needless to say, you're going to need a little coordination and balance to carry this off. Instructors start you on a beach at Kanahā, where the big boys go. Lessons range from two-hour introductory classes to five-day advanced "flight school." If you're an old salt, pick up tips and equipment from the companies below.

ON THE SIDELINES

Few places lay claim to as many windsurfing tournaments as Maui. In March the **Hawaiian Pro Am Windsurfing** competition gets under way. In April the **Da Kine Hawaiian Pro Am** lures top wind-surfers, and in October the **Aloha Classic World Wave Sailing Championships** takes place. All are held at Hoʻokipa Bay, right outside the town of Pāʻia. For competitions featuring amateurs as well as professionals, check out the **Maui Race Series** (☎ 808/877–2111), six events held at Kanahā Beach in Kahului in summer.

Best Spots

After **Hoʻokipa Bay** (⊠ 2 mi past Pāʻia on Hāna Hwy.) was discovered by windsurfers three decades ago, this windy beach 10 mi east of Kahu-lui gained an international reputation. The spot is blessed with optimal wave-sailing wind and sea conditions, and can offer the ultimate aerial experience.

In summer the windsurfing crowd heads south to **Kalepolepo Beach** (⊠ S. Kīhei Rd. near Ohukai St.). Trade winds build in strength and by afternoon a swarm of dragonfly sails can be seen skimming the white-caps, with the West Maui mountains as a backdrop.

A great site for speed, **Kanahā Beach Park** (⊠ Behind Kahului Airport) is dedicated to beginners in the morning hours, before the waves and wind really get roaring. After 11 AM, the professionals choose from their quiver of sails the size and shape best suited for the day's demands. This beach tends to have smaller waves and forceful winds—sometimes send-ing sailors flying at 40 knots. ■ TIP→ **If you aren't ready to go pro, this is a great place for a picnic while you watch from the beach.**

Equipment Rental & Lessons

Action Sports Maui. The quirky, friendly professionals here will meet you at Kanahā, outfit you with your sail and board, and guide you through your first "jibe" or turn. They promise your learning time will be cut in half. Don't be afraid to ask lots of questions. Lessons are held at 9 AM every morning except Sunday at Kanahā, and start at $79 for a 2½-hour class. ⊠ *415 Dairy Rd., Kahului* ☎ *808/871–5857* ⊕ *www. actionsportsmaui.com.*

Hi Tech Surf & Sports. Known locally as Maui's finest windsurfing school, Hawaiian Sailboarding Techniques (HST) (located in Hi Tech) brings

CLOSE UP

The Humpback's Winter Home

THE HUMPBACK WHALES' attraction to Maui is legendary. More than half the Pacific's humpback population winters in Hawai'i, especially in the waters around the Valley Isle, where mothers can be seen just a few hundred feet offshore training their young calves in the fine points of whale etiquette. Watching from shore it's easy to catch sight of whales spouting, or even breaching—when they leap almost entirely out of the sea, slapping back onto the water with a huge splash.

At one time there were thousands of the huge mammals, but a history of overhunting and marine pollution dwindled the world population to about 1,500. In 1966 humpbacks were put on the endangered species list. Hunting or harassing whales is illegal in the waters of most nations, and in the United States, boats and airplanes are restricted from getting too close. The word is still out, however, on the effects military sonar testing has on the marine mammals.

Marine biologists believe the humpbacks (much like the humans) keep returning to Hawai'i because of its warmth. Having fattened themselves in subarctic waters all summer, the whales migrate south in the winter to breed, and a rebounding population of thousands cruise Maui waters. Winter is calving time, and the young whales, born with little blubber, probably couldn't survive in the frigid Alaskan waters. No one has ever seen a whale give birth here, but experts know that calving is their main winter activity, since the 1- and 2-ton youngsters suddenly appear while the whales are in residence.

The first sighting of a humpback whale spout each season is exciting and reassuring for locals on Maui. A collective sigh of relief can be heard, "Ah, they've returned." In the not-so-far distance, flukes and flippers can be seen rising above the ocean's surface. It's hard not to anthropomorphize the tail-waving, it looks like such an amiable, human gesture. Each fluke is uniquely patterned, like a human's fingerprint, and used to identify the giants as they travel halfway around the globe and back.

you quality instruction by skilled sailors. Founded by Alan Cadiz, an accomplished World Cup Pro, the school sets high standards for a safe, quality windsurfing experience. Hi Tech itself offers excellent equipment rentals; $45 gets you a board, two sails, a mast, and roof racks for 24 hours. ⊠ *425 Koloa, Kahului* ☎ *808/877–2111* ⊕ *www.htmaui.com.*

Second Wind. Located in Kahului, this company rents boards with two sails for $43 per day. Boards with three sails go for $48 per day. ⊠ *11 Hāna Hwy., Kahului* ☎ *808/877–7467.*

Whale-Watching

From November through April, whale-watching becomes one of the most popular activities on Maui. Boats leave the wharves at Lahaina and Māʻalaea in search of humpbacks, allowing you to enjoy the awe-inspiring size of these creatures in closer proximity. As it's almost impossible *not* to see whales in winter on Maui, you'll want to prioritize: is adventure or comfort your aim? If close encounters with the giants of the deep are your desire, pick a smaller boat that promises sightings. If an impromptu marine-biology lesson sounds fun, go with the Pacific Whale Foundation. Two-hour forays into the whales' world start at $20. For those wanting to sip mai tais as whales cruise calmly by, stick with a sunset cruise on a boat with open bar and pūpūs ($40 and up). ■ TIP→ Afternoon trips are generally rougher because the wind picks up, but some say this is when the most surface action occurs.

Every captain aims to please during whale season, getting as close as legally possible (100 yards). Crew members know when a whale is about to dive (after several waves of its heart-shape tail) but rarely can predict breaches (when the whale hurls itself up and almost entirely out of the water). Prime viewing space (on the upper and lower decks, around the railings) is limited, so boats can feel crowded even when half-full. If you don't want to squeeze in beside strangers, opt for a smaller boat with less bookings. Don't forget to bring sunscreen, sunglasses, light long sleeves, and a hat you can secure. Winter weather is less predictable, and at times, can be extreme, especially as the wind picks up. Arrive early to find parking.

Best Spots

From December 15 to May 1 the Pacific Whale Foundation has naturalists stationed in two places—on the rooftop of their headquarters and at the scenic viewpoint at **McGregor Point Lookout** (⊠ Between mile markers 7 and 8 on Honoapi'ilani Hwy., Rte. 30). Just like the commuting traffic, whales cruise along the *pali*, or cliff side, of West Maui's Honoapi'ilani highway all day long. ■ TIP→ Make sure to park safely before craning your neck to see them.

The northern end of **Keawakapu Beach** (⊠ S. Kīhei Rd. near Kilohana Dr.) seems to be a whale magnet. Situate yourself on the sand or at the nearby restaurant, and you're bound to see a mama whale patiently teaching her calf the exact technique of flipper-waving.

Boats & Charters

Kiele V. The Hyatt Regency Maui's *Kiele V,* a 55-foot luxury catamaran, does seasonal whale-watching excursions as well as daily snorkel trips, and afternoon cocktail sails. A comfortable ride, the cat leaves from Kā'anapali Beach, which is more fun than the harbor. The trip costs $55 per adult and includes pūpūs and an open bar. ⊠ *200 Nohea Kai Dr., Lahaina* ☎ 808/667-4727.

★ ♻ **Pacific Whale Foundation.** This nonprofit organization pioneered whale-watching back in 1979 and now runs four boats, with 15 trips daily. As the most recognizable name in whale-watching, the crew (with a certified marine biologist on-board) offers insights into whale behavior (do they *really* know what those tail flicks mean?) and suggests ways for you to help save marine life worldwide. The best part about these trips is the underwater hydrophone that allows you to actually listen to the whales sing. Trips meet at the Foundation's store, where you can buy whale paraphernalia, snacks, and coffee—a real bonus for 8 AM trips.

Passengers are then herded much like migrating whales down to the harbor. These trips are more affordable than others, but you'll be sharing the boat with about 100 people in stadium seating. Once you catch sight of the wildlife up-close, however, you can't help but be thrilled. ✉ *Māʻalaea Harbor* ☎ *800/942–5311 or 808/249–8811* ⊕ *www. pacificwhale.org.*

GOLF, HIKING & OTHER ADVENTURES

Updated by
Elaine Gast

You may come to Maui to sprawl out on the sand, but it won't take long before you realize there's much more to Maui than the beach. The island's interior is vast and varied—a mecca of rain forest, valley, waterfalls, and mountains that provide a whirlwind of options for action and adventure. Whether you're riding horseback or backroading it on an ATV, there's plenty to keep you busy.

ATV Tours

Haleakalā ATV Tours. Haleakalā ATV Tours explore the mountainside in their own way: propelled through the forest on 350 cc, four-wheel-drive, Honda Rancher all-terrain vehicles. The adventures begin at Haleakalā Ranch and rev right up to the pristine Waikamoi rain-forest preserve. Kids under 15 ride alongside in the exciting Argo Conquest, an eight-wheel amphibious vehicle. Two-hour trips go for $90, and 3½-hour trips are $135. Haleakalā ATV Tours is now offering combination ATV and Zipline tours with Skyline Eco Adventures on Monday and Thursday for $177. ☎ *808/661–0288* ⊕ *www.atvmaui.com.*

Biking

Maui County biking is safer and more convenient than in the past, but long distances and mountainous terrain keep it from being a practical mode of travel. Still, painted bike lanes enable riders to travel all the way from Mākena to Kapalua, and you'll see hardy souls battling the trade winds under the hot Maui sun.

Several companies offer guided downhill bike tours from the top of Mt. Haleakalā all the way to the coast. From peak to sea level it's 38 mi total with only about 400 yards of actual pedaling required. This activity is a great way to see the summit of the world's largest dormant volcano and enjoy an easy, gravity-induced bike ride, but isn't for those not confident in their ability to handle a bike. The ride is inherently dangerous due to the slope, sharp turns, and the fact that you're riding down an actual road with cars on it. That said, the guided bike companies do take every safety precaution. A few companies are now offering unguided (or as they like to say "self-guided") tours where they provide you with the bike and transportation to the top and then you're free to descend at your own pace. Sunrise is downright brisk at the summit, so dress in layers.

Best Spots
Though it's changing, at present there are few truly good spots to ride on Maui. Street bikers will want to head out to scenic **Thompson Road**

(✉ Off Rte. 37, Kula Hwy., Keokea). It's quiet, gently curvy, and flanked by gorgeous views on both sides. Plus, because it's at a higher elevation, the air temperature is cooler and the wind lighter. The coast back down toward Kahului is worth the ride up. Mountain bikers can head up to **Polipoli Forest** (✉ Off Rte. 377, end of Waipoli Rd.). A bumpy trail leads through an unlikely forest of conifers. You'll likely forget you're in Hawaii, and the downhill run will give you a ride you won't soon forget.

Bike Rentals & Guided Trips

Haleakalā Bike Company. If you're thinking about an unguided Haleakalā bike trip, consider one of the trips offered by this company. Meet at the Old Haiku Cannery and take their van shuttle to the top. Along the way you'll learn about the history of the island, the volcano, and other Hawaiiana. Unlike the guided trips, food is not included although there are several spots along the way down to stop, rest, and eat. The simple, mostly downhill route takes you right back to the cannery where you started. HBC offers bike sales, rentals, and services as well. ✉ *810 Ha'ikū Rd., Suite 120, Haiku* ☎ *808/575–9575, 888/922–2453* ⊕ *www.bikemaui.com.*

Island Biker. This is the premiere bike shop on Maui when it comes to rental, sales, and service. They offer 2005 Specialized standard front-shock bikes, road bikes, and full suspension mountain bikes. Daily or weekly rates range $35–$140, and include a helmet, pump, water bottle, and flat-repair kit. They can suggest various routes appropriate for mountain or road biking, or you can join them in a bi-weekly group ride. ✉ *415 Dairy Rd., Kahului* ☎ *808/877–7744* ⊕ *www.islandbikermaui.com.*

Maui Downhill. If biking down the side of Haleakalā sounds like fun, several companies are ready to book you a tour. Maui Downhill vans will pick you up at your resort, shuttle you to the mountaintop, help you onto a bike, and follow you as you coast down through clouds and gorgeous scenery into the town of Pāia. Haleakalā summit trips available for sunrise or midday, sunset half trips from the crater to Kula are also offered. Lunch or breakfast is included, depending on your trip's start time; treks cost $150, discounts available for Internet bookings. ✉ *199 Dairy Rd., Kahului 96732* ☎ *808/871–2155 or 800/535–2453* ⊕ *www.mauidownhill.net.*

West Maui Cycles. Servicing the west side of the island, WMC offers an assortment of cycles including front-suspension Giant bikes for $40 per day ($160 per week) and Cannondale road bikes for $50 per day ($200 per week). Sales and service available. ✉ *1087 Limahana St., Lahaina* ☎ *808/661–9005.*

Golf

Maui's natural beauty and surroundings offer some of the most jaw-dropping vistas imaginable on a golf course. Holes run across small bays, past craggy lava outcrops, and up into cool, forested mountains. Most courses feature mesmerizing ocean views, some close enough to feel the salt in the air. And although many of the courses are affiliated with resorts (and therefore a little pricier), the general public courses are no less impressive. Green fees listed here are the highest course rates per round on weekdays and weekends. Discounts are often available for resort guests and for those who book tee times on the Web. Rental clubs may or may not be included with green fees. Twilight fees are usually offered; call individual courses for information.

Kā'anapali Resort. The Kā'anapali North Course (1962) is one of three in Hawai'i designed by Robert Trent Jones Sr., the godfather of modern golf architecture. The greens average a whopping 10,000 square feet, necessary because of the often-severe undulation. The par-4 18th hole (into the prevailing trade breezes, with out-of-bounds on the left, and a lake on the right) is notoriously tough. The South Course shares similar seaside-into-the-hills terrain, but is rated a couple of strokes easier, mostly because putts are less treacherous. ☒ *2290 Kā'anapali Pkwy., Lahaina* ☎ *808/661–3691* ⊕ *www.kaanapali-golf.com* ⅄ *North Course: 18 holes. 6136 yds. Par 71. Green Fee: $160. South Course: 18 holes. 6067 yds. Par 71. Green Fee: $130* ☞ *Facilities: Driving range, putting green, rental clubs, golf carts, lessons, restaurant, bar.*

Fodor'sChoice **Kapalua Resort.** Perhaps Hawai'i's best known golf resort and Maui's
★ crown jewel, Kapalua hosts the PGA Tour's first event each January: the Mercedes Championships at the Plantation Course at Kapalua. Ben Crenshaw and Bill Coore (1991) tried to incorporate traditional shot values in a very nontraditional site. The par-5 18th, for instance, plays 663 yards from the back tees (600 yards from the resort tees). The hole drops 170 feet in elevation, narrowing as it goes to a partially guarded green, and plays downwind and down-grain. Despite the longer-than-usual distance, the slope is great enough to reach the green with two well-struck shots—a truly unbelievable finish to a course that will challenge, frustrate, and reward the patient golfer.

The Bay Course (Arnold Palmer and Francis Duane, 1975) is the most traditional of Kapalua's triad, with gentle rolling fairways and generous greens. The most memorable hole is the par-3 fifth, with a tee shot that must carry a turquoise finger of Onelua Bay. The Village Course at Kapalua (Palmer and Ed Seay, 1980) winds high into the West Maui Mountains through historic stands of Cook pines and eucalyptus, then out through pineapple fields and tall grasses. The sixth hole is particularly dramatic: the tee is 100 feet above the fairway, with a dense stand of pines to the left and a lake to the right. **The Kapalua Golf Academy** (☒ 1000 Office Rd. ☎ 808/669–6500) offers 23 acres of practice turf and 11 teeing areas, a special golf fitness gym, and an instructional bay with video analysis. Each course has a separate clubhouse. **The Bay Course:** ☒ *300 Kapalua Dr., Kapalua* ☎ *808/669–8820* ⊕ *www. kapaluamaui.com/golf* ⅄ *18 holes. 6,051 yds. Par 72. Green Fee: $200* ☞ *Facilities: Driving range, putting green, rental clubs, pro shop, lessons, restaurant, bar.* **The Plantation Course:** ☒ *2000 Plantation Club Dr., Kapalua* ☎ *808/669–8877* ⊕ *www.kapaluamaui.com/golf* ⅄ *18*

BEFORE YOU HIT THE 1ST TEE . . .

Golf is golf, and Hawai'i is part of the United States, but island golf nevertheless has its own quirks. Here are a few tips to make your golf experience in the Islands more pleasant.

- All resort courses and many daily fee courses provide rental clubs. In many cases, they're the latest lines from top manufacturers. This is true for both men and women, as well as left-handers, which means you don't have to schlepp clubs across the Pacific.

- Come spikeless—very few Hawai'i courses still permit metal spikes. And most of the resort courses require a collared shirt.

- Maui is notorious for its trade winds. Consider playing early if you want to avoid the wind, and remember that while it'll frustrate you at times and make club selection difficult, you may very well see some of your longest drives ever.

- In theory you can play golf in Hawai'i 365 days a year, but there's a reason the Hawaiian Islands are so green. An umbrella and light jacket can come in handy.

- Unless you play a muni or certain daily fee courses, plan on taking a cart. Riding carts are mandatory at most courses and are included in the green fees.

holes. 6547 yds. Par 73. Green Fee: $250 ☞ Facilities: Driving range, putting green, golf carts, pull carts, rental clubs, pro shop, golf academy/lessons, restaurant, bar. **The Village Course:** ✉ 2000 Village Rd., Kapalua ☎ 808/669–8835 ⊕ www.kapaluamaui.com/golf ⌘ 18 holes. 5753 yds. Par 70. Green Fee: $185 ☞ Facilities: Driving range, putting green, golf carts, pull carts, rental clubs, pro shop, golf academy/lessons, restaurant, bar.

Makena Resort. Robert Trent Jones Jr. and Don Knotts (not the Barney Fife actor) built the first course at Mākena in 1981. A decade later Jones was asked to create 18 totally new holes and blend them with the existing course. The resulting North and South courses—sculpted from the lava flows on the western flank of Haleakalā—offer quick greens with lots of breaks, and plenty of scenic distractions. On the North Course, the fourth is a picturesque inland par-3, with the green guarded on the right by a pond. The sixth is an excellent example of option golf: the fairway is sliced up the middle by a gaping ravine, which must sooner or later be crossed to reach the green. Although trees frame most holes on the North Course, the South Course is more open. This means it plays somewhat easier off the tee, but the greens are trickier. The par-4 16th is another sight to see, with the Pacific running along the left side. ✉ 5415 Mākena Alanui, Mākena ☎ 808/879–3344 ⊕ www.princeresortshawaii.com ⌘ North Course: 18 holes. 6567 yds. Par 72. Green Fee: $180. South Course: 18 holes. 6630 yds. Par 72. Green Fee: $180 ☞ Facilities: Driving range, putting green, golf carts, rental clubs, pro shop, golf academy/lessons, restaurant, bar.

★ **Wailea.** Wailea is one of just two Hawai'i resorts to offer three different courses: Gold, Emerald, and Blue. Designed by Robert Trent Jones Jr., these courses share similar terrain, carved into the leeward slopes of Haleakalā. Although the ocean does not come into play, its beauty is visible on almost every hole. ■ TIP➜ **Remember putts break dramatically toward the ocean.**

Host to the Championship Senior Skins Game in February, the Gold Course at Wailea (1993) is all trees and lava and regarded as the hardest of the three courses. The trick here is to note even subtle changes in elevation. The par-3 eighth, for example, plays from an elevated tee across a lava ravine to a large, well-bunkered green framed by palm trees, the blue sea, and tiny Molokini. The course has been labeled a thinking player's course because it demands strategy and careful club selection. The Emerald Course at Wailea (1994) has lots of flowers and bunkering away from greens. This by no means suggests that it plays easy. A bunker well in front of a green disguises the distance to the hole. Likewise, the Emerald's extensive flower beds are designed to be dangerous distractions because of their beauty. The Gold and Emerald share a clubhouse, practice facility, and 19th hole. Judging elevation change is also key at Wailea's first course, the Blue Course (Arthur Jack Snyder, 1971). Fairways and greens tend to be wider and more forgiving than on the Gold or Emerald, and run through colorful flora that includes hibiscus, wiliwili, bougainvillea, and plumeria. **Blue Course:** ✉ *120 Kaukahi St., Wailea* ☎ *808/875–5155* ⊕ *www.waileagolf.com* ⅄ *18 holes. 6765 yds. Par 72. Green Fee: $175.* ⌗ *Facilities: Driving range, putting green, golf carts, rental clubs, pro shop, golf academy/lessons, restaurant, bar.* **Gold and Emerald Courses:** ✉ *100 Wailea Golf Club Dr., Wailea* ☎ *808/875–7450* ⊕ *www.waileagolf.com* ⅄ *Gold Course: 18 holes. 6653 yds. Par 72. Green Fee: $185. Emerald Course: 18 holes. 6407 yds. Par 72. Green Fee: $185* ⌗ *Facilities: Driving range, putting green, golf carts, rental clubs, pro shop, golf academy/lessons, restaurant, bar.*

The Dunes at Maui Lani. This is Robin Nelson (1999) at his minimalist best, a bit of British links in the middle of the Pacific. Holes run through ancient, lightly wooded sand dunes, 5 mi inland from Kahului Harbor. Thanks to the natural humps and slopes of the dunes, Nelson had to move very little dirt and created a natural beauty. During the design phase he visited Ireland, and not so coincidentally the par-3 third looks a lot like the Dell at Lahinch: a white dune on the right sloping down into a deep bunker and partially obscuring the right side of the green—just one of several blind to semiblind shots here. Popular with residents, this course has won several awards including "Best 35 New Courses in America" by Golf Magazine and "Five Best Kept Secret Golf Courses in America" by Golf Digest. ✉ *1333 Maui Lani Pkwy., Kahului* ☎ *808/ 873–0422* ⊕ *www.dunesatmauilani.com* ⅄ *18 holes. 6841 yds. Par 72. Green Fee: $100* ⌗ *Facilities: Driving range, putting green, golf carts, rental clubs, pro shop, golf academy/lessons, restaurant, bar.*

Pukalani Golf Course. Located 1,110 feet above sea level, Pukalani (Bob. E. and Robert L. Baldock, 1979) provides one of the finest vistas in all Hawai'i. Holes run up, down, and across the slopes of Haleakalā. The trade wind tends to come up in the late morning and afternoon. This—combined with frequent elevation change—makes club selection a test. The fairways tend to be wide, but greens are undulous and quick. ⊠ *360 Pukalani St., Pukalani* ☎ *808/572–1314* ⊕ *www.pukalanigolf.com* ⚑ *18 holes. 6945 yds. Par 72. Green Fee: $60* ☞ *Facilities: Driving range, putting green, rental clubs, golf carts, restaurant, bar.*

Hang Gliding

Hang Gliding Maui. Armin Engert will take you on an instructional powered hang-gliding trip out of Hāna Airport in East Maui. With more than 7,500 hours in flight and a perfect safety record, Armin flies you 1,000 feet over Maui's most beautiful coast. A 30-minute flight lesson costs $115, and a 60-minute lesson is $190. This is easily one of the coolest things you can do in Hāna. Snapshots of your flight from a wing-mounted camera cost an additional $25. ⊠ *Hāna Airport, Hāna* ☎ *808/ 572–6557* ⊕ *www.hangglidingmaui.com.*

Proflyght Paragliding. Proflyght is the only paragliding outfit on Maui to offer solo, tandem, and instruction at Polipoli State Park. The leeward slope of Haleakalā lends itself perfectly to paragliding with breathtaking scenery and upcountry air currents that increase and rise throughout the day. Polipoli creates tremendous thermals that allow one to peacefully descend 3,000 feet to the landing zone. Owner–pilot Dexter Clearwater boasts a perfect safety record with tandems and student pilots since taking over the company in 2002. Ask and Dexter will bring along his flying duck Chuckie or his paragliding pound puppie Daisy. Prices start at $175, with full certification available. ⊠ *Polipoli State Park, Kula* ☎ *808/874–5433* ⊕ *www.paraglidehawaii.com.*

Helicopter Tours

Helicopter flight-seeing excursions can take you over the West Maui Mountains, Hāna, and Haleakalā Crater. This is a beautiful, exciting way to see the island, and the *only* way to see some of its most dramatic areas and waterfalls. Tour prices usually include a videotape of your trip so you can relive the experience at home. Prices run from about $125 for a half-hour rain-forest tour to almost $400 for a two-hour mega-experience that includes a champagne toast on landing. Generally the 45–50 minute flights are the best value, and if you're willing to chance it, considerable discounts may be available if you call last minute.

Blue Hawaiian Helicopters. Blue Hawaiian has provided aerial adventures in Hawai'i since 1985, and has been integral in some of the filming Hollywood has done on Maui. Its ASTAR helicopters are air-conditioned and have noise-blocking headsets for all passengers. Flights are 30–65 minutes and cost $125–$280. They also offer a fly–drive special to Hāna with Temptation Tours limo vans. ⊠ *Kahului Heliport, Hangar 105, Kahului* ☎ *808/871–8844* ⊕ *www.bluehawaiian.com.*

Sunshine Helicopters. Sunshine offers tours of Maui and Moloka'i, as well as the Big Island, in its *Black Beauty* ASTAR or WhisperStar aircraft. A pilot-narrated videotape of your actual flight is available for purchase. Prices are $150–$370 for 30–65 minutes. First-class seating is available for a fee. ⊠ *Kahului Heliport, Hangar 107, Kahului* ☎ *808/871–0722 or 800/544–2520* ⊕ *www.sunshinehelicopters.com.*

Hiking

Hikes on Maui range from coastal seashore to verdant rain forest to alpine desert. Orchids, hibiscus, ginger, heliconia, and anthuriums grow wild on many trails, and exotic fruits like mountain apple, lilikoi, thimble-berry, and strawberry guava provide refreshing snacks for hikers. Ironically, much of what you see in lower altitude forests is alien, brought to Hawai'i at one time or another by someone hoping to improve upon nature. Plants like straw-berry guava and ginger may be tasty, but they outcompete native forest plants and have become serious, problematic weeds.

The best hikes get you out of the imported landscaping and into the truly exotic wilderness. Hawai'i possesses some of the world's rarest plants, insects, and birds. Pocket field guides are available at most grocery or drug stores and can really illuminate your walk. Before you know it you'll be nudging your companion and pointing out trees that look like something out of a Dr. Suess book. If you watch the right branches quietly you can spot the same honeycreepers or happy-faced spiders scientists have spent their lives studying.

> ### KEEP IN MIND
>
> Wear sturdy shoes while hiking; you'll want to spare your ankles from a crash course in loose lava rock. When hiking near streams or waterfalls, be extremely cautious, flash floods can occur at any time. Do not drink stream water or swim in streams if you have open cuts; bacteria and parasites are not the souvenir you want to take home. Exposure poses the main danger. Wear sunscreen, a hat, and layered clothing, and be sure to drink plenty of water (even if you don't feel thirsty). At upper elevations, the weather is guaranteed to be extreme—alternately chilly or blazing.

Best Spots

Fodor'sChoice ★ Going into **Haleakalā Crater**—the best hiking on the island—is like going to a different planet. In the early 1960s NASA actually brought moon-suited astronauts here to practice "walking on the moon." You'll traverse black sand and wild lava formations, follow the trail of blooming 'ahinahina (silverswords), watch for nēnē (Hawaiian geese), and witness tremendous views of big sky and burnt-red cliffs. There are 30 mi of moderate to strenuous trails, two camping areas, and three cabins. If you're in shape, you can do a day hike descending from the summit (along Sliding Sands Trail) to the crater floor. Be sure to ask a ranger about water availability before starting your hike. Bring plenty of warm, layered clothing. It may be scorching hot during the day, but it can get very chilly after dark. If you have time, consider camping here amid the cinder cones, lava flows, and all that loud silence.

⇨ *For more information see* Haleakalā National Park *earlier in this chapter.*

'**Ohe'o Gulch** (✉ Rte. 31, 10 mi past Hāna town) is a branch of Haleakalā National Park. Famous for its "sacred" pools (the area is sometimes called the "Seven Sacred Pools"), the cascading gulch is the starting point of one of Maui's best hikes—the 2-mi trek upstream to the 400-foot **Waimoku Falls.** Follow signs from the parking lot up the road, past the bridge overlook, and uphill into the forest. Along the way you can take side trips and swim in the stream's basalt-lined pools. The trail bridges a sensational gorge and passes onto a boardwalk through a mystifying forest of giant bamboo. This stomp through muddy and rocky terrain takes around three hours to fully enjoy. It's best done early in the morning, before the touring crowds arrive (though it can never truly be called crowded). A $10 national park fee applies, which is valid for one week and can be used at Haleakalā's summit as well. Down at the grassy sea cliffs, you can camp, no permit required, although you can stay only three nights. Toilets, grills, and tables are available here, but there's no water and open fires aren't allowed.

A good hiking spot—and something totally unexpected on a tropical island—is **Polipoli Forest.** During the Great Depression the government began a program to reforest the mountain, and soon cedar, pine, cypress, and even redwood took hold. It's cold and foggy here, and often wet or at least misty. To reach the forest, take Route 37 all the way out to the far end of Kula. Then turn left at Route 377. After about a half mile, turn right at Waipoli Road. First you'll encounter switchbacks; after that the road is just plain bad, but passable. There are wonderful trails, a small campground, and a cabin that you can rent from the Division of State Parks. Write far in advance for the **cabin** (✉ Box 1049, Wailuku 96793 ☎ 808/244–4354); for the campground, you can wait until you arrive in Wailuku and visit the **Division of State Parks** (✉ 54 High St. ☎ 808/984–8109).

A much neglected hike is the coastal **Hoapili Trail** (✉ Follow Mākena Alanui to end of paved road, walk through parking lot along dirt road, follow signs) beyond the 'Āhihi-Kīn'au Natural Area Reserve. Named after a bygone Hawaiian king, it follows the shoreline, threading through the remains of ancient Hawaiian villages. The once-thriving community was displaced by one of Maui's last lava flows. Later, King Hoapili was responsible for overseeing the creation of an island-wide highway. This remaining section, a wide path of stacked lava rocks, is a marvel to look at and walk on, though it's not the easiest surface for the ankles. (It's rumored to have once been covered in grass.) You can wander over to the Hanamanioa lighthouse, or quietly ponder the rough life of the ancients. Wear sturdy shoes and bring extra water. This is brutal territory with little shade and no facilities. Beautiful, yes. Accommodating, no.

You can take one of several easy hikes from the parking lot at '**Īao Valley State Park** (✉ Western end of Rte. 32, Wailuku). Cross 'Īao Stream and explore the junglelike area past the curious '**Īao Needle**, a spire that rises more than 2,000 feet from the valley floor. This park has a beautiful network of trails that snake through the deep valley. You can pause in the garden of Hawaiian heritage plants and marvel at the local youngsters hurling themselves from the bridge into the chilly stream water with yelps of delight.

Guided Hikes

★ **Hike Maui.** Hike Maui is the oldest hiking company on the Islands, its rain forest, mountain ridge, crater, coastline, and archaeological-snorkel hikes are led by such knowledgeable folk as ethnobotanists and marine biologists. Prices range from $65 to $150 for hikes of 3 to 10 hours, including lunch. They also offer a private Heli Hike and Waterfalls for upward of $2,000, giving you everything you came to Maui to see. Hike Maui supplies waterproof day packs, rain ponchos, first-aid gear, water bottles, and transportation to the site. ☎ 808/879–5270 ⊕ *www. hikemaui.com.*

Maui Eco Adventures. For excursions into remote areas, Maui Eco Adventures is your choice. The ecologically minded company leads hikes into private or otherwise inaccessible areas. Hikes, which can be combined with kayaking, mountain biking, or sailing trips, explore botanically rich valleys in Kahakuloa and East Maui, as well as Hanā, Haleakalā, and more. Guides are botanists, mountaineers, boat captains, and backcountry chefs. Most excursions are $120–$150. ✉ *180 Dickenson St., Suite 101, Lahaina* ☎ *808/661–7720 or 877/661–7720* ⊕ *www.ecomaui.com.*

Maui Hiking Safaris. Hikes with Maui Hiking Safaries are limited to groups of eight or less. Excursions include hikes to waterfalls, Haleakalā, rain forests, and more. You can choose any two hikes to customize your own full-day tour. Hikes range from $60 to $129. ✉ *273 Leolani Pl., Pukalani* ☎ *808/573–0168 or 888/445–3963* ⊕ *www.mauihikingsafaris.com.*

Sierra Club. A great avenue into the island's untrammeled wilderness is Maui's chapter of the Sierra Club. Rather than venturing out on your own, join one of the club's hikes into pristine forests and valley isle watersheds, or along ancient coastal paths. Several hikes a month are led by informative naturalists who carry first-aid kits and arrange waivers to access private land. Some outings include volunteer service, but most are just for fun. Bring your own food and water, sturdy shoes, and a suggested donation of $5—a true bargain. ✉ *Box 791180, Pā'ia* ☎ *808/ 573–4147* ⊕ *www.hi.sierraclub.org/maui.*

Horseback Riding

Several companies on Maui offer horseback riding that's far more appealing than the typical hour-long trudge over a dull trail with 50 other horses.

★ **Maui Stables.** Hawaiian-owned and run, this company provides a trip back in time, to an era when life moved more slowly and reverently—though galloping is allowed, if you're able to handle your horse! Educational tours begin at the stable in remote Kipahulu (near Hāna), and pass through several historic Hawaiian sites. Before heading up into the forest, your guides intone the words to a traditional *oli*, or chant, asking for permission to enter. By the time you reach the mountain pasture overlooking Waimoku Falls, you'll feel lucky to have been a part of the tradition. Both morning and afternoon rides are available at $150 per rider. ⊠ *Between mile markers 40 and 41 on Hwy. 37, Hāna* ☎ *808/ 248–7799* ⊕ *www.mauistables.com.*

Mendes Ranch. Family-owned and run, Mendes operates out of the beautiful ranchland of Kahakuloa on the windward slopes of the West Maui Mountains. Two-hour morning and afternoon trail rides ($110) are available with an optional barbecue lunch ($20). Cowboys will take you cantering up rolling pastures into the lush rain forest to view some of Maui's biggest waterfalls. Mendes caters to weddings and parties and offers private trail rides on request. Should you need accommodations they have a home and bunk for rent right on the property. ⊠ *Hwy. 340, Wailuku* ☎ *808/244–7320 or 808/871–8222* ⊕ *www.mendesranch.com.*

Pi`iholo Ranch. The local wranglers here will lead you on a rousing ride through family ranchlands—up hillside pastures, beneath a eucalyptus canopy, and past many native trees. Morning picnic rides are 3½ hours and include lunch. Afternoon rides are two hours. Their well-kept horses navigate the challenging terrain easily, but hold on when deer pass by! Prices are $120–$160. Private rides and lessons are available. ⊠ *End of Waiahiwi Rd., Makawao* ☎ *808/357–5544 or 866/572–5544* ⊕ *www. piiholo.com.*

Tennis

Most courts charge by the hour but will let players continue after their initial hour for free, provided no one is waiting. In addition to the facilities listed below, many hotels and condos have courts open to nonguests for a fee. The best free courts are the five at the **Lahaina Civic Center** (⊠ 1840 Honoapi`ilani Hwy., Lahaina ☎ 808/661–4685), near Wahikuli State Park. They're available on a first-come, first-served basis.

Kapalua Tennis Garden. This complex, home to the Kapalua Tennis Club, serves the Kapalua Resort with 10 courts, four lighted for night play, and a pro shop. You'll pay $12 an hour if you're a guest, $15 if you're not. ⊠ *100 Kapalua Dr., Kapalua* ☎ *808/669–5677.*

Wailea Tennis Club. The club has 11 Plexipave courts (its famed grass courts are, sadly, a thing of the past), lessons, rentals, and ball machines. On weekday mornings clinics are given to help you improve your ground strokes, serve, volley, or doubles strategy. Rates are $12 per hour, per person, with three lighted courts available for night play. ⊠ *131 Wailea Ike Pl., Kīhei* ☎ *808/879–1958 or 800/332–1614.*

SHOPPING

By Shannon
Wianecki

Whether you're searching for a dashboard hula dancer or an original Curtis Wilson Cost painting, you can find it on Front Street in Lahaina or at the Shops at Wailea. Art sales are huge in the resort areas, where artists regularly show up to promote their work. Alongside the flashy galleries are standards like Quicksilver and ABC store, where you can stock up on swim trunks, sunscreen, and flip-flops.

Don't miss the great boutiques lining the streets of small towns like Pā'ia and Makawao. You can purchase boutique fashions and art while strolling through these charming, quieter communities. Notably, several local designers—Tamara Catz, Sig Zane, and Maui Girl—all produce top-quality island fashions. In the neighboring galleries, local artisans turn out gorgeous work in a range of prices. Special souvenirs include rare hardwood bowls and boxes, prints of sea life, Hawaiian quilts, and blown glass.

> **BEST MADE-ON-MAUI GIFTS**
>
> - *Koa* jewelry boxes from **Maui Hands.**
> - Fish-shape sushi platters and bamboo chopsticks from the **Maui Crafts Guild.**
> - Black pearl pendant from **Maui Divers.**
> - Handmade Hawaiian quilt from **Hāna Coast Gallery.**
> - Fresh plumeria lei, made by you!

Specialty food products—pineapples, coconuts, or Maui onions—and Made in Maui jams and jellies make great, less-expensive souvenirs. Cook Kwee's Maui Cookies have gained a following, as have Maui Potato Chips. Coffee sellers now offer Maui-grown-and-roasted beans alongside the better-known Kona varieties. Remember that fresh fruit must be inspected by the U.S. Department of Agriculture before it can leave the state, so it's safest to buy a box that has already passed inspection.

Business hours for individual shops on the island are usually 9 to 5, seven days a week. Shops on Front Street and shopping centers tend to stay open later (until 9 or 10 on weekends).

West Maui

Shopping Centers

Lahaina Cannery Mall. In a building reminiscent of an old pineapple cannery are 50 shops and an active stage. The mall hosts free events year-round (like the International Jazz Festival). Recommended stops include Na Hoku, purveyor of striking Hawaiian heirloom jewelry and pearls; Totally Hawaiian Gift Gallery; and Kite Fantasy, one of the best kite shops on Maui. An events schedule is on the Web site. ⊠ *1221 Honoapi'ilani Hwy., Lahaina* ☏ *808/661–5304.*

Lahaina Center. Island department store Hilo Hattie Fashion Center anchors the complex and puts on a free hula show at 2 PM every Wednesday and Friday. In addition to Hard Rock Cafe, Banana Republic, and a four-screen cinema, you can find a replica of an ancient Hawaiian village complete with three full-size thatch huts built with 10,000 feet of Big Island 'ōhi'a wood, 20 tons of *pili* grass, and more than 4 mi of hand-woven coconut *senit* (twine). There's all that *and* validated parking. ⊠ *900 Front St., Lahaina* ☏ *808/667–9216.*

Whalers Village. Chic Whalers Village has a whaling museum and more than 50 restaurants and shops. Upscale haunts include Louis Vuitton, Ferragamo, Versace, and Chanel Boutique. The complex also offers some interesting diversions: Hawaiian artisans display their crafts daily; hula dancers perform on an outdoor stage weeknights from 7 to 8; and three films spotlighting whales and marine history are shown daily for free at the Whale Center of the Pacific. ⊠ *2435 Kā'anapali Pkwy., Kā'anapali* ☎ *808/661–4567.*

Clothing

Hilo Hattie Fashion Center. Hawai'i's largest manufacturer of aloha shirts and *mu'umu'u* also carries brightly colored blouses, skirts, and children's clothing. ⊠ *Lahaina Center, 900 Front St., Lahaina* ☎ *808/661–8457.*

Honolua Surf Company. If you're not in the mood for a matching aloha shirt and *mu'umu'u* ensemble, check out this surf shop—popular with young men and women for surf trunks, casual clothing, and accessories. ⊠ *845 Front St., Lahaina* ☎ *808/661–8848.*

Maggie Coulombe. Maggie Coulombe's cutting-edge fashions have the style of SoHo and the heat of the Islands. The svelte, body-clinging designs are unique and definitely worth a look. ⊠ *505 Front St., Lahaina* ☎ *808/662–0696.*

Galleries

Lahaina Galleries. Works of both national and international artists are displayed at the gallery's two locations in West Maui. ⊠ *828 Front St., Lahaina* ☎ *808/667–2152* ⊠ *Kapalua Resort, Bay Dr., Kapalua* ☎ *808/ 669–0202.*

Lahaina Printsellers Ltd. Hawai'i's largest selection of original antique maps and prints pertaining to Hawai'i and the Pacific is available here. You can also buy museum-quality reproductions and original oil paintings from the Pacific Artists Guild. A second, smaller shop is at 505 Front Street. ⊠ *Whalers Village, 2435 Kā'anapali Pkwy., Kā'anapali* ☎ *808/ 667–7617.*

Martin Lawrence Galleries. Martin Lawrence displays the works of noted mainland artists, including Andy Warhol and Keith Haring, in a bright and friendly gallery. ⊠ *Lahaina Market Pl., Front St. and Lahainaluna Rd., Lahaina* ☎ *808/661–1788.*

Village Gallery. This gallery, with two locations on the island, showcases the works of such popular local artists as Betty Hay Freeland, Wailehua Gray, Margaret Bedell, George Allen, Joyce Clark, Pamela Andelin, Stephen Burr, and Macario Pascual. ⊠ *120 Dickenson St., Lahaina* ☎ *808/661–4402* ⊠ *Ritz-Carlton, 1 Ritz-Carlton Dr., Kapalua* ☎ *808/ 669–1800.*

Jewelry

Jessica's Gems. Jessica's has a good selection of Hawaiian heirloom jewelry, and its Lahaina store specializes in black pearls. ⊠ *Whalers Village, 2435 Kā'anapali Pkwy., Kā'anapali* ☎ *808/661–4223* ⊠ *858 Front St., Lahaina* ☎ *808/661–9200.*

Lahaina Scrimshaw. Here you can buy brooches, rings, pendants, cuff links, tie tacks, and collector's items adorned with intricately carved sailors' art. ⊠ *845A Front St., Lahaina* ☎ *808/661–8820* ⊠ *Whalers Village, 2435 Kā'anapali Pkwy., Kā'anapali* ☎ *808/661–4034.*

Maui Divers. This company has been crafting gold and coral into jewelry for more than 20 years. ⊠ *640 Front St., Lahaina* ☎ *808/661–0988.*

The South Shore

Shopping Centers

Azeka Place Shopping Center. Azeka II, on the *mauka* (toward the mountains) side of South Kīhei Road, has Longs Drugs (the place for slippers), the Coffee Store (the place for iced mochas), Who Cut the Cheese (the place for aged gouda), and the Nail Shop (the place for shaping, waxing, and tweezing). Azeka I, the older half on the *makai* side of the street, has a decent Vietnamese restaurant and Kīhei's post office. ⊠ *1280 S. Kīhei Rd., Kīhei.*

Rainbow Mall. This mall is one-stop shopping for condo guests—it offers video rentals, Hawaiian gifts, plate lunches, and a liquor store. ⊠*2439 S. Kīhei Rd., Kīhei.*

The Shops at Wailea. Stylish, upscale, and close to most of the resorts, this mall brings high fashion to Wailea. Luxury boutiques such as Gucci, Fendi, Cos Bar, and Tiffany & Co. have shops, as do less-expensive chains like Gap, Guess, and Tommy Bahama's. Several good restaurants face the ocean, and regular Wednesday-night events include live entertainment, art exhibits, and fashion shows. ⊠ *3750 Wailea Alanui Dr., Wailea* ☎ *808/891–6770.*

Kīhei Kalama Village Marketplace. This is a fun place to investigate. Shaded outdoor stalls sell everything from printed and hand-painted T-shirts and sundresses to jewelry, pottery, wood carvings, fruit, and gaudily painted coconut husks—some, but not all, made by local craftspeople. ⊠ *1941 S. Kīhei Rd., Kīhei* ☎ *808/879–6610.*

Clothing

Hilo Hattie Fashion Center. Hawai'i's largest manufacturer of aloha shirts and *mu'umu'u* also carries brightly colored blouses, skirts, and children's clothing. ⊠ *297 Pi'ikea Ave., Kīhei* ☎ *808/875–4545.*

Honolua Surf Company. If you're in the mood for colorful print tees and sundresses, check out this surf shop. It's popular with young men and women for surf trunks, casual clothing, and accessories. ⊠ *2411 S. Kīhei Rd., Kīhei* ☎ *808/874–0999.*

Nell. Far better than typical resort boutiques, this expansive shop at the Fairmont Kea Lani carries truly stylish resort clothing for women. If you've recently spied a pretty bracelet on a celebrity in a magazine, there's a good chance you can find it here. ⊠ *Fairmont Kea Lani, 4100 Wailea Alanui Dr., Wailea* ☎ *808/875–4100.*

Sisters & Company. Opened by four sisters, this little shop has a lot to offer—current brand-name clothing such as Tamara Catz and ener-chi, locally made jewelry, beach sandals, and gifts. Sister No. 3, Rhonda, runs a tiny, ultrahip hair salon in back. ⊠ *1913 S. Kīhei Rd., Kīhei* ☎ *808/875–9888.*

Tommy Bahama's. It's hard to find a man on Maui who *isn't* wearing a TB-logo aloha shirt. For better or worse, here's where you can get yours. Make sure to grab a Barbados Brownie on the way out at the restaurant, which is attached to the shop. ⊠ *The Shops at Wailea, 3750 Wailea Alanui Dr., Wailea* ☎ *808/879–7828.*

Central Maui

Shopping Centers

Ka'ahumanu Center. This is Maui's largest mall with 75 stores, a movie theater, an active stage, and a food court. The mall's interesting rooftop, composed of a series of manta ray–like umbrella shades, is easily spotted. Stop at Camellia Seed Shop for what the locals call "crack seed," a delicacy made from dried fruits, nuts, and lots of sugar. Other stops here include mall standards such as Macy's, Gap, and American Eagle Outfitters. ⊠ *275 Ka'ahumanu Ave., Kahului* ☎ *808/877–3369.*

Maui Marketplace. On the busy stretch of Dairy Road, just outside the Kahului Airport, this behemoth marketplace couldn't be more conveniently located. The 20-acre complex houses several outlet stores and big retailers, such as Pier One Imports, Sports Authority, and Borders Books & Music. Sample local food at the Kau Kau Corner food court. ⊠ *270 Dairy Rd., Kahului* ☎ *808/873–0400.*

Clothing

Hi-Tech. Stop here immediately after deplaning to stock up on surf trunks, windsurfing gear, bikinis, and sundresses. ⊠ *425 Koloa Rd., Kahului* ☎ *808/877–2111.*

★ **Sig Zane.** Local clothing designer Sig Zane draws inspiration from island botanical treasures—literally. His sketches of Hawaiian flowers such as *puakenikeni* and *maile* decorate the brightly colored fabrics featured in his shop. The aloha shirts and dresses here are works of art—original and not too flashy. ⊠ *53 Market St., Wailuku* ☎ *808/249–8997.*

Food Specialties

Maui Coffee Roasters. This café and roasting house near Kahului Airport is the best stop for Kona and island coffees. The salespeople give good advice and will ship items. You even get a free cup of joe in a signature to-go cup when you buy a pound of coffee. ⊠ *444 Hāna Hwy., Unit B, Kahului* ☎ *808/877–2877.*

Upcountry, the North Shore & Hāna

Clothing

Biasa Rose. This boutique offers hip island styles for the whole family. The owners have also created unique gifts—pillows, napkins, photo albums—with batik fabrics they've acquired while traveling through Indonesia. ⊠ *104 Hāna Hwy., Pā'ia* ☎ *808/579–8602.*

Collections. This eclectic boutique is brimming with pretty jewelry, humorous gift cards, Italian bags and sandals, yoga wear, and Asian print silks. ⊠ *3677 Baldwin Ave., Makawao* ☎ *808/572–0781.*

Moonbow Tropics. If you're looking for an aloha shirt that won't look out of place on the mainland, make a stop at this little store, which sells the best-quality shirts on the island. ⊠ *36 Baldwin Rd., Pā'ia* ☎ *808/579–8592.*

★ **Tamara Catz.** This Maui designer already has a worldwide following, and her sarongs and super-stylish beachwear have been featured in many fashion magazines. If you're looking for a sequined bikini or a delicately embroidered sundress, this is the place to check out. ⊠ *83 Hāna Hwy., Pā'ia* ☏ *808/579–9184.*

Galleries

FodorśChoice **Maui Crafts Guild.** This is one of the more interesting galleries on Maui.
★ Set in a two-story wooden building alongside the highway, the Guild is crammed with treasures. Resident artists craft everything in the store—from Norfolk-pine bowls to raku (Japanese lead-glazed) pottery to original sculpture. The prices are surprisingly low. Upstairs, gorgeous pieces of handcrafted hardwood furniture are on display. ⊠ *43 Hāna Hwy., Pā'ia* ☏ *808/579–9697.*

★ **Maui Hands.** This gallery shows work by dozens of local artists, including *paniolo*-theme lithographs by Sharon Shigekawa, who knows whereof she paints: she rides each year in the Kaupō Roundup. ⊠ *3620 Baldwin Ave., Makawao* ☏ *808/572–5194.*

★ **Hāna Coast Gallery.** One of the best places to shop on the island, this 3,000-square-foot gallery has fine art and jewelry on consignment from local artists. ⊠ *Hotel Hāna-Maui, Hāna Hwy., Hāna* ☏ *808/248–8636 or 800/637–0188.*

Jewelry

Master Touch Gallery. The exterior of this shop is as rustic as all the old buildings of Makawao, so there's no way to prepare yourself for the elegance of the handcrafted jewelry displayed within. Owner David Sacco truly has the master touch. ⊠ *3655 Baldwin Ave., Makawao* ☏ *808/572–6000.*

Swimwear

FodorśChoice **Maui Girl.** This is *the* place for swimwear, cover-ups, beach hats, and san-
★ dals. Maui Girl designs its own suits and imports teenier versions from Brazil as well. Tops and bottoms can be purchased separately, greatly increasing your chances of finding a suit that actually fits. ⊠ *13 Baldwin Ave., Pā'ia* ☏ *808/579–9266.*

Grocery Stores on Maui

Foodland. In Kīhei town center, this is the most convenient supermarket for those staying in Wailea. It's open round-the-clock. ⊠ *1881 S. Kīhei Rd., Kīhei* ☏ *808/879–9350.*

Lahaina Square Shopping Center Foodland. This Foodland serves West Maui and is open daily from 6 AM to midnight. ⊠ *840 Waine'e St., Lahaina* ☏ *808/661–0975.*

Mana Foods. Stock up on local fish and grass-fed beef for your barbecue here. You can find the best selection of organic produce on the island, as well as a great bakery and deli at this typically crowded health-food store. ⊠ *49 Baldwin Ave., Pā'ia* ☏ *808/579–8078.*

Safeway. Safeway has three stores on the island open 24 hours daily. ⊠ *Lahaina Cannery Mall, 1221 Honoapi'ilani Hwy., Lahaina* ☏ *808/667–4392* ⊠ *170 E. Kamehameha Ave., Kahului* ☏ *808/877–3377* ⊠ *277 Piikea Ave., Kīhei* ☏ *808/891–9120.*

SPAS

By Shannon
Wianecki

Maui has recently become a spa paradise. Nearly every resort has jumped aboard the fitness–beauty bandwagon, giving spa-goers more choices than ever before.

Traditional Swedish massage and European facials anchor most spa menus, though you'll also find shiatsu, ayurveda, aromatherapy, and other body treatments drawn from cultures across the globe. *Lomi Lomi*, traditional Hawaiian massage involving powerful strokes down the length of the body, is a regional specialty passed down through generations. Many treatments incorporate local plants and flowers. *Awapuhi*, or Hawaiian ginger, and *noni*, a pungent-smelling fruit, are regularly used for their therapeutic benefits. *Limu*, or seaweed, and even coffee is employed in rousing salt scrubs and soaks. And this is just the beginning.

In spas on Maui, the emphasis is definitely on relaxation. But if you're craving your fitness routine, there should be no trouble continuing it here—or even ramping it up on the advanced equipment available to most resort guests. Complementing sightseeing with early-morning walks, meditation, fitness classes, treatments, and beauty services can deepen the relaxing effects of your vacation.

The Spa at Four Seasons Resort. The Four Seasons' hawklike attention to detail is reflected here. Thoughtful gestures like fresh flowers beneath the massage table (to give you something to stare at) and a choice of music relax you before your treatment even begins. The spa is genuinely stylish and serene, and the therapists are among the best. If you're looking to lounge all day here though, it's a bit small. For a private, outdoor experience, the oceanfront massage *hales* (structures) are particularly charming and well worth the extra $25. ✉ *3900 Wailea Alanui Dr., Wailea* ☎ *808/874–8000 or 800/334–6284* ⊕ *www.fourseasons.com* ☞ *$125 50-minute massage, $370 3-treatment packages* ⎈ *Hair salon, steam room. Gym with: cardiovascular machines, free weights, weight-training equipment. Services: aromatherapy, body wraps, facials, hydrotherapy, massage. Classes and programs: aquaerobics, meditation, personal training, Pilates, Spinning, tai chi, yoga.*

Fodor'sChoice
★

Spa Grande, Grand Wailea. Built to satisfy an indulgent Japanese billionaire, this 50,000-square-foot spa makes others seem like well-appointed closets. Slathered in honey and wrapped up in the steam room (if you go for the Aliʻi honey steam wrap), you'll feel like royalty. All treatments include a loofah scrub and a trip to the *termé*, a hydrother-

> ## BUDGET-FRIENDLY SPAS
>
> If hotel spa prices are a little intimidating, try **Spa Luna** (✉ 810 Hāʻiku Rd., Hāʻiku ☎ 808/575–2440), a day spa, which is also an aesthetician's school. In the former Hāʻiku Cannery, it offers services ranging from massage to microdermabrasion. You can opt for professional services, but the student clinics are the real story here. The students are subject to rigorous training, and their services are offered at a fraction of the regular cost ($25 for a 50-minute massage).

apy circuit including a Roman Jacuzzi, furo bath, plunge pool, powerful waterfall and Swiss jet showers, and five therapeutic baths. (Soak for 10 minutes in the moor mud to relieve sunburn or jellyfish stings.) Plan to arrive an hour before your treatment to fully enjoy the baths. The termé is available separately for $55 ($80 for nonhotel guests). At times—especially during the holidays—this wonderland can be crowded. ⊠ *3850 Wailea Alanui Dr., Wailea* ☎ *808/875–1234 or 800/888–6100* ⊕ *www.grandwailea.com* ☞ *$145 50-minute massage, $325 half-day spa packages* ⚲ *Hair salon, hot tub, sauna, steam room. Gym with: cardiovascular machines, free weights, racquetball, weight-training equipment. Services: aromatherapy, body wraps, facials, hydrotherapy, massage, Vichy shower. Classes and programs: aquaerobics, cycling, Pilates, qigong, yoga.*

The Spa at Hotel Hāna Maui. A bamboo gate opens into an outdoor sanctuary with a lava-rock pool and hot tub; at first glimpse this spa seems to have been organically grown, not built. The decor here can hardly be called decor—it's an abundant, living garden. Taro varieties, orchids, and ferns still wet from Hāna's frequent downpours nourish the spirit as you rest with a cup of jasmine tea, or take an invigorating dip in the plunge pool. Signature aromatherapy treatments utilize *Honua*, the spa's own sumptuous blend of sandalwood, coconut, ginger, and vanilla orchid essences. Daily yoga classes round out a perfectly relaxing experience. ⊠ *3850 Wailea Alanui Dr., Wailea* ☎ *808/875–1234 or 800/888–6100* ⊕ *www.hotelhanamaui.com* ☞ *$125 60-minute massage, $250 spa packages* ⚲ *Hair salon, hot tubs (indoor and outdoor), sauna, steam room. Gym with: cardiovascular machines, free weights, weight-training equipment. Services: aromatherapy, body wraps, facials, hydrotherapy, massage. Classes and programs: meditation, Pilates, yoga.*

Spa Kea Lani, Fairmont Kea Lani Hotel Suites & Villas. Once one of the island's nicest, this tiny spa is scheduled for a major renovation. We anticipate great things. Until then, opt for a poolside massage—treatments by the divinely serene adult pool can be reserved on the spot. If the pool feels too exposed, we recommend the spa's Citrus Glow treatment: a private hydrotherapy treatment followed by an exfoliating massage. ⊠ *4100 Wailea Alanui Dr., Wailea* ☎ *808/875–4100 or 800/659–4100* ⊕ *www.kealani.com* ☞ *$120 55-minute massage, $295 spa packages* ⚲ *Hair salon, steam room. Gym with: cardiovascular machines, free weights, weight-training equipment. Services: aromatherapy, body wraps, facials, hydrotherapy, massage, Vichy shower. Classes and programs: aquaerobics, yoga.*

Spa Moana, Hyatt Regency Maui. Spa Moana's oceanfront salon has a million-dollar view; it's a perfect place to beautify before your wedding or special anniversary. An older facility, it's still spacious and well-appointed, offering numerous innovative treatments such as the Ka'anapali Coffee Scrub or the Maui Sugar Scrub, in addition to traditional Swedish and Thai massage, reiki, and shiatsu. For body treatments, the oceanfront rooms are a tad too warm—request one in back. In conjunction with Spa Moana, the Maui Wellness Institute offers two-

2

day programs including workshops on kinesiology, feng shui, sex, and chocolate. Er . . . yum. ⊠ *200 Nohea Kai Dr., Lahaina* ☎ *808/661– 1234 or 800/233–1234* ⊕ *www.hyatt.com* ☞ *$150 50-minute massage, $420 all-day spa packages* ⚹ *Hair salon, hot tub, sauna, steam room. Gym with: cardiovascular machines, free weights, weight-training equipment. Services: aromatherapy, body wraps, facials, hydrotherapy, massage, Vichy shower. Classes and programs: aquaerobics, Pilates, tai chi, yoga.*

Waihua, Ritz-Carlton, Kapalua. If the stress of traveling has fried your nerves (or even if it hasn't), book a Waihua signature treatment such as "Harmony" or "Family Relations," which employs aromatherapy, hot stones, and massage. High-quality, handcrafted products enhance treatments inspired by Hawaiian culture, such as the *lomi lomi* massage with healing plant essences followed by a salt foot scrub. The newly refurbished facility lacks some of the other spas' amenities but does offer superb services and a well-stocked boutique. Attention fitness junkies: personal DVD players are attached to the state-of-the-art cardiovascular machines. ⊠ *1 Ritz-Carlton Dr., Kapalua* ☎ *808/669–6200 or 800/262–8440* ⊕ *www. ritzcarlton.com* ☞ *$120 60-minute massage, $320 half-day spa packages* ⚹ *Hair salon, sauna, steam room. Gym with: cardiovascular machines, free weights, weight-training equipment. Services: aromatherapy, body wraps, facials, massage. Classes and programs: aquaerobics, nutrition, yoga.*

The Spa at the Westin Maui. An exquisite 80-minute Lavender Body Butter treatment is the star of this spa's menu, thanks to a partnership with a local lavender farm. Other options include cabana massage (for couples, too) and water lily sunburn relief with green tea. The brand-new facility is flawless, and it's worth getting a treatment just to sip lavender lemonade in the posh ocean-view waiting room (it's coed, so keep your robe tightly tied). The open-air yoga studio and the gym offer energizing workouts. Bridal parties can request a private area within the salon. ⊠ *Westin Ka'anapali, 2365 Ka'anapali Pkwy., Ka'anapali* ☎ *808/ 667–2525* ⊕ *www.westinmaui.com* ☞ *$115 50-minute massage, $137–$411 day-spa packages* ⚹ *Hair salon, hot tub, sauna, steam room. Gym with: cardiovascular machines, free weights, weight-training equipment. Services: aromatherapy, body wraps, facials, hydrotherapy, massage, Vichy shower. Classes and programs: aquaerobics, yoga.*

ENTERTAINMENT & NIGHTLIFE

By Elaine Gast

Looking for wild island nightlife? We can't promise you'll find it here. Maui has little of Waikīkī's after-hours decadence, and the club scene (if you want to call it that) can be quirky, depending on the season and the day of the week. But this quiet island can surprise you with a big-name concert, outdoor festival, or special event, and it seems the whole island shows up for the party. Aside from lū'au shows, dinner cruises, and tiki-lighted cocktail hours, you can usually find some down-home DJ-spinning, or the strum of acoustic at your nearest watering hole. Lahaina and Kīhei are your best bets for action. On the right night, both towns stir with activity, and if you don't like one scene, there's always next door. Pick up the free *Maui Time Weekly,* or Thursday's edition of the *Maui News,* where you'll find a listing of all your after-dark options, island-wide.

The **Maui Arts & Cultural Center** (✉ One Cameron Way, near harbor on Kahului Beach Rd., Kahului ☎ 808/242–2787) is the hub of all high-brow arts and quality performances. Their events calendar features everything from rock to reggae to Hawaiian slack key, international dance and circus troupes, political and literary lectures, art films, cult classics—you name it. Each Wednesday (and occasionally Friday) evenings, the MACC (as it's locally known) hosts movie selections from the Maui Film Festival. The complex includes the 1,200 Castle Theater, a 4,000-seat amphitheater for large outdoor concerts, a 350-seat McCoy Theater for plays and recitals, and a courtyard café offering preshow dining and drinks. For information on current events, check the **Events Box Office** (☎ 808/242–7469) or the *Maui News.*

Entertainment

Lū'au

The Feast at Lele. "Lele" is an older, more traditional name for Lahaina. This feast redefines the lū'au by crossing it with island-style fine dining in an intimate beach setting. Each course of this succulent sit-down meal expresses the spirit of specific island culture—Hawaiian, Samoan, Tongan, Tahitian—and don't forget dessert. Dramatic Polynesian entertainment accompanies the dinner, along with excellent wine and liquor selections. This is the most expensive lū'au on the island for a reason: Lele is top-notch. ✉ *505 Front St., Lahaina* ☎ *808/667–5353* ⚑ *Reservations essential* ⊕ *www.feastatlele.com* 🍴 *$99 adult, $69 child* ☼ *Nightly at sunset.*

Fodor'sChoice **Old Lahaina Lū'au.** Many consider this the best lū'au on Maui; it's certainly the most traditional. Located right on the water, at the northern end of town, the Old Lahaina Lū'au is small, personal, and as authentic as it gets. Sitting either at a table or on a *lauhala* mat, you'll dine on all-you-can-eat Hawaiian cuisine: pork *lau lau,* ahi poke, *lomi lomi* salmon, Maui-style mahimahi, *haupia* (coconut pudding), and more. At sunset the show begins a historical journey that relays key periods in Hawai'i's history, from the arrival of the Polynesians to the influence of the missionaries and, later, tourism. The tanned, talented performers will charm you with their music, chanting, and variety of hula styles (modern and *kahiko,* the ancient way of communicating with the gods). But if it's fire dancers you want to see, you won't find them here, as they aren't considered traditional. Although it's performed nightly, this lū'au sells out regularly. Make your reservations when planning your trip to Maui. You can cancel up until 10 AM the day of the scheduled show. ✉ *1251 Front St.,* makai *of Lahaina Cannery Mall, Lahaina* ☎ *808/667–1998* ⚑ *Reservations essential* ⊕ *www.oldlahainaluau.com* 🍴 *$85 adult, $55 child* ☼ *Nightly at 5:15 PM in winter, 5:45 PM in summer.*

Renaissance Wailea Sunset Beach Lū'au. Held on the manicured greens of Wailea, the Renaissance offers a good show and an even better spread. You'll find an open bar and standard lū'au fare, plus some extras—kālua pork, teriyaki steak, grilled fish, and an outstanding dessert tray (try the chocolate macadamia tarts). As long as you don't mind the corny jokes, the show is festive and flashy, especially the Samoan fire-knife dance finale. ✉ *3350 Wailea Alanui Dr., Wailea* ☎ *888/349–7888* ⊕ *www.renaissancewaileabeachluau.com* ✍ *Reservations essential* 🎟 *$65 adult, $30 child* ☉ *Wed. and Fri. 5:30 PM.*

Dinner & Sunset Cruises

There's no better place to see the sun set on the Pacific than from one of Maui's many boat tours. You can find a tour to fit your mood, anything from a quiet, sit-down dinner, to a festive, beer-swigging booze cruise. Dinner cruises typically feature music and are generally packed—which is great if you're feeling social, but you might have to fight for a good seat. You can usually get a much better meal at one of the local restaurants. Most nondinner cruises offer *pūpūs* (appetizers) and an open bar. Winds are consistent in summer, but variable in winter—sometimes making for a rocky ride. If you're worried about sea sickness, you might consider a catamaran, which is much more stable than a mono-hull. Take Dramamine before the trip, and if you feel sick, sit in the shade (but not inside the cabin), place a cold rag or ice on the back of your neck, and *breathe* as you look at the horizon. Tours leave from Mā'alaea or Lahaina harbors. Be sure to arrive at least 15 minutes early.

Kaulana **Cocktail Cruise.** This two-hour sunset cruise prides itself on its live music and festive atmosphere. Accommodating up to 100 people, the cruise generally attracts a younger, more boisterous crowd. *Pūpūs,* such as meatballs, smoked salmon, and teriyaki pineapple are served, and the open bar includes frozen drinks. ✉ *Lahaina Harbor, Lahaina* ☎ *808/667–9595* ⊕ *www.kaulana-of-maui.com* 🎟 *$49* ☉ *Weekdays 5–7:30 PM.*

Paragon **Champagne Sunset Sail.** This 47-foot catamaran brings you a performance sail within a personal setting. Limited to groups of 24 (with private charters available), you can spread out on deck and enjoy the gentle trade winds. An easygoing, attentive crew will serve you hot and cold *pūpūs,* such as grilled chicken skewers, spring rolls, and a veggie platter, along with beer, wine, mai tais, and champagne at sunset. This is one of the best trips around. ✉ *Loading Dock, Lahaina Harbor* ☎ *808/244–2087* ⊕ *www.sailmaui.com* 🎟 *$44* ☉ *Mon., Wed., Fri. evenings; call for check-in times.*

Pride **Charters.** A 65-foot catamaran built specifically for Maui's waters, the *Pride of Maui* has a spacious cabin, dance floor, and large upper deck for unobstructed viewing. Evening cruises include cocktails and a buffet of *pūpūs* such as grilled chicken, beef and veggie kebabs, and warm Asian wontons. ✉ *Mā'alaea Harbor, Mā'alaea* ☎ *877/867–7433* ⊕ *www.prideofmaui.com* 🎟 *$47* ☉ *Tues. and Sat. 5–7:30 PM.*

Spirit of Lahaina **Cocktail or Dinner Cruise.** This double-deck, 65-foot catamaran offers you a choice of a full dinner cruise, featuring freshly grilled steak, mahimahi, and shrimp, or a cocktail cruise with appetizers, drinks, and dessert. Both cruises feature contemporary Hawaiian music and hula show. ✉ *Slip 4, Lahaina Harbor* ☎ *808/662–4477*

⊕ *www.spiritoflahaina.com* ✉ *$69 dinner cruise, $49 cocktail cruise* ⊙ *Daily 5–7:15 PM.*

Film & Theater

In the heat of the afternoon, a theater may feel like paradise. There are megaplexes showing first-run movies in Kukui Mall (Kīhei), Lahaina Center, and Maui Mall and Kaʻahumanu Shopping Center (Kahului). For live theater, check local papers for events and showtimes.

Maui Film Festival. In this ongoing celebration, the Maui Arts & Cultural Center features art-quality films every Wednesday (and sometimes Friday) evening at 5 and 7:30 PM, accompanied by live music, dining, and poetry in the Candlelight Café. In summer an international weeklong festival attracts big-name celebrities to Maui for cinema under the stars. ☎ *808/572–3456 recorded program information* ⊕ *www.mauifilmfestival.com.*

☾ ★ **"ʻUlalena" at Maui Theater.** One of Maui's hottest tickets, "ʻUlalena" is a 75-minute musical extravaganza that is well received by audiences and Hawaiian-culture experts alike. Cirque de Soleil–inspired, the ensemble cast (20 singer-dancers and a five-musician orchestra) mixes native rhythms and stories with acrobatic performance. High-tech stage wizardry gives an inspiring introduction to island culture. It has auditorium seating, and beer and wine are for sale at the concession stand. There are dinner-theater packages in conjunction with top Lahaina restaurants. ✉ *878 Front St., Lahaina* ☎ *808/661–9913 or 877/688–4800* ✍ *Reservations essential* ✉ *$48–$68* ⊙ *Tues.–Sat. at 6:30 PM.*

Warren & Annabelle's. This is one show not to miss—it's serious comedy with an amazing sleight-of-hand. Magician Warren Gibson entices his guests into his swank nightclub with red carpets and a gleaming mahogany bar, and plies them with à la carte appetizers (coconut shrimp, crab cakes), desserts (rum cake, crème brûlée), and "smoking cocktails." Then, he performs table-side magic while his ghostly assistant, Annabelle, tickles the ivories. This is a nightclub, so no one under 21 is allowed. ✉ *Lahaina Center, 900 Front St.* ☎ *808/667–6244* ✍ *Reservations essential* ✉ *$45 or $75, including food and drinks* ⊙ *Mon.–Sat. at 5.*

Bars & Clubs

Your best bet when it comes to bars on Maui? If you walk by and it sounds like it's happening, go in. If you want to scope out your options in advance, be sure to check the free *Maui Time Weekly,* found at most stores and restaurants, to find out who's playing where. The *Maui News* also publishes an entertainment schedule in its Thursday edition of the "Maui Scene." With an open mind (and a little luck), you can usually find a good scene for fun.

West Maui

Hard Rock Cafe. You've seen one Hard Rock Cafe, you've seen them all. However, Maui's Hard Rock brings you Reggae Monday, featuring our beloved local reggae star Marty Dread. $5 cover, 10 PM. ✉ *Lahaina Center, 900 Front St., Lahaina* ☎ *808/667–7400.*

Longhi's. This upscale, open-air restaurant is the spot on Friday nights, when there's usually live music and a bumping dance floor. Here you'll mingle with what locals call Maui's beautiful people, so be sure to dress your casual best. $5 cover, 10 PM. ✉ *Lahaina Center, 888 Front St., next to Hard Rock Cafe, Lahaina* ☎ *808/667–2288.*

Moose McGillycuddy's. The Moose offers no-cover live or DJ music on most nights, drawing a young, mostly single crowd who come for the burgers, beer, and dance floor beats. ✉ *844 Front St., Lahaina* ☎ *808/667–7758.*

> ## WHAT'S A LAVA FLOW?
>
> Can't decide between a pina colada or strawberry daiquiri? Go with a Lava Flow—a mix of light rum, coconut and pineapple juice, and a banana, with a swirl of strawberry puree. Add a wedge of fresh pineapple and a paper umbrella, and mmm . . . good. Try one at Lulu's in Kīhei.

Paradice Bluz. Live local bands and comedians frequent the stage at this popular, underground West Side hangout. This place is as close to a real night club as you'll find in Lahaina. It's dark and smoky, with a swanky lounge area, pool tables, and a decent lineup of bands and DJs. Expect to pay a hefty cover ($12–$20). ✉ *744 Front St., Lahaina* ☎ *808/667–5299.*

The Sly Mongoose. Off the beaten tourist path, the Sly Mongoose is the seediest dive bar in town, and one of the friendliest. The bartender will know your name and half your life history inside of 10 minutes, and she makes the strongest mai tai on the island. ✉ *1036 Limahana Pl., Lahaina* ☎ *808/661–8097.*

The South Shore

Hapa's Brewhaus & Restaurant. You can almost never go wrong with Hapa's. Famed local performer Willi K. owns Monday nights at this club, which has a large stage, a roomy dance floor, good sound, and a wild array of spinning disco lights. The place gets packed on other nights as well, offering a constant influx of hip-hop, reggae, sometimes even punk and metal. Tuesday is Ultra Fab techno night (gay-friendly), and Wednesday is half-price ladies night. When it's not crowded, there's always televised sports and tasty brews. ✉ *Lipoa Center, 41 E. Lipoa St., Kīhei* ☎ *808/879–9001.*

Lulu's. Lulu's could be your favorite bar in any beach town. It's a second-story, open-air tiki and sports bar, with a pool table, small stage, and dance floor to boot. The most popular night is Salsa Thursday, with dancing and lessons until 11. Friday is country night; Saturday is house. ✉ *1945 S. Kīhei Rd., Kīhei* ☎ *808/879–9944.*

★ **Mulligan's on the Blue.** Frothy pints of Guinness and late-night fish-and-chips—who could ask for more? Sunday nights feature foot-stomping Irish jams that will have you dancing a jig, and singing something about "a whiskey for me-johnny." Twice weekly, Mulligan's also brings you the more mellow *Wailea Nights,* an inspired dinner show performed by members of the band Hapa. ✉ *Blue Golf Course, 100 Kaukahi St., Wailea* ☎ *808/874–1131.*

Tsunami's. Located in one of Maui's most elite resorts, Tsunami's scene feels chic and electric. You can dance to DJ hip-hop, house, techno, and Top 40—or occasional live music. The place packs in a sophisticated crowd that spins on the dance floor under laser-beam lights. Weekend nights are the best, from 9:30 to 1. The dress code is strictly enforced—no jeans or shirts without a collar. $10 cover. ⊠ *Grand Wailea, 3850 Wailea Alanui Dr., Wailea* ☎ *808/875–1234.*

Upcountry & the North Shore

Casanova Italian Restaurant & Deli. Casanova can bring in some big acts, which in the past have included Kool and the Gang, Los Lobos, and Taj Majal. Most Friday and Saturday nights, though, it attracts a hip, local scene with live bands and eclectic DJs spinning house, funk, and world music. Don't miss the costume theme nights. Wednesday is for Wild Wahines (code for ladies drink half price), which can be more on the smarmy side. Cover $5–$15. ⊠ *1188 Makawao Ave., Makawao* ☎ *808/ 572–0220.*

Charley's. The closest thing to country Maui has to offer, Charley's is a down-home, divey bar in the heart of Pa'ia. It recently expanded its offerings to include disco, house, industry, and lounge nights. If you're lucky, you might even see Willy Nelson hanging here. ⊠ *142 Hāna Hwy., Pa'ia* ☎ *808/579–9453.*

Jacque's. Jacque's was once voted by locals as the "best place to see suspiciously beautiful people from around the world." On Friday nights, the crowd spills onto the cozy streets of Pa'ia, as funky DJs spin Latino, world lounge, salsa, and live jazz. $5, 10 PM. ⊠ *120 Hāna Hwy., Pa'ia* ☎ *808/579-8844.*

WHERE TO EAT

By Shannon Wianecki

In the early 1990s, a few rebel Hawai'i chefs boycotted expensive produce from the mainland and started sourcing local ingredients. Mixing the spoils of Polynesia with classic European or Asian preparations, they spawned such dishes as *'ahi* (yellowfin tuna) carpaccio, breadfruit soufflé, and *liliko'i* (passion fruit) cheesecake. Hawai'i regional cuisine was born. Many of its innovators—Bev Gannon of Hali'imaile General Store, Roy Yamaguchi of Roy's, and Peter Merriman of Hula Grill, to name a few—continue to raise the culinary bar around the state. Savvy restaurateurs have followed their lead, and now most restaurants offer tasting menus with excellent wine lists. Maui's outstanding natural resources—prime agricultural land and the adjoining Pacific Ocean—fill menus with healthy options, so feel free to indulge. Fresh fish selections, bursting ripe produce, and simple, stylized presentations characterize the very best. Expect to eat well at any price.

If you're hankering for ethnic or local-style cooking try wandering into the less-touristy areas such as Wailuku or Kahului. A good Hawaiian "plate lunch" will fulfill your daily requirement of carbohydrates: macaroni salad, two scoops of rice, and an entrée of, say, curry stew, teriyaki beef, or *kālua* (roasted in an underground oven) pig and cabbage.

Reservations are usually unnecessary, but it's never a bad idea to phone ahead to book a table. Restaurants are open daily unless otherwise specified. Generally, dinner is served from 5 to 9 PM. Casual dress—an aloha shirt and pants for men and a simple dress or pants for women—are acceptable in all establishments.

WHAT IT COSTS				
$$$$	$$$	$$	$	¢
RESTAURANTS over $35	$27–$35	$18–$26	$10–$17	under $10

Prices are for one main course at dinner.

West Maui

American

★ **$-$$** ✕ **Lahaina Coolers.** This breezy little café with a surfboard hanging from its ceiling serves such tantalizing fare as Evil Jungle Pasta (pasta with grilled chicken in spicy Thai peanut sauce) and linguine with prawns, basil, garlic, and cream. It also has pizzas, steaks, burgers, and desserts such as a chocolate taco filled with tropical fruit and berry salsa. Pastas are made fresh in-house. Don't be surprised to see a local fisherman walk through or a harbor captain reeling in a hearty breakfast. ☒ *180 Dickenson St., Lahaina* ☎ *808/661-7082* ▭ *AE, MC, V. $11-$26.*

¢ ✕ **The Gazebo Restaurant.** Even locals will stand in line up to half-an-hour for a table overlooking the beach at this restaurant, an actual open-air gazebo. The food is standard diner fare, but it's thoughtfully prepared. Breakfast choices include macadamia-nut pancakes and Portuguese sausage omelets. There are satisfying burgers and salads at lunch. The friendly hotel staff puts out coffee for those waiting in line. ☒ *Nāpili Shores Resort, 5315 Lower Honoapiʻilani Hwy., Nāpili* ☎ *808/669-5621* ▭ *No credit cards* ☉ *No dinner. $3-$9.*

Continental

$$$-$$$$ ✕ **Son'z.** Chef Aaron Placourakis, formerly of Sarento's, Nick's, and Aaron's atop Ala Moana (on Oʻahu) has taken over the Hyatt's beloved Swan Court. Now you can sample one of 3,000 bottles of wine (from the largest cellar in the state) while shielding your sourdough roll from the staring eyes of the swans. Outstanding steak and seafood dishes are featured. ☒ *Hyatt Regency Maui, Kāʻanapali Beach Resort, 200 Nohea Kai Dr., Kāʻanapali* ☎ *808/661-1234* ▭ *AE, D, DC, MC, V. $28-$45.*

Eclectic

$-$$$ ✕ **Café Sauvage.** This eclectic little restaurant is in a courtyard on Front Street. The atmosphere is not as intimate or elegant as some of its neighboring, oceanfront restaurants, but the food is excellent and the prices are surprisingly low. Specialties include peppered ʻahi tuna, cajun seared scallops, and a petite filet mignon wrapped in bacon and served with truffle butter and red wine sauce. The Seafood Sampler, which includes the fish of the day, tempura prawns, lobster ravioli, soup or salad, dessert and coffee, is a great deal. ☒ *844 Front St., Lahaina* ☎ *808/661-7600* ▭ *AE, MC, V. $16-$27.*

★ **¢-$** ✕ **Mala Ocean Tavern.** Perched above the tide-tossed rocks, this breezy "ocean tavern" is wholly satisfying. The menu, divided between *mala* (garden) and *moana* (ocean), is composed of small plates. The flatbread is crisp

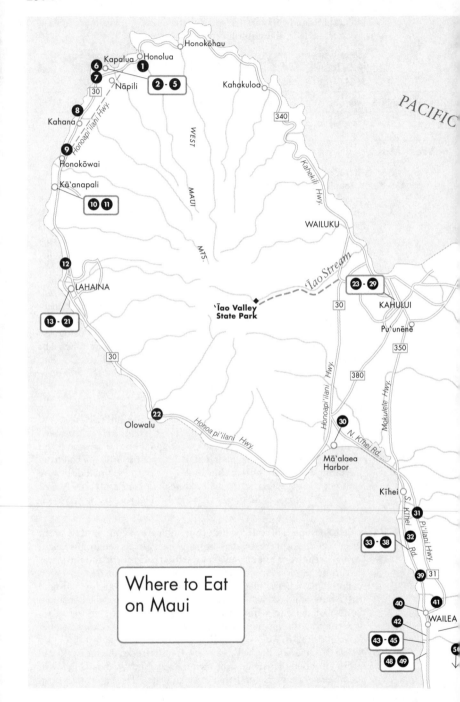

Honokōhau

Kapalua ○Honolua
6
7 ○Nāpili
1
2 · **5**

Kahakuloa

30

8
Kahana ○
WEST

9
Honokōwai
MAUI

Kā'anapali
MTS.
WAILUKU
340

10 **11**

Kahekili Hwy.

12
'Īao Stream

○LAHAINA
23 · **29**

'Īao Valley
State Park
30
KAHULUI

13 · **21**
Pu'unēnē

30
350

22
380

Olowalu
Honoa pi'ilani Hwy.
Honoapi'ilani Hwy.

30

N. Kīhei Rd.

Mā'alaea
Harbor

Kīhei ○
31

33 · **38**
32

Pi'ilani Hwy.

39 31

40
41

42
WAILEA

43 · **45**

48 **49**
50

PACIFIC

Where to Eat on Maui

2

PACIFIC OCEAN

and flavorful, the hefty Kobe burger drips with Maytag bleu cheese. Best of all is the calamari, lightly battered and fried with lemon slices, dipped in a spicy pesto. In the evening, the small bar is a coveted hangout. ✉ *1307 Front St., Lahaina* 🕾 *808/661–9394* ▭ *AE, MC, V. $9–$15.*

French

$$$–$$$$ ✕ **Chez Paul.** Since 1975 this tiny roadside restaurant between Lahaina and Māʻalaea in Olowalu has been serving excellent French cuisine to a packed house of repeat customers. Such dishes as fresh local fish poached in white wine with shallots, cream, and capers typify the classical menu. If you can't resist foie gras, this is the place to have it. The restaurant's offbeat exterior belies the fine art, linen-draped tables, and wine cellar. Don't blink or you'll miss this small group of buildings huddled in the middle of nowhere. ✉ *Honoapiʻilani Hwy., 4 mi south of Lahaina, Olowalu* 🕾 *808/661–3843* ⌲ *Reservations essential* ▭ *AE, D, MC, V* ☽ *No lunch. $29–$45.*

$$$–$$$$ ✕ **Gerard's.** Owner and celebrated chef Gerard Reversade started cook-
★ ing at the age of 10, and at 12 he was baking croissants. He honors the French tradition with such exquisitely prepared dishes as rack of lamb in mint crust with thyme jus, and venison cutlets in a port sauce with confit of chestnuts, walnuts, fennel, and pearl onions. The menu changes once a year, but many favorites—such as the sinfully good crème brûlée—remain. A first-class wine list, a lovely room, and celebrity-spotting round out the experience. ✉ *Plantation Inn, 174 Lahainaluna Rd., Lahaina* 🕾 *808/661–8939* ▭ *AE, D, DC, MC, V* ☽ *No lunch. $28–$47.*

Hawaiian–Pacific Rim

★ **$$$–$$$$** ✕ **The Banyan Tree.** If you've never tried foie gras ice cream, don't be shy. The menu is daring but delectable. Nothing is prepared as it should be: the priciest dish, lobster and scallops, is a salad, and the fish of Hawaiian royalty, *moi*, is served atop Indian-spice lentils with a yogurt sauce. We recommend placing your evening's fate in the care of the chef. The tasting menus and wine pairings provide an epicurean experience to be savored long afterward in memory. The open-beam restaurant's subdued atmosphere is charged with the sounds of live world music. ✉ *Ritz-Carlton, Kapalua, 1 Ritz-Carlton Dr., Kapalua* 🕾 *808/669–6200* ▭ *AE, D, DC, MC, V. $32–$48.*

$$–$$$$ ✕ **David Paul's Lahaina Grill.** Though the restaurant's namesake is only
FodorsChoice a consultant now, David Paul's is still a favorite. Beautifully designed,
★ it's adjacent to the elegant Lahaina Inn in a historic building on Lahainaluna Road. The restaurant has an extensive wine cellar, an in-house bakery, and splashy artwork decorating the walls. The house sommelier's suggestions keep up with the celebrated menu. Try the signature tequila shrimp and firecracker rice along with the scrumptious triple-berry pie. Demi portions are available at the bar. ✉ *127 Lahainaluna Rd., Lahaina* 🕾 *808/667–5117* ▭ *AE, DC, MC, V. $26–$42.*

$$–$$$ ✕ **Plantation House Restaurant.** It's hard to decide which is better here, the food or the view. Misty hills, grassy volcanic ridges lined with pine trees, and fairways that appear to drop off into the ocean provide an idyllic setting. The specialty is fresh island fish prepared according to different "tastes"—Upcountry Maui, Asian-Pacific, Provence, and others. The breeze through the large shuttered windows can be cool, so you may want to bring a sweater or sit by the fireplace. Breakfast here is a luxurious way to start your day. ✉ *Plantation Course Clubhouse, 2000 Plantation Club Dr., past Kapalua* ☎ *808/669–6299* ▭ *AE, MC, V. $18–$32.*

$$–$$$ ✕ **Roy's Kahana Bar & Grill.** Roy Yamaguchi's own sake brand ("Y") and Hawaiian fusion specialties, such as shrimp with sweet-and-spicy chili sauce and miso yaki butterfish, keep regulars returning for more. Locals know to order the incomparable chocolate soufflé immediately after being seated. Both restaurants, in Kahana and Kīhei, are in supermarket parking lots—it's not the view that excites, it's the food. ✉ *Kahana Gateway Shopping Center, 4405 Honoapi'ilani Hwy., Kahana* ☎ *808/669–6999* ✉ *Safeway Shopping Center, 303 Piikea Ave., Kīhei* ☎ *808/891–1120* ▭ *AE, D, DC, MC, V. $25–$31.*

$–$$$ ✕ **Hula Grill.** Genial chef-restaurateur Peter Merriman's bustling, family-oriented restaurant is in a re-created 1930s Hawaiian beach house, and every table has an ocean view. You can also dine on the beach, toes in the sand, at the Barefoot Bar, where Hawaiian entertainment is presented every evening. South Pacific snapper is baked with tomato, chili, and cumin aioli and served with a black bean, Maui onion, and avocado relish. Spareribs are steamed in banana leaves, then grilled with mango barbecue sauce over mesquitelike *kiawe* wood. ✉ *Whalers Village, 2435 Kā'anapali Pkwy., Kā'anapali* ☎ *808/667–6636* ▭ *AE, DC, MC, V. $17–$32.*

$–$$$ ✕ **Pineapple Grill.** Chef Joey Macadangdang heads the kitchen of Kapalua's newest restaurant. Hawai'i regional cuisine finds superb expression here, in dishes like the porcini-dusted *opakapaka* with *yuzu* velouté. The braised short ribs are garnished with just enough Maui pineapple relish to heighten hidden lemongrass and anise flavors. But don't get attached to anything on the menu—Chef Joey likes to reinvent it regularly. If the weather isn't too cold, the outdoor tables facing the West Maui mountains can be even nicer than those with an ocean view. ✉ *200 Kapalua Dr., Kapalua* ☎ *808/669–9600* ▭ *AE, MC, V. $17–$32.*

¢–$ ✕ **Aloha Mixed Plate.** Set right on the ocean, this funky open-air bar and restaurant is a great place for "'ono grinds"—good food in Hawaiian slang. Crispy coconut prawns, taro burgers, shoyu chicken, and kahlua pork are favorite island comfort foods (these are the things local kids daydream about when they're sent away to college). You too can indulge in these Hawaiian treats at this awesome outdoor location. ✉ *1286 Front St., Lahaina* ☎ *808/661–3322* ▭ *AE, D, DC, MC, V. $5–$13.*

¢–$ ✕ **Honokowai Okazuya.** Don't expect to sit down at this miniature restaurant sandwiched between a dive shop and a salon—this is strictly a take-out joint. You can order local plate lunches, Chinese, vegetarian, or sandwiches. The spicy eggplant is delicious, and the fresh chow fun noodles are bought up quickly. ✉ *3600-D Lower Honoapi'ilani Hwy., Lahaina* ☎ *808/665–0512* ▭ *No credit cards* ☉ *Closed Sun. and daily 2:30–4:30. $7–$11.*

Italian

$–$$$$ ✕ **VINO.** D. K. Kodama, the culinary mastermind behind Sansei, teamed up with Master Sommelier Chuck Furuya to create a strange child—an Italian tapas restaurant with a Japanese twist. The results have been hailed as, well, masterful. Set on the Kapalua golf course, the restaurant's active, somewhat noisy atmosphere encourages experimentation. Small plates of lamb chops, osso buco, or plump shrimp atop Asian noodles with truffle butter are sure to tempt. Wines are served in Riedel stemware; flights can be sampled at the bar. ⊠ *2000 Village Rd., Kapalua* ☏ *808/661–8466* ⊟ *AE, D, DC, MC, V. $10–$50.*

$$–$$$ ✕ **Longhi's.** A Lahaina establishment, Longhi's has been around since 1976, serving great Italian pasta as well as sandwiches, seafood,

> ### SO YOU DON'T LIKE SUSHI?
>
> On Maui, there's a sushi restaurant for everyone—even those who don't like sushi. Sansei has the most diverse menu: everything from lobster ravioli to sea urchin. People love designer rolls such as "69"—*unagi* eel slathered in sweet sauce paired with crab, or "caterpillar"—avocado and tuna wrapped around rice, complete with radish-sprout antennae.

beef, and chicken dishes. The pasta is homemade, and the in-house bakery turns out breakfast pastries, desserts, and fresh bread. Even on a warm day, you won't need air-conditioning with two spacious, breezy, open-air levels to choose from. The black-and-white tile floors are a classic touch. There's a second restaurant on the South Shore, at the Shops at Wailea. ⊠ *888 Front St., Lahaina* ☏ *808/667–2288* ⊠ *The Shops at Wailea, 3750 Wailea Alanui Dr., Wailea* ☏ *808/891–8883* ⊟ *AE, D, DC, MC, V. $25–$35.*

¢–$ ✕ **Penne Pasta.** Heaping plates of flavorful pasta and low-key, unintrusive service make this restaurant the perfect alternative to an expensive night out in Lahaina. The osso buco (Thursday's special) is sumptuous, and the traditional salade niçoise overflows with generous portions of olives, peppers, garlic 'ahi, and potatoes. Couples should split a salad and entrée, as portions are large. ⊠ *180 Dickenson St., Lahaina* ☏ *808/661–6633* ⊟ *AE, D, DC, MC, V* ⊘ *No lunch weekends. $7–$15.*

Japanese

$–$$$$ ✕ **Kai.** Master sushi chef Tadashi Yoshino sits at the helm of this intimate, ocean-view sushi bar, hidden behind the Lobby bar at the Ritz-Carlton, Kapalua. The menu includes sushi and hot Japanese entrées, but your best bet is to let Chef Yoshino design the meal. He might have yellowtail cheeks, fresh sea urchin, and raw lobster. He also makes lobster-head soup, a Japanese comfort food. ⊠ *Ritz-Carlton, Kapalua, 1 Ritz-Carlton Dr., Kapalua* ☏ *808/669–6200* ⊟ *AE, D, DC, MC, V. $10–$50.*

¢–$$$ ✕ **Sansei.** One of the best-loved restaurants on the island, Sansei is
Fodor'sChoice Japanese with a Hawaiian twist. Inspired dishes include panko-crusted
★ 'ahi, spicy fried calamari, mango-and-crab-salad roll, and a decadent foie gras nigiri sushi. Desserts often use local fruit; the Kula-persimmon crème brûlée is stunning. Both locations are now popular karaoke hangouts, serving late-night sushi at half price. ⊠ *Kapalua Shops, 115 Bay Dr., Kapalua* ☏ *808/666–6286* ⊠ *Kīhei Town Center, 1881 S. Kīhei Rd., Kīhei* ☏ *808/879–0004* ⊟ *AE, D, MC, V* ⊘ *No lunch. $8–$30.*

Mexican

¢–$ ✕ **Cilantro.** At last! Mexican food to brag about on the West Side. The flavors of Old Mexico are given new life here, where the tortillas are hand-pressed and no fewer than nine chilies are used to create the salsas. Rotisserie chicken tacos with jicama slaw are both mouthwatering and healthy. The Mother Clucker flautas with crema fresca and jalepeño jelly are not to be missed. Look for owner Paris Nabavi's collection of dead soldiers—tortilla presses worn from duty, now hand-painted and displayed up on the wall. ⊠ *In Old Lahaina Center, 170 Papalaua Ave., Lahaina* ☎ *808/667–5444* ⊟ *AE, MC, V. $7–$15.*

Seafood

$$–$$$$ ✕ **Pacific'O.** You can sit outdoors at umbrella-shaded tables near the water's edge, or find a spot in the breezy, marble-floor interior. The exciting menu features fresh 'ahi-and-ono tempura, in which the two kinds of fish are wrapped around *tobiko* (flying-fish roe), then wrapped in nori, and wok-fried. There's a great lamb dish, too—a whole rack of sweet New Zealand lamb, sesame-crusted and served with roasted macadamia sauce and Hawaiian chutney. Live jazz is played Thursday through Saturday from 9 to midnight. ⊠ *505 Front St., Lahaina* ☎ *808/667–4341* ⊟ *AE, D, DC, MC, V. $22–$40.*

The South Shore

American

$$–$$$$ ✕ **Joe's Bar & Grill.** Owners Joe and Bev Gannon, who run the immensely popular Hāli'imaile General Store, have brought their flair for food home to roost in this comfortable treetop-level restaurant at the Wailea Tennis Club, where you can dine while watching court action from a balcony seat. With friendly service and such dishes as New York strip steak with caramelized onions, wild mushrooms, and Gorgonzola cheese crumble, there are lots of reasons to stop in at this hidden spot. ⊠ *131 Wailea Ike Pl., Wailea* ☎ *808/875–7767* ⊟ *AE, MC, V. $20–$38.*

$–$$$ ✕ **Seawatch.** The Plantation House's South Shore sister restaurant has an equally good view, and almost as delicious a menu. Breakfast is especially nice here—the outdoor seating is cool in the morning, overlooking the parade of boats heading out to Molokini. The crab-cake Benedicts are a well-loved standard. Avoid seats above their private catering section, which can be noisy. ⊠ *100 Golf Club Dr., Wailea* ☎ *808/875–8080* ⊟ *AE, D, DC, MC, V. $16–$28.*

¢–$$$ ✕ **Tastings Wine Bar & Grill.** A wedge of a restaurant, this tiny epicurean mecca is tucked in behind a number of rowdy bars on South Kīhei Road. The owner-chef hails from Healdsburg, California, and he brought his highly regarded restaurant with him. The menu features tastings of oysters, risotto, lamb chops, and seared *opakapaka* (Hawaiian pink snapper) with a number of well-chosen wines by the bottle or glass. At the bar you can rub elbows with chefs and waiters from the island's best restaurants who come to spend their hard-earned tips here. ⊠ *1913 S. Kīhei Rd., Kīhei* ☎ *808/879–8711* ⊕ ⊟ *AE, D, DC, MC, V. $8–$27.*

$–$$ ✕ **Maui Onion.** Forget the overrated Cheeseburger in Paradise in Lahaina—Maui Onion has the best burgers on the island, hands down, and phenomenal onion rings as well. They coat the onions in pancake batter, dip them in panko, then fry them until they're golden brown. ⊠ *Renaissance Wailea, 3550 Wailea Alanui Dr., Wailea* ☎ *808/879–4900* ⊟ *AE, D, DC, MC, V. $10–$24.*

¢–$ ✕ **Kihei Caffe.** People-watching is fun over a cup of coffee at this casual breakfast and lunch joint. Hearty, affordable portions will prepare you for a day of surfing across the street at Kalama Park. The bowl-shaped egg scramble is tasty and almost enough for two. The resident rooster may come a-beggin' for some of your muffin. ⊠ *1945 S. Kīhei Rd., Kīhei* ☎ *808/879–2230* ⊟ *MC, V. $6–$10.*

Hawaiian–Pacific Rim

$$$–$$$$ ✕ **Humuhumunukunukuāpua'a.** Wrestle with the restaurant's formidable name—the name of the state fish—or simply watch the fish swim by in the 2,100-gallon tank at the bar. The thatch-roof building actually floats on a lagoon, creating an atmosphere that tends to outshine the food. We recommend skipping the dining room and enjoying *pūpū* at the bar. Try their signature 'ahi traps (delectable chunks of seared fish on lemongrass stalks) with an over-the-top cocktail. If you do try the dining room, you can fetch your own spiny lobster (which is best simply grilled) from a cage below the water's surface or try *laulau,* a traditional Hawaiian preparation of fish or meat steamed in leaves. ⊠ *Grand Wailea Resort, 3850 Wailea Alanui Dr., Wailea* ☎ *808/875–1234* ⊟ *AE, D, DC, MC, V. $28–$38.*

★ $$$–$$$$ ✕ **Spago.** Celebrity chef and owner Wolfgang Puck wisely brought his fame to this gorgeous locale. Giant sea-anemone prints, modern-art-inspired lamps, and views of the shoreline give diners something to look at while waiting. The solid menu delivers with dishes like seared scallops with asparagus and *pohole* (fiddlehead fern) shoots, and "chinois" lamb chops with Hunan eggplant. The beef dish, with braised celery, Armagnac, and horseradish potatoes, may be the island's priciest—but devotees swear it's worth every cent. ⊠ *Four Seasons Resort, 3900 Wailea Alanui Dr., Wailea* ☎ *808/879–2999* ⊟ *AE, D, DC, MC, V* ⊘ *No lunch. $29–$57.*

Irish

¢–$$ ✕ **Mulligan's on the Blue.** If you're hankering for bangers and mash or shepherd's pie, stop in at this pub on Wailea's Blue golf course. You'll be greeted by a nearly all-Irish staff, and before you know it, you'll be sipping a heady pint of Guinness. The Wailea Nights dinner show is outstanding—and a terrific deal to boot. Breakfast is a good value for the area, and the view is one of the best. ⊠ *100 Kaukahi St., Wailea* ☎ *808/ 874–1131* ⊟ *AE, D, DC, MC, V. $6–$18.*

Italian

$$$–$$$$ ✕ **Sarento's on the Beach.** The beachfront setting at this South Maui Italian restaurant is irresistible. Chef George Gomes, formerly of A Pacific Café, heads the kitchen. The menu features both traditional dishes—like penne Calabrese and seafood *fra diavolo*—as well as inventions such as swordfish saltimbocca, a strangely successful entrée with a prosciutto, Bel Paese cheese, radicchio, and porcini-mushroom sauce. The wine list includes some affordable finds. ⊠ *2980 S. Kīhei Rd., Kīhei* ☎ *808/875–7555* ⊟ *AE, D, DC, MC, V* ⊘ *No lunch. $27–$41.*

$$–$$$$
Fodor'sChoice
★
× **Capische?** Hidden up at the quiet Blue Diamond Resort, this restaurant is one local patrons would like kept secret. A circular stone atrium gives way to a small piano lounge, where you can find the best sunset view on the island. You can count on the freshness of the ingredients in superb dishes like the quail saltimbocca, and the saffron *vongole*—a colorful affair of squid-ink pasta and spicy saffron broth. Tables nestled in the downstairs garden have a peek at the "chef's cave" where a different region of Italy is explored each month. Intimate and well conceived, Capische, with its seductive flavors and ambience, ensures a romantic night out. ⊠ *Blue Diamond Resort, 555 Kaukahi St., Wailea* ☎ *808/879-2224* ▤ *AE, D, DC, MC, V* ☺ *No lunch. $26–$45.*

> **BEST BETS FOR *KEIKI* (KIDS)**
>
> **Hula Grill** (Kāʻanapali). You and your kids can dangle your feet in the sand at the "Barefoot Bar" fronting Kāʻanapali Beach.
> **Longhi's** (Lahaina, South Shore). Which kid doesn't love pasta? Though Longhi's doesn't have a *keiki* or kid's menu, the kitchen will whip up tyke-size noodle dishes on request.
> **Maui Ocean Center** (South Shore). What was the best exhibit? The manta ray? The jellyfish? Decide over sandwiches and shakes at the aquarium's café.
> **Sugar Cane Train** (Lahaina). Why not wow the kids with a barbecue dinner aboard Maui's famed Sugar Cane Train?

$$–$$$$ × **Ferraro's.** Overlooking Wailea Beach, this outdoor restaurant is beautiful both day and night. For lunch, indulge in a lobster and grapefruit sandwich—we haven't found its superior yet. At dinner begin your feast with the lump meat crab gazpacho and make use of the wine list's excellent Italian offerings. The service here is unparalleled. Occasionally you can catch celebrities gossiping at the bar. ⊠ *Four Seasons Resort Maui, Wailea Alanui Dr., Wailea* ☎ *808/874-8000* ▤ *AE, D, DC, MC, V. $26–$40.*

$–$$$ × **Caffe Ciao.** Caffe Ciao brings Italy to the Fairmont Kea Lani. Authentic, fresh gnocchi and lobster risotto taste especially delicious in the open-air café, which overlooks the swimming pool. For casual European fare, try the poached-tuna salad, grilled panini, or pizza from the wood-burning oven. Locals have long known Caffe Ciao's sister deli as the sole source for discerning palates: delectable pastries, tapenades, mustards, and even $50 bottles of truffle oil. ⊠ *Fairmont Kea Lani, 4100 Wailea Alanui Dr., Wailea* ☎ *808/875-4100* ▤ *AE, D, DC, MC, V. $13–$32.*

Japanese

¢–$$ × **Hirohachi.** A stone's throw from the flashier Sansei, Hirohachi has been serving authentic Japanese fare for years. Owner Hiro has discerning taste, he buys only the best from local fishermen and imports many ingredients from Japan. Order with confidence even if you can't read the Japanese specials posted on the wall; everything on the menu is high quality. ⊠ *1881 S. Kīhei Rd., Kīhei* ☎ *808/875-7474* ▤ *AE, MC, V* ☺ *Closed Mon. $6–$18.*

Seafood

$$$–$$$$ ✕ **Nick's Fishmarket Maui.** This romantic spot serves fresh seafood using the simplest preparations: mahimahi with Kula-corn relish, ʻahi pepper fillet, and *opakapaka* (Hawaiian pink snapper) with rock shrimp in a lemon-butter-caper sauce, to name a few. Everyone seems to love the Greek Maui Wowie salad made with local onions, tomatoes, avocado, feta cheese, and bay shrimp. Service is somewhat formal, but it befits the beautiful food presentations and extensive wine list. ✉ *Fairmont Kea Lani, 4100 Wailea Alanui Dr., Wailea* ☎ *808/879–7224* 🗖 *AE, D, DC, MC, V* ☉ *No lunch. $27–$49.*

$$–$$$$ ✕ **Waterfront Restaurant.** At this harborside establishment, fresh fish is prepared in a host of sumptuous ways: baked in buttered parchment paper; imprisoned in ribbons of angel-hair potato; or topped with tomato salsa, smoked chili pepper, and avocado. The varied menu also lists an outstanding rack of lamb and veal scaloppini. Visitors like to come early to dine at sunset on the outdoor patio. Enter Māʻalaea at the Maui Ocean Center and then follow the blue WATERFRONT RESTAURANT signs to the third condominium. ✉ *50 Hauʻoli St., Māʻalaea* ☎ *808/244–9028* 🗖 *AE, D, DC, MC, V* ☉ *No lunch. $19–$53.*

Thai

¢–$ ✕ **Thai Cuisine.** Fragrant tea and coconut-ginger chicken soup begin a satisfying meal at this excellent Thai restaurant. The care that goes into the decor here (reflected in the glittering Buddhist shrines, fancy napkin folds, and matching blue china) also applies to the cuisine. The lean and moist meat of the red-curry duck rivals similar dishes at resort restaurants, and the fried bananas with ice cream are wonderful. ✉ *In Kukui Mall, 1819 S. Kīhei Rd., Kīhei* ☎ *808/875–0839* 🗖 *AE, D, DC, MC, V. $8–$17.*

Vegetarian

¢–$ ✕ **Joy's Place.** You may see Joy in the back, whipping up one of her fantastic, vitamin-packed soups. Her glowing skin and smile are testaments to her healthful, culinary wizardry. Try a sandwich or green leaf wrap filled with veggies and a creamy spread. If you have a hint of a cold, a spicy potion is available to ward it off. ✉ *In Island Surf Bldg., 1993 S. Kīhei Rd., Suite 17, Kīhei* ☎ *808/879–9258* 🗖 *MC, V. $4–$14.*

Central Maui

American

¢ ✕ **Maui Bake Shop.** Wonderful breads baked in old brick ovens (dating to 1935), hearty lunch fare, and irresistible desserts make this a popular spot in Central Maui. Baker José Krall was trained in France, and his wife, Claire, is a Maui native whose friendly face you can often see when you walk in. Standouts include the focaccia and homemade soups. ✉ *2092 Vineyard St., Wailuku* ☎ *808/242–0064* 🗖 *AE, D, MC, V* ☉ *Closed Sun. No dinner. $4–$8.*

Chinese

¢–$ ✕ **Dragon Dragon.** Whether you're a party of 10 or 2, this is the place to share seafood-tofu soup, spareribs with garlic sauce, or fresh Dungeness crab with four sauces. Tasteful, simple decor complements the solid menu. The restaurant shares parking with the Maui Megaplex and makes a great pre- or post-movie stop. ⊠ *Maui Mall, 70 E. Kaahumanu Ave., Kahului* ☎ *808/893–1628* ▭ *AE, D, MC, V. $6–$17.*

Hawaiian

¢–$ ✕ **A.K.'s Café.** Nearly hidden between auto-body shops and karaoke bars is this wonderful, bright café. Affordable, tasty entrées such as grilled tenderloin with wild mushrooms or garlic-crusted ono with ginger relish come with a choice of two sides. The flavorful dishes are healthy, too—Chef Elaine Rothermal previously instructed island nutritionists on how to prepare health-conscious versions of local favorites. Try the Hawaiian french-fried sweet potatoes, the steamed *ulu* (breadfruit), or the poi. ⊠ *1237 Lower Main, Wailuku* ☎ *808/244–8774* ▭ *D, MC, V* ⊗ *Closed Sun. $4–$14.*

Italian

¢–$$$ ✕ **Marco's Grill & Deli.** This convenient eatery outside Kahului Airport (look for the green awning) serves reliable Italian food that's slightly overpriced. Homemade pastas appear on the extensive menu, along with an unforgettably good Reuben sandwich and the best tiramisu on the island. The local business crowd fills the place for breakfast, lunch, and dinner. The Kīhei branch is in a gorgeous new building with a grand piano. ⊠ *444 Hāna Hwy., Kahului* ☎ *808/877–4446* ⊠ *1445 S. Kīhei Rd., Kīhei* ☎ *808/874–4041* ▭ *AE, D, DC, MC, V. $7–$27.*

Thai

¢–$ ✕ **Saeng's Thai Cuisine.** Choosing a dish from the six-page menu here requires determination, but the food is worth the effort, and most dishes can be tailored to your taste buds: hot, medium, or mild. Begin with spring rolls and a dipping sauce, move on to such entrées as Evil Prince Chicken (cooked in coconut sauce with Thai herbs), or red-curry shrimp, and finish up with tea and tapioca pudding. Asian artifacts, flowers, and a waterfall decorate the dining room, and tables on a veranda satisfy lovers of the outdoors. ⊠ *2119 Vineyard St., Wailuku* ☎ *808/244–1567* ▭ *AE, MC, V. $8–$13.*

Vietnamese

¢–$$ ✕ **A Saigon Café.** The only storefront sign announcing this small, delightful hideaway is one reading OPEN. Once you find it, treat yourself to *banh hoi chao tom,* more commonly known as "shrimp pops burritos" (ground marinated shrimp, steamed and grilled on a stick of sugarcane). Fresh island fish is always available and vegetarian fare is well represented—try the green-papaya salad. The white interior serves as a backdrop for Vietnamese carvings in this otherwise unadorned space. Background music includes one-hit wonders from the early '70s. ⊠ *1792 Main St., Wailuku* ☎ *808/243–9560* ▭ *D, MC, V. $9–$19.*

¢ ✕ **Ba Le.** Tucked into the mall's food court is the best, cheapest fast food on the island. The famous soups, or *pho,* come laden with seafood or rare beef, fresh basil, bean sprouts, and lime. Tasty sandwiches are served on crisp French rolls—lemongrass chicken is a favorite. The word is out, so the place gets busy at lunchtime, though the wait is never long. ⊠ *Kau Kau Corner food court, Maui Marketplace, 270 Dairy Rd., Kahului* ☎ *808/877–2400* ▭ *AE, D, DC, MC, V. $4–$8.*

Upcountry

Hawaiian–Pacific Rim

★ $–$$$ ✕ **Hāli'imaile General Store.** What do you do with a lofty wooden building surrounded by sugarcane and pineapple fields that was a tiny town's camp store in the 1920s? If you're Bev and Joe Gannon, you invent a legendary restaurant. The Szechuan barbecued salmon and Hunan-style rack of lamb are classics, as is the sashimi napoleon appetizer: a tower of crispy wontons layered with 'ahi and salmon. Pastry chef Teresa Gannon makes an unbelievable pineapple upside-down cake. The restaurant even has its own cookbook. ✉ *900 Hāli'imaile Rd., take left exit halfway up Haleakalā Hwy., Hāli'imaile* ☎ *808/572–2666* ⊟ *MC, V. $15–$35.*

Italian

$–$$$ ✕ **Casanova Italian Restaurant & Deli.** This family-owned Italian dinner house is an Upcountry institution. The pizzas, baked in a brick wood-burning oven imported from Italy, are the best on the island, especially the *tartufo,* or truffle oil pizza. The daytime deli serves outstanding sandwiches and espresso. After dining hours, local and visiting entertainers heat up the dance floor. ✉ *1188 Makawao Ave., Makawao* ☎ *808/572–0220* ⊟ *D, DC, MC, V. $13–$33.*

Mexican

¢–$$ ✕ **Polli's.** This Mexican restaurant not only offers standards such as enchiladas, chimichangas, and fajitas but will also prepare any item on the menu with seasoned tofu or vegetarian taco mix—and the meatless dishes are just as good as the real thing. A special treat are the *bunuelos*—light pastries topped with cinnamon, maple syrup, and ice cream. The intimate interior is plastered with colorful sombreros and other cantina knickknacks. ✉ *1202 Makawao Ave., Makawao* ☎ *808/572–7808* ⊟ *AE, D, DC, MC, V. $8–$18.*

¢ ✕ **Maui's Fresh Tamales.** The owner of this tiny tamale haven can sometimes be seen surrounded by towers of fresh Kula corn. From these she makes indisputably "Maui's best tamales." Her daily specials—chipotle pork or chicken mole—are divine. This is a great spot to grab a bite to eat while touring Upcountry. ✉ *In Pukalani Sq., 81 Makawao Ave., Pukalani* ☎ *808/573–2998* ⊙ *Closes at 6 PM. $3–$7.*

Steak

$$–$$$ ✕ **Makawao Steak House.** A restored 1927 house on the slopes of Haleakalā is the setting for this *paniolo* restaurant, which serves consistently good prime rib, rack of lamb, and fresh fish. Three fireplaces, friendly service, and an intimate lounge create a cozy, welcoming atmosphere. ✉ *3612 Baldwin Ave., Makawao* ☎ *808/572–8711* ⊟ *D, DC, MC, V* ⊙ *No lunch. $18–$28.*

The North Shore

American

¢–$$ ✕ **Colleen's.** Hidden up a jungly road in Hā'iku, this is the neighborhood hangout for windsurfers, yoga teachers, and just plain beautiful people. For breakfast, the pastries tend to be jam-packed with berries and nuts, rather than butter and flakiness. Sandwiches are especially good, served on giant slices of homemade bread. For dinner you can't go wrong with the beef tenderloin salad or a piping hot pizza. ⊠ *In Hā'iku Cannery, 810 Kokomo Rd., Hā'iku* ☎ *808/575–9211* ▭ *AE, DC, MC, V. $7–$19.*

¢–$$ ✕ **Pā'ia Fishmarket Restaurant.** The line leading up to the counter of this tiny corner fish market attests to the popularity of the tasty fish sandwiches. Bench seating is somewhat grimy (you aren't the only one to have enjoyed fries here) but you really won't find a better fish sandwich. Don't bother with the other menu items—go for your choice of fillet served on a soft bun with a dollop of slaw and some grated cheese. As we say in Hawai'i, 'ono! ⊠ *2A Baldwin Ave., Pā'ia* ☎ *808/579–8030* ▭ *AE, DC, MC, V. $7–$19.*

Eclectic

$–$$ ✕ **Jacque's.** Jacque, an amiable French chef, won the hearts of the windsurfing crowd when he opened this hip, ramshackle bar and restaurant. French-Caribbean dishes like Jacque's Crispy Little Poulet (chicken) reveal the owner's expertise. The outdoor seating can be a little chilly at times; coveted spots at the sushi bar inside are snatched up quickly. ⊠ *120 Hāna Hwy., Pā'ia* ☎ *808/579–8844* ▭ *AE, D, MC, V. $11–$22.*

¢–$ ✕ **Café Des Amis.** Papier-mâché wrestlers pop out from the walls at this small creperie. French crêpes with Gruyère, and Indian wraps with lentil curry are among the choices, all served with wild greens and sour cream or chutney on the side. The giant curry bowls are mild but tasty, served with delicious chutney. For dessert there are crêpes, of course, filled with chocolate, Nutella, cane sugar, or banana. ⊠ *42 Baldwin Ave., Pā'ia* ☎ *808/579–6323* ▭ *AE, D, MC, V. $6–$11.*

Mexican

¢–$$$ ✕ **Milagro's.** Delicious fish tacos are found at this corner hangout, along with a selection of fine tequilas. Latin fusion recipes ignite fresh fish and vegetables. The location at the junction of Baldwin Avenue and Hāna Highway makes people-watching under the awning shade a lot of fun. Lunch and happy hour (3–5) are the best values; the prices jump at dinnertime. ⊠ *3 Baldwin Ave., Pā'ia* ☎ *808/579–8755* ▭ *AE, D, DC, MC, V. $8–$29.*

Seafood

★ $$$–$$$$ ✕ **Mama's Fish House.** For years Mama's has been *the* destination for special occasions. A stone- and shell-engraved path leads you up to what would be, in an ideal world, a good friend's house. The Hawaiian nautical theme is hospitable and fun—the menu even names which boat reeled in your fish. But, sadly, fame has gone to this restaurant's head. Prices bulged while portions shrank and dinner reservations start at 4:30 PM. If you're willing to fork over the cash, the daily catch baked in a creamy caper sauce or steamed in traditional lū'au leaves is still worth trying. Mama's is marked by a tiny fishing boat perched above the entrance about 1½ mi east of Pā'ia on Hāna Highway. ⊠ *799 Poho Pl., Kū'au* ☎ *808/579–8488* ⌂ *Reservations essential* ▭ *AE, D, DC, MC, V. $32–$48.*

WHERE TO STAY

By Shannon Wianecki

Maui's accommodations come in three sizes: small, medium, and gargantuan. Small B&Bs are personal and charming—often a few rooms or a cottage beside the owner's own home. They open a window into authentic island life. Medium-size condominiums are less personal (you won't see the owner out trimming the bougainvillea) but highly functional—great for longer stays or families who want no-fuss digs. The resorts are out of this world. They do their best to improve on nature, trying to re-create what is beautiful about Maui. And their best is pretty amazing. Opulent gardens, fantasy swimming pools with slides (some with swim-up bars), waterfalls, spas, and championship golf courses make it hard to work up the willpower to leave the resort and go see the real thing.

So, where to go for what? The resorts are clustered along the leeward (west and south) shores, meaning they are hot and sunny in summer and hot and sunny in winter, with periodic downpours. Kāʻanapali (in West Maui), the grande dame, is the original resort community and has the most action, feeding off the old whaler's haunt, Lahaina town. Kapalua, farther north, is more private and serene, and catches a bit more wind and rain. On the South Shore, posh Wailea has excellent beaches and designer golf courses, each with a distinct personality.

If you're willing to compromise on luxury, you can find convenient condos on the West Side, (in Nāpili or Kahana) or on the South Shore (in Kīhei). Many are oceanfront and offer the amenities of a hotel suite without the cost. Furnishings can be a little scruffy, however, and rarely do condos have central air-conditioning—something to consider if you aren't used to sleeping in humidity.

Most of the accommodations elsewhere on the island—say, Upcountry or in Hāna—are B&Bs or vacation rentals. Few offer breakfast, but most deliver ample seclusion and a countryside experience. Some are extravagant, million-dollar ocean-view properties that you can really write home about. Others are humble guest rooms with cozy furnishings that make you feel right at home. ■ TIP→ **If you're booking off the Internet, it pays to fact-check. Questions to ask before making the deposit: how far from the airport/beach/shops is it? Will I have a private bathroom and kitchen? Is there a phone and TV in the room?** Every owner thinks their vacation rental is a slice of heaven; whether you agree depends on your expectations.

WHAT IT COSTS				
$$$$	$$$	$$	$	¢
HOTELS over $340	$261–$340	$181–$260	$100–$180	under $100

Hotel prices are for two people in a standard double room in high season. Condo price categories reflect studio and one-bedroom rates.

West Maui

West Maui is a long string of small communities, beginning with Lahaina at the south end and meandering into Kāʻanapali, Honokowai,

Kahana, Nāpili, and Kapalua. Here's the breakdown on what's where: Lahaina is the business district with all the shops, shows, restaurants, historic buildings, churches, and rowdy side streets. Kā'anapali is all glitz: fancy resorts set on Kā'anapali Beach. Honokowai, Kahana, and Nāpili are quiet little nooks characterized by comfortable condos built in the late 1960s. All face the same direction, and get the same consistently hot, humid weather. Kapalua, at the northern tip, faces windward, and has a cooler climate and slightly more rain.

Hotels & Resorts

$$$$ 🏨 **Hyatt Regency Maui.** Fantasy landscaping with splashing waterfalls, swim-through grottoes, a lagoonlike swimming pool, and a 130-foot waterslide wows guests of all ages at this active Kā'anapali resort. Stroll through the lobby past museum-quality art, brilliant parrots, and . . . South African penguins (like we said, fantasy). It's not necessarily Hawaiian, but it is photogenic. At the southern end of Kā'anapali Beach, this resort is in the midst of the action. Also on the premises is Spa Moana, an oceanfront, full-service facility. ⊠ *200 Nohea Kai Dr., Kā'anapali 96761* ☎ *808/661–1234 or 800/233–1234* 🖷 *808/667–4499* ⊕ *www.maui. hyatt.com* ⇨ *815 rooms* ♿ *A/C, 4 restaurants, in-room data ports, in-room safes, cable TV with movies and video games, 2 18-hole golf courses, 6 tennis courts, pool, health club, spa, beach, 6 bars, library, children's programs (ages 3–12), no-smoking floors* ⊟ *AE, D, DC, MC, V.* *$400–$660.*

★ **$$$$** 🏨 **Ritz-Carlton, Kapalua.** If butler-drawn baths and brocade drapery are your cup of tea, book a room at this elegant hillside property. Although not set directly on the sand, the resort does command views of D. T. Fleming Beach, and Honolua Bay—and the multilevel pool and two hot tubs are open 24 hours. The grounds are private and secluded, despite being in the midst of Kapalua's collection of hotels, shops, restaurants, and golf courses. A full-time cultural adviser, Clifford Nae'ole, educates employees and guests alike in Hawaiian traditions. Tuesday night slack key guitar performances are not to be missed. This is a great jumping-off point for golfers—privileges are available at three championship courses, and the island of Lāna'i, with its two renowned courses is a quick ferry ride away. The dining is outstanding here; the decor needs some attention. ⊠ *1 Ritz-Carlton Dr., Kapalua 96761* ☎ *808/669–6200 or 800/262–8440* 🖷 *808/665–0026* ⊕ *www.ritzcarlton.com/resorts/kapalua* ⇨ *548 rooms* ♿ *A/C, 3 restaurants, in-room data ports, in-room safes, cable TV with movies, golf privileges, 10 tennis courts, pool, health club, hair salon, beach, lobby lounge, shops, spa, children's programs (ages 5–12), laundry service, business services* ⊟ *AE, D, DC, MC, V. $395–$705.*

WHERE TO STAY IN WEST MAUI

HOTEL NAME	Worth Noting	Cost $	Pools	Beach	Golf Course	Tennis Courts	Gym	Spa	Children's Programs	Rooms	Restaurants	Other	Location
Hotels & Resorts													
5 Hyatt Regency Maui	130-ft water slide	400–660	1	yes	yes	6	yes	yes	3–12	815	4		Kā'anapali
8 Kā'anapali Beach Hotel	Hula & lei-making classes	185–610	1	yes	priv.					430	3		Kā'anapali
4 Lahaina Inn	Historic property	125–175								12		no TVs	Lahaina
12 Mauian Hotel	On Nāpili Bay	145–195	1	yes						44		no TVs	Nāpili
3 Plantation Inn	Gerard's restaurant	170–265	1							18	1		Lahaina
★ 14 Ritz-Carlton, Kapalua	Banyan Tree restaurant	395–705	1	yes	priv.	10	yes	yes	5–12	548	3	shops	Kapalua
9 Sheraton Maui	Nightly torch-lighting ritual	360–640	1	yes		3	yes	yes	5–12	510	2		Kā'anapali
7 Westin Maui Resort	The Heavenly Spa	360–700	5	yes	priv.		yes	yes	0–12	761	3		Kā'anapali
Condos													
6 Kā'anapali Ali'i	Great location	360–540	2	yes	yes	6				264		kitchen	Kā'anapali
10 Mahina Surf	Free parking and phone	130–210	1							50		kitchen	Māhinahina
★ 13 Nāpili Kai Beach Club	Outstanding beach	250–450	4	yes					6–12	162		kitchen	Nāpili
11 Sands of Kahana	Kid's putting green	225–265	2	yes		3				162		kitchen	Kahana
B&Bs & Vacation Rentals													
2 Bambula Inn	Studio apartments	85–125								2		kitchen	Lahaina
1 Ho'oilo House	Private outdoor showers	245	1							5		no kids	Lahaina

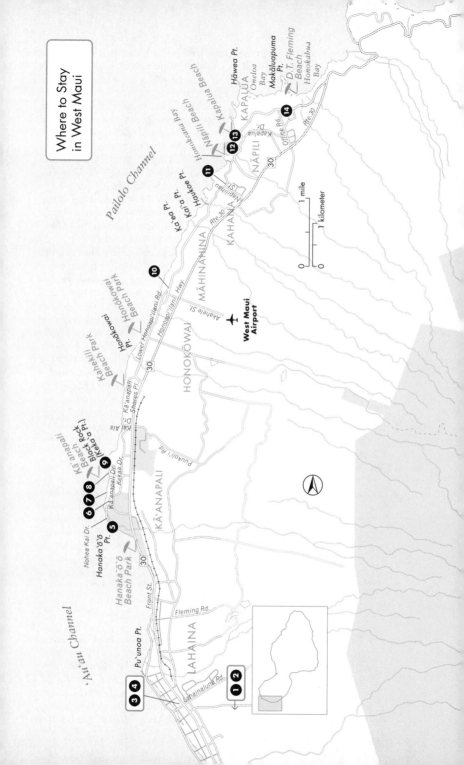

Where to Stay in West Maui

'Au'au Channel

Pailolo Channel

LAHAINA

KĀ'ANAPALI

HONOKŌWAI

MĀHINAHINA

KAHANA

NĀPILI

KAPALUA

West Maui Airport

Pu'unoa Pt.
Hanaka'ō'ō Beach Park
Hanaka'ō'ō Pt.
Nohea Kai Dr.
Kā'anapali Beach
Black Rock (Keka'a Pt.)
Kā'anapali Dr.
Kekaa Dr.
Kai Ala Dr.
Kā'anapali Shores Pt.
Kahekili Beach Park
Honokōwai Pt.
Honokōwai Beach Park
Kai'a Pt.
Ka'ea Pt.
Haukoe Pt.
Honokeana Bay
Nāpili Beach
Kapalua Beach
Hāwea Pt.
Omeloa Bay
Makāluapuma Pt.
D.T. Fleming Beach
Honokahua Bay

Front St.
Lahainaluna Rd.
Fleming Rd.
Puʻukoliʻi Rd.
Lower Honoapiʻilani Rd.
Honoapiʻilani Hwy.
Akahele St.
Nāpilihau St.
Office Rd.
Kapalua Dr.
Rte. 30
30

1 mile
1 kilometer

1 2
3 4
5
6 7 8
9
10
11
12 13
14

$$$$ ⌂ **Sheraton Maui.** Set among dense gardens on Kāʻanapali's best stretch of beach, the Sheraton offers a quieter, more understated atmosphere than its neighboring resorts. The open-air lobby has a crisp, cool look with minimal furnishings and decor, and sweeping views of the pool area and beach. The majority of the spacious rooms come with ocean views; only one of the six buildings has rooms with mountain or garden views. The swimming pool looks like a natural lagoon, with rock waterways and wooden bridges. Best of all, the hotel sits next to the 80-foot-high "Black Rock," from which divers leap in a nightly torch-lighting ritual. ✉ *2605 Kāʻanapali Pkwy., Kāʻanapali 97671* 🕾 *808/661–0031 or 888/ 488–3535* 🖷 *808/661–0458* ⊕ *www.starwood.com/hawaii* 🖙 *510 rooms* ⚘ *A/C, 2 restaurants, in-room safes, refrigerators, 3 tennis courts, pool, health club, hair salon, hot tub, spa, beach, lobby lounge, children's programs (ages 5–12), laundry facilities, Internet room, business services* ▤ *AE, D, DC, MC, V. $360–$640.*

$$$$ ⌂ **The Westin Maui Resort & Spa.** The cascading waterfall in the lobby of this hotel gives way to an "aquatic playground" with five heated swimming pools, abundant waterfalls (15 at last count), lagoons complete with pink flamingos, and a premier beach. The water features combined with a spa and fitness center, and privileges at two 18-hole golf courses make this an active resort—great for families. Relaxation is by no means forgotten. Elegant dark-wood furnishings in the rooms accentuate the crisp linens of "Heavenly Beds." Rooms in the Beach Tower are newer but slightly smaller than those in the Ocean Tower. The 13,000-square-foot Heavenly Spa features 11 treatment rooms and a yoga studio. ✉ *2365 Kāʻanapali Pkwy., Kāʻanapali 96761* 🕾 *808/667–2525 or 888/ 488–3535* 🖷 *808/661–5831* ⊕ *www.starwood.com/hawaii* 🖙 *761 rooms* ⚘ *3 restaurants, cable TV with movies, golf privileges, 5 pools, health club, hair salon, hot tubs, spa, beach, lobby lounge, babysitting, children's programs (infant–12), Internet room, meeting rooms* ▤ *AE, D, DC, MC, V. $360–$700.*

$$–$$$$ ⌂ **Kāʻanapali Beach Hotel.** This attractive, old-fashioned hotel is full of aloha. Locals say that it's one of the few resorts on the island where visitors can get a true Hawaiian experience. The vintage-style Mixed Plate restaurant, known locally for its native cuisine program, has displays honoring the many cultural traditions represented by the staff: the employees themselves contributed the artifacts. The spacious rooms are simply decorated in wicker and rattan and face the beach beyond the courtyard. There are complimentary classes in authentic hula dancing, lei making, and ʻukulele playing. ✉ *2525 Kāʻanapali Pkwy., Kāʻanapali 96761* 🕾 *808/661–0011 or 800/262–8450* 🖷 *808/667–5978* ⊕ *www. kbhmaui.com* 🖙 *430 rooms* ⚘ *A/C, 3 restaurants, in-room safes, cable TV with movies, golf privileges, pool, beach, lobby lounge* ▤ *AE, D, DC, MC, V. $185–$610.*

$–$$$ ⌂ **Plantation Inn.** Tucked into a corner of a busy street in the heart of Lahaina, the Plantation Inn's charm is what sets it apart. Filled with Victorian and Asian furnishings, it's reminiscent of a southern plantation home. Secluded lānai draped with hanging plants face a central courtyard, pool, and a garden pavilion perfect for morning coffee. Each guest room or suite is decorated differently, with hardwood floors, French doors, slightly dowdy antiques, and four-poster beds. (We think number 10 is nicest.) Suites have kitchenettes and whirlpool baths. A generous breakfast is included in the room rate, and one of Hawai'i's best French restaurants, Gerard's, is on-site. Breakfast, coupled with free parking in downtown Lahaina makes this a truly great value, even if it's 10 minutes from the beach. ⊠ *174 Lahainaluna Rd., Lahaina 96761* ☎ *808/ 667–9225 or 800/433–6815* 🖷 *808/667–9293* ⊕ *www.theplantationinn. com* 🛏 *18 rooms* ♿ *A/C, restaurant, fans, refrigerators, cable TV, pool, hot tub* ▭ *AE, MC, V. $170–$265.*

$–$$ 🏨 **Mauian Hotel.** If you're looking for a quiet place to stay, this nostalgic hotel way out in Nāpili may be for you. The rooms have neither TVs nor phones—such noisy devices are relegated to the 'Ohana Room, where a Continental breakfast is served daily. The simple two-story buildings date from 1959, but have been renovated with bright islander furnishings. Rooms include well-equipped kitchens. Best of all, the 2-acre property opens out onto lovely Nāpili Bay. ⊠ *5441 Lower Honoapi'ilani Hwy., Nāpili 96761* ☎ *808/669–6205 or 800/367–5034* 🖷 *808/669– 0129* ⊕ *www.mauian.com* 🛏 *44 rooms* ♿ *A/C, kitchens, pool, beach, hair salon, shuffleboard, laundry facilities, Internet room; no room phones, no room TVs* ▭ *AE, D, MC, V. $145–$195.*

$ 🏨 **Lahaina Inn.** This antique jewel right in the heart of town is classic Lahaina—a two-story wooden building that will transport you back to the turn of the 20th century. The nine small rooms and three suites shine with authentic period furnishings, including quilted bedcovers, antique lamps, and Oriental carpets. You can while away the hours in a wicker chair on your balcony, sipping coffee and watching Old Lahaina town come to life. The renowned restaurant, David Paul's, is downstairs. ⊠ *127 Lahainaluna Rd., Lahaina 96761* ☎ *808/661–0577 or 800/669–3444* 🖷 *808/667–9480* ⊕ *www.lahainainn.com* 🛏 *9 rooms, 3 suites* ♿ *A/C, Internet room; no room TVs, no smoking* ▭ *AE, D, MC, V. $125–$175.*

Condos

$$$$ 🏨 **Kā'anapali Ali'i.** Four 11-story buildings are laid out so well that the feeling of seclusion you'll enjoy may make you forget you're in a condo complex. Instead of tiny units, you'll be installed in an ample one- or two-bedroom apartment. All units have great amenities: a chaise in an alcove, a sunken living room, a whirlpool, and a separate dining room, though some of the furnishings are dated. The Kā'anapali Ali'i is maintained like a hotel, with daily maid service, an activities desk, and a 24-hour front-desk service. ⊠ *50 Nohea Kai Dr., Kā'anapali 96761* ☎ *808/667– 1400 or 800/642–6284* 🖷 *808/661– 1025* ⊕ *www.classicresorts.com*

CONDO COMFORTS

Foodland. This large grocery store should have everything you need, including video rentals and a Starbucks. ⊠ *Old Lahaina Center, 845 Waine'e St., Lahaina* ☎ *808/661– 0975.*

Gaby's Pizzeria and Deli. The friendly folks here will toss a pie for takeout. ⊠ *505 Front St., Lahaina* ☎ *808/661–8112.*

The Maui Fish Market. It's worth stopping by this little fish market for an oyster or a cup of fresh-fish chowder. You can also get live lobsters and fillets marinated for your barbecue. ⊠ *4405 Lower Honoapi'ilani Hwy., Honokowai* ☎ *808/665–9895.*

🛏 *264 units* ⚒ *A/C, in-room safes, kitchens, 18-hole golf course, 6 tennis courts, 2 pools, sauna, beach, laundry facilities* ▭ *AE, D, DC, MC, V. 1-bedroom $360–$540, 2-bedroom $490–$760.*

★ **$$–$$$$** 🏨 **Nāpili Kai Beach Club.** On 10 beautiful beachfront acres—the beach here is one of the best on the West Side for swimming and snorkeling—the Nāpili Kai draws a loyal following. Hawaiian-style rooms are done in seafoam and mauve, with rattan furniture; shoji doors open onto the lānai. The rooms closest to the beach have no air-conditioning, but ceiling fans usually suffice. "Hotel" rooms have only mini-refrigerators and coffeemakers, while studios and suites have fully equipped kitchenettes. This is a family-friendly place, with children's programs and free classes in hula and lei making. Packages that include a car, breakfast, and other extras are available if you stay five nights or longer. ✉ *5900 Lower Honoapiʻilani Hwy., Nāpili 96761* ☎ *808/669–6271 or 800/367–5030* 📠 *808/669–5740* ⊕ *www.napilikai.com* 🛏 *162 units* ⚒ *A/C in some rooms, in-room data ports, fans, kitchenettes, cable TV, 2 putting greens, 4 pools, exercise equipment, hot tub, beach, shuffleboard, children's programs (ages 6–12), dry cleaning, concierge* ▭ *AE, MC, V. Hotel room $200–$290, studios $250–$325, 1-bedroom $385–$450, 2-bedroom $555–$700.*

$$ 🏨 **Sands of Kahana.** Meandering gardens, spacious rooms, and an on-site restaurant distinguish this large condominium complex. Primarily a time-share property, a few units are available as vacation rentals. The upper floors benefit from their height—matchless ocean views stretch away from private lānai. The oceanfront penthouse, which accommodates up to eight, is a bargain at $435 during peak season. Kids can enjoy their own pool area near a putting green and ponds filled with giant koi. Raul Bermudez, the restaurant's chef, took first place in the 2004 "Taste of Lahaina" festival. ✉ *4299 Lower Honoapiʻilani Hwy., Kahana 96761* ☎ *808/669–0423 or 800/669–0400* 📠 *808/669–8409* ⊕ *www. sands-of-kahana.com* 🛏 *162 units* ⚒ *A/C in some rooms, restaurant, BBQs, in-room data ports, fans, kitchens, cable TV, putting green, 3 tennis courts, 2 pools, hot tub, beach, volleyball, concierge* ▭ *AE, MC, V. 1-bedroom $225–$265, 2-bedroom $325–$375, 3-bedroom $435.*

$–$$ 🏨 **Mahina Surf.** Mahina Surf stands out from the many condo complexes lining the ocean-side stretch of Honoapiʻilani Highway by being both well managed and affordable. You won't be charged fees for parking, check-out, or local phone use, and discount car rentals are available. The individually owned units are typically overdecorated, but each one has a well-equipped kitchen and an excellent ocean view. The quiet complex is a short amble away from Honokowai's grocery shopping, beaches, and restaurants. ✉ *4057 Lower Honoapiʻilani Hwy., Mahinahina 96761* ☎ *808/669–6068 or 800/367–6086* 📠 *808/669–4534* ⊕ *www. mahinasurf.com* 🛏 *50 units* ⚒ *BBQs, fans, kitchens, cable TV, some in-room broadband, in-room safes, pool, concierge, laundry facilities* ▭ *AE, MC, V. 1-bedroom $130–$210, 2-bedroom $160–$240.*

B&Bs & Vacation Rentals

$$ 🏨 **Hoʻoilo House.** If you really want to treat yourself to a luxurious getaway, spend a few nights at this Bali-inspired B&B. In the foothills of the West Maui Mountains, just south of Lahaina town, this stunning property brings the words "quiet perfection" to mind. As you enter the house your eye is immediately drawn to the immense glass doors that open onto a small but sparkling pool and a breathtaking view of the Pacific. Almost all of the furnishings and the materials used to build the house were imported from Bali. Two "conversation tables" in the common area are filled with Balinese cushions, providing great spots to snack, chat, or just relax. Each room is uniquely decorated and features traditional Balinese doors with mother-of-pearl inlay, a custom bed, a private lānai, a huge bathroom with a giant bathtub, and best of all—a private outdoor shower. ⊠ *138 Awaiku St., Lahaina 96761* ☎ *808/667–6669* 🖷 *808/661–7857* ⊕ *www.hooilohouse.com* ⇥ *5 rooms* ♿ *A/C, fans, Wi-Fi, in-room safes, cable TV, pool, massage; no kids, no smoking* ▭ *AE, MC, V. $245, 3-night minimum.*

¢–$ 🏠 **Bambula Inn.** This casual sprawling house in a quiet Lahaina residential area has two studio apartments, one attached to the house and one freestanding. No breakfast is served; this is a move-in-and-hang-out beach house. Just across the street is a small beach, and moored just offshore is a sailboat hand-built by the owner. He likes to take his guests out for whale-watching and sunset sails, no charge. He also provides snorkel equipment. This is a friendly, easygoing way to visit Lahaina. ⊠ *518 Ilikahi St., Lahaina 96761* ☎ *808/667–6753 or 800/544–5524* 🖷 *808/667–0979* ⊕ *www.bambula.com* ⇥ *2 studios* ♿ *A/C in some rooms, fans, kitchens, kitchenettes, cable TV* ▭ *AE, D, MC, V. $85–$125.*

The South Shore

The South Shore is composed of two main communities: resort-filled Wailea and down-to-earth Kīhei. In general, the farther south you go, the fancier the accommodations get. ■ TIP→ **North Kīhei tends to have great prices but the windy beaches are scattered with seaweed. (Not a problem if you don't mind driving 5–10 minutes to save a few bucks.)** As you travel down South Kīhei Road, you can find condos both on and off inviting beach parks, and close to shops and restaurants. Once you hit Wailea, the opulence quotient takes a giant leap—perfectly groomed resorts gather around Wailea and Polo beaches. This resort wonderland mimics (some say improves upon) Kā'anapali. The two communities continuously compete over which is more exclusive and which has better weather—in our opinion it's a definite draw.

Hotels & Resorts

$$$$ 🏠 **Fairmont Kea Lani Hotel Suites & Villas.** Gleaming white spires and tiled

Fodor'sChoice   archways are the hallmark of this stunning resort. Spacious suites have

★   microwaves, stereos, and marble bathrooms. But the villas are the real lure. Each is two-story, has a private plunge pool, two (or three) large bedrooms, a laundry room, and a fully equipped kitchen—barbecue and margarita blender included. Best of all, maid service does the dishes. A fantastic haven for families, the villas are side by side in a sort of miniature neighborhood. Request one on the end, with an upstairs sundeck. The resort offers good dining choices, a gourmet deli, and a small, almost private beach. ⊠ *4100 Wailea Alanui Dr., Wailea 96753* ☎ *808/875–4100 or 800/882–4100* 🖷 *808/875–1200* ⊕ *www.kealani.com* ⇥ *413 suites, 37 villas* ♿ *A/C, 3 restaurants, in-room data ports, mi-*

WHERE TO STAY ON THE SOUTH SHORE

HOTEL NAME	Worth Noting	Cost $	Pools	Beach	Golf Course	Tennis Courts	Gym	Spa	Children's Programs	Rooms	Restaurants	Other	Location
Hotels & Resorts													
★ ❸ Fairmont Kea Lani Hotel Suites & Villas	Villas available	385–665	3	yes	priv.		yes	yes	5-12	450	3	shops	Wailea
★ ❹ Four Seasons Resort	Luxurious	365–890	1	yes	priv.	2	yes	yes	5-12	380	3		Wailea
❺ Grand Wailea	Spa Grande	485	3	yes	priv.	2	yes	yes	5-12	779	5	shops	Wailea
⓭ Mana Kai Maui	Great prices	100–135	1	yes						98			Kihei
⓯ Maui Coast Hotel	Beach across the street	145–235	1			2				379	2		Kihei
❶ Maui Prince	Secluded beach	335–525	2	yes	yes	6			5-12	310	4		Mākena
❼ Renaissance Wailea Beach Resort	VIP club available	309–419	2	yes			yes		5-12	345	3		Wailea
Condos													
★ ⓬ Hale Hui Kai	Oceanfront lounge	275	1	yes						40		kitchen	Kihei
⓮ Kama'ole Sands	Beach across the street	195–275	1			4				309	1	kitchen	Kihei
⓰ Maui Sunseeker Resort	Beach across the street	115–135								4		kitchen	Kihei
❷ Polo Beach Club	Location, location, location	360–385	1	yes	priv.					71		kitchen	Wailea
❽ Wailea 'Ekahi	Studios available	210–510	4	yes	priv.					300		kitchen	Wailea
❻ Wailea 'Elua	Gated community	270–925	2	yes	priv.					150		kitchen	Wailea
❿ Wailea 'Ekolu	Good prices	180–260	2	no	priv.					160		kitchen	Wailea
B&Bs & Vacation Rentals													
❾ Amanda and George's Wonderful Wailea	1-BR suite	120	2			4				1		kitchen	Wailea
⓫ Eva Villa	360° views from rooftop	130–150	1							3		kitchen	Wailea

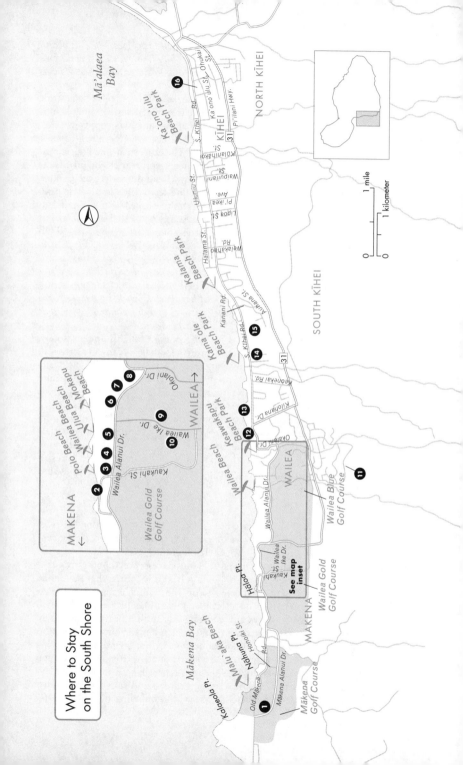

Where to Stay on the South Shore

Māʻalaea Bay

Mākena Bay

Kalaeola Pt.
Maluʻaka Beach
Nahuna Pt.
Honoiki St.

Old Mākena Rd.

Mākena Alanui Dr.

Mākena Golf Course

MAKENA

WAILEA

Wailea Gold Golf Course

Hāloa Pt.

Kaukahi St.
Wailea Ike Dr.

See map inset

Wailea Alanui Dr.

WAILEA

Wailea Blue Golf Course

Okolani Dr.

KĪHEI

Keawakapu Beach Park
Kamaʻole Beach Park
Kalama Park
Beach Park

Wailea Beach

Kilohana Dr.
Keonekai Rd.
S. Kīhei Rd.
ʻAuhana St.
Kanani Rd.
Halama St.
Weiakahao Rd.
Lipoa St.
Prʻikea Ave.
Waipulani St.
ʻUlulu St.
Kolanihakoi St.
S. Kīhei Rd.
Kaʻono ʻulu St.
Ohukai St.
Pīʻilani Hwy.

Kaʻono ʻulu Beach Park

NORTH KĪHEI

SOUTH KĪHEI

31

Map inset (MAKENA / WAILEA)

MAKENA →

**← Polo Beach Beach
Wailea Beach
ʻUlua Mokapu Beach**

Wailea Alanui Dr.

Kaukahi St.
Wailea Ike Dr.

Wailea Gold Golf Course

Okolani Dr.

WAILEA →

0   1 mile
0   1 kilometer

crowaves, refrigerators, in-room VCRs, golf privileges, 3 pools, health club, hair salon, hot tubs, spa, beach, lobby lounge, shops, children's programs (ages 5–12) ▭ AE, D, DC, MC, V. Suites $385–$665, villas $1,600–$2,800.

$$$$

Fodor'sChoice
★

✉ **Four Seasons Resort.** Impeccably stylish, subdued, and relaxing describe most Four Seasons properties; this one fronting award-winning Wailea beach is no exception. Thoughtful luxuries—like Evian spritzers poolside and room-service attendants who toast your bread in-room—earned this Maui favorite its reputation. The property has an understated elegance, with beautiful floral arrangements, courtyards, and private cabanas. Most rooms have an ocean view (avoid those over the parking lot in the North Tower) and you can find terry robes and whole-bean coffee grinders in each. Choose between three excellent restaurants, including Wolfgang Puck's Spago. The recently renovated spa is small but expertly staffed. Honeymooners: request Suite 301, with its round tub and private lawn. ✉ 3900 Wailea Alanui Dr., Wailea 96753 ☎ 808/874–8000 or 800/334–6284 🖷 808/874–6449 ⊕ www.fourseasons.com/maui ⇨ 380 rooms ⚬ A/C, 3 restaurants, in-room data ports, in-room safes, refrigerators, cable TV with movies and video games, golf privileges, 2 tennis courts, pool, health club, spa, beach, bike rental, badminton, croquet, volleyball, 3 bars, recreation room, children's programs (ages 5–12) ▭ AE, D, DC, MC, V. $365–$890.

$$$$

✉ **Grand Wailea.** "Grand" is no exaggeration for this opulent sunny, 40-acre resort. Elaborate water features include a "canyon riverpool" with slides, caves, a Tarzan swing, and a water elevator. Tropical garden paths meander past artwork by Léger, Warhol, Picasso, Botero, and noted Hawaiian artists—sculptures even hide in waterfalls. Spacious ocean-view rooms are outfitted with stuffed chaises, comfortable desks, and oversize marble bathrooms. Spa Grande, the island's most comprehensive spa facility, offers you everything from mineral baths to massage. For kids, Camp Grande has a full-size soda fountain, game room, and movie theater. Although not the place to go for quiet or for especially attentive service, the property is astounding. ✉ 3850 Wailea Alanui Dr., Wailea 96753 ☎ 808/875–1234 or 800/888–6100 🖷 808/874–2442 ⊕ www.grandwailea.com ⇨ 779 rooms ⚬ A/C, 5 restaurants, in-room data ports, in-room safes, cable TV with movies, golf privileges, 3 pools, health club, hair salon, indoor and outdoor hot tubs, spa, beach, racquetball, 6 bars, nightclub, recreation room, shops, children's programs (ages 5–12) ▭ AE, D, DC, MC, V. $485.

$$$–$$$$

✉ **Maui Prince.** This isn't the most luxurious resort on the South Shore—it could actually use a face-lift—but it has many pluses that more than make up for the somewhat dated decor. The location is superb. Just south of Mākena, the hotel is on a secluded piece of land surrounded by two magnificent golf courses and abutting a beautiful, near-private beach. The pool area is simple (two round pools), but surrounded by beautiful gardens that are quiet and understated compared to the other big resorts. The attention given to service is apparent from the minute you walk into the open-air lobby—the staff is excellent. Rooms on five levels all have ocean views (in varying degrees) and surround the courtyard, which has a Japanese garden with a bubbling stream. ✉ 5400

Mākena Alanui Rd., Mākena 96753 ☎ *808/874–1111 or 800/321–6284* 📠 *808/879–8763* ⊕ *www.princeresortshawaii.com* ⤻ *310 rooms* ⚬ *A/C, 4 restaurants, in-room safes, some in-room VCRs, 2 18-hole golf courses, 6 tennis courts, 2 pools, exercise equipment, hot tub, beach, badminton, croquet, shuffleboard, children's programs (ages 5–12), business services, meeting rooms* ▤ *AE, DC, MC, V. $335–$525.*

$$$–$$$$ ▦ **Renaissance Wailea Beach Resort.** Most of the rooms here are positioned on fantastic Mōkapu Beach. A giant ceremonial canoe enhances the lobby area. Outside you can find exotic gardens, waterfalls, and reflecting ponds. A decent value package offers discounts at the restaurants and the hotel's own lū'au, performed on-site three nights a week. The VIP Mōkapu Beach Club building has 26 luxury accommodations closest to the beach, and its own concierge, pool, and beach cabanas. Mōkapu Beach Club guests also have access to nearby golf and tennis facilities. ✉ *3550 Wailea Alanui Dr., Wailea 96753* ☎ *808/879–4900 or 800/992–4532* 📠 *808/874–6128* ⊕ *www.renaissancehotels.com* ⤻ *345 rooms* ⚬ *A/C, 3 restaurants, in-room data ports, refrigerators, cable TV with movies and video games, 2 pools, health club, hot tub, beach, basketball, Ping-Pong, shuffleboard, lobby lounge, children's programs (ages 5–12)* ▤ *AE, D, DC, MC, V. $309–$419.*

$–$$$ ▦ **Mana Kai Maui.** This unsung hero of South Maui hotels may be older than its competitors, but that only means it's closer to the beach—beautiful Keawakapu. Hotel rooms with air-conditioning are remarkably affordable for the location. Two-room condos with private lānai benefit from the hotel amenities, such as daily maid service and discounts at the oceanfront restaurant downstairs. Shoji screens and bamboo furniture complement the marvelous ocean views, which in winter are punctuated by the visiting humpback whales. ✉ *2960 S. Kīhei Rd., Kīhei 96753* ☎ *808/879–2778 or 800/367–5242* 📠 *808/879–7825* ⊕ *www.crhmaui.com* ⤻ *49 hotel rooms, 49 1-bedroom condos* ⚬ *A/C, restaurant, in-room safes, refrigerators, cable TV, pool, hair salon, hot tub, beach, meeting rooms* ▤ *AE, D, DC, MC, V. Hotel rooms $100–$135, condos $180–$310.*

$–$$ ▦ **Maui Coast Hotel.** You might never notice this elegant hotel because it's set back off the street. The standard rooms are fine—very clean and modern—but the best deal is to pay a little more for one of the suites. In these you'll get an enjoyable amount of space and jet nozzles in the bathtub. You can sample nightly entertainment by the large, heated pool or work out in the new fitness center until 10 PM. The 6-mi-long stretch of Kama'ole Beach I, II, and III is across the street. ✉ *2259 S. Kīhei Rd., Kīhei 96753* ☎ *808/874–6284, 800/895–6284, or 800/426–0670* 📠 *808/875–4731* ⊕ *www.westcoasthotels.com* ⤻ *265 rooms, 114 suites* ⚬ *A/C, 2 restaurants, in-room safes, refrigerators, cable TV with movies, 2 tennis courts, pool, exercise equipment, hot tubs, dry cleaning, laundry service* ▤ *AE, D, DC, MC, V. $145–$235.*

Condos

$$$$ ▦ **Polo Beach Club.** This wonderful, old eight-story property lording over a hidden section of Polo beach somehow manages to stay under the radar. From your giant corner window, you can look down at the famed Kea Lani villas, and know you've scored the same great locale at a fraction of the price. Individually owned apartments are well-cared for and feature top-of-the-line amenities, such as stainless-steel kitchens, marble floors, and valuable artwork. The property is no-smoking and an underground parking garage keeps vehicles out of the blazing Kīhei sun. ⊠ *3750 Wailea Alanui Dr., Wailea 96753* ☎ *808/879–1595 or 800/ 367–5246* 🖷 *808/874–3554* ⊕ *www.drhmaui.com* 🛏 *71 units* ⚘ *A/C, fans, Wi-Fi, kitchens, cable TV, in-room VCRs, pool, hot tub, tennis privileges, beach, golf privileges, laundry facilities; no smoking* ⊟ *AE, MC, V. 1-bedroom $360–$385, 2-bedroom $430–$570.*

$$–$$$$
Fodor'sChoice
★

🛏 **Wailea 'Ekahi, 'Elua, and 'Ekolu.** The Wailea Resort started out with three upscale condominium complexes named, appropriately, 'Ekahi, 'Elua, and 'Ekolu (One, Two, and Three). The individually owned units, managed by Destination Resorts Hawai'i, represent some of the best values in this high-class neighborhood. All benefit from daily housekeeping, air-conditioning, high-speed Internet, free long distance, lush landscaping, and preferential play at the neighboring world-class golf courses and tennis courts. You're likely to find custom appliances and sleek furnishings befitting the million-dollar locale. ■ TIP→ **The concierges here will stock your fridge with groceries—even hard-to-find dietary items—for a nominal fee.** 'Ekolu, farthest from the water, is the most affordable, and benefits from a hillside view; 'Ekahi is a large V-shape property focusing on Keawakapu beach; 'Elua has 24-security security and overlooks Ulua beach. ⊠ *3750 Wailea Alanui Dr., Wailea 96753* ☎ *808/879–1595 or 800/367–5246* 🖷 *808/874–3554* ⊕ *www.drhmaui.com* 🛏 *594 units* ⚘ *A/C, fans, Wi-Fi, kitchens, cable TV, in-room VCRs, 8 pools, hot tubs, tennis privileges, 2 beaches, golf privileges, laundry facilities* ⊟ *AE, MC, V. Studios $210, 1-bedroom $180–$550, 2-bedroom $215–$725, 3-bedroom $655–$925.*

★ **$$$**

🛏 **Hale Hui Kai.** Bargain hunters who stumble across this small three-story condo complex will think they've died and gone to heaven. The beachfront units are older, but many of them have been renovated. Some have marble countertops in the kitchens and all have outstanding views. But never mind the interior, you'll want to spend all of your time outdoors—in the shady lava-rock lobby that overlooks a small pool perfect for kids, or on gorgeous Keawakapu beach just steps away. Light sleepers should avoid the rooms just above the neighboring restaurant, Sarento's, but definitely stop in there for dinner. ⊠ *115 S. Kīhei Rd., Kīhei 96753* ☎ *808/879–1219 or 800/809–6284* 🖷 *808/879–0600* ⊕ *www.beachbreeze.com* 🛏 *40 units* ⚘ *Fans, kitchens, cable TV,*

CONDO COMFORTS

Eskimo Candy. Stop here for fresh fish or fish-and-chips. ⊠ *2665 Wai Wai Pl., Kīhei* ☎ *808/879–5686.*

Premiere Video. With two locations, this is the best video store around. ⊠ *North Kīhei, 357 Huku Lii Pl.* ☎ *808/875–0500* ⊠ *South Kīhei, 2439 S. Kīhei Rd.* ☎ *808/ 875-1113.*

Safeway. Find every variety of grocery at this giant superstore. ⊠ *277 Piikea Ave., Kīhei* ☎ *808/ 891-9120.*

Who Cut the Cheese. This shop has great party foods: *fromage,* fancy balsamics, and wines. ⊠ *Azeka Marketplace, 1279 S. Kīhei Rd., Suite 309* ☎ *808/874–3930.*

in-room VCRs, in-room safes, pool, beach, laundry facilities ☰ *AE, D, DC, MC, V. 1-bedroom $275, 2-bedroom $275–$375.*

$$–$$$ ▦ **Kamaʻole Sands.** "Kam" Sands is a good choice for the active traveler; there are tennis and volleyball courts to keep you in shape, and the ideal family beach (Kamaʻole III) waits across the street. Eleven four-story buildings wrap around 15 acres of grassy slopes with swimming pools, a small waterfall, and barbecues. Condos are equipped with modern conveniences, but there's a relaxed, almost retro feel to the place. All units have kitchens, laundry facilities, and private lānai. The property has a 24-hour front desk and an activities desk. ▪ TIP➔ **Attention homeowners: privately owned house-trade options are available at www. kamaole-sands.com.** ✉ *2695 S. Kīhei Rd., Kīhei 96753* ☎ *808/874–8700 or 800/367–5004* 🖷 *808/879–3273* ⊕ *www.castleresorts.com/KSM* ⤳ *309 units* ♿ *A/C in some rooms, restaurant, fans, in-room data ports, kitchens, some cable TV, some in-room VCRs, 4 tennis courts, pool, hot tubs, wading pool, volleyball* ☰ *AE, D, DC, MC, V. 1-bedroom $195–$275, 2-bedroom $275–$375, 3-bedroom $485.*

$ ▦ **Maui Sunseeker Resort.** The care put into this property is noticeable from the sign on the road. This small North Kīhei hotel is a great value for the area and is private and relaxed. You can opt for a simple but attractively furnished studio, one-bedroom, or two-bedroom penthouse; all have kitchenettes and full baths, as well as barbecues. The 4-mi stretch of beach across the street isn't the best for swimming, but it's great for strolling and watching windsurfers, whales (in winter), and sunsets. ✉ *551 S. Kīhei Rd., Kīhei 96753* ☎ *808/879–1261 or 800/532–6284* 🖷 *808/ 874–3877* ⊕ *www.mauisunseeker.com* ⤳ *4 units* ♿ *A/C, kitchenettes, cable TV, some in-room VCRs, hot tub, laundry facilities, Internet room* ☰ *MC, V. Studios $115, 1-bedroom $135, 2-bedroom $165; 3-night minimum.*

B&Bs & Vacation Rentals

$ ▦ **Amanda and George's Wonderful Wailea Condominium.** Exceptionally tasteful decor (a king-size bed, a leather couch, lovely artwork) makes this one-bedroom suite live up to its name. The views are nice, and the location is outstanding—on the Blue golf course, it's a quick drive (or seven-minute jog) to South Maui's best beaches, restaurants, and shops. The kitchen and bathroom are well-appointed and spotless. Amenities include use of the two pools and Jacuzzis on the grounds and access to the famed Wailea Tennis Club. ✉ *At Grand Champions, Wailea Ike Pl. #25, Wailea 96753* ☎ *808/891–2214* ⊕ *www.travelmaui.com/condo rental/wailea* ⤳ *1 suite* ♿ *A/C, BBQ, fans, kitchen, cable TV, 2 pools, hot tubs, 4 tennis courts, laundry facilities; no smoking* ☰ *No credit cards. $120, 5-night minimum.*

$ ▦ **Eva Villa.** A waterfall and lilies provide an elegant welcome at this B&B in the residential neighborhood above Wailea. Three modern, 600-square-foot suites come furnished with queen-size beds and sleeper sofas, kitchens stocked with Continental breakfasts, and access to the pool and Jacuzzi. Rick and Dale Pounds, the congenial owners who live on-property, even provide guests with a farewell CD of island photos and music. The real treasure, however, is the 360-degree ocean and mountain view from the rooftop patio, accompanied by a telescope. ✉ *815*

Kumulani Dr., Wailea 96753 ☎ *808/874–6407* ⊕ *www.mauibnb.com* ⤶ *3 suites* ⟁ *BBQ, fans, kitchens, cable TV, pool, hot tub, laundry facilities, Internet room. $130–$150.*

Central Maui

Kahului and Wailuku, the industrial centers that make up Central Maui, are not known for their lavish accommodations. The exceptions, of course, make the rule, and the few listed below meet some travelers' needs perfectly.

B&Bs & Vacation Rentals

$ ⊞ **Old Wailuku Inn.** This historic home, built in 1924, may be the ultimate Hawaiian B&B. Each room is decorated with the theme of a Hawaiian flower, and the flower motif is worked into the heirloom Hawaiian quilt on each bed. Other features include 10-foot ceilings, floors of native hardwoods, and (depending on the room) delightful bathtubs and Swiss jet showers. The first-floor rooms have private gardens. A hearty breakfast is included. ⊠ *2199 Kahoʻokele St., Wailuku 96793* ☎ *808/ 244–5897 or 800/305–4899* ⊕ *www.mauiinn.com* ⤶ *7 rooms* ⟁ *A/ C, in-room data ports, some cable TV, in-room VCRs, library, business services* ▤ *AE, D, DC, MC, V. $120–$180.*

¢ ⊞ **Banana Bungalow Maui Hostel.** A typical lively and cosmopolitan hostel, Banana Bungalow offers the cheapest accommodations on the island. Private rooms have one queen or two single beds; bathrooms are down the hall. Dorm rooms are available for $22 per night. Free daily tours to waterfalls, beaches, and Haleakalā Crater make this a stellar deal. (Yes, the tours are *free.*) The property's amenities include free high-speed Internet access in the common room, kitchen privileges, a Jacuzzi, and banana trees ripe for the picking. Though it's tucked in a slightly rough-around-the-edges corner of Wailuku, the old building has splendid mountain views. ⊠ *310 N. Market St., Wailuku 96793* ☎ *808/244– 5090 or 800/846–7835* ⊕ *www.mauihostel.com* ⤶ *38 rooms* ⟁ *BBQ, kitchen, laundry facilities, Internet room; no A/C* ▤ *MC, V. Dorm rooms $22, private rooms $44–$66.*

Upcountry

Upcountry accommodations (in Kula, Makawao, and Haliʻimaile) are on country estates and are generally small, privately owned vacation rentals, or B&Bs. At high elevation, these lodgings offer splendid views of the island, temperate weather, and a getting away from it all feeling— which is actually the case, as most shops and restaurants are a fair drive away, and beaches even farther. You'll definitely need a car.

Hotels & Resorts

$ ⊞ **Kula Lodge.** This hotel isn't typical for Hawaiʻi: the lodge inexplicably resembles a chalet in the Swiss Alps, and two units even have gas fireplaces. Charming and cozy in spite of the nontropical ambience, it's a good spot for a romantic stay. Units are in two wooden cabins; four have lofts in addition to the ample bed space downstairs. On 3 acres, the lodge has startling views of Haleakalā and two coasts, enhanced by the surrounding tropical gardens. The property has an art gallery and a protea store that will pack flowers for you to take home. ✉ *Haleakalā Hwy., Rte. 377* ⬠ *R.R. 1, Box 475, Kula 96790* ☎ *808/878–2517 or 800/233–1535* 🖷 *808/878–2518* ⊕ *www.kulalodge.com* ↪ *5 units* ⚘ *Restaurant, shop; no A/C, no room phones, no room TVs* ⊟ *AE, MC, V. $110–$165.*

B&Bs & Vacation Rentals

$$–$$$ 🏠 **Aloha Cottages.** The two secluded cottages on this property, the Bali Bungalow and the Thai Treehouse, are perfect for honeymooners or anyone else seeking a romantic getaway. The property abounds with tropical plants allowing each cottage complete privacy. Intricate woodwork and furnishings, all imported from Bali, add a touch of exoticism to the interiors. Each cottage has a large comfortable bed, fully equipped kitchen, and outdoor hot tub on a private lānai. Ranjana, your hostess, is happy to assist you with planning activities and booking restaurants. She can also arrange for a private massage, yoga lessons, or even a candlelight dinner in the "Lotus House" on the property. The restaurants and shops of Makawao are a short drive away. ✉ *1879 Olinda Rd., Makawao 96768* ☎ *808/573–8500* ⊕ *www.alohacottage.com* ↪ *2 rooms* ⚘ *Fans, kitchens, in-room data ports, cable TV, in-room VCRs, outdoor hot tubs; no A/C, no kids, no smoking* ⊟ *MC, V. $245–$275, 3-night minimum.*

$$ 🏠 **The Star Lookout.** Hidden away halfway up Haleakalā, this charming 100-year-old perch is an ideal getaway. With a view of most of the Valley Isle, this retreat is remote, serene, and deliciously temperate—you'll want to snuggle up, rather than blast the air-conditioning. Up to six people can be accommodated in this inventively designed house, but four is more comfortable, and two is downright romantic. Snipping a few fresh herbs from the garden will make cooking while on vacation all the more fun. ✉ *622 Thompson Rd., Keokea* ☎ *907/346–8028* ⊕ *www.starlookout.com* ↪ *1 house* ⚘ *Kitchen, cable TV, in-room VCR, hot tub; no A/C* ⊟ *No credit cards. $200.*

$–$$ 🏠 **Olinda Country Cottages & Inn.** This restored Tudor home and adjacent cottages are so far up Olinda Road above Makawao you'll keep thinking you must have passed them. The Inn, which sits amid an 8½-acre protea farm surrounded by forest and some wonderful hiking trails, has five accommodations: two upstairs bedrooms with private baths; the downstairs Pineapple Sweet; a romantic cottage, which looks like a dollhouse from the outside; and best of all, Hidden Cottage, which has a private hot tub. Bring warm clothes—the mountain air can be chilly. Breakfast is served in the common living room. ✉ *2660 Olinda Rd., Olinda 96768* ☎🖷 *808/572–1453* ☎ *800/932–3435* ⊕ *www.mauibnbcottages.com* ↪ *3 rooms, 2 cottages* ⚘ *Some cable TV; no A/C, no smoking* ⊟ *No credit cards. $140–$245, 2- to 3-night minimum.*

CONDO COMFORTS

Head to **Pukalani Terrace Center** (✉ 55 Pukalani St., Pukalani) for pizza, a bank, post office, hardware store, and Starbucks. There's also a **Foodland** (☎ 808/572-0674), which has fresh sushi and a good seafood section in addition to the usual grocery store fare, and **Paradise Video** (☎ 808/572-6200).

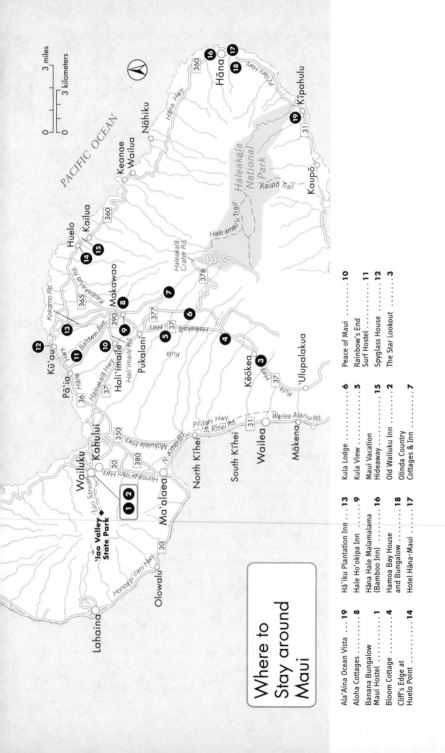

Where to Stay around Maui

PACIFIC OCEAN

Haleakalā National Park

Kaupō Trail

Hale amau'u Trail

$ 📺 **Bloom Cottage.** The name comes from the abundance of roses and other flowers that surround this well-run, classic B&B. The property consists of a main house and separate cottage. This is life in the slow lane, with quiet, privacy, and a living room fireplace for when the evenings are nippy. The furnishings are very Ralph Lauren, with a cowhide flourish suited to this ranch-country locale. The 1906 house has three rooms and is good for four to six people willing to share a single bathroom. The cottage is ideal for a couple. ✉ *229 Kula Hwy., Kula 96790* ☎ *808/579–8282* 📠 *661/ 393–5015* ⊕ *www.hookipa.com/bloom_cottage.html* 🛏 *1 house, 1 cottage* ⟐ *Kitchens, cable TV, in-room VCRs, laundry facilities; no A/C, no smoking* ▭ *AE, D, MC, V. $125–$165, 3-night minimum.*

¢–$ 📺 **Hale Ho'okipa Inn.** This handsome 1924 Craftsman-style house in the heart of Makawao town is a good base for excursions to the crater or to Hāna. The owner has furnished it with antiques and fine art, and allows guests to peruse her voluminous library of Hawai'i-related books. The house is divided into three single rooms, each prettier than the next, and the South Wing, which sleeps four and includes the kitchen. There's also a separate cottage on the property, which sleeps two to four. All rooms have private claw-foot baths. This inn has a distinct plantation-era feel with squeaky wooden floors and period furnishings to boot. ✉ *32 Pakani Pl., Makawao 96768* ☎ *808/572–6698* 📠 *808/572–2580* ⊕ *www.maui-bed-and-breakfast.com* 🛏 *3 rooms, 1 2-bedroom suite, 1 cottage* ⟐ *A/C in some rooms, cable TV, library* ▭ *No credit cards. $95–$145.*

¢–$ 📺 **Peace of Maui.** This Upcountry getaway is ideal for budget-minded travelers who want to be out and active all day. Well situated for accessing the rest of the island, it's only 15 minutes from Kahului and less than 10 from Pāia, Ha'ikū, and Makawao. Six modest double rooms in a "lodge" have pantries and mini-refrigerators. The kitchen, two bathrooms, and living room are shared. An amply equipped separate cottage (including fresh-cut flowers) sleeps four to six and overlooks the North Shore and the West Maui Mountains. You'll have sweeping views of rainbow-washed pineapple fields here. If you're lucky, the family dog will sit near the Jacuzzi while you relax after a hard day's adventuring. ✉ *1290 Hali'imaile Rd., Hali'imaile 96768* ☎ *808/572–5045 or 888/ 475–5045* ⊕ *www.peaceofmaui.com* 🛏 *6 rooms with shared bath, 1 cottage* ⟐ *Refrigerators, cable TV, hot tub, Internet room; no A/C* ▭ *No credit cards. $55–$100.*

¢ 📺 **Kula View.** This affordable home-away-from-home sits in peaceful, rural Kula. At an elevation of 2,000 feet, the climate is pleasantly temperate. Guests stay in the entire upper floor of a tastefully decorated house with a private entrance, deck, and gardens. A commanding view of Haleakalā stretches beyond the French doors. The hostess provides an amenity basket, a very popular Continental breakfast, advice on touring, and even beach towels or warm clothes for your crater trip. ✉ *600 Holopuni Rd., Kula 96790* ☎ *808/878–6736* ⊕ *www.kulaview.com* 🛏 *1 room* ⟐ *Kitchenette; no A/C* ▭ *No credit cards. $95.*

The North Shore

A string of unique accommodations starts in the North Shore surf town of Pā'ia, passes through tiny Ku'au, then winds along the rain-forested Hāna Highway through Hā'iku and Huelo. Many are oceanfront—not necessarily beachfront—with tropical gardens overflowing with ginger, bananas, and papayas. Some have heart-stopping views or the type of solitude that seeps in, easing your tension before you know it. Several have muddy driveways and nightly bug symphonies. This is a rain forest, after all. Brief, powerful down pours let loose frequently here, especially in Hā'iku and Huelo.

You'll need a car to enjoy staying on the North Shore.

B&Bs & Vacation Rentals

$–$$$ 🖥 **Cliff's Edge at Huelo Point.** Perched on a 300-foot cliff overlooking Waipio Bay, you can sometimes spot turtles swimming below this 2-acre multimillion-dollar estate. The guesthouses are resplendent, with well-equipped kitchens, entertainment systems, and large bathtubs. But it's the heart-stopping views from the private hot tubs that keep regulars coming back. The brand-new Bali cottage is wildly popular, decked out entirely in elegant Balinese imports. In the main house, the Penthouse and King suite each have breathtaking views, private entrances, lānai, and kitchenettes. You're free to pick fruit and flowers from the lush grounds. You'll be far from it all out here, in a remote paradise. ✉ Door of Faith Rd., Huelo ✎ Box 1095, Hā'iku 96708 ☎ 808/572–4530 ⊕ www.cliffsedge. com ⇆ 2 rooms, 2 houses ⚘ Wi-Fi, kitchens, cable TV, BBQ, pool, hot tubs; no kids under 13 ⊟ AE, MC, V. Rooms $165–$195, guesthouses $300–$325; 3-night minimum.

¢–$ 🖥 **Hā'iku Plantation Inn.** Water lilies and a shade tree bedecked in orchids greet you at this forested bend in the road. A remnant of Hā'iku's plantation history, this gracious estate was built in 1870 for the company doctor. A feeling of wellness persists—revered Hawaiian healer Kahu Lyons Na'one teaches traditional medicine and ho'oponopono, literally "making right," on-site. A small massage hale stands beside a thatched roof gazebo in a lush garden of ulu (breadfruit), lilikoi (passion fruit), sugarcane, bananas, and pineapple. Rooms are uncluttered and charming with private baths; the Plumeria room has a claw-foot tub. ✉ 555 Hā'iku Rd., Hā'iku ☎ 808/575–7500 ⊕ www.haikuplantation.com ⇆ 5 rooms ⚘ Cable TV, kitchen, library, hot tub, fitness classes, massage; no A/C ⊟ AE, MC, V. $99–$129.

¢–$ 🖥 **Maui Vacation Hideaway.** The warm ocean breeze rolls through these pretty rentals, shooing the mosquitoes away. The decor is both whimsical and calming—expect colorfully painted walls and sheer curtains.

The saltwater pool is fed by a waterfall. Fully equipped kitchens and Wi-Fi make these studios an ideal home away from home. Allergy-prone travelers can relax here—no chemicals or pesticides are used on the property. This is a perfect spot if you want quiet, gorgeous scenery, and don't mind being a fair drive from civilization. ✉ *240 N. Holokai Rd., Hā'iku* ☎ *808/572–2775* ⊠ *808/573–2775* ⊕ *www.mauivacationhideaway.com* ➭ *3 rooms* ⚲ *Fans, Wi-Fi, kitchens, cable TV, in-room VCRs, pool, laundry facilities; no A/C. $90–$125, 3-night minimum.*

¢–$ 🏠 **Spyglass House.** This eccentric old beach property is somewhere Pippi Longstocking might have lived after cashing in her pirate father's gold: splendid views of the Pacific, stained-glass windows, wood floors, even a room called the "Crow's Nest." Rooms in the main house are a tad classier and larger, with better views than those in the Dolphin house, but all are nice. The two houses can be rented together, accommodating up to 20 for special occasions. Your hostess, Poni, is a singer-songwriter and avid surfer who may fill you in on the weekly surf report. ✉ *367 Hāna Hwy., Kūau* ☎ *808/579–8608 or 800/475–6695* ⊕ *www.spyglassmaui.com* ➭ *6 rooms* ⚲ *Kitchen, hot tub; no A/C* ▤ *MC, V* ⦿ *BP. Rooms $85–$150.*

¢ 🏠 **Rainbow's End Surf Hostel.** "Rainbow" is right: the kitchen in this colorful hostel is painted a cheery fuschia with lime trim. A quick stroll from Pā'ia's shops, beaches, and restaurants, this active place is a cheap headquarters for surfers and adventurers. A giant wooden longboard decorates the hallway and surfboards can be stored out back. Free Internet access is available in the cozy (if sometimes hot) common area. Built in the 1940s, the home's shared bathrooms and kitchen areas are humble, but never dirty. Make sure to get a room with a good cross-breeze; the midday heat can be stifling. ✉ *221 Baldwin Ave., Pā'ia* ☎ *808/579–9057* ⊕ *www.mauigateway.com/~riki* ➭ *3 four-person dorm rooms, 3 private rooms* ⚲ *Kitchen, cable TV with VCR, Internet room; no A/C. $25 dorm rooms, $55 private rooms.*

Hāna

Why stay in Hāna when it's so far from everything? In a world where everything moves at high speed, Hāna still travels on horseback, ambling along slowly enough to smell the fragrant vines hanging from the trees. But old-fashioned and remote do not mean tame—this is a wild coast, known for heart-stopping scenery and passionate downpours. Leave city expectations behind: the single grocery may run out of milk, and the only videos to rent may be several years old. The dining options are slim. ■ **TIP→** If you're staying for several days, or at a vacation

> ### SHOPPING IN HĀNA
>
> **Hasegawa General Store.** The one-stop shopping option in Hāna is charming, old, ramshackle Hasegawa's. Buy fishing tackle, hot dogs, ice cream, and eggs here. You can rent videos and buy the newspaper, which isn't always delivered on time. Check out the bulletin board for local events. Be sure to take a Hasegawa T-shirt home with you as proof of your stay out in heavenly Hāna. ✉ *5165 Hāna Hwy.* ☎ *808/248–8231.*

rental, stock up on groceries before you head out to Hāna. Even with these inconveniences, Hāna is a place you won't want to miss.

Hotels & Resorts

$$$–$$$$

Fodor's Choice

★

🏨 **Hotel Hāna-Maui.** Tranquillity envelops Hotel Hāna's ranch setting, with its unobstructed views of the Pacific. Small, secluded, and quietly luxurious, this property is a departure from the usual resort destinations. Spacious rooms (680 to 830 square feet) have bleached-wood floors, authentic kapa-print fabric furnishings, and sumptuously stocked minibars at no extra cost. Spa suites and a heated *watsu* (massage performed in warm water) pool complement a state-of-the-art spa-and-fitness center. The Sea Ranch Cottages with individual hot tubs are the best value. Horses nibble wild grass on the sea cliff nearby. A shuttle takes you to beautiful Hāmoa Beach. ⊠ *Hāna Hwy.* ✆ *Box 9, Hāna 96713* ☎ *808/248–8211 or 800/321–4262* 🖷 *808/248–7264* ⊕ *www. hotelhanamaui.com* 🛏 *19 rooms, 47 cottages, 1 house* ♿ *A/C, 2 restaurants, 2 tennis courts, 2 pools, gym, hot tub, spa, beach, horseback riding, bar, library, Internet room; no room TVs* ⊟ *AE, D, DC, MC, V.* *$295–$725.*

B&Bs & Vacation Rentals

$$

🏨 **Hamoa Bay House & Bungalow.** This Balinese-inspired property is sensuous and secluded—a private sanctuary in a fragrant jungle. There are two buildings: the main house is 1,300 square feet and contains two bedrooms; one of them is a suite set apart by a breezeway. There are a screened veranda with an ocean view and an outdoor lava-rock shower accessible to all guests. The 600-square-foot bungalow is a treetop perch with a giant bamboo bed and a hot tub on the veranda. Hamoa Beach is a short walk away. ⊠ *Hāna Hwy.* ✆ *Box 773, Hāna 96713* ☎ *808/248–7884* 🖷 *808/248–7047* ⊕ *www.hamoabay.com* 🛏 *1 house, 1 bungalow* ♿ *Kitchen, in-room VCRs, laundry facilities; no kids under 14, no smoking* ⊟ *No credit cards.* *$195–$250, 3-night minimum.*

$–$$

🏨 **Hāna Hale Malamalama (Bamboo Inn).** If you're looking for the amenities and activities of a resort, you won't be happy here. But if you want lots of nature and little distraction, this place is perfect. The two duplexes and three cottages overlook a natural spring-fed fish pond and the remains of a *heiau* (an ancient Hawaiian stone platform once used as a place of worship). A black-sand beach, surrounded by lush tropical forest is steps away. Accommodations are simple but clean with rustic bamboo furniture, full kitchens, large bathrooms, and private lānai. Don't be surprised to find a few ants, they come with all the scenery. A Continental breakfast is served in the "lobby," a Polynesian-style, open-air hut. The roar of the ocean and the rustling of palm trees adds a soothing backdrop to the stunning setting. This is paradise as nature meant it to be. ✆ *Box 374, Hāna 96713* ☎ *808/248–8211* ⊕ *www.hanahale. com* 🛏 *4 rooms, 3 cottages* ♿ *BBQs, fans, in-room data ports, kitchens,*

BED-AND-BREAKFASTS

Additional B&Bs on Maui can be found by contacting **Bed & Breakfast Hawai'i** (☎ 808/733–1632 ⊕ www.bandb-hawaii.com), or **Bed and Breakfast Honolulu** (☎ 808/595–7533 or 800/288–4666 ⊕ www.hawaiibnb.com).

cable TV, in-room DVD players, Internet room, no-smoking rooms; no A/C ⊟ *MC, V. $135–$250.*

$ 🏠 **Ala'Aina Ocean Vista.** This B&B is on the grounds of an old banana plantation past 'Ohe'o Gulch (about a 40-minute drive from Hāna). Banana trees still populate the property alongside mango, papaya, and avocado trees. There's also a Balinese garden, complete with a lotus-shape pond. The single room has a private lānai with an outdoor kitchenette, outdoor shower (there's a regular shower in the room as well), and astonishing views of the coastline. Sam and Mercury, a mother-daughter team, live in the main house on-site and are available to give tips and advice about exploring the area. This is a simple, back-to-nature kind of spot, perfect for a couple who wants some time alone away from everything. ⊠ *Off Hwy. 31, 10 mi past Hāna* ⟲ *SR 184-A, Hāna 96713* ☎ *808/248–7824 or 877/216–1733* ⊕ *www.hanabedandbreakfast.com* ⤴ *1 room* ♿ *BBQ, kitchenette, in-room TV/VCR with movies; no A/C* ⊟ *No credit cards. $165, 2-night minimum.*

MAUI ESSENTIALS

Transportation

BY AIR

You can fly to Maui from the mainland United States or from Honolulu. Flight time from the West Coast to Maui is about 5 hours; from the Midwest, expect about an 8-hour flight; and coming from the East Coast will take about 10 hours, not including layovers. Maui is the most visited of the Neighbor Islands and therefore the easiest to connect to on an interisland flight. Honolulu–Kahului is one of the most heavily traveled air routes in the nation.

AIRPORTS & CARRIERS · The Kahului Airport is Maui's only airport with direct service from the mainland. It's smallish and easy to navigate; the main disadvantage is its distance from the major resort destinations. A wide range of airlines now fly nonstop from various West Coast terminals to Kahului. (Las Vegas is an especially Hawai'i-friendly hub.) Fewer airlines fly interisland: Hawaiian Airlines, Aloha Airlines, and Island Air are the main carriers. Interisland flights leave several times throughout the day for about $75 one way. Small air taxis also fly interisland–a good choice for those who don't mind 6-seaters and want to avoid the main terminals. ⇨ *See* Smart Travel Tips *at the front of this guide for airline contact information.*

If you're staying in West Maui, you might choose to fly into the Kapalua–West Maui Airport. The little airport only accomodates small planes. Tiny Hāna in East Maui has a single airstrip, served by commuter planes from Honolulu and charter flights from Kahului and Kapalua. Flying here is a great option if you want to avoid the long and windy drive to Hāna from one of the other airports.

TO & FROM THE AIRPORTS · The best way to get from the airport to your destination—and to see the island itself—is in your own rental car. Most major car-rental companies have desks or courtesy phones at each airport and can provide a map and directions to your hotel. It will take you about an hour, with traffic in your favor, to get from Kahului Airport to a hotel in Kapalua or Kā'anapali and 30 to 40 minutes to go to Kīhei or Wailea.

Maui has around two-dozen taxi companies that make infrequent passes through the Kahului and Kapalua-West Maui airports. If you don't see a cab, you can call La Bella Taxi for island-wide service from the airport. Call Kīhei Taxi if you're staying in the Kīhei, Wailea, or Mākena area. Charges from Kahului Airport to Kā'anapali run about $75; to Lahaina, about $70; and to Wailea, about $53.

If you're flying into Hāna Airport and staying at the Hotel Hāna-Maui, your flight will be met by a hotel van. If you have reserved a rental car, the agent will usually know your arrival time and meet you. Otherwise you can call Dollar Rent A Car to pick you up.

🚗 **Dollar Rent A Car** ☎ 800/800-4000. **Kīhei Taxi** ☎ 808/879-3000. **La Bella Taxi** ☎ 808/242-8011.

BY BUS & SHUTTLE

Maui has a limited bus system, run in conjunction with a private company, Roberts Hawai'i. Passengers can travel among Wailuku, Kā'anapali, Kahului, Kapalua, Kīhei, Wailea, Mā'alaea, and Lahaina. Inexpensive one-way, round-trip, and all-day passes are available.

If you're staying in the right hotel or condo, there are a few shuttles that can get you around the area. Akina Bus Service ferries Wailea resort passengers to and from the Shops at Wailea, free of charge, hourly from 8 AM to 10 PM. The free Kā'anapali Trolley Shuttle runs within the resort area between 9 AM and 11 PM and stops automatically at all hotels and at condos when requested. All Kā'anapali hotels have copies of schedules.

🚌 **Roberts Hawai'i** ☎ 808/871-4838 ⊕ www.co.maui.hi.us/bus. **Akina Bus Service** ☎ 808/879-2828 ⊕ www.akinatours.com.

BY CAR

To really see the island, you'll need a car. Maui has bad roads in beautiful places. Roads generally have two lanes, and sometimes only one—ancient highways that bridge staggering valleys in testimony to their bygone engineers. Maui's landscape is extraordinarily diverse for such a small island. Your sense of place (and the weather) will seem to change every few miles. If you drive to the summit of Haleakalā, you can rise from palm-lined beaches to the rare world inhabited by silverswords in less than two hours. On the Road to Hāna, you'll drive into and out of the rain, with rainbows that seem to land on the hood of your car. Maui's two difficult roads are Hāna Highway (Rte. 36) and an 8-mi scenic stretch between Kapalua and Wailuku. If you're going to attempt the partially paved, patched, and bumpy road between Hāna and 'Ulupalakua, take a four-wheel-drive vehicle. Be forewarned: rental-car companies prohibit travel on roads they've determined might damage the car. If you break down, you're on your own for repairs.

CAR RENTAL   During peak seasons—summer, and Christmas through Easter—be sure to reserve your car well ahead of time. Expect to pay about $35–$40 a day—before taxes, insurance, and extras—for a compact car from one of the major companies. You can get a less-expensive deal from one of the locally owned budget companies. There's a $3 daily road tax on all rental cars in Hawai'i.

Budget, Dollar, and National have courtesy phones at the Kapalua–West Maui Airport; Hertz and Alamo are nearby. All of the above, plus Avis, have desks at or near Maui's major airport in Kahului. Quite a few locally owned companies rent cars on Maui, including Aloha Rent-A-Car, which will pick you up at Kahului Airport or leave a vehicle for you if your flight comes in after-hours.

Aloha Rent-A-Car ☎ 808/877-4477 or 877/452-5642.

MOPED RENTAL To rent a moped, you need to be 20 years of age, and have a driver's licence and credit card. Be especially careful navigating roads where there are no designated bicycle lanes. Note that helmets are optional on Maui, but eye protection is not.

Hula Hogs in Kīhei can outfit you with a moped for $50 a day. On the West Side, Aloha Toys Exotic Cars is a little pricier, and specializes in exotic auto rentals, Jeeps, Harleys, and mopeds.

Aloha Toys Exotic Cars ✉ 640 Front St., Lahaina ☎ 808/891-0888. **Hula Hogs** ✉ Azeka Place, 1279 Kīhei Rd., Kīhei ☎ 808/875-7433.

BY FERRY

There is daily ferry service between Lahaina, Maui, and Mānele Bay, Lāna'i with Expeditions Lāna'i Ferry. The 9-mi crossing costs $50 cash (or $52 if you pay with a credit card) round-trip, per person and takes about 45 minutes or so, depending on ocean conditions (which can make this trip a rough one). Moloka'i Ferry offers twice-daily ferry service between Lahaina, Maui and Kaunakakai, Moloka'i. Travel time is about 90 minutes each way and the round-trip fare is $40 per person. Reservations are recommended for both ferries.

Expeditions Lāna'i Ferry ☎ 800/695-2624 ⊕ www.go-lanai.com. **Molokai Ferry** ☎ 866/307-6524 ⊕ www.molokaiferry.com.

BY TAXI

You'd be smart to use taxis just for the areas in which they're located. The county rate is $3 a mile, and most destinations are spread out over long distances. For short hops between hotels and restaurants, taxis can be a convenient way to go, but you'll have to call ahead. Even busy West Maui doesn't have curbside taxi service.

Ali'i Cab covers West Maui. Arthur's Limousine Service offers a chauffeured super-stretch Lincoln complete with bar and two TVs for $122 per hour. Arthur's fleet also includes less grandiose Lincoln Town Cars for $91 per hour with a two-hour minimum. Classy Taxi offers limos, convertibles, and a 1929 Model A Ford Phaeton for a regular cab's fare. Kīhei Taxi serves Central Maui. Wailea Limousine Service provides vans, Cadillacs, and limousines on the South Shore. Despite the name, they also service the Lahaina area.

Ali'i Cab ☎ 808/661-3688. **Arthur's Limousine Service** ☎ 808/871-5555 or 877/ 408-9559. **Classy Taxi** ☎ 808/665-0003. **Kīhei Taxi** ☎ 808/879-3000. **Wailea Limousine Service** ☎ 808/875-4114, 808/661-4114 in Lahaina.

Contacts & Resources

EMERGENCIES

In an emergency, dial **911** to reach an ambulance, the police, or the fire department.

For emergency road service, there's a Honolulu-based AAA. A dispatcher will send a tow truck, but you will need to tell the driver where to take your car. Don't forget to carry your membership card with you.

For medical assistance in West Maui, call Doctors on Call. Or try West Maui Health Care Center, a walk-in clinic at Whalers Village. It's open daily from 8 AM to 10 PM. Kīhei Clinic Medical Services in South Maui is geared to working with visitors in Kīhei and Wailea.

🏥 Doctors **Doctors on Call** ✉ Hyatt Regency Maui, Nāpili Tower, Suite 100, 200 Nohea Kai Dr., Lahaina ☎ 808/667-7676. **Kīhei Clinic Medical Services** ✉ 2349 S. Kīhei Rd., Suite D, Kīhei ☎808/879-1440. **West Maui Health Care Center** ✉2435 Kā'anapali Pkwy., Suite H-7, Kā'anapali ☎ 808/667-9721.

🏥 Emergency Services **AAA** ☎ 800/222-4357. **Coast Guard Rescue Center** ☎ 800/552-6458.

🏥 Hospitals **Hāna Medical Center** ✉ 4590 Hāna Hwy., Hāna ☎ 808/248-8294. **Kula Hospital** ✉ 100 Keokea Hwy., Kula ☎ 808/878-1221. **Maui Memorial Hospital** ✉ 221 Mahalani St., Wailuku ☎ 808/244-9056.

🏥 Pharmacies **Kīhei Professional Pharmacy** ✉ 41 E. Lipoa Kīhei ☎ 808/879-8499. **Kmart Stores** ✉ 424 Dairy Rd., Kahului ☎ 808/871-5677. **Valley Isle Pharmacy** ✉ 130 Prison St., Lahaina ☎ 808/661-4747.

VISITOR INFORMATION

Before you go, contact the Hawai'i Visitors & Convention Bureau (HVCB) for general information, free brochures that include an accommodations and car-rental guide, and an entertainment and dining guide containing one-line descriptions of bureau members. Take a virtual visit to the islands on the Web, which can be most helpful in planning many aspects of your vacation. The HVCB site has a calendar section that allows you to see what local events are in place during the time of your stay.

🏥 **Hawai'i Visitors & Convention Bureau** ✉ 2270 Kalakaua Ave., Suite 801, Honolulu 96815 ☎ 808/923-1811, 800/464-2924 for brochures ⊕ www.gohawaii.com. In the U.K. contact the **Hawai'i Visitors & Convention Bureau** ☎ 36 Southwark Bridge Rd., London SE1 9EU ☎ 020/7202-6384 🖷 020/7928-0722 ⊕ www.gohawaii.com.

The Big Island of Hawai'i

Pu' uhonua O Hōnaunau (Place of Refuge) Park

WORD OF MOUTH

"We've been several times, but never get tired of Volcanoes National Park. The lava flows are always fascinating. Evening trips are best, but take long pants, good shoes, and a flashlight."

–Spokaneman

"We loved the Big Island. [It] has mountains, rainforest, waterfalls, volcanoes, coffee plantations, quirky villages, ranches, very nice restaurants. I felt it represented the 'real' Hawai'i."

–shorebrau

WELCOME TO THE BIG ISLAND

TOP 5
Reasons to Go

① **Hawai'i Volcanoes National Park:** Catch the nighttime lava fireworks at the end of Chain of Craters Road.

② **Waipi'o Valley:** Experience a real-life secret garden, the remote spot known as the Valley of the Kings.

③ **Kealakekua Bay Double Feature:** Kayak past spinner dolphins to the Captain Cook Monument, then go snorkeling along the fabulous coral reef.

④ **The Heavens:** Stargaze through gigantic telescopes on snow-topped Mauna Kea.

⑤ **Hidden Beaches:** Discover one of the Kohala Coast's lesser-known gems.

■ **TIP→** Directions on the island are often given as mauka (toward the mountains) and makai (toward the ocean).

The sparkling turquoise Kohala Coast is where all those long Hawaiian white-sand beaches are found, and the expensive resorts that go with them.

Kailua-Kona is a seaside town bustling with tourists.

In South Kona, younger residents and transplants have turned defunct coffee farms into lively art communities overlooking beautiful Kealakekua Bay.

'Upolu Pt.
Hāwī
POLOLU VALLEY
270
250
Kawaihae
Ka'ahumanu
Waikoloa
Kohala Coast
Belt
190
Queen
Hawai'i
Kona International Airport
19
Kalaoa
Mount Hualālai 8,271 ft
Kailua-Kona
Kailua Bay
Captain Cook
Kealakekua Bay
11
Hawai'i
Belt Rd.
SOUTH KONA
Māmalahoa
11

0   10 mi
0   10 km

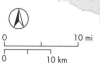

Getting Oriented

You could fit all of the other Hawaiian Islands onto the Big Island and still have a little room left over—hence the clever name. Locals refer to the island by side: Kona side to the west and Hilo side to the east. Most of the resorts, condos, and restaurants are crammed into 30 miles of the sunny Kona side, while the rainy, tropical Hilo side is much more local and residential.

Ranches sprawl across the cool, upland meadows surrounding Waimea (Kamuela). This is *paniolo* (cowboy) country.

Waterfalls, dramatic cliffs, ancient hidden valleys, the greenest green you'll ever see, rain forests, and flowers you didn't know existed await on the Hāmākua Coast.

The rainy side of the island takes its name from the large fishing town of Hilo, nicknamed the City of Rainbows.

Puna, the part of the island most recently covered by lava, has brand-new, jet-black beaches punctuated with volcanically-heated hot springs.

WAIPIO VALLEY

240

19

Waimea (Kamuela)

Hawai'i

Belt Rd.

HĀMĀKUA COAST

Mauna Kea 13,796 ft

200

Hilo Bay

Hilo

11 Hilo International Airport (General Lyman Field)

Saddle Rd.

Hwy.

Stainback

130

Mauna Loa 13,679 ft

Pāhoa

132

PUNA

Volcano Village

130

Kīlauea Crater

Kīlaueā 4,096 ft

Hawai'i Volcanoes National Park

11

Belt Rd.

Hawai'i

Hwy.

South Pt. (Ka Lae)

Hawai'i Volcanoes National Park is growing, as active Kīlauea Volcano sends lava spilling into the ocean, creating new land. The nearest village is Volcano.

BIG ISLAND PLANNER

When You Arrive

The Big Island's two airports are directly across the island from each other. Kona International Airport on the west side is about a 10-minute drive from Kailua-Kona and 30 to 45 minutes from the Kohala Coast. On the east side, Hilo International Airport, 2 mi from downtown Hilo, is about 40 minutes from Volcanoes National Park. ■ TIP➔ The shortest, best route between Hilo and Kailua-Kona is the northern route, a 96-mi, 2½-hour drive. No time? Take a 20-minute flight on Island Air.

Manta Rays

The Big Island is known for its scuba diving, and the visibility is amazing. The island's manta rays were scarce for awhile, but they are slowly returning. If you book a nighttime manta-ray dive, you will probably actually see some, and it's an experience not to be missed.

Will I See Flowing Lava?

The best time to see lava is at night. However, you may or may not see flowing lava. Anyone who tries to tell you they can guarantee it or predict it is lying or trying to sell you something. Your best bet is to call the visitor center at the national park before you head out; even at that you could be pleasantly surprised or utterly disappointed. Keep in mind that the volcano is a pretty amazing sight even if it's not spewing fire.

Fitting It All In

Yes, it's big, and yes, there's a lot to see. If you're short on time, consider flying into one airport and out of the other. That will give you the opportunity to see both sides of the island without ever having to go backwards. Decide what sort of note you'd rather end on to determine your route—if you'd prefer to spend your last few days sleeping on the beach, go from east to west; if hiking through rain forests and showering in waterfalls sounds like a better way to end the trip, move from west to east. If you're short on time, head straight for Hawai'i Volcanoes National Park and briefly visit Hilo before traveling the Hāmākua Coast route and making your new base in Kailua-Kona.

Car Rentals

You will need a car on the Big Island. Get a four-wheel-drive vehicle if you're at all interested in exploring. Some of the island's best sights (and most beautiful beaches) are at the end of rough or unpaved roads.

TIPS➔

■ Talk to the agency in advance if you want to pick up a car at one airport and drop it off at the other. Though they allow this, most charge an additional fee of up to $50. If you arrange it ahead of time, they can often be talked into waiving the fee.

■ Most agencies make you sign an agreement that you won't drive on the Saddle Road, the path to Mauna Kea and its observatories. Though smoothly paved, the Saddle Road is remote, winding, unlighted, and bereft of gas stations. Alamo, Budget, Dollar, and Harper Rentals let you drive it in their four-wheel-drive vehicles.

Timing Is Everything

You can see humpback whales clearly off the western coast of the island from about January until May. Technically, whale season is from November to May, but the migration doesn't really get going until January. The few scattered sightings in November and December are usually young males showing off. The Merrie Monarch Festival brings a full week of hula, both ancient and modern, to Hilo, beginning the week after Easter. Fish stories abound in Kailua-Kona every August during the week-long Hawaiian International Billfish Tournament. The Ironman Triathlon takes place every October in Kailua-Kona. Consider volunteering—you'll be inspired, and it's a great party.

Surfing

The Big Island is not known for its surf, but that doesn't mean that there isn't any, or that there aren't plenty of local surfers. Surf's up in winter, down in summer; the beautiful peaceful beach you went to last summer could be a rough and rowdy surfer beach in the winter.

Keep the Kids Happy

With a little advance planning, you can please your smallest critics. If you're renting a condo in Kailua-Kona, ask if they have a pool and, if so, how large it is. Many of the condo complexes have pools that are about the size of your bathtub. Make advance reservations for family favorites, like *Fair Winds* snorkel cruises to Kealakekua Bay (they've got a sweet slide off the back of the boat) or the *Atlantis VII* submarine (it can be a bit pricey, but you really do see things you couldn't otherwise see, plus submarines are just cool).

Will It Rain?

The Kona side of the Big Island is arid and hot, with mile upon mile of black lava fields lining a shimmering coastline. The Hilo side, on the other hand, gets roughly 130 inches of rain a year, so the chances of getting rained on while driving along the Hāmākua Coast to Hilo are pretty high. That said, it tends to rain in the morning on the Hilo side and clear up by afternoon, leaving a handful of rainbows behind.

Guided Activities

The Kona Coast has long been famous for its deep-sea fishing, and late summer to early fall is peak season. The Big Island is also rapidly building a reputation as the golfers' island.

ACTIVITY	COST
Aerial Tours	$115–$370
Deep-Sea Fishing	$400–$800
Golf	$62–$195
Kayak Tours	$65–$135
Lū'au	$62–$76
Snorkel Cruises	$80–$100
Surfing Lessons	$90–$125
Whale-Watching	$60–$70

1-Day Itineraries

The following one-day itineraries will take you to our favorite spots on the island.

A Day (or Two) at Hawai'i Volcanoes National Park

The volcano is not to be missed. How often do you have the chance to see earth being formed? Call ahead of time to check the lava activity and plan your time accordingly. If the volcano is very active, go straight to the lava flow area. If it's less active, find out the best times of day for seeing what lava flow there is and head to the active flows at that time. And don't forget that there's a lot more to see in the park. Hike on the Kīlauea Iki trail, a 4-mile loop that takes you down through volcanic rain forests and then across the floor of a small vent, and check out the Thurston Lava Tube. Just before sunset, head down to the ocean via Chain of Craters Road; this is the best spot to see the nighttime lava show. Consider staying a night in Volcano Village, especially if your home base is on the Kona side. It will give you the time to explore, without having to rush off for the long (over 2 hours), dark drive back to Kona.

Waipi'o Valley

Completely off the grid today, it's hard to believe that Waipi'o Valley was once home to a thriving little village, not to mention early Hawaiian royalty. Waipi'o is a uniquely Big Island experience—untouched nature and a mystifying bit of island history. It's best to book a tour to see the valley either on horseback or from a jeep. Most tours last from two to four hours.

Hāmākua Coast

This jagged stretch of coastline along the eastern side of the island embodies all things tropical. There are waterfalls galore, and the trees and plants are thick and bright green. It's wet, but it tends to rain most in the mornings and clear up in the afternoons. Plan to spend some time driving down the tiny roads that dart off the main highway. Anywhere you see a gulch there's a waterfall waiting to be discovered. And keep your eyes peeled for rainbows.

Kohala Beach Day

Chances are that one of the main reasons you came to Hawai'i was to lie on the beach and work on your tan—do the whole island vacation thing. You will not be disappointed with the Kohala Coast. Hāpuna Beach has powdery soft white sand and crystal-clear blue water. Or get an early start and hike into one of the Kohala Coast's unmarked beaches, like Kua Bay or Makalawena. Either way, end the day at a seaside restaurant in Kawaihae or Kailua-Kona, watching the sunset and sipping a mai tai.

Paniolo Country

Upcountry Waimea is not what pops to mind when you think "Hawai'i"—rolling green hills, a chill in the morning, and ranches. Stop first at the old sugarcane town of Hāwī or at Pololū Valley. Then take Kohala Mountain Road (Highway 250) up the hill to Waimea, stopping along the way to snap pictures of the incredible view. There are several ranches in Waimea where you can go horseback or ATV riding. Plan on staying for dinner at one of Waimea's top-notch restaurants.

■ *For more details see* Exploring and Beaches *on the Big Island in this chapter.*

Written by
Peter Serafin &
Amy
Westervelt

Updated by
Amy
Westervelt

ALTHOUGH DEVELOPMENT HAS RUN WILD on the Big Island as of late, it manages to maintain an Old Hawai'i feel, with tourism concentrated on its sunny northwest coast. From its active volcano seeping lava into the ocean to its white-sand beaches and its verdant green valleys, waterfalls, and rainbows, the Big Island delivers everything the postcards promise and then some. Sea turtles and manta rays make their homes here, and Mark Twain wrote some of his best prose in the moonlike southern region. Long after his death, artists, travelers, and locals continue to seek inspiration from the cliffs, lava, hidden valleys, ancient wisdom, and tranquil waters of Hawai'i.

The Big Island is indeed big, and the largest of the Islands by far at 4,038 square miles. Even with recent development, the Big Island's population remains low (163,000), and only 2% of the island's 2.57 million acres is classified as urban.

Geology

Home to 11 climate zones (missing only tundra), this is the land of fire (thanks to active Kīlauea Volcano) and ice (compliments of not-so-active Mauna Kea, topped with snow and expensive telescopes). At just under a million years old, Hawai'i is the youngest of the Hawaiian islands. The east rift zone on Kīlauea has been spewing lava intermittently since January 3, 1983. Mauna Loa's explosions caused some changes back in 1984, and she's due to blow again any minute. Though these two are the only of the island's five considered active, the others haven't been pronounced officially dead just yet.

Flora & Fauna

Sugar was the main agricultural and economic staple of all the Islands, but especially the Big Island. The drive along the Hāmākua Coast from Hilo illustrates recent agricultural developments on the island. Sugarcane stalks have been replaced by orchards of macadamia-nut trees, eucalyptus, and specialty crops (from lettuce to strawberries). Macadamia nuts on the Big Island supply 90% of the state's yield, and coffee continues to be big business, dominating the mountains above Kealakekua Bay. Orchids keep farmers from Honoka'a to Pāhoa afloat, and small organic farms produce meat, fruits, vegetables, and even goat cheese for high-end resort restaurants.

History

Though no longer home to the capital, the state's history is nonetheless rooted in that of its namesake island, Hawai'i. Kamehameha, the greatest king in Hawaiian history and the man credited with uniting the Islands, was born here, raised in Waipi'o Valley, and died peacefully in Kailua-Kona. The other man who most affected the history of Hawai'i, Captain James Cook, spent the bulk of his time here, docked in Kealakekua Bay (he landed first in Kaua'i, but had little contact with the natives there). Thus it was here that Western influence was first felt, and from here that it spread to the rest of the Islands.

On the Big Island Today

The Big Island is in a period of great change. In the last few years, Wal-Mart, Kmart, and Costco opened; development went wild; and real estate prices skyrocketed. These sorts of things make locals unhappy. Work is underway to counteract some of the poorly planned development of the island. New developments are required by law to consult with a Hawaiian cultural expert, and most of the island's hotels have a Hawaiian historian on staff to teach visitors about the ancient customs and keep developers from breaking with Hawaiian traditions any more than is absolutely necessary.

Ocean Reefs & Currents

The Big Island offers some of the best diving and snorkeling in the world, and even edges out its Neighbor Islands as the favorite feeding ground of manta rays and the nesting place of the Hawaiian sea turtle. The manta ray population had decreased in the 1990s, but has returned thanks to active conservation efforts. The best way to see these bizarre and amazing creatures is on a night dive. The sea turtle's favorite nesting place is the island's larges black-sand beach, Punalu'u. The turtles are used to people and will likely swim right up to you—no touching please!

EXPLORING THE BIG ISLAND

The first secret to enjoying the Big Island: rent a car, ideally one with four-wheel drive. The second: stay more than three days, or return again and again to really explore this fascinating place. With 266 mi of coastline made up of white coral, black lava, and a dusting of green-olivine beaches, interspersed with lava cliffs, emerald gorges, and splashing waterfalls, the Big Island can be overwhelming. Depending on the number of days you have available, it would be best to divide your time between the Hilo and Kona sides of the island in order to take in the attractions of each.

The Kohala District & Waimea

North of Kona International Airport, along Highway 19, brightly colored bougainvillea stands out in relief against miles of black lava fields stretching as far as the eye can see. Most of the lava flows, spreading from the mountain to the sea, are from the last eruptions of Mt. Hualālai, in 1800 and 1801. They are interrupted only by the green oases of irrigated golf courses surrounding the glamorous luxury resorts along the Kona-Kohala Coast. Kohala is a microcosm of the Big Island as a whole, both in terms of people—wealthy travelers seeing the sights, locals commuting in to work at the resorts from nearby villages, and both local and foreign artists reviving old sugar plantation towns—and land, from the arid coast to the lush valley of Pololū and the rolling hills of Waimea's farm country. The island's best beaches are here, as are the best restaurants, some excellent hiking, and the only destination spas on the island. During the winter months, glistening humpback whales cleave the waters just offshore. If you had only a weekend to spend on the Big Island, this is where you'd want to do it.

You could spend all day checking out Kohala and Waimea, passing lava-covered flatlands and lush mountain pastures. If you're short on time, head either straight for Waimea to visit the Parker Ranch Museum or to Hāwī and Kapaʻau to see the beautiful Pololū Valley and to experience the dramatic history of these sugar towns.

Main Attractions

⑤ Hāwī and Kapaʻau. These two neighboring villages thrived during plantation days. There were hotels, saloons, and theaters—even a railroad. Today, both towns are blos-

soming once again, thanks to strong local communities and an influx of artists keen on honoring the towns' past. Old historic buildings have been restored and now hold shops, galleries, and eateries. In Kapaʻau, browse through the Hawaiian collection of **Kohala Book Shop** (⌧ 54-3885 Akoni Pule Hwy. ☎ 808/889–6400 ⊕ www.kohalabooks.com), the second-largest bookstore in the state. ⌧ *Hwy. 270, North Kohala.*

NEED A BREAK?

If you're looking for something sweet, **Tropical Dreams** (⌧ Hāwī ☎ 808/889–5577) makes ice cream that is *da kine* (translation: awesome, amazing—pick any superlative).

⑧ Kohala Mountain Road Lookout. The lookout here provides a splendid view of the Kohala Coast and Kawaihae Harbor far below. On clear days, you can see well beyond the resorts. It's one of the most scenic spots on the island and great for a picnic. Often, thick mists drift in, casting an eerie feeling. ⌧ *Kohala Mountain Rd., Hwy. 250.*

★ ④ Moʻokini Heiau. This National Historic Landmark, an isolated *heiau* (an ancient place of worship), is so impressive in size it may give you goose bumps. Its foundations date to about AD 480, but the high priest Paʻao from Tahiti expanded it several centuries later to offer sacrifices to please his gods. You can still see the lava slab where hundreds of people were killed, which gives this place a truly haunted feel. A nearby sign marks the place where Kamehameha I was born in 1758. The area is now part of the Kohala Historical Sites State Monument. ⌧ *Turn off Hwy. 270 at sign for ʻUpolu Airport, near Hāwī, and hike or drive in a four-wheel-drive vehicle 1½ mi southwest* ☎ *808/974–6200.*

⑪ Parker Ranch Visitor Center & Museum. The center chronicles the life of John Palmer Parker (and his descendants), who founded Parker Ranch in 1847. Parker married the granddaughter of King Kamehameha and bought 2 acres of land from the king for the sum of $10. Purchase your tickets here for the **Parker Ranch Historic Homes,** a couple of miles south of town. The original family residence, Mānā, is built entirely from native woods such as koa. Puʻopelu, added to the estate in 1879, was the residence of Richard Smart, a sixth-generation Parker who expanded the house to make room for his European art collection. On Friday, Hawaiian crafts demonstrations take place at the homes. A wagon ride allows you a comfortable, albeit old-fashioned, visit to the pastures. Also available are horseback rides and walking tours. ⌧ *Parker Ranch Shopping Center, 67-1185 Māmalahoa Hwy., Waimea* ☎ *808/885–7655 or 808/*

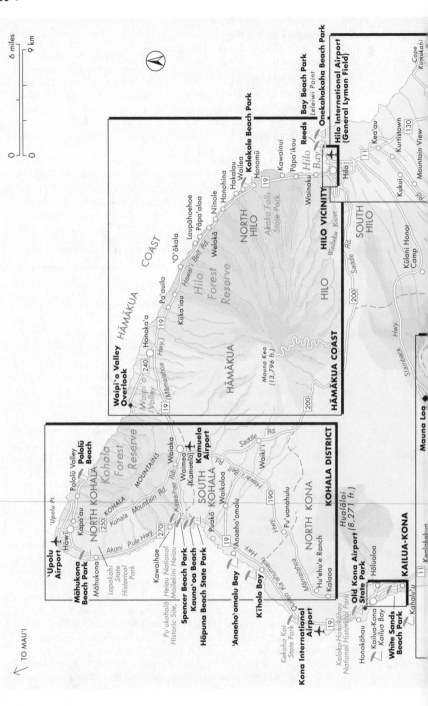

6 miles
9 km

TO MAU'I

'Upolu Airport
'Upolu Pt.
Māhukona Beach Park
Māhukona
Kapa'au
Hāwī
Pololū Valley
Pololū Beach
NORTH KOHALA
Kohala Forest Reserve
KOHALA MOUNTAINS
Lapakahi State Historical Park
Kawaihae
Kohala Mountain Rd.
Akoni Pule Hwy.
Pu'ukoholā Heiau National Historic Site, Mailekini Heiau
Spencer Beach Park
Kauna'oa Beach
Hāpuna Beach State Park
Kawaihae Rd.
Waimea (Kamuela)
Waioka
Kamuela Airport
SOUTH KOHALA
Puakō
'Anaeho'omalu
Waikoloa
250
270
19
KOHALA DISTRICT

'Anaeho'omalu Bay
Kīholo Bay
Mamalahoa Hwy.
Queen Ka'ahumanu Hwy.
190
Hwy.
Pu'uanahulu
NORTH KONA
Hualālai (8,271 ft.)
Waiki'i
Saddle Rd.
Hu'ehu'e Ranch
Kalaoa
Kona International Airport
Kekaha Kai State Park
19
Kaloko-Honokōhau National Historical Park
Honokōhau
Old Kona Airport State Park
Kailua-Kona Kailua Bay
White Sands Beach Park
KAILUA-KONA
Hōlualoa
11
Keauhou
Kahalu'u

Mauna Loa

Waipi'o Valley
HĀMĀKUA
COAST
Waipi'o Valley Overlook
Waipi'o Valley
Honoka'a
240
19
(Māmalahoa Hwy.)
Pa'auilo
19
Kūka'iau
'O'ōkala
Hawai'i Belt Rd.
Weloka
Laupāhoehoe
Pāpa'aloa
Ninole
NORTH HILO
Honohina
Hakalau
Wailea
Kawainui
Papa'ikou
Honomū
Akaka Falls State Park
Kolekole Beach Park
19
Mauna Kea (13,796 ft.)
HĀMĀKUA
Hilo Forest Reserve
200
Saddle Rd.
HILO
Wainaku
Wailuku River
Hilo Bay
Reeds Bay Beach Park
HILO VICINITY
Hilo
Hilo International Airport (General Lyman Field)
Leleiwi Point
Onekahakaha Beach Park
Cape Kumukahi

SOUTH HILO
HĀMĀKUA COAST
Kūlani Honor Camp
Stainback Hwy.
200
Saddle Rd.
Kea'au
Kurtistown
Mountain View
Kukui
Kukui Rd.
130
11

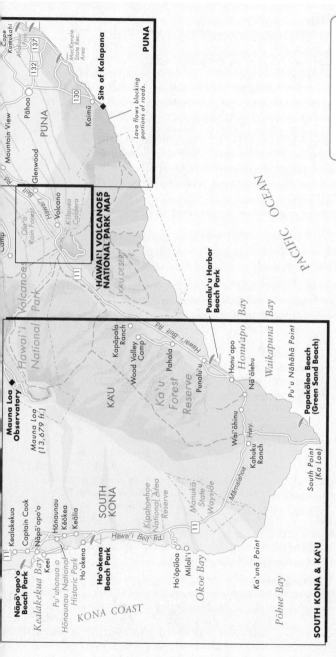

The Big Island of Hawai'i

PUNA

Cape Kumukahi
137
132
MacKenzie State Rec. Area
Pāhoa
PUNA
130
Mountain View
Glenwood
Site of Kalapana
Kaimū
Lava flows blocking portions of roads.

Volcano
Kīlauea Caldera
Ola'a Rain Forest

HAWAI'I VOLCANOES NATIONAL PARK MAP

11

Hawai'i National Park

Mauna Loa Observatory ◆

Kapāpala Ranch

Wood Valley Camp

KA'U

Pahala

Mauna Loa (13,679 ft.)

Ka'ū Forest Reserve

Punalu'u

Punalu'u Harbor Beach Park

Honu'apo

Honu'apo Bay

Nā'ālehu

Waikapuna Bay

Wai'ōhinu

Pu'u Nāhāhā Point

Papakōlea Beach (Green Sand Beach)

Kahuku Ranch

South Point (Ka Lae)

Kealakekua
Captain Cook
Nāpō'opo'o
Keei
Hōnaunau
Kēōkea
Keālia
Ho'okena

SOUTH KONA

Kīpahoehoe Natural Area Reserve

Mānuka State Wayside

11

Ka'unā Point

Ho'ōpūloa
Miloli'i
Okoe Bay

Pōhue Bay

SOUTH KONA & KA'U

Nāpō'opo'o Beach Park

Kealakekua Bay

Pu'uhonua o Hōnaunau National Historic Park

Ho'okena Beach Park

KONA COAST

PACIFIC OCEAN

KA'U DESERT

Hawai'i Belt Rd.

Mamalāhoa

Kahuku Hwy.

Volcanoes National Park

Hawai'i Belt Rd.

Graffiti

YOU WILL NO DOUBT NOTICE that the black-lava fields lining Highway 19 from Kona International Airport into Kailua-Kona or out to the Kohala resorts are littered with white-coral graffiti. This has been going on for decades, and locals still get a kick out of it, as do tourists. The first thing everyone asks is "where do the white rocks come from?" and the answer is this: they're bits of coral and they come from the ocean. Now that we've figured out that coral isn't totally expendable, no one starts from scratch anymore. If you want to write a message in the lava, you've got to use the coral that's already out there. This means that no one's message lasts for long, but that's all part of the fun. Some local couples even have a tradition of writing their names in the same spot on the lava fields every year on their anniversary.

885–5433, 800/262–7290 toll-free ⊕ www.parkerranch.com ✉ Museum $6.50, homes $8.50, both $14 ⊘ Museum Mon.–Sat. 9–5, homes daily 10–5.

❼ Pololū Valley. A steep trail leads through this lush green valley and down to Pololū Beach, which edges a rugged coastline ribboned by silver waterfalls. The valleys beyond provide water for the Kohala Ditch, the ingenious project that once brought water to the area's sugar plantations. Some of the former ditch trails have become inaccessible and dangerous. A kayak cruise through the old irrigation ditch, offered by tour operators, reveals more of this dramatic part of Kohala history. **Hawai'i Forest and Trail** (☎ 808/331–8505 or 800/464–1993 ⊕ www.hawaii-forest.com) leads half-day hikes into the valley. ✉ End of Hwy. 270.

★ ❶ Pu'ukoholā Heiau National Historic Site. In 1790 a prophet told King Kamehameha I to build a *heiau* on top of Pu'ukoholā (Hill of the Whale) and dedicate it to the war god Kūkā'ilimoku by sacrificing his principal rival, Keōua Kūahu'ula. By doing so the king would achieve his goal of conquering the Hawaiian Islands. The prophecy came true in 1810. A short walk over arid landscape leads from the visitor center to **Pu'ukoholā Heiau** and to **Mailekini Heiau**, a navigational aid constructed about 1550. An even older temple, dedicated to the shark gods, lies submerged just offshore. The center organizes Hawaiian arts-and-crafts programs on a regular basis. ✉ Hwy. 270, Kawaihae ☎ 808/882–7218 ⊕ www.nps.gov ✉ Free ⊘ Daily 7:30–4.

Also Worth Seeing

⓬ 'Imiola Congregational Church. Stop here to admire the dark koa interior and the unusual wooden calabashes hanging from the ceiling. Be careful not to walk in while a service is in progress, as the front entry of this church, which was established in 1832 and rebuilt in 1857, is behind the pulpit. ✉ Off Hwy. 19, along famous "church row," Waimea ☎ 808/885–4987.

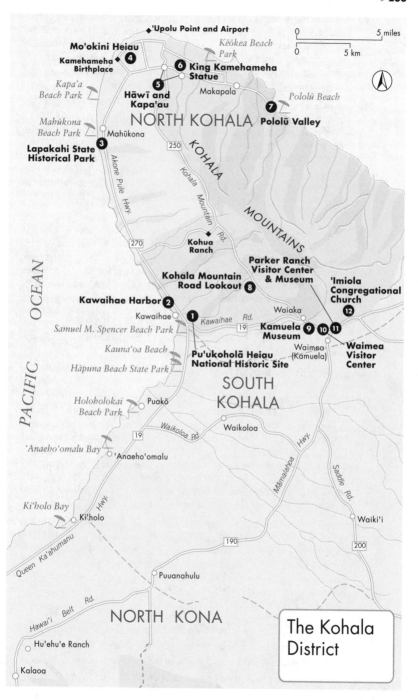

◆ 'Upolu Point and Airport

Kēōkea Beach Park

0   5 miles

0   5 km

Mo'okini Heiau ❹

Kamehameha Birthplace ◆

❻ **King Kamehameha Statue**

❺

Makapala

Hāwī and Kapa'au

Kapa'a Beach Park

Pololū Beach

NORTH KOHALA

❼ **Pololū Valley**

Mahūkona Beach Park

Mahūkona

❸

250

KOHALA

Lapakahi State Historical Park

Akone Pule Hwy.

270

Kohala Mountain Rd.

MOUNTAINS

◆ **Kohua Ranch**

Parker Ranch Visitor Center & Museum

'Imiola Congregational Church ⓬

Kohala Mountain Road Lookout ❽

Waiaka

Kawaihae Harbor ❷

Kawaihae ❶ Kawaihae Rd.

19

Kamuela Museum ❾ ❿ ⑪

Waimea Visitor Center

PACIFIC OCEAN

Samuel M. Spencer Beach Park

Kauna'oa Beach

Pu'ukoholā Heiau National Historic Site

Waimea (Kāmuela)

Hāpuna Beach State Park

SOUTH KOHALA

Holoholokai Beach Park

Puakō

Waikoloa Rd.

Waikoloa

19

Māmalahoa Hwy.

Saddle Rd.

'Anaeho'omalu Bay

'Anaeho'omalu

Ki'holo Bay

Ki'holo

Waiki'i

190

200

Queen Ka'ahumanu Hwy.

Puuanahulu

Hawai'i Belt Rd.

NORTH KONA

Hu'ehu'e Ranch

Kalaoa

The Kohala District

9 **Kamuela Museum.** This small private museum has a fascinating collection of artifacts from Hawai'i and around the world. The eclectic collection includes Hawaiian weapons and a satiny-smooth koa table that once graced 'Iolani Palace in Honolulu. There are also period furniture pieces, artwork, and military and war memorabilia. ⊠ *Hwys. 19 and 250, Waimea* ☎ *808/885–4724* ☜ *$5* ⏱ *Daily 8–4.*

2 **Kawaihae Harbor.** This commercial harbor, where in 1793 the first cattle came ashore, is a hub of activity. It's especially busy on weekends, when paddlers and local fishing boats float on the waves. Second in size only to Hilo Harbor on the east coast, the harbor is often home to the *Makali'i*, one of three Hawaiian sailing canoes. King Kamehameha I and his men launched their canoes from here when they set out to conquer the islands. ■ TIP➔ There are several restaurants with nice sunset views in Kawaihae should you be nearby at dinnertime. ⊠ *Kawaihae Harbor Rd. off Hwy. 270.*

6 **King Kamehameha Statue.** This is the original of the statue in front of the Judiciary Building on King Street in Honolulu. It was cast in Florence in 1880 but lost at sea when the German ship transporting it sank near the Falkland Islands. A replica was shipped to Honolulu. Two years later an American sea captain found the original in a Port Stanley (Falkland Islands) junk yard and brought it to the Big Island. The legislature voted to erect it near Kamehameha's birthplace. Every year, on King Kamehameha Day (June 11), a magnificent abundance of floral lei adorns the image of Hawai'i's great king. It's in front of the old Kohala Courthouse next to the highway. ⊠ *Hwy. 270, Kapa'au.*

★ **3** **Lapakahi State Historical Park.** A self-guided, 1-mi walking tour leads through the ruins of the once-prosperous fishing village Koai'e, which dates as far back as the 15th century. Displays illustrate early Hawaiian fishing and farming techniques, salt gathering, games, and legends. A park guide is often on-site to answer questions. Since the shoreline near the state park is an officially designated Marine Life Conservation District, and part of the site itself is considered sacred, swimming is discouraged. For some reason a distinction is made between swimming and snorkeling, which is fortunate because the snorkeling here is superb. ⊠ *Hwy. 270, between Kawaihae and Māhukona, North Kohala* ☎ *808/974–6200 or 808/882–6207* ☜ *Free* ⏱ *Daily 8–4.*

10 **Waimea Visitor Center.** The 1909 Lindsey House—a restored ranch cabin listed on the Hawai'i Register of Historic Places—serves as a visitor center. Part of the Waimea Preservation Association, it offers detailed information on Kohala's many historic and cultural sites. ⊠ *65-1291 Kawaihae Rd., behind High Country Traders, Waimea* ☎ *808/885–6707* ⊕ *www.northhawaii.net* ⏱ *Mon.–Sat. 9:30–4:30.*

> **NEED A BREAK?**
>
> At **Aioli's** (⊠ 'Opelo Plaza, Hwy. 19 and 'Opelo Rd., Waimea ☎ 808/885–6325) you can pick up ready-to-go box lunches or opt for a custom-made sandwich. They also offer a delicious bistro menu that changes often to make use of local produce and fresh fish. If you're in the mood for a steaming latte and a warm pastry, stop by **Waimea Coffee & Company** (⊠ Parker Sq., 65-1279 Kawai-

hae Rd., Waimea ☎ 808/885–4472), sit out on their veranda, and try to believe you're in Hawai'i and not West Virginia.

Kailua-Kona

A surprising number of historic sites are tucked amongst the open-air restaurants and trinket shops that line Ali'i Drive, the main drag of Kailua-Kona. Not just your average touristy seaside village, Kailua-Kona is where King Kamehameha I died in 1819 and where his successor, King Liholiho, broke the ancient *kapu* (roughly translating as "forbidden," it was the name for the strict code of conduct islanders were compelled to follow). The following year, on April 4, 1820, the first Christian missionaries came ashore here, changing the Islands forever. If you want to know more about the village's fascinating past, arrange for a 75-minute guided walking tour with the **Kona Historical Society** (⊠ 81-6551 Māmalahoa Hwy. ☎ 808/323–3222 ⊕ www.konahistorical.org).

> ### WHERE DO I PARK?
>
> The easiest place to park your car is at King Kamehameha's Kona Beach Hotel ($3). Some free parking is also available: when you enter Kailua via Palani Road (Highway 190), turn left onto Kuakini Highway; drive for a half block, and turn right into the small marked parking lot. Walk *makai* (toward the ocean) on Likana Lane a half block to Ali'i Drive and you'll be in the heart of Kailua-Kona.

Kailua-Kona enjoys year-round sunshine—except for the rare deluge. Mornings offer cooler weather, smaller crowds, and more birds singing in the banyan trees, but afternoon outings are great for cool drinks while gazing out over the ocean.

Main Attractions

★ ⑯ **Hulihe'e Palace.** Fronted by a wrought-iron gate decorated with an elaborate crest, Hulihe'e Palace is one of only three royal palaces in America. The two-story residence was built by Governor John Adams Kuakini in 1838, a year after he completed Moku'aikaua Church. During the 1880s it served as King David Kalākaua's summer palace. It's constructed of local materials, including lava, coral, koa wood, and 'ōhi'a timber. The oversize doors and furniture bear witness to the size of some of the Hawaiian people. On weekday afternoons hula schools rehearse on the grounds. Hulihe'e Palace is operated by the Daughters of Hawai'i, a nonprofit focused on maintaining the heritage of the Islands. Free concerts are given regularly. ■ TIP➔ **For you crazy romantics planning a Hawai'i wedding, Hulihe'e Palace is available for receptions.** ⊠ *75-5718 Ali'i Dr.* ☎ *808/329–1877* ⊕ *www.huliheepalace.org* ☜ *$5* ☉ *Weekdays 9–4, weekends 10–4.*

⑱ **Kona Inn Shopping Village.** Originally a hotel, the Kona Inn was built in 1928 to woo a new wave of wealthy travelers. As newer condos and resorts opened along the Kona and Kohala coasts, it lost much of its appeal. It was transformed into a mall with dozens of clothing boutiques, art galleries, gift shops, and island-style eateries. Broad lawns with coconut trees on the ocean side are lovely for afternoon picnics. Prior to

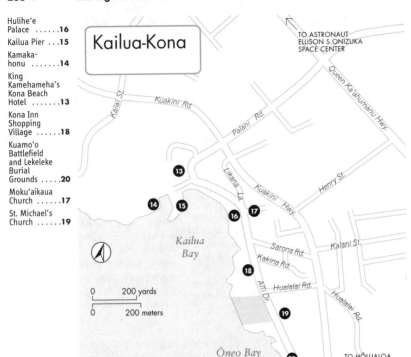

the construction of the inn, the personal *heiau* of King Liholiho stood on this shore. ✉ *75-5744 Ali'i Dr.*

OFF THE BEATEN PATH

HŌLUALOA – Hugging the hillside above Kealakekua Bay, the tiny village of Hōlualoa is just up Hualālai Road from Kailua-Kona. A charming surprise, it's the kind of place where locals sit on their porches or in front of the stores and shoot the breeze all day long. It's comprised almost entirely of galleries in which all types of artists, from woodworkers to jewelry-makers and more traditional painters, work in their studios in back and sell the finished product up front. Formerly coffee country, there are still quite a few coffee farms offering free tours and cups of joe. Duck into the only café in town, the cleverly named **Hōluakoa Cafe** (✉ 76-5900 Mamalahoa Hwy. ☎ 808/322–2233), and grab a cup to sip while you stroll through town.

Also Worth Seeing

⑮ Kailua Pier. Though most fishing boats use Honokōhau Harbor, this pier dating from 1918 is still a hub of ocean activity. Outrigger canoe teams practice, and tour boats depart. Each October close to 1,500 international athletes swim 2⁴⁄10 mi from the pier to begin the grueling Ironman Triathlon competition. Along the seawall children daily cast their lines. For youngsters, a bamboo pole and hook are easy to come by, and plenty of locals are willing to give pointers. ✉ *Next to King Kamehameha's Kona Beach Hotel; seawall is between Kailua Pier and Huliheʻe Palace on Aliʻi Dr.*

★ ⓴ **Kamakahonu.** King Kamehameha I spent his last years, from 1812 to 1819, near what is now King Kamehameha's Kona Beach Hotel. Part of what was once a 4-acre homestead complete with several houses and religious sites has been swallowed by Kailua Pier, but a replica of the temple, **Ahuʻena Heiau,** keeps history alive. Free tours start from King Kamehameha's Kona Beach Hotel. ✉ *75-5660 Palani Rd.* ☎ *808/329–2911* 🖅 *Free* 🕙 *Tours weekdays at 1:30.*

⓭ **King Kamehameha's Kona Beach Hotel.** Stroll through the high-ceiling lobby of this Kailua-Kona fixture to view displays of Hawaiian artifacts and mounted marlin from Hawaiian International Billfish tournaments (from when Kailua Pier was still the weigh-in point). These "granders," marlin weighing 1,000 pounds or more, are the big attraction here. Classes in Hawaiian arts and crafts are given regularly. ✉ *75-5660 Palani Rd.* ☎ *808/329–2911 or 800/367–6060* ⊕ *www.konabeachhotel.com.*

⓴ **Kuamoʻo Battlefield and Lekeleke Burial Grounds.** In 1819 an estimated 300 Hawaiians were killed on this vast, black-lava field. After the death of his father, Kamehameha I, Liholiho was crowned king; shortly thereafter he ate at the table of women, thereby breaking an ancient *kapu* (taboo). Chief Kekuaokalani, with radically different views about religious traditions, unsuccessfully challenged King Liholiho in battle. The site of the battle is now filled with terraced graves. ✉ *South end of Aliʻi Dr.*

★ ⓱ **Mokuʻaikaua Church.** A thatch hut, erected on this site by missionaries in 1820, served as the first Christian church on the Islands. A more permanent structure was built in 1836 with black stone from an abandoned *heiau.* The stone was mortared with white coral and topped by an impressive steeple. Inside, behind a panel of gleaming koa wood, is a model of the brig *Thaddeus.* ✉ *75-5713 Aliʻi Dr.* ☎ *808/329–0655.*

⓳ **St. Michael's Church.** The site of Kona's first Catholic church, built in 1840, is marked by a small thatch structure to the left of the present church, which dates from 1850. In front of the church a coral grotto shrine holds 2,500 coral heads, harvested in 1940, when preservation was not yet an issue. ✉ *75-5769 Aliʻi Dr.* ☎ *808/326–7771.*

NEED A BREAK?	The laid-back **Island Lava Java** (✉ 75-5799 Aliʻi Dr. ☎ 808/327–2161), in the Aliʻ Sunset Plaza, has great coffee and the best and biggest cinnamon rolls on the island. In the afternoon stop by for fresh fish or *kālua* pig tacos, sandwiches, fruit smoothies, and ice cream. The large outdoor seating area has a bird's-eye view of the ocean. Locals hang out here to read the paper, play board games, or just watch the surf.

South Kona & Kealakekua Bay

South of Kailua-Kona, Highway 11 hugs splendid coastlines, leaving busy streets behind. A detour along the winding narrow roads in the moun-

COFFEE-FARM TOURS

Several coffee farms around the South Kona and Upcountry Kona coffee-belt area from Hōlualoa to Hōnaunau welcome visitors. You'll learn about the whole process, from green beans to packaging. Often, macadamia nuts are for sale, and the brew, of course, is always ready. Some tours are self-guided, and most are free, with the exception of Kona Coffee Living History Farm.

Bay View Coffee Farm. ⇨ Exploring South Kona & Kealakekua Bay

Greenwell Farms. ✉ 81-6581 Māmalahoa Hwy., Kealakekua ☎ 808/323-2862.

Hōlualoa-Kona Coffee Company. ✉ 77-6261 Old Māmalahoa Hwy., Hwy. 180, Hōlualoa ☎ 808/322-9937 or 800/334-0348.

Kona Coffee Living History Farm (D. Uchida Farm). ⇨ Exploring South Kona & Kealakekua Bay

Royal Kona Coffee Museum & Coffee Mill. ✉ 83-5427 Māmalahoa Hwy., next to tree house in Hōnaunau ☎ 808/328-2511.

tains above takes you straight to the heart of coffee country where lush plantations and jaw-dropping views offer a taste of what Hawai'i was like before the resorts took over. Take a tour at one of the coffee farms to find out what the big deal is about Kona coffee, and snag a free sample while you're at it. A half-hour back on the highway will lead you to magical Kealakekua Bay, where Captain James Cook arrived in 1778, changing the Islands forever. Hawaiian spinner dolphins frolic in the bay, now a marine preserve nestled alongside impossibly high green cliffs more reminiscent of Ireland than posters of Hawai'i. Snorkeling is superb here, as it's a protected marine reserve, so you may want to bring your gear and spend an hour or so exploring the coral reefs. This is also a nice kayaking spot, as the bay is extremely calm, and kayaks are available for rent from a dozen or so vendors.

The winding road above Kealakekua Bay is home to a quaint little painted church, as well as several reasonably priced B&Bs with stunning views. The communities surrounding the bay (Kainaliu and Captain Cook) are brimming with local and transplanted artists, making them great places to stop for a meal, some unique gifts, or an afternoon stroll.

Main Attractions

㉓ Captain Cook Monument. No one knows for sure what happened on February 14, 1779, when English explorer Captain James Cook was killed on this spot. He had chosen Kealakekua Bay as a landing place in November 1778. Cook, arriving during the celebration of Makahiki, the harvest season, was welcomed at first. Some Hawaiians saw him as an incarnation of the god Lono. Cook's party sailed away in February 1779, but a freak storm off the Kona Coast forced his damaged ship back to Kealakekua Bay. The Hawaiians were not so welcoming this time, and various confrontations arose between them and Cook's sailors. The theft of a longboat brought Cook and an armed party ashore to reclaim it. One thing led to another: shots were fired, daggers and spears were thrown, and Captain Cook fell, mortally wounded. Strangely enough, this didn't deter other Westerners from visiting the Islands; Captain James Cook and his party had effectively introduced the Hawaiian Islands to the world. Soon after, Western influences arrived on Hawai'i's shores: whalers, sailors, traders, missionaries, and more, and they brought with them crime, debauchery, alcohol, disease, and a world unknown to the Hawaiians. A 27-foot-high obelisk marks the spot where Captain Cook died on the shore of Kealakekua Bay. Locals like to point out that the land the monument sits on is British territory (to clarify: the British government owns the land that the monument occupies, but it's still U.S. territory). The three-hour 2½-mi hike to get to the monument begins at the trailhead 100 yards off Highway 11 on Nāpō'opo'o Road. Look for the downslope trail opposite three large royal palm trees.

㉑ Kealakekua Bay. This is one of the most beautiful spots on the island. Fodor'sChoice Dramatic cliffs surround crystal-clear, turquoise water chock-full of
★ stunning coral and tropical fish. Before the arrival of Captain Cook in the late 18th century, this now tranquil state marine park and sanctuary lay at the center of Hawaiian life. Historians consider Kealakekua Bay to be the birthplace of the post-contact era.

The term "beach" is used a bit liberally for **Nāpō'opo'o Beach,** on the south side of the bay. There's no real beach to speak of, but there are easy ways to enter the water. To the left of the parking lot is an old cement pier that serves as a great ladder for swimmers going into or coming out of the bay. This is a nice place to swim as it's well protected from weather or currents, so the water is almost always calm and clear.
■ TIP→ **Be very careful entering the bay from near the Captain Cook Monument, as stepping on coral or a sea urchin can be extremely painful to you and devastating to them. Remember that this is a protected marine reserve.** Excellent snorkel cruises can be booked through Fair Wind Cruises (⇨ *See* Snorkeling *later in this chapter*), the only company allowed to dock in Kealakekua. ⊠ *Bottom of Nāpō'opo'o Rd.*

NEED A BREAK? | Before or after winding down Nāpō'opo'o Road, treat yourself to awesome views of Kealakekua Bay at the **Coffee Shack** (⊠ 83-5799 Māmalahoa Hwy. ☎ 808/ 328-9555 ⊕ www.coffeeshack.com), a deli and pizza place with just nine tables on an open, breezy lānai. The bread is home-baked, the eggs benedict is a local breakfast favorite, the sandwiches are generous, and the staff is friendly.

★ ㉔ **Pu'uhonua O Hōnaunau (Place of Refuge).** This 180-acre National Historic Park was once considered a place of refuge. It was a safe haven for women in times of war as well as for *kapu* breakers, criminals, and prisoners of war—anyone who could get inside the 1,000-foot-long wall, which was 10 feet high and 17 feet thick, could avoid punishment. **Hale-o-Keawe Heiau,** built in 1650 as the burial place of King Kamehameha I's ancestor Keawe, has been restored. South of the park, tide pools offer another delight—most notably the crowd of sea turtles feeding there regularly. Demonstrations of poi pounding, canoe making, and local games

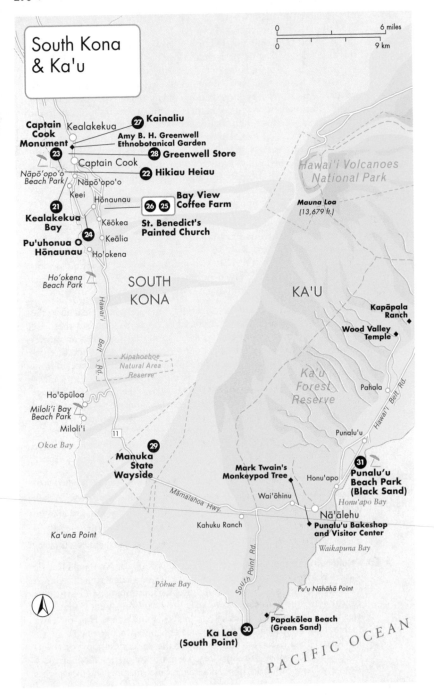

South Kona & Ka'u

27 **Kainaliu**

Captain Cook Monument Kealakekua

Amy B. H. Greenwell Ethnobotanical Garden

23

Captain Cook

28 **Greenwell Store**

Nāpō'opo'o Beach Park

Nāpō'opo'o

22 **Hikiau Heiau**

Keei

Hōnaunau

26 25 **Bay View Coffee Farm**

21

Kēōkea

St. Benedict's Painted Church

Kealakekua Bay

24

Keālia

Pu'uhonua O Hōnaunau

Ho'okena

Ho'okena Beach Park

SOUTH KONA

Hawai'i Volcanoes National Park

Mauna Loa *(13,679 ft.)*

KA'U

Kapāpala Ranch

Wood Valley Temple

Hawai'i Belt Rd.

Hawai'i Belt Rd.

Kīpāhoehoe Natural Area Reserve

Ka'u Forest Reserve

Pāhala

Ho'ōpūloa

Miloli'i Bay Beach Park

Miloli'i

11

Punalu'u

Okoe Bay

29 **Manuka State Wayside**

Mark Twain's Monkeypod Tree

Honu'apo

31 **Punalu'u Beach Park (Black Sand)**

Māmalahoa Hwy.

Wai'ōhinu

Honu'apo Bay

Nā'ālehu

Ka'unā Point

Kahuku Ranch

Punalu'u Bakeshop and Visitor Center

Waikapuna Bay

South Point Rd.

Pōhue Bay

Pu'u Nāhāhā Point

Papakōlea Beach (Green Sand)

Ka Lae (South Point)

30

PACIFIC OCEAN

0   6 miles
0   9 km

are occasionally scheduled. ⊠ *Rte. 160, about 20 mi south of Kailua-Kona* ☏ *808/328–2288* ⊕ *www.nps.gov/puho* ⊠ *$3–$5* ⊙ *Park Mon.–Thurs. 6 AM–8 PM, Fri.–Sun. 6 AM–11 PM; visitor center daily 8 AM–4:30 PM.*

Also Worth Seeing

Amy B. H. Greenwell Ethnobotanical Garden. Often overlooked, this garden fosters a wealth of Hawaiian cultural traditions. On 12 acres grow 250 types of plants that were typical in an early Hawaiian *ahupua'a*, a pie-shape land division that ran from the mountains to the sea. Call to find out about guided tours or drop in between 8:30 AM and 5 PM. ⊠ *82-6188 Māalahoa Hwy., Captain Cook* ☏ *808/323–3318* ⊕ *www.bishopmuseum.org/greenwell.*

㉖ Bay View Coffee Farm. Most of the coffee farms on the island offer tours, and this place has one of the better ones—mostly because the coffee is really good. The tour lasts about an hour; it's interesting, even if you're not into coffee. ⊠ *½ mi past St. Benedict's Painted Church, 83-5249 Painted Church Rd., Hōnaunau* ☏ *808/328–9658* ⊠ *Free* ⊙ *Daily 9–5.*

㉘ Greenwell Store. Established in 1850, the homestead of Henry N. Greenwell served as cattle ranch, sheep station, store, post office, and family home all in one. Now, all that remains is the 1875 stone structure, which is listed on the National Register of Historic Places. It houses a fascinating museum that has exhibits on ranching and coffee farming. It's also headquarters for the **Kona Historical Society,** which organizes walking tours of Kailua-Kona. ⊠ *81-6551 Māmalahoa Hwy.* ☏ *808/323–3222* ⊕ *www.konahistorical.org* ⊠ *Donations accepted* ⊙ *Weekdays 9–3.*

㉒ Hikiau Heiau. This stone platform was once an impressive temple dedicated to the god Lono. When Captain Cook arrived in 1778, ceremonies in his honor were held here. ⊠ *Bottom of Nāpō'opo'o Rd.*

㉗ Kainaliu. Like many of the Big Island's old plantation towns, Kainaliu is experiencing a bit of a renaissance. In addition to a ribbon of funky old stores, many of them traditional Japanese family-operated shops, a handful of new galleries and shops have sprung up in the last couple of years. Browse around Oshima's, established in 1926, and Kimura's, established in 1927, to find authentic Japanese goods beyond tourist trinkets, then pop into Cafe Nasturtium for a tasty vegetarian snack. Cross the street to peek into the 1932 Aloha Theatre, where community-theater actors might be practicing a Broadway revue. ⊠ *Hwy. 11, mile markers 112–114.*

Kona Coffee Living History Farm. Known as the D. Uchida Farm, this site is on the National Register of Historic Places. Completely restored by the Kona Historical Society, it includes a 1913 farmhouse surrounded by coffee trees, a Japanese bathhouse, *kuriba* (coffee-processing mill), and *hoshidana* (traditional drying platform). Tours of the farm are available by reservation only and cost $20. ⊠ *81-6551 Māmalahoa Hwy., Kealakekua* ☏ *808/323–3222* ⊕ *www.konahistorical.org.*

㉕ St. Benedict's Painted Church. The walls, columns, and ceiling of this Roman Catholic church depict colorful biblical scenes through the paintbrush of Belgian-born priest Father Velghe. Mass is still held every weekend. The view of Kealakekua Bay from the entrance is amazing. ⊠ *Painted Church Rd. off Hwy. 160, Hōnaunau* ☎ *808/328–2227.*

Ka'u & Ka Lae (South Point)

The most desolate region of the island, Ka'u is nonetheless home to some spectacular sights. Mark Twain wrote some of his finest prose here, where macadamia-nut farms, green-sand beaches, and tiny villages offer as-yet largely undiscovered beauty. The 50-mi drive from Kailua-Kona to windswept South Point, where the first Polynesians came ashore as early as AD 750, winds away from the ocean through a surreal moonscape of lava-covered forests. Past South Point, glimpses of the ocean return and hidden Green Sand Beach tempts hikers to stop awhile before the highway narrows and returns to the coast, passing verdant cattle pastures and sheer cliffs on the way to the black-sand beach of Punalu'u, the nesting place of the Hawaiian sea turtle.

The drive from Kailua-Kona to Ka Lae is a long one (roughly 2½ hours), but there are a few interesting stops. It's a good idea to fill up on gasoline and pack some snacks, as there are few amenities along the way.

Main Attractions

★ **㉚ Ka Lae (South Point).** Windswept Ka Lae is the southernmost point of land in the United States. A few abandoned structures were used in the 19th and early 20th centuries to lower cattle and produce to ships anchored below the cliffs. It's thought that the first Polynesians came ashore here. Check out the old canoe-mooring holes that are carved through the rocks, possibly by settlers from Tahiti as early as AD 750. Some artifacts, thought to have been left by early voyagers who never settled here, date to AD 300. Driving down to the point, you pass Kama'oa Wind Farm; although the rows of windmill turbines are still fueled by the nearly constant winds sweeping across this coastal plain, the equipment and facilities are falling into disrepair due to neglect. Indeed, some of the windmills no longer turn at all. Continue down the road (parts at the end are unpaved, but driveable), bear left when the road forks and park in the lot at the end; walk past the boat hoists toward the little lighthouse. South Point is just past the lighthouse at the southernmost cliff. ■ TIP→ Don't leave anything of value in your car, and you don't have to pay for parking. It's a free, public park, so anyone trying to charge you is running some sort of scam. ⊠ *Turn right past mile marker 70 on Māmalahoa Hwy., then drive 12 mi down South Point Rd.*

NEED A BREAK?

Punalu'u Bakeshop & Visitor Center (⊠ Māmalahoa Hwy. at Kaalaiki Rd., Na'alehu ☎ 808/929–7343 ☉ Daily 9–5) is a bit of a tourist trap, but it's also a good spot to grab a snack before heading back out on the road. Try some Portuguese sweet bread or a homemade ice-cream sandwich paired with some local Ka'u coffee (that's right, not Kona, but equally tasty).

Papakōlea Beach (Green Sand Beach). It takes awhile to get down and even longer to get back, but where else are you going to see green sand? Add to that the fact that the rock formations surrounding the beach are surreally beautiful, and this is a detour worth taking. ⊠ *2½ mi northeast of South Point.*

③ Punalu'u Beach Park (Black Sand Beach). This easily accessed beach is well worth at least a short stop for two reasons: it's a beautiful black-sand beach, and it's where the Hawaiian sea turtles like to nest so the water's swarming with them. The turtles are used to people by now, and have no problem swimming right alongside you. ⊠ *Turn right down driveway into beach off Hwy. 11 south. Beach is well marked off hwy.*

Also Worth Seeing

㉙ Manuka State Wayside. This dry, upland forest spreads across several lava flows. A rugged trail follows a 2-mi loop past a pit crater and winds around ancient trees such as *hau* and *kukui*. This is an okay spot to wander through the well-maintained arboretum, snap a few photos of the eerie forest, and let the kids scramble around trees so large they can't get their arms around them, but we don't recommend spending too much time here, especially if you're planning on driving all the way down to South Point. The pathways are not well maintained, but restrooms, picnic areas, and telephones are available. ⊠ *Hwy. 11, north of mile marker 81* ☎ *808/974–6200* ⊠ *Free* ☉ *Daily 7–7.*

OFF THE BEATEN PATH

PAHALA – About 16 mi east of Na'lehu, beyond Punalu'u Beach Park, Highway 11 flashes past this little town. You'll miss it if you blink. Pahala is a perfect example of a sugar-plantation town. Behind it, along a wide cane road, you enter Wood Valley, once a prosperous community, now just a road heavily scented by eucalyptus trees, coffee blossoms, and night-blooming jasmine. Here you'll find **Wood Valley Temple** (☎ 808/928–8539), a quiet Tibetan Buddhist retreat that welcomes guests who seek serenity and solitude.

Hawai'i Volcanoes National Park | **See Page 294**

Hilo

When compared to Kailua-Kona, Hilo is often described as "the real Hawai'i." For some reason, life does seem more Hawaiian on this side of the island. Hilo is a quaint, traditional Hawaiian fishing village stretching from the banks of the Wailuku River to Hilo Bay, where a few hotels line stately Banyan Drive. As with many historic American cities, the wonderful old buildings that make up Hilo's downtown have recently been spruced up as part of a revitalization effort. Nearby, the 30-acre Lili'uokalani Gardens, a formal Japanese garden with arched bridges and waterways, was created in the early 1900s to honor the area's

Continued on page 303

NORTHEAST RIFT ZONE

Kīlauea Volcano Summit (4096 ft.)

'OLA'A FOREST

Mauna Loa Summit (13,679 ft.)

Kīpuka Puaulu

Volcano Village

SOUTHWEST RIFT ZONE

Kīlauea Caldera

Kīlauea Visitors Center

EAST RIFT ZONE

Hawai'i Belt Hwy

Pu'u 'Ō'ō (Source of Current Eruption)

Current Lava Flows

11

KA'U DESERT

Chain of Craters Rd

HILINA PALI

HOLEI PALI

Holei Sea Arch

Ka'ena Point

Apua Point

PACIFIC OCEAN

0   10 mi
0   15 km

HAWAI'I VOLCANOES NATIONAL PARK

It's nothing short of miraculous. Kīlauea Volcano is adding new land to the Big Island. Not hundreds of thousands of years ago—today. Molten lava meets the ocean, cools, and solidifies into a brand-new stretch of coastline. It's fire and water, creation at its most elemental. What makes it even more amazing? You can watch it happen right in front of you. If you do nothing else on the Big Island, do the volcano.

Kīlauea, youngest and most rambunctious of the Hawaiian volcanoes, erupted at its summit from the 19th century through the 1950s. Since then, the top of the volcano has been more or less quiet, frequently shrouded in mists. Its eastern side, on the other hand, has been percolating, sending lava spilling into the ocean. The current eruption has been ongoing since January 3, 1983, primarily from Pu'u 'Ō'ō Vent. The lava flows are generally steady and slow, appearing and disappearing from view. And the volcano doesn't only create, it destroys. In 1990, a lava flow engulfed and demolished the coastal town of Kalapana.

Exploring the surface of the world's most active volcano—from the moonscape craters at the summit to the red lava flows on the coast—is the ultimate ecotour.

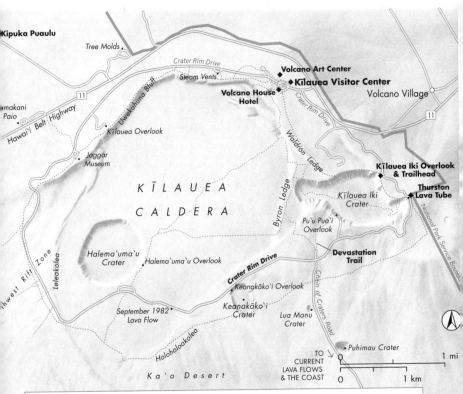

THE SUMMIT: CALDERA & CRATERS

At the summit of Kīlauea is a massive grey pit (2 mi long and 3 mi wide) encircled by plumes of sulfuric smoke. The size of this main caldera, not to mention its uncanny resemblance to those old Apollo moon photos, makes for an eerie, awe-inspiring spot. Within and around the caldera are several smaller craters. Although the summit does not currently have any active lava flows, signs of devastation—black fields of lava, dried in folds and ripples of rock; burnt-out forests; steaming sulfur vents—are everywhere, as are signs of rebirth—scrubby vegetation taking root, fern forests, and even the endangered *nēnē*.

Keep in Mind: As you explore Kīlauea, remember that it is dwarfed by neighboring Mauna Loa, the national park's other volcano and the world's most massive. Mauna Loa's last eruption was in 1984, and scientists believe another is due. The summit is difficult to reach, but you will most likely walk on some part of this volcano during your visit to the Big Island, as it encompasses nearly half of the island.

CAUTION

Yellow, acrid-smelling sulfur banks and gaping vents emitting warm steam are found throughout the cool environs of the park. Pregnant women and anyone with heart or respiratory problems should avoid both the sulfur banks and the noxious fumes.

EXPERIENCING THE SUMMIT

Wear comfortable shoes because the best way to experience the wonder of this place is to hike it. Even a short stroll can take you deep into a primeval landscape. The summit is easy to navigate; trailheads and overlooks are signposted off Crater Rim Drive.

1ST STOP: KĪLAUEA VISITOR CENTER
808/985–6010, Daily 7:45–5.

Always check the status of the current lava flows first. Don't get caught on the summit when the lava is bubbling on the coast. The summit is amazing, but as it's currently dormant, it will be there when you're ready for it. Plus rangers know the inside scoop on summit trails.

While you're there: Check out **Volcano House** (808/967–7321). This remarkable old lodge peers impudently down into Kīlauea from its perch on the caldera's rim. The 1941 building itself is sadly showing wear and tear, but there's usually a blaze in the stone fireplace. Skip the food, but don't miss the views.

Take a look at the work of Big Island photographers, artists, and craftspeople at the **Volcano Art Center** (808/967–7565, www.volcanoartcenter.org, daily 9–5).

Kīlauea Iki Trail

DRIVING TOUR OF CRATER RIM DRIVE
Distance: 11 mi • Time: 1–3 hrs.

Crater Rim Drive circles Kīlauea Caldera and Kīlauea Iki Crater, providing panoramic vistas of vast lava deserts, steam vents, and forests all along the way. The drive loops back to the visitor center. This is a must-do to get a sense of the size and scope of the caldera.

BEST TRAILS

Sandalwood Trail.
Distance: 1.5 mi • Time: 1–1½ hrs.
Difficulty: Easy.

A loop trail winds through rain forest, and past steam vents with views of Kilauea Caldera, Halemaʻumaʻu Crater, and Mauna Loa. If you start on the Earthquake Trail, you'll see the portion of Crater Rim drive that fell into the crater during the 1983 earthquake.

Thurston Lava Tube Trail.
Distance: 3 mi • Time: 45 min. Difficulty: Easy.

A lava tube is the tunnel formed when the surface of a lava flow cools and solidifies, and the still-molten interior drains away. A paved trail leads from the parking lot through the rain forest to the Thurston tube entrance, which resembles an old coal mine. A 15-minute walk inside takes you through narrow tunnels and fairly large rooms. Bring a flashlight for everyone in your group and hike the secondary cave that goes back another 330 yards.

Kīlauea Iki Trail.
Distance: 4 mi • Time: 2–3 hrs.
Difficulty: Moderate.
Elevation Change: 400 ft.

This could be the best hike on the Big Island. You descend through lush rain forest, cross the hardened (and surprisingly flat) lava lake, then climb up the other side to the crater rim. If it seems quiet, consider that Kīlauea Iki was geysering lava as recently as 1959.

EXPLORING THE CURRENT LAVA FLOWS

Pu'u 'Ō'ō Vent is the source of the current lava flows at Kīlauea Volcano. Lava has been flowing from this crater on the eastern face of the volcano since 1983. The eruption has created over 560 acres of land, covered 8.9 mi of coastal highway, and destroyed over 150 structures. The coastal town of Kalapana (in Puna) was engulfed in 1990. Lava flows have covered a vast swath of the mountainside and coast, leaving behind a stark, treeless plain.

The chance to see red–hot, flowing lava is most likely what you're here for. Plan to be on the coast at sunset to maximize your chances of catching the show. Chain of Craters Road is the only way into and out of this area of the park; trailheads and overlooks are signposted along its length.

1ST STOP: KĪLAUEA VISITOR CENTER
808/985–6010, Daily 7:45–5.

Make a quick stop here. It's a long drive down to the coast—make sure that's where the action is before you set out.

DRIVING DOWN CHAIN OF CRATERS ROAD
Distance: 38 mi • Time: 2 hrs.
No food, water, or gasoline is available.

Chain of Craters Road descends 3,700 feet from the fern forests and thick stands of 'ōhi'a at the steaming summit to the starkly barren, lava-covered beaches of the Kalapana Coast. The road passes by or near several small craters on the side of the volcano on its way down to the ocean. Lava flow from one of them, Mauna Ulu, forced the rerouting of this road back in 1974. You can still see steam rising occasionally from Mauna Ulu, so keep an eye out (on your left as you head down toward the coast). You can also see the path of lava from past eruptions zigzagging this way and that down the mountainside, as well as panoramic glimpses of the coast and ocean below. The road ends at the point where it was engulfed in a 1983 flow. The pavement disappears beneath folds and rolls of hardened lava. A NO PARKING sign sticks forlornly out of the tumbled rock. Rangers set up a mobile information booth and portable toilets here.

THE LAVA HIKE
Distance: Variable • Time: Variable.

At the end of Chain of Craters Road, you can (with Madame Pele's consent) see flowing lava up close. If you've got a GPS, this is the place for it—there are no marked trails, the terrain is quite uneven, and you're on your own. Although you can hike any time of the day, the best time is just before dusk, so that you'll be on the flow to see the red glow of any lava flowing off the cliffs or into the ocean.

Park rangers man the mobile information shack at the end of the road until an hour or two after dark. Check with them before setting out about conditions and hazards. Because lava flows are unpredictable, it's impossible to say how long a hike to flowing lava will take, but if you leave at dusk figure to be back around midnight (give or take a couple of hours).

CAUTION

When lava enters the sea it produces huge clouds of white steam. Stay out of them. They contain (among other harmful gases) hydrofluoric acid, which can etch glass (like camera lenses and eyeglasses, to say nothing of what it can do to your lungs). Do not get too close to the ocean. This is brand-new land and unstable lava benches can (and do) break off and drop into the ocean.

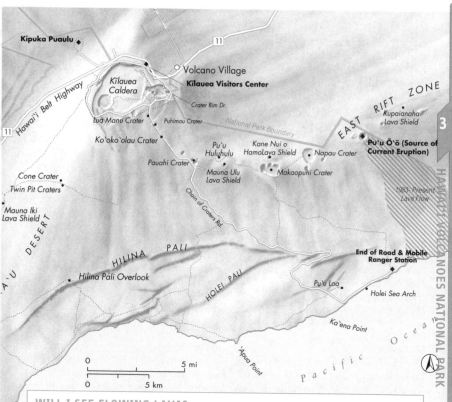

Kipuka Puaulu

11

Volcano Village

Kīlauea Visitors Center

Kīlauea
Caldera

Hawai'i Belt Highway

Crater Rim Dr.

EAST RIFT ZONE

11

Lua Manu Crater   Puhimau Crater

National Park Boundary

Kupaianaha
Lava Shield

Ko'oko'olau Crater

Kane Nui o
Hamolaya Shield

**Pu'u Ō'ō (Source of
Current Eruption)**

Pu'u
Huluhulu

Napau Crater

Pauahi Crater

Cone Crater

Mauna Ulu
Lava Shield

Makaopuhi Crater

Twin Pit Craters

Chain of Craters Rd.

1983–Present
Lava Flow

Mauna Iki
Lava Shield

HILINA   PALI

KA'U   DESERT

HOLEI PALI

**End of Road & Mobile
Ranger Station**

Hilina Pali Overlook

Pu'u Loa

Holei Sea Arch

Ka'ena Point

Pacific Ocean

'Apua Point

0   5 mi

0   5 km

HAWAI'I VOLCANOES NATIONAL PARK

3

WILL I SEE FLOWING LAVA?

You may or may not see flowing lava. Conditions change daily. You might be able to see red lava from the end of Chain of Craters Road, or you might have to hike to it. If it's really gushing, you'll be able to see it during the day. If, however, as is typically the case, it's just sort of seeping, then the best time to see it is at night. Lava flows beneath the surface can shine through the crust in the dark of night.

PLANNING YOUR TRIP TO THE VOLCANO

■ **Stay the night.** We strongly recommend staying the night. There is more than enough to fill a day and a half. And you signficantly improve your chances of seeing red lava if you are there at night. (⇨ *See Where to Stay later in this chapter.*)

■ **Always stop in at Kīlauea Visitor Center first.**

■ **Go for at least two hikes or walks** (one on the summit and one on the coast).

Park Information

CONTACT:
Hawai'i Volcanoes National Park
P.O. Box 52
Hawai'i National Park, HI 96718
808/985–6000
www.nps.gov/havo
Hours: Open 24 hours a day
Admission: $10 per car for seven days

GETTING HERE:
It's a 45-minute drive from Hilo to the park. The drive from Kailua-Kona is three hours one way (another reason to stay the night); the southern route (via South Point) is quickest from the Kona Side.

WHAT TO BRING:
Dress in layers. Take a sweater (or a jacket in winter), as temperatures get nippy at the summit's 4,000-foot elevation, and maybe a poncho for the occasional downpour. It's much hotter and windier on the coast; wear sunscreen and a hat. Pack a lunch. Volcano Village is too far from the park to be convenient midday, and food at Volcano House is forgettable tour-group fare.

If your hiking plans are more ambitious than a short walk, there's more to pack. Wear sturdy shoes. You can go in tennis shoes (though the lava will do a number on the soles), but hiking boots are much better. Forget about hiking in sandals or flip-flops. Wear sunscreen and maybe a hat. Bring plenty of water (2–3 liters per person) and energy bars or other snacks. If you plan to hike to the shoreline lava flow at dusk or dawn, flashlights (with extra batteries) are mandatory for everyone in your group.

HEALTH & SAFETY:
With very few exceptions, the entire park is open to visitors, and, in the ever-changing eruption conditions, only the fool enters into closed areas or ignores posted warnings. The risk of injury from falling into a lava crack is real, as is the threat of becoming disoriented and lost due to volcanic fumes, smoke, and haze clouds. This is a dangerous place, and signs are posted for a reason. Be sure to follow all rules and posted signs and markers, and don't wander off by yourself.

GUIDED HIKES:
If you plan to do the park in a single day and if you are coming from the Kona side, consider booking your excursion with an outfitter.

National Park Ranger Programs. Tours vary; information is posted at the visitor center by 9 each morning. Register a week in advance for the Wednesday wild-cave hike.

Hawai'i Forest and Trail. 808/331–8505 or 800/464–1993, www.hawaii-forest.com.

Hawaiian Walkways. 808/775–0372 or 800/457–7759, www.hawaiianwalkways.com.

Airplane & Helicopter Tours

There's nothing quite like the aerial view of lava flowing into the ocean with clouds of steam billowing into the air. Aerial tours have unfortunately become a controversial subject. The park service requests that tour helicopters avoid flying directly over certain sites that are

Pu'u Ō'o Cone, Kīlauea Volcano

of religious significance to native Hawaiians. A few unscrupulous operators, however, ignore these requests and even advertise better safety records than they've actually earned. Be smart when booking your tour, and ask the right questions: How close will I get to the surface of a lava flow? (FAA regulations mandate an altitude of 500 feet.) Do you fly over Halema'uma'u or Kīlauea caldera? (Culturally sensitive areas to be avoided.) Do you have 2-way headsets so passengers can talk with the pilot? (Very desirable.) Book a tour from Hilo airport, if possible. It's much cheaper as you won't pay to fly from Kona over the relatively boring landscape on the way.

Mauna Loa Helicopters. 73-310 U'u Street, Kailua-Kona, 808/334–0234, www.maunaloahelicopters.com.

Mokulele Flight Service. 808/326–7070 or 866/260–7070, www.mokulele.com.

Sunshine Helicopters. Helipad at the Hāpuna Beach Prince Hotel and Hilo Airport, 808/882–1223, 808/969–7506, or 800/469–3000, www.sunshinehelicopters.com.

Volcano Village

If you plan to stay the night or are just hungry for a good meal, Volcano Village is your destination. With two country stores, a couple of family-run restaurants, a post office, and a hardware store, this little village of a few thousand souls nestled at the edge of the volcano's summit is Mayberry in the rain forest. Stop by the Sunday-morning farmers' market at Cooper Center on Wright Road, across from the firehouse (the community pitched in to build both structures).

ALSO NEAR THE PARK:

Akatsuka Orchid Gardens. Tour one of the largest orchid collections in Hawai'i. The cool volcano climate provides the ideal conditions for cultivation. The shop sells plants and cut flowers and can ship to anywhere in the world. Hwy. 11, just past mile marker 22, 808/967–8234 or 888/967–6669, www.akatsukaorchid.com, free, daily 8:30–5.

Kīpuka Puaulu. A *kīpuka* is a forested island surrounded by a sea of lava. This 100-acre mesic forest is also known as Bird Park; native birds, such as the 'apapane and the 'elepaio, call from their hiding places in the thick canopy. Drive southwest on Highway 11 from the park to the next right and turn onto Mauna Loa Road. You'll see a sign marked TREE MOLDS. Each chimneylike formation was created when molten lava hardened around a tree, burning it away in the process. About 2 mi in, you can take a self-guided mile-long walk around Kīpuka Puaulu. Hawai'i Volcanoes National Park.

Volcano Winery. This unusual winery creates white table wines from Symphony grapes, as well as honey wines, a red Pele Delight, Guava or Passion Chablis, and Volcano Blush. Experiments with traditional varietals such as pinot noir are underway. 35 Pi'imauna Dr., 808/967–7772, www.volcanowinery.com, daily 10–5:30.

YOUR HOSTESS, MADAME PELE

Hawai'i is full of myths and legends that have been passed down from the ancients, but the Big Island is the only one with its own mercurial, vengeful, gin-guzzling goddess, Pele. Kīlauea, specifically Halema'uma'u Crater, is her home.

It's said that, before every eruption, Pele appears in human form as a wrinkled old woman walking along isolated back roads. Those who offer her a ride return home to find a river of boiling magma abruptly halted inches from their property or diverted around their houses. Those who pass her by find their homes devastated by molten lava.

And she doesn't just mess with the natives, so don't think you're off the hook. Madame Pele wreaks havoc on the lives of those who take lava rock from the island, and that includes green, black, or even white sand that came from lava. You can't help the bits that make it into your shoes and suits, but don't even think about taking any extra. People have been returning rocks and sand to the Big Island for years after suffering health problems, bizarre accidents, and any number of other problems thought to be the curse of Pele. Nine times out of 10 when they bring the lava back, their luck changes. If you see lei and gin bottles scattered on the ground around a crater, those are gifts for Pele.

Some forms of lava take their names from the goddess. **Pele's hair,** thin strands of volcanic glass drawn out from molten lava, resembles golden-blond hair. Solidified, round, jet-black bits of volcanic glass (molten lava that cools quickly) are known as **Pele's tears.** They are often found at the end of strands of Pele's hair.

Tales of Pele also wind around many of the remarkable plants that flourish in her home. **Ohi'a Lehua,** the most common of the Park's native trees, has blossoms, called Lehua, that range from dark red to light yellow. Legends say that Pele fell in love with a local boy called Ohi'a, who was already in love with a beautiful young girl called Lehua. Pele asked Ohi'a to be her husband, but he refused and professed his undying love for Lehua. Angry, Pele turned Ohi'a into an ugly grey tree. The rest of the gods were unable to bring Ohi'a back to life, so they turned Lehua into a blossom on the same tree. It is still believed that picking a Lehua blossom will bring rain (tears from above for separating the lovers).

Of the several different varieties of 'ohelo found around Kīlauea, the most common is a small bush with serrated leaves and juicy berries ranging from yellow to red. The 'ohelo is believed to be the embodiment of Hi'iaka, one of Pele's sisters. Its berries are sacred to Pele, and today there are those who will not eat the fruit and who will not even pass through the Kīlauea area without making an offering of 'ohelo to Pele.

Skylight, Kīlauea Volcano

Japanese sugar-plantation laborers. It also became a safety zone after a devastating tidal wave swept away businesses and homes on May 22, 1960, killing 60 people.

Though the center of government and commerce for the island, Hilo is primarily a residential town. Mansions with yards of lush tropical foliage surround older wooden houses with rusty corrugated roofs. It's a friendly community, populated primarily by descendants of the contract laborers—Japanese, Chinese, Filipino, Puerto Rican, and Portuguese—brought in to work the sugarcane fields during the 1800s. With a population of almost 50,000 in the entire district, Hilo is the fourth-largest city in the state and home to the University of Hawai'i at Hilo.

With an average rainfall of 130 inches per year, it's easy to see why Hilo's yards are so green, and buildings so weather-worn. But when the sun shines and the snow glistens on Mauna Kea, 25 mi in the distance, the town sparkles. Most days the rain blows away by noon, leaving behind the colorful arches that earn Hilo its nickname: the City of Rainbows.

Rain or shine, Hilo is best experienced from one of the area's terrific B&Bs, most of which are housed in historic family homes. The whole town has fewer than 1,000 hotel rooms, and they tend to be pretty funky, standing in stark contrast to the modern luxe resorts on the Kohala Coast.

Main Attractions

★ ❹ **Banyan Drive.** The more than 50 leafy banyan trees with aerial roots dangling from their limbs were planted some 60 to 70 years ago by visiting celebrities. You'll find such names as Amelia Earhart and Franklin Delano Roosevelt on plaques affixed to the trees. ⊠ *Begin at Hawai'i Naniloa Resort, 93 Banyan Dr.*

★ ❹ **Hilo Farmers' Market.** An abundant and colorful market draws farmers and shoppers from all over the island. Two days a week, bright orchids, anthuriums, and birds-of-paradise create a feast for the eyes, while exotic vegetables, tropical fruits, and baked goods create a feast for the stomach. Don't dawdle, as it closes in the early afternoon. ⊠ *Mamo and Kamehameha Sts.* ⊘ *Wed. and Sat. 6:30 AM–2:30 PM.*

★ ❹ **Lili'uokalani Gardens.** Fish-filled ponds, stone lanterns, half-moon bridges, elegant pagodas, and a ceremonial teahouse make this 30-acre park a favorite Sunday destination. It was designed to honor Hawai'i's first Japanese immigrants. The surrounding area used to be a busy residential neighborhood until a tsunami in 1960 swept the buildings away, taking the lives of 60 people in the process. ⊠ *Banyan Dr. at Lihiwai St.* ☎ *808/961–8311.*

❹ **Pe'epe'e Falls.** Four separate streams fall into a series of circular pools, forming the Pe'epe'e Falls. The resulting turbulent action—best seen after a good rain—has earned this stretch of the Wailuku River the name Boiling Pots. ⊠ *3 mi northwest*

NO SWIMMING
There's no swimming allowed in the pools at Pe'epe'e Falls, or anywhere in the Wailuku River due to dangerous currents and undertows.

Hilo Vicinity

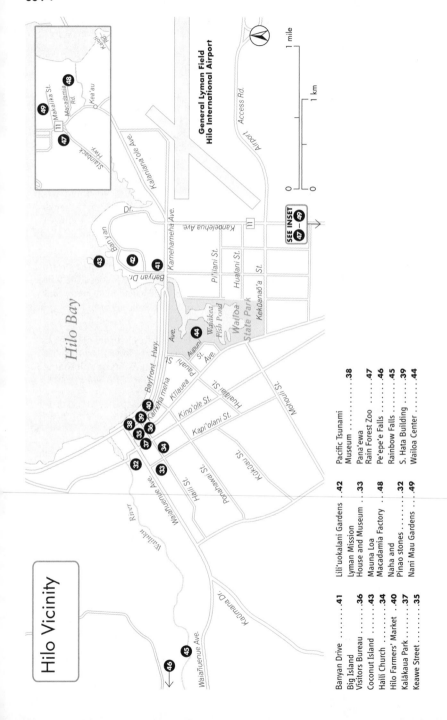

Hilo Bay

Wailuku River

Wai‘anuenue Ave.

Kaumana Dr.

Waiānuenue Ave.

Ponahawai St.

Haili St.

Kalākaua Ave.

Keawe St.

Kino‘ole St.

Kamehameha Ave.

Kīlauea Ave.

Kamehameha Ave.

Pauahi St.

‘Aupuni St.

Bayfront Hwy.

Banyan Dr.

Banyan Dr.

Kamehameha Ave.

Kanoelehua Ave.

Kalaniana‘ole Ave.

Kalaniana‘ole Ave.

Kūkūau St.

Kapi‘olani St.

Kekūanaō‘a St.

Hualālai St.

Hualani St.

Pi‘ilani St.

Mohouli St.

Waiākea Fish Pond

Wailoa State Park

General Lyman Field
Hilo International Airport

Airport Access Rd.

Kea‘au

Keaau Rd.

Makaʻika St.

Macadamia Rd.

Saddleback Hwy.

Stainback Hwy.

SEE INSET 47 — 49

0   1 mile

0   1 km

Banyan Drive **41**
Big Island
Visitors Bureau **36**
Coconut Island **43**
Haili Church **34**
Hilo Farmers' Market . . **40**
Kalākaua Park **37**
Keawe Street **35**

Lili‘uokalani Gardens . . **42**
Lyman Mission
House and Museum . . **33**
Mauna Loa
Macadamia Factory . . **48**
Naha and
Pinao stones **32**
Nani Mau Gardens . . . **49**

Pacific Tsunami
Museum **38**
Pana‘ewa
Rain Forest Zoo **47**
Pe‘epe‘e Falls **46**
Rainbow Falls **45**
S. Hata Building **39**
Wailoa Center **44**

of Hilo on Waiānuenue Ave.; keep to right when road splits and look for a green sign for Boiling Pots.

★ **45** **Rainbow Falls.** After a hard rain, these falls thunder into the Wailuku River gorge. If the sun peeks out in the morning hours, rainbows form above the mist. ✉ *Take Waiānuenue Ave. west of town 1 mi; when road forks, stay on right of Waiānuenue Ave.; look for Hawaiian warrior sign.*

Also Worth Seeing

36 **Big Island Visitors Bureau.** Marked by a red-and-white Hawaiian warrior sign, the bureau is worth a visit for brochures, maps, and up-to-date, friendly insider advice. ✉ *250 Keawe St., at Haili St.* ☎ *808/961–5797* ⊕ *www.bigisland.org* ⊙ *Weekdays 8–4:30.*

★ **43** **Coconut Island.** This small island, just offshore from Liliʻuokalani Gardens, is accessible via a footbridge. It was considered a place of healing in ancient times. Today children play in the tide pools while fisherfolk try their luck. ✉ *Liliʻuokalani Gardens, Banyan Dr.*

34 **Haili Church.** This church was originally constructed in 1859 by New England missionaries, but the church steeple was rebuilt in 1979 following a fire. Haili Church is known for its choir, which sings hymns in Hawaiian during services. ✉ *211 Haili St.* ☎ *808/935-4847.*

37 **Kalākaua Park.** King Kalākaua, who revived the hula, was the inspiration for Hilo's Merrie Monarch Festival. The park is named in his honor. A bronze statue, erected in 1988, depicts the king with a taro leaf in his left hand to signify the Hawaiian peoples' bond with the land. The park also features a huge spreading banyan tree and small fishponds, but no picnic or recreation facilities. In a local tradition, families that have had recent funerals often leave leftover floral displays and funeral wreaths along the fishpond walkway as a way of honoring and celebrating their loved ones. It makes for a unique and colorful display. ✉ *Kalākaua and Kinoʻole Sts.*

NEED A BREAK?

For breads and sandwiches, soups, mouthwatering apple pies, croissants, and biscotti, O'Keefe & Sons Bread Bakers (✉ 374 Kinoʻole St. ☎ 808/934-9334) is the place to go. The tiny retail shop is filled with specialties such as five-grain sourdough, banana bread, and cinnamon toast.

35 **Keawe Street.** Buildings here have been restored to their original 1920s and '30s plantation styles. Although most shopping is along Kamehameha Avenue, the ambience on Keawe Street offers a nostalgic sampling of Hilo as it might have been 80 years ago.

33 **Lyman Mission House & Museum.** Built in 1839 for David and Sarah Lyman, Congregationalist missionaries, the Lyman House is the oldest frame building on the island. In the adjacent museum, dedicated in 1973, there's a realistic magma chamber and exhibits on the islands' formation. There's also an interesting section on Hawaiian flora and fauna. The gift shop sells Hawaiian books, cards, gifts, and music. ✉ *276 Haili St.* ☎ *808/935-5021* ⊕ *www.lymanmuseum.org* 🎟 *$10* ⊙ *Mon.–Sat. 9:30–4:30.*

48 Mauna Loa Macadamia Factory. Acres of macadamia trees lead to a processing plant with viewing windows. A videotape depicts the harvesting and preparation of the nuts, and there are free samples in the visitor center. Children can run off their energy on the nature trail. Feel free to pack your own picnic lunch. ⊠ *Macadamia Rd. off Hwy. 11, 5 mi south of Hilo* ☎ *808/966–8618* ⊕ *www.maunaloa.com* ۞ *Daily 8:30–5:30.*

32 Naha and Pinao stones. These two huge, oblong stones are legendary. The Pinao stone is purportedly an entrance pillar of an ancient temple built near the Wailuku River. Kamehameha I is said to have moved the 5,000-pound Naha stone when he was still in his teens. Legend decreed that he who did so would become king of all the islands. They're in front of the Hilo Public Library. ⊠ *300 Waiānuenue Ave.*

★ **49 Nani Mau Gardens.** The name means "forever beautiful" in Hawaiian, and that's a good description of this 20-acre botanical garden filled with several varieties of fruit trees and hundreds of varieties of ginger, orchids, anthuriums, and other exotic plants. A botanical museum details the history of Hawaiian flora. Guided tours by tram are available. ⊠ *421 Makalika St., off Hwy. 11* ☎ *808/959–3500* ⊕ *www.nanimau.com* ☞ *$10, tram tour $15* ۞ *Daily 8–5.*

☾ 38 Pacific Tsunami Museum. A memorial to all those who lost their lives in the tragedies that have struck this side of the island, this small museum offers a poignant history of tsunamis. In a 1931 C. W. Dickey–designed building—the former home of the First Hawaiian Bank—you'll find an interactive computer center, a science room, a theater, a replica of Old Hilo Town, a *keiki* (children's) corner, and a knowledgeable, friendly staff. In the background, a striking quilt tells a silent story. ⊠ *130 Kamehameha Ave.* ☎ *808/935–0926* ⊕ *www.tsunami.org* ☞ *$7* ۞ *Mon.–Sat. 9–4.*

☾ 47 Pana`ewa Rain Forest Zoo. Children enjoy the spider monkeys, the pygmy hippopotamus, and the white tiger in this quiet zoo, which also hosts native Hawaiian species such as the state bird, the nēnē, Hawaiian goose. It's the only rain-forest zoo in the United States. The trails have been paved, but you should take an umbrella for protection from the frequent showers. ⊠ *Stainback Hwy. off Hwy. 11* ☎ *808/959–7224* ⊕ *www.hilozoo.com* ☞ *Free* ۞ *Daily 9–4.*

39 S. Hata Building. Erected as a general store in 1912 by Sadanosuke Hata and his family, this historic structure now houses shops, restaurants, offices, and a museum called Mokupapapa: Discovery Center for Hawai`i's Remote Coral Reefs. During World War II the Hatas were interned and the building confiscated by the U.S. government. When the war was over, a daughter repurchased it for $100,000. A beautiful example of Renaissance-revival architecture, it won an award from the state for the authenticity of its restoration. ⊠ *308 Kamehameha Ave., at Mamo St.*

44 Wailoa Center. This circular exhibition center, adjacent to Wailoa State Park, has shows by local artists that change monthly. There's also a photographic exhibit of the 1946 and 1960 tidal waves. Just in front of the center is a 12-foot-high bronze statue of King Kamehameha I, made in Italy in the late 1980s. Check out his gold Roman sandals. ⊠ *Pi`opi`o*

WALKING AROUND HILO

Put on some comfortable shoes, because Hilo is best explored on foot. All of the downtown destinations are within easy walking distance of each other. Start your excursion in front of the public library, on Waiānuenue Avenue, four blocks from Kamehameha Avenue. Here, you'll find the ponderous **Naha and Pinao stones,** which legend says King Kamehameha I was able to lift as a teenager, thus foretelling that someday he would be a powerful king. Cross the road to walk southeast along Kapi'olani Street, and turn right on Haili Street to visit the historic **Lyman Mission House & Museum.** Back on Haili Street, follow this busy road toward the ocean; on your right you'll pass **Haili Church.**

Soon you'll reach **Keawe Street** with its plantation-style architecture. Stop at the **Big Island Visitors Bureau** on the right-hand corner for maps and brochures before taking a left. You'll bump into Kalākaua Street; for a quick respite turn left and rest on the benches in **Kalākaua Park.**

Continue *makai* on Kalākaua Street to visit the **Pacific Tsunami Museum** on the corner of Kalākaua and Kamehameha Avenue. After heading three blocks east, you'll come across the **S. Hata Building,** which has interesting shops and restaurants and the Mokupapapa: Discovery Center for Hawaii's Remote Coral Reefs Museum. Just next door, on either side of Mamo Street, is the **Hilo Farmers' Market.**

St. off Kamehameha Ave. ☎ *808/933–0416* ⊗ *Mon., Tues., Thurs., and Fri. 8:30–4:30, Wed. noon–4:30, Sat. 9:30–3.*

Hāmākua Coast

The spectacular waterfalls, mysterious jungles, emerald fields, and stunning ocean vistas along Highway 19 northwest of Hilo are collectively referred to as the Hilo–Hāmākua Heritage Coast. Brown signs featuring a sugarcane tassel reflect the area's history: thousands of acres of sugarcane are now idle, with no industry to support since "King Sugar" left the island in the early 1990s. The 45-mi drive winds through little plantation towns, Pāpa'ikou, Laupāhoehoe, and Pa'auilo among them. It's a great place to wander off the main road and see "real" Hawai'i— untouched valleys, overgrown banyan trees, tiny coastal villages. In particular, the "Heritage Drive," a 4-mi loop just off the main highway, is well worth the detour. Once back on Highway 19, you'll pass the road to Honoka'a, which leads to the end of the road bordering Waipi'o Valley, ancient home to Hawaiian royalty. The isolated valley floor has maintained the ways of old Hawai'i, with taro patches, wild horses, and a handful of houses.

If you've stopped to explore the quiet little villages with wooden boardwalks and dogs dozing in backyards, or if you've spent several hours in Waipi'o Valley, night will undoubtedly be falling by the time you've had your fill of the Hāmākua Coast. Don't worry: the return to Hilo via High-

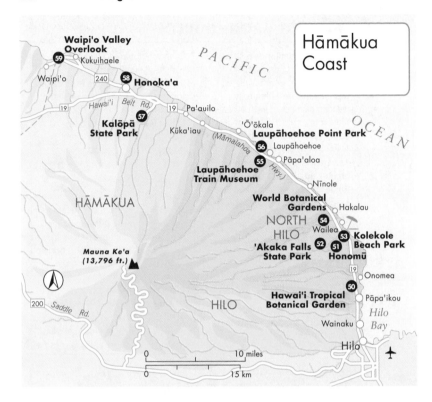

Hāmākua Coast

Waipi'o Valley Overlook — 59
Kukuihaele
Waipi'o
240
Honoka'a — 58
Hawai'i Belt Rd.
19
Pa'auilo
Kalōpā State Park — 57
Kūka'iau
(Māmalahoa)
'Ō'ōkala
Laupāhoehoe Point Park — 56
Laupāhoehoe
Pāpa'aloa — 55
Laupāhoehoe Train Museum
Nīnole
HĀMĀKUA
World Botanical Gardens — 54
Hakalau
NORTH HILO
Wailea
Kolekole Beach Park — 53
'Akaka Falls State Park — 52
Honomū — 51
Mauna Ke'a (13,796 ft.)
19
Onomea
Hawai'i Tropical Botanical Garden — 50
Pāpa'ikou
HILO
200 Saddle Rd.
Wainaku
Hilo Bay
Hilo
PACIFIC OCEAN

0 ⎯ 10 miles
0 ⎯ 15 km

way 19 only takes about an hour, or you can continue on the same road to stop for dinner in Waimea (30 minutes) before heading back to the Kohala Coast resorts (another 25 to 45 minutes).

Main Attractions

★ 52 **'Akaka Falls State Park.** A meandering 10-minute loop trail takes you to the best spots to see the two cascades, **'Akaka** and **Kahuna.** The 400-foot Kahuna Falls is on the lower end of the trail. The majestic upper 'Akaka Falls drops more than 442 feet, tumbling far below into a pool drained by Kolekole Stream amid a profusion of fragrant white, yellow, and red torch ginger. ⊠ *4 mi inland off Hwy. 19, near Honomū* ☎ *808/974–6200* ⊡ *Free* ☉ *Daily 7–7.*

Fodor'sChoice **Mauna Ke'a.** Mauna Ke'a is the antithesis of the typical island experi-
★ ence. Freezing temperatures and arctic conditions are common at the summit, and snowstorms can occur year-round. It's also home to Lake Waiau, one of the highest lakes in the world. The summit—at 13,796 feet—is reputedly the clearest place in the world for viewing the night sky; it's also an outstanding place to see the sun rise and set. To get there, you'll need a four-wheel-drive vehicle. Make sure to stop at the **Onizuka Center for International Astronomy Visitor Information Station** (☎ 808/961–2180 ⊕ www.ifa.hawaii.edu/info/vis ☉ Daily 9 AM–10 PM), at a

9,300-foot elevation. On weekends the Onizuka Center offers escorted summit tours, heading up the mountain in a caravan. Reservations are not required for the free tours, which depart at 1 PM. The center is the best amateur observation site on the planet, with three telescopes and a knowledgeable staff. It hosts nightly stargazing sessions from 6 to 10. To get here from Hilo, which is about 34 mi away, take Highway 200 (Saddle Road), and turn right at mile marker 28 onto the John A. Burns Way, which is the access road to the summit.

If you haven't rented a four-wheel-drive vehicle, don't want to deal with driving to the summit, or don't want to leave until you see the stars (the Onizuka Center tour gets everyone off the summit no later than a half hour after sunset), consider booking a tour. All of the ones listed here provide parkas, as well as telescopes, and meals; excursion fees range from about $90 to $165. **Arnott's Lodge & Hiking Adventures** (☎ 808/969–7097 ⊕ www.arnottslodge.com) leaves from Hilo and is a bit cheaper than the others. **Hawai'i Forest & Trail** (☎ 808/331–8505 or 800/464–1993 ⊕ www.hawaii-forest.com) stops for dinner along the way at a historic ranch. **Mauna Kea Summit Adventures** (☎ 808/322–2366 ⊕ www.maunakea.com) specializes in tours to the mountain. It was the first company to do so, so it has a bit more cred than the rest of the pack.

■ TIP→ Whether you're hiking or driving to the summit, take the change in altitude seriously—don't overexert yourself, especially at the top. Note that scuba divers must wait at least 24 hours before attempting a trip to the summit to avoid getting the bends.

Waipi'o Valley. Though completely off the grid today, Waipi'o was once the center of Hawaiian life; somewhere between 4,000 and 20,000 people made it their home between the 13th and 17th centuries. In 1780 Kamehameha I was singled out here as a future ruler by reigning chiefs. In 1791 he fought Kahekili in his first naval battle at the mouth of the valley. In 1823 the first white visitors found 1,500 people living in this Eden-like environment amid fruit trees, banana groves, taro fields, and fishponds. The 1946 tidal wave drove most residents to higher ground. Now, as then, waterfalls frame the landscape, but the valley has become one of the most isolated places in the state. To preserve this pristine part of the island, commercial transportation permits are limited—only four outfits offer organized valley trips—and Sunday the valley rests. The walk down into the valley is less than a mile—start at the four-wheel-drive road leading down from the lookout point—but keep in mind, the climb back up is strenuous in the hot sun.

If climbing back out of the valley is not an appealing prospect, or if your time is limited, consider taking a guided tour. Costs range from about $40 to $145, depending on the company. **Waipi'o Ridge Stables** (☎ 808/775–7291 ⊕ www.waipioridgestables.com) and **Na'alapa Stables** (☎ 808/775–0419 ⊕ www.naalapastables.com) offer horseback riding trips down into the Waipi'o Valley. Other outfitters include **Waipi'o Rim Backroad Adventures** (☎ 808/775–1122 or 877/757–1414 ⊕ www.topofwaipio.com), which leads tours of the valley. **Waipi'o Valley Shuttle** (☎ 808/775–7121 ⊕ www.waipiovalleytour.com) drives those afraid of wrecking their rental cars into the valley and around to the waterfalls. **Waipi'o Valley Wagon Tours** (☎ 808/775–9518 🌐 www.waipiovalleywagontours.com) takes you on a 1½-hour tour through the valley in mule-drawn wagons.

★ (59) **Waipi'o Valley Overlook.** Bounded by 2,000-foot cliffs, the Valley of the Kings was once a favorite retreat of Hawaiian royalty. Waterfalls drop 1,200 feet from the Kohala Mountains to the valley floor. Horses roam narrow trails and rocky streams. Sheer cliffs make access difficult. Only four-wheel-drive vehicles should attempt the steep road from the overlook. A crescent of black sand makes it a popular spot for surfers. **TIP→ Continued overuse of the beach area and lack of sanitary facilities have caused serious unhealthy conditions to persist since 2003. Until it's cleaned up we don't recommend getting into the water.** ✉ *Follow Hwy. 240 8 mi northwest of Honoka'a.*

Also Worth Seeing

★ (50) **Hawai'i Tropical Botanical Garden.** Eight miles north of Hilo, stunning coastline views appear around each curve of the 4-mi scenic jungle drive that accesses the privately owned nature preserve beside Onomea Bay. Paved pathways in the 17-acre botanical garden lead past ponds, waterfalls, and more than 2,000 species of plants and flowers, including palms, bromeliads, ginger, heleconia, orchids, and ornamentals. ✉ *27-717 Old Māmalahoa Hwy., Pāpa'ikou* ☎ *808/964–5233* 🌐 *www.hawaiigarden.com* 🎫 *$15* 🕓 *Daily 9–4.*

(58) **Honoka'a.** In 1881 Australian William Purvis planted the first macadamia-nut trees in Hawai'i near what is now this funky little town. But Honoka'a's true heyday came when sugar was king in the early part of the 20th century. During World War II, this was the place for soldiers stationed around Waimea to cut loose. Its historic buildings are home today to little eateries and stores crammed with knickknacks, second-hand goods, and antiques. ✉ *Mamane St., Hwy. 240.*

NEED A BREAK?

A quick stop at Tex Drive-In (✉ 45-690 Pakalana St. and Hwy. 19 ☎ 808/775–0598) will give you a chance to taste the snack that made it famous: *malasada*, a puffy, doughy doughnut without a hole. These deep-fried beauties are best eaten hot. They also come in cream-filled versions, including vanilla, chocolate, and coconut.

(51) **Honomū.** A plantation past is reflected in the wooden boardwalks and tin-roof buildings of this small, struggling town. It's fun to poke through old, dusty shops such as Glass from the Past, where you'll find an assortment of old bottles. The Woodshop Gallery/Café showcases local artists. ✉ *2 mi inland from Hwy. 19 en route to 'Akaka Falls State Park.*

★ (57) **Kalōpā State Park.** Past the old plantation town of Pa'auilo, at a cool elevation of 2,000 feet, lies this 100-acre state park. There's a lush forested area with picnic tables and restrooms, and an easy ¾-mi loop trail with additional paths in the adjacent forest reserve. Small signs identify some of the plants. ✉ *12 mi north of Laupāhoehoe and 3 mi inland off Hwy. 19* ☎ *808/775–8852* 🎫 *Free* 🕓 *Daily 7–7 or by permit.*

③ **Kolekole Beach Park.** This rocky beach on the Kolekole River offers an idyllic setting for a barbecue or picnic. A large banyan tree leans over the river, and its rope swing is a hit with local kids during lazy summer days. An old train bridge crosses the river where it empties into the ocean. The surf can be rough, so only experienced swimmers should venture past the river's mouth. Back on the road, a scenic drive takes you from the top of the park through the old town of Wailea back to Highway 19. ⊠ *Off Hwy. 19* ☎ *808/961–8311* 🎫 *Free* ☉ *Daily 7 AM–sunset.*

⑤⑥ **Laupāhoehoe Point Park.** Come here to watch the surf pound the jagged black rocks at the base of the stunning point. This is not a safe place for swimming, however. Still vivid in the minds of longtime area residents is the 1946 tragedy in which 21 schoolchildren and three teachers were swept to sea by a tidal wave. ⊠ *On northeast coastline, Hwy. 19,* makai *side, north of Laupāhoehoe* ☎ *808/961–8311* 🎫 *Free* ☉ *Daily 7 AM–sunset.*

⑤⑤ **Laupāhoehoe Train Museum.** Behind the stone-loading platform of the once-famous Hilo Railroad, constructed around the turn of the 20th century, the former manager's house is a poignant reminder of the era when sugar was the local cash crop. The railroad, one of the most expensive built in its time, was washed away by the tidal wave of 1946. Today one of the old engines is running again on a short Y-track at the museum. ⊠ *Hwy. 19, Laupāhoehoe* ☎ *808/962–6300* 🎫 *$3* ☉ *Weekdays 9–4:30, weekends 10–2.*

♻ ⑤④ **World Botanical Gardens.** About 300 acres of former sugarcane land are slowly giving way to a botanical center, which includes native Hawaiian plants such as orchids, palms, gingers, hibiscus, and heliconias. In the 10-acre arboretum children love to wind their way through a maze made of shrubs. From within the gardens you have access to splendid views of one of the prettiest waterfalls on the isle, triple-tiered **Umauma Falls.** You may feel a little bit cheated, since it's $8 per person, but unfortunately this is the only place to see Umauma without some pretty rigorous hiking and scrambling. ⊠ *Hwy. 19, from Hilo just past mile marker 16* ☎ *808/963–5427* ⊕ *www.wbgi.com* 🎫 *$8* ☉ *Mon.–Sat. 9–5:30.*

Puna

The Puna District is a wild place in every sense of the word. The jagged black coastline is changing all the time; the trees are growing out of control to form canopies over the few paved roads; the land is dirt-cheap and there are no building codes; and the people, well, there's something about living in an area that could be destroyed by lava at any moment (as Kalapana was just a decade or so ago) that makes the laws of modern society seem silly. So it is that Puna has its well-deserved reputation as the "outlaw" region of the Big Island. That said, it's a unique place that's well worth a detour, especially if you're in this part of the island anyway. There are volcanically heated springs, tide pools bursting with interesting sea life, and some mighty fine people-watching opportunities in Pāhoa, a funky little town that the outlaws call home. This is also farm country (yes, that kind of farm, but also the legal sort).

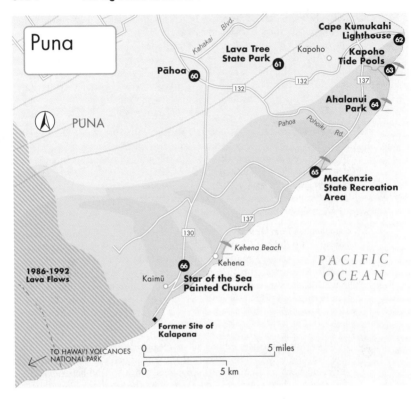

Local farmers grow everything from orchids and anthuriums to papayas, bananas, and macadamia nuts. Several of the island's larger, rural residential subdivisions are between Kea'au and Pāhoa, including Hawaiian Paradise Park, Orchidland Estates, Hawaiian Acres, Hawaiian Beaches, and others.

The roads connecting Pāhoa to Kapoho and the Kalapana coast form a loop that's about 25 mi long; driving times are from two to three hours, depending on the number of stops you make and the length of time at each stop. There are long stretches of the road that may be completely isolated at any given point; this can be a little scary at night, but beautiful and tranquil during the day.

Main Attractions

64 Ahalanui Park. This park was established with a federal grant in the mid-1990s to replace those lost to the lava flows at Kalapana. It's 2½ mi south of the intersection of highways 132 and 137 on the Kapoho Coast, southeast of Pāhoa town. There's a half-acre pond fed by thermal freshwater springs mixed with seawater, which makes for a relaxing soak. ■ TIP→ There have been occasional reports of bacterial contamination by the health department. Check with on-duty lifeguards and follow any posted advisory signs. Facilities include portable restrooms, outdoor showers,

BIG ISLAND SIGHTSEEING TOURS

Guided tours on the island are great for specific things: seeing Mauna Kea, exploring Waipi'o Valley, maybe even touring Volcanoes National Park (especially if your time is short). Sticking to a guided tour the whole time, though, would not be a great idea. Half the fun of the island is in exploring it on your own. Plus, if you stick to a guided tour, you'll only see the major tourist attractions, none of the Big Island's many hidden treasures.

Local tour-bus operators conduct volcano tours and circle-island tours, with pickup at the major resorts. Costs range from $38 to $68, depending on pickup location.

The circle-island tour is a full 12-hour day, but Jack's and Polynesian Adventure Tours also offer half-day tours to the volcano, Mauna Kea observatory, and around Kailua-Kona.

Jack's Tours. ☎ 808/329-2555 in Kona, 808/961-6666 in Hilo, 800/442-5557 ⊕ www.jackstours.com.

Polynesian Adventure Tours. ☎ 808/329-8008 in Kona, 800/622-3011 ⊕ www.polyad.com.

Roberts Hawai'i. ☎ 808/329-1688 in Kona, 808/966-5483 in Hilo, 800/831-5541 ⊕ www.robertshawaii.com.

and picnic tables; no drinking water is available. ⊠ *Hwy. 137, 2½ mi south of junction of Hwy. 132, Puna.*

62 Cape Kumukahi Lighthouse. The lighthouse, 1½ mi east of the intersection of highways 132 and 137, was miraculously unharmed during the 1960 volcano eruption here that destroyed the town of Kapoho. The lava flowed directly up to the lighthouse's base but instead of pushing it over, actually flowed around it. According to Hawaiian legend, Pele, the volcano goddess, protected the Hawaiian fisherfolk by sparing the lighthouse. The lighthouse itself is a simple metal-frame structure with a light on top, similar to a tall electric-line transmission tower. Seeing the hardened lava flows skirting directly around the lighthouse is worth the visit. ⊠ *Past intersection of Hwys. 132 and 137, Kapoho.*

63 Kapoho Tide Pools. This network of tide pools at the end of Kapoho-Kai Road are great for a swim or a snorkel, or even just a beautiful view of new coastline. Some of the pools are volcanically heated, so if your back's a little sore from exploring the island, stop for a 10-minute soak and you can feel better immediately. Take the road to the end, turn left and park. Some of the pools are on private property, but those closest to the ocean, Wai'ōpae (ponds), are open to all. ⊠ *End of Kapoho-Kai Rd., off Hwy. 137.*

60 Pāhoa. Sort of like an outlaw town from the Wild West, but with renegade Hawaiians instead of cowboys, this little town is all wooden boardwalks and rickety buildings. The secondhand stores, tie-dye clothing boutiques, and art galleries in quaint old buildings are fun to wander through, but Pāhoa is not the best spot to go wandering around at night. Pāhoa's main street boasts a handful of island eateries, the best of which is Luquin's Mexican Restaurant. ■ TIP→ If you're here in the evening, listen for the sound of the ubiquitous Kukio frogs; farmers consider them a pest both for the effect they have on crops and because they continuously let out the loudest, shrillest squeaks you've ever heard. ⊠ *Turn southeast onto Hwy. 130 at Kea'au, drive 11 mi to right turn marked Pāhoa.*

Also Worth Seeing

61 **Lava Tree State Park.** Tree molds that rise like blackened smokestacks formed here in 1790 when a lava flow swept through the 'ōhi'a forest. Some reach as high as 12 feet. The meandering trail provides close-up looks at some of Hawaii's tropical plants and trees. There are restrooms and a couple of picnic pavilions and tables. ■ TIP→ Mosquitoes like to live here in abundance, so be sure to bring repellent. ⊠ *Hwy. 132, Puna District* ☎ 808/974–6200 ⊠ *Free* ⊙ *Daily 30 min before sunrise–30 min after sunset.*

65 **MacKenzie State Recreation Area.** This is a coastal park located on rocky shoreline cliffs in a breezy, cool ironwood grove. There are picnic tables, restrooms, and a tent-camping area; bring your own drinking water. The park is significant for the restored section of the old "King's Highway" trail system, which circled the coast in the era before Hawai'i was discovered by the Western world. In those days, tribal kings and chiefs used these trails to connect the coastal villages, allowing them to collect taxes and maintain control over the people. Short hikes of an hour or less are possible along the existing sections of the rough rocky trail. There are views of rugged coast, rocky beach, and coastal dry forest. ⊠ *Hwy. 137, Puna District.*

66 **Star of the Sea Painted Church.** This historic church, now a community center, was moved to its present location in 1990 just ahead of the advancing lava flow that destroyed the Kalapana area. The church, which dates from the 1930s, was built by a Belgian Catholic missionary priest, Father Evarest Gielen, who also did the detailed paintings on the church's interior. Though similar in style, the Star of the Sea and St. Benedict's were actually painted by two different Belgian Catholic missionary priests. Star of the Sea also has several lovely stained-glass windows. ⊠ *Hwy. 130, 1 mi north of Kalapana.*

BEACHES

Don't believe anyone who tells you that the Big Island lacks beaches.

It's not so much that the Big Island has fewer than the other islands, just that there's more island so getting to the beaches can be slightly less convenient. That said, there are plenty of those perfect white beaches you think of when you hear "Hawai'i," and the added bonus of black- and green-sand beaches, thanks to the age of the island and its active volcanoes. New beaches appear—and disappear—regularly. In 1989 a black-sand beach, Kamoamoa, formed when molten lava shattered as it hit cold ocean waters; it was closed by new lava flows in 1992.

The bulk of the island's beaches are on the northwest part of the island, along the Kohala Coast. Black-sand beaches and green-sand beaches are in the southern region, along the coast nearest the volcano. On the eastern side of the island, beaches tend to be of the rocky-coast–surging-surf variety, but there are still a few worth visiting, and this is where the Hawaiian shoreline is at its most picturesque.

Kohala Coast

This is where all the white sandy beaches are, and also, understandably, where all the resorts are on the island. The resorts are required to offer public access to at least part of their beach, so don't be frightened off by a guard shack and a fancy sign. The resort beaches aside, there are some real hidden gems on the Kohala coast accessible only by boat, four-wheel drive, or a 15–20-minute hike. It's well worth the effort to get to at least one of these. The beaches here are listed in order from north (farthest from Kona) to south.

Pololū Beach. While you're in the Pololū Valley, leave time to hike down to Pololū Beach. Follow the trail at the end of Highway 270, the northernmost point of the island. The black-sand beach below is absolutely beautiful, surrounded by jagged green cliffs and huge black-sand dunes. ■ TIP→ **The surf is almost always rough and the currents are strong, so it's not an ideal spot for swimming or snorkeling.** The hike's not easy going back up, but there are plenty of spots to stop for a rest. ⌧ *End of Hwy. 270* ⌁ *No facilities.*

Spencer Beach Park. This spot is popular with local families because of its reef-protected waters. It's safe for swimming year-round, which makes it an excellent spot for a lazy day at the beach. The water is clear, but there aren't loads of fish here, so it's not a great snorkeling spot. It's a smaller beach, gently sloping with white sand and a few pebbles. You can walk from here to Pu'ukoholā Heiau National Historic Site. ⌧ *Off Hwy. 270, uphill from Kawaihae Harbor* ☎ *808/961–8311* ⌁ *Lifeguard, toilets, showers, picnic tables, grills, parking lot.*

FodorśChoice **Kauna'oa Beach.** Hands-down one of the most ★ beautiful beaches on the island, Kauna'oa is a white crescent of sand. The beach, at the Mauna Kea Beach Hotel, slopes very gradually. It's a great place for snorkeling. ■ TIP→ **Currents can be strong, and powerful winter waves can be dangerous, so be careful.** Beachgoers are welcome at the hotel's waterfront café, where there's a restroom. Public parking

BEACHES KEY	
🚻	*Restroom*
🚿	*Showers*
🏄	*Surfing*
🤿	*Snorkel/Scuba*
🚼	*Good for kids*
🅿	*Parking*

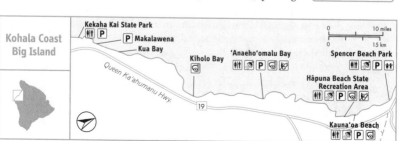

Kohala Coast Big Island

Kekaha Kai State Park
🚻 🅿 🅿 Makalawena
Kua Bay
Kīholo Bay 🤿   'Anaeho'omalu Bay 🚻 🚿 🅿 🤿 🏄   Spencer Beach Park 🚻 🚿 🅿 🚼

Queen Ka'ahumanu Hwy.

0 ——— 10 miles
0 ——— 15 km

Hāpuna Beach State Recreation Area 🚻 🚿 🅿 🤿 🏄

19

Kauna'oa Beach 🚻 🚿 🅿 🤿

is limited to only 30 spots, so it's best to arrive before 10 AM. ✉ *Off Hwy. 19; entry through gate to Mauna Kea Beach Resort* ☞ *Lifeguard, toilets, showers, parking lot.*

Fodor'sChoice
★
Hāpuna Beach State Recreation Area. Guidebooks always say it's a toss-up between Hāpuna and Kauna'oa for "best beach" on the island, but, although Kauna'oa is beautiful, most locals give the prize to Hāpuna. First of all, there's loads of parking so you don't have to get here at dawn. Second, though a tiny section of the beach is (grudgingly) given over to the Hāpuna Prince Hotel a few years back, it doesn't feel like the hotel's property. The beach itself is a long (½-mi), white, perfect crescent, wide enough to hold half the island on a holiday weekend. The turquoise water is very calm in summer, with just enough rolling waves to make bodysurfing or boogie boarding fun. ■ TIP→ In winter, surf can be very rough. There's some excellent snorkeling around the jagged rocks that border the beach on either side, but a strong current means it's only for experienced swimmers. Hāpuna tends to get a little windy in the late afternoon; even that can have a benefit, as everyone else leaves just in time to give you a private, perfect sunset. ✉ *Hwy. 19, near mile marker 69, at Hāpuna Beach Prince Hotel* ☎ 808/974–6200 ☞ *Lifeguard, toilets, showers, food concession, picnic tables, grills/firepits, parking lot.*

★ **'Anaeho'omalu Beach (A-Bay).** This expansive beach, at the Waikoloa Beach Marriott, is perfect for swimming, windsurfing, snorkeling, and diving. It's a well-protected bay, so even when surf is rough on the rest of the island, it's fairly calm here. Snorkel gear, kayaks, and boogie boards are available for rent at the north end. Be sure to wander around the ancient fishponds and petroglyph fields. There's a trail that runs along the shoreline leading to the Hilton Waikoloa that passes a few busy tide pools. Not a good barefoot walk, though—between the lava rock and the coral, you'll regret leaving your shoes on the beach mat. ✉ *Follow Waikoloa Beach Dr. to Kings' Shops, then turn left; parking lot and beach right-of-way south of Waikoloa Beach Marriott* ☞ *Toilets, showers, food concession, picnic tables, parking lot.*

Kīholo Bay. A new gravel road to the shoreline makes Kīholo Bay an absolute must-see (previously you'd have to hike over lava for 20 minutes). Thanks to Mauna Loa, what was once the site of King Kamehameha's gigantic fish pond is now several freshwater ponds encircling a beautiful little bay. The water's a bit cold and hazy because of the mix of fresh and salty water, but there are tons of green sea turtles here, and the snorkeling is great. If you follow the shoreline southwest toward Kona, just past the big yellow house is another public beach where you'll find some naturally occurring freshwater pools inside a lava tube. This area, called Queen's Bath, is as cool as it sounds. ✉ *Hwy. 19, gravel road between mile markers 82 and 83* ☞ *No facilities.*

Kua Bay. Locals are pretty unhappy about the newly paved road leading to Kua Bay, the northernmost beach in the stretch of coast that comprises Kekaha Kai (Kona Coast) State Park. At one time you had to hike over a few miles of unmarked, rocky trail to get here, which kept

BEACH SAFETY

Note that many beaches have dangerous undertows. Rip currents and pounding shore breaks may cause serious risk anywhere at any time. The west side tends to be calmer, but still the surf gets rough in winter. Few public beaches have lifeguards. To be safe, try to stick to those with lifeguards, keep an eye out for warning signs, and get into the water only when you see other swimmers. (The presence of surfers is not an indication that the area is safe for swimmers.) If you're still not sure, ask the lifeguard on duty.

Finally, remember that black or green sand is not a souvenir. There's only so much, and everyone wants to enjoy these spots for years to come. Plus, they are technically the remnants of lava, and everyone knows that Madame Pele will put a serious curse on the head of anyone who removes lava from the island.

many people out. It's easy to understand why the locals would be so protective. This is one of the most beautiful bays you will ever see—the water is crystal clear, deep aquamarine, and peaceful in summer. Rocky shores on either side keep the beach from getting too windy in the afternoon. ■ TIP➡ **The surf here can get very rough in winter.** ⊠ *Hwy. 19, north of mile marker 88* ☞ *No facilities.*

Makalawena. Also at Kekaha Kai (Kona Coast) State Park, Makalawena is a long white crescent, dotted with little coves and surrounded by dunes and trees. If it weren't so hard to get to, this would be the unanimous choice for best beach on the island. The sand is powdery fine, the water is perfect, and the place is deserted because of the whole "it's hard to get to" thing. You either have to rent a boat and anchor there, walk 20 minutes over a lava trail, or take a brutal four-wheel-drive jaunt over the lava. (You still have to walk the last 5 to 10 minutes.) But it's worth it. Makalawena is more than just a great beach—it's a truly magical place. An afternoon here is a recipe for delirious happiness. Sometimes people are so happy they just want to frolic around naked. Did we mention that there are wild goats hanging around? There's a freshwater pond that beats hosing off at one of those water-spigot showers at the marked public beaches. ⊠ *Hwy. 19, between mile markers 88 and 89; if you're walking, park in lot at Kekaha Kai (Kona Coast) State Park and follow footpath along the shore* ☞ *No facilities.*

Kekaha Kai (Kona Coast) State Park. Beyond the park's entrance, at the end of two 1½-mi-long unpaved roads, you can find two sandy beaches: Mahai'ula to the south, and Ka'elehuluhulu to the north. In calm weather, they're great for swimming. You can hike along a historic 4½-mi trail from one to the other, but be prepared for the heat and bring lots of drinking water. ⊠ *Hwy. 19, sign about 2 mi north of Keāhole–Kona International Airport marks rough road.* ☎ *808/327–4958 or 808/974–6200* ☞ *Parking lot at entrance, Mahai'ula: Toilets, picnic area; Ka'elehuluhulu: No facilities.*

Kailua-Kona

Most of the coastline around Kona is rocky, so there aren't the white sandy beaches found in Kohala. What you will discover, though, is excellent snorkeling and scuba diving, some calm swimming spots, and decent surf conditions.

Kaloko–Honokōhau National Historical Park. This 1,160-acre park near Honokōhau Harbor has three beaches, all good for swimming. **'Ai'opio** (☞ Toilets), a few yards north of the harbor, is a small beach with calm, protected swimming areas (good for kids) and great snorkeling in the water near the archaeological site of Hale o Mono. **Honokōhau Beach** (☞ No facilities) a ¾-mi stretch with ruins of ancient fishponds, is also north of the harbor. At the north end of the beach, a historic trail leads *mauka* (toward the mountain) across the lava to a pleasant freshwater pool called Queen's Bath. A Hawaiian settlement until the 19th century, the area is being developed as a cultural and historical site. **'Alula** (☞ No facilities) is a slip of white sand at the south end of the harbor, a short walk over lava to the left of the harbor entrance. For information about the park, visit its headquarters, a 5- to 10-minute drive away. ⊠ *74-425 Kealakehe Pkwy. off Hwy. 19* ☎ *808/329–6881* ⊕ *www.nps.gov* ☼ *Park road gate 8 AM–3:30 PM* ☞ *Toilets, food concession, parking lot.*

Old Kona Airport State Recreation Area. The unused runway—great for jogging—is still visible above this palm-tree-lined beach at Kailua Park. The beach has a sheltered, sandy inlet with tide pools for children, but for adults it's better for snorkeling than swimming. An offshore surfing break known as Old Airport is popular with local surfers. ⊠ *North end of Kuakini Hwy., Kailua-Kona* ☎ *808/327–4958 or 808/974–6200* ☞ *Toilets, showers, picnic tables, parking lot.*

☝ **Kailua Bay & Kamakahonu Beach.** Next to King Kamehameha's Kona Beach Hotel, this little square of white sand is the only beach in downtown Kailua-Kona. Protected by the harbor, the calm water makes this a perfect spot for kids; for adults it's a great place for a swim and a lazy beach day. The water is surprisingly clear for being surrounded by an active pier. Snorkeling can be good, especially if you move south from the beach. There's a kiosk with snorkeling and kayaking equipment rentals. ■ TIP→ A little family of sea turtles likes to hang out next to the seawall, so keep an eye out. ⊠ *Ali'i Dr.* ☞ *Toilets.*

White Sands, Magic Sands, or Disappearing Sands Beach. Now you see it, now you don't. Overnight, winter waves wash away this small white-sand beach on Aliʻi Drive just south of Kailua-Kona. In summer you'll know you've found it when you see the body- and board surfers. Though not really a great beach, this is a really popular summer hangout for young locals. ✉ *Aliʻi Dr., 4½ mi south of Kailua-Kona* ☎ *808/961–8311* ☞ *Lifeguard, toilets, showers, food concession, parking lot.*

Kahaluʻu Beach Park. This spot was a favorite of King Kalākaua, whose summer cottage is on the grounds of the neighboring Outrigger Keauhou Beach Resort. Kahaluʻu is popular with commoners, too, and on weekends it gets crowded. This is, however, one of the best snorkeling spots on the island—it's a good place to see fish up close, as they are used to snorkelers. ■ TIP→ **Beware—a strong riptide during high surf pulls swimmers away from shore.** A narrow path takes you directly to the hotel's beach bar, which serves sandwiches and plate lunches. ✉ *Aliʻi Dr., 5½ mi south of Kailua-Kona* ☎ *808/961–8311* ☞ *Lifeguard, toilets, showers, food concession, picnic tables, parking lot.*

South Kona & Kaʻū

You wouldn't expect to find sparkling white-sand beaches in the moonscape of South Kona and Kaʻū, and you won't. What you will find is something a bit more rare and well worth the visit: black- and green-sand beaches. Rent a four-wheel-drive vehicle if you plan on hitting the beach in this region. Beaches are listed here from north to south.

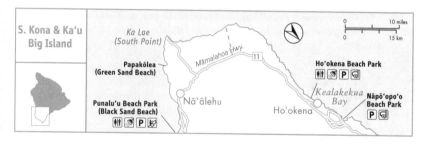

Nāpōʻopoʻo Beach Park. There's no real beach here, but don't let that deter you—this is a great spot. Kealakekua Bay is protected by impossibly high green cliffs, so the water's always very calm and clear. Swimming is great here, but bring a mask along, as the snorkeling in this marine reserve is amazing; your chances of seeing Hawaiian spinner dolphins are very good, especially if you come in the early morning. If you enter the water from the short pier at the left side of the parking lot, you'll see coral and fish almost immediately. This is also a great kayaking spot, and several stands along the highway rent kayaks, in addition to snorkel gear. Another great way to enjoy this marine preserve is to take a snorkel, scuba, or glass-bottom boat tour from Keauhou Bay. Fair Wind Cruises is the only operation allowed to dock in Kealakekua Bay. ✉ *End of Nāpōʻopoʻo Rd., off Hwy. 11, Kealakekua Bay* ☎ *808/961–8311* ☞ *Parking lot.*

Hoʻokena Beach Park. Driving south from Kealakekua Bay, you'll see the sign for Hoʻokena Beach Park. The road down to the beach is narrow and steep, but the views are great. (Plus you'll feel like you're venturing off the beaten path.) The beach is on the small side and is mostly frequented by the people from the nearby village; it's rarely crowded, except on weekends. By Hawaiian standards, this is an average beach (the water's nice for swimming, and there's a bit of snorkeling but nothing amazing), but that still makes it great for the rest of us. Plus it's the only white-sand beach on this part of the island. ✉ *2-mi drive down road bordered by ruins of stone wall off Hwy. 11, 23 mi south of Kailua-Kona* ☎ *808/961–8311* ⚲ *Toilets, showers, picnic tables, parking lot.*

★ **Papakōlea Beach (Green Sand Beach).** You'll need good hiking shoes and a four-wheel-drive vehicle to get to this green crescent, one of the most unusual beaches on the island. The beach lies at the base of Pu'u o Mahana, at Mahana Bay, where a cinder cone formed during an early eruption of Mauna Loa. The greenish tint is caused by an accumulation of olivine that forms in volcanic eruptions. ■ TIP→ Swimming can be dangerous the farther you get from shore, especially when it's windy, which is fairly often. In calm water close to the shore, however, the aquamarine surf feels great, and the landscape is totally surreal. Take the road toward the left at the end of the paved road to Ka Lae (South Point). Park at the end of the road and follow the trail along the shoreline. Anyone trying to charge you for parking is running a scam. ✉ *2½ mi northeast of South Point, off Hwy. 11* ⚲ *No facilities.*

★ **Punalu'u Beach Park (Black Sand Beach).** The endangered Hawaiian green sea turtle nests in the black sand of this beautiful and easily accessible beach. You can see the turtles feeding on the seaweed along the surfbreak. They're used to people, and will swim along right next to you. (Resist the urge to touch them, though.) At the northern end of the beach near the boat ramp lie the ruins of a flat sacrificial stone. This area used to be a sugar port until the tidal wave of 1946 destroyed the buildings. ■ TIP→ Although you'll see a few local surfers riding the waves, offshore rip currents are extremely dangerous. Inland is a memorial to Henry 'Ōpūkaha'ia. In 1809, when he was 17, 'Ōpūkaha'ia swam out to a furtrading ship in the harbor and asked to sign up as a cabin boy. When he reached New England, he entered the Foreign Mission School in Connecticut, but he died of typhoid fever in 1818. His dream of bringing Christianity to the Islands inspired the American Board of Missionaries to send the first Protestant missionaries to Hawai'i in 1820. ✉ *Hwy. 11, 27 mi south of Hawai'i Volcanoes National Park* ☎ *808/961–8311* ⚲ *Toilets across road, showers, grills, firepits, parking lot.*

Hilo

Hilo isn't exactly known for its beautiful white beaches. However, there are a few gems, and plenty of opportunities to dip into streams and waterfalls if the ocean is being uncooperative. Beaches are listed from north to south.

Reeds Bay Beach Park. Safe swimming, proximity to downtown Hilo, and a freshwater-fed swimming hole called "the Ice Pond" are the enticements of this cove. ✉ *Banyan Dr. and Kalaniana'ole Ave., Hilo* ☎ *808/ 961–8311* ⚲ *Toilets, showers, parking lot.*

Leleiwi Beach Park and Richardson Ocean Park. There's hardly any sand here, but these two beaches make up one beautiful spot—laced with bays, inlets, lagoons, and pretty parks. The grassy area is ideal for picnics. Snorkeling can be great, as turtles and dolphins frequent this area. ⊠ *2349 Kalaniana'ole Ave., 4 mi east of Hilo* ☎ *808/961–8311* ☞ *Lifeguard (on weekends), picnic tables, parking lot.*

Hāmākua Coast

Kolekole Beach Park. The Kolekole River meets the ocean at this small beach between 'Akaka and Umauma Falls. Although there's a rocky shoreline, the river is calm and great for swimming. There's even a rope swing tied to a banyan tree on the opposite side. Local surfers like this spot in the winter. ■ TIP➡ **Where the river meets the ocean, the surf is rough and the currents strong. Only very experienced swimmers should venture here.** ⊠ *Off Hwy. 19* ☎ *808/961–8311* ✉ *Free* ☉ *Daily 7 AM–sunset* ☞ *Toilets, showers, picnic tables, grills, parking lot.*

Puna

As the region closest to Kīlauea, Puna's few beaches have some unique attributes—swaths of black sand, volcano-heated springs, and a coastline that is beyond dramatic (sheer walls of lava rock dropping into the bluest ocean you've ever seen). Beaches here are listed in order from north to south along Highway 137.

Kapoho Tide Pools. Snorkelers will find tons of coral and the fish who feed off it in this network of tide pools at the end of Kapoho-Kai Road. Take the road to the end, then turn left and park. Some of the pools have been turned into private swimming pools; those closest to the ocean are open to all. The pools are usually very calm, and some are volcanically heated. It's best to come during the week, as the pools can get crowded on the weekend. ⊠ *End of Kapoho-Kai Road, off Hwy. 137* ☞ *No facilities.*

Ahalanui Park. This 3-acre beach park, also known as Pū'āla'a, has a ½-acre pond heated by volcanic steam. There's nothing like swimming in this warm pool, but the nearby ocean is rough. ■ TIP➡ **Since 2003 the thermal pool has had bacterial-contamination problems; check with the lifeguard–attendant on safety and heed all posted signs.** ⊠ *Hwy. 137, 2½ mi south of junction of Hwy. 132* ☎ *808/961–8311* ☞ *Lifeguard, toilets, showers, picnic tables, grills.*

WATER ACTIVITIES & TOURS

The waters surrounding Hawai'i are some of the world's greatest natural playgrounds. The boating, sailing, snorkeling, scuba diving, and deep-sea fishing are among the best anywhere, and the surfing isn't bad if you know where to go. As a general rule, the waves are gentler here than on other Islands, but there are a few things to be aware of before heading to the shore. First, don't turn your back on the ocean. It's unlikely, but if conditions are right a wave could come along and slam you face first into the sand or drag you out to sea. Conditions can change quickly, so keep your eyes open. Second, realize that ultimately you must keep yourself safe. We strongly encourage you to obey lifeguards and park rangers stationed on the beaches of the Big Island—it could save your trip, or even your life.

Boogie Boarding & Bodysurfing

According to the movies, in the Old West there was always friction between cattle ranchers and sheep ranchers. Some will say the same situation exists between surfers and boogie boarders. Sure, there's some good-natured trash-talking between the groups, but nothing more. The truth is, boogie boarding is a blast. The only surfers who don't do it are hardcore surfing purists, and almost none of that type live on this island.

Novice boogie boarders should use smooth-bottom boards, wear protective clothing (or at least T-shirts), and catch shore waves only. You'll need a pair of short fins to get out to the bigger waves offshore (not recommended for newbies). As for bodysurfing, just catch a wave and make like Superman going faster than a speeding bullet.

Best Spots

When conditions are right, **Hāpuna Beach State Recreation Area** (⊠ Hwy. 19, near mile marker 69) is fabulous. The water is very calm in summer, with just enough rolling waves for bodysurfing or boogie boarding. But this beach north of Kailua-Kona isn't known as the "broken-neck capital" for nothing. Ask the lifeguards about conditions before heading into the water. ■ TIP➜ Remember that if almost no one is in the water, there's a good reason for it.

Much of the sand at **White Sands, Magic Sands, or Disappearing Sands Beach Park** (⊠ Ali'i Dr., 4½ mi south of Kailua-Kona) washes out to sea and forms a sandbar just offshore. This causes the waves to break in a way that's great for intermediate or advanced boogie boarding. No wonder the Magic Sands Bodysurfing Contest, which brings out hard-core bodysurfers each winter, is held here. This small beach can get pretty crowded. ■ TIP➜ There can be nasty rip currents at high tide. If you're not using fins, wear reef shoes because of the rocks.

Equipment Rentals

Equipment rental shacks are all over the place. Boogie board rental rates are $5 to $8 per day or $15 to $20 per week.

Deep-Sea Fishing

Along the Kona Coast you can find some of the world's most exciting "blue-water" fishing. Although July, August, and September are peak months, with the best fishing and a number of tournaments, charter fishing goes on year-round. You don't have to compete to experience the thrill of landing a Pacific blue marlin or other big-game fish. More than 60 charter boats, averaging 26 to 58 feet, are available for hire, most of them out of **Honokōhau Harbor,** north of Kailua-Kona.

Prices vary but generally range $400–$500 for a half-day charter and $600–$800 for a full day. If fuel prices continue increasing, expect charter costs to rise. Most boats are licensed to take up to six passengers, in addition to the crew. Tackle, bait, and ice are furnished, but you'll usually have to bring your own lunch. You won't be able to keep your catch although if you ask, many captains will send you home with a few fillets.

> **ON THE SIDELINES**
>
> Kona hosts a variety of fishing tournaments, but the Big Kahuna is the **Hawaiian International Billfish Tournament** (☎ 808/329-6155 ⊕ www.konabillfish.com), held in August since 1959. Billfish, of course, are majestic marlin. If you're in town, you'll find a number of tournament-related activities. Pay attention to the list of winners, as it helps you choose which boat to charter.

Big fish are weighed in daily at **Honokōhau Harbor's Fuel Dock.** Show up at 11 AM to watch the weigh-in of the day's catch from the morning charters, or 3:30 PM for the afternoon charters. If you're lucky you'll get to see a "grander" weighing in at 1,000-plus pounds. A surprising number of these are caught just outside Kona Harbor. ■ TIP➔ **On Kona's Waterfront Row look for the "Grander's Wall" of anglers with their prizes.**

Booking Agencies

Before you sign up with anyone, think about the kind of trip you want. Looking for a romantic cruise? A rockin' good time with your buddies? Serious fishing in one of the "secret spots"? A family-friendly excursion? Be sure to describe your expectations so your booking agent can match you with a captain and a boat that suits your style.

Honokōhau Harbor Charter Desk. With 50 boats on the books, this place can take care of almost anyone. You can make arrangements through your hotel activity desk, but we suggest you go down to the desk at the harbor and look things over for yourself. ⊠ *74-381 Kealahe Pkwy., Kailua-Kona* ☎ *808/329–5735* ⊕ *www.charterdesk.com.*

Boats & Charters

Pamela Big Game Fishing. This family-operated company has been in the business since 1967. The 38-foot *Pamela* is captained by either Peter Hoogs or his son. They've also got an informative Web site with information on sportfishing. ☎ *808/329–3600 or 800/762–7546* ⊕ *www.konabiggamefishing.com.*

Charter Locker. This fleet of four boats ranging from 38 to 53 feet is a good bet for both novices and experts. Operating since 1964, Charter Locker is one of the respected old-timers at Honokohau Harbor. ☎ *808/ 326–2553* ⊕ *www.charterlocker.com.*

Reel Action Light-Tackle Sportfishing. Attention fishing fanatics: this outfit takes only two people per trip on its 25-foot open-console boat. You can bottom fish, reef fish, or fly-fish—as well as go after the granders. No e-mail, no fax, and no nonsense. Call to make reservations. ☎ *808/ 325–6811.*

Jet Skiing

Kailua Bay in Kona has generally calm waters that are perfect for jet skiing.

Aloha Jet Ski Rentals. The only outfitter on the island charges $85 an hour for a Jet Ski that can accommodate up to three passengers. Drivers must be at least 16, and must stay in a designated area south of the pier. Ask about an early-bird discount. ⊠ *Kailua Pier, across from King Kamehameha's Kona Beach Hotel, Kailua-Kona* ☎ 808/329–2754 ⊕ *www. mauiwatersports.com.*

Kayaking

Kayaks are great for observing Hawai'i's diverse marine life and serene shores. When you venture out, however, be sure to respect Hawai'i's waters. Almost a third of marine mammals here are unique to the Big Island. Coral reefs are endangered, so many bays are protected marine reserves. A reputable kayak shop can brief you on proper conduct and recommend places with manageable currents.

Best Spots

The likelihood of seeing dolphins makes **Kealakekua Bay** (⊠ Bottom of Nāpō'opo'o Rd., south of Kailua-Kona) one of the most popular kayak spots on the Big Island. The bay is usually calm, and the kayaking is not difficult—except during high surf. If you're there in the morning you're likely to see spinner dolphins. Depending on your strength and enthusiasm, you'll cross the bay in 30–60 minutes and put in at the ancient canoe landing about 50 yards to the left of the **Captain Cook Monument.** The monument marks the landfall of Captain James Cook in 1778, the first European to visit Hawai'i. The coral around the monument itself is too fragile to land a kayak, but it makes for fabulous snorkeling.

> **DOLPHINS AT REST**
>
> Kealakekua Bay is a designated marine refuge where the dolphins return to rest after feeding. Kayakers occasionally pursue the dolphins in an aggressive way. Because of the actions of a few, some environmental activists are working to close the bay to all kayakers. Those who charge after dolphins may be videotaped and have complaints filed against them (as well as suffer the ephemeral but very real consequences of behaving without the aloha spirit). If you behave in a calm, nonthreatening manner, the dolphins are very likely to come to you.

There are several rental outfitters on Highway 11 between mile markers 110 and 113. There's also one unofficial stand at the shore, at the house on the corner just across from the parking lot. After you've loaded your kayak onto the roof of your car, follow the 2-mi road down the rather steep hill to the parking lot below. There are usually local guys who will set up your kayak and get you into (and out of) of the water; tips of between $5 and $10 are encouraged, expected, and appreciated.

Ōneo Bay (✉ Ali'i Dr., south of Kailua-Kona) is usually quite a placid place to kayak. It's easy to get to and great for all skill levels. If you can't find a parking spot along Ali'i Drive, there's a parking lot across the street near the farmers' market.

Hilo Bay (✉ 2349 Kalaniana'ole Ave., about 4 mi east of Hilo) is a favorite kayak spot. The best place to put in is at **Richardson's Ocean Beach Park.** Most afternoons you can share the bay with local paddling clubs. Stay inside the breakwater unless the ocean is calm (or you're feeling unusually adventurous). Conditions range from extremely calm to quite choppy.

Equipment Rentals & Tours

Flumin' Da Ditch. When King Sugar ruled this island, immigrant Japanese, Chinese, Portuguese, and Filipino plantation workers built irrigation ditches to bring water to the crops. Generations of adventurous plantation kids grabbed their inner tubes or anything else that floated and went "flumin' da ditch"—gently floating through pitch-dark tunnels and emerging in an unspoiled rainforest. Today guides will take you on a kayak tour through the 22½-mi irrigation system of the historic Kohala Sugar Plantation. This is a nonstrenuous activity appropriate for almost everyone. The guides are well-informed about local history—from the plantation economy to the story of King Kamehameha I, who was born nearby and went on to unify all the islands into a single kingdom. Rates are $98 per person. ✉ 55-519 Hāwī Rd., off Hwy. 250, Hāwī ☎ 808/889–6922 or 877/449–6922 ⊕ www.flumindaditch.com.

Kona Boys. On the highway above Kealakekua Bay, this full-service outfitter handles kayaks, boogie boards, and related equipment. Single-seat kayaks are $27, doubles $47, clear bottoms $79. Dive kayaks with a well for an air tank are also available. They also lead guided trips to Kealakekua (½ day for $135 per person), as well as customized overnight camping–kayaking trips to Miloli'i, Pololū, or our favorite, Waipi'o Valley. ✉ 79-7539 Mamalahoa Hwy., Kealakekua ☎ 808/328–1234 ⊕ www.konaboys.com.

Ocean Safari's Kayak Adventures. On the 3½-hour tours that begin in Keauhou Bay, you can visit sea caves along the coast, then swim ashore for a snack and perhaps some cliff jumping. The kayaks are on the beach so you don't have to hassle with transporting them. The cost is $64 per person. A two-hour dolphin–whale tour leaves at 7 AM on Tuesday. It's $30 per person. ✉ End of Kamehameha III Rd., Kailua-Kona ☎ 808/326–4699 ⊕ www.oceansafariskayaks.com.

Kiteboarding

⇨ *See* Windsurfing & Kiteboarding *below.*

Sailing

Hawaiian Sailing Adventures. Captain Casey Cho takes you on a 2½-hour cruise off the Kohala Coast on the *Hahalua Lele* (Flying Manta Ray), his traditional wooden double-hull Hawaiian canoe. Sail, snorkel, or troll for deep-sea fish and talk about Hawaiian history and legends. Cruises ($95 per person) depart from the Fairmont Orchid Hawai'i on Pauoa Bay. ☎ *808/885–2000* ⊕ *www.hawaiiankineadventures.com.*

Maile Charters. Ralph Blancato and Kalia Potter offer unique around-the-Islands sailing adventures that range from half-day excursions to five-day journeys to Maui, Moloka'i, or Lāna'i. Private cabins and hot showers keep you comfortable, and island-style meals keep you satisfied. Fees start at $590 for six passengers for a half-day charter to $5,000 for five days. ⊠ *Kawaihae Harbor, Kawaihae* ☎ *808/326–5174 or 800/726–7245* ⊕ *www.adventuresailing.com.*

Scuba Diving

With its steep undersea drop-offs, the Big Island has some of the most dramatic diving in the Hawaiian islands. Although there's diving on the Hilo side, the Kona coast is much better. Two-tank dives average $100–$150 depending on whether you're already certified and whether you're diving from a boat or from shore. Instruction with PADI, SDI, or TDI certification in three to five days costs $400–$650. Most instructors rent out dive equipment and snorkel gear, and many rent underwater cameras. A few organize otherworldly manta-ray dives at night, or whale-watching cruises in season.

Best Spots

Hāpuna Beach State Recreation Area (⊠ Hwy. 19, near mile marker 69) in Kohala can be a good shore dive. **Plane Wreck Point,** off Keāhole Point, is for expert divers only. Damselfish, fantail, and filefish hover around in the shadows.

Dive boats come to **Pu'uhonua O Hōnaunau (Place of Refuge)** (⊠ Rte. 160, about 20 mi south of Kailua-Kona ⊕ www.nps.gov/puho) for the steep drop-offs and dramatic views. You can also get in the water from the shore on the north end.

Equipment Rentals & Dive Tours

There are quite a few good dive shops on the Kona coast. Most are happy to take on all customers, but a few focus on specific types of trips.

★ **Aloha Dive Company.** Native-born Hawaiian and PADI master dive instructor Mike Nakamachi, together with wife Buffy (a registered nurse and PADI dive instructor) and Earl Kam (a videographer and PADI dive master) have been instructing since 1990. Although they'll take anybody, they're biased in favor of experienced divers who want unique locations and know how to take care of themselves in deep water. Their boat is fast enough to bring you places other companies can't reach. They're fun people with great attitudes and operate the only true *kamāʻaina* (Hawaiʻi born-and-raised) outfitter around. ☎ *800/708–5662 or 808/ 325–5560* ⊕ *www.alohadive.com.*

Body Glove Cruises. This company offers primarily snorkel cruises but can also accommodate several divers. It's a good choice for families where at least one member is a certified diver and the rest want to snorkel. A 55-foot catamaran sets off from the Kailua Pier daily for a 4½-hour dive and snorkel cruise, which includes breakfast and a buffet lunch. Snorkelers pay $94 per adult and $54 per child, plus an additional $53 per certified diver who needs equipment (you'll get a single tank). ⊠ *Kailua Pier, Kailua-Kona* ☎ *808/326–7122 or 800/551–8911* ⊕ *www. bodyglovehawaii.com.*

Jack's Diving Locker. The best place for novice and intermediate divers (certified to 60 feet), Jack's Diving Locker has trained and certified tens of thousands of divers since opening in 1981. The company has two boats that can each take 12 divers. It does a good job looking out for customers and protecting the coral reef. Before each charter the dive master briefs divers on various options and then everyone votes on where to go. Jack's also runs the biggest dive shop on the island, and has classrooms and a dive pool for beginning instruction. ■ TIP➔ **Kona's best dive bargain for newbies is the introductory shore dive from Kailua Pier for $55.** ⊠ *75-5813 Aliʻi Dr., Kailua-Kona* ☎ *800/345–4807 or 808/329–7585* ⊕ *www. jacksdivinglocker.com.*

★ **Ocean Eco Tours.** Ecofriendly and full-service, this outfit is eager to share a wealth of knowledge. It's close to a number of good reefs and other prime locations. ⊠ *Honokōhau Harbor, 74-425 Kealakehe Pkwy., Kailua-Kona* ☎ *808/324–7873* ⊕ *www.oceanecotours.com.*

Snorkeling

Although the snorkeling on the Hilo side is passable (except for the Kapoho tide pools, which are stunning), the real action is on the Kona side where colorful tropical fish frequent the lava outcroppings and coral reefs. It's easy to arrange a do-it-yourself snorkeling tour by renting masks and snorkels from any of the many diving outfits in Kailua-Kona or at the resorts.

Many snorkel cruises are also available. Shop for prices at kayak, scuba, and sailing outfitters; ask about the size of the boat, and be sure you know what equipment and food is included. Also find out what the extras (mask defogger, dry bags, or underwater cameras) will cost.

Best Spots

★ **Kealakekua Bay** (⊠ Bottom of Nāpōʻopoʻo Rd., south of Kailua-Kona) is, hands down, the best snorkel spot on the island, with fabulous coral reefs around the Captain Cook monument and generally calm waters. Besides, you'll probably get to swim with dolphins. Overland access is difficult, so you'll want to kayak across the bay to get to the monument. ■ TIP➔ Be on the lookout for kayakers who might not notice you swimming beneath them.

Continued on page 330

SNORKELING IN HAWAI'I

The waters surrounding the Hawaiian Islands are filled with life—from giant manta rays cruising off the Big Island's Kona Coast to humpback whales giving birth in Maui's Mā'alaea Bay. Dip your head beneath the surface to experience a spectacularly colorful world: pairs of milletseed butterflyfish dart back and forth, red-lipped parrotfish snack on coral algae, and spotted eagle rays flap past like silent spaceships. Sea turtles bask at the surface while tiny wrasses give them the equivalent of a shave and a haircut. The water quality is typically outstanding; many sites afford 30 foot-plus visibility. On snorkel cruises, you can often stare from the boat rail right down to the bottom.

Certainly few destinations are as accommodating to every level of snorkeler as Hawai'i. Beginners can tromp in from sandy beaches while more advanced divers descend to shipwrecks, reefs, craters, and sea arches just offshore. Because of Hawai'i's extreme isolation, the island chain has fewer fish species than Fiji or the Caribbean—but many of the fish that are here exist nowhere else. The Hawaiian waters are home to the highest percentage of endemic fish in the world.

The key to enjoying the underwater world is slowing down. Look carefully. Listen. You might hear the strange crackling sound of shrimp tunneling through coral, or you may hear whales singing to one another during winter. A shy octopus may drift along the ocean's floor beneath you. If you're hooked, pick up a waterproof fish key from Long's Drugs. You can brag later that you've looked the Hawaiian turkeyfish in the eye.

Picasso Triggerfish	Milletseed Butterflyfish*	Yellow Tang
Moorish Idol	Hawaiian Whitespotted Toby*	Saddleback Wrasse*
Red-lipped Parrotfish	Hawaiian Turkeyfish*	Zebra Moray Eel
Stocky Hawkfish	Green Sea Turtle	Spotted Eagle Ray

*endemic to Hawai'i

3

SNORKELING IN HAWAI'I

POLYNESIA'S FIRST CELESTIAL NAVIGATORS: HONU

Honu is the Hawaiian name for two native sea turtles, the hawksbill and the green sea turtle. Little is known about these dinosaur-age marine reptiles, though snorkelers regularly see them foraging for *limu* (seaweed) and the occasional jellyfish in Hawaiian waters. Most female honu nest in the uninhabited Northwestern Hawaiian Islands, but a few sociable ladies nest on Maui beaches. Scientists suspect that they navigate the seas via magnetism—sensing the earth's poles. Amazingly, they will journey up to 800 mi to nest—it's believed that they return to their own birth sites. After about 60 days of incubation, nestlings emerge from the sand at night and find their way back to the sea by the light of the stars.

The snorkeling just north of the boat launch at **Pu'uhonua O Hōnaunau (Place of Refuge)** (⊠ Rte. 160, about 20 mi south of Kailua-Kona ⊕ www. nps.gov/puho) is almost as good as Kealakekua Bay, and it's much easier to reach. It's also a popular scuba diving spot.

White Sands, Magic Sands, or Disappearing Sands Beach Park (⊠ Ali'i Dr., 4½ mi south of Kailua-Kona) is a great place for beginning and intermediate snorkelers. In winter it's also a good place to see whales.

Kapoho Tide Pools (⊠ End of Kapoho-Kai Road, off Hwy. 137) has the best snorkeling on the Hilo side. Fingers of lava from the 1960 flow (that destroyed the town of Kapoho) jut into the sea to form a network of tide pools. Conditions near the shore are excellent for beginners, and challenging enough farther out for experienced snorkelers.

Cruises & Equipment Rentals

Captain Zodiac Raft Expedition. The exciting four-hour trip on an inflatable raft takes you along the Kona Coast to explore gaping lava-tube caves, search for dolphins and turtles, and snorkel around Kealakekua Bay. The cost is $80. ⊠ *Honokōhau Harbor, Kailua-Kona* ☎ *808/329–3199* ⊕ *www.captainzodiac.com.*

★ **Fair Wind Cruises.** This outfit offers both a 4½-hour morning snorkeling and 3½-hour afternoon excursions to Kealakekua Bay, and a new luxury cruise that sails into three different secret snorkeling spots a day. Snorkel gear included (ask about prescription masks), but bring your own towel. On morning cruises you'll get a Continental breakfast and a barbecue lunch. These trips are great for families with small kids (lots of pint-size flotation equipment), and they provide underwater viewing devices for those who don't want to use a mask–snorkel setup. Morning snorkel cruises cost $99 for adults and $59 for kids—afternoons are cheaper, but you're less likely to see dolphins in the bay. ⊠ *78-7130 Kaleiopapa St., Keauhou Bay, Kailua-Kona* ☎ *808/322–2788 or 800/ 677–9461* ⊕ *www.fair-wind.com.*

Snorkel Bob's. You're likely to see his wacky ads in your airline inflight magazine. The company actually delivers what it promises, and you can make reservations online before beginning your trip. ⊠ *75-5831 Kahakai St., Kailua-Kona* ☎ *808/329–0770* ⊕ *www.snorkelbob.com.*

Snuba

Snuba—a cross between scuba and snorkeling—is a great choice for non-scuba divers who want to go a step beyond snorkeling. You and an instructor dive off a raft attached to a 25-foot hose and regulator; you can dive as deep as 20 feet or so. This is a good way to explore reefs a bit deeper than you can get to by snorkeling.

Snuba Big Island. Rendezvous with your instructor across from King Kamehameha's Kona Beach Hotel in Kailua-Kona for 30 minutes of instruction and a one-hour dive in Kailua Bay ($79 per person). Boat dives lasting three hours leave from Honakahou Harbor ($120 per person). You can also dive in Kealakekua Bay. ☎ *808/326–7446* ⊕ *www. snubabigisland.com.*

Submarine Tours

🕭 *Atlantis VII* **Submarine.** Want to stay dry while exploring the undersea
Fodor'sChoice world? Climb aboard the 48-foot *Atlantis VII* submarine anchored off
★ Kailua Pier, across from King Kamehameha's Kona Beach Hotel in
Kailua-Kona. A large glass dome in the bow and 13 viewing ports on
the sides allow clear views of the aquatic world more than 100 feet down.
This is a great trip for kids and nonswimmers. Each one-hour voyage
costs $79.99 for adults and $42 for children under 12. The company
also operates on Oʻahu and Maui. ☎ *808/329–6626 or 800/548–6262*
⊕ *www.atlantisadventures.com.*

Surfing

You won't find the world-class waves of Oʻahu or Maui on the Big Island, but there are decent waves and a thriving surf culture. Expect high
surf in winter and much calmer activity during summer. The surf scene
is much more active on the Kona side.

Your best bet on the Kona side is **Kahaluʻu Beach Park** (⊠ Aliʻi Dr., 5½
mi south of Kailua-Kona). On the east side, try **Honoliʻi Cove** (⊠ Access
road off Hwy. 19, just past mile marker 4).

Surf Shops & Schools

Pacific Vibrations. ⊠ *75-5702 Linana La., at Aliʻi Dr. a block south of
Kailua Pier, Kailua-Kona* ☎ *808/329–4140.*

Orchid Land Surf Shop. ⊠ *262 Kamehameha Ave., Hilo* ☎ *808/935–1522*
⊕ *www.orchidlandsurf.com.*

Whale-Watching

Each winter humpback whales migrate from the waters off Alaska to
the warm Hawaiian ocean to give birth and care for their newborns.
Recent reports indicate that the whale population is on the upswing—
a few years ago one even ventured into the mouth of Hilo Harbor, which
marine biologists say is quite rare. Humpbacks are spotted here from
early December through the end of April, but other species can be seen
year-round. Most ocean tour companies offer whale outings during the
season, but two owner–operators do it full time. They are much more
familiar with whale behavior and you're more likely to have a quality
whale-watching experience. ■ TIP→ **If you take the morning cruise, you're
likely to see dolphins as well.**

Captain Dan McSweeney's Year-Round Whale Watching Adventures. This
is probably the most experienced small operation on the island. Captain Dan McSweeney offers three-hour trips on his 40-foot boat. In addition to humpbacks in the winter, he'll show you some of the six other
whale species that live off the Kona Coast year-round. Three-hour tours
cost $60 per adult and $40 for kids under 12 (snacks and juices included).
McSweeney guarantees you'll see a whale or he'll take you out again
free. ⊠ *Honokōhau Harbor, Kailua-Kona* ☎ *808/322–0028 or 888/942–
5376* ⊕ *www.ilovewhales.com.*

Living Ocean Adventure. Captain Tom Bottrell leads whale-watching excursions (combined with deep-sea fishing, if desired) for up to six people on the *Spinner,* his 31-foot fishing boat. Standard 3½-hour tours cost $70 (bottled water is included, but you have to bring your own snacks). Full- and half-day charters also available for small groups. ☎ *808/325–5556* ⊕ *www.livingoceanadventures.com.*

Windsurfing & Kiteboarding

Windsurfers trim their sails along the Big Island's Kohala Coast. In the new sport of kiteboarding (also known as kite surfing), you are pulled along by a kite attached to your surfboard. Great fun, but tougher to learn than windsurfing.

One of the best windsurfing–kiteboarding locations on the Big Island is at **'Anaeho'omalu Beach** (⊠ Follow Waikoloa Beach Dr. to Kings' Shops, then turn left) in North Kohala. The beach is near the Waikoloa Beach Marriott.

Equipment Rentals & Lessons

Ocean Sports. This concession rents boards and teaches windsurfing on the beach. ⊠ *Waikoloa Beach Resort* ☎ *808/886–6666 or 888/724–5234* ⊕ *www.hawaiioceansports.com.*

GOLF, HIKING & OTHER ADVENTURES

Aerial Tours

⇨ *See also* Hawai'i Volcanoes National Park, *earlier in this chapter.*

There's nothing quite like the aerial view of a waterfall that drops a couple thousand feet into multiple pools, or seeing lava flow to the ocean, where clouds of steam billow into the air. Most outfitters provide a worthwhile service, but a few unscrupulous operators have tarnished the image of the whole industry and earned the wrath of local communities. Rogue pilots will buzz communities in violation of FAA rules. How to get the best experience for your money? ■ TIP➔ **Before you hire a company, be a savvy traveler and ask the right questions. Do they have two-way headsets so you can talk with the pilot? What kind of aircraft do they fly? The best touring 'copters are Eco-Stars, Hughes, and AStars.**

Big Island Air. Big Island Air operates 1½- to 2-hour plane tours out of Kona International Airport. ⊠ *Kona International Airport* ☎ *808/329–4868 or 800/303–8868.*

Mokulele Flight Service. For a fixed-wing air tour, contact Kawehi Inaba, a native Hawaiian who was bitten by the flight bug when she worked the counter at Aloha Airlines. She went on to earn her commercial pilot's license. Her company offers 45-minute volcano–waterfall tours from Hilo and two-hour circle-the-island tours from Kona. You can also book interisland charters. ☎ *808/326–7070 or 866/260–7070* ⊕ *www. mokulele.com.*

Sunshine Helicopters. You can buy a video of your 30-minute, 45-minute, or 2-hour group tour. Rates are $110–$330 per person. ⊠ *Helipad at*

Hāpuna Beach Prince Hotel and Hilo Airport ☏ *808/882–1223, 808/ 969–7506, or 800/469–3000* ⊕ *www.sunshinehelicopters.com.*

Paradise Helicopters. Paradise also operates from Kona, but your best bet is flying out of Hilo on its four-passenger MD-500 aircraft. Everyone has a window seat in these highly maneuverable helicopters, and you can even select the "doors off" option for better viewing. Communicate with the friendly and knowledgeable pilots over two-way headsets. ⊠ *Hilo Airport, Kona Airport* ☏ *808/969–7392* ⊕ *www. paradisecopters.com.*

ATV Tours

A different way to experience the Big Island's rugged coastline and wild ranch lands is through an off-road adventure. At higher elevations, weather can be nippy and rainy, but views can be awesome. You can ride in your own all-terrain vehicle or share a Hummer. Protective gear is provided. Prices range from $85 to $125 per person, depending on tour length and specifics.

ATV Outfitters Hawai'i. ⊠ *Old Sakamoto Store, Hwy. 270, Kapa'au* ☏ *808/889–6000 or 888/288–7288* ⊕ *www.outfittershawaii.com.*

HMV Tours. ⊠ *Hwy. 250, Hāwī* ☏ *808/889–6922 or 877/449–6922* ⊕ *www.hmvtours.com.*

Kahuā Ranch ATV Rides. ⊠ *Hwy. 250, 10 mi north of Waimea* ☏ *808/ 882–7954 or 808/882–4646* ⊕ *www.kahuaranch.com.*

Kukui ATV & Adventures. ⊠ *Kukuihaele* ☏ *808/775–1701 or 877/757– 1414* ⊕ *www.topofwaipio.com.*

Biking

Fodor'sChoice *Mountain Bike* magazine voted **Kulani Trails** the best ride in the state.
★ To reach the trailhead from the intersection of Highway 11 and Highway 19, take Highway 19 south about 4 mi, then turn right onto Stainback Highway and continue on 2½ mi, then turn right at the Waiakea Arboretum. Park near the gate. This technically demanding ride, which passes majestic eucalyptus trees, is for advanced cyclists. ■ TIP➔ For other suggested rides see the Web site run by **Alternative Hawai'i** (⊕ www. alternative-hawaii.com/activity/biecotrb.htm).

The **Old Puna Trail** (⊠ Trailhead: From Hwy. 130, take Kaloli Rd. to Beach Rd.) is a 10½-mi ride through the subtropical jungle in Puna, one of the island's most isolated areas. You'll start out on a cinder road, which becomes a four-wheel-drive trail. If it's rained recently, you'll have to deal with some puddles—the first few of which you'll gingerly avoid until you give in and go barreling through the rest of them for the sheer fun of it. This is a great ride for all abilities that takes about 90 minutes.

Guided Rides

Kona Coast Cycling Tours. Kona Coast leads a number of different tours. See the Big Island up close on a tour that includes the Kohala Coast, the Hāmākua Coast, and the historic Māmalahoa Highway. Custom tours

Ironman & Friends

Run annually since 1978, the **Ironman Triathlon World Championship** (☎ 808/329-0063 ⊕ www. ironmanlive.com) is the granddaddy of them all. For about a week prior to Race Day (the third Saturday of October), Kailua-Kona takes on the air of an Olympic Village as top athletes from across the globe arrive to compete for glory and $580,000 in prize money at the world's premiere swim/bike/run endurance event. To watch these 1,800 competitors push themselves to the ultimate in this grueling event is an inspiring testament to the human spirit. The competition starts at Kailua Pier with a 2.4-mi open-water swim, immediately followed by a 112-mi bicycle ride, then a 26.2-mi marathon. The Ironman wouldn't happen without the 7,000 volunteers who donate their time and services. To volunteer, register online at the Ironman Web site.

The **Honu Half-Ironman Triathlon** (☎ 808/329-0063 ⊕ www. honuhalfironman.com) in early June is an Ironman "farm-team event." Participants swim at Hāpuna beach, bike the Ironman course, and run on the Mauna Lani resort grounds.

Supermen/women do the Ironman. A few notches down on the difficulty scale, but still extremely challenging, is the **Manna-Man Eco-Biathlon** (☎ 808/989-3655 ⊕ www. bigislandraceschedule.com), held the last Sunday in March. The race occurs in and around Kealakeua Bay. You're required to either wear or carry your shoes while swimming (points are given for creative ways to keep 'em with you, and you're penalized for leaving equipment or trash anywhere on the racecourse).

How about racing on an active volcano? No, you're not trying to outrun flowing lava (which is actually not much of a challenge, given the speed at which it usually travels). The **Kīlauea Volcano Wilderness Runs** (☎ 808/967-8222 ⊕ www. volcanoartcenter.org) includes a marathon, 10-mi and 5-mi races, and a noncompetitive 5-mi run-walk. This July event is held completely within Hawai'i Volcanoes National Park.

For the most current race information, check out the **Big Island Race Schedule** (⊕ www. bigislandraceschedule.com/Race Links.html).

---

are also available. Rates for standard tours range from $50 to $150. ✉ 74-5588 Pawai Pl., Suite 1, Kailua-Kona 96740 ☎ 808/327–1133 or 877/592–2453 ⊕ www.cyclekona.com.

Mauna Kea Mountain Bikes. Daily tours down the upper slopes of Mauna Kea—chances are you'll start out in the snow—and downhill along the Kohala Mountains, are offered by this company. Tour prices range from $50 to $115. You can also rent a bike to explore on your own. ⊡ Box 44672, Kamuela 96743 ☎ 808/883–0130 or 888/682–8687 ⊕ www. bikehawaii.com/maunakea.

Bike Shops & Clubs

If you want to strike out on your own, there are several rental shops in Kailua-Kona and a couple in Waimea and Hilo. Resorts rent bicycles that can be used around the properties. Most outfitters listed can provide a bicycle rack for your car.

Big Island Mountain Bike Association. This nonprofit has tons of information on biking the Big Island. Its slogan is "Take only pictures and leave only your tracks." They provide maps and detailed descriptions of rides for all ability levels. ⊕ *www.interpac.net/~mtbike.*

C&S Outfitters. Close to trails that flank the slopes of Mauna Kea, this shop has both road and mountain bikes, as well as accessories and repair services. These folks have a wealth of knowledge about the island's biking trails. Plus they rent kayaks and can equip you for paintball and archery sports held at a nearby range. ⊠ *64-1066 Māmalahoa Hwy., Waimea 96743* ☎ *808/885–5005.*

Hawaiian Pedals. At this shop in Kailua-Kona, road and mountain bike rentals start at $15 for five hours or $20 for the day. ⊠ *Kona Inn Shopping Village, 75-5744 Ali'i Dr., Kailua-Kona* ☎ *808/329–2294* ⊕ *www.hpbikeworks.com.*

Golf

For golfers, the Big Island is a big deal—starting with Mauna Kea, which opened in 1964 and remains one of the state's top courses. Black lava and deep blue sea are the predominant themes on the island. Most of the best courses are concentrated along the Kona Coast, statistically the sunniest spot in the Hawaiian archipelago.

★ **Big Island Country Club.** Set 2,000 feet above sea level on the slopes of Mauna Kea, the Big Island Country Club is rather out of the way but well worth the drive. Pete and Perry Dye (1997) created a gem that plays through an upland woodlands—more than 2,500 trees line the fairways. On the par-5 15th, a giant tree in the middle of the fairway must be avoided with the second shot. Five lakes and a meandering natural mountain stream mean water comes into play on nine holes. The most dramatic is on the par-3 17th, where Dye creates a knockoff of his infamous 17th at the TPC at Sawgrass. ⊠ *71-1420 Māmalahoa Hwy., Kailua-Kona* ☎ *808/325–5044* ⊕ *www.intrawest.com* ⅄ *18 holes. 7034 yds. Par 72. Green Fee: $99* ☞ *Facilities: Driving range, putting green, rental clubs, golf carts, pro shop, lessons.*

★ **Hualālai Resort.** Named for the volcanic peak that is the target off the first tee, the Nicklaus Course at Hualālai is semiprivate, open only to guests of the adjacent Four Seasons Resort Hualālai. From the forward and resort tees, this is perhaps Jack Nicklaus' most friendly course in Hawai'i, but the back tees play a full mile longer. The par-3 17th plays across convoluted lava to a seaside green, and the view from the tee is so lovely, you may be tempted to just relax on the koa bench and enjoy the scenery. ⊠ *100 Ka'ūpūlehu Dr., Kohala Coast* ☎ *808/325–8480* ⊕ *www.fourseasons.com/hualalai* ⅄ *18 holes. 7117 yds. Par 72. Green Fee: $185* ☞ *Facilities: Driving range, putting green, pull carts, golf carts, rental clubs, lessons, pro shop, restaurant, bar.*

★ **Kona Country Club.** This venerable country club offers two very different tests with the aptly named Ocean and Ali'i Mountain courses. The Ocean Course (William F. Bell, 1967) is a bit like playing through a coconut plantation, with a few remarkable lava features—such as the "blowhole" in front of the par-4 13th, where sea water propelled through a lava tube erupts like a geyser. The Ali'i Mountain Course (front nine, William F. Bell, 1983: back nine, Robin Nelson and Rodney Wright, 1992) plays a couple of strokes tougher than the Ocean and is the most delightful split personality you may ever encounter. Both nines share breathtaking views of Keauhou Bay, and elevation change is a factor in most shots. The most dramatic view on the front nine is from the tee of the par-3 5th hole, one of the best golf vistas in Hawai'i. The green seems perched on the edge of the earth, with what only seems to be a sheer 500-foot drop just beyond the fringe. The back nine is links-style, with less elevation change—except for the par-3 14th, which drops 100 feet from tee to green, over a lake. The routing, the sight lines and framing of greens, and the risk-reward factors on each hole make this one of the single best nines in Hawai'i. ✉ *78-7000 Ali'i Dr., Kailua-Kona* ☎ *808/322–2595* ⊕ *www.konagolf.com* ⚑ *Ocean Course: 18 holes. 6806 yds. Par 72. Green Fee: $155. Mountain Course: 18 holes. 6673 yds. Par 72. Green Fee: $89* ⚐ *Facilities: Driving range, putting green, golf carts, rental clubs, lessons, restaurant, bar.*

Mākālei Country Club. Set on the slopes of Hualālai, at an elevation of 2,900 feet, Mākālei is one of the rare Hawai'i courses with bent-grass putting greens, which means they're quick and without the grain associated with bermuda greens. Former PGA Tour official Dick Nugent (1994) designed holes that play through thick forest and open to provide wide ocean views. Elevation change is a factor on many holes, especially the par-3 15th, with the tee 80 feet above the green. ✉ *72-3890 Hawai'i Belt Rd., Kailua-Kona* ☎ *808/325–6625* ⚑ *18 holes. 7041 yds. Par 72. Green Fee: $110* ⚐ *Facilities: Driving range, putting green, golf carts, rental clubs, pro shop, lessons, restaurant.*

Fodor'sChoice **Mauna Kea Beach Resort.** Mauna Kea Golf Course isn't just a golf course,
★ it's a landmark, an icon, a national treasure. Robert Trent Jones Sr., who designed more than 500 courses around the world, rated Mauna Kea among his three best. Built on a 5,000-year-old lava flow, an essential part of Mauna Kea's greatness is the way Jones insinuated holes into the landscape. Only two fairways, holes five and six, are parallel. Mauna Kea is a classic championship design, somewhat forgiving off the tee but quite stern about approach shots. Although No. 3, which plays across a blue bay from rocky promontory to promontory, gets all the photo ops, the toughest par-3 is the 11th. Arnold Palmer and Ed Seay created the resort's second course, Hāpuna, in 1992. Unlike seaside Mauna Kea, Hāpuna is a links-style course that rises to 600 feet elevation, providing views of the ocean and elevation-change challenges. Trees are a factor

LAVA HAZARDS

Lava tends to be razor-sharp and not good for the life of golf balls, or golf shoes. If you hit a ball into the black stuff, consider it an offering to Madame Pele, goddess of lava, and drop another one.

on most holes at Mauna Kea, but they seldom are at Hāpuna. Palmer-Seay put a premium on accuracy off the tee, and are more forgiving with approaches. The two courses have separate clubhouses. **Hāpuna Golf Course:** ✉ *62-100 Kaunaʻoa Dr., Kohala Coast* ☎ *808/880–3000* ⊕ *www.hapunabeachprincehotel.com* 🏌 *18 holes. 6534 yds. Par 72. Green Fee: $145* ☞ *Facilities: Driving range, putting green, golf carts, rental clubs, pro shop, lessons, restaurant, bar.* **Mauna Kea Golf Course:** ✉ *62-100 Mauna Kea Beach Dr., Kohala Coast* ☎ *808/882–5400* ⊕ *www.maunakearesort.com* 🏌 *18 holes. 6737 yds. Par 72. Green Fee: $195* ☞ *Facilities: Driving range, putting green, golf carts, rental clubs, pro shop, lessons, restaurant, bar.*

Fodor'sChoice ★ **Mauna Lani Resort.** Black lava flows, lush green turf, white sand, and the Pacific's multihues of blue define the 36 holes at Mauna Lani. The South Course includes the par-3 15th across a turquoise bay, one of the most photographed holes in Hawaiʻi. But it shares "signature hole" honors with the seventh. A long par-3, it plays downhill over convoluted patches of black lava, with the Pacific immediately to the left and a dune to the right. The North Course plays a couple of shots tougher. Its most distinctive hole is the 17th, a par-3 with the green set in a lava pit 50 feet deep. The shot from an elevated tee must carry a pillar of lava that rises from the pit and partially blocks your view of the green. ✉ *68-1310 Mauna Lani Dr., Kohala Coast* ☎ *808/885–6655* ⊕ *www.maunalani.com* 🏌 *North Course: 18 holes. 6601 yds. Par 72. Green Fee: $195. South Course: 18 holes. 6436 yds. Par 72. Green Fee: $195* ☞ *Facilities: Driving range, putting green, golf carts, rental clubs, pro shop, lessons, restaurant, bar.*

Volcano Golf & Country Club. Located just outside Volcanoes National Park—and barely a stout drive from Halemaʻumaʻu Crater—Volcano is by far Hawaiʻi's highest course. At 4,200 feet elevation, shots tend to fly a bit farther than at sea level, even in the often cool, misty air. Because of the elevation and climate, Volcano is one of the few Hawaiʻi courses with bent-grass putting greens. The course is mostly flat and holes play through stands of Norfolk pines, flowering *lehua* trees, and multitrunk *hau* trees. The uphill par-4 15th doglegs through a tangle of *hau*. ✉ *Piʻi Mauna Dr., off Hwy. 11, Volcanoes National Park* ☎ *808/967–7331* ⊕ *www.volcanogolfshop.com* 🏌 *18 holes. 6106 yds. Par 72. Green Fee: $62* ☞ *Facilities: Driving range, putting green, golf carts, rental clubs, restaurant, bar.*

Fodor'sChoice ★ **Waikoloa Beach Resort.** Robert Trent Jones Jr. built the Beach Course at Waikoloa (1981) on an old flow of crinkly *aʻā* lava, which he used to create holes that are as artful as they are challenging. The third tee, for instance, is set at the base of a towering mound of lava. The par-5 12th plays through a chute of black lava to an oceanside green, the blue sea on the right coming into play on the second and third shots. At the King's Course at Waikoloa (1990), Tom Weiskopf and Jay Morrish built a very links-esque track. It turns out lava's natural humps and declivities remarkably replicate the contours of seaside Scotland. But there are a few island twists—such as seven lakes. This is "option golf" as Weiskopf and Morrish provide different risk-reward tactics on each hole. Beach and King's have separate clubhouses. **Beach Course:** ✉ *1020 Keana Pl., Waikoloa* ☎ *808/886–6060* ⊕ *www.waikoloagolf.com* ⚐ *18 holes. 6566 yds. Par 70. Green Fee: $175* ☞ *Facilities: Driving range, putting green, golf carts, rental clubs, lessons, restaurant, bar.* **Kings' Course:** ✉ *600 Waikoloa Beach Dr., Waikoloa* ☎ *808/886–7888* ⊕ *www. waikoloagolf.com* ⚐ *18 holes. 6594 yds. Par 72. Green Fee: $175* ☞ *Facilities: Driving range, putting green, golf carts, rental clubs, lessons, restaurant, bar.*

Waikoloa Village Golf Course. A 20-minute drive from Waikoloa Beach Resort, Robert Trent Jones Jr.'s Waikoloa Village (1972) is not affiliated with the resort. It is, however, the site of the annual Waikoloa Open, one of the most prestigious tournaments in Hawai'i. Holes run across rolling hills with sweeping mountain and ocean views. ✉ *68-1792 Melia St., Waikoloa* ☎ *808/883–9621* ⊕ *www.waikoloa.org* ⚐ *18 holes. 6230 yds. Par 72. Green Fee: $100* ☞ *Facilities: Driving range, putting green, golf carts, rental clubs, lessons, restaurant, bar.*

Hiking

⇨ *See also* Hawai'i Volcanoes National Park, *earlier in this chapter.*

Meteorologists classify the world's weather into 23 climates. Twenty-one are here on the Big Island, and you can experience as many of them as you like. The ancient Hawaiians blazed many trails across their archipelago, and many of these paths can still be used today. Part of the King's Trail at 'Anaeho'omalu winds through a field of lava rocks covered with prehistoric carvings meant to communicate stories of births, deaths, marriages, and other family events. Plus, the serenity of remote beaches, such as Papakōlea Beach (Green Sand Beach), is accessible only to hikers.

For information on all Big Island's state parks, contact the **Department of Land and Natural Resources, State Parks Division** (✉ 75 Aupuni St., Hilo 96720 ☎ 808/974–6200 ⊕ www.hawaii.gov/dlnr/dsp/hawaii.html).

Best Spots

The **Mauna Kea Trail** (✉ Trailhead at Onizuka Visitors Center) ascends from the visitor center (9,200 feet) to the 13,000-foot summit. The difficult, four-hour trek rewards the hardy with glimpses of endangered species, a stunning view of the primeval Lake Waiau, and a fabulous vantage point from the top of the world (you look down on the sunset). Because of the difficulty of the trail and the low-oxygen environment, it's a very tough hike even for the most fit. At these altitudes, you must drink plenty of water. Also, wear warm clothes and sunglasses, and put on plenty of sunscreen. This trek is not recommended for children under 16, pregnant women, or those with respiratory problems.

At **Kekaha Kai (Kona Coast) State Park** (✉ Hwy. 19, sign about 2 mi north of Keāhole–Kona International Airport marks rough road), two 1½-mi-long unpaved roads lead to the Mahai'ula Beach and Kua Bay sections of the park. Mahai'ula has a sandy beach with a picnic area. A 4½-mi hike north along the Ala Kahakai historic coastal trail leads to Kua Bay. Midway, a hike to the summit of Pu'u Ku'ili, a 342-foot high cinder cone, offers an excellent view of the coastline. It's dry and hot with no drinking water, so be sure to pack sunscreen and bottled water.

Guided Hikes

To get to some of the best trails and places, it's worth going with a skilled guide. Costs range from $75 to $180, and hikes include picnic meals and gear such as binoculars, ponchos, and walking sticks. The outfitters mentioned here also offer customized adventure tours.

Hawai'i Forest & Trail. Expert naturalist guides take you to 500-foot Kalopa Falls in North Kohala, through the 4,000-year-old craters at Mount Hualālai (the volcano that created all those lava fields along the coast), and on bird-watching expeditions throughout the island. In addition to its other expeditions, the company offers tours in Pinzgauers (Austrian all-terrain vehicles) that are perfect for groups, especially those that include off-road junkies. It offer tours into lava tubes and through normally inaccessible areas of Hawai'i Volcanoes National Park. ☎ *808/ 331–8505 or 800/464–1993* ⊕ *www.hawaii-forest.com.*

Hawaiian Walkways. Hawaiian Walkways conducts several tours—waterfall hikes, coastal adventures, flora and fauna explorations, and jaunts through Hawai'i Volcanoes National Park—as well as custom-designed trips. ☎ *808/775–0372 or 800/457–7759* ⊕ *www. hawaiianwalkways.com.*

Horseback Riding

With its *paniolo* (cowboy) heritage, the Big Island is a great place for equestrians. Riders can gallop through green Upcountry pastures, ride to Kealakekua Bay to see the Captain Cook Monument, or saunter into Waipi'o Valley for a taste of old Hawai'i. In addition to the companies listed below, the Mauna Kea Beach Hotel maintains stables in Waimea.

King's Trail Rides O'Kona. Riders take a 4½-hour excursion to the Captain Cook Monument in Kealakekua Bay for snorkeling. (All your gear is provided, except for fins and reef walkers). The cost is $135 to $150. ⊠ *Hwy. 11, mile marker 111, Kealakekua* ☎ *808/323–2388* ⊕ *www. konacowboy.com.*

Na'alapa Stables. This company is a good bet, especially for novice riders. The horses are well trained, and the stable is well run. Rides through the Waipi'o Valley cross freshwater streams and pass a black-sand beach. Rides depart twice daily from Waipi'o Valley Artworks. ⊠ *Off Hwy. 240, Kukuihaele* ☎ *808/775-0419* ⊕ *www.naalapastables.com.*

Waipi'o Ridge Stables. Two different rides around the rim of Waipi'o Valley are offered—a 2½-hour trek for $75 and a 5-hour hidden-waterfall adventure for $145. Riders meet at Waipi'o Valley Artworks. ⊠ *Off Hwy. 240, Kukuihaele* ☎ *808/775–1007 or 877/757–1414* ⊕ *www. waipioridgestables.com.*

Skiing

Where else but Hawai'i can you surf, snorkel, and snow ski on the same day? In winter, the 13,796-foot Mauna Kea (Hawaiian for "white mountain") has snow at higher elevations—and along with that, skiing. No lifts, no manicured slopes, no faux-Alpine lodges, no apres-ski nightlife—but the chance to ski some of the most remote (and let's face it, unlikely) runs on earth. Some people even have been known to use boogie board as sleds, but we don't recommend it. As long as you're up there, fill your cooler with the white stuff for a snowball fight on the beach with local kids.

Ski Guides Hawaiʻi. ⌂ *Box 1954, Kamuela 96743* ☎ *808/885–4188, 808/884–5131 off-season* ⊕ *www.skihawaii.com.*

Tennis

Many of the island's resorts allow nonguests to play for a fee. They also rent rackets, balls, and shoes. On the Kohala Coast, try the Fairmont Orchid Hawaiʻi, the Mauna Kea Beach Hotel, Hilton Waikoloa Village, and Waikoloa Beach Marriott. In Kailua-Kona there's the Ohana Keauhou Beach Resort, King Kamehameha's Kona Beach Hotel, and the Royal Kona Resort.

Contact the **County of Hawaiʻi Department of Parks and Recreation** (✉ 25 Aupuni St., Hilo 96720 ☎ 808/961–8311 ⊕ www.hawaii-county.com/directory/dir_parks.htm) for information on all public courts.

In Kailua-Kona, you can play for free at the **Kailua Playground** (✉ 75-5794 Kuakini Hwy., Kailua-Kona ☎ 808/886–1655). Tennis courts are available at **Old Kona Airport State Recreation Area** (✉ North end of Kuakini Hwy., Kailua-Kona ☎ 808/327–4958 or 808/974–6200).

> ### ON THE SIDELINES
>
> The world's best players compete in January in the **United States Tennis Association Challenger** (☎ 518/274-1674) on the courts of Hilton Waikoloa Village.

On the Hilo side, there's a small fee to play on the eight courts (three lighted for night play) at **Hilo Tennis Stadium** (✉ Hoʻolulu County Park, Piʻilani and Kalanikoa Sts., Hilo ☎ 808/961–8720).

SHOPPING

Residents like to complain that there isn't much to shop for on the Big Island, but unless you're searching for winter coats or high-tech toys, you can find plenty to deplete your pocketbook. Kailua-Kona has a range of souvenirs from far-flung corners of the globe. Resorts along the Kohala Coast have high-quality clothing and accessories. Galleries and boutiques, many showcasing the work of local artists, fill historic buildings in Waimea and North Kohala. Hotel shops generally offer the most attractive and original resort wear, but prices run higher than elsewhere.

In general, stores and shopping centers on the Big Island open at 9 or 10 AM and close by 6 PM. Hilo's Prince Kūhiō Shopping Plaza stays open until 9 weekdays. In Kona, most shops in shopping plazas that are geared to tourists remain open until 9. Big outlets such as KTA are open until midnight.

Kohala

Shopping Centers

Kawaihae Harbor Center. This harborside shopping plaza houses a dive shop, a bathing-suit store, restaurants, and art galleries, including the Harbor Gallery. ✉ *Hwy. 270, Kawaihae.*

King's Shops at Waikoloa Village. Here you can find fine stores such as Under the Koa Tree, with its upscale gift items crafted by artisans, along with high-end outlets such as DFS Galleria and Louis Vuitton and several other specialty resort shops and boutiques. At the other end of the spectrum, there are also a couple of convenience stores here, but the prices are stiff. ✉ *250 Waikoloa Beach Dr., Waikoloa* ☎ *808/886–8811.*

Books & Maps

Kohala Book Shop. In the historic Old Nanbu Hotel, the state's largest used-book store contains one of the most complete Hawaiian and Pacific collections. There are also some rare first editions. ✉ *54-3885 Akoni Pule Hwy., Kapa'au* ☎ *808/889–6400.*

Clothing

As Hāwī Turns. This North Kohala shop, in the historic 1932 Toyama Building, adds a sophisticated touch to resort wear with items made of hand-painted silk. There are vintage and secondhand treasures as well. ✉ *Akoni Pule Hwy., Hāwī* ☎ *808/889–5023.*

Hawaiian Arts & Crafts

Remote North Kohala has a remarkable number of galleries in its old restored plantation buildings.

Ackerman Fine Art Gallery. Painter Gary Ackerman; his wife, Yesan; and their daughter, Camille, have a fine and varied collection of gifts for sale in their side-by-side gallery and gift shop near the King Kamehameha statue. ✉ *54-3878 Akoni Pule Hwy., Kapa'au* ☎ *808/889–5971.*

Elements Jewelry & Fine Crafts. Be sure to stop at the Old Nanbu Hotel, built in 1898. In the front window of his store, John Flynn creates exquisite jewelry such as delicate silver lei and gold waterfalls. The shop also showcases carefully chosen gifts, including unusual ceramics and glass. ✉ *54-3885 Akoni Pule Hwy., Kapa'au* ☎ *808/889–0760.*

Gallery at Bamboo. Inside the Bamboo Restaurant, this gallery seduces visitors with elegant koa-wood pieces such as rocking chairs and writing desks. It also has a wealth of gift items such as boxes, jewelry, and Hawaiian wrapping paper. ✉ *Hwy. 270, Hāwī* ☎ *808/889–1441.*

Nanbu Gallery. Here you can admire the paintings of owner Patrick Sweeney and other island artists. ✉ *54-3885 Akoni Pule Hwy., Kapa'au* ☎ *808/889–0997.*

Rankin Gallery. Watercolorist and oil painter Patrick Louis Rankin runs this shop in the old Wo On Store, next to the Chinese community and social hall, the Tong Wo Society. ✉ *53-4380 Akoni Pule Hwy., Kapa'au* ☎ *808/889–6849.*

Swerdlow Art Gallery. It's worth a stop here to browse the tropically inspired artworks of resident artist Sue Swerdlow. ✉ *54-3862 Akoni Pule Hwy., Kapa'au* ☎ *808/889–0002.*

Tropical Flowers

Na Pua O Kohala. At this North Kohala flower shop, you can order lei or let owner Johanna Bard help you create a memorable bouquet. She'll ship your selections for you. ⊠ *55-3413 Akoni Pule Hwy., Hāwī* ☎ *808/ 889–5541 or 877/889–5571.*

Waimea

Shopping Centers

Parker Ranch Center. With a snazzy ranch-style motif, this shopping hub's anchors include a supermarket, coffee shop, natural foods store, and some clothing boutiques. The Parker Ranch Store and Parker Ranch Visitor Center and Museum are also here. ⊠ *67-1185 Māmalahoa Hwy., Waimea.*

Parker Square. Browse around boutiques here and in the adjacent **High Country Traders,** where you may find hand-stitched Hawaiian quilts. ⊠ *65-1279 Kawaihae Rd., Waimea* ☎ *808/331–1000.*

Waimea Center. Here you can find an eclectic mix of stores, including a gift shop, a large supermarket, and a travel service called Without Boundaries. ⊠ *65-1158 Māmalahoa Hwy., Waimea.*

Hawaiian Arts & Crafts

Dan DeLuz's Woods. Master bowl-turner Dan DeLuz creates works of art from 50 types of exotic wood grown on the Big Island. The shop features a variety of items—from picture frames to jewelry boxes—made from koa, monkeypod, mango, kiawe, and other fine local hardwoods. Dan's wife, Mary Lou, operates the Koa Shop Kaffee restaurant next door. There's a another branch south of Hilo in Kurtistown. ⊠ *64-1013 Māmalahoa Hwy., Waimea* ☎ *808/885–5856* ⊠ *Hwy. 19, Kurtistown* ☎ *808/968–6607.*

Gallery of Great Things. At this Parker Square shop, you might fall in love with the Ni'ihau shell lei ranging from $150 to $7,000. More affordable are koa mirrors and other high-quality artifacts from around the Pacific basin. ⊠ *65-1279 Kawaihae Rd., Waimea* ☎ *808/885–7706.*

Harbor Gallery. For fine art, furniture, and decorative pieces made with koa and other native woods, be sure to stop here. The gallery is next to Harbor Grill. ⊠ *Kawaihae Harbor Center, Hwy. 270, Kawaihae* ☎ *808/ 882–1510.*

Mauna Kea Galleries. The specialty here is rare vintage collectibles, including hula dolls, prints, and koa furniture. ⊠ *65-1298 Kawaihae Rd., Waimea* ☎ *808/887–2244.*

Kailua-Kona

Shopping Centers

Coconut Grove Marketplace. Just south of Kona Inn Shopping Village, this meandering labyrinth of airy buildings hides coffee shops, boutiques, ethnic restaurants, and an exquisite gallery. ⊠ *75-5795–75-5825 Ali'i Dr.* ☎ *808/326–2555.*

Crossroads Shopping Center. Shopping in Kailua-Kona has begun to go the way of mainland cities at this complex with Borders Books & Music, Safeway, Wal-Mart and an eclectic collection of restaurants. ✉ 75-1000 Henry St. ☎ 808/329–4822.

Keauhou Shopping Center. About 5 mi south of Kailua-Kona, the stores and boutiques here include KTA Superstore, Long's Drugs, and Alapaki's Hawaiian Gifts. ✉ 78-6831 Ali'i Dr. ☎ 808/322–3000.

Kona Inn Shopping Village. On the *makai* side of Ali'i Drive in the heart of Kailua-Kona, extending for an entire block along Kailua Bay, the village is crammed with boutiques selling bright beach wraps and knickknacks. ✉ 75-5744 Ali'i Dr. ☎ 808/329–6573.

Makalapua Center. Just north of Kona, off Highway 19, islanders find bargains at Kmart at this prodigious mall. Of more interest might be the large Macy's; although a mainland chain, it keeps nice selections in apparel and gifts from local vendors. ✉ Kamakaeha Ave. at Hwy. 19, south of Kailua-Kona.

Books
Middle Earth Bookshoppe. This is a great independent bookstore with superb maps and an esoteric collection of literary works. ✉ 75-5719 Ali'i Dr., Kailua-Kona ☎ 808/329–2123.

Candies & Chocolates
Kailua Candy Company. The chocolate here is made with locally grown cacao beans from the Original Hawaiian Chocolate Factory. Of course, tasting is part of the fun. Through a glass wall you can watch the chocolate artists at work. ✉ 74-5563 Kaiwi St., Kailua-Kona ☎ 808/329–2522.

Clothing
A'ama Surf & Sport. This boutique has some cool button-ups for men, along with unbelievably cute suits for women in a variety of unusual styles and fabrics. There's a new branch on Henry, across the street from the Crossroads Shopping Center. ✉ 75-5741 Kuakini Hwy. ☎ 808/326–7890 ✉ 75-1002 Henry St. ☎ 808/326–7890.

Coconut Willie. The only shop downtown to shun beachwear in favor of trendier threads for women, Coconut Willie sells mainland standards like Free People tops, Seven jeans, and Juicy sweats. ✉ Kona Inn Shopping Village, 75-5744 Ali'i Dr. ☎ 808/329–6573.

Flamingo's. Stop by this little shop to browse vintage clothing and antique jewelry. ✉ Kona Inn Shopping Village, 75-5744 Ali'i Dr. ☎ 808/329–4122.

★ **Hilo Hattie.** The well-known clothier matches his-and-her aloha wear and carries a huge selection of casual clothes, slippers, jewelry, and souvenirs. Call for free transportation from nearby hotels. ✉ 75-5597 Palani Rd., Kopiko Plaza, Kailua-Kona ☎ 808/329–7200.

Honolua Surf Company. Locals have been complaining forever that you can't find "cool" clothes on the Big Island. That's finally changed as stores like this one have begun following the fashion trends. Honolua Surf Company has hip casual wear along with the more expected inventory of Roxie shorts and suits. ⊠ *Kona Inn Shopping Village* ☎ *808/329–1001.*

Island Salsa. You'll find plenty of tropical toppers, as well as cute souvenir T-shirts, at this little shop. ⊠ *Kona Inn Shopping Village, 75-5744 Ali'i Dr.* ☎ *808/329–9279.*

Paradise Found. In the upcountry town of Kainaliu, as well as in two of Kailua-Kona's shopping centers, this reputable spot carries contemporary silk and rayon clothing. ⊠ *Māmalahoa Hwy. 11, Kainaliu* ☎ *808/322–2111* ⊠ *Lanihau Center, 75-5595 Palani Rd., Kailua-Kona* ☎ *808/329–2221* ⊠ *Keauhou Shopping Center, 78-6831 Ali'i Dr., Kailua-Kona* ☎ *808/324–1177.*

Sirena. Kealakekua is home to the first high-end designer boutique on the Big Island. Sirena carries squeal-worthy contemporary clothing from designers like Carlos Miele, Barbara Bui, and Catherine Malandrino. If these names are familiar, we don't need to tell you to expect high prices. ⊠ *79-7491 Māmalahoa Hwy., Kealakekua* ☎ *808/322–3900.*

Hawaiian Arts & Crafts

Alapaki's Hawaiian Gifts. For hula instruments, intricate feather headbands, and other original art, look no further than this popular shop. ⊠ *Keauhou Shopping Village, 78-6831 Ali'i Dr.* ☎ *808/322–2007.*

Hōlualoa Gallery. In the little coffee town of Hōlualoa, this is one of several excellent galleries that crowd the narrow street. It carries stunning raku (Japanese lead-glazed pottery). ⊠ *76-5921 Māmalahoa Hwy., Hōlualoa* ☎ *808/322–8484.*

★ **Kimura's Lauhala Shop.** Men can pick up an authentic *lauhala* hat here for some stylish sun protection. ⊠ *Māmalahoa Hwy., Hōlualoa* ☎ *808/324–0053.*

Kona Arts Center. There's an entire community of artists at work in this complex; feel free to drop in if the doors are open. ⊠ *Māmalahoa Hwy., Hōlualoa.*

★ **Made on the Big Island.** This place is geared to cruise-ship passengers with little time on their hands. It's a one-stop shopping for traditional island gifts. You can find quite a few treasures here, such as koa boxes and bonsai trees that may be exported. ⊠ *King Kamehameha's Kona Beach Hotel, 75-5660 Palani Rd.* ☎ *808/326–4949.*

Markets

Ali'i Gardens Market Place. More a flea market than a farmers' market, this cluster of vendor stalls has everything from beautiful tropical flowers to locally grown coffee. It's open Wednesday to Sunday. ⊠ *75-6129 Ali'i Dr., 1½ mi south of Kona Inn Shopping Village, Kailua-Kona* ☎ *808/334–1381.*

Kona Inn Farmers' Market. The low-key farmers' market is filled with produce, coffee, and macadamia nuts from around the region. It's held in the parking lot of the Kona Inn Shopping Village on Wednesday and Saturday from 7 AM until 3 PM. ⊠ *75-7544 Ali'i Dr., park at Kona Inn Shopping Village parking lot, Kailua-Kona.*

Hilo

Shopping Centers

Hilo Shopping Center. This rather dated shopping plaza has several air-conditioned shops and restaurants. Great cookies, cakes, and baked goodies are at Lanky's Pastries. There's plenty of free parking. ⊠ *Kekuanaoa St. at Kīlauea Ave., Hilo.*

Prince Kūhiō Shopping Plaza. Hilo's most comprehensive mall, Prince Kūhiō Shopping Plaza is where you can find Macy's for fashion, Safeway for food, and Longs Drugs for just about everything else, along with several other shops and boutiques. ⊠ *111 E. Puainako St., at Hwy. 11, Hilo* ☎ *808/959–3555.*

Waiakea Center. Here you can find a Borders Books & Music, Island Naturals, and a Wal-Mart. If all the shopping makes you hungry, there's also a food court. ⊠ *Maka'ala St. and Kanoelehua Ave., across from Prince Kūhiō Shopping Plaza, at Hwy. 11, Hilo* ☎ *808/792–7225.*

Books & Magazines

Basically Books. This shop stocks one of Hawai'i's largest selections of maps and charts, including topographical and relief maps. It also has Hawaiiana books, with great choices for children. ⊠ *160 Kamehameha Ave., Hilo* ☎ *808/961–0144 or 800/903–6277.*

Candies & Chocolate

★ **Big Island Candies.** This chocolate factory lets you tour and taste before you buy. ⊠ *585 Hinano St., Hilo* ☎ *808/935–8890.*

Clothing

★ **Hilo Hattie.** The well-known clothier matches his-and-her aloha wear and carries a huge selection of casual clothes, slippers, jewelry, and souvenirs. Call for free transportation from selected hotels. ⊠ *Prince Kūhiō Shopping Plaza, 111 E. Puainako St., Hilo* ☎ *808/961–3077.*

★ **Sig Zane Designs.** This acclaimed boutique sells distinctive island wearables with bold colors and motifs. ⊠ *122 Kamehameha Ave., Hilo* ☎ *808/935–7077.*

Gifts

Dragon Mama. Step into this spot to find authentic Japanese fabrics, futons, and antiques. ⊠ *266 Kamehameha Ave., Hilo* ☎ *808/934–9081.*

Ets'ko. You'll find Japanese tea sets, exquisite ceramics, and affordable bamboo ware here. ⊠ *35 Waiānuenue Ave., Hilo* ☎ *808/961–3778.*

Fuku-Bonsai Cultural Center. In addition to selling and shipping miniature *brassaia lava* plantings and other bonsai plants, this place on the way to Volcano has interesting exhibits of different ethnic styles of pruning. ⊠ *Ola'a Rd., Kurtistown* ☎ *808/982–9880.*

Hoaloha. If you're driving north from Hilo, take time to browse through this shop and pick up a colorful *pareu* (beach wrap). ⊠ *Last Chance Store, off Hwy. 240, Kukuihaele* ☎ *808/775–0502.*

Most Irresistible Shop. This place lives up to its name by stocking unique gifts from around the Pacific, be it coconut-flavored butter or whimsical wind chimes. ✉ *256 Kamehameha Ave.* ☎ *808/935–9644* ✉ *Prince Kūhiō Shopping Plaza, 111 E. Puainako St., at Hwy. 11, Hilo* ☎ *808/ 959–6515.*

Waipi`o Valley Artworks. In this remote gallery you can find finely crafted wooden bowls, koa furniture, paintings, and jewelry—all made by local artists. ✉ *Off Hwy. 240, Kukuihaele* ☎ *808/775–0958.*

Markets

★ **Hilo Farmers' Market.** The farmers here sell a profusion of tropical flowers, high-quality produce, and macadamia nuts. This colorful, open-air market—the most popular in the state—opens for business Wednesday and Saturday from 6:30 AM to 2:30 PM. ✉ *Kamehameha Ave. and Mamo St., Hilo.*

Hāmākua Coast

Shopping Centers

Kaloko Industrial Park. Developed for local consumers, this shopping plaza has outlets such as Costco Warehouse and Home Depot. It's useful for off-the-beaten-path finds. ✉ *Off Hwy. 19 and Hina Lani St., near Keāhole-Kona International Airport.*

SPAS

Hawaiian Rainforest Salon & Spa at the Waikoloa Marriott. The Marriott recently added a bunch of treatments to its spa menu, which adds to the appeal of this reasonable resort on the Kohala Coast. Although treatments like the Smooth and Sunkissed body treatment (an exfoliating scrub, followed by bronzer that makes sure you don't frighten anyone on the beach) are appealing, none are as spectacular as the standard ocean-side massage. Their therapists are highly skilled, and their tables are right on one of the prettiest beaches on the coast. One caveat: this is not the place to get your hair cut on vacation. ✉ *69-275 Waikoloa Beach Dr., Waikoloa* ☎ *808/886–7727* ⊕ *www.marriott.com* ☞ *$80–$100, 50- to 80-min massage. Gym with: cardiovascular machines. Services: body scrubs and wraps, facials, massages. Classes and programs: aerobics, yoga.*

**Ho`ōla Spa at the Sheraton Keauhou Bay.** The Sheraton Keauhou Bay occupies one of the prettier corners of the island, with an unbeatable view from most parts of the hotel. The Ho`ōla Spa, which opened in 2005, takes full advantage of its location with several windows facing the bay. The spa menu includes a variety of locally influenced treatments. The warm lava-rock massage is a little slice of heaven, and the facials are relaxing and rejuvenating. The packages are an excellent deal, combining several services for far less than you would pay à la carte. For couples, the spa offers an ocean-side massage that takes place on a balcony overlooking the water, folowed by a dip in a whirlpool bath. ✉ *78-128 Ehukai St., Kailua-Kona* ☎ *808/930–4900* ⊕ *www.sheratonkeauhou. com* ☞ *$110, 50-min massage. Facilities: hair salon, hot tub, sauna,* *steam room. Services: aromatherapy, body scrubs and wraps, facials, massages, waxing.*

Kalona Salon & Spa at the Outrigger Keauhou Beach Resort. This spa is a great place to get a massage or body treatment for much less than you'd likely pay at the big resorts. Though not quite as nice as the bigger facilities, it's simple and clean, on the ocean, and staffed with well-trained therapists. The spa offers facials using its own line of products made from island ingredients. Be careful if you have touchy skin. ⊠ *78-6740 Ali'i Dr., Kailua-Kona* ☎ *808/322–3441 or 800/462–6262* ⊕ *www. outrigger.com* ☞ *$80 massage. Services: facials, massage.*

★ **Kohala Sports Club & Spa at the Hilton Waikoloa Village.** The orchids that run riot in the rain forests of the Big Island suffuse the signature treatments at the Kohala Sports Club & Spa. By the end of the Orchid Isle Wrap, you're completely immersed in the scent and in bone-deep relaxation. The island's volcanic character is also expressed in several treatments, as well as in the design of the lava-rock soaking tubs. Locker rooms are outfitted with private changing rooms for the modest and a wealth of beauty and bath products for the adventurous. The extensive hair and nail salon could satisfy even Bridezilla with its updo consultations and luxe pedicure stations. The nearby ocean-side cabanas are the perfect venue for massage on the beach. The fitness center is well-equipped, but group classes that roam across the beautifully manicured resort grounds—like tai chi on the lawn or walking meditation at Buddha Point—are much more appealing. ⊠ *Hilton Waikoloa Village, 425 Waikoloa Beach Dr., Kohala Coast* ☎ *808/886–2828 or 800/445–8667* ⊕ *www.kohalaspa. com* ☞ *$135–$145 50-min massage, $180 body wrap, $145 facial. Hair salon, hot tubs (indoor and outdoor), sauna, steam room. Gym with: cardiovascular machines, free weights, weight-training equipment. Services: acupuncture, aromatherapy, body scrubs and wraps, facials, hydromassage, massage. Classes and programs: body sculpting, fitness analysis, personal training, Pilates, Spinning, step aerobics, tai chi, yoga.*

Mauna Kea Beach Hotel. Lacking a specific theme or high-end design concept, the spa at the Mauna Kea is not as flashy as its neighbors. Massages are good but not great. The best thing going here is the body treatment menu, with unusual options like the aloe and herbal wrap (which combats cellulite) in addition to island standards like the sea salt body glow. You can use the gym at the Hāpuna Golf Course's clubhouse, accessible via a free shuttle. ⊠ *62-100 Mauna Kea Beach Dr., Kohala Coast* ☎ *808/882–7222* ⊕ *www.maunakeabeachhotel.com* ☞ *$96–$100, 50-min massage. Hair salon, sauna, steam room. Services: aromatherapy, body treatments, facials, massage. Classes and programs: aerobics.*

Fodor's Choice **Mauna Lani Spa.** If you're looking for a one-of-a-kind experience, this
★ is your destination. Most treatments take place in outdoor, bamboo-floor *hales* surrounded by lava rock. Incredible therapists offer a mix of the old standbys (*lomi lomi* massage, moisturizing facials) and innovative treatments, many of which are heavily influenced by ancient traditions and incorporate local products. One exfoliating body treatment is self-

administered in one of the outdoor saunas—a great choice for people who aren't too keen on therapists seeing them in their birthday suits. Watsu therapy takes place in an amazing pool filled by the adjacent lava tube. Meant to re-create the feeling of being in a womb, the hour-long therapy is essentially an underwater massage. You feel totally weightless, thanks to some artfully applied weights and the buoyancy of the warm salt water. It's a great treatment for people with disabilities that keep them from enjoying a traditional massage. The aesthetic treatments on the menu incorporate high-end products from Epicuran and Emminence, so a facial will have a real and lasting therapeutic effect on your skin. The spa also offers a full regimen of fitness and yoga classes, as well as more mainland-style procedures like Botox and Restylane injections. ⊠ *Mauna Lani Resort, 68-1400 Mauna Lani Dr., Kohala Coast* ☎ *808/885–6622* ⊕ *www.maunalani.com* ☞ *$125, 50-min massage, $150–$265 facials, $60 lava sauna, $140–$190 watsu. Hair salon, hot tubs (indoor and outdoor), sauna, steam room. Gym with: cardiovascular machines, free weights, weight-training equipment. Services: aquatic therapy, baths, body wraps, Botox, facials, massage, Restylane, scrubs. Classes and programs: aerobics, kickboxing, personal training, Pilates, Spinning, weight training, yoga.*

Paul Brown Salon & Spa at the Hāpuna Beach Prince Hotel. It's not unusual for wealthy locals to drive an hour each way to get their hair cut here. Paul Brown has been in the business for 30 years, and he now has three locations in Hawai'i. Hair is still the specialty here, but it's not just a salon. The full-service spa—nicely designed to let in lots of light—has an extensive menu of massages, facials, and body treatments. You feel safe having anything done here—Brown and his staff really know their stuff. The well-run facility even has a trained practitioner who administers expert acupuncture treatments. It's the best place for waxing in case you didn't have time before you left home. You can use the gym at the Hāpuna Golf Course's clubhouse, accessible via a free shuttle. ⊠ *62-100 Kauna'oa Dr., Kohala* ☎ *808/880–1111 or 800/882–6060* ⊕ *www.princeresortshawaii.com* ☞ *$100, 50-min massage; $85, 50-min facials; $100–$150 acupuncture. Hair salon, sauna, steam room. Services: acupuncture, body wraps, facials, massage. Classes and programs: aerobics, yoga.*

Spa Without Walls at the Fairmont Orchid Hawai'i. This is possibly the best massage on the island, partially due to having the best setting. Massages at the Spa Without Walls are either facing the ocean or a waterfall. Though most people will probably opt for the ocean, both settings are absolutely peaceful. There are other great treatments as well, including facials, fragrant herbal wraps, and coffee and vanilla scrubs, but the massages are the best thing going. ⊠ *Fairmont Orchid Hawai'i, 1 N. Kanikū Dr., Kohala Coast* ☎ *808/885–2000* ⊕ *www.fairmont.com* ☞ *$129, 50-min massage, $150 facial, $120 body treatment. Sauna, steam room. Gym with: cardiovascular machines, free weights, weight-training equipment. Services: baths, body wraps, facials, massage, scrubs. Classes and programs: aquaerobics, guided walks, meditation, personal training, yoga.*

ENTERTAINMENT & NIGHTLIFE

If you're the sort of person who doesn't come alive until after dark, you're going to be lonely on the Big Island. Blame it on the plantation heritage. People did their cane-raising in the morning.

Entertainment

Hula

★ For hula lovers, the biggest show of the year and the largest event of its kind in the world is the annual **Merrie Monarch Hula Festival** (✉ Hawai'i Naniloa Resort, 93 Banyan Dr., Hilo 96720 ☎ 808/935–9168 ⊕ www. naniloaresort.com). Honoring the legacy of King David Kalākaua, Hawai'i's last king, the festival is staged in Hilo at the spacious Edith Kanaka'ole Stadium during the first week following Easter Sunday. Hula *hālau* compete in various classes of ancient and modern dance styles. You need to reserve accommodations and tickets up to a year in advance.

Lū'au & Polynesian Revues

KOHALA COAST & WAIKOLOA

Hilton Waikoloa Village. The Hilton seats 400 people outdoors at the Kamehameha Court, where the acclaimed Polynesian group Tihati performs a lively show. A buffet dinner provides samplings of Hawaiian food as well as fish, beef, and chicken to appeal to all tastes. ✉ *425 Waikoloa Beach Dr., Waikoloa* ☎ *808/886–1234* ⊕ *www.hiltonwaikoloavillage. com* 🍴 *$74* ◷ *Fri. at 6.*

Mauna Kea Beach Hotel. Once a week, on the gracious North Pointe Lū'au Grounds of the Mauna Kea Beach Hotel, you can sample the best of Hawaiian cuisine while listening to the enchanting songs of Nani Lim. Every Tuesday, chefs come together here to create a traditional Hawaiian *pa'ina* (dinner feast), which includes the classic *kālua* (roasted in an underground oven) pig. ✉ *62-100 Mauna Kea Beach Dr., Kohala Coast* ☎ *808/882–7222* ⊕ *www.maunakeabeachhotel.com* 🍴 *$76* ◷ *Tues. at 6.*

Waikoloa Beach Marriott. At this celebration, entertainment includes a Samoan fire dance as well as songs and dances of various Pacific cultures. Traditional Hawaiian dishes are served alongside more familiar fare. ✉ *69-275 Waikoloa Beach Dr., Waikoloa* ☎ *808/886–6789* ⊕ *www.marriott. com* 🍴 *$67, including open bar* ◷ *Wed. and Sun. 5–8:30.*

KAILUA-KONA

King Kamehameha's Kona Beach Hotel. Witness the royal court arrive by canoe at the Island Breeze Lū'au, a beachfront event, which includes a 22-item buffet, an open bar, and a show. ✉ *75-5660 Palani Rd., Kailua-Kona* ☎ *808/326–4969 or 808/329–8111* ⊕ *www.islandbreezeluau.com* 🍴 *$62.50* ◷ *Tues.–Thurs. and Sun. 5:30–8:30.*

★ **Kona Village Resort.** In its utter isolation, the lū'au here is one of the most authentic and traditional on the Islands. As in other lū'au, activities include the steaming of a whole pig in the *imu* (ground oven). A Polynesian show on a stage over a lagoon is magical. ✉ *Queen Ka'ahumanu Hwy., 6 mi north of Kona International Airport, Kailua-Kona* ☎ *808/325–5555 or 808/325–4273* ⊕ *www.konavillage.com* 🍴 *$84, including open bar* ◷ *Fri. from 5; walking tour at 5:30, imu ceremony at 6:30, dinner at 7, show at 8.*

Hawai'i's Hippy Hippy Shake

LEGENDS IMMORTALIZE LAKA as the goddess of hula, portraying her as a gentle deity who journeyed from island to island, sharing the dance with all who were willing to learn. Laka's graceful movements, spiritual and layered with meaning, brought to life the history, the traditions, and the genealogy of the islanders. Ultimately taught by parents to children and by *kumu* (teachers) to students, the hula preserved the culture of these ancient peoples without a written language.

Some legends trace the origins of hula to Moloka'i, where a family named La'ila'i was said to have established the dance at Ka'ana. Eventually the youngest sister of the fifth generation of La'ila'i was given the name Laka, and she carried the dance to all the Islands in the Hawaiian chain.

Another legend credits Hi'iaka, the volcano goddess Pele's youngest sister, as having danced the first hula in the *hala* groves of Puna on the Big Island. Hi'iaka and possibly even Pele were thought to have learned the dance from Hōpoe, a mortal and a poet also credited as the originator of the dance.

In any case, hula thrived until the arrival of puritanical New England missionaries, who with the support of Queen Ka'ahumanu, an early Christian convert, attempted to ban the dance as an immoral activity throughout the 19th century.

Though hula may not have been publicly performed, it remained a spiritual and poetic art form, as well as a lively celebration of life presented during special celebrations in many Hawaiian homes. David Kalākaua, the popular "Merrie Monarch" who was king from 1874 to 1891, revived the hula. Dancers were called to perform at official functions.

Gradually, ancient hula, called *kahiko*, was replaced with a lively, updated form of dance called *'auana* (modern). Modern costumes of fresh ti-leaf or raffia skirts replaced the voluminous *pa'u* skirts made of *kapa* (cloth made of beaten bark), and the music became more melodic, as opposed to earlier chanted routines accompanied by *pahu* (drums), *'ili 'ili* (rocks used as castanets), and other percussion instruments. Such tunes as "Lovely Hula Hands," "Little Grass Shack," and the "Hawaiian Wedding Song" are considered hula *'auana*. Dancers might wear graceful *holomu'u* with short trains or ti-leaf skirts with coconut bra tops.

In 1963 the Merrie Monarch Festival was established in Hilo on the Big Island and has since become the most prestigious hula competition in the state. It's staged annually the weekend after Easter, and contestants of various *halau* (hula schools) from Hawai'i and the mainland compete in the categories of Miss Aloha Hula, hula *kahiko* (ancient), and hula *'auana* (modern). For more information, contact the **Merrie Monarch Hula Festival** (✉ Hawai'i Naniloa Resort, 93 Banyan Dr., Hilo 96720 ☎ 808/935-9168 ⊕ www. naniloaresort.com).

Royal Kona Resort. This resort lights lūʻau torches for a full Polynesian show and a Hawaiian-style oceanfront buffet three times a week. ⊠ *75-5852 Aliʻi Dr., Kailua-Kona* ☎ *808/329–3111 Ext. 4* ⊕ *www.konaluau. com* ⊠ *$62* ⊙ *Mon., Wed., Fri., and Sat. at 5.*

Sunset Cruises

★ **Captain Beans' Polynesian Dinner Cruise.** This is the ever-popular standby in sunset dinner cruises. You can't miss it—as the sun sets, look out over the water and you'll see a big gaudy boat with distinctive orange sails. This cruise is corny, and dinner is nothing special, but it's an experience, with unlimited drinks and a Hawaiian show. This is for adults only. ⊠ *Kailua Pier, Kailua-Kona* ☎ *808/329–2955 or 800/831–5541* ⊕ *www. robertshawaii.com* ⊠ *$60* ⊙ *Tues.–Sun. at 5:15.*

Bars & Clubs

Kohala District

Honu Bar. This elegant spot at the Mauna Lani Bay Hotel & Bungalows has a nice dance floor for weekend revelry. Delicious appetizers, imported cigars, and fine cognacs make this a popular gathering spot on the Kohala Coast. ⊠ *68-1400 Mauna Lani Dr., Kohala Coast* ☎ *808/885–6622.*

Malolo Lounge. A favorite after-work spot for employees from the surrounding hotels, this lounge in the Hilton Waikoloa Village offers decent live music (usually jazz), friendly bartenders, and a pool table. ⊠ *425 Waikoloa Beach Dr., Waikoloa* ☎ *808/886–1234.*

Polo Bar. This wood-paneled watering hole in the Fairmont Orchid Hawaiʻi has a huge lānai and a great view. Bartenders are great, service is impeccable. The crowd's not rowdy, so it's a great place for an early evening cocktail or an after-dinner port. ⊠ *1 N. Kanikū Dr., Kohala Coast* ☎ *808/885–2000.*

Kailua-Kona

Huggo's on the Rocks. Jazz, country, and even rock bands perform at this popular restaurant, so call ahead to find out what's on. Outside, people often dance in the sand to Hawaiian songs. ⊠ *75-5828 Kahakai Rd., at Aliʻi Dr., Kailua-Kona* ☎ *808/329–1493.*

Lulu's. On weekends, the young crowd gyrates until late in the evening to hot dance music—hip-hop, R&B, and rock—spun by a professional DJ. ⊠ *75-5819 Aliʻi Dr., Kailua-Kona* ☎ *808/331–2633.*

Oceans Sports Bar & Grill. This is the current hot spot in Kona—a sports bar in the back of the Coconut Grove Marketplace. There's a pool table

BEST SUNSET MAI TAIS

Huggo's on the Rocks (Kailua-Kona). Literally on the rocks, this sand-floored bar has strong drinks and live music Friday and Saturday.

Kawaihae Harbor Grill (Kohala). Views off the deck of the upstairs Seafood Bar, great food in the restaurant next door, and well-poured drinks.

Kona Inn (Kailua-Kona). Wide, unobstructed view, in the middle of downtown, best mai tais on the island.

Waiʻoli Lounge in the Hilo Hawaiian Hotel (Hilo). A nice view of Coconut Island, live music most nights and karaoke others.

and an outdoor patio, and this place really gets hopping on most weekend evenings. ⊠ *Coconut Grove Marketplace, 75-5811 Ali'i Dr., Kailua-Kona* ☎ *808/327–9494.*

Hilo

Ho'omalimali Lounge. This lounge and dance club at the Hawai'i Naniloa Resort in Hilo competes with the crashing surf on Friday and Saturday night with live music until midnight. ⊠ *93 Banyan Dr., Hilo* ☎ *808/ 969–3333.*

WHERE TO EAT

Hotels along the Kohala Coast invest in celebrated chefs who know how to make a meal memorable. Cutting-edge chefs use the freshest local ingredients, creating intriguing blends of flavors that reflect the island's varied cultural backgrounds. Events such as the Great Waikoloa Food, Wine and Music Fest at the Hilton Waikoloa Village, and Cuisines of the Sun at the Mauna Lani Bay Hotel draw hundreds of guests to starlighted open-air dinners celebrating the bounty of the isle's land and waters.

As the bulk of Big Island tourism is on the Kona coast, the majority of restaurants are here as well, and they tend to be a bit pricey. There are also some great choices in Upcountry Waimea, North Kohala (in Kawaihae and Hāwī, both a short drive from the resort area) and on the east side of the island in Hilo. Less populated areas like Ka'ū, the Hāmākua Coast, and Puna offer limited choices for dinner, but usually at least one or two spots that do a decent plate lunch. A handful of excellent little eateries have recently cropped up in Kainaliu, near Kealakekua Bay. As more and more young people move into this area they are opening up their own businesses, from funky clothing boutiques to organic cafés.

WHAT IT COSTS				
$$$$	**$$$**	**$$**	**$**	**¢**
RESTAURANTS over $35	$27–$35	$18–$26	$10–$17	under $10

Prices are for one main course at dinner.

Kohala

American–Casual

$–$$$ ✕ **Café Pesto.** This branch of Café Pesto, in the quaint harbor town of Kawaihae, is just as popular as its sibling in Hilo. Exotic pizzas (with chili-grilled shrimp, shiitake mushrooms, and cilantro crème fraîche, for example), Asian-inspired pastas and risottos, and fresh seafood reflect the ethnic diversity of the island. Local microbrews and a full-service bar make this a good place to end the evening. ⊠ *Kawaihae Harbor Center, Hwy. 270, Kawaihae* ☎ *808/882–1071* ☐ *AE, D, DC, MC, V. $10–$29.*

$–$$ ✕ **Kawaihae Harbor Grill & Seafood Bar.** This little restaurant is always packed—there's something about the crisp green-and-white, 1850s building that draws people in. That and the fact that it smells way too good to pass up if you're hungry. The food is not adventurous but very good; fresh island fish, chicken, and ribs, all served in hearty portions. Inside, it's all vintage Hawaiana—old records, a surfboard, and hula skirts. The Seafood Bar is upstairs in a separate structure that also dates from the 1850s, and it has been a hot spot since it opened in 2003. The bar is a good place to wait until your table is ready, or to feast from the all-*pūpū* (appetizers) menu. ⊠ *Kawaihae Harbor, Hwy. 270, Kawaihae* ☎ *808/882–1368* ▤ *MC, V. $10–$24.*

Chinese

¢–$$$$ ✗ **Grand Palace Chinese Restaurant.** A reasonably priced alternative in a land of hotel dining, this restaurant offers dishes from most regions, including such standards as egg foo yung, wonton soup, chicken with snow peas, and beef with broccoli. More adventurous dishes include sautéed local seafood, lobster, and sizzling shrimp with garlic sauce. Etched-glass panels are a nice embellishment. ⊠ *King's Shops at Waikoloa Village, 250 Waikoloa Beach Dr., Kohala Coast* ☎ *808/886–6668* ▤ *AE, DC, MC, V. $9–$40.*

Contemporary–Hawaiian

$$$$ ✗ **Hale Samoa at Kona Village Resort.** Formal and romantic, this Kona Village restaurant has a magical atmosphere, especially at sunset. In a Samoan setting with screens and candles, you can feast on five-course prix-fixe dinners that change daily. Specialties may include papaya-and-coconut bisque, duck stuffed with andouille sausage, or wok-charred prime strip loin. Reservations can be made only on the day you want to dine. ⊠ *Kona Village Resort, Hwy. 19, 12 mi north of Kailua-Kona, North Kona Coast* ☎ *808/325–5555* ⚠ *Reservations essential* ▤ *AE, DC, MC, V* ⊘ *Closed Wed., Fri., and 1st wk in Dec. $65–$90.*

★ $$$–$$$$ ✗ **The Batik at Mauna Kea Beach Hotel.** For the hotel's elegant signature restaurant—with its glass-enclosed, split-level waterfront dining room—executive chef Thomas Woods combines French-Mediterranean elements with Indonesian influences to create dazzling dishes such as a macadamia-nut-crusted ono with lemongrass-coconut emulsion. Most of the staff has been here for 15 years, so the service is seamless. ⊠ *Mauna Kea Beach Hotel, 62-100 Mauna Kea Beach Dr., Kohala Coast* ☎ *808/882–5810* ▤ *AE, D, DC, MC, V* ⊘ *Closed Mon. and Tues. $31–$48.*

$$$–$$$$ ✗ **Brown's Beach House at the Fairmont Orchid Hawai'i.** This waterfront
Fodor'sChoice wonder is well worth the splurge—the menu is inventive (but not too
★ inventive), and the wine list is excellent. Though you can order steak here, the seafood is really where it's happening. Their crab-crusted ono is a little piece of heaven, sitting on clouds of wasabi mashed potatoes. Leave room for dessert; the sweets change regularly, but they're always worth the indulgence. Local musicians play nightly on the grassy knoll outside. ⊠ *Fairmont Orchid Hawai'i, 1 N. Kanikū Dr., Kohala Coast* ☎ *808/885–2000* ▤ *AE, D, DC, MC, V* ⊘ *No lunch. $31–$50.*

$$$–$$$$ ✗ **Kamuela Provision Company at the Hilton Waikoloa Village.** Quiet guitar music, tables set along a breezy lānai, and a sweeping view of the Kohala-Kona coastline are the perfect accompaniments to the elegant

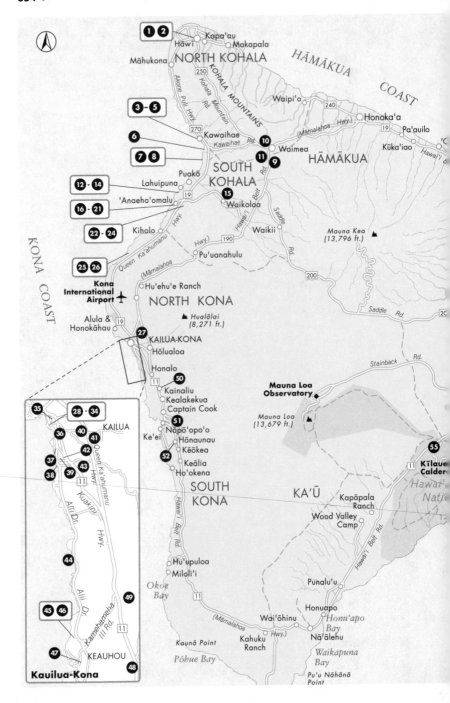

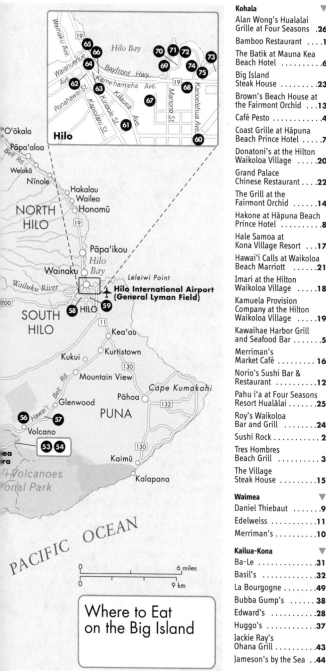

Hilo

19
65
66
64
62
63
61
70 71 72 73
69
74
75
68
67
60

Hilo Bay
Wainaku Ave.
Waianuenue Ave.
Bayfront Hwy.
Kamehameha Ave.
Ponahawai St.
Kapiolani St.
Kinoole St.
Kilauea Ave.
Kanoelehua Ave.
Manono St.

'O'ōkala
Pāpa'aloa
Welokā
Nīnole
Hakalau
Wailea
Honomū

NORTH HILO
19

Pāpa'ikou
Hilo Bay
Wainaku
Hilo Bay
Leleiwi Point

Wailuku River
200

SOUTH HILO
58 HILO 59
11

Hilo International Airport
(General Lyman Field)

Kea'au
Kukui
Kurtistown
130
Mountain View
Glenwood
Pāhoa
132
56 57
Volcano
PUNA
53 54
Kaimū

Cape Kumakahi

Kalapana

PACIFIC OCEAN

0   6 miles
0   9 km

**Where to Eat
on the Big Island**

yet down-to-earth Hawai'i regional cuisine. Popular are the bouillabaisse with *nori crostini* and the Parker Ranch rib-eye steak with green peppercorn sauce. This is a great place to sip cocktails—the adjacent Wine Bar makes for a romantic evening in itself, with an appetizer menu and more than 40 labels available by the glass. ⊠ *Hilton Waikoloa Village, 425 Waikoloa Beach Dr., Kohala Coast* ☎ *808/886–1234* ▤ *AE, D, DC, MC, V* ⊗ *No lunch. $28–$52.*

★ $$–$$$$ ✕ **Alan Wong's Hualalai Grille at the Four Seasons Resort Hualālai.** The menu changes regularly, depending on availability of local produce, fish, and meat, but expect the sort of "fusion" fare you'd find in a top-notch New York or San Francisco restaurant. The added bonus is that you can sit outside and enjoy a balmy breezes. The food is surprisingly reasonable for what you get and where you're eating. You could easily make a meal out of a selection of pūpū. The wine list is extensive and well-chosen, and servers are extremely well-versed and helpful. ⊠ *Four Seasons Resort Hualālai, 100 Ka'ūpūlehu Dr., North Kona Coast* ⌕ *Reservations essential* ▤ *AE, DC, MC, V* ⊗ *Closed Wed., Fri., and 1st wk in Dec. $18–$90.*

★ $$–$$$$ ✕ **Coast Grille at Hāpuna Beach Prince Hotel.** This is a beautiful spot, with high ceilings and a lānai overlooking the ocean. It offers perhaps the best seafood menu on the island, including loads of fresh oysters and creative Pacific Rim dishes like pan-seared *opah* (moonfish) in cardamom sauce and, when available, delicate farm-raised moi, in ancient times enjoyed only by chiefs. Don't overlook the appetizer sampler with seared 'ahi and tempura sushi, and save room for warm Valrhona chocolate cake. If you're in the mood for an early dinner (before 6:30 PM), Coast Grille has a selection of very reasonably priced three-course prix-fixe meals. ⊠ *Hāpuna Beach Prince Hotel, 62-100 Kauna'oa Dr., Kohala Coast* ☎ *808/880–3192* ▤ *AE, D, DC, MC, V* ⊗ *No lunch. $18–$36.*

$$–$$$$ ✕ **Hawai'i Calls at Waikoloa Beach Marriott.** With its retro art calling to mind the '20s to the '50s, Hawai'i Calls offers a nostalgic taste of the islands. The menu, however, is contemporary and fresh, changing seasonally, with specialties such as moi, seared crispy and served with coconut rice, pickled ginger, and spicy cucumber salad. Don't miss the macadamia-chocolate tart with vanilla ice cream. The spacious outdoor setting is lovely—ask for a table near the koi pond and waterfall—and a great place to watch the sun set as tiki torches light up the gardens. The adjacent Clipper Lounge serves tropical drinks and features a bistro menu. ⊠ *Waikoloa Beach Marriott, 69-275 Waikoloa Beach Dr., Kohala Coast* ☎ *808/886–6789* ▤ *AE, D, DC, MC, V. $20–$42.*

$$–$$$$ ✕ **Pahu i'a at the Four Seasons Resort Hualālai.** *Pahu i'a* means "aquarium," so it's fitting that a 9- by 4-foot aquarium in the entrance casts
Fodor's Choice   a dreamy light through this exquisite restaurant. Presentation is para-
★   mount—tables are beautifully set, with handblown glassware—and the food tastes as good as it looks. Asian-influenced dishes stand out for their layers of flavor. Don't miss the three sashimi and three caviar appetizers, or the crispy whole moi served with Asian slaw, black beans, and sweet chili-lime vinaigrette. Breakfast is also superb; there's a buffet, as well as a menu. Their lemon ricotta pancakes are so good they should be illegal. Reserve a table on the patio and you may be able to

spot whales while dining. At sunset, the oceanfront tables in the upstairs Lava Lounge are an excellent spot to take it all in. ⊠ *Four Seasons Resort Hualālai, 100 Kaʻūpūlehu Dr., North Kona Coast* ☎ *808/325–8000* 🖃 *AE, D, DC, MC, V* ☺ *No lunch. $25–$48.*

$$–$$$ ✕ **Roy's Waikoloa Bar & Grill.** You can easily fill up on the enormous selection of appetizers at Roy Yamaguchi's cool and classy place overlooking a lake. If you want a full meal, try the blackened island ʻahi with spicy soy-mustard-butter sauce, or jade-pesto steamed Hawaiian whitefish with cilantro, ginger, and garlic. An extensive wine-by-the-glass list offers good pairing options. Be forewarned that the place tends to get noisy. ⊠ *King's Shops at Waikoloa Village, 250 Waikoloa Beach Dr., Kohala Coast* ☎ *808/886–4321* ⊕ *www.roysrestaurant.com* 🖃 *AE, D, DC, MC, V. $18–$29.*

$–$$$ ✕ **Bamboo Restaurant.** It's out of the way, but the food at this spot in the heart of Hāwī is good and the service has a country flair. Creative entrées feature fresh island fish prepared several ways. The Thai-style fish, for example, combines lemongrass, Kaffir lime leaves, and coconut milk—best washed down with a passion-fruit margarita or passion-fruit iced tea. Bamboo finishes, bold artwork, and an old unfinished wooden floor make the restaurant cozy. Local musicians entertain on Friday and Saturday night. ⊠ *Hwy. 270, Hāwī* ☎ *808/889–5555* 🖃 *MC, V* ☺ *Closed Mon. No dinner Sun. $15–$28.*

Italian

★ $$–$$$$ ✕ **Donatoni's at the Hilton Waikoloa Village.** This romantic restaurant overlooking the boat canal resembles an Italian villa and serves scrumptious dishes with the subtle sauces of northern Italy. From mahimahi with marinated artichokes to fettuccine with Hawaiian lobster, this intimate place sets out to please. Be sure to look over the Italian wine and champagne list. ⊠ *425 Waikoloa Beach Dr., Kohala Coast* ☎ *808/886–1234* 🖃 *AE, D, DC, MC, V* ☺ *No lunch. $18–$46.*

¢–$ ✕ **Merriman's Market Café.** From Peter Merriman, one of Hawaiʻi's star chefs, comes a more affordable alternative to his upscale Waimea and Maui restaurants. The simple but delicious Mediterranean-influenced menu includes a variety of pasta dishes, tasty appetizers, and some of the island's best salads. Its huge patio has quickly become a favorite for locals and visitors alike, which means you could have a bit of a wait for a table. ⊠ *King's Shops at Waikoloa Village, 250 Waikoloa Beach Dr., Kohala Coast* ☎ *808/886–1700* 🖃 *AE, MC, V. $9–$16.*

Japanese

$$$–$$$$ ✕ **Hakone Steakhouse & Sushi Bar at the Hāpuna Beach Prince Hotel.** It's hard not to start whispering in this tranquil and graceful restaurant. Choose from exquisite Japanese sukiyaki, *shabu shabu* (thin slices of beef cooked in broth), and the selections at the elaborate sushi bar. The broad selection of sake (try a sakitini, a martini made with sake) is guaranteed to enliven your meal. The best time to visit is on a Friday or Saturday night when the restaurant serves a great dinner buffet. ⊠ *Hāpuna Beach Prince Hotel, 62-100 Kaunaʻoa Dr., Kohala Coast* ☎ *808/880–3192* 🖃 *AE, D, DC, MC, V* ☺ *No lunch. $34–$45.*

$$–$$$$ ✕ **Imari at the Hilton Waikoloa Village.** This elegant restaurant, complete with waterfalls and a teahouse, serves sukiyaki and tempura aimed to please mainland tastes. Beyond the impressive display of Imari porcelain at the entrance, you can find *teppanyaki* (beef or shrimp cooked table-side), shabu shabu (beef and vegetables in broth), and an outstanding sushi bar. Impeccable service by kimono-clad waitresses adds to the quiet refinement. ⊠ *425 Waikoloa Beach Dr., Kohala Coast* ☎ *808/886–1234* ▭ *AE, D, DC, MC, V* ⊗ *No lunch. $25–$52.*

$$–$$$ ✗ **Norio's Sushi Bar & Restaurant.** Sashimi and sushi are lovingly prepared with the freshest possible fish (both from the ocean and from the numerous aqua farms at the nearby National Energy Laboratory). The flounder, 'ahi, and abalone are not to be missed. Some equally delicious hot dishes include baked sea scallops and miso butterfish. The assortment of tropical drinks is tasty, as is the sinfully good chocolate fondue, served with an assortment of tropical fruits. ⊠ *Fairmont Orchid Hawai'i, 1 N. Kaniku Dr., Kohala Coast* ☎ *808/885–2000* ▭ *AE, D, DC, MC, V* ⊗ *Closed Tues. and Wed. No lunch. $20–$30.*

$$–$$$ ✗ **Sushi Rock.** In Hāwī's funky Without Boundaries, Sushi Rock offers both the island's freshest raw fish (including lots of new-wave California-style rolls and a terrific Hawaiian-style ceviche), and a variety of cooked seafood, noodle dishes, and salads. Everything is served beautifully either at the sushi bar, at one of the handful of indoor tables, or on the covered back patio. There's also a full bar. ⊠ *55-3435 Akoni Pule Hwy., Hāwī* ☎ *808/889–5900* ▭ *AE, DC, MC, V* ⊗ *No lunch. $20–$30.*

Mexican

$–$$ ✗ **Tres Hombres Beach Grill.** The food is decent, if a bit pricey, but what you come here for are the marvelous margaritas. They're in all sorts of tropical flavors, including *lillikoi* (passion fruit). Lunch is the usual Mexican combination platters (tacos, enchiladas, chiles rellenos) as well as burgers and sandwiches. Dinner entrées include fresh fish, killer fajitas, bean-and-rice combinations, and steaks. ⊠ *Kawaihae Harbor Center, Hwy. 270, Kawaihae* ☎ *808/882–1031* ▭ *MC, V. $11–$20.*

Steak Houses

★ **$$$$** ✗ **The Grill at the Fairmont Orchid Hawai'i.** Set back from the beach, the Grill is a martini-and-filet-mignon kind of place. The menu is heavier on meats (leaving the seafood to the nearby Brown's Beach House), and you'd be hard-pressed to find a better steak on the island. The service is impeccable, the wine list superb, and the macadamia-nut pie may be the best dessert we've ever had. Open-air seating is available, and the tables are still close enough to the ocean to catch the breeze. ⊠ *Fairmont Orchid Hawai'i, 1 N. Kanikū Dr., Kohala Coast* ☎ *808/885–2000* ⌂ *Reservations essential* ▭ *AE, D, DC, MC, V. $36–$59.*

BEST BREAKFAST

Bubba Gump's (Kailua-Kona). A chain with the best outdoor seating in Kailua-Kona and cinnamon-raisin French toast.

Café 100 (Hilo). Local destination for *loco moco* on the Hilo side.

Ken's House of Pancakes (Hilo). Like IHOP, but with Spam.

Kona Bay Beach Club (Kailua-Kona). Excellent, varied menu, served on a huge outdoor deck; delicious Mexican breakfasts.

Pahu i'a at the Four Seasons Hualālai (Kohala). Hands-down the best fancy brunch on the island.

$–$$$$ ✕ **Big Island Steak House.** This is a good old-fashioned steak house with a bit of Blue Hawai'i kitsch thrown in. This place is always a safe bet if you're in the mood for meat, and the portions are huge. Seafood is also on the menu, but why order scallops at a steak house? There's also a bar and an outdoor dining area overlooking a lake. ⊠ *King's Shops at Waikoloa Village, 250 Waikoloa Beach Dr., Kohala Coast* ☎ *808/ 886–8805* ▤ *AE, D, MC, V* ⊘ *No lunch. $15–$43.*

$–$$$ ✕ **The Village Steak House.** Sunset views overlooking the golf course and steaks are the highlights here. Start with *pūpū* like skewered shrimp, crab cakes, or Hawaiian-Chinese mushrooms. Steaks come in all sizes and include filet mignon, New York strip, T-bone, and porterhouse. Other entrées include fresh island fish, chicken with orange sauce, baby back ribs with passion fruit–hoisin sauce, pork chops with pineapple, and curry-coconut prawns. There's a quiet, comfortable clubhouse atmosphere. Reservations are recommended. ⊠ *68-1792 Melia St., Waikoloa* ☎ *808/ 883–9644* ▤ *AE, D, MC, V* ⊘ *Closed Mon. $15–$30.*

Waimea

Contemporary

$$–$$$$ ✕ **Daniel Thiebaut.** The building that once held the historic Chock In Store, which catered to the ranching community beginning in 1900, has been transformed into an eatery with five dining areas. The store's redwood countertop now serves as one long community dining table. Collectibles abound, such as antique porcelain pieces. Chef Daniel Thiebaut's French-Asian creations include an amazing appetizer of sweet-corn crab cake with a lemongrass, coconut, and lobster sauce. Other signature dishes include Hunan-style rack of lamb served with eggplant compote, and Big Island goat cheese. ⊠ *65-1259 Kawaihae Rd., Waimea* ☎ *808/ 887–2200* ▤ *AE, D, DC, MC, V. $20–$40.*

★ **$$–$$$** ✕ **Merriman's.** This is the signature restaurant of Peter Merriman, one of the pioneers of Hawai'i regional cuisine. Merriman's is the home of the original wok-charred 'ahi, usually served with buttery Wainaku corn. If you prefer meat, try the Kahuā Ranch lamb, raised to the restaurant's specifications, or opt for the prime Kansas City Cut steak, grilled to order. The wine list includes 22 selections poured by the glass, and the staff is refreshingly knowledgeable. For true foodies, Merriman's now offers a farmers' market tour—four hours spent browsing around local ranches and food stands, culminating in a fantastic five-course meal using produce and meat bought throughout the day. ⊠ *'Opelo Plaza, 65-1227 'Opelo Rd., Waimea* ☎ *808/885–6822* ✍ *Reservations essential* ▤ *AE, MC, V. $20–$33.*

German

★ **$$–$$$$** ✕ **Edelweiss.** An authentic German *gasthaus* right in the middle of Hawai'i, Edelweiss is truly a great place. Fear not if you don't see anything you want on the menu; there are 15 to 20 daily specials that your server will rattle off without batting an eye. No one can figure out how (or why) they do it. The rack of lamb is always good, and anything ending in schnitzel is a safe bet, as are items ending in brat or braten. The chicken cordon bleu is large enough and rich enough for two. Soup (al-

The Plate Lunch Tradition

TO EXPERIENCE ISLAND HISTORY FIRST-HAND, take a seat at one of Hawaiʻi's ubiquitous "plate lunch" eateries, and order a segmented Styrofoam plate piled with rice, macaroni salad, and maybe some fiery pickled vegetable condiment. On the sugar plantations, native Hawaiians and immigrant workers from many different countries ate together in the fields, sharing food from their kaukau kits, the utilitarian version of the Japanese *bento* lunchbox. From this melting pot came the vibrant language of pidgin and its equivalent in food: the plate lunch.

At beaches and events, you can probably see a few tiny kitchens-on-wheels, another excellent venue for sampling plate lunch. These portable restaurants are descendants of lunch wagons that began selling food to plantation workers in the 1930s. Try the deep-fried chicken *katsu* (rolled in Japanese panko flour and spices). The marinated beef teriyaki is another good choice, as is miso butterfish. The noodle soup, *saimin*, with its Japanese fish stock and Chinese red-tinted barbecue pork, is a distinctly local medley. Koreans have contributed spicy barbecue *kal-bi* ribs, often served with chili-laden *kimchi* (pickled cabbage). Portuguese bean soup and tangy Filipino *adobo* stew are also favorites. The most popular Hawaiian contribution to the plate lunch is the *laulau*, a mix of meat and fish and young taro leaves, wrapped in more taro leaves and steamed.

most always what sounds like a weird combination turns out to be a real treat), salad, and coffee or tea are included in dinner prices. The wine list is decent, but c'mon, get the Hefeweizen. You won't have room for dessert with the size of their portions, but you're not missing much. If you're a potato pancake fan, call two days ahead and the kitchen will whip up a batch for you. ⊠ *Hwy. 19, Waimea* ☎ *808/885–6800* ⌂ *Reservations essential* ▭ *MC, V* ⊗ *Closed Sun. and Mon. and Sept. $21–$56.*

Kailua-Kona

American–Casual

$$–$$$ ✕ **Jameson's by the Sea.** If you can't get a table outside, Jameson's is not really worth the trip. Make sure to reserve one in advance—the waves actually splash your feet while you eat. The traditional Continental fare is decent but not amazing; fresh fish is always the best bet. ⊠ *77-6452 Aliʻi Dr., Kailua-Kona* ☎ *808/329–3195* ▭ *AE, D, DC, MC, V* ⊗ *No lunch weekends. $21–$27.*

$–$$ ✕ **Jackie Ray's Ohana Grill.** Uphill from downtown Kailua-Kona, this bright green open-air restaurant is a popular lunch destination. The chicken sandwich with avocado and Swiss is an excellent combination of flavors, and the fries are crisped to perfection. Some inventive salads and fresh fish dishes make this place worth the slight detour out of town. ⊠ *Pottery Terrace, 75-5995 Kuakini Hwy., Kailua-Kona* ▭ *MC, V. $10–$20.*

$-$$ ✕ **Rooster's.** Tucked behind some shops, an information kiosk, and table upon table of trinkets, it's easy to see why Rooster's is still such a well-kept secret. The food is best described as comfort food, but the chef adds plenty of inventive twists to old standbys like ribs and fried chicken. The dining room is small and cozy—it could even be described as romantic if Hawai'i has put you in that frame of mind. The wine list is great, focusing on an assortment of well-chosen California varietals. There's live jazz on Friday and Saturday that is surprisingly good and not at all intrusive. Once the secret's out it will probably be hard to get a table. ⊠ *Ali'i Dr., underneath Hula Cafe* ☎ 808/327–9453 ☰ *AE, MC, V* ⊗ *No lunch. $15–$25.*

¢-$ ✕ **Bubba Gump's.** Okay, it's a chain, and a chain that centers around a Tom Hanks movie, no less. Get over it. For starters, it has one of the largest oceanfront patios on the island. And the food's not bad, once you get past the silly names. Anything with popcorn shrimp in it is good, and the "Run Chicken Run" salad (a combination of chicken, Gorgonzola cheese, walnuts, and cranberries) is the perfect size for lunch. The place does a great breakfast, too, with strong coffee and plenty of options, from the cream-cheese stuffed French toast to bacon and eggs. ⊠ *75-5776 Ali'i Dr., Kailua-Kona* ☎ 808/331–8442 ☰ *MC, V. $7–$12.*

¢-$ ✕ **Kona Bay Beach Club.** This corner of Kona's waterfront complex has been cursed for over a decade, with a variety of restaurants opening and closing within a year. The Kona Bay Beach Club is turning the tide with good service, a tasteful redesign of the interior that maximizes its ocean view, and a menu that does everything well. Giving Bubba Gump's a run for its money, Kona Bay's view is just slightly better, and the coffee and breakfast menu win hands down. ⊠ *75-5770 Ali'i Dr. in Waterfront Row complex, Kailua-Kona* ☰ *MC, V. $7–$15.*

¢-$ ✕ **Kona Brewing Company & Brewpub.** One of the better additions to Kailua-Kona's restaurant and bar scene, Kona Brewing Company has an excellent and varied menu including pulled-pork quesadillas, gourmet pizzas, and a killer spinach salad with Gorgonzola cheese, macadamia nuts, all topped with strawberry dressing. Go for the beer tasting menu—it's six of the eight microbrews in miniature glasses that are roughly equivalent to two regular-size mugs. ⊠ *75-5629 Kuakini Hwy., just past Palani intersection on right, Kailua-Kona* ☎ 808/329–2739 ☰ *MC, V. $9–$15.*

¢-$ ✕ **Quinn's Almost By the Sea.** Okay, Quinn's is a bit of a dive. That said, it does have a few things going for it—the best ono sandwiches on the island, for example. It's open until 11 PM, later than any other restaurant in Kailua-Kona (except Denny's). If time gets away from you on a drive to South Point, Quinn's is awaiting your return with a cheap beer and a basket of excellent calamari. You can also have a beer at the funky bar filled with fishermen. ⊠ *75-5655A Palani Rd., Kailua-Kona* ☎ 808/ 329–3822 ☰ *MC, V. $8–$15.*

Contemporary

$$-$$$$ ✕ **Edward's.** Offering fresh seafood prepared with Mediterranean flair and an extensive wine list in a new oceanfront location downtown (in the Waterfront Row building on Ali'i Drive), Edward's is about to give Huggo's a run for their "best fine dining in town" money. The restaurant is also open for breakfast and lunch, but dinner is the best bet (prices at lunch are a bit high), especially if you call ahead and reserve an ocean-side table at sunset. ⊠ *Kanaloa at Kona, Waterfront Row, Upstairs, Kailua-Kona* ☎ 808/324–1434 ▤ *MC, V. $25–$50.*

$–$$$ ✕ **Huggo's.** This is the only restaurant in town with prices and atmosphere comparable to the splurge restaurants at the Kohala-coast resorts. Open windows extend out over the rocks at the ocean's edge, and at night you can almost touch the manta rays drawn to the spotlights. Relax with a cocktail for two and feast on fresh local seafood; the catch changes daily, and the nightly chef's special is always a good bet. **Huggo's on the Rocks,** next door, is a great outdoor bar with a floor of sand; it's become Kailua-Kona's hot spot for drinks and live music on Friday nights. ⊠ *75-5828 Kahakai Rd., off Ali'i Dr., Kailua-Kona* ☎ 808/329–1493 ▤ *AE, D, DC, MC, V. $15–$30.*

$–$$$ ✕ **Tropics Café at the Royal Kona Resort.** From the open-air dining room, you have a lovely view of boats bobbing in Kailua Bay. The restaurant serves daily breakfast buffets and is open nightly for à la carte dinners, but the place is best known for its ample seafood and prime-rib buffets on Tuesday, Friday, and Saturday nights—a good value for big eaters. The resort is within walking distance of downtown Kailua-Kona. ⊠ *75-5852 Ali'i Dr., Kailua-Kona* ☎ 808/329–3111 ▤ *AE, D, DC, MC, V. $11–$30.*

$–$$ ✕ **Kai at the Sheraton Keauhou Bay.** Aside from the lobby, this restaurant is the best-looking part of the Sheraton Keauhou Bay. Facing Keauhou Bay, Kai has a primo view. The enormous windows are left open most of the time, making it almost feel like an outdoor restaurant. The menu is limited, but each entrée is good, from the fresh local fish to the hormone-free chicken. Everything is prepared with that fusion of Pacific Rim and Continental that makes up Hawaiian cuisine. The seared 'ahi appetizer is not to be missed. Breakfast is a good bet as well; very reasonable, great buffet, and the view during the daytime is just about perfect. ⊠ *78-128 Ehukai St., Kailua-Kona* ☎ 808/930–4900 ▤ *AE, MC, V. $13–$25.*

$–$$ ✕ **O's.** Chef Amy Ferguson-Ota combines Southwestern flavors with Hawaiian regional cuisine and a touch of French cooking. There are noodles of all types, in all shapes, from all ethnic backgrounds—be they as delicate spring rolls, as a crisp garnish to an exquisite salad, or as orecchiette in Ota's tuna casserole with wok-seared spiced 'ahi and shiitake cream. ⊠ *Crossroads Shopping Center, 75-1129 Henry St., Kailua-Kona* ☎ 808/329–9222 ▤ *AE, D, DC, MC, V. $15–$22.*

French

$$–$$$ ✕ **La Bourgogne.** A genial husband-and-wife team owns this relaxing, country-style bistro with dark-wood walls and private, romantic booths. The traditional French menu has classics such as escargots, beef with a cabernet sauvignon sauce, rack of lamb with roasted garlic and rosemary, and a less-traditional venison with a pomegranate glaze. Call well in advance for reservations. ⊠ *77-6400 Nālani St., Kailua-Kona* ☎ 808/ 329–6711 ⚑ *Reservations essential* ▤ *AE, D, DC, MC, V* ☺ *Closed Sun. and Mon. No lunch. $20–$32.*

$ ✕ **Peaberry & Galette.** This little creperie is a welcome addition to the neighborhood. It serves Illy espresso, excellent sweet and savory crepes, and rich desserts like lemon cheesecake and chocolate mousse that are made fresh daily. It's got a cool, urban-café vibe, and is a nice place to hang for a bit if you're waiting for a film at the theater next door, or just feel like taking a break from paradise to sip a decent espresso and flip through the latest *W.* ⊠ *Keauhou Shopping Center, 78-6740 Makolea St., Kailua-Kona* ☎ 808/322–6020 ⊟ *MC, V. $10–$15.*

Hawaiian Fast Food

¢ ✕ **Ba-Le.** Comparable to Kona Mix Plate in terms of prices, food quality, and local cred, Ba-Le serves a great plate lunch. It also has tasty Vietnamese-influenced food, such as their popular croissant sandwiches stuffed with mint, lemongrass, sprouts, and your choice from a variety of Vietnamese-style meats. There are 20 other shops throughout the state, but it's Hawaiian-owned and operated, so the place doesn't feel like a chain. ⊠ *Kona Coast Shopping Center, 74-5588 Palani Rd., Kailua-Kona* ☎ 808/327–1212 ⊟ *No credit cards. $5–$7.*

¢ ✕ **Kona Mix Plate.** Don't be surprised if you find yourself rubbing elbows with lots of hungry locals at this inconspicuous Kona lunch spot. The antithesis of a tourist trap, this casual island favorite with fluorescent lighting and wooden tables is all about the food. Try the teriyaki chicken, shrimp tempura, or *katsu*—a chicken breast fried with bread crumbs and served with a sweet sauce. ⊠ *341 Palani St., Kailua-Kona* ☎ 808/329–8104 ⊟ *No credit cards* ⊙ *Closed Sun. $5–$7.*

Italian

$–$$$ ✕ **Basil's.** This tiny traditional trattoria is nothing special, really—the tablecloths are checkered, the candles are in chianti bottles, there's spaghetti on the menu, and it always feels a little hot and greasy inside. That said, the pizza is decent, the beer's cheap, and you can't beat the location. It's on Ali'i Drive in downtown Kailua-Kona, right across the street from the ocean. ⊠ *75-5707 Ali'i Dr., Kailua-Kona* ☎ 808/326–7836 ⊟ *MC, V. $12–$30.*

Japanese

$–$$$ ✕ **Kenichi Pacific.** With its black-lacquer tables and lipstick-red banquettes, Kenichi's seems a little out of place in this small strip mall. The location keeps many tourists from finding it, even though it's been open for several years now. This is where everyone in Kailua-Kona goes when they feel like splurging on top-notch sushi. It's a little on the spendy side, but it's worth it. The sashimi is so fresh it melts in your mouth, and the signature rolls are inventive and tasty. For vegetarians, the Austin roll—tempura asparagus—is fish-free and delicious. ⊠ *Keauhou Shopping Center, 78-6831 Ali'i Dr., Kailua-Kona* ☎ 808/322–9140 ⊟ *No credit cards. $17–$30.*

Mexican

$–$$ ✕ **Pancho & Lefty's.** Across the street from the Kona Village Shopping Center, Pancho & Lefty's is a typical Tex-Mex place—great for nachos and margaritas (watch out, they pour 'em strong) on a lazy afternoon. Some of the items on the menu are expensive, and some of the combos are described exactly the same way in other sections of the menu for less, so read carefully. ⊠ *75-5719 Ali'i Dr., Kailua-Kona* ☎ 808/326–2171 ⊟ *MC, V. $12–$18.*

¢ ✕ **Tacos El Unico.** At last, good Mexican food at reasonable prices on the Big Island. You can find an array of soft-taco choices (beef and chicken, among others), burritos, quesadillas, and great homemade tamales. Order at the counter, take a seat outside at one of a dozen yellow tables with blue umbrellas, and enjoy all the good flavors served up in those red plastic baskets. ⊠ *Kona Marketplace, 75-5729 Ali'i Dr., Kailua-Kona* ☎ *808/326–4033* ▭ *No credit cards. $3–$7.*

Thai

¢–$ ✕ **Orchid Thai Cuisine.** This reasonably priced, family-run restaurant is off the beaten track in a small strip mall. It's cheerfully decorated with purple-and-gold fabrics, and orchids (real and fake) abound. Entrées range from basic curries (red, green, yellow, and "evil") to barbecue hen with lemongrass and garlic. Don't miss the tasty summer rolls. Top off your meal with a desert of mango and sticky rice. ⊠ *77-5563 Kaiwi St., Suite B 27–28, Kailua-Kona* ☎ *808/327–9437* ▭ *MC, V* ☉ *Closed Sun. $7–$14.*

¢–$ ✕ **Thai Rin Restaurant.** The Thai owner at this old-timer in Ali'i Sunset Plaza is likely to take your order, cook it, and bring it to your table himself. The menu includes five curries, a green-papaya salad, and a popular platter that combines spring rolls, satay, beef salad, and *tom yum* (lemongrass soup). ⊠ *75-5799 Ali'i Dr., Kailua-Kona* ☎ *808/329–2929* ▭ *AE, D, DC, MC, V. $9–$17.*

South Kona

American–Casual

¢–$$ ✕ **Ke'ei Café.** This casual restaurant is in a plantation-style building 15 minutes south of Kona. Delicious dinners with Brazilian, Asian, and European flavors utilize fresh ingredients provided by local farmers. Try the Thai red curry or wok-seared 'ahi accompanied by a selection from the extensive wine list. ⊠ *Hwy. 11, ½ mi south of Kainaliu, Hōnaunau* ☎ *808/328–8451* ⌔ *Reservations essential* ▭ *No credit cards* ☉ *Closed Sun. and Mon. $9–$19.*

¢–$ ✕ **Café Nasturtium.** This café is tucked into a cheerful little red-orange house in Kainaliu, about 10-minutes from Kailua-Kona. They've planted signs before and after the restaurant, so you'll know when it's coming up and when you've passed it. They serve only organic food here, some of it vegan and all of it very good, from soups made fresh daily to 'ahi tuna sandwiches to homemade *lilikoi* (passion fruit) sorbet. The back patio is sunny and green, with flowers and vines climbing the walls. The downside: service is painfully slow, and the hours are erratic. Call ahead to make sure it's open. ⊠ *Hwy. 11, Kainaliu* ☎ *808/322–5083* ▭ *MC, V* ☉ *Closed weekends. $9–$15.*

★ ¢–$ ✕ **Manago Hotel.** About 20-minutes south of Kailua-Kona, Manago is a time-warp experience. A vintage neon sign identifies the hotel, and Formica tables, ceiling fans, and venetian blinds add to the flavor of this film-noir spot. The T-shirts (which are great if you need to bring back a gift for anyone) brag that the place has the best pork chops in town, and it's not false advertising. The fresh fish is excellent as well, especially ono and butterfish. Unless you request otherwise, the fish is all sautéed with a special butter-soy sauce concoction (always good, don't worry). Meals come with rice for the table (served family style, of course) and an assortment of side dishes that change from time to time. ✉ 82-6155 *Māmalahoa Hwy., Captain Cook* ☎ 808/323–2642 ▬ *D, DC, MC, V* ⊙ *Closed Mon. $7–$12.*

Japanese

¢–$ ✕ **Teshima's.** Locals show up at Teshima's whenever they're in the mood for fresh sashimi, puffy shrimp tempura, or *hekka* (beef and vegetables cooked in an iron pot) at a reasonable price. You might also want to try a *teishoku* (tray) of assorted Japanese delicacies. The service is laid-back and friendly. The restaurant is 15-minutes south of Kailua-Kona. ✉ *Māmalahoa Hwy., Honalo* ☎ 808/322–9140 ▬ *No credit cards. $8–$16.*

Volcano

American–Casual

¢–$$ ✕ **Lava Rock Café.** For a decent meal, a drink, or Internet access, head to the Lava Rock, which serves breakfast and lunch daily and dinner Tuesday through Saturday in a breezy, pinewood-lattice setting. Dishes range from chicken salad to New York steak, beverages from cappuccino to wine. ✉ *Old Volcano Hwy., behind Kīlauea General Store, Volcano* ☎ 808/967–8526 ⊙ *No dinner Sun.* ▬ *MC, V. $7–$18.*

¢–$ ✕ **Volcano Golf & Country Club.** A local favorite for its large portions and classic, greasy breakfasts. Stop by for a breakfast burger (with fried egg, cheese, and your choice of meat) and a cup of local coffee. If it's lunchtime, you can't beat the burgers. ✉ *Pi'i Mauna Dr., off Hwy. 11, Volcano* ☎ 808/967–8228 ⊙ *No dinner* ▬ *MC, V. $5–$12.*

Contemporary

$–$$$$ ✕ **Kīlauea Lodge.** Chef Albert Jeyte combines contemporary trends with traditional cooking styles from the mainland, France, and his native Hamburg, Germany. Entrées include venison, duck à l'orange with an apricot-mustard glaze, and authentic *hasenpfeffer* (braised rabbit) served with Jeyte's signature sauerbraten. Built in 1937 as a YMCA camp, the restaurant still has the original "Friendship Fireplace" made from stones from around the world. The roaring fire, koa-wood tables, and warm lighting make the sunny main building feel like a lodge. ✉ *Old Volcano Hwy., Volcano Village* ☎ 808/967–7366 ▬ *AE, MC, V* ⊙ *No lunch. $17–$38.*

Italian

$–$$ ✕ **Kiawe Kitchen.** Everyone around here says the same thing: "Kiawe has awesome pizza, but it's a little expensive for pizza." And it's true—the wood-fired pizza has a perfect thin crust and an authentic Italian taste, but you have to be prepared to spend around $15 on a typical pie. Food options are limited in this area, though. Go for it. ✉ *19-4005 Old Volcano Rd., Volcano* ☎ 808/967–7711 ▬ *MC, V* ⊙ *Closed Wed. $15–$25.*

Thai

¢–$ ✕ **Thai Thai Restaurant.** The food is authentic, and the prices are reasonable at this little Volcano Village find. A steaming-hot plate of curry or a dish of pad thai noodles is the perfect antidote to a chilly day on the volcano. The chicken satay is excellent—the peanut dipping sauce the perfect match of sweet and spicy. Be careful when you order, as "medium" is more than spicy enough even for hard-core chili addicts. The service is warm and friendly. ⊠ *19-4084 Old Volcano Rd., Volcano* ☎ *808/ 967–7969* ⊙ *No lunch* ▤ *MC, V. $9–$16.*

Hilo

American–Casual

$–$$$ ✕ **Café Pesto.** Both branches of Café Pesto—here and in Kawaihae—are equally popular. Fresh local seafood is one of the best reasons to stop by for dinner. Local microbrews and a full-service bar make this a good place to end the evening. ⊠ *308 Kamehameha Ave., Hilo* ☎ *808/969– 6640* ▤ *AE, D, DC, MC, V. $10–$29.*

$–$$$ ✕ **The Seaside.** The Nakagawa family has been running this eatery since the early 1920s. The latest son to manage the place has spruced it up a bit with tablecloths and candles, but the decor is still bare-bones. No matter, since it serves some of the freshest fish on the island. (Not a surprise, as the fish come from the restaurant's own aqua farm.) Islanders travel great distances for the fried *āholehole* (young Hawaiian flagtail). Not a fish eater? Try the grilled lamb chops, chicken, or prime rib. Arrive before sunset and request a table on the patio for a view of the egrets roosting around the fish ponds. ⊠ *1790 Kalaniana'ole Ave., Hilo* ☎ *808/ 935–8825* ▤ *AE, DC, MC, V* ⊙ *Closed Mon. No lunch. $11–$27.*

$–$$ ✕ **Harrington's.** A great view and a daily happy hour make this steak-and-seafood restaurant on Reed's Bay a popular place. You can't go wrong with either the catch of the day served in a tangy citrus-wasabi beurre blanc or the peppercorn steak. The garlic-laced Slavic steak is a specialty of the house. For lunch try the Harrington's burger, served with cream-cheese aioli. ⊠ *135 Kalaniana'ole Ave., Hilo* ☎ *808/961–4966* ▤ *MC, V. $16–$25.*

$–$$ ✕ **Queen's Court at the Hilo Hawaiian Hotel.** Queen's Court is known for one thing: buffets. On the weekends the spread includes seafood (Friday and Saturday) and Hawaiian fare (Sunday), but during the week it's prime rib every night. The prime rib's not great, but the seafood specialties are. ⊠ *1730 Kamehameha Ave., Hilo* ☎ *808/935–8711* ▤ *AE, D, DC, MC, V. $16–$25.*

¢–$$ ✕ **Hilo Bay Café.** Not the greatest setting (in a strip mall that contains Office Max and Wal-Mart), but fantastic food. When in season, the out-of-this-world heirloom tomato salad puts any mainland variation to shame. The vegan offerings, which range from garlic fries to pot pie, are good enough to seduce meat-eaters. Other excellent options include cheese fondue, pepper steak, roasted chicken breast stuffed with pine nuts and garlic cream cheese, and any of the salads (the beet salad is a stand-out). Prices are exceedingly reasonable. ⊠ *315 Makaala St., Hilo* ☎ *808/935–4939* ▤ *AE, DC, MC, V. $7–$20.*

¢–$$ ✕ **Uncle Billy's.** Uncle Billy's is pure Hawaiian kitsch—right out of 1930s Hollywood—but the thatch roofs, tinkling capiz-shell wind chimes, and Tahitian-print curtains add to the fun, as does a free nightly hula show. The show and the ambience are the reasons to visit; the food is so-so. Choose from mahimahi meunière, teriyaki chicken, and local specialties. ⊠ *Hilo Bay Hotel, 87 Banyan Dr., Hilo* ☎ *808/935–0861* ☰ *AE, D, DC, MC, V* ☺ *No lunch. $9–$25.*

¢–$ ✕ **Ken's House of Pancakes.** For years this 24-hour coffee shop between the airport and the hotels along Banyan Drive has been a gathering place for Hilo residents. As its name implies, Ken's serves good pancakes, but there are about 180 other items to from which to choose. Wednesday is prime rib night. ⊠ *1730 Kamehameha Ave., Hilo* ☎ *808/935–8711* ☰ *AE, D, DC, MC, V. $8–$15.*

Contemporary

★ $–$$$ ✕ **Restaurant Kaikodo.** Now that the service has improved, Kaikodo is back on top of its game. Slight changes have improved the menu. The salmon sauteed in miso butter and served with crab on buckwheat noodles is excellent, but most nights the best bet is the seafood special. It's always something caught locally and prepared in an inventive way. The lamb and steak dishes are also excellent. Desserts are good, too. ⊠ *60 Keawe St., Hilo* ☎ *808/961–2558* ☰ *AE, D, DC, MC, V. $16–$35.*

Hawaiian Fast Food

¢–$ ✕ **Café 100.** This popular local restaurant is famous for its tasty *loco moco,* prepared in more than a dozen ways, and its dirt-cheap breakfast and lunch specials. (You can stuff yourself for $3 if you order right.) If you're looking for a salad, keep walking. ⊠ *969 Kīlauea Ave., Hilo* ☎ *808/935–8683* ☰ *No credit cards. $5–$10.*

¢–$ ✕ **Kūhiō Grille.** There's no ambience to speak of, and water is served in unbreakable plastic, but if you're searching for local fare—that eclectic and undefinable fusion of ethnic cuisines—Kūhiō Grille is a must. Sam Araki serves a 1-pound *laulau* (a steamed bundle of taro leaves and pork) that is worth the trip. This diner at the edge of Hilo's largest mall opens at 6 AM. ⊠ *Prince Kūhiō Shopping Plaza, 111 E. Puainako St., at Hwy. 11* ☎ *808/959–2336* ☰ *AE, MC, V. $5–$14.*

¢ ✕ **Ba-Le.** This place serves a great plate lunch, but people come here for the tasty sandwiches—mixtures of mint, lemongrass, sprouts, and your choice of Vietnamese-style meats served on a croissant or crusty French bread. ⊠ *111 E. Puainako, Hilo* ☎ *808/959–1300* ☰ *No credit cards. $5–$7.*

¢ ✕ **Blane's Drive-In.** With a vast menu second only to Ken's House of Pancakes, Blane's serves up everything from standard hamburgers to chicken *katsu.* There's a mean plate lunch with tons of fresh fish for only $7. The slow-cooked homemade chili and sticky white rice is a meal in itself, and costs less than $3. ⊠ *217 Wainuenue Ave., Hilo* ☎ *808/969–9494* ☰ *No credit cards. $2–$7.*

Italian

$–$$$ ✕ **Pescatore.** With dim lights, stately high-back chairs, and dark-wood paneling, Pescatore conjures up an Italian trattoria. The surprisingly authentic Italian cuisine includes items like lasagne, chicken marsala, and chicken or veal parmigiana. Lunch consists of Italian-style sandwiches; breakfast, served on weekends only, features omelets and crepes. Families love the pastas made to please choosy children. ⊠ *235 Keawe St., at Haili St., Hilo* ☎ *808/969–9090* ☰ *AE, D, DC, MC, V. $15–$29.*

Japanese

$–$$$ ✕ **Nihon Restaurant.** This open, airy dining room has a great view of Hilo Bay. Servers are dressed in colorful kimonos, and Japanese art and music add to the ambience. The menu offers a wide choice of authentic Japanese cuisine including beef, pork, chicken, and seafood dishes. Try the soba noodles, the teriyaki steak, and the grilled butterfish marinated in a rich miso-soy sauce. A sushi bar provides a full range of wonderful and varied sushi and sashimi. The restaurant is adjacent to the Lili'uokalani Gardens. ✉ *123 Lihiwai St., Hilo* ☎ *808/969–1133* ⊟ *AE, MC, V* ⊗ *Closed Sun. $12–$30.*

¢–$ ✕ **Miyo's.** Tucked behind a karaoke bar at the Waiakea Villas Hotel, Miyo's large open dining room overlooks a beautiful pond. The menu focuses on fresh and delicious sashimi, complemented by fluffy tempura and not-too-sweet teriyaki. Each dish is served on a platter with salad, miso soup, and rice. Most meals are under $10, making Miyo's a terrific find. ✉*400 Hualani St., Hilo* ☎*808/935–2273* ⊟*MC, V* ⊗ *Closed Sun. $8–$15.*

Mexican

¢–$ ✕ **Island Cantina.** They make the guacamole at your table at this excellent Mexican eatery. The enchiladas are soft and fresh, and the nachos are piled high with gooey cheese, beans, and sour cream. There are also Mexican-influenced fish dishes. The only drawback is the lack of margaritas (they're waiting on a liquor license), but for the time being you can BYOB. ✉ *110 Kalākaua St., Hilo* ☎ *808/969–7009* ⊟ *D, DC, MC, V. $6–$15.*

Thai

¢–$ ✕ **Naung Mai.** There's not much to this downtown eatery: five tables, three booths, and owner Alisa Rung Khongnok hard at work in the kitchen. It's a bit hard to find, but fresh, reasonably priced meals make it worth seeking out. It may be the best Thai food on the island. For those who like to pair spicy curry with cold beer, feel free to pick up a six-pack at the grocery store up the street. Naung Mai charges $2 for glasses. ✉ *86 Kīlauea Ave., Hilo* ☎ *808/934–7540* ⊟ *MC, V* ⊗ *Closed Sun. No lunch Wed. or Sat. $8–$11.*

¢–$ ✕ **Royal Siam.** A downtown Hilo fixture, this authentic Thai eatery offers little ambience. But you don't need a dramatic view when you can choose from a menu that includes five kinds of curries and plenty of stir-fried meals. The tangy stir-fried garlic shrimp with coconut milk and wild mushrooms is particularly good. ✉ *70 Mamo St., Hilo* ☎ *808/961–6100* ⊟ *AE, D, DC, MC, V* ⊗ *Closed Sun. $7–$12.*

WHERE TO STAY

You'll almost always be able to find a room on the Big Island, but you might not get your first choice if you wait until the last minute. Make reservations six months to a year in advance if you're visiting during the winter season (December 15 through April 15). The week after Easter Sunday, when the Merrie Monarch Festival is in full swing, all of Hilo's rooms are booked. Kailua-Kona is packed in mid-October during the Ironman World Triathlon Championship. (Even tougher than trying to find a room at these times is trying to find a rental car.)

There are literally hundreds of vacation condo rentals in Kailua-Kona, and along the Kohala Coast, which is a good way to get more space and save some money by eating in (although it's easy to amass a huge bill at the grocery store, so you still have to be careful).

Hotel package deals are often available in all price categories and may include a rental car, meals, spa treatments, golf, and other activities. Children under 17 can sometimes stay for free. Check with a travel agent or visit the listed Web sites.

If you choose a B&B, inn, or an out-of-the-way hotel, explain your expectations fully and ask plenty of questions before booking. Be clear about your travel and location needs. Some places require stays of two or three days. When booking, ask about car-rental arrangements, as many B&B networks offer discounted rates. No matter where you stay, you'll want to rent a car—preferably one with four-wheel drive. This is imperative for getting to some of the best beaches and really seeing the island.

Members of the Big Island–based Hawai'i Island Bed & Breakfast Association are listed with phone numbers and rates in a comprehensive online brochure. In order to join this network, B&Bs must be evaluated and meet fairly stringent minimum requirements.

Bed & Breakfast Honolulu (Statewide) (☎ 800/288–4666 🖷 808/595–7533 ⊕ www.hawaiibnb.com). **Hawai'i Island Bed & Breakfast Association** (⊕ www.stayhawaii.com). **Hawai'i's Best Bed & Breakfasts** (☎ 808/985–7488 or 800/262–9912 🖷 808/967–8610 ⊕ www.bestbnb.com).

For information on camping at county parks, including Spencer Beach Park, contact the **Department of Parks and Recreation** (✉ 25 Aupuni St., Hilo 96720 ☎ 808/961–8311 ⊕ www.hawaii-county.com).

WHAT IT COSTS				
$$$$	**$$$**	**$$**	**$**	**¢**
HOTELS over $340	$261–$340	$181–$260	$100–$180	under $100

Pices are for two people in a standard double room in high season. Condo price categories reflect studio and one-bedroom rates.

Kohala Coast

Hotels & Resorts

★ ☉ **$$$$** 🖾 **Four Seasons Resort Hualālai.** Beautiful views everywhere, polished wood floors, warm earth and cool white tones, and Hawaiian artwork make Hualālai a peaceful retreat. Ground-level rooms have outdoor garden showers. Bungalows are large and cozy, with down comforters and spacious slate-floor bathrooms. One of the five pools, called King's Pond, is a brackish water pond with loads of fish and two manta rays that guests have the opportunity to feed daily. The main infinity pool looks like something out of an ad for an expensive liquor—it's long and peaceful, surrounded by cabanas and palm trees with a clear view to the ocean beyond. The on-site Hawaiian Cultural Center honors the

WHERE TO STAY: KOHALA COAST & WAIMEA

Hotels & Resorts

★ HOTEL NAME	Worth Noting	Cost $	Pools	Beach	Golf Course	Tennis Courts	Gym	Spa	Children's Programs	Rooms	Restaurants	Other	Location
★ ⑥ Fairmont Orchid Hawai'i	Great restaurants	309–559	1	yes	yes	10	yes	yes	5–12	540	4		Kohala Coast
★ ① Four Seasons Hualālai	Impeccable service	560–775	5	yes	yes	8	yes	yes	5–12	274	3		Kohala Coast
⑨ Hāpuna Beach Prince	Outstanding beach	360–650	1	yes	yes	13	yes	yes	5–12	350	5		Kohala Coast
★ ③ Hilton Waikoloa Village	Dolphin Quest	199–649	3	yes	yes	8	yes	yes	5–12	1,297	9	shops	Kohala Coast
★ ② Kona Village Resort	Thatch-roof bungalows	530–940	2	yes	yes	3	yes	yes	6–17	125	2	no A/C	Kohala Coast
★ ⑩ Mauna Kea Beach Hotel	Great lū'au	370–650	1	yes	yes	13	yes	yes	5–12	310	5		Kohala Coast
★ ⑦ Mauna Lani Bay Hotel & Bungalows	One-of-a-kind spa	395–850	1	yes	yes	16	yes	yes	5–12	350	6		Kohala Coast
④ Waikoloa Beach Marriott	Good deal	254–445	1	yes	yes	6	yes	yes	5–12	545	1		Kohala Coast
⑮ Waimea Country Lodge	Some kitchenettes	101–127								21		no A/C	Waimea

Condos

★ HOTEL NAME	Worth Noting	Cost $	Pools	Beach	Golf Course	Tennis Courts	Gym	Spa	Children's Programs	Rooms	Restaurants	Other	Location
⑤ ResortQuest Shores	Borders a golf course	285–345	1			2				75		kitchens	Kohala Coast
⑧ Mauna Lani Point	Ocean front	326–415	1		priv.					61		kitchens	Kohala Coast

B&Bs & Vacation Rentals

★ HOTEL NAME	Worth Noting	Cost $	Pools	Beach	Golf Course	Tennis Courts	Gym	Spa	Children's Programs	Rooms	Restaurants	Other	Location
⑯ Aaah, The Views!	Some kitchens	80–155										sauna	Waimea
⑫ Hale Ho'onanea	Kitchenettes	100–130								3		no A/C	Kawaihae
⑬ Jacaranda Inn	1897 ranch house	159–225								9		no A/C	Waimea
⑭ Kamuela Inn	Good deal	60–85								31		no A/C	Waimea
⑪ Kohala Ranch	Walk to Hāpuna beach	150–1,130	some			some							Kohala Coast

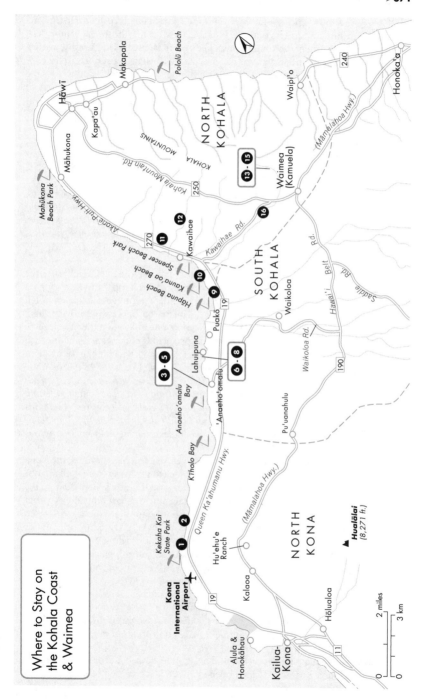

Where to Stay on the Kohala Coast & Waimea

grounds' spiritual heritage, and the sports club and spa offer top-rate health and fitness options. Hualālai's golf course hosts the Senior PGA Tournament of Champions. The resort is super kid-friendly, with a great activities program. The downside is this: despite efforts to the contrary, the Four Seasons doesn't feel much like Hawai'i; add to that the number of guests who will be squawking on their cell phones next to you at the pool (despite the sign reading NO CELL PHONES), and the too-good-to-be-true cheeriness of the staff with their near-constant "Aloha" greetings, and you can see why some folks avoid this place. Still, it's beautiful, the restaurants are dazzling, the rooms are more than comfortable, and the service is definitely of Four Seasons quality. ⊠ *100 Ka'ūpūlehu Dr.,* ✎ *Box 1269, Kailua-Kona 96745* ☎ *808/325–8000, 800/819–5053, or 888/340–5662* ⛶ *808/325–8200* ⊕ *www.fourseasons.com* ⇨ *243 rooms, 31 suites* ⚲ *3 restaurants, A/C, in-room broadband, in-room safes, cable TV with movies, in-room DVD players, 18-hole golf course, 8 tennis courts, 5 pools, health club, spa, beach, 2 bars, recreation room, babysitting, children's programs (ages 5–12), laundry service, business services, airport shuttle, no-smoking rooms* ▭ *AE, DC, MC, V.* $560–$775.

$$$$ 🏨 **Hāpuna Beach Prince Hotel.** Often cheaper than its neighbors, the Hāpuna Beach Prince is no less luxurious and happens to be sitting on a corner of the best beach on the island. Very much a business hotel, rooms at the Hāpuna are spacious, with marble bathrooms, private lānai, and at least partial views of the ocean. Meandering pathways lead to restaurants, beach facilities, and a spectacular golf course. A hiking trail and a frequent shuttle connect Hāpuna with its partner, the Mauna Kea Beach Hotel. ⊠ *62-100 Kauna'oa Dr., Kohala Coast 96743* ☎ *808/880–1111 or 800/882–6060* ⛶ *808/880–3112* ⊕ *www.princeresortshawaii. com* ⇨ *314 rooms, 36 suites* ⚲ *5 restaurants, A/C, in-room broadband, refrigerators, cable TV with movies, 18-hole golf course, 13 tennis courts, pool, health club, hair salon, hot tub, spa, beach, 2 bars, children's programs (ages 5–12), business services, no-smoking rooms* ▭ *AE, D, DC, MC, V.* $360–$650.

★ **$$$$** 🏨 **Kona Village Resort.** Without phones, televisions, or radios, the Kona Village is a time warp—the perfect place to get away from it all in your own thatch-roof *hale* (house) near the resort's sandy beach. Built on the grounds of an ancient Hawaiian village, the modern bungalows reflect styles of South Seas cultures—Tahitian, Samoan, Maori, Fijian, or Hawaiian. The extra-large Royal rooms have private hot tubs. Rates include all meals, an authentic Polynesian Friday-night lū'au, ground tours, tennis, sports activities, and rides in the resort's glass-bottom boat. Children's programs are not available in May or September. ⊠ *Queen Ka'ahumanu Hwy., Box 1299, Kailua-Kona 96745* ☎ *808/325–5555 or 800/367–5290* ⛶ *808/325–5124* ⊕ *www.konavillage.com* ⇨ *125 bungalows* ⚲ *2 restaurants, fans, 3 tennis courts, 2 pools, health club, hot tub, beach, boating, 3 bars, children's programs (ages 6–17), business services, airport shuttle; no A/C, no room phones, no room TVs* ▭ *AE, DC, MC, V.* $530–$940.

★ **$$$$** 🏨 **Mauna Kea Beach Hotel.** The grande dame of Kohala Coast, the Mauna Kea Beach Hotel opened in 1965. It has long been regarded as one of the world's premier vacation resort hotels. It borders one of the islands' finest white-sand beaches, Kauna'oa. Rare works of art, such as a 7th-century Buddha, enhance walkways and open spaces. The rooms have a fresh look with pastel tones and natural woods. Although it's an older hotel, the Mauna Kea has maintained an old-money feel that, coupled with the traditional Hawaiian vibe and the amazing beach, is hard to beat. Shuttles operate between the Mauna Kea and the adjacent Hāpuna Beach Prince Hotel, allowing guests to use the facilities at both hotels. ⊠ *62-100 Mauna Kea Beach Dr., Kohala Coast 96743* ☎ *808/882–7222 or 800/882–6060* 🖷 *808/880–3112* ⊕ *www. princeresortshawaii.com* ⟿ *300 rooms, 10 suites* ⚅ *5 restaurants, A/C, in-room broadband, in-room safes, refrigerators, cable TV, 2 18-hole golf courses, 13 tennis courts, pool, health club, hair salon, spa, beach, children's programs (age 5–12), business services, no-smoking rooms* ▭ *AE, D, DC, MC, V. $370–$650.*

★ $$$$ ⬚ **Mauna Lani Bay Hotel & Bungalows.** This is one of the oldest, and still one of the most beautiful, resorts on the island. The open-air lobby has astronomically high ceilings. The vast majority of the recently renovated rooms have ocean views, and all have a large lānai. The resort is known for its two spectacular golf courses and the award-winning spa. None of the restaurants would qualify as phenomenal (although CanoeHouse is beautiful and has won many awards) and all are a bit pricey, but many other restaurants are right up the road. ⊠ *68-1400 Mauna Lani Dr., Kohala Coast 96743* ☎ *808/885–6622 or 800/367–2323* 🖷 *808/885–1484* ⊕ *www.maunalani.com* ⟿ *335 rooms, 10 suites, 5 bungalows* ⚅ *6 restaurants, A/C, in-room broadband, Wi-Fi, in-room safes, mini-bars, refrigerators, cable TV, in-room VCRs, 2 18-hole golf courses, 16 tennis courts, pool, gym, spa, 5 bars, children's programs (ages 5–12), business services, no-smoking rooms* ▭ *AE, D, DC, MC, V. $395–$850.*

$$$–$$$$ ⬚ **Fairmont Orchid Hawai'i.** The Fairmont is an elegant, old-school FodorsChoice hotel—rooms are tasteful, the lobby is enormous with lots of marble ★ and sweeping ocean views, service is impeccable, and the restaurants are all top-notch. The grounds are expansive, lush, and well-maintained. This is one of the island's largest resorts, and its romantic botanical gardens and waterfall ponds stretch along 32 beachfront acres. Though it used to charge a "resort fee" for things like the morning paper and yoga classes, it now offers a $40 activity pass good for your entire stay that gets you access to all sorts of classes, equipment rentals, and various other amenities. The resort also offers 2½-hour voyages aboard an authentic Polynesian double-hull sailing canoe, the *Hahalua Lele*, or "Flying Manta Ray." The "Gold Floor" includes free breakfast and a daily wine and hors d'oeuvres hour. This can be especially useful for breakfast, as there's nearly always a wait for a table at the restaurant. ⊠ *1 N. Kanikū Dr., Kohala Coast 96743* ☎ *808/885–2000 or 800/845–9905* 🖷 *808/885–8886* ⊕ *www.fairmont.com* ⟿ *486 rooms, 54 suites* ⚅ *4 restaurants, A/C, in-room safes, minibars, cable TV with movies and video games, in-room broadband, 2 18-hole golf courses, 10 tennis courts, pool, health club, hair salon, spa, beach, snorkeling, boating, basketball, volleyball, 4 bars, shops, children's programs (ages 5–12), business services; no smoking* ▭ *AE, D, DC, MC, V. $309–$559.*

$$–$$$$ **Hilton Waikoloa Village.** Dolphins chirp in the lagoon; a pint-size
Fodor'sChoice daredevil zooms down the 175-foot waterslide; a bride poses on the grand
★ staircase; a fire-bearing runner lights the torches along the seaside path
at sunset—these are the scenes that greet you at this 62-acre playground
of a resort. Shaded pathways lined with a multimillion-dollar Pacific Is-
land art collection connect the three tall buildings; Swiss-made trams
and Disney-engineered boats shuttle the weary (in another nod to Dis-
ney, employees access the various areas of the resort via underground
tunnels). The stars of **Dolphin Quest** (☎ 800/248–3316 ⊕ www.
dolphinquest.org) are the resort's pride and joy; reserve in advance for
an interactive learning session. Though there's no ocean beach, there's
a seaside trail to 'Anaeho'omalu Bay. An artificial sand beach borders
the 4-acre resort lagoon. Large, modern rooms in neutral tones have pri-
vate lānai. Be sure to leave your room with plenty of time before any
appointment, or you'll learn to appreciate the size of this place as you
sprint past the tram. Brides-to-be take note: this is one-stop shopping;
the resort has a wedding planning office, cakes, flowers, photography,
and even fireworks and a "Just Married" boat ride. ⊠ *425 Waikoloa
Beach Dr., Waikoloa 96738* ☎ *808/886–1234 or 800/445–8667* 🖷 *808/
886–2900* ⊕ *www.hiltonwaikoloavillage.com* 🛏 *1,240 rooms, 57
suites* ⚎ *10 restaurants, room service, A/C, in-room broadband, in-room
safes, minibars, cable TV with movies, 2 18-hole golf courses, 8 tennis
courts, 3 pools, health club, spa, beach, snorkeling, bike rentals, rac-
quetball, volleyball, 9 bars, shops, babysitting, children's programs
(ages 5–12), laundry facilities, laundry service, business services, car rental,
no-smoking rooms* ⊟ *AE, D, DC, MC, V. $199–$649.*

$$–$$$$ **Waikoloa Beach Marriott.** The most affordable resort on the Kohala
Coast, the Waikoloa Beach Marriott covers 15 acres and encompasses
ancient fishponds, historic trails, and petroglyph fields. All rooms have
Hawaiian art and bamboo-type furnishings. The oversize cabana rooms
overlook the lagoon. Reliable dining is available at the Hawai'i Calls
restaurant. The Hawaiian Rainforest Salon & Spa offers a full range of
treatments. Bordering the white-sand beach of 'Anaeho'omalu Bay, the
hotel has a range of ocean activities, including wedding-vow renewals
on a catamaran. ⊠ *69-275 Waikoloa Beach Dr., Waikoloa 96738*
☎ *808/886–6789 or 800/688–7444* 🖷 *808/886–1554* ⊕ *www.marriott.
com* 🛏 *523 rooms, 22 suites* ⚎ *Restaurant, A/C, in-room broadband,
refrigerators, cable TV with movies and video games, 2 18-hole golf
courses, 6 tennis courts, pool, health club, hair salon, spa, beach, 2 bars,
children's programs (ages 5–12), laundry facilities, business services, no-
smoking rooms* ⊟ *AE, D, DC, MC, V. $254–$445.*

Condos

Along the Kohala Coast, most of the available condos are associated with
the resorts and can be booked through the resort reservations desk.

$$$–$$$$ **Mauna Lani Point Condominiums.** Surrounded by the emerald greens
of a world-class ocean-side golf course, spacious two-story suites offer
a private, independent home away from home. The privately owned units,
individually decorated according to the owners' tastes, have European
cabinets and oversize soaking tubs in the main bedrooms. The pool has
a little waterfall. You're just a few steps away from the Mauna Lani Bay

Hotel and Bungalows, where you have access to golf, tennis, spa facilities, and restaurants. ⊠ *68-1050 Mauna Lani Point Dr., Kohala Coast 96743* ☎ *808/885–5022 or 800/ 642–6284* ☐ *808/885–5015* ⊕ *www.classicresorts.com* ⟲ *61 units* ⚬ *BBQs, A/C, fans, some kitchens, some kitchenettes, golf privileges, pool, hot tub, sauna* ⊟ *AE, DC, MC, V. 1-bedroom $326–$415, 2-bedroom $426–$555.*

$$$–$$$$ ⌷ **ResortQuest Shores at Waikoloa.** These red-tile-roof villas are set amid landscaped lagoons and waterfalls at the edge of the championship Waikoloa Village Golf Course. The spacious villas and condo units— the ground floor and upper floor are available separately—are privately owned, so all furnishings are different. Sliding glass doors open onto large lānai. Picture windows look out on rolling green fairways. All have complete kitchens with washer-dryer units and come with maid service. Check the Web site for deals; separate rates are quoted for online booking. ⊠ *69-1035 Keana Pl., Waikoloa 96738* ☎ *808/886– 5001 or 800/922–7866* ☐ *808/922–8785* ⊕ *www.resortquesthawaii. com* ⟲ *75 units* ⚬ *A/C, fans, kitchens, 2 tennis courts, pool, hot tub, shop, laundry facilities* ⊟ *AE, D, DC, MC, V. 1-bedroom $285–$345, 2-bedroom $330–$400.*

B&Bs & Vacation Rentals

$–$$$$ ⌷ **Kohala Ranch.** Several homes in this upscale gated community do double duty as vacation rentals. Prices range greatly, from $150 a night for a small house with an ocean view to $1,000 a night for a huge mansion on a hill with a private tennis court and pool. This is a fantastic location—close to the island's best beaches, to the resorts, and to the airport. ⊠ *Kohala Ranch, Hwy. 19, north of Waikoloa, Kohala Coast* ⊕ *www.vrbo.com or www.hawaiianbeachrentals.com* ⟲ *Number of units varies* ⚬ *A/C, kitchens, cable TV* ⊟ *AE, MC, V. $150–$1,130.*

$ ⌷ **Hale Ho'onanea.** The Hawaiian translation of this comfortable home's name is "House of Relaxation." It sits on 3 acres in the Kohala Estates hills, above the ocean. From here you can watch the sun rise over Mauna Kea and set over the Pacific, and view the sparkling beauty of Hawai'i's night sky. It's minutes away from dining and shopping at Waimea and the attractions of the Kohala Coast. Continental breakfast is included in the rates. There's a two-night minimum if you book less than a week in advance; $25 fee applied to single-night bookings made within seven days of arrival. ⊠ *Kohala Estates, 59-513 Ala Kahua Dr., Kawaihae 96743* ☎ *808/882–1653 or 877/882–1653* ☐ *808/882–1653* ⊕ *www.houseofrelaxation.com* ⟲ *3 suites* ⚬ *Kitchenettes, cable TV, library; no A/C* ⊟ *MC, V. $100–$130.*

CONDO COMFORTS

There are fewer stores and takeout options on the Kohala Coast, but, as the condos are all associated with resorts, most of your needs will be met. If you require anything not provided by the management, the **King's Shops at Waikoloa Village** (⊠ 250 Waikoloa Beach Dr., Waikoloa ☎ 808/886–8811) is the place to go. There's a small grocery store, a liquor store, and a couple of decent takeout options. It's not exactly cheap, but you're paying for the convenience of not having to drive into town.

Waimea

Hotels & Resorts

$ 🏨 **Waimea Country Lodge.** In the heart of cowboy country, this modest lodge offers views of the green, rolling slopes of Mauna Kea. It's so quiet you forget you're close to busy Waimea. The rooms are adequate and clean, with Hawaiian quilts lending an authentic touch. A Continental breakfast is included in the rate, and you can charge meals at Merriman's and Paniolo Country Inn to your room. ✉ 65-1210 Lindsey Rd., Waimea ✐ Box 2559, Kamuela 96743 ☎ 808/885–4100 or 800/367–5004 🖷 808/885–6711 ⊕ www.castleresorts.com/WCL ⏎ 21 rooms ♿ In-room data ports, some kitchenettes, cable TV with movies, no-smoking rooms; no A/C ⊟ AE, D, DC, MC, V ⏀ CP. $101–$127.

B&Bs & Vacation Rentals

$–$$ 🏨 **Jacaranda Inn.** Built in 1897, this sprawling estate was once the home of the manager of Parker Ranch. Charming inside and out, it's been re-decorated in hues of raspberry and lavender with lots of koa wood accents. Most of the rooms have hot tubs. The units are booked under two separate plans. Plan A includes daily maid service, full breakfasts, and a bottle of wine; Plan B is simpler, with Continental breakfast and less service. ✉ 65-1444 Kawaihae Rd., Waimea 96743 ☎ 808/885–8813 🖷 808/885–6096 ⊕ www.jacarandainn.com ⏎ 8 suites, 1 cottage ♿ Hot tubs, billiards, recreation room; no A/C, no room phones, no room TVs, no smoking ⊟ MC, V. $159–$225, cottage $350.

¢–$ 🏨 **Aaah, The Views!** This tranquil and pretty stream-side mountain home in upcountry Waimea is lovingly tended by owners Erika and Derek Stuart. Rooms are clean and bright, with lots of windows to enjoy the views. The Dream Room is actually an apartment, with a full kitchen, private deck, and hot tub. The house has a sauna and a yoga room (private lessons available), and there's even wireless Internet access. ✉ 66-1773 Alaneo St., off Akulani, just past mile marker 60 on Hwy. 19, Waimea ☎ 808/885–3455 ⊕ www.aaahtheviews.com ⏎ 4 rooms ♿ Wi-Fi, some kitchens, microwaves, refrigerators, cable TV, no-smoking rooms ⊟ No credit cards. $80–$155.

¢ 🏨 **Kamuela Inn.** The rooms at this unpretentious, peaceful inn, just 20 minutes from the beaches, are clean and comfortable. Small lānai look out over the inn's gardens. Depending on your needs, you can choose anything from a no-nonsense single bedroom to two connecting penthouse suites with a lānai and full kitchen. ✉ 65-1300 Kawaihae Rd., Box 1994, Waimea 96743 ☎ 808/885–4243 or 800/555–8968 🖷 808/885–8857 ⊕ www.kamuelainn.com ⏎ 20 rooms, 11 suites ♿ Some kitchenettes, cable TV; no A/C, no phones in some rooms ⊟ AE, D, DC, MC, V. $60–$85.

Kailua-Kona

Hotels & Resorts

$$$–$$$$ 🏨 **Sheraton Keauhou Bay Resort & Spa.** This hotel on the edge of Keauhou Bay has been restored to glory. The lobby is particularly stunning, and the well-designed restaurant Kai serves a limited but excellent menu. The pool, which can only be described as massive, is one of the coolest on the island, with a slide, waterfalls, and an ocean view. The rooms, though, are less impressive, and they seem to have scrimped on the details (rough sheets and bathrooms that don't look like they've updated). The newly opened spa offers a full-service menu and an oceanfront location. ☒ *78-128 Ehukai St., Kailua-Kona 96740* ☎ *808/930–4900* 🖷 *808/930–4800* ⊕ *www.sheratonkeauhou.com* ⤳ *511 rooms, 10 suites* ☼ *Restaurant, A/C, in-room data ports, Wi-Fi, in-room safes, refrigerators, cable TV with movies, 2 tennis courts, pool, health club, beach, volleyball, bar, playground, business services, no-smoking rooms* ▭ *AE, D, DC, MC, V. $325–$460.*

HAWAI'I ON A BUDGET

Kona Tiki Hotel (Kailua-Kona). Oceanfront, all rooms have ocean views, walking distance to downtown.

Manago Hotel (South Kona). Historic, Japanese theme, clean, some oceanfront rooms, super reasonable, excellent restaurant.

Nāmakani Paio Cabins (Volcano Village). Close to the Volcano, cheap, clean, recently renovated.

Royal Kona Resort (Kailua-Kona). Old-school Hawai'i, oceanfront, great bar, good package deals, close to downtown Kailua-Kona.

$$–$$$$ 🏨 **Royal Kona Resort.** This is a great option if you're on a budget. The resort has seen better days, but the owners are finally doing a bit of renovation. The location is great, the lobby and restaurants are right on the water, and lānai-front rooms are decked out in Hawaiian kitsch. The resort is within walking distance of Kailua-Kona and across from numerous shops and restaurants. Artificial streams and a private lagoon with a sandy beach set the stage for carefree tropical living. The resort hosts a weekly lū'au with Polynesian entertainment. Make sure to book online, where the rates can be 50% less than the rack rates. ☒ *75-5852 Ali'i Dr., Kailua-Kona 96740* ☎ *808/329–3111 or 800/222–5642* 🖷 *808/329–9532* ⊕ *www.royalkona.com* ⤳ *452 rooms, 8 suites* ☼ *Restaurant, A/C, in-room safes, refrigerators, cable TV with movies, in-room data ports, 4 tennis courts, pool, health club, hair salon, spa, beach, bar, laundry facilities, Internet room, no-smoking rooms* ▭ *AE, D, DC, MC, V. $210–$385.*

$–$$ 🏨 **King Kamehameha's Kona Beach Hotel.** Rooms here are not particularly special (the fifth- and sixth-floor oceanfront rooms are best), and the hotel itself is not aging gracefully. What you get instead of the luxury of the upscale resorts is a bit of local history, a reasonable rate, and a great central location. It's on a small white-sand beach and a calm swimming bay next to Kailua Pier. You can explore the lush grounds and historic Ahu'ena Heiau, which King Kamehameha I had reconstructed in the early 1800s. The hotel serves an ample champagne brunch every Sunday and hosts a fabulous beachfront Polynesian lū'au several nights a week. ☒ *75-5660 Palani Rd., Kailua-Kona 96740* ☎ *808/329–2911 or 800/367–6060* 🖷 *808/329–4602* ⊕ *www.konabeachhotel.com* ⤳ *455 rooms* ☼ *2 restaurants, A/C, in-room data ports, in-room safes, cable TV with movies, tennis courts, pool, hair salon, hot tub, sauna, beach, 2 bars, shops, laundry facilities, laundry service, travel services* ▭ *AE, D, DC, MC, V. $170–$250.*

WHERE TO STAY: KONA COAST & UPCOUNTRY

★ HOTEL NAME	Cost $	Worth Noting	Pools	Beach	Golf Course	Tennis Courts	Gym	Spa	Children's Programs	Rooms	Restaurants	Other	Location
Hotels & Resorts													
⑫ King Kamehameha's	170–250	Great lūʻau	1	yes		1				455	2	shops	Kailua-Kona
⑪ Kona Seaside Hotel	60–120	Across from Kailua Bay	2				yes			224			Kailua-Kona
⑨ Kona Tiki Hotel	61–84	Oceanfront bargain	1							15		no A/C	Kailua-Kona
⑩ Royal Kona Resort	210–385	Good deal	1	yes		4	yes			460	1		Kailua-Kona
⑥ Sheraton Keauhou Bay	325–460	Cool pool	1	yes		2	yes	yes		521	1		Kailua-Kona
Condos													
⑤ Kanaloa at Kona	169–265	Borders country club	3			2				166	1	kitchens	Kailua-Kona
⑧ Kona Bali Kai	75–125	Near beach and town	1							62		kitchens	Kailua-Kona
⑦ Kona Magic Sands	85–112	Ocean views	1							37	1	kitchens	Kailua-Kona
B&Bs & Vacation Rentals													
③ Aloha Guesthouse	140–250	Ocean views								5			Captain Cook
⑮ Nancy's Hideaway	115–135	Private entrances										no A/C	Kailua-Kona
② Bougainvillea B&B	70–75	Remote and secluded	1							3			South Point
⑭ Hale Hualalai	135	Gourmet breakfast										no A/C	Kailua-Kona
① Hale Oʻluna	85–125									2		no A/C	Pahala
⑬ Hōlualoa Inn	175–205	Elegant B&B	1							6		no A/C	Hōlualoa
④ Manago Hotel	31–70	Old Hawaiʻi vibe								64	1	no A/C	Captain Cook

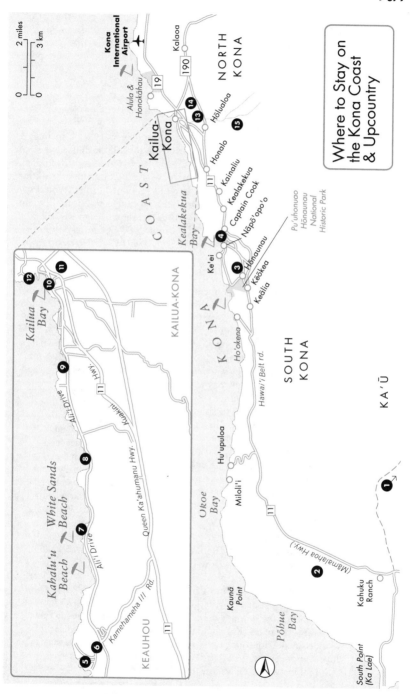

Where to Stay on
the Kona Coast
& Upcountry

¢–$ 🏨 **Kona Seaside Hotel.** If you're on a budget, desire a central location, and don't need a spacious room or lavish bath, you'll feel at home in this casual hotel. It's on a busy intersection, right across the street from Kailua Bay. Rooms nearest the street are built around a private pool. The staff is very friendly. ⊠ *75-5646 Palani Rd., Kailua-Kona 96740* ☎ *808/329–2455 or 800/560–5558* 🖷 *808/329–6157* ⊕ *www. konaseasidehotel.com* ⤳ *223 rooms, 1 suite* ♿ *A/C, fans, refrigerators, cable TV, 2 pools, gym, bar, laundry facilities, no-smoking rooms* ▤ *AE, D, DC, MC, V. $60–$120.*

¢ 🏨 **Kona Tiki Hotel.** The best thing about this three-story walk-up budget hotel, about a mile south of Kailua-Kona, is that all the units have lānai right next to the ocean. The rooms are modest but pleasantly decorated. You can sunbathe by the seaside pool, where a Continental breakfast is served. Some would call this place old-fashioned; others would say it's local and the best deal in town, with glorious sunsets no different from those at the resorts. ⊠ *75-5968 Ali'i Dr., Kailua-Kona 96745* ☎ *808/ 329–1425* 🖷 *808/327–9402* ⤳ *15 rooms* ♿ *BBQ, fans, refrigerators, pool, beach; no A/C, no room phones, no room TVs* ▤ *No credit cards. $61–$84.*

Condos

When booking a condo, remember that most are individually owned and that most owners oursource the rental process. Renters make arrangements through property management companies. **Property Network** (⊠ 75-5799 B-3 Ali'i Dr., Kailua-Kona 96740 ☎ 808/329–7977 🖷 808/329–1200 ⊕ www.hawaii-kona.com) looks after the majority of the vacation rentals on the Kona side of the island. With more than 250 units in nearly every condo complex along Ali'i Drive, Property Network can find exactly what you're looking for, whether you're on a budget or looking to splurge on a deluxe oceanfront villa. You can also browse the Web site for photos of available units to find the perfect one. **Maryl Realty** (☎ 808/845–7559 ⊕ www. marylrealty.com) is another great place to find quality vacation rentals throughout the island.

$–$$$ 🏨 **Kanaloa at Kona.** The 16-acre grounds provide a peaceful and verdant background for this low-rise condominium complex bordering the Keauhou-Kona Country Club. It's walking distance to the golf course but a five-minute drive to the nearest beaches (Kahalu'u and White Sands). Large one-, two-, and three-bedroom apartments have koawood cabinetwork and washer-dry-

---

CONDO COMFORTS

Crossroads Shopping Center. The **Safeway** here is the cleanest, largest, and best-stocked store on the island. It's right next to **Kona Natural Foods,** so you can supplement with local organic produce and other tasty treats. There's also a **Coldstone Creamery** in this shopping center, so dessert is taken care of, too. ⊠ *75-1000 Henry St., Kailua-Kona.*

Blockbuster. ⊠ *Kona Coast Shopping Center, 74-5588 Palani Rd., Kailua-Kona* ☎ *808/326–7694.* Pizza-wise, **Kona Brewing Company** is best if you're willing to go pick it up. Otherwise, **Domino's** (☎ 808/329–9500) is actually good here.

ers; oceanfront villas have private hot tubs. ✉ *78-261 Manukai St., Kailua-Kona 96740* ☎ *808/322–9625, 808/322–2272, or 800/688–7444* 🖷 *808/322–3818* ⊕ *www.outrigger.com* ↘ *166 units* ♿ *A/C in some rooms, in-room safes, kitchenettes, 2 tennis courts, 3 pools, hot tub, bar, laundry facilities* ▭ *AE, D, DC, MC, V. 1-bedroom $169–$265, 2-bedroom $185–$315.*

¢–$ ▦ **Kona Bali Kai.** These slightly older condominium units, spread out through three low-rises on the ocean side of Ali'i Drive, have a pretty good location. They're just a couple of minutes from Kailua-Kona and walking-distance to popular White Sands beach. And they're great for families. Kitchens are fully equipped, and there's a little convenience store. If you can afford it, choose an oceanfront unit for the luxury of quiet sunsets. ✉ *76-6246 Ali'i Dr., Kailua-Kona 96740* ☎ *808/329–9381 or 800/535–0085* 🖷 *808/326–6056* ⊕ *www.marcresorts.com* ↘ *62 units* ♿ *BBQ, A/C in some rooms, fans, kitchens, in-room VCRs, pool, hair salon, hot tub, shop, laundry facilities* ▭ *AE, D, DC, MC, V. Studios $75–$95, 1-bedroom $100–$125, 2-bedroom $135–$167.*

¢–$ ▦ **Kona Magic Sands.** Cradled between two small beaches, this condo complex is great for swimmers and sunbathers in summer (the sand at Magic Sands washes away in winter). Units vary because they're individually owned, but all are oceanfront, spacious, and light. Some units have enclosed lānai, and all have an ocean view. ✉ *77-6452 Ali'i Dr., Kailua-Kona 96740* ☎ *808/329–9393 or 800/622–5348* 🖷 *808/326–4137* ⊕ *www.konahawaii.com* ↘ *37 units* ♿ *Restaurant, A/C in some rooms, kitchens, kitchenettes, pool, bar* ▭ *MC, V. Studios $85–$112.*

B&Bs & Vacation Rentals

$–$$ ▦ **Hōlualoa Inn.** Six spacious rooms are available in this cedar home on a 40-acre Upcountry orchard estate, 4 mi above Kailua Bay. The artists' town of Hōlualoa is steps away. The Balinese suite, one of the nicest here, has wraparound windows with stunning views. A lavish breakfast includes estate-grown coffee as well as homemade breads and macadamia-nut butter. Rooftop gazebos inspire quiet, relaxing moments, and for stargazers there's a telescope. ✉ *76-5932 Māmalahoa Hwy., Box 222, Hōlualoa 96725* ☎ *808/324–1121 or 800/392–1812* 🖷 *808/322–2472* ⊕ *www.holualoainn.com* ↘ *6 rooms* ♿ *Fans, pool, hot tub, billiards; no A/C, no room TVs, no kids under 13, no smoking* ▭ *AE, D, DC, MC, V. $175–$205.*

$ ▦ **Hale Hualalai.** Near the artsy village of Hōlualoa, Hale Hualalai has four suites with exposed beams, hardwood floors, hot tubs, and private lānai. Perhaps the most memorable aspect of Hale Hualalai is the food—owner Lonn Armour was a professional chef for 20 years, and cooks up a breakfast that puts other B&B offerings to shame. ✉ *74-4968 Māmalahoa Hwy., Hōlualoa 96725* ☎ *808/326–2909* ⊕ *www.hale-hualalai.com* ↘ *6 rooms* ♿ *Refrigerators, hot tub; no A/C, no room phones* ▭ *No credit cards. $135.*

$ ▦ **Nancy's Hideaway.** A few miles up the hill from Kailua-Kona, this charming cottage and studio offer modern comforts and ocean views. Each has its own entrance, a lānai, and a wet bar. The cottage stands alone; the studio is attached to the main house, but is very private.

Breakfast is served in the rooms to give guests their privacy. This place is ideal for couples, but not for families with kids. ☒ *73-1530 Uanani Pl., Kailua-Kona 96740* ☎ *808/325–3132 or 866/325–3132* 🖷 *808/325–3132* ⊕ *www.nancyshideaway.com* ⤣ *6 rooms* ⌂ *Cable TV, in-room VCRs; no A/C, no kids under 13, no smoking* ▭ *MC, V. $115–$135.*

South Kona & Ka'u

$–$$ 🖼 **Aloha Guesthouse.** In the hills above Kealakekua Bay, Aloha Guesthouse offers quiet elegance, complete privacy, and ocean views from every room. With a focus on nature, the house is furnished in earth tones. The bath products are 100% organic, and the yummy full breakfasts are as close to organic as they can muster. Common areas include a kitchenette for guests who want to cook their own meals, as well as a high-definition television, a DVD library, and a computer with high-speed Internet. ☒ *Old Tobacco Rd., off Hwy. 11 near mile marker 104, Captain Cook* ☎ *808/328–8955* ⊕ *www.alohaguesthouse.com* ⤣ *5 rooms* ⌂ *Wi-Fi, refrigerators, cable TV, some in-room DVD players, hot tub, Internet room* ▭ *AE, MC, V. $140–$250.*

¢–$ 🖼 **Hale O'Luna.** At this vacation house in the old plantation village of Pahala, you can rent just a room or the whole place, depending on the size of your group. The pretty, quiet house has a full kitchen for the use of all guests. The house has hardwood floors, authentic antiques, and a fully stocked library. Pahala is not an exciting place, but you are close to the black-sand beach of Punalu'u Beach Park, Hawai'i Volcanoes National Park, and some of the lesser-known sights of the area like Wood Temple. ☒ *96-3181 Pikake St., Pahala* ☎ *808/928–8144* ⊕ *www.pahala.info* ⤣ *2 rooms* ⌂ *Library; no A/C, no room TVs* ▭ *No credit cards. $85–$125.*

¢ 🖼 **Bougainvillea Bed & Breakfast.** This large country home is in a remote area close to Green Point and the Ka'u District. It's close to hiking trails, black- and green-sand beaches, and Hawai'i Volcanoes National Park. Breakfast is served on the lānai. There are restaurants, a coin laundry, a grocery store, and a gas station nearby. ☒ *Hwy. 11, between mile markers 77 and 78, Box 6045, Ocean View 96737* ☎ *808/929–7089 or 800/688–1763* ⊕ *hi-inns.com/bouga* ⤣ *3 rooms* ⌂ *A/C, in-room VCRs, pool, hot tub, massage* ▭ *MC, V. $70–$75.*

¢ 🖼 **Manago Hotel.** This historic hotel is a good option if you want to escape the touristy thing but still be close to everything on the island. Don't let the front TV room creep you out—you have not checked into an old folks' home. The place has an authentic Hawai'i vibe, and the restaurant is one of the best on the island. Dwight Manago—whose grandparents, Kinzo and Osame Manago, built the main building in 1917—has maintained one Japanese-style room with tatami mats and a *furo*, a traditional Japanese bath. The other rooms are nothing special, but those in the newer wing have great views high above the Kona Coast. ☒ *81-6155 Māmalahoa Hwy., Box 145, Captain Cook 96704* ☎ *808/323–2642* 🖷 *808/323–3451* ⊕ *www.managohotel.com* ⤣ *64 rooms, 42 with bath* ⌂ *Restaurant, bar; no A/C, no room TVs* ▭ *D, MC, V. $31–$70.*

Where to Stay Hilo Side & Volcano

Volcano

Hotels & Resorts

¢–$$ ⊡ **Volcano House.** On the very rim of a volcano, this place has knock-out views of Kīlauea Caldera that make it worth a visit even if you're not staying here. It's the only lodging option (except for cabins and camp-sites) within Hawai'i Volcanoes National Park. Book a crater-view room as far from the busy dining room area as possible. Alas, the 1941 hotel is looking a bit worn, with tired carpeting and '50s-era furnishings. ⊠ *Crater Rim Dr., Box 53, Hawai'i Volcanoes National Park, 96718* ☎ *808/967–7321* 🖶 *808/967–8429* 🔊 *42 rooms* ⚬ *Restaurant, shop; no A/C* ⊟ *AE, D, DC, MC, V. $95–$225.*

$ ⊡ **Inn at Volcano.** At this boutique resort, afternoon tea is served before a fireplace. A candlelit breakfast under a glittering chandelier adds a touch of elegance. The Inn's two-story Treehouse Suite ($299), with wraparound windows, a marble wet bar, and a fireplace, gives one the impression of floating on the tops of the trees. ⊠ *Wright Rd., Volcano Village 96785* ☎ *808/967–7786 or 800/937–7786* 🖶 *808/967–8660* ⊕ *www.volcano-hawaii.com* 🔊 *6 rooms* ⚬ *Cable TV, in-room VCRs, hot tubs* ⊟ *AE, D, DC, MC, V. $139–$159.*

★ $ ⊡ **Kīlauea Lodge.** A mile from the entrance of Hawai'i Volcanoes National Park, this inn dating from the 1930s is tastefully furnished with European antiques. Rooms have rich quilts and Hawaiian photographs, as well as their own wood-burning fireplaces. A charming one-bedroom cottage with a gas fireplace and a private balcony are perfect for romance. Cottages off the main property include Pīi Mauna House, on the fairway of the Volcano Golf Course. Rates include breakfast. ⊠ *Old Volcano Hwy., 1 mi northeast of Volcano Store* ⬡ *Box 116, Volcano Village 96785* ☎ *808/967–7366* 🖶 *808/967–7367* ⊕ *www.kilauealodge.com* 🔊 *11 rooms, 3 cottages* ⚬ *Restaurant, dining room, hot tub, shop; no A/C, no TV in some rooms, no smoking* ⊟ *AE, MC, V. $140–$165.*

B&Bs & Vacation Rentals

¢–$$$$ ⊡ **Chalet Kīlauea Collection.** The Collection comprises five inns and lodges and five vacation houses in and around Volcano Village; the theme rooms, suites, and vacation homes range from no-frills dorm-style bedrooms in a funky old house to a plantation mansion with its own six-person hot tub. Among its reasonably priced offerings are the **Volcano Bed & Breakfast** ($49–$69 double-occupancy room), which has a communal kitchen and fireplace. ⊠ *Wright Rd., Volcano Village 96785* ☎ *808/967–7786 or 800/937–7786* 🖶 *808/967–8660* ⊕ *www.volcano-hawaii.com* 🔊 *11 rooms, 9 suites, 5 houses* ⚬ *Some kitchens, some microwaves, cable TV with movies; no A/C, no phones in some rooms, no smoking* ⊟ *AE, D, DC, MC, V. $49–$399.*

¢–$$ ⊡ **Volcano Places.** A collection of lovely vacation homes, the accommodations range from a simple cottage in the rain forest to a stunning Craftsman-style house with its own spa room. Many can accommodate up to eight people comfortably. All come equipped with full kitchens. ☎ *808/967–7990* ⊕ *www.volcanoplaces.com* 🔊 *3 cottages* ⚬ *A/C, kitchens, refrigerators, some in-room VCRs, hot tubs* ⊟ *MC, V. $95–$250.*

$ ⊞ **Hydrangea Cottage & Mountain House.** You'll find this landscaped estate about a mile from Hawai'i Volcanoes National Park. The one-bedroom cottage has a wraparound porch and floor-to-ceiling windows looking out over giant tree ferns. The Mountain house has two living rooms and three bedrooms filled with antique furnishings. Each bedroom has its own bath. Both units have kitchens, and breakfast fixings are provided. ☐ *Box 563, Waimea 96743* ☎ *808/262–8133* ⇒ *1 house, 1 cottage* △ *Kitchen, cable TV, in-room VCRs, laundry facilities; no A/C* ⊟ *No credit cards. 1-bedroom cottage $125–$150, 3-bedroom house $375–$450.*

$ ⊞ **Volcano Teapot Cottage.** A near-perfect spot for couples seeking a romantic getaway, this cute red-and-white cottage is completely private. The claw-foot bathtub, hot tub, and fireplace add to the general coziness. Breakfast is included, and the restaurants in Volcano Village are nearby. ⊠ *19-3820 Old Volcano Hwy., Volcano Village* ☐ *Box 511, Volcano 96785* ☎ *808/967–7112* ⊕ *www.volcanoteapot.com* ⇒ *1 cottage* △ *Kitchen, hot tub, in-room VCR* ⊟ *No credit cards. $175.*

¢–$ ⊞ **Hale Ohia Cottages.** A stately and comfortable Queen Anne–style mansion, Hale Ohia was built in the 1930s as a summer place for a wealthy Scotsman. The namesake Ohia cottage, large enough for a family, has a full kitchen. The Ihilani cottage is the cushiest of the cottages; built into an old water tank, it's naturally lighted, beautifully designed, and completely private. Breakfast (including homemade bread made with bananas, macadamia nuts, and cranberries) is left in your refrigerator while you're away in the afternoon so that you can enjoy it at your leisure in the morning. This place does everything possible to make you feel at home. ⊠ *Hale Ohia Rd., off Hwy. 11* ☎ *808/967–7986* ⊕ *www. haleohia.com* ⇒ *4 rooms, 3 cottages, 1 suite* △ *Some kitchenettes, some microwaves, some refrigerators, hot tub, no-smoking rooms; no A/C, no room phones* ⊟ *MC, V. $95–$159.*

¢–$ ⊞ **My Island Bed & Breakfast Inn.** Gordon and Joann Morse, along with their daughter Ki'i, opened their historic home and 7-acre botanical estate to visitors in 1985. The oldest in Volcano, it was built in 1886 by the Lyman missionary family. Three rooms, sharing two baths, are in the main house. Scattered around the area are three garden apartments and five fully equipped guesthouses. You won't start the day hungry after a deluxe all-you-can-eat breakfast. ⊠ *19-3896 Old Volcano Hwy., Volcano Village* ☐ *Box 100, Volcano 96785* ☎ *808/967–7216 or 808/967– 7110* 📠 *808/967–7719* ⊕ *www.myislandinnhawaii.com* ⇒ *6 rooms, 3 with bath; 5 guesthouses* △ *Library; no A/C, no phones in some rooms, no TV in some rooms, no smoking* ⊟ *MC, V. $70–$105.*

Cabins

¢ ⊞ **Nāmakani Paio Cabins.** These recently remodeled cabins, managed by Volcano House, are definitely for those who are into roughing it. The simple cabins are at the end of a long, deserted road. Inexpensive and clean, each has a double bed, two bunk beds, and electric lights. Bring extra blankets, as it gets cold at night. Each cabin also has a grill outside, but you must bring your own firewood. ⊠ *Volcano House, Box 53, Hawai'i Volcanoes National Park, Volcano Village* ☎ *808/967–7321* 📠 *808/967–8429* ⇒ *10 cabins* △ *BBQs; no A/C, no room phones, no room TVs* ⊟ *MC, V. $45.*

Hilo

Hotels & Resorts

★ **$–$$$$** ☒ **Hilo Hawaiian Hotel.** This older hotel, with large bay-front rooms offering spectacular views of Mauna Kea and Coconut Island, is one of the most pleasant lodgings on Hilo Bay. Streetside rooms overlook the golf course. Most accommodations have private lānai, and kitchenettes are available in some one-bedroom suites. Views of the bay are showcased in the Queen's Court dining room, and the Wai'oli Lounge has entertainment Thursday through Saturday. ⊠ *71 Banyan Dr., Hilo 96720* ☎ *808/935–9361, 800/367–5004 from mainland, 800/272–5275 interisland* 🖷 *808/961–9642* ⊕ *www.hilohawaiian.com* 🛏 *286 rooms, 6 suites* ⟡ *Restaurant, A/C, in-room data ports, some kitchenettes, refrigerators, cable TV, pool, bar, laundry facilities, no-smoking rooms* ▤ *AE, D, DC, MC, V. $135–$385.*

★ **¢** ☒ **Dolphin Bay Hotel.** A glowing lava flow sign marks the office and bespeaks owner John Alexander's passion for the volcano. Stunning lava pictures adorn the common area, and Alexander is a great source of information for visiting the park and for exploring the back roads of Hilo. Units in the 1950s-style motor lodge are modest, but they are clean and inexpensive. Coffee and fresh fruit are offered daily. Four blocks from Hilo Bay, in a residential area called Pu'ue'o, the hotel borders a verdant 2-acre Hawaiian garden with jungle trails and shady places to rest. Guests of the hotel return repeatedly, and it's ideal for families who seek a home base. ⊠ *333 'Iliahi St., Hilo 96720* ☎ *808/935–1466* 🖷 *808/935–1523* ⊕ *www.dolphinbayhotel.com* 🛏 *13 rooms, 4 1-bedroom units, 1 2-bedroom unit* ⟡ *Fans, kitchens, kitchenettes, microwaves; no A/C, no room phones, no room TVs* ▤ *MC, V. $66–$99.*

¢ ☒ **Hilo Bay Hotel.** Funky and cheap—enough said. This is a popular stopover for those who enjoy proprietor Uncle Billy Kimo's Hawaiian hospitality. A nightly hula show and entertainment during dinner at Uncle Billy's restaurant are part of the fun. ⊠ *87 Banyan Dr., Hilo 96720* ☎ *808/935–0861, 800/367–5102 from the mainland, 800/442–5841 interisland* 🖷 *808/935–7903* ⊕ *www.unclebilly.com* 🛏 *145 rooms* ⟡ *Restaurant, A/C, some kitchenettes, refrigerators, pool, bar, laundry facilities, Internet room, no-smoking rooms* ▤ *AE, D, DC, MC, V. $84–$94.*

B&Bs & Vacation Rentals

★ **$$** ☒ **Shipman House Bed & Breakfast Inn.** You'll have a choice between three rooms in the "castle"—the turreted main house dating from 1899—or two rooms in a separate cottage. The B&B is on 5½ verdant acres on Reed's Island; the house is furnished with antique koa and period pieces, some dating from the days when Queen Lili'uokalani came to tea. On Tuesday night, an authentic hula school practices Hawai'i's ancient dances in the house. Barbara (part of the Shipman family) and her husband Gary are friendly hosts with a vast knowledge of the area and the rest of the island; they're also excellent cooks, which means you should try absolutely everything at breakfast. ⊠ *131 Kaiulani St., Hilo 96720* ☎ *808/934–8002 or 800/627–8447* 🖷 *808/934–8002* ⊕ *www.hilo-hawaii.com* 🛏 *3 rooms, 2 cottage rooms* ⟡ *Fans, refrigerators, library; no A/C, no room phones, no room TVs, no kids, no smoking* ▤ *AE, MC, V. $199–$219.*

$ ⊡ **Hale Kai.** On a bluff above Hilo Bay, this 5,400-square-foot modern home is 2 mi from downtown Hilo. The four impeccable rooms with patios and the private loft that is ideal for families have grand ocean views and are within earshot of lapping waves. Fresh flowers add a warm, European touch. The Norwegian-Hawaiian hosts, Evonne and Paul Bjornen, serve a delightful breakfast—fruit, bread, and special egg dishes—on an outdoor deck or in the kitchen's bay-window dining area. ⊠ *111 Honoli'i Pali St., Hilo 96720* ☎ *808/935–6330* 🖷 *808/935–8439* ⊕ *www.halekaihawaii.com* 📷 *4 rooms, 1 suite* ⚬ *A/C, fans, cable TV, pool, hot tub, laundry service; no kids, no smoking* ▤ *No credit cards.* *$115–$140.*

$ ⊡ **Waterfalls Inn Bed & Breakfast.** This elegant old family home is in the exclusive Reed's Bay neighborhood, just a few blocks from downtown Hilo. Relaxation is the key here. Bounded on two sides by tropical streams and forest, there's no noise except the gentle gurgle of the stream. The 1916-era home has been carefully restored, retaining the original light fixtures, fine 'ōhi'a wood flooring, antique furniture, and some original bath fixtures. You'll find lots of room to unwind in the expansive glassed-in lānai. Breakfast (George always whips up a warm and wonderful treat) is served in the large dining room. Business travelers enjoy easy access to town, government offices, and the University of Hawai'i at Hilo. There's a $20 additional fee for one-night stays. ⊠ *240 Kaiulani St., Hilo 96720* ☎ *808/969–3407* ⊕ *www.waterfallsinn.com* 📷 *4 suites* ⚬ *Wi-Fi, refrigerators, cable TV, in-room DVD/VCR players; no A/C, no kids under 6* ▤ *AE, MC, V. $130–$175.*

> ## BED & BREAKFAST, HAWAIIAN STYLE
>
> **Hōlualoa Inn** (Kailua-Kona). Gorgeous wood floors, quiet location, beautiful coffee-country views, close to the quaint artist's community of Hōlualoa.
>
> **Jacaranda Inn** (Waimea). Charming, country-style, Jacuzzis, walking distance to all the best restaurants in Waimea.
>
> **Waianuhea** (Hāmākua Coast). Stunning views, hot tub, completely off the grid, beautiful architecture, delicious hors d'oeuvres and wine tasting nightly.
>
> **Waterfalls Inn** (Hilo). Quiet and stately, in the nicest neighborhood in Hilo, walking distance to downtown.

Hāmākua Coast

$–$$$$ ⊡ **The Palms Cliff House Inn.** This handsome Victorian-style mansion, 15 mi north of Hilo, is perched on the sea cliffs 150 feet above the crashing surf of the tropical Hāmākua Coast. You can pick tropical fruit and macadamia nuts from the gardens of the 3½-acre estate. Individually decorated rooms have private lānai. Suites include double hot tubs (the one in Room 8 is in the window with a stunning view of the coast), but there's also a communal hot tub in the garden. A husband-and-wife team serve breakfast with pride on the veranda overlooking the cliffs; meals generally include fresh-baked muffins, locally grown fruit, a warm egg or meat dish (they always ask about food allergies or dietary restrictions ahead of time) and, of course, fantastic local coffee. Dinner is available

FodorsChoice ★

on request. They can help you plan activities, including hula lessons. ✉ *28-3514 Māmalahoa Hwy., Honomū 96728* ☎ *808/963–6076* 🖷 *808/963–6316* ⊕ *www.palmscliffhouse.com* ⇌ *2 rooms, 6 suites* ⚭ *A/ C in some rooms, fans, in-room data ports, in-room safes, cable TV, in-room DVD players, hot tub; no kids under 12, no smoking* ☰ *AE, D, DC, MC, V. $175–$375.*

$–$$$$ 🏨 **Waianuhea.** Waianuhea defines Hawaiian country elegance. Fully self-contained, this gorgeous country home sits in a forested area on the Hāmākua Coast. The four guest rooms and large suite have tasteful color schemes and lavish furnishings and there is contemporary artwork throughout. The large common room with its stunning ocean views and lava-rock fireplace is a big attraction, especially at the wine tasting and hors d'oeuvres hour each evening. Stroll the flower garden and fruit orchards. The house has solar-electric power. ✉ *45-3503 Kahana Dr., Honoka'a 96727* ☎ *888/775–2577 or 808/775–1118* 🖷 *888/296–6302* ⊕ *www.waianuhea.com* ⇌ *5 rooms* ⚭ *Cable TV, in-room DVD players, Internet room; no A/C, no smoking* ☰ *AE, D, MC, V. $170–$350.*

¢–$ 🏨 **Waipi'o Wayside.** Nestled amid the avocado and kukui trees of a plantation estate, this serene inn provides a retreat close to the Waipi'o Valley. Jacqueline Horne has given each room its own character with, for example, rare Chinese antiques or patchwork quilts. A sprawling garden has an orchid-covered deck and a little gazebo has hammocks to help you indulge your lazy side. ✉ *Waipi'o Valley Rd., Hwy. 240, Honoka'a 96727* ☎ *808/775–0275 or 800/833–8849* 🖷 *808/775–0275* ⊕ *www.waipiowayside.com* ⇌ *5 rooms* ⚭ *In-room data ports; no A/C, no room phones, no room TVs, no smoking* ☰ *MC, V* ⦿ *CP. $95–$170.*

¢ 🏨 **Hotel Honoka'a Club.** This bargain hotel is 45 minutes from Hilo and close to Waipi'o Valley. Rustic rooms range from lower-level dormitory-style units—bring your own sleeping bag—to upper-story rooms with private baths, ocean views, and a complimentary Continental breakfast. ✉ *45-3480 Māmane St., Box 247, Honoka'a 96727* ☎ *808/775–0678 or 800/808–0678* ⊕ *www.hotelhono.com* ⇌ *13 rooms, 5 dorm-style rooms* ⚭ *Restaurant, Wi-Fi; no A/C, no room phones, no TV in some rooms, no smoking* ☰ *MC, V. Dorm rooms $18–$38, standard rooms $50–$75.*

Puna

$–$$ 🏨 **Kalani Oceanside Retreat.** This lodging sponsors numerous meditation and yoga classes in addition to programs on Hawaiian culture, healing, and gay relationships. Accommodations include campsites, shared rooms, cottage units with shared kitchens, lodge rooms, and private, luxurious tree-house units. Bathing suits are optional both on the nearby beach and at the Olympic-size pool. There's a thermal spring nearby. Even the driveway is beautiful, and the grounds are lush and well-kept. The food is good, too, but a bit pricey considering it's served cafeteria style. Full meal plans are available at an additional charge. ✉ *Pāhoa-Beach Rd., Hwy. 137, R.R. 2, Box 4500, Pāhoa 96778* ☎ *808/965–7828 or 800/800–6886* 🖷 *808/965–0527* ⊕ *www.kalani.com* ⇌ *24* *rooms with shared bath, 9 cottages, 4 tree-house units, 3 guesthouse rooms ⌂ Fans, some refrigerators, tennis court, pool, hair salon, hot tub, sauna, laundry facilities, laundry service, no-smoking rooms; no A/ C, no room TVs* ☰ *AE, D, MC, V. $110–$240.*

¢–$ 🏨 **Bed & Breakfast Mountain View.** This modern home is surrounded by rolling forest and farmland. The secluded 4-acre estate has extensive floral gardens and a fishpond. Owners Linus and Jane Chao are longtime Big Island art educators and have an art studio on the lower level where they teach classes. Some special packages include art lessons. The house itself is a virtual art gallery with varied displays in oil, acrylic, watercolor, and Oriental brush paintings. ⊠ *South Kulani Rd., Kurtistown 96760* ☎ *808/968–6868 or 888/698–9896* 🖷 *808/968–7017* ⊕ *www. bbmtview.com* ⌁ *4 rooms, 2 with shared bath ⌂ Fishing, billiards, laundry facilities; no A/C, no TV in some rooms, no kids under 5* ☰ *MC, V. $55–$110.*

¢–$ 🏨 **Yoga Oasis.** This center, on 26 tropical acres, has a bit of a commune feel. With its exposed redwood beams, Balinese doorways, and imported art, it draws those who seek relaxation and rejuvenation, and perhaps a free yoga lesson or two. A 1,600-square-foot state-of-the-art yoga and gymnastics space, with 18-foot ceilings, crowns this friendly retreat. You're close to hot springs and black-sand beaches, and the volcano is a 45-minute drive away. Bathrooms are shared. ⊠ *Pohoiki Rd., Box 1935, Pāhoa 96778* ☎ *808/965–8460 or 800/274–4446* ⊕ *www. yogaoasis.org* ⌁ *5 rooms with shared bath, 4 bungalows, 1 cottage ⌂ Some fans, massage, laundry service; no A/C, no room phones, no room TVs, no smoking* ☰ *MC, V. $35–$145.*

BIG ISLAND ESSENTIALS

Transportation

BY AIR

CARRIERS   You can fly direct to Hilo International Airport and Kona International Airport from other islands as well as from the Mainland. United offers flights from San Francisco and Los Angeles to Kona International Airport. ATA has new non-stop flight from Oakland, CA to Hilo International Airport. If you're willing to change planes on O'ahu or Maui, you can get here from anywhere. Hawaiian Airlines, for example, flies from San Diego, San Francisco, Portland, Phoenix, Las Vegas, Los Angeles, and Seattle from Honolulu. Aloha Airlines has daily trips from Oakland, Orange County, Burbank, Phoenix, Vancouver, and Las Vegas.

Aloha and Hawaiian airlines offer 40-minute flights from Honolulu to either Hilo or Kona. Fares are $160 to $220. Charters are available through Pacific Wings, which flies eight-passenger Cessna 402C-8 aircraft.

Island Air, Aloha Airline's commuter carrier, flies between Hilo and Kona for only $20—a great option for those who want to fly into one airport and out of another. Island Air also offers frequent flights from Kona to smaller destinations, including Lāna'i, Moloka'i, and Kapalua. ⇨ *See* Smart Travel Tips *for airline contact information.*

🔋 Charter Information: **Pacific Wings** ☎ 888/575-4546 or 808/873-0877 ⊕ www. pacificwings.com

AIRPORTS The Big Island has two main airports: Hilo International Airport and Kona International Airport. If you're staying on the west side of the island, fly into Kona. If you're staying on the eastern side, in Hilo or near Volcano, fly into Hilo. Waimea-Kohala Airport, near Waimea, is a small airstrip used by charter planes companies.

🔋 **Kona International Airport (KOA)** ☎ 808/329-3423. **Hilo International Airport (ITO)** ✉ General Lyman Field ☎ 808/934-5838 visitor information. **Waimea-Kohala Airport (MUE)** ☎ 808/887-8126.

TO & FROM KONA INTERNATIONAL AIRPORT Kona International Airport is about 7 mi (a 10-minute drive) from Kailua-Kona. The Keauhou resort area stretches another 6 mi to the south beyond Kailua. It takes about 30 to 45 minutes by car to reach the upscale resorts along the North Kona-Kohala Coast. If you're staying in the Waimea area, expect an hour's drive north from Kona.

Limousine service with a chauffeur who serves as a personal guide is $100 or more an hour, with a two-hour minimum. A few have all the extras—bar, televisions, and narrated tours.

If you're staying in Kailua or at the Keauhou resort area south of the airport, check with your hotel to see if shuttle service is available. There's no regularly scheduled shuttle service from Kona, although private service is offered by the Kohala Coast resorts, and by a local shuttle company. The rates for both shuttles depend on the distance, but are less than taxi fare. Check-in for the resort shuttles is at the Kohala Coast Resort Association counters at the Aloha and Hawaiian airlines arrival areas. SpeediShuttle arranges shared rides from Kona International Airport for $10 per person each way, but you must call ahead of time.

Taxi fares start at about $20 for transport to King Kamehameha's Kona Beach Hotel and are slightly more expensive for other Kailua-Kona hotels and condos. Taxi fares to Kohala Coast resorts range from $45 to $65. Several taxis offer guided tours.

🔋 **Aloha Taxi** ☎ 808/325-5448. **Elsa Taxi** ☎ 808/887-6446. **Luana Limousine** ☎ 808/326-5466. **Kona Airport Taxi** ☎ 808/329-7779. **Paradise Taxi** ☎ 808/329-1234. **SpeediShuttle** ☎ 808/329-5433.

TO & FROM HILO INTERNATIONAL AIRPORT Hilo International Airport is 2 mi from the hotels along Hilo's Banyan Drive. If you have chosen a B&B closer to Hawai'i Volcanoes National Park, plan on a 40-minute drive. If you're staying in the Waimea area, expect an hour's drive.

Limousine service starts at $100 an hour, with a two-hour minimum. Taxis to Hilo's Banyan Drive charge about $10 to $12. There's no regularly scheduled shuttle service from Hilo.

🔋 **A-1 Bob's Taxi** ☎ 808/959-4800. **Hilo Harry's Taxi** ☎ 808/935-7091.

BY BUS

Ali'i Shuttle operates buses between Keauhou Bay and Kailua-Kona Monday to Saturday, 8:30 AM to 7 PM. The shuttle connects all major hotels, attractions, and shopping centers along Ali'i Drive. The cost is $3.

The Hele-On bus, operated by the Hawai'i County Mass Transit Agency, travels around the island, with fares varying depending on the route. Visitors staying in Hilo, can take advantage of the Transit Agency's Shared Ride Taxi program which provides door-to-door transportation in the area. A one-way fare is $2 and a book of 15 coupons can be purchased for $30.

Ali'i Shuttle ☎ 808/938-1112. **Hele-On Bus** ☎ 808/961-8744 ⊕ www.hawaii-county.com/mass_transit/transit_main.htm.

BY CAR

You need a car to see the sights of the Big Island. Even if you're solely interested in relaxing at your self-contained megaresort, you may want to rent a car to drive to Kailua-Kona or to the restaurants in Waimea. We highly recommend that you rent a four-wheel-drive vehicle—there are several sights that are only reachable this way, and many of those that are accessible with regular cars are more easily reached with four-wheel drive.

Although there are several rental companies, cars can be scarce during holiday weekends, special events (especially the Ironman Triathlon in October), and during peak seasons from mid-December through mid-March. It's best to book well in advance.

CAR RENTAL Alamo, Avis, Budget, Dollar, Enterprise, Hertz, National, and Thrifty have offices on the Big Island, and all but Thrifty have locations at both Kona and Hilo airports. Ask about additional fees for picking up a car at one location and dropping it off at the other. Companies charge up to $50 for the convenience, but if you arrange it ahead of time they often waive the fee.

To get the best rate on a rental car, book it in conjunction with an interisland flight on Hawaiian or Aloha Airlines, or ask your travel agent to check out room-and-car packages. Drivers must be 25 years or older.

Most agencies make you sign an agreement that you won't drive on Saddle Road between Hilo and Waimea. This is a holdover from when it was actually dangerous. Now it's paved and not bumpy, although it still has no lighting, gas stations, or emergency phones. If you're thinking about stargazing, take the road up to Mauna Kea off Saddle Road for the clearest views. Alamo, Budget, Dollar, and Harper Rentals let you do this in their four-wheel-drive vehicles. *See* Smart Travel Tips ⇨ *for car rental company contact information.*

BY TAXI

To get from the airport to Kailua-Kona will cost you about $30 by taxi, and to get to the Kohala Coast resorts will be $15–$30 depending on which resort you're staying at (the Four Seasons is closest to the airport, while the Fairmont and the Mauna Lani are farther away). It costs an average of $50 each way from the Kohala Coast into Kailua-Kona town by taxi. Several companies advertise guided tours by taxi, but it's an expensive way to travel, with a trip around the island totaling about $350.

Contacts & Resources

EMERGENCIES

Dial **911** in an emergency to reach the police, fire department, or an ambulance. Call one of the hospitals listed for a doctor or dentist close to you. The Volcano Update Hotline provides 24-hour recorded information.

🚹 Emergency Services **Police** ☎ 808/935–3311. **Poison Control Center** ☎ 800/362–3585. **Volcano Update Hotline** ☎ 808/985–6000.

🚹 Hospitals **Hilo Medical Center** ✉ 1190 Waiānuenue Ave., Hilo ☎ 808/974–4700. **Kona Community Hospital** ✉ Hwy. 11 at Hau Kapila St., Kealakekua ☎ 808/322–9311. **Kona-Kohala Medical Associates** ✉ 75-137 Hualalai Rd., Kailua-Kona ☎ 808/329–1346. **North Hawai'i Community Hospital** ✉ 67-1125 Māmalahoa Hwy., Waimea ☎ 808/885–4444.

MEDIA

🚹 Bookstores **Basically Books** ✉ 160 Kamehameha Ave., Hilo ☎ 808/961–0144 or 800/903–6277 ⊕ www.basicallybooks.com. **Borders Books & Music** ✉ 75-1000 Henry St., Kailua-Kona ☎ 808/331–1668 ✉ 301 Maka'ala, Hilo ☎ 808/933–1410. **Middle Earth Bookshoppe** ✉ 75-5719 Ali'i Dr., Kailua-Kona ☎ 808/329–2123.

VISITOR INFORMATION

🚹 **Big Island Visitors Bureau** ✉ 250 Keawe St., Hilo 96720 ☎ 808/961–5797 🖶 808/961–2126 ✉ King's Shops at Waikoloa Village, 250 Waikoloa Beach Dr., B12, Waikoloa 96738 ☎ 808/886–1655 ⊕ www.bigisland.org. **Destination Hilo** ✉ 2109F Kaiwiki Rd., Hilo 96720 ☎ 808/935–5294 ⊕ www.destinationhilo.org. **Destination Kona Coast** 🗐 Box 2850, Kailua-Kona 96745 ☎ 808/329–6748 ⊕ www.destinationkonacoast.com. **Hawai'i Island's Magazine** ⊕ www.hawaii-island.com. **Hawai'i Visitors and Convention Bureau** ⊕ www.gohawaii.com. **Kohala Coast Resort Association** ✉ 69-275 Waikoloa Beach Dr., Waikoloa 96743 ☎ 808/886–4915 or 800/318–3637 ⊕ www.kkra.org. **Weather** ☎ 808/961–5582.

Kaua'i

Shipwreck Beach, South Shore (Poi'pū area)

WORD OF MOUTH

"I loved Kaua'i. Particularly Hanalei Bay. Absolutely magical. We snorkeled at Tunnels, hiked Nā Pali, kayaked and swam in the river, caught the sunset and had drinks at Princeville (a must!). I loved the roosters!"   —surlygirl

"Kaua'i [is] definitely the most lush, green, and 'natural' of the islands we've visited . . . I think if we went back I would like to rent a house and really get off the beaten path a little more."
                                                                              —Erin74

WELCOME TO KAUA'I

TOP 5
Reasons to Go

1. **Nā Pali Coast:** On foot, by boat, or by air---explore what is unargubly one of the most beautiful stretches of coastline in all Hawai'i.

2. **Kalalau Trail:** Hawai'i's ultimate adventure hike will test your endurance but reward you with lush tropical vegetation, white-sand beaches, and unforgettable views.

3. **Kayaking:** Kaua'i is a mecca for kayakers, with four rivers plus the spectacular coastline to explore.

4. **Waimea Canyon:** Dramatic, colorful rock formations and frequent rainbows make this natural wonder one of Kaua'i's most stunning features.

5. **Birds:** Birds thrive on Kaua'i, especially at the Kīlauea Point National Wildlife Refuge.

■ TIP→ On Kaua'i, the directions *mauka* (toward the mountains) and *makai* (toward the ocean) are often used. Locals tend to refer to highways by name rather than by number.

Dry, sunny, and sleepy, the West Side includes the historic towns of Hanapēpē, Waimea, and Kekaha. This area is ideal for outdoor adventurers because it's the entryway to the Waimea Canyon and Kōke'e State Park, and the departure point for most Nā Pali Coast boat trips.

NĀ PALI COAST
Kalalau Trail
Kōke'e State Park
550
WAIMEA CANYON
WEST SIDE
552
550
50
Kaulakahi Channel
Kekaha
Waimea
TO NI'IHAU
50
'Ele'e
Hanapēpē
Hanapēpē Bay

0   8 mi
0   8 km

Getting Oriented

Despite its small size—550 square mi—Kaua'i has four distinct regions, each with its own unique characteristics. The windward coast, which catches the prevailing trade winds, consists of the North Shore and East Side, while the drier leeward coast encompasses the South and West sides. One main road nearly encircles the island, except for a 15-mi stretch of sheer cliffs comprising Nā Pali Coast.

Dreamy beaches, green mountains, breathtaking scenery, and abundant rain, waterfalls, and rainbows characterize the North Shore, which includes the towns of Kīlauea, Princeville, and Hanalei.

The East Side is Kaua'i's commercial and residential hub, dominated by the island's largest town, Kapa'a. The airport, harbor, and government offices are found in the county seat of Līhu'e.

Peaceful landscapes, sunny weather, and beaches that rank among the best in the world make the South Side the resort capital of Kaua'i. The Po'ipū resort area is here along with the main towns of Kōloa, Lāwa'i, and Kalāheo.

4

KAUA'I PLANNER

When You Arrive

All commercial flights land at Līhu'e Airport, about 3 mi east of Līhu'e town. A rental car is the best way to get to your hotel, though taxis and some hotel shuttles are available. From the airport it will take you about 15 to 25 minutes to drive to Wailua or Kapa'a, 30 to 40 minutes to reach Po'ipū, and 45 minutes to an hour to get to Princeville or Hanalei.

Car Rentals

Unless you plan to stay strictly at a resort or do all of your sightseeing as part of guided tours, you'll need a rental car. You can take the bus, but they tend to be slow and don't go everywhere.

■ TIPS➔ **You most likely won't need a four-wheel-drive vehicle anywhere on the island, so save yourself the money. And while convertibles look fun, the frequent, intermittent rain showers and intense tropical sun make hardtops a better (and cheaper) choice. ■ Reserve your vehicle in advance, especially during the Christmas holidays. This will not only ensure that you get a car, but also that you get the best rates. Kaua'i has some of the highest gas prices in the islands.**

Timing Is Everything

If you're a beach lover, keep in mind that big surf can make many North Shore beaches unswimmable during winter months, while the South Side gets its large swells in summer. If you want to see the humpback whales, February is the best month, though they arrive as early as December and a few may still be around in early April. In the winter, Nā Pali Coast boat tours are sometimes rerouted due to high seas, and the Kalalau Trail can become very wet and muddy or, at times, impassable. Kayaking Nā Pali during winter is simply not an option. If you have your heart set on visiting Kaua'i's famed coast you may want to visit in the drier, warmer months (May–September).

Will It Rain?

Kaua'i is beautiful in every season, but if you must have good beach weather you should plan to visit between June and October. The rainy season runs from November through February, with the windward or east and north areas of the island receiving most of the rainfall. Nights can be chilly from November through March. Rain is possible throughout the year, of course, but it rarely rains everywhere on the island at once. If it's raining where you are, the best thing to do is head to another side of the island, usually south or west.

Guided Activities

When it comes to kayaking, Kaua'i is the island of choice. It's the only island with navigable rivers. A boat tour along Nā Pali Coast is another unique-to-Kaua'i experience. This chart lists rough prices for Kaua'i's top guided activities.

ACTIVITY	COST
Aerial Tours	$125–$370
Boat tours	$80–$175
Deep Sea Fishing	$120–$575
Golf	$8–$195
Lū'au	$58–$95
Kayaking Tours	$60–$200
Scuba Diving	$110–$395
Snorkel Cruises	$80–$175
Surfing Lessons	$55–$150
Whale-Watching	$59–$69

1-Day Itineraries

So much to do, so little time, is a common lament among visitors who think they can see Kaua'i in a day or two. To sample the highlights, try some of the following one-day itineraries.

Waimea Canyon & Kōke'e State Park.
Start early, pack a picnic, and head up the mountain for some of the loveliest scenery on the island. Stop at the scenic overlooks and peer into the colorful chasm of Waimea Canyon, then continue on to the cool forests of Kōke'e. Spend the afternoon hiking, then cruise down to Salt Pond Beach Park and watch the sunset.

Wailua River & Kapa'a.
Whether you rent a kayak, take a guided tour, or board one of the motor boats, spend the morning traversing the Wailua River. You'll pass through lush tropical foliage and wind up at the Fern Grotto. Afterward, drive up Kuamo'o Road to 'Ōpaeka'a Falls, then head into Kapa'a for lunch and a bit of shopping in one of the many boutiques and galleries on the northern edge of town.

Sweet History.
Start at the Kaua'i Museum in Līhu'e for an overview of island history, then tour Grove Farm Homestead to get a feel of country life in bygone days. As you head west on Kaumuali'i Highway, stop in at Kilohana Plantation and check out the mansion. Continue on to Kaumakani, the dusty little camp town on the West Side, where you can take a guided tour of the island's last sugar plantation, owned by Gay & Robinson. After viewing the fields and seeing how cane is processed into granulated sugar, head east to Kōloa town, site of Kaua'i's first plantation. Browse the shops in the historic buildings that line the charming main street, or zip over to Po'ipū Beach, where you can wash off the dust with a refreshing swim before dinner.

Beaches & Birds.
Load up the kids and head for Lydgate State Park on the East Side, where they can enjoy Kamalani Playground and everyone can swim and snorkel. For lunch, grab a bite to eat as you drive north through Kapa'a. Relax and enjoy the scenery as you continue to the Kīlauea Point National Wildlife Refuge, where you can watch seabirds soar and perhaps spot whales and dolphins cavorting offshore. Continue north to Hanalei Bay, where you can swim, boogie board, or jog on the beach. If the waves are huge, stay out of the water and check out the surfing scene. As the sun sinks and the mountains turn rosy, pick up a pizza and drive back to your hotel while the kids snooze in the back seat.

■ *For more details, see* Exploring; Beaches; Water Activities & Tours; *and* Golf, Hiking & Other Activities *on Kaua'i in this chapter.*

Ways to Save

■ Save on produce and flowers by shopping at the farmers' markets held on different days of the week all around the island.

■ Stock up on gas and groceries in Kapa'a and Līhu'e if you're staying on the North Shore or South Side, as prices go up farther from town.

■ Book guided activities, such as Nā Pali Coast boat tours, on the Internet. Individual outfitters' Web sites usually offer discounts for those who book online.

■ Reserve the smallest car for your needs to save money on gas and rental fees.

Written by
Joan Conrow
& Kim
Steutermann
Rogers

Updated by
Kim
Steutermann
Rogers

EVEN A NICKNAME LIKE "THE GARDEN ISLAND" fails to do justice to Kaua'i's beauty. Verdant trees grow canopies over the island's few roads, brooding mountains are framed by long, sandy beaches, coral reefs, and sheer sea cliffs. For years, Kaua'i managed to resist the rampant growth occurring elsewhere in the state. Its reputation for rain deterred tourists, and devastating hurricanes in 1982 and 1992 discouraged development. Currently, a proliferation of new construction offers irrefutable proof that Kaua'i has been discovered, but life here remains simple, and the locals are determined to keep it that way.

The oldest of the Hawaiian islands, Kaua'i also holds the dubious honor of being "the wettest place on Earth," thanks to its 460-inch average annual rainfall. At 558 square miles it is the fourth-largest island, and its population remains low at 54,200.

Geology

Kaua'i is the oldest and northernmost of the main Hawaiian Islands. Five million years of wind and rain have worked their magic, sculpting fluted sea cliffs and whittling away at the cinder cones and caldera that prove its volcanic origin. Foremost among these is Wai'ale'ale, one of the wettest spots on Earth. Its 480-inch annual rainfall feeds the mighty Wailua River, the only navigable waterway in Hawai'i. The vast Alaka'i Swamp soaks up rain like a sponge, releasing it slowly into the watershed that gives Kaua'i its emerald sheen.

Flora & Fauna

Kaua'i offers some of the best birding in the state, due in part to the absence of the mongoose. Many nēnē (endangered Hawaiian state bird) reared in captivity have been successfully released here, along with an endangered forest bird called the puai'ohi. The island is also home to a large colony of migratory nesting seabirds, and has two refuges protecting endangered Hawaiian water birds. Kaua'i's most noticeable fowl, however, is the wild chicken. A cross between jungle fowl (moa) brought by the Polynesians, and domestic chickens and fighting cocks that escaped during the last two hurricanes, they are everywhere, and the roosters crow when they feel like it, not just at dawn. Consider yourself warned.

History

Kaua'i's residents have had a reputation for independence since ancient times. Called "the separate kingdom," Kaua'i alone resisted King Kamehameha's charge to unite the Hawaiian Islands. In fact, it was only by kidnapping Kaua'i's king, Kaumuali'i, and forcing him to marry Kamehameha's widow that the Garden Isle was joined to the rest of Hawai'i. That spirit lives on today as Kaua'i residents resist the lure of tourism dollars captivating the rest of the islands. Local building rules maintain that no structure may be taller than a coconut tree, and Kaua'i's capital city Līhu'e is still more small town than city.

On Kaua'i Today

Kaua'i can't keep the rest of the world at bay forever. The island was just starting to develop when Hurricane Iniki hit in 1992. At the time, many people credited the hurricane with preserving Kaua'i. Now, 15 years later, cruise ships are docking off the coast, development is back on track, and there are several condos and resorts going up all around the island. That said, the island's natural beauty is still its greatest asset and residents are determined to preserve it. Luckily, the increasing popularity of ecotourism on the island means they can do so without losing out on tourist dollars.

Legends & Mythology: The Menehune

Although all of the island's have a few stories about the menehune—magical little people who accomplished great big feats—Kaua'i is believed to be their home base. The Menehune Fishpond, above Nāwilwili Harbor, is a prime example of their work. The story goes that the large pond (initially 25 mi in diameter) was built in one night by thousands of menehune passing stones from hand to hand. A spy disrupted their work in the middle of the night, leaving two gaps that are still visible today (drive to the pond on Hulemalu Road, or kayak up Huleia Stream).

EXPLORING KAUA'I

The main road tracing Kaua'i's perimeter takes you past much more scenery than would seem possible on one small island. Chiseled mountains, thundering waterfalls, misty hillsides, dreamy beaches, lush vegetation, and quaint small towns comprise the physical landscape. And there's plenty to do, as well as see: plantation villages, a historic lighthouse, wildlife refuges, a fern grotto, a colorful canyon, and deep rivers are all easily explored.

■ TIP→ **While exploring the island, try to take advantage of the many roadside scenic overlooks to pull off and take in the constantly changing view. And don't try to pack too much into one day.** Kaua'i is small, but travel is slow. The island's sights are divided into four geographic areas, in clockwise order: the North Shore, the East Side, the South Shore, and the West Side.

The North Shore

The North Shore of Kaua'i includes the environs of Kīlauea, Princeville, Hanalei and Hā'ena. Traveling north on Route 56, the coastal highway crosses the Wailua River and the busy towns of Wailua and Kapa'a before emerging into a decidedly rural and scenic landscape, with expansive views of the island's rugged interior mountains. As the two-lane highway turns west and narrows, it winds through spectacular scenery and passes the posh resort community of Princeville before dropping down into Hanalei Valley. Here it narrows further and becomes a federally recognized scenic roadway, replete with one-lane bridges (the local etiquette is for five or six cars to cross at a time, before yielding to those on the other side), hairpin turns, and heart-stopping coastal vistas. The road ends at Kē'ē, where the ethereal rain forests and fluted sea cliffs of Nā Pali Coast Wilderness State Park begin.

In winter Kaua'i's North Shore receives more rainfall than other areas of the island. Don't let this deter you from visiting. The clouds drift over the mountains of Nā Molokama creating a mysterious mood and then,

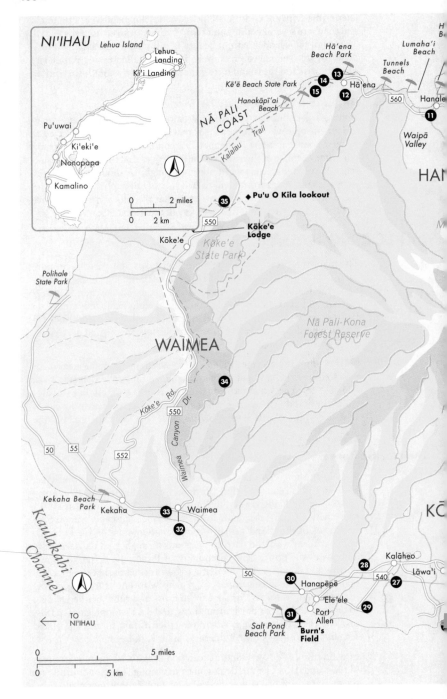

Kaua'i

in a blink, disappear, and you're rewarded with mountains laced with a dozen waterfalls or more. The views of the mountain—as well as the sunsets over the ocean—from The Living Room, adjacent to the lobby of the Princeville Resort, are fantastic.

The North Shore attracts all kinds. It was once home, or so they say, to a mythical people, called Menehune (⇨ *see* Maniniholo Dry Cave). In the late 1960s, Howard Taylor, brother to actress Elizabeth Taylor, allowed a few men to camp on his property. They invited friends who invited more friends until the number reached well over 100 and the area became known as "Taylor Camp." Some lived in tents, others under tarps, a good number even built make-shift tree houses. Eventually, state officials bulldozed the camp. Today, the North Shore attracts the likes of Taylor's sister—Hollywood celebrities—and surfers. In fact, Andy Irons, three-time world surfing champion, grew up riding waves along the North Shore; when he's not traversing the globe in search of waves, he lives and surfs here.

Main Attractions

Hanalei. Crossing the historic one-lane bridge into Hanalei reveals old-world Hawai'i, including working taro farms, poi making, and evenings of throwing horseshoes at Black Pot Beach Park—found unmarked (as most everything is on Kaua'i) at the east end of Hanalei Bay Beach Park. Although the current real estate boom on Kaua'i has attracted mainland millionaires building estate homes on the few remaining parcels of land in Hanalei, there's still plenty to see and do. It's *the* gathering place on the North Shore. Restaurants, shops, and people-watching top the list here, and you won't find a single brand name, chain or big-box store around—unless you count surf brands like Quiksilver and Billabong. The beach and river offer swimming, snorkeling, boogie boarding, surfing, and kayaking. Those hanging around at sunset often congregate at the Hanalei Pavilion where a husband-and-wife, slack-key-guitar-playing combo are long-time fixtures. There's an old rumor that the local newspaper, the *Garden Island,* recently quashed, that says Hanalei was the inspiration for the song *Puff the Magic Dragon* performed by the 1960s singing sensation Peter, Paul & Mary. Even with the newspaper's exposé, Hawai'i Movie Tours (⇨ *see* Sightseeing Tours *later in this chapter*) caps off their day-long visit of famous Kaua'i movie sites on the Hanalei Pier with a guide pointing out the shape of the dragon carved into the mountains encircling the town. ⊠ *Rte. 560, 3 mi north of Princeville Shopping Center.*

❿ Hanalei Valley Overlook. Dramatic mountains and a patchwork of neat taro farms bisected by the wide Hanalei River make this one of Hawai'i's most picturesque sights. The fertile Hanalei Valley has been planted in taro since perhaps AD 700, save for a century-long foray into rice that ended in 1960. (The historic Haraguchi Rice Mill is all that remains of the era.) Many taro farmers lease land within the 900-acre Hanalei National Wildlife Refuge, helping to provide wetland habitat for four species of endangered Hawaiian water birds. ⊠ *Rte. 56, across from Foodland, Princeville.*

Hiking the Kalalau Trail

See Page 443

9 Kīlauea Point National Wildlife Refuge & Kīlauea Lighthouse. A beacon for sea traffic since it was built in 1913, this National Historic Landmark has the largest clamshell lens of any lighthouse in the world. It's within a national wildlife refuge, where thousands of seabirds soar on the trade winds and nest on the steep ocean cliffs. Endangered *nēnē* geese, red-footed boobies, Laysan albatross, wedge-tailed shearwaters, white- and red-tailed tropicbirds, great frigatebirds, Pacific golden plovers (all identified on educational signboards) along with native plants, dolphins, humpback whales, huge winter surf, and gorgeous views of the North Shore add to the drama of this special place, making it well worth the modest entry fee. The gift shop has a great selection of books about the island's natural history and an array of unique merchandise, with all proceeds benefitting education and preservation efforts. ⊠ *Kīlauea Lighthouse Rd., Kīlauea* ☎ *808/828–0168* ⊕ *www.fws.gov/pacificislands/ wnwr/kkilaueanwr.html* ⊠ *$3* ☉ *Daily 10–4.*

Fodor'sChoice
★

NEED A BREAK?

Banana Joe's Tropical Fruit Stand (⊠ Just north of turnoff to Kīlauea, past mile marker 23, Kīlauea ☎ 808/828–1092 ⊕ www.bananajoekauai.com) occupies a rustic yellow shelter on the *mauka* side of Route 56, past the turnoff to Kīlauea. Owners Joe and Cindy Halasey make refreshing frosties and smoothies from tropical fruits, including their own bananas. They also sell dried fruits, flower lei, and a very good selection of locally grown fruits and fresh vegetables. It's a great place to try seasonal specialties and things you likely won't find in the produce section back home.

★ ☺ **7** Na 'Aina Kai. One small sign along the highway is all that promotes this one-time private garden gone awry. Ed and Joyce Doty's love for plants and art now spans 240 acres, includes 13 different gardens, a hardwood plantation, a canyon, lagoons, Japanese teahouse, a poinciana maze, waterfall, and a sandy beach. Throughout are more than 70 bronze sculptures, reputedly one of the nation's largest collections. Now a nonprofit organization, the latest project is a children's garden with a 16-foot-tall Jack and the Beanstalk bronze sculpture, gecko maze, treehouse, kid-size train and, a tropical jungle. Located in a residential neighborhood and hoping to maintain good neighborly relations, the garden limits tours (guided only). Tour lengths vary from 1½ to 5 hours. Reservations strongly recommended. ⊠ *Rte. 56 north of mile marker 21, turn* makai *on Wailapa Rd. and follow signs* ☎ *808/828–0525* ⊕ *www.naainakai. org* ⊠ *$25 for 1½-hr stroll to $70 for 5-hr hiking tour* ☉ *Tues.–Fri., call ahead for hours.*

Also Worth Seeing

★ **15** Kē'ē Beach State Park. This stunning, and often overcrowded, beach marks the start of majestic Nā Pali Coast. The 11-mi **Kalalau Trail** begins near the parking lot, drawing day hikers and backpackers (⇨ *see* Hiking the

Kalalau Trail *later in this chapter*). Another path leads from the sand to a stone hula platform dedicated to **Laka**, the goddess of hula, which has been in use since ancient times. This is a sacred site that should be approached with respect; it's inappropriate for visitors to leave offerings at this altar tended by students in a local hula *halau* (school). Local etiquette suggests observing from a distance. Most folks head straight for the sandy beach and its idyllic lagoon, which is great for snorkeling when the sea is calm. ⊠ *Drive to western end of Rte. 560.*

⑧ Kīlauea. A former plantation town, Kīlauea town itself maintains its rural flavor in the midst of the unrelenting gentrification encroaching it. Especially noteworthy are its historic lava-rock buildings, including **Christ Memorial Episcopal Church** on Kolo Street and the Kong Lung Company on Keneke Street, now an expensive shop. ⊠ *Rte. 56, mile marker 23.*

⑬ Limahuli Garden. Narrow Limahuli Valley, with its fluted mountain peaks and ancient stone taro terraces, creates an unparalled setting for this botanical garden and nature preserve. Dedicated to protecting native plants and unusual varieties of taro, it represents the principles of conservation and stewardship held by its founder, Charles "Chipper" Wichman. Limahuli's priomordial beauty and strong *mana* (spiritual power) eclipse the extensive botanical collection. It's one of the most gorgeous spots on Kaua'i and the crown jewel of the National Tropical Botanical Garden, which Wichman now heads. Call ahead to reserve a guided tour, or tour on your own. Be sure to check out the quality gift shop and revolutionary compost toilet and be prepared for walking a somewhat steep hillside. ⊠ *Rte. 560, Hā'ena* ☎ *808/826–1053* ⊕ *www.ntbg.org* ⊡ *Self-guided tour $10, guided tour $15* ☉ *Tues.–Fri. and Sun. 9:30–4.*

⑫ Maniniholo Dry Cave. According to legend, Maniniholo was the head fisherman of the Menehune, the possibly real, possibly mythical first inhabitants of the island. As they were preparing to leave Kaua'i and return home (wherever that was), Maniniholo called some of his workers to Hā'ena to collect food from the reef. They gathered so much that they couldn't carry it all, and left some near the ocean cliffs, with plans to retrieve it the following day. It all disappeared during the night, however, and Maniniholo realized that imps living in the rock fissures were the culprits. He and his men dug into the cliff to find and destroy the imps, leaving behind the cave that now bears his name. Across the highway from Maniniholo Dry Cave is **Hā'ena State Park.** ⇨ *See* Beaches *later in this chapter.* ⊠ *Rte. 560, Hā'ena.*

⑭ Waikapala'e and Waikanaloa Wet Caves. Said to have been dug by Pele, goddess of fire, these watering holes used to be clear, clean, and great for swimming. Now stagnant, they're nevertheless a photogenic example of the many haunting natural landmarks of Kaua'i's North Shore. Waikanaloa is visible right beside the highway. Across the road from a small parking area, a five-minute uphill walk leads to Waikapala'e. ⊠ *Western end of Rte. 560.*

⑪ Wai'oli Mission House. This 1837 home was built by missionaries Lucy and Abner Wilcox. Its tidy New England architecture and formal koa-wood furnishings epitomize the prim and proper missionary influence, while the informative guided tours offer a fascinating peek into the private lives of the island's first white residents. Half-hour guided tours are available. ⊠ *Kūhiō Hwy., Hanalei* ☎ *808/245–3202* 🖂 *Donations accepted* ⊙ *Tues., Thurs., and Sat. 9–3.*

The East Side

The East Side encompasses Līhu'e, Wailua, and Kapa'a; it's also known as the "Coconut Coast," as there was once a coconut plantation where today's aptly named Coconut Marketplace is located. A small grove still exists on both sides of the highway. *Mauka*, a fenced herd of goats keep the grass tended; on the *makai* side, you can walk through the grove, although it's best not to walk directly under the trees. Falling coconuts hit hard. Līhu'e is the county seat and the whole East Side is the island's center of commerce, so early morning and late afternoon drive times (or rush hour) can get congested. (Because there's only one main road, if there's a serious traffic accident the entire roadway may be closed, with no way around. Not to worry; it's a rarity.) Continuing straight from the airport, the road leads to the middle of Līhu'e. To the left and right are fast-food restaurants, Wal-Mart, Kmart, Borders Books & Music, and a variety of county and state buildings.

Turn to the right out of the airport for the road to Wailua. A bridge—under which the culturally significant Wailua River gently flows—marks the beginning of town. Wailua is comprised of a few restaurants and shops, a few midrange resorts along the coastline and a housing community *mauka*. It quickly blends into Kapa'a; there's no real demarcation. Kapa'a houses the two biggest grocery stores on the island, side by side: Foodland and Safeway. It also offers plenty of dining and shopping options. Old Town Kapa'a was once a plantation town, which is no surprise—most larger towns on Kaua'i once were—however this one didn't disappear with the sugar mill and pineapple cannery. Old Town Kapa'a is made up of a collection of wooden-front shops, some built by plantation workers and still run by their progeny today.

Main Attractions

🔟 Kaua'i Museum. Maintaining a stately presence on Rice Street, the historic museum building is easy to find. It features a permanent display, "The Story of Kaua'i," which provides a competent overview of the Garden Island and Ni'ihau, tracing the islands' geology, mythology, and cultural history. Local artists are represented in changing exhibits in the second-floor Mezzanine Gallery. The gift shop alone is worth a visit, with a fine collection of authentic Ni'ihau shell lei, feather hatband lei, hand-turned wooden bowls, reference books, and other quality arts, crafts, and gifts, many of them locally made. ⊠ *4428 Rice St., Līhu'e* ☎ *808/245–6931* 🖂 *$7* ⊙ *Weekdays 9–4, Sat. 10–4.*

2 Lydgate State Park. The park, named for the Reverend J. M. Lydgate, founder of the Līhu'e English Union Church, has a large children-designed and community-built playground, pavilion, and picnic area. It also houses the remains of an ancient site where commoners who broke

Continued on page 408

HAWAI'I' S PLANTS 101

Hawai'i is a bounty of rainbow-colored flowers and plants. The evening air is scented with their fragrance. Just look at the front yard of almost any home, travel any road, or visit any local park and you'll see a spectacular array of colored blossoms and leaves. What most visitors don't know is that the plants they are seeing are not native to Hawai'i; rather, they were introduced during the last two centuries as ornamental plants, or for timber, shade, or fruit.

Hawai'i boasts every climate on the planet, excluding the two most extreme: arctic tundra and arid desert. The Islands have wine-growing regions, cactus-speckled ranchlands, icy mountaintops, and the rainiest forests on earth.

Plants introduced from around the world thrive here. The lush lowland valleys along the windward coasts are predominantly populated by non-native trees including yellow- and red-fruited **guava**, silvery leafed **kukui**, and orange-flowered **tulip trees**.

The colorful **plumeria flower**, very fragrant and commonly used in lei making, and the

giant multicolored **hibiscus flower**, are both used by many women as hair adornments, and are two of the most common plants found around homes and hotels. The umbrella-like **monkeypod tree** from Central America provides shade in many of Hawai'i's parks including Kapiolani Park in Honolulu. Hawai'i's largest tree, found in Lahaina, Maui, is a giant **banyan tree**. Its canopy and massive support roots cover several acres. The native **o'hia tree**, with it's brilliant red brush-like flowers, and the **hapu'u**, a giant tree fern, are common in Hawai'i's forests and are also used ornamentally in gardens and around homes.

Bougainvillea

Guava

Monkeypod Tree

Banyan Tree

O'hia Lehua

Tulip Tree

Plumeria

Pandanus

Hibiscus

Anthurium

Kukui Tree

Hapu'u Okina

DID YOU KNOW?

Over 2,200 plant species are found in the Hawaiian Islands, but only about 1,000 are native. Of these, 282 are so rare, they are endangered. Hawai'i's endemic plants evolved from ancestral seeds arriving on the Islands over thousands of years as baggage on birds, floating on ocean currents, or drifting on winds from continents thousands of miles away. Once here, these plants evolved in isolation, creating many new species known nowhere else in the world.

a royal taboo could seek refuge from punishment. It's part of an extensive complex of sacred archaeological sites that runs from Wai'ale'ale to the sea, underscoring the significance of this region to the ancient Hawaiians. ✉ *South of Wailua River turn* makai *off Rte. 56 onto Leho Dr. and left onto Nalu Rd.* ⧉ *Free* ☉ *Daily, dawn–dusk.*

★ ❺ **'Ōpaeka'a Falls.** The mighty Wailua River produces many dramatic waterfalls, and 'Ōpaeka'a (pronounced oh-pie-kah-ah) is one of the best. It plunges hundreds of feet to the pool below and can be easily viewed from a scenic overlook with ample parking. 'Ōpaeka'a means "rolling shrimp," which refers to tasty native crustaceans that were once so abundant they could be seen tumbling in the falls. ✉ *Rte. 580, Kuamo'o Rd., Wailua.*

❹ **Poli'ahu Heiau.** Storyboards near this ancient *heiau* (sacred site) recount the significance of the sacred structures found along the Wailua River. It's unknown exactly how the ancient Hawaiians used Poli'ahu Heiau— one of the largest pre-Christian temples on the island—but legend says it was built by the Menehune because of the unusual stonework found in its walled enclosures. From this site, drive downhill toward the ocean to **pōhaku hānau**, a two-piece birthing stone said to confer special blessings on all children born there, and **pōhaku piko**, whose crevices were a repository for umbilical cords left by parents seeking a clue to their child's destiny, which reportedly was foretold by how his cord fared in the rock. Some Hawaiians feel these sacred stones shouldn't be viewed as tourist attractions. Treat them with respect: never stand or sit on the rocks, or leave any offerings. ✉ *Rte. 580, Kuamo'o Rd., Wailua.*

❶ **Wailua Falls.** You may recognize this impressive cascade from the opening sequences of the *Fantasy Island* television series. Kaua'i has plenty of noteworthy waterfalls, but this one is especially picturesque, easy to find, and easy to photograph. ✉ *End of Rte. 583, Ma'alo Rd., 4 mi west of Rte. 56.*

Also Worth Seeing

⓳ **Alekoko (Menehune) Fishpond.** No one knows who built this aquaculture structure in the Hule'ia River. Legend attributes it to the Menehune, a possibly real, possibly mythical ancient race of people known for their small stature, industrious nature, and superb stoneworking skills. Volcanic rock was cut and fit together into massive walls 4 feet thick and 5 feet high, forming an enclosure for raising mullet and other freshwater fish that has endured for centuries. Strangely enough, it is currently for sale for $12 million. ✉ *Hulemalu Rd., Niumalu.*

❸ **Fern Grotto.** This yawning lava tube swathed in lush fishtail ferns is 3 miles upriver. Although it's part of a state park, the state leased the landing concession to two motorboat companies that offer rather campy tours. Recently, Sonny Waialeale lost his concession and the state confiscated his boats when he refused to pay his concession fees, claiming an inherent right as a native Hawaiian to use the river. Smith's Motor Boat Services is now the only way to legally see the grotto, recently refurbished under a state tourism grant. You can access the entrance with a kayak, but if boats are there, you won't be allowed to land. ✉ *Depart from*

Wailua Marina on mauka *side of Rte. 56, just south of Wailua River*
☎ 808/821–6892 ☒ *$20* ☽ *Daily 9–3:30.*

★ ❷⓪ **Grove Farm Homestead.** Guided tours of this carefully restored 80-acre
country estate offer a fascinating, and authentic, look at how upper-class
Caucasians experienced plantation life in the mid-19th century. The tour
focuses on the original home, built by the Wilcox family in 1860 and
filled with a quirky collection of classic Hawaiiana. You can also see
the workers' quarters, farm animals, orchards, and gardens that reflect
the practical, self-sufficient lifestyle of the island's earliest Western inhabitants. Tours of the homestead are conducted twice a day, three days
per week. To protect the historic building and its furnishings, tours may
be canceled on very wet days. ■ TIP➜ With a six-person limit per tour, reservations are essential and young children are not encouraged. ☒ *Rte. 58, Nāwiliwili Rd., Līhu'e* ☎ *808/245–3202* ☒ *$5* ☽ *Tours Mon., Wed., and Thurs.
at 10 and 1.*

☾ ❷① **Kilohana Plantation.** This estate dates back to 1896, when plantation manager Albert Spencer Wilcox first developed it as a working cattle ranch.
His nephew, Gaylord Parke Wilcox, took over in 1936, building Kaua'i's
first mansion. Today the 16,000-square-foot, Tudor-style home houses
specialty shops, art galleries, and Gaylord's, a pretty restaurant with courtyard seating. Nearly half the original furnishings remain, and the gardens and orchards were replanted according to the original plans. You
can tour the grounds for free; children enjoy visiting the farm animals.
Horse-drawn carriage rides are available, or you can tour the old Grove
Farm Plantation in a sugarcane wagon pulled by Clydesdales. Beginning
the summer of 2006, a train will run 2½ mi through 104 acres of lands
representing the agricultural story of Kaua'i—then and now. ☒ *3-2087
Kaumuali'i Hwy., Rte. 50, Līhu'e* ☎ *808/245–5608* ☽ *Mon.–Sat.
9:30–9:30, Sun. 9:30–5.*

❶⓺ **Līhu'e.** The commercial and political center of Kaua'i County, which includes the islands of Kaua'i and Ni'ihau, Līhu'e is home to the island's
major airport, harbor, and hospital. This is where you can find the state
and county offices that issue camping and hiking permits, and the same
fast-food eateries and big-box stores that blight the mainland. The
county is seeking help in reviving the downtown; for now, once your
business is done, there's little reason to linger in lackluster Līhu'e.
☒ *Rtes. 56 and 50.*

❶⓼ **Nāwiliwili.** The commercial harbor at Nāwiliwili is a major port of call
for container ships, U.S. Navy vessels, and passenger cruise lines. Anglers and recreational boaters use the nearby small boat harbor. This is
the main departure point for deep-sea fishing charters. There's protected
swimming at Kalapakī Bay, fronting the Marriott resort, although the
water quality is questionable at times. With the recent increase in docking cruise ships, Anchor Cove Shopping Center and Harbor Mall have
refurbished and offer a good selection of shops and restaurants. ☒ Makai
end of Wa'apā Rd., Līhu'e.

❻ **Sleeping Giant.** Although its true name is Nounou, this landmark mountain ridge is better known as the Sleeping Giant because of its resem-

blance to a very large man sleeping on his back. Legends differ on whether the giant is Puni, who was accidentally killed by rocks launched at invading canoes by the Menehune, or Nunui, a gentle creature who has not yet awakened from the nap he took centuries ago after building a massive temple and enjoying a big feast. ⊠ *Mauka Rte. 56, about 1 mi north of Wailua River, backing Kapa'a.*

NEED A BREAK? Stop in at **Lotus Root** (⊠ 4-1384 Kuhio Hwy, Kapa'a ☎ 808/823–6658), an offshoot of the wildly popular vegan restaurant Blossoming Lotus, for a healthy and yummy snack. This juice bar and bakery serves pizza, breakfast burritos, and outta-this-world Cloud Nine, a juice concoction made with papaya, macadamia nuts, dates, coconut milk, and vanilla rooibos tea.

☺ **Smith's Tropical Paradise.** Nestled up next to Wailua Marina along the mighty Wailua River, this 30-acre botanical and cultural garden offers a glimpse of exotic foliage, including fruit orchards, a bamboo rain forest, and tropical lagoons. Take the tram and enjoy a narrated tour or stroll along the mile-long pathways. It's a popular spot for wedding receptions and other large events, and its three-times-weekly lū'au is one of the island's oldest and best. ■ TIP→ It's very difficult to make a northbound turn onto Kūhiō Highway from this road, so it's best to stop in when you're Līhu'e-bound. ⊠ *Just south of Wailua River,* mauka, *on Rte. 56., Kapa'a* ☎ *808/821–6895* ⤳ *$5.25* ☉ *Daily 8:30–4.*

The South Shore

As you follow the main road south from Līhu'e, the landscape becomes lush and densely vegetated before giving way to drier conditions that characterize Po'ipū, the South Side's major resort area. Po'ipū owes much of its popularity to a steady supply of sunshine and a string of sandy beaches, although the beaches are smaller and more covelike compared to West Side beaches. With its extensive selection of accommodations, services, and activities, it attracts more visitors than any other region on Kaua'i. Both Po'ipū and nearby Kōloa (site of Kaua'i's first sugar mill) can be reached via Route 520 (Maluhia Road) from the Līhu'e area. Route 520 is known locally as Tree Tunnel Road due to the stand of eucalyptus trees lining the road that were planted at the turn of the 20th century. It's a distinctive way to announce, "You are now on vacation," for there's a definite feel of leisure in the air here. There's still plenty to do—snorkel, bike, walk, horseback ride, take ATV tours, surf, scuba dive, shop, and dine—everything you'd want on a tropical vacation. From the west, Route 530 (Kōloa Road) slips into downtown Kōloa, a string of fun shops and restaurants, at an intersection with the only gas station on the South Shore.

Main Attractions

㉒ **Kōloa.** Hawai's lucrative foray into sugar was born in this sleepy town, where the first sugar was milled back in 1830. You can still see the mill's old stone smokestack. Little else remains, save for the charming plantation-style buildings that have kept Kōloa from becoming a tacky tourist trap for Po'ipū-bound visitors. The original small-town ambience has been preserved by converting historic structures along the main street into boutiques, restaurants, and shops. Placards describe the original tenants and life in the old mill town. Look for Kōloa Fish Market, which offers poke and sashimi takeout, and Progressive Expressions, a popular local surf shop. ⊠ *Rte. 520.*

㉕ National Tropical Botanical Gardens (NTBG). Tucked away in Lāwa'i Valley, these gardens include lands and a cottage once used by Hawai'i's Queen Emma for a summer retreat. Visitors can take a self-guided tour of the rambling 252-acre **McBryde Gardens** to see and learn about plants collected from throughout the tropics. The 100-acre **Allerton Gardens,** which can be visited only on a guided tour, artfully display statues and water features that were originally developed as part of a private estate. A secluded cove known as Lāwa'i Kai can be reached through Allerton Gardens (only on tour, with no time for romping around in the sand); the beach is otherwise largely inaccessible to the public. Reservations are required for tours of Allerton Gardens, but not for the self-guided tours of McBryde Gardens. The visitor center has a high-quality gift shop with botany-theme merchandise.

Besides harboring and propagating rare and endangered plants from Hawai'i and elsewhere, NTBG functions as a scientific research and education center. The organization also operates gardens in Limahuli, on Kaua'i's north shore, and in Hāna, on Maui's east shore. ⊠ *Lāwa'i Rd., across from Spouting Horn parking lot, Po'ipū* ☎ *808/742–2623* ⊕ *www.ntbg.org* ⌑ *Self-guided tour (McBryde) $15, guided tour (Allerton) $30* ☉ *McBryde Gardens Mon.–Sat. 9:30–5, Allerton Gardens tours Mon.–Sat. at 9, 10, 1, and 2, Sun. at 10 and 1:30.*

㉖ Spouting Horn. If the conditions are right, you can see a natural blowhole in the reef behaving like Old Faithful, shooting salt water high into the air. It's most dramatic during big summer swells, which force large quantities of water through an ancient lava tube with great force. ■ **TIP➔ Stay on the paved walkways as rocks can be slippery and wave action unpredictable.** Vendors hawk inexpensive souvenirs and other items in the parking lot. You may find good deals on shell jewelry, but ask for a certificate of authenticity to ensure it's a genuine Ni'ihau shell lei before paying the higher price that these intricate creations command. ⊠ *At end of Lāwa'i Rd., Po'ipū.*

Also Worth Seeing

㉓ Po'ipū. Po'ipū has emerged as Kaua'i's top visitor destination, thanks to its generally sunny weather and a string of golden-sand beaches dotted with oceanfront lodgings, including the Sheraton Kaua'i Resort and a half dozen condominium projects. More and more homes in the area are converting to private vacation rentals and B&Bs. (This trend across the island has created a shortage of affordable housing for residents.) Beaches are user-friendly, with protected waters for *keiki* (children) and novice snorkelers, lifeguards, clean restrooms, covered pavilions, and a sweet coastal promenade ideal for leisurely strolls. Some experts even rank Po'ipū Beach Park number one in the nation. That may be a bit of an overstatement, although it certainly does warrant high accolades.

SUNSHINE MARKETS

If you want to rub elbows with the locals and purchase fresh produce and flowers at very reasonable prices, head for Sunshine Markets, also known as Kauaʻi's farmers' markets. These busy markets are held weekly, usually in the afternoon, at locations all around the island. They're good fun, and they support small, neighborhood farmers. Arrive a little early, bring dollar bills to speed up transactions and plastic shopping bags to carry your produce, and be prepared for some pushy shoppers. Farmers are usually happy to educate visitors about unfamiliar fruits and veggies, especially when the crowd thins. For more information, contact **Sunshine Markets** (📞 808/241-6303 ⊕ www.kauai.gov).

North Shore: ✉ Waipa, mauka of Rte. 560 north of Hanalei after mile marker 3 ◷ Tues. 2 pm ✉ Kīlauea Neighborhood Center, on Keneke St. in Kīlauea ◷ Thurs. 4:30 pm ✉ Hanalei Community Center ◷ Sat. 9:30 am.

East Side: ✉ Vidinha Stadium, Līhuʻe, 1/2 mi south of airport on Rte. 51 ◷ Fri. 3 pm ✉ Wailua Homesteads Park, Wailua, turn *mauka* on Kuamoʻo Rd., drive 2½ mi, turn right on Rte. 581/Olohena Rd., drive 1/2 mi ◷ Tues. 3 pm ✉ Kapaʻa, turn *mauka* on Rte. 581/Olohena Rd for 1 block ◷ Wed. 3 pm.

South Shore: ✉ Ballpark, Kōloa, north of intersection of Kōloa Road and Rte. 520 ◷ Mon. noon.

■ TIP→ Don't bother looking for downtown Poʻipū; there is no definitive town center. ✉ *Rte. 520.*

㉔ Prince Kūhiō Park. A triangle of grass behind the Prince Kūhiō condominiums honors the birthplace of Kauaʻi's beloved Prince Jonah Kūhiō Kalanianaʻole. Known for his kind nature and good deeds, he lost his chance at the throne when Americans staged an illegal overthrow of Queen Liliʻuokalani in 1893 and toppled Hawaiʻi's constitutional monarchy. This is a great place to view wave riders surfing a popular break known as "PKs," and to watch the sun sink into the Pacific. ✉ *Lāwaʻi Rd., Poʻipū.*

The West Side

Exploring the West Side is akin to visiting an entirely different world. The landscape is dramatic and colorful: a patchwork of green, blue, black, and orange. The weather is hot and dry, the beaches are long, the sand is dark. Niʻihau, a private island where only Hawaiians may live, can be glimpsed offshore. This is rural Kauaʻi, where sugar is making its last stand and taro is still cultivated in the fertile valleys. The lifestyle is slow and traditional, with many folks fishing and hunting to supplement their diets. Here and there modern industry has intruded into this pastoral scene: huge generators turn oil into electricity at Port Allen; scientists cultivate experimental crops of genetically engineered plants in Kekaha; the Navy launches rockets at Mānā to test the "Star Wars" missile defense system; and NASA mans a tracking station in the wilds of Koke'e. It's a region of contrasts that simply shouldn't be missed.

Heading west you pass through a string of tiny towns, plantation camps, and historical sites, each with a story to tell of centuries past. There's Hanapēpē, whose coastal salt ponds have been harvested since ancient times; Kaumakani, where the sugar industry still clings to life; Fort Elisabeth, from which an enterprising Russian tried to take over the island in the early 1800s; and Waimea, where Captain Cook made his first landing in the Islands, forever changing the face of Hawai'i.

From Waimea town you can head up into the mountains, skirting the rim of magnificent Waimea Canyon and climbing higher still until you reach the cool, often-misty forests of Kōke'e State Park. From the vantage point at the top of this gemlike island, 3,200 to 4,200 feet above sea level, you can gaze into the deep verdant valleys of the North Shore and Nā Pali Coast. This is where the "real" Kaua'i can still be found: the native plants, insects, and birds that are found nowhere else on Earth.

Main Attractions

30 Hanapēpē. In the 1980s Hanapēpē was fast becoming a ghost town, its farm-based economy mirroring the decline of agriculture. Today it's a burgeoning art colony, with galleries, crafts studios, and a lively art-theme street fair on Friday nights. The main street has a new vibrancy enhanced by the restoration of several historic buildings. The emergence of Kaua'i Coffee as a major West Side crop and expanded activities at Port Allen, now the main departure point for tour boats, also gave the town's economy a boost. ⊠ *Rte. 50.*

★ **35 Kalalau Lookout.** At the end of the road, high above Waimea Canyon, Kalalau Lookout marks the start of a 1-mi (one-way) hike to **Pu'u o Kila lookout.** On a clear day at either spot you can look down at a dreamy landscape of gaping valleys, sawtooth ridges, waterfalls, and turquoise seas, where whales can be seen spouting and breaching during the winter months. If clouds obscure the spectacle, don't despair. They tend to blow through fast, giving you time to snap that photo of a lifetime before the next cloud bank drifts in. You may spot wild goats clambering on the sheer, rocky cliffs, and white tropic birds soaring gracefully on the thermals, their long tails streaming behind them. If it's very clear to the northwest, look for the shining sands of Kalalau Beach, gleaming like golden threads against the deep blue of the Pacific. ⊠ *Waimea Canyon Dr., 4 mi north of Kōke'e State Park.*

★ **Kōke'e State Park.** This 4,345-acre wilderness park is 4,000 feet above sea level, an elevation that affords you breathtaking views in all directions. You can gain a deeper appreciation of the island's rugged terrain and dramatic beauty from this vantage point. Large tracts of native ōhi'a and koa forest cover much of the terrain, along with many varieties of exotic plants. Hikers can follow a 45-mi network of trails through diverse landscapes that feel wonderfully remote—until the tour helicopters pass overhead. (⇨ See Hiking, *later in this chapter.*)

Kōke'e Natural History Museum is a great place to start your visit. The friendly staff is knowledgeable about trail conditions and weather, while informative displays and a good selection of reference books can teach you more about the unique attributes of the native flora and fauna. You may also find that special memento or gift you've been looking for. ✉ *Rte. 550* ☎ *808/335–9975* ✉ *Donations accepted* ⊙ *Daily 10–4.*

34 Waimea Canyon. Carved over countless centuries by the mighty Waimea River and the forces of wind and rain, this dramatic gorge is aptly nicknamed the "Grand Canyon of the Pacific." Hiking and hunting trails wind through the canyon, which is 3,600 feet deep, 2 mi wide, and 10 mi long. The cliff sides have been sharply eroded, exposing swatches of colorful soil. The deep red, brown, and green hues are constantly changing in the sun, and frequent rainbows and waterfalls enhance the natural beauty. This is one of Kaua'i's prettiest spots, and it's worth stopping at both the **Pu'u ka Pele** and **Pu'u hinahina** lookouts to savor the views. Clean public restrooms and plenty of parking are at both lookouts.

Fodor'sChoice
★

Also Worth Seeing

28 Hanapēpē Valley and Canyon Lookout. This dramatic divide and fertile river valley once housed a thriving Hawaiian community of taro farmers, with some of the ancient fields still in cultivation today. From the lookout you can take in the farms on the valley floor with the majestic mountains as a backdrop. ✉ *Rte. 50.*

NEED A BREAK?
You can savor fresh baked goods and coffee drinks at the spiffy black-and-white bar, or dine on wholesome vegetarian fare and fish at **Hanapēpē Café** (✉ 3830 Hanapēpē Rd., Hanapēpē ☎ 808/335–5011).

29 Kaua'i Coffee Visitor Center and Museum. Two restored camp houses, dating from the days when sugar was the main agricultural crop on the Islands, have been converted into a museum, visitor center, and gift shop. About 3,400 acres of McBryde sugar land have become Hawai'i's largest coffee plantation. You can walk among the trees, view old grinders and roasters, watch a video to learn how coffee is processed, sample various estate roasts, and check out the gift store. On the way to Waimea Canyon in 'Ele'ele, take Highway 50 and veer right onto Highway 540, west of Kalāheo. The center is 2½ mi from the Highway 50 turnoff. ✉ 870 *Halawili Rd.* ☎ *808/335–3237* ⊕ *www.kauaicoffee.com* ✉ *Free* ⊙ *Daily 9–5.*

27 Kukuiolono Park. Translated as "light of the god Lono," Kukuiolono has serene Japanese gardens, a display of significant Hawaiian stones, and spectacular panoramic views. This quiet hilltop park is one of Kaua'i's most scenic areas and an ideal picnic spot. There's also a small golf course. ✉ *Pāpālina Rd., Kalāheo* ☎ *808/332–9151* ✉ *Free* ⊙ *Daily 6:30–6:30.*

31 Salt Pond Beach Park. This popular park lies just west of some privately owned salt ponds where Hawaiians continue the traditional practice of harvesting salt (valued for its culinary and medicinal properties). They let the sun evaporate the seawater in mud-lined drying beds, then gather the salt left behind. You can't visit the ponds, but the beach park's protected swimming cove and camp grounds are worth a stop. ✉ *Lele Rd., Hanapēpē.*

KAUA'I SIGHTSEEING TOURS

Tours are great when you want to relax and let someone else do the driving. You also gain a better sense of what it's like to actually live on this green gem in the Pacific.

Aloha Kaua'i Tours. You get *way* off the beaten track on these 4WD van excursions. There's the half-day Backroads Tour covering haul-cane roads in the Grove Farm Plantation. The full-day Aloha Kaua'i Tour starts with the Backroads Tour and spends the other half day covering Waimea Canyon. These are roads you can traverse on your own, but the tour will teach you about the plants and birds in Waimea Canyon and Kōke'e State Park. The half-day Rainforest Tour follows the Wailua River to its source, Mt. Wai'ale'ale. The expert guides are some of the best on the island. Rates are $70, $125 and $68, respectively. ✉ *Check in at Kilohana Plantation on Rte. 50 in Puhi, Līhu'e* ☎ *808/ 245-6400 or 800/452-1113* ⊕ *www. alohakauaitours.com.*

Gay and Robinson Tours. The island's last sugar grower offers tours of its plantation and factory. You go into the fields to hear about how cane is grown and processed, and you learn about the history of sugar in Hawai'i. One highlight is viewing coastal areas otherwise closed to the public. Tours are offered weekdays at 8:45 and 12:45 for $30. ☎ *808/335-2824* ⊕ *www. gandrtours-kauai.com.*

Hawai'i Movie Tours. Minibuses with in-van TV monitors let you see the scenes of films while visiting the locations used for the filming of *Jurassic Park, Raiders of the Lost Ark, South Pacific, Blue Hawaii, Gilligan's Island,* and other Hollywood hits. The standard land tour is $111. ✉ *4-885 Kūhiō Hwy., Kapa'a* ☎ *808/822-1192 or 800/ 628-8432* ⊕ *www.hawaiimovietour. com.*

Kaua'i Island Tours. A good general tour company, Kaua'i Island Tours will arrange charter tours around Kaua'i in anything from a passenger car to a 57-person bus. ☎ *808/245-4777 or 800/733-4777.*

Plantation Lifestyles Walking Tour. To see a rapidly vanishing lifestyle that once dominated life in Hawai'i, take a tour through the residential area of a real mill camp. In the shadow of an old sugar mill, the dirt lanes of the 70-year-old camp are shaded by fruit trees and tropical gardens. Sometimes elderly residents come to say aloha to touring guests. Reservations are needed for the complimentary two-hour tour that begins at 9:30 AM every Monday at the West Kaua'i Visitor Center. ☎ *808/338-1332.*

Roberts Hawai'i Tours. The Round-the-Island Tour, sometimes called the Wailua River–Waimea Canyon Tour, gives a good overview of the island including Fort Elisabeth, 'Ōpaeka'a Falls, and Alekoko (Menehune) Fishpond. Guests are transported in air-conditioned, 17-passenger minivans. The $63 trip includes a boat ride up the Wailua River to the Fern Grotto, and a visit to the lookouts above Waimea Canyon. ☎ *808/245-9101 or 800/831-5541* ⊕ *www. robertshawaii.com.*

4

32 **Waimea.** This serene, pretty town has played a major role in Hawaiian history since 1778, when Captain James Cook became the first European to set foot on the Hawaiian Islands. Waimea was also the place where Kaua'i's King Kaumuali'i acquiesced to King Kamehameha's unification drive in 1810, averting a bloody war. The town hosted the first Christian missionaries, who hauled in massive timbers and limestone blocks to build the sturdy Waimea Christian Hawaiian and Foreign Church in 1846. It's one of many lovely historic buildings preserved by residents who take great pride in their heritage and history. The town itself has the look of the Old West and the feel of Old Hawai'i, with a lifestyle that's decidedly laid-back. Waimea beaches are sunny and sandy, but near-shore waters are often murky with runoff from the Waimea River. It's an ideal place for a refreshment break while sightseeing on the West Side. ☒ *Rte. 50.*

33 **West Kaua'i Visitor and Technology Center.** Local photos and informational computers with touch screens bring the island's history and attractions to life. ☒ *9565 Kaumuali'i Hwy. (Rte. 50), Waimea* ☎ *808/338–1332* ⊕ *www.kauaidiscovery.com* ✉ *Free* ☉ *Mon.–Sat. 9–5, Sun. 9–2.*

BEACHES

Kaua'i has more sandy beaches per mile of coastline than any other Hawaiian island, and if you've seen one, you certainly haven't seen them all. Each beach is unique unto itself, for that day, that hour. Conditions, scenery, and intrigue can change throughout the day and certainly throughout the year, transforming, say, a tranquil lakelike ocean setting in summer into monstrous waves drawing internationally ranked surfers from around the world in winter.

Kaua'i is encircled by a variety of beaches. There are sandy beaches, rocky beaches, wide beaches, narrow beaches, skinny beaches, and alcoves. Generally speaking, surf kicks up on the North Shore in winter and the South Shore in summer, although summer's southern swells aren't nearly as frequent or big as the northern winter swells.

All beaches are public, but their accessibility varies greatly. Some require an easy half-mile stroll, some require a four-wheel-drive vehicle, others require boulder-hopping, and one takes an entire day of serious hiking. And then there are those "drive-in" beaches onto which you can literally pull up and park your car. ■ TIP→ **Kaua'i is not Disneyland, so don't expect much signage to help you along the way. One of the top-ranked beaches in all the world—Hanalei—doesn't have a single sign in town directing you to the beach.**

We've divided the island's best beaches into four sections in clockwise order: the North Shore, the East Side, the South Shore, and the West Side. We'll take you from the road's end on the North Shore to the road's end on the West Side, and a bit beyond. If you think of the island as a clock, the North Shore beaches start at about 11; the East Side beaches start around 2, the South Side beaches at 5, and the West Side beaches around 7.

BEACH SAFETY

Kaua'i's waters are beguiling. The Pacific Ocean, despite its tranquil-sounding name, is a *real* ocean deserving real respect. Dangerous conditions can occur at any time of the year at any beach, even in normal surf conditions and under clear, sunny skies. Remember, not all beaches have lifeguards—even those with lifeguard stands aren't necessarily staffed all day or even year-round. The Hawaiian Lifeguard Association recommends that you:

Only swim when a lifeguard is present.

Don't go swimming alone.

Only dive in water you know is deep.

Before swimming, always ask the lifeguard about water conditions.

Watch for beach safety signs, and always heed them.

If you're ever unsure if the water is safe, don't go in.

We offer two additional tips:

Never turn your back on the ocean.

If lava rock boulders are wet, stay off them. Another wave may wash in and knock you down at a moment's notice.

The North Shore

If you've ever dreamed of Hawai'i, you've dreamed of Kaua'i's North Shore. Lush, tropical, abundant are just a few words to describe this rugged and dramatic area. And the views to the sea aren't the only attraction—the inland views of velvety green valley folds and carved mountain peaks will take your breath away. Rain is the reason for all the greenery on the North Shore and winter is the rainy season. Not to worry though, it rarely rains *everywhere* on the island at one time. The rule of thumb is to head south or west when it rains in the north.

The waves on the North Shore can be big—and we mean huge—in winter, drawing crowds to witness nature's spectacle. By contrast, in summer the waters can be completely serene. The beaches below are listed in order—west to east—from Hanakāpī'ai to Kalihi Wai. ■ TIP→ **Remember to gear up before you head to the beach.** Try one-stop shopping at

BEACHES KEY

🚻	Restroom
🚿	Showers
🏄	Surfing
🤿	Snorkel/Scuba
👪	Good for kids
P	Parking

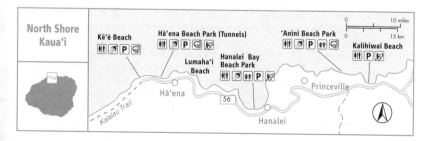

North Shore Kaua'i

Kē'ē Beach 🚻 🚿 P 🤿

Hā'ena Beach Park (Tunnels) 🚻 🚿 P 🤿 🏄

Lumaha'i Beach

Hanalei Bay Beach Park 🚻 🚿 👪 P 🏄

'Anini Beach Park 🚻 🚿 P 👪 🤿

Kalihiwai Beach 🚻 P 🏄

Hā'ena

56

Kalalau Trail

Princeville

Hanalei

0 — 10 miles
0 — 15 km

Ching Young Village in Hanalei, which has several stores that will fill your trunk with goodies such as snorkel gear, surf and body boards, beach chairs, umbrellas, snacks, coolers, and more.

FodorsChoice **Hanakāpī'ai Beach.** ⇨ *For more information, see* Hiking the Kalalau
★ Trail, *later in this chapter.*

★ **Kē'ē Beach.** Highway 560 on the North Shore literally dead ends at this beach, which is also the trailhead for the famous Kalalau Trail and the site of an ancient *heiau* (a stone platform used as a place of worship) dedicated to hula. The beach is protected by an offshore reef—except during high surf—creating a small, sandy bottom lagoon and making it a popular snorkel destination. If there's a current, it's usually found on the western edge of the beach as the incoming tide ebbs back out to sea. Makana (a prominent peak also known as Bali Hai after the block-buster musical *South Pacific*) is so artfully arranged, you definitely want to capture the memory, so don't forget your camera. The popularity of this beach makes parking difficult; but, it's worth the struggle. ■ TIP➜**Start extra early or, better yet, arrive at the end of the day, in time to witness otherworldly sunsets sidelighting Nā Pali Coast.** ✉ *End of Rte. 560, 7 mi west of Hanalei* ☞ *Toilets, showers, parking lot.*

Hā'ena Beach Park. This is a drive-up beach park popular with campers year-round. The wide bay here—named Mākua and commonly known as Tunnels—is bordered by two large reef systems creating quite favorable waves for surfing during peak winter conditions. In July and August this same beach is usually transformed into lakelike conditions and snorkelers enjoy the variety of fish life found in a hook-shape reef made up of underwater lava tubes, on the east end of the bay. ■ TIP➜**During the summer months only, this is the premier snorkel site on Kaua'i.** It's not unusual to find a couple food vendors parked here selling sandwiches and drinks out of their converted bread vans. ✉ *Near end of Rte. 560, across from lava tube sea caves, after stream crossing* ☞ *Lifeguard, toilets, showers, food concession, picnic tables, grills/firepits, parking lot, camping.*

Lumaha'i Beach. Famous because it's the beach where Nurse Nellie washed that man out of her hair in *South Pacific*, Lumaha'i Beach's setting is all you've ever dreamed Hawai'i to be. That's the drawing card and if you're adventurous and safety-conscious, a visit here is definitely worth it. The challenges are, it's hard to find, there's little parking, and there's a steep hike in; too many people misjudge the waves, even those never intending to step foot in the water. There's a year-round surge of onshore waves, massive sand movements (especially around the river mouth), and a steep foreshore assaulted by strong currents. Like the mythical creature from the deep, rogue waves have actually washed up on lava rock outcroppings and pulled sightseers out to sea. Lumaha'i Beach has the second-highest drowning rate on Kaua'i, behind Hanakāpī'ai. Our advice: look from the safety of the scenic overlook or walk on *dry* sand only; play in the water at another beach. ✉ *On winding section of Rte. 560 west of Hanalei, east of mile marker 5. Park on makai side of road and walk down steep path to beach* ☞ *No facilities.*

★ ☺ **Hanalei Bay Beach Park.** This 2-mi, crescent-shape beach surrounds a spacious bay that is quintessential Hawai'i. After gazing out to sea and realizing you have truly arrived in paradise, look landward. The site of the mountains, ribboned with waterfalls, will take your breath away. In winter Hanalei Bay boasts some of the biggest onshore surf breaks in the state, attracting world-class surfers. Luckily, the beach is wide enough to have safe real estate for your beach towel even in winter. In summer the bay is transformed—calm waters lap the beach, sailboats moor in the bay, and outrigger canoe paddlers ply the sea. Pack the cooler, haul out the beach umbrellas, and don't forget the beach toys, Hanalei Bay is definitely worth scheduling for an entire day, maybe two. ⊠ *In Hanalei, turn* makai *at Aku Rd. and drive 1 block to Weli Weli Rd. Parking areas are on* makai *side of Weli Weli Rd.* ☞ *Lifeguard, toilets, showers, picnic tables, grills/firepits, parking lot, camping.*

☺ **'Anini Beach Park.** A great family park, 'Anini is unique in that it features one of the longest and widest fringing reefs in all Hawai'i creating a shallow lagoon that is good for snorkeling and quite safe in all but the highest of winter surf. The reef follows the shoreline for some 2 mi and extends 1,600 feet offshore at its widest point. During times of low tide—usually occurring around the full moon of the summer months—much of the reef is exposed. 'Anini is unarguably the windsurfing mecca on Kaua'i, even for beginners, and it's also attracting the newest athletes of wave riding: kiteboarders. On Sunday afternoons in summer, polo matches in the fields behind the beach park draw a sizeable crowd. ■ TIP➔ Try the "Sara Special" at the lone food vendor here—'Anini Beach Lunch Shak, which is really a lunch wagon. ⊠ *Turn* makai *off Rte. 56 onto Kalihi Wai Rd., on Hanalei side of Kalihi Wai Bridge; follow road left to reach 'Anini Rd. and beach* ☞ *Toilets, showers, food concession, picnic tables, grills/firepits, parking lot, camping.*

Kalihiwai Beach. A winding road leads down a cliff face to this picture-perfect beach. A jewel of the North Shore, Kalihiwai Beach is on par with Hanalei, just without the waterfall-ribbon backdrop. It's another one of those drive-up beaches, so it's very accessible. Most people park on the sand under the grove of ironwood trees. Families set up camp for the day at the west end of the beach, near the stream, where young kids like to splash and older kids like to boogie board. This is also a good spot to disembark for a kayaking adventure up the stream. It's not a long paddle but it is calm, so it's perfect for beginning paddlers. (Haul in your own; there's none for rent on the beach.) On the eastern edge of the beach, from which the road descends, there's a locals' favorite surf spot during winter's high surf. The onshore break can be dangerous during this time. During the calmer months of summer, Kalihi Wai Beach is a good choice for beginning board riders and swimmers. ⊠ *Turn* makai *off Rte. 56 onto Kalihi Wai Rd., on Kilauea side of Kalihi Wai Bridge* ☞ *Toilets, parking lot.*

The East Side

The East Side of the island is considered the windward side, a term you'll often hear in weather forecasts. It simply means the side of the island receiving onshore winds. The wind helps break down rock into sand, so there are plenty of beaches here. Unfortunately, only a few of those beaches are protected, so many are not ideal for beginning oceangoers, though they are perfect for long sunrise ambles. On super windy-days, kiteboarders sail along the east shore, sometimes jumping waves and performing acrobatic maneuvers in the air.

The beaches below are listed in order from Keālia in the north to Kalapakī in the south. ■ TIP➔ **Fill your cooler with sandwiches and drinks at Safeway or Foodland in Kapa'a before you hit the sand.** Snorkel and other beach gear is available at Seasport Divers, Snorkel Bob's, and Play Dirty, among others.

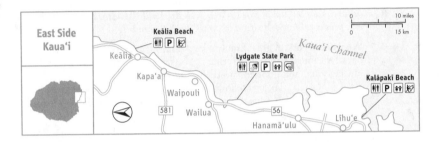

Keālia Beach. A half-mile long and adjacent to the highway heading north out of Kapa'a, Keālia Beach attracts body boarders and surfers year-round (possibly because the local high school is just up the hill). Keālia is not generally a great beach for swimming or snorkeling, the waters are usually rough and the waves crumbly due to an onshore break (no protecting reef) and northeasterly trade winds. A scenic lookout on the southern end, accessed off the highway, is a superb location for saluting the morning sunrise or spotting whales during winter. A level dirt road follows the coastline north and is one of the most scenic coastal trails on the island for walking, running, and biking. ■ TIP➔ **The toilets here are the portable kind, located by the lifeguard stand.** ⊠ *At mile marker 10 on Rte. 56* ☞ *Lifeguard, toilets, parking lot.*

🐚 **Lydgate State Park.** This is hands-down the best family beach park on Kaua'i. The waters off the beach are protected by a hand-built breakwater creating two boulder-enclosed saltwater pools for safe swimming and snorkeling just about year-round. The smaller of the two is perfect for *keiki* (children). Behind the beach is Kamalani Playground—designed by the children of Kaua'i and built by the community. Children of all ages, that includes you, enjoy the swings, lava-tube slides, tree house, and more. Picnic tables abound in the park and a large covered pavilion is available by permit for celebrations. Recently, Kamalani Bridge was built, again by the community and again based on the children's design, as a second playground south of the original. (The two are united by a walking path that will some day go all the way to Anahola Beach Park.) A second, smaller pavilion is the newest addition to the park—built near the bridge—and is surrounded by campsites, perfect for group outings. ■ TIP→ **This park is perennially popular; the quietest times to visit are early mornings and weekdays.** ✉ *Just south of Wailua River, turn* makai *off Rte. 56 onto Lehu Dr. and left onto Nalu Rd.* ☞ *Lifeguard, toilets, showers, picnic tables, grills/firepits, playground, parking lot, camping.*

☺ **Kalapakī Beach.** Five minutes south of the airport in Līhu'e, you'll find this wide, sandy-bottom beach fronting the Kaua'i Marriott. One of the big attractions is that this beach is almost always safe from rip currents and undertow because it's situated around the back side of a peninsula, in its own cove. There are tons of activities here, including all the usual water sports—beginning and intermediate surfing, body boarding, body-surfing, and swimming—plus, there are two outrigger canoe clubs paddling in the bay and the Nāwiliwili Yacht Club's boats sailing around the harbor. Kalapakī is the only place on Kaua'i where sailboats—in this case Hobe Cats—are available for rent (at Kaua'i Beach Boys, which fronts the beach next to Duke's Canoe Club restaurant). Visitors can also rent snorkel gear, surfboards, body boards, and kayaks. A volleyball court on the beach is often used by a loosely organized group of local players; visitors are always welcome. Duke's Canoe Club restaurant is one of only a couple restaurants on the island actually located on a beach; the restaurant's lower level is casual, even welcoming beach attire and sandy feet, perfect for lunch or an afternoon cocktail. ✉ *Off Wapa'a Rd., which runs from Līhu'e to Nāwiliwili* ☞ *Toilets, food concession, picnic tables, grills/firepits, playground, parking lot.*

The South Shore

The South Shore's primary access road is Highway 520, a tree-lined, two-lane, windy road. As you drive along it, there's a sense of tunneling down a rabbit hole into another world, à la Alice. And the South Shore is certainly a wonderland. On average, it only rains 30 inches per year, so if you're looking for fun in the sun, this is a good place to start. The beaches with their powdery-fine sand are consistently good year-round, except during high surf, which, if it hits at all, will be in summer. If you want solitude, this isn't it; if you want excitement—well, as much excitement as quiet Kaua'i offers—this is the place for you.

The beaches below are listed in order from Māhā'ulepū west to Po'ipū Beach Park. ■ TIP→ **The best places to gear up for the beach are Nukumoi Surf Co. across from Po'ipū Beach, and Seasport Divers at the junction to Spouting Horn on Po'ipū Road.**

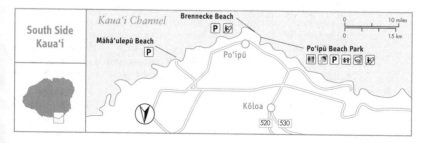

Māhā'ulepū Beach. This 2-mi stretch of coast with its sand dunes, limestone hills, sinkholes, and caves is unlike any other on Kaua'i. Remains of a large, ancient settlement, evidence of great battles, and the discovery of a now underwater petroglyph field indicate Hawaiians lived in this area as early as 700 AD. ■ TIP→ Māhā'ulepū's coastline is unprotected and rocky, which makes venturing into the ocean hazardous. There are three beach areas with bits of sandy-bottom swimming; however, we think the best way to experience Māhā'ulepū is simply by roaming, especially at sunrise. ⊠ *Continue on Po'ipū Rd. past Hyatt Regency (it turns into dirt road) to T-intersection and turn makai; road ends at beach parking area* ☞ *Parking lot.*

Brennecke Beach. Pending surf and tides, there's little beach here on the eastern end of Po'ipū Beach Park; however, Brennecke Beach is synonymous on the island with board and bodysurfing, thanks to its shallow sand bar and reliable shore break. Because the beach is small and often congested, surf boards are prohibited near shore. The water on the rocky, eastern edge of the beach is a good place to see the endangered green sea turtles noshing on plants growing on the rocks. ⊠ *Turn makai off Po'ipū Rd. onto Ho'owili Rd., then left onto Ho'one Rd.; beach is at intersection with Kuai Rd.* ☞ *Food concession, parking lot.*

© **Po'ipū Beach Park.** The most popular beach on the South Side, and perhaps on all of Kaua'i, is Po'ipū Beach Park. The snorkeling's good, the body boarding's good, the surfing's good, the swimming's good, and because the sun is almost always shining, that's good, too. The beach can be crowded at times, especially on weekends and holidays, but that just makes people-watching that much more fun. You'll see *keiki* (kids) experiencing the ocean for the first time; snorkelers trying to walk with their flippers on; 'ukulele players; birthday party revelers; young and old; visitors and locals. Even the endangered Hawaiian monk seal may make an appearance. ⊠ *From Po'ipū Rd., turn right on Ho'one Rd.* ☞ *Lifeguard, toilets, showers, food, picnic tables, grills/firepits, playground, parking lot.*

Fodor'sChoice
★

The West Side

While Kaua'i's North Shore is characterized by the color green, the West Side's coloring is red. When you look closer, you'll see the red is dirt, which happens to have a high iron content. With little vegetation on the West Side, the red dirt is everywhere—in the air, a thin layer on the car, even in the river. In fact, the only river on the West Side is named "Waimea" which means "reddish water." The West Side of the island receives hardly enough rainfall year-round to water a cactus, and because it's also the leeward side, there are hardly any tropical breezes. That translates to sunny and hot with long, languorous, and practically deserted beaches. You'd think the leeward waters—untouched by wind—would be calm; but there's no offshore reef system, so the waters are not as inviting as one would like. ■ TIP→ The best place to gear up for the beaches on the West Side is on the south or east shores. While there's some catering to visitors here, there's not much!

© **Salt Pond Beach Park.** A great family spot, Salt Pond Beach Park features a naturally made, shallow swimming pond behind a curling finger of rock where *keiki* (children) splash and snorkel. This pool is generally

Seal-Spotting on the South Side

WHEN STROLLING on one of Kaua'i's lovely beaches, don't be surprised if you find yourself in the rare company of Hawaiian monk seals. These are among the most endangered of all marine mammals, with perhaps fewer than 1,500 remaining. They primarily inhabit the northwestern Hawaiian islands, although more are showing their sweet faces on the main Hawaiian islands, especially on Kaua'i. They're fond of hauling out on the beach for a long snooze in the sun, especially after a night of gorging themselves on fish. They need this time to rest and digest, safe from predators.

During the past several summers, female seals have birthed young in the calm waters of Kaua'i's Po'ipū Beach, where they have stayed to nurse their pups for up to six weeks. It

seems the seals enjoy this particular beach for the same reasons we do: it's shallow and partially protected.

If you're lucky enough to see a monk seal, keep your distance and let it be. Although they may haul out near people, they still want and need their space. Stay several hundred feet away, and forget photos unless you've got a zoom lens. It's illegal to do anything that causes a monk seal to change its behavior, with penalties that include big fines and even jail time. In the water, seals may appear to want to play. It's their curious nature. Don't try to play with them. They are wild animals—mammals, in fact, with teeth. If you have concerns about the health or safety of a seal, or just want more information, contact the **Kaua'i Monk Seal Watch Program** (☎ 808/246–2860 ⊕ www.kauaimonkseal.com).

safe except during a large south swell, which usually occurs in summer, if at all. The center and western edge of the beach are popular with body boarders and bodysurfers. On a cultural note, the flat stretch of land to the east of the beach is the last spot in Hawai'i where ponds are utilized to harvest salt in the dry heat of summer. The beach park is popular with locals and can get crowded on weekends and holidays. ⊠ *From Rte. 50 in Hanapēpē, turn* makai *onto Lele Rd., Rte. 543* ⊂ *Lifeguard, toilets, showers, picnic tables, grills/firepits, parking lot, camping.*

★ **Polihale State Park.** The longest stretch of beach in Hawai'i starts in Kekaha and ends about 15 mi away at the start of Nā Pali Coast. Nā Pali end of the beach is the 5-mi-long, 140-acre Polihale State Park. In addition to being long, this beach is 300 feet wide in places and backed by sand dunes 50 to 100 feet tall. Polihale is a remote beach accessed via a 5-mi haul cane road (4WD preferred, not required) at the end of Route 50 in Kekaha. ■ **TIP→** Be sure to start the day with a full tank of gas and a cooler filled with food and drink. Many locals wheel their 4WD vehicles up and over the sand dunes right onto the beach; but don't try this in a rental car, you're sure to get stuck and found in violation of your rental car agreement.

On weekends and holidays Polihale is a popular locals' camping location, but even on busy days this beach is never crowded. On days of high surf, experts only surf the waves. In general, the water here is extremely rough and not recommended for recreation; however, there's one small fringing reef, called Queen's Pond, where swimming is usually safe. Neighboring Polihale Beach is the Pacific Missile Range Facility (PMRF), operated by the U.S. Navy. Since September 11, 2001, access to the beaches fronting PMRF is restricted. ⊠ *Drive to end of Rte. 50 and continue on dirt road; several access points along the way* ☞ *Toilets, showers, picnic tables, grills/firepits, parking lot, camping.*

WATER ACTIVITIES & TOURS

Boat Tours

FodorśChoice
★

One of the best ways to experience Nā Pali Coast is by boat. There are numerous boat tour operators, and, quite frankly, they all do a good job. The most important thing is to match your group's personality with the personality of the boat. If you like thrills and adventure, the rubber, inflatable rafts—often called Zodiacs, which Jacques Cousteau made famous and which the U.S. Coast Guard uses—will entice you. They're fast and sure to leave you drenched. If you prefer a smoother, more leisurely ride, then the large catamarans are the way to go.

You'll also have to decide whether you want to go on the morning tour, which includes a deli lunch and a stop for snorkeling, or the afternoon tour, which does not stop to snorkel but does include a sunset over the ocean. The 5½-hour morning tour with snorkeling is more popular with families and those who love dolphins. You don't have to be an expert snorkeler or have any experience whatsoever to snorkel, as long as you're a quick learner. There will be some snorkel instruction, but not much. Hawaiian spinner dolphins are so prolific in the mornings that some tour companies guarantee you'll see them, although you can't get in the water and swim with them. The 3½-hour afternoon tour is more popular with nonsnorklers and photographers interested in capturing the setting sunlight on the coast.

Most tour companies operate seven days a week (schedules may vary by season), and offer both morning snorkeling and afternoon sightseeing tours of Nā Pali Coast. Most companies do not allow pregnant women, people with bad backs or other serious health concerns, or children under age four.

Catamaran Tours
Blue Dolphin Charters. This company operates 63-foot and 65-foot sailing (rarely raised and always motoring) catamarans designed with three decks of spacious seating with great

WEATHER

If it's raining where you're staying, that doesn't mean it's raining over the water, so don't be scared away from a boat tour. Besides, it's not the rain that should concern you, it's the wind. The wind, especially from due north and south, creates surface chop and makes for rough riding. Larger craft are designed to handle winter's ocean swells, however, so unless there are monster waves out there, your tour should depart without a hitch. If the water is too rough, your boat captain may reroute to calmer waters.

visibility. ■ TIP➔ **The lower deck is best for shade-seekers.** Upgrades from snorkeling to scuba diving—no need for certification—are available, but the diving is really best for beginners or people who need a refresher course. On Tuesday and Friday a tour of Nā Pali Coast includes a detour across the channel to Ni'ihau for snorkeling and diving. Blue Dolphin likes to say they have the best mai tais "off the island," and, truth is, they probably do. Prices range from $99 to $175. ⊠ *In Port Allen Marina Center. Turn* makai *onto Rte. 541 off Rte. 50, at 'Ele'ele* ☎ *808/ 335–5553 or 877/511–1311* ⊕ *www.kauaiboats.com.*

Catamaran Kahanu. This Hawaiian-owned-and-operated company has been in business since 1985 and runs a 36-foot power catamaran with 18-passenger seating. The boat is smaller than most, and may feel a tad crowded, but the tour feels more personal, with a laid-back, 'ohana style. Guests can learn the ancient cultural practice of weaving on board. There's no alcohol allowed. Prices range from $95 to $115. ⊠ *From Rte. 50, turn left on Rte. 541 at 'Ele'ele, proceed just past Port Allen Marina Center, turn right at sign; check-in booth on left* ☎ *808/645–6176 or 888/ 213–7711* ⊕ *www.catamarankahanu.com.*

HoloHolo Charters. Choose between a 48-foot sailing (wind contingent and always motoring) catamaran trip to Nā Pali Coast, and a 65-foot powered catamaran trip to the island of Ni'ihau. Both boats have large cabins and little outside seating. Originators of the Ni'ihau tour, Holo-Holo Charters built their 65-foot powered catamaran with a wide beam to reduce side-to-side motion, and twin 425 HP turbo diesel engines specifically for the 17-mi channel crossing to Ni'ihau. Prices range from $89 to $169. ⊠ *Check in at Port Allen Marina Center. Turn* makai *onto Rte. 541 off Rte. 50, at 'Ele'ele* ☎ *808/335–0815 or 800/848–6130* ⊕ *www. holoholocharters.com.*

Kaua'i Sea Tours. This company operates a 61-foot sailing catamaran designed almost identically to that of Blue Dolphin Charters—hence, with all the same benefits. They also have upgrades from snorkeling to intro-to-scuba-diving lessons. Snorkeling tours anchor at Nūalolo Kai (a great snorkeling spot); and in summer, guests are offered a shuttle ride to shore on an inflatable raft and a tour of an ancient fishing village—a unique cultural experience. Prices range from $95 to $144. ⊠ *Turn* makai *off Rte. 50 onto Rte. 541 at 'Ele'ele and left at Aka Ula Rd. Office on right* ☎ *808/ 826–7254 or 800/733–7997* ⊕ *www. kauaiseatours.com.*

Inflatable Raft Tours

Nā Pali Explorer. Owned by a woman of Hawaiian descent, these tours are

THE ROLLING & REELING OCEAN

As anyone who's been on a boat in Kaua'i's waters knows, the Pacific Ocean isn't always so pacific. Even lifelong Navy men have admitted to feeling queasy on a Nā Pali boat tour. Some people think the bigger the boat the better, but studies show the lowest incidence of seasickness occurs on the rubber inflatable rafts. It may have something to do with being closer to the water and moving in a natural rhythm with the waves. If you think you're going to get sick, motion sickness tablets are probably a good idea.

operated out of Waimea, a tad closer to Nā Pali Coast than most of the catamaran tours. The company operates two inflatable rubber rafts: a 48-foot, 35-passenger craft with an onboard toilet, freshwater shower, shade canopy, and seating in the stern (which is surprisingly smooth and comfortable) and bow (which is where the fun is); and a 26-foot, 16-passenger craft for the all-out fun and thrills of a white-knuckle ride in the bow. Both stop at Nūalolo Kai for snorkeling; in summer the smaller vessel ties up onshore for a tour of the ancient fishing village. Rates range from $79 to $125, and charters are available. ⊠ *Follow Rte. 50 west to Waimea; office* mauka *after crossing river, 9935 Kaumuali'i Hwy., Waimea 96796* ☎ *808/338–9999 or 877/335–9909* ⊕ *www.napali-explorer.com.*

Kaua'i Sea Tours. This company also offers snorkel and nonsnorkel tours in an inflatable rubber raft. ⇨ *See* Catamaran Tours.

River Boat Tours to Fern Grotto

This 2½-mi, upriver trip culminates at a yawning lava tube that is covered with enormous fishtail ferns. During the boat ride, guitar and 'ukulele players regale you with Hawaiian melodies and tell the history of the river. It's a kitschy bit of Hawaiiana; worth the little money ($20) and short time required. Flat-bottom, 150-passenger riverboats (that rarely fill up) depart from Wailua Marina at the mouth of the Wailua River. Round-trip excursions take 1½ hours, including time to walk around the grotto and environs. Tours run every half hour from 9 AM to 3 PM daily. Reservations are not required. Contact **Smith's Motor Boat Services** (☎ 808/821–6892 ⊕ www.smithskauai.com) for more information.

Boogie Boarding & Bodysurfing

The most natural form of wave riding is bodysurfing, a popular sport on Kaua'i, because of its many shore breaks. Wave riders of this style stand waist-deep in the water, facing shore, and swim madly as a wave picks them up and breaks. It's great fun and requires no special skills and absolutely no equipment other than a swimsuit. The next step up is boogie boarding, also called body boarding. In this case, wave riders lie with their upper body on a foam board about half the length of a traditional surf board and kick as the wave propels them toward shore. Again, this is easy to pick up, and there are many places to practice. The locals wear short-finned flippers to help them catch waves, although they are not necessary for and even hamper beginners. It's worth spending a few minutes watching these experts as they spin, twirl, and flip—that's right—while they slip down the face of the wave. Of course, all beach safety precautions apply and just because you see wave riders of any kind in the water doesn't mean it's safe. Any snorkel gear outfitter (⇨ *see* Snorkeling) also rents body boards.

Best Spots

Some of our favorite bodysurfing and body boarding beaches are **Brennecke, Wailua, Keālia, Kalihi Wai,** and **Hanalei.** ⇨ *For directions, see* Beaches, *earlier in this chapter.*

Deep-Sea Fishing

Simply step aboard and cast your line for mahimahi, 'ahi, ono, and marlin. That's about how quickly the fishing—mostly trolling with lures—begins on Kaua'i. The water gets deep quickly here, so there's less cruising time to fishing grounds. Of course, your captain may elect to cruise to a hot location where he's had good luck lately.

There are oodles of charter fishermen around; most depart from Nāwiliwili Harbor in Līhu'e and most use lures instead of live bait. Inquire about each boat's fish policy, that is, what happens to the fish if any are caught. Some boats keep all; others will give you enough for a meal or two. On shared charters, ask about the maximum passenger count and about the fishing rotation; you'll want to make sure everyone gets a fair shot at reeling in the big one. Another option is to book a private charter. Shared and private charters run four, six, and eight hours in length.

Boats & Charters

Captain Don's Sport Fishing & Ocean Adventure. Captain Don is very flexible—he'll stop to snorkel or whale-watch if that's what the group (four to six) wants. Saltwater fly-fishermen (bring your own gear) are welcome. He'll even fish for bait and let you keep part of whatever you catch. Rates start at $125 for shared; $525 for private charters. ⊠ *Nāwiliwili Harbor* ☎ *808/639–3012* ⊕ *www.captaindonsfishing.com.*

Hana Pa'a. The advantage with Hana Pa'a is that they take fewer people (minimum two, maximum four), but you pay for it. Rates start at $200 for shared, $575 for private charters. Their fish policy is flexible. ⊠ *Nāwiliwili Harbor* ☎ *808/823–6031 or 866/776–3474* ⊕ *www.fishkauai.com.*

North Shore Charters. This is a great choice for anyone staying on the North Shore, although conditions may get iffy in the winter. The owner-operator—there are no hired hands running the boat—will fish for live bait or bottom fish if passengers are interested. You'll get to keep a share of whatever you catch. The boat carries four to six passengers and is also available for narrated tours of Nā Pali Coast. Rates are $120 for shared, $675–$700 for private charters. ⊠ *'Anini Beach Boat Ramp* ☎ *808/828–1379 or 877/728–1379.*

Kayaking

★ Kaua'i is the only Hawaiian island with navigable rivers. As the oldest inhabited island in the chain, Kaua'i has had more time for wind and water erosion to deepen and widen cracks into streams and streams into rivers. Because this is a small island, the rivers aren't long, and there are no rapids; that makes them perfectly safe for kayakers of all levels, even beginners.

For more advanced paddlers, there aren't many places in the world more beautiful for sea kayaking than Nā Pali Coast. If this is your draw to Kaua'i, plan your vacation for the summer months when the seas are at their calmest.

■ TIP→ Tour and kayak rental reservations are recommended at least a week in advance during peak summer and holiday seasons. In general, tours and rentals are available year-round, Monday through Saturday. Pack a swimsuit, sunscreen, a hat, bug repellent, water shoes (sport sandals, aqua socks, old tennis shoes), and motion sickness medication if you're planning on sea kayaking.

Best Spots for River Kayaking

Tour outfitters operate on the Hulēʻia, Wailua, and Hanalei rivers with guided tours that combine hiking to waterfalls and snorkeling. Another option is renting kayaks and heading out on your own. There are advantages and disadvantages to each, but it boils down as follows:

If you want to swim at the base of a remote, 100-foot waterfall, sign up for a five-hour kayak (4 mi round-trip) and hiking (2 mi round-trip) tour of the **Wailua River**; it includes a dramatic waterfall that is best accessed with the aid of a guide, so you don't get lost. ■ TIP→ Remember that it's dangerous to swim directly under waterfalls no matter how good a water massage may sound. Rocks and logs are known to plunge down, especially after heavy rains.

If you want to kayak on your own, choose the **Hanalei River**; it's most scenic from the kayak itself—there are no trails to hike. And better yet, a rental company (Kayak Kauaʻi, ⇨ see Kayak Rentals & Tours) is right on the river—no hauling kayaks on top of your car.

If you're not sure of your kayaking abilities, head to the **Hulēʻia River**; 3½-hour tours include easy paddling upriver, a nature walk through a rain forest with a cascading waterfall, a rope swing for playing Tarzan and Jane, and a ride back down river—into the wind—on a motorized, double-hull canoe.

As for the kayaks themselves, most companies use the two-person, sit-on-top style that are quite buoyant—no Eskimo rolls required. The only possible danger comes in the form of communication. The kayaks seat two people, which means you'll share the work (good) with a spouse, child, parent, friend, or guide (the potential danger part). On the river, the two-person kayaks are known as "divorce boats." Counseling is not included in the tour price.

Best Spots for Sea Kayaking

In its second year and second issue, *National Geographic Adventure* ranked kayaking **Nā Pali Coast** second on its list of "America's Best 100 Adventures," right behind rafting the Colorado River through the Grand Canyon. That pretty much says it all. It's the adventure of a lifetime in one day—involving eight hours of paddling. Although it's good to have some kayaking experience, feel comfortable on the water, and be reasonably fit, it doesn't require the preparation, stamina, or fortitude of, say, climbing Mt. Everest. Tours run May through September, ocean conditions permitting. In the winter months sea-kayaking tours operate on the **South Shore**—beautiful, but not Nā Pali.

Kayak Rentals & Tours

Kayak Kauaʻi. Based in Hanalei, this company offers guided tours on the Hanalei and Wailua rivers, and along Nā Pali Coast. They have a shop right on the Hanalei River for kayak rentals and camping gear. The guided Hanalei River Kayak and Snorkel Tour starts at the shop and heads downriver, so there's not much to see of the river valley. (For that, rent a kayak on your own.) Instead, this three-hour tour paddles down to the river mouth where the river meets the sea. Then, it's a short paddle around a point to snorkel at either Puʻu Poa Beach or, conditions permitting, a bit farther at Hideaways Beach. This is a great choice if you want to try your paddle at a bit of ocean kayaking.

A second location in Kapaʻa (only open during check-in times) is the base for Wailua River guided tours and kayak rentals; it's not right on the river, however, so shuttling is involved. For rentals, the company provides the hauling gear necessary for your rental car. Guided tours range from $60 to $200. Kayak rentals range from $28 to $75. ⊠ *Hanalei: 1 mi past Hanalei bridge, on makai side* ⊠ *Kapaʻa: south end of Coconut Marketplace near movie theaters* ☎ *808/826–9844 or 800/437–3507* ⊕ *www.kayakkauai.com.*

Nā Pali Kayak. A couple of longtime guides for Kayak Kauaʻi ventured out on their own a few years back to create this company that focuses solely on sea kayaking—Nā Pali Coast in summer, as the name implies and the South Shore in winter (during peak times only). These guys are highly experienced and still highly enthusiastic about their livelihood. Prices start at $175. You can also rent kayaks; price range from $35 to $70. ⊠ *5-575 Kūhiō Hwy., next to Postcards Café* ☎ *808/826–6900 or 866/977–6900* ⊕ *www.napalikayak.com.*

☺ **Outfitters Kauaʻi.** This well-established tour outfitter operates year-round river-kayak tours on the Hulēʻia and Wailua rivers; as well as sea-kayaking tours along Nā Pali Coast in summer and the South Side in winter. They're always coming up with new adventures and their latest is the **Kipu Safari.** This all-day adventure starts with kayaking up the Hulēʻia River, and includes a rope swing over a swimming hole, a wagon ride through a working cattle ranch, a picnic lunch by a private waterfall, hiking, and a "zip" across the river (strap on a harness, clip into a cable and zip across the river). It ends with a ride on a motorized, double-hull canoe. It's a great tour for the family, because no one ever gets bored. The Kipu Safari costs $155; other guided tours range from $94 to $185. ⊠ *2827-A Poʻipū Rd., Poʻipū 96756* ☎ *808/742–9667 or 888/742–9886* ⊕ *www.outfitterskauai.com.*

Wailua Kayak & Canoe. This is the only purveyor of kayak rentals on the Wailua River, which means no hauling your kayak on top of your car (a definite plus). Rates are $45 for a single; $75 for a double. ⊠ *Across from Wailua Beach, turn mauka at Kuamoʻo Rd. and take first left, 169 Wailua Rd., Kapaʻa* ☎ *808/821–1188.*

Kiteboarding

The latest wave-riding craze to hit the islands is **kiteboarding.** As the name implies, there's a kite and a board involved. The board you strap on your feet; the kite is attached to a harness around your waist. Steering is accomplished with a rod that's attached to the harness and the kite. Depending on conditions and the desires of the kiteboarder, the kite is played out some 30 to 100 feet in the air. The result is a cross between waterskiing—without the boat—and windsurfing. Speeds are fast and aerobatic maneuvers are involved. If you're a surfer of any kind, you might like to give this a try. (We highly recommend a lesson; besides, there's no rental gear available on the island.) Otherwise, you might find it more fun to watch. The most popular year-round spot for kiteboarding is **Kapa'a Beach Park** due to its reliable northeast trade winds.

'Anini Beach Windsurfing. The certified kiteboarding instructors here give five-hour lessons for $400 for one person or $600 for two. Lessons are usually held at Hanalei Bay and are only available when conditions allow. Call for reservations. ⊠ *Meet at beach, Hanalei* ☎ *808/826–9463.*

■ TIP➔ **Many visitors come to Kaua'i dreaming of parasailing. If that's you, make a stop at Maui or the Big Island. There's no parasailing on Kaua'i.**

Scuba Diving

The majority of scuba diving on Kaua'i occurs on the South Side. Boat and shore dives are available, although boat sites surpass the shore sites for a couple of reasons. First, they're deeper and exhibit the complete symbiotic relationship of a reef system; and, second, the visibility is better a little further off shore.

The dive operators below offer a full range of services, including certification dives, referral dives, boat dives, shore dives, night dives, and drift dives. ■ TIP➔ **As for certification, we recommend completing your confined-water training and classroom testing before arriving on island; that way, you'll spend less time training and more time diving.**

Best Spots

The best and safest scuba-diving sites are accessed by boat on the South Side of the island, right off the shores of Po'ipū. The captain selects the actual site based on ocean conditions of the day; **Sheraton Caverns, General Store,** and **Brennecke's Ledge** are good picks. Beginners may prefer shore dives, which are best at **Kōloa Landing** on the South Side year-round and **Mākua (Tunnels) Beach** on the North Shore in the calm summer months. Keep in mind though, you'll have to haul your gear a ways down the beach.

For the advanced diver, the island of Ni'ihau—across an open ocean channel in deep and crystal-clear waters—beckons and rewards, usually, with some big fish. Seasport Divers and Bubbles Below venture the 17 mi across the channel in summer when the crossing is smoothest. Divers can expect deep dives, walls, and strong currents at Ni'ihau where conditions can change rapidly. To make the long journey worthwhile, three dives and Nitrox are included.

Dive Tours & Equipment Rentals

Bubbles Below. Marine ecology is the emphasis here. This company discovered some pristine dive sites on the West Side of the island where white-tip reef sharks are common—and other divers are not. Ocean conditions permitting, they offer Ni'ihau, Nā Pali, and North Shore dives year-round (thanks to the addition of a 32-foot powered catamaran). A bonus on these tours is the Grinds pizza served up between dives. There's a charge of $110 for a standard two-tank boat dive; up to $25 extra for rental gear. ✉ *Port Allen Small Boat Harbor; turn makai onto Rte. 541 from Rte. 50 in 'Ele'ele* 🕿 *808/332–7333 or 866/524–6268* ⊕ *www. bubblesbelowkauai.com.*

Sacred Seas Scuba. This company specializes in shore diving only, typically at Kōloa Landing (year-round) and Tunnels (summers). They're not only geared toward beginning divers—for whom they provide a very thorough and gentle certification program—they also offer night dives and scooter (think James Bond) dives. Certified divers can participate in turtle surveys for the National Marine Fisheries. Their main emphasis is a detailed review of marine biology, like pointing out rare dragon eel and harlequin shrimp tucked away in pockets of coral. Rates range from $69 for a one-tank, certified dive to $395 for certification. ✉ *P.O. box 1874, Kapaa* 🕿 *877/441–3483 or 808/635–7327* ⊕ *www. sacredseasscuba.com.*

Seasport Divers. Rated highly by readers of Rodale's *Scuba Diving* magazine, Seasport Divers' 48-foot *Anela Kai* tops the chart for dive boat luxury. The company does a brisk business, which means they won't cancel at the last minute because of a lack of reservations—like some other companies. They also run a good-size dive shop for purchase and rentals. Ni'ihau trips are available in summer. All trips leave from Kukuiula Harbor in Po'ipū. Rates start at $110 for a two-tank boat dive; $20 extra for rental gear. ✉ *Check-in office on Po'ipū Rd. just north of Lāwa'i Rd. turnoff to Spouting Horn. Look for yellow submarine in parking lot, 2827 Po'ipū Rd., Po'ipū* 🕿 *808/742–9303 or 800/685–5889* ⊕ *www.seasportdivers.com.*

Snorkeling

Generally speaking, the calmest water and best snorkeling can be found on Kaua'i's North Shore in summer and South Shore in winter. The East Side, known as the windward side, has year-round, prevalent northeast trade winds that make snorkeling unpredictable, although there are some good pockets. The best snorkeling on the West Side is accessible only by boat.

A word on feeding fish: don't. As Captain Ted with HoloHolo Charters says, fish have survived and

---

TIPS ON SAFE SNORKELING

Mike Hopkins with SeaFun Kaua'i, suggests these tips for safe snorkeling:

- Snorkel with a buddy and stay together.

- Ask the lifeguard about conditions, especially currents, before getting in the water.

- Plan your entry and exit points before getting in the water.

- Swim into the current on entering and then ride the current back to your exit point.

- Look up periodically to gauge your location with a reference point on land.

- When in doubt, try a guided tour.

populated reefs for much longer than we have been donning goggles and staring at them; they will continue to do so without our intervention. Besides, fish food messes up the reef and—one thing always leads to another—can eliminate a once-pristine reef environment.

Best Spots

Just because we say these are good places to snorkel doesn't mean the exact moment you arrive, the fish will flock—they are wild, after all. The beaches here are listed in clockwise fashion starting on the North Shore.

The search for **Tunnels (Mākua)** (⊠ At Hā'ena Beach Park, near end of Rte. 560, across from lava-tube sea caves, after stream crossing) is as tricky as the snorkeling. Park at Hā'ena Beach Park and walk east—away from Nā Pali Coast—until you see a sand channel entrance in the water, almost at the point. Once you get here, the reward is fantastic. The name of this beach comes from the many underwater lava tubes, which always attract marine life. The shore is mostly beach rock interrupted by three sand channels. You'll want to enter and exit at one of these channels (or risk stepping on a sea urchin or scraping your stomach on the reef). Follow the sand channel to a drop-off; the snorkeling along here is always full of nice surprises. Expect a current running east to west. ■ TIP➜ Snorkeling here in winter can be hazardous; summer is the best and safest time for snorkeling.

🕓 **Lydgate Beach Park** (⊠ Just south of Wailua River, turn *makai* off Rte. 56 onto Lehu Dr. and left onto Nalu Rd.) is the absolute safest place to snorkel on Kaua'i. With its lava-rock wall creating a protected swimming pool, this is the perfect spot for beginners, young and old. The fish are so tame here it's almost like swimming in a saltwater aquarium.

You'll generally find good, year-round snorkeling at **Po'ipū Beach Park** (⊠ From Po'ipū Rd., turn right on Ho'one Rd.), except during summer's south swells (which are not nearly as frequent as winter's north swells). The best snorkeling fronts the Marriott Waiohai Beach Club. Stay inside the crescent shape created by the sand bar and rocky point. The current runs east to west.

Don't pack the beach umbrella, beach mats, or cooler for snorkeling at **Beach House (Lāwa'i Beach)** (⊠ *Makai* side of Lāwa'i Rd.; park on road in front of Lāwa'i Beach Resort). Just bring your snorkel gear. The beach—named after its neighbor the Beach House restaurant (yum)—is on the road to Spouting Horn. It's a small slip of sand during low tide and a rocky shoreline during high tide; however, it's right by the road's edge, and its rocky coastline and somewhat rocky bottom make it great for snorkeling. Enter and exit in the sand channel (not over the rocky reef) that lines up with the Lāwa'i Beach Resort's center atrium. Stay within the rocky points anchoring each end of the beach. The current runs east to west.

★ **Nu'alolo Kai** was once an ancient Hawaiian fishpond and is now the best snorkeling along Nā Pali Coast (and perhaps on all of Kaua'i). The only way to access it is by boat, and only a few Nā Pali snorkel tour operators are permitted to do so. We recommend Nā Pali Explorer and Kaua'i Sea Tours (⇨ *see* Boat Tours).

The Forbidden Isle

SEVENTEEN MILES from Kaua'i, across the Kaulakahi Channel, lies the privately owned island of Ni'ihau. It's known as the "Forbidden Isle" because access is limited to the Robinson family, which owns it, and the 200 or so native Hawaiians who were born there.

Ni'ihau was bought from King Kamehameha in 1864 by a Scottish widow, Eliza Sinclair. Sinclair was introduced to the island after an unusually wet winter; she saw nothing but green pastures and thought it would be an ideal place to raise cattle. The cost was $10,000. It was a real deal, or so Sinclair thought.

Unfortunately, Ni'ihau's usual rainfall is about 12 inches a year, and the land soon returned to its normal desertlike state. Regardless, Sinclair did not abandon her venture and today the island and ranching operation are owned by Bruce Robinson, Eliza Sinclair's great-great-grandson.

Visits to the island are restricted to custom hunting expeditions and flightseeing tours through Ni'ihau Helicopter. Tours depart from Kaumakani and avoid the western coastline, especially the village of Pu'uwai. There's a four-passenger minimum for each flight, and reservations are essential. A picnic lunch on a secluded Ni'ihau beach is included, with time for swimming, beachcombing, and snorkeling. The half-day tour is $325 per person.

For more information contact **Ni'ihau Tours** (☐ Box 690370, Makaweli 96769 ☎ 808/335–3500 or 877/441–3500 ⊕ www.niihau.us)

Fodor'sChoice ★ With little river runoff and hardly any boat traffic, the waters off the island of **Ni'ihau** are some of the clearest in all Hawai'i and that's good for snorkeling. Like Nu'alolo Kai, the only way to snorkel here is to sign on with one of the two tour boats venturing across a sometimes rough open ocean channel: Blue Dolphin Charters and HoloHolo (⇨ *see* Boat Tours). Sammy the Monk Seal likes to hang out behind Lehua Rock off the north end of Ni'ihau and swim with the snorkelers.

Guided Snorkel Tours

SeaFun Kaua'i. This guided snorkel tour, for beginners and intermediates, is led by a marine expert. Not only is there excellent "how-to" instruction, but the guide actually gets in the water with you and identifies marine life. You're guaranteed to spot a plethora of critters you'd never see on your own. This is a land-based operation and the only one of its kind on Kaua'i. (Don't think those snorkel cruises are guided snorkel tours, they rarely are. A member of the boat's crew serves as lifeguard, not a marine life *guide*.) A half-day tour includes all your snorkel gear—and a wetsuit to keep you warm—and stops at two snorkel locations, chosen based on ocean conditions. The cost is $80. ⊠ *Check in at Kilohana Plantation in Puhi, next to Kaua'i Community College* ☎ *808/245–6400 or 800/452–1113* ⊕ *www.alohakauaitours.com.*

Surfing

Good old stand-up surfing is alive and well on Kaua'i, especially in winter's high surf season on the North Shore. If you're new to the sport, we highly recommend taking a lesson. Not only will this ensure you're up and riding waves in no time, instructors will provide the right board for your experience and size, help you time a wave, and give you a push to get your momentum going. If you're experienced and want to hit the waves on your own, most surf shops rent boards for all levels—from beginners to advanced.

Best Spots

Perennial-favorite beginning surf spots include **Po'ipū Beach** (the area fronting the Marriott Waiohai Beach Club); **Hanalei Bay** (the area next to the Hanalei Pier); and the stream end of **Kalapakī Beach**. More advanced surfers move down the beach in Hanalei to an area fronting a grove of pine trees known as *"Pine Trees."* When the trade winds die, the north ends of **Wailua** and **Keālia** beaches are teeming with surfers. Breaks off **Po'ipū** and **Beach House/Lāwa'i Beach** attract intermediates year-round. During high surf, the break on the cliff side of **Kalihi Wai** is for experts only. ⇨ *See* Beaches, *earlier in this chapter, for complete beach information and directions.*

Lessons

Blue Seas Surf School. Surfer and instructor Charlie Smith specializes in beginners (especially children) and will go anywhere on the island to find just the right surf. His soft-top, long boards are very stable, making it easier to stand up. Rates start at $65 for a one-and-a-half-hour lesson. ⊠ *Meet at beach; location varies pending surf conditions* ☎ *808/634–6979* ⊕ *www.blueseassurfingschool.com.*

Margo Oberg Surfing School. Seven-time world surfing champion Margo Oberg runs a surf school that meets on the beach in front of the Sheraton Kaua'i in Po'ipū. Lessons are $55 for two hours, though she herself rarely teaches any more. ⊠ *Po'ipū Beach* ☎ *808/332–6100* ⊕ *www.surfonkauai.com.*

Titus Kinimaka Hawaiian School of Surfing. Famed as a pioneer of big-wave surfing, this Hawaiian believes in giving back to his sport. Beginning, intermediate, and "extreme" lessons, including tow-in, are available. If you want to learn to surf from a living legend, this is the man. ■ **TIP→ He does employ some other instructors, so if you want Titus, be sure to ask for him.** Rates are $65 for a 90-minute group lesson; $100 to $120 per hour for a private lesson; $150 for a one-hour, tow-in lesson. A surf DVD is included with each lesson. ⊠ *Meets at various beaches* ☎ *808/652–1116.*

Surf Board Rentals

Progressive Expressions. ⊠ *On Kōloa Rd. in Old Kōloa Town* ☎ *808/742–6041.*

Tamba Surf Company. ⊠ *Mauka on north end of Hwy. 56, 4-1543 Kūhiō Hwy., Kapa'a* ☎ *808/823–6942.*

Hanalei Surf Company. ⊠ *Mauka at Hanalei Center, 5-5161 Kūhiō Hwy., Hanalei* ☎ *808/826–9000.*

Whale-Watching

Every winter North Pacific humpback whales swim some 3,000 mi over 30 days, give or take a few, from Alaska to Hawai'i. Whales arrive as early as November and sometimes stay through April, though they seem to be most populous in February and March. They come to Hawai'i to breed, calve, and nurse their young.

Although humpbacks spend more than 90% of their lives underwater, they can be very active above water while they're in Hawai'i. Here are a few maneuvers you may see:

- Blow: the expulsion of air that looks like a geyser of water.
- Spy hop: the raising of just the whale's head out of the water, as if to take a look around.
- Tail slap: the repetitive slap of the tail, or fluke, on the surface of the water.
- Pec slap: the repetitive slap of one or both fins on the surface of the water.
- Fluke up dive: the waving of the tail above water as the whale slowly rolls under water to dive.
- Breach: the launching of the entire whale's body out of the water.

Of course, nothing beats seeing a whale up close. During the season, any boat on the water is looking for whales; they're hard to avoid, whether the tour is labeled whale-watching or not. Several boat operators will add two-hour, afternoon whale-watching tours during the season that run on the South Shore (not Nā Pali). Operators include **Blue Dolphin, Catamaran Kahanu, HoloHolo,** and **Nā Pali Explorer** (⇨ *see* Boat Tours). There are a few lookout spots around the island with good land-based viewing: Kīlauea Lighthouse on the North Shore, the Kapa'a Scenic Overlook just north of Kapa'a town on the East Side, and the cliffs to the east of Keoneloa (Shipwreck) Beach on the South Shore.

Windsurfing

Windsurfing on Kaua'i isn't nearly as popular as it is on Maui; however, 'Anini Beach Park is the place if you're going to windsurf or play the spectator. Rentals and lessons are available from **Windsurf Kaua'i** (☎ 808/828–6838). Lessons run $85 for three hours; rentals run $25 for one hour, and up to $75 for the day. The instructor will meet you on 'Anini Beach.

GOLF, HIKING & OTHER ADVENTURES

Aerial Tours

Fodor'sChoice
★ From the air, the Garden Isle blossoms with views you cannot see by land, on foot, or from the sea. In an hour you can see waterfalls, craters, and other places that are inaccessible even by hiking trails (some say that 70% or more of the island is inaccessible). The majority of flights

depart from the Līhu'e airport and follow a clockwise pattern around the island. ■ TIP→ **If you plan to take an aerial tour, it's a good idea to fly when you first arrive, rather than saving it for the end of your trip.** It will help you visualize what's where on the island and it may help you decide what you want to see from a closer vantage point during your stay. Many companies advertise a low-price 30- or 40-minute tour, which they rarely fly, so don't expect to book a flight at the advertised rate. The most popular flight is 60 minutes long.

Helicopter Tours

Blue Hawaiian Helicopters. The newest helicopter company to the island is not new to Hawai'i, having flown for 20 years on Maui and Big Island. They are the only company on Kaua'i flying the latest in helicopter technology, the Eco-Star, costing $1.8 million. It has 23% more interior space for its six passengers, has unparalleled viewing, and offers a few extra safety features none of the other helicopters on the island have. As the name implies, the helicopter is a bit more environmentally friendly, with a 50% noise reduction rate. Their flights run a tad shorter than others (approximately 50 minutes instead of the 55 to 65 minutes that others tout), although the flight feels very complete. The rate is $210. A DVD of your actual tour is available for $25 additional. ⊠ *Harbor Mall in Nāwiliwili, Līhu'e* ☎ *808/245–5800 or 800/745–2583* ⊕ *www. bluehawaiian.com.*

Inter-Island Helicopters. This company flies four-seater Hughes 500 helicopters *with the doors off.* It can get chilly at higher elevations, so bring a sweater and wear long pants. They offer a spectacular tour that includes landing by a waterfall for a picnic and swim. Tours depart from Hanapēpē's Port Allen Airport. Prices range from $185 to $250 per person. ⊠ *From Rte. 50, turn makai onto Rte. 543 in Hanapēpē* ☎ *808/ 335–5009 or 800/656–5009* ⊕ *www.interislandhelicopters.com.*

Safari Helicopters. This company flies the "Super" ASTAR helicopter, which offers floor-to-ceiling windows on its doors, four roof windows, and Bose X-Generation headphones. Two-way microphones allow passengers to converse with the pilot. Prices start at $194; a DVD is $25 extra. ⊠ *3225 Akahi St., Līhu'e* ☎ *808/246–0136 or 800/326–3356* ⊕ *www. safariair.com.*

Will Squyres Helicopter Tours. The majority of this company's pilots were born and raised in Hawai'i, making them excellent tour guides. In an interesting move, Will Squyres removed its two-way microphones, eliminating the possibility of one passenger hogging the airwaves. Prices start at $189. ⊠ *3222 Kūhiō Hwy., Līhu'e* ☎ *808/245–8881 or 888/245– 4354* ⊕ *www.helicopters-hawaii.com.*

Plane Tours

Kaua'i Aero Tours. This tour is really a flying lesson in a Citabria tail dragger that was designed specifically for aerobatics. You can take the stick or let your pilot handle the controls. The aerobatics roll on until you say stop. The plane can only take one passenger at a time. Tours last 30 to 60 minutes; prices range from $125 to $165. ⊠ *Līhu'e Airport* ☎ *808/639–9893.*

Tropical Bi-Planes. This company flies a Waco biplane, built in 2002 based on a 1936 design. An open cockpit and staggered wing design means there's nothing between you and the sights. The plane can carry two passengers in front and flies at an altitude of 1,000 feet, at about 85 mph. The hourly rate is $371 for two people. ⊠ *Lihu'e Airport Commuter Terminal* ☎ *808/246–9123* ⊕ *www.tropicalbiplanes.com.*

ATV Tours

Although all the beaches on the island are public, much of the interior land—once sugar and pineapple plantations—is privately owned. This is really a shame, because the valleys and mountains that make up the vast interior of the island easily rival the beaches in sheer beauty. The good news is some tour operators have agreements with landowners making exploration possible, albeit a bit bumpy, and unless you have back troubles, that's half the fun.

Kaua'i ATV Tours. This is *the* thing to do when it rains on Kaua'i. Consider it an extreme mud bath. Kaua'i ATV in Kōloa is the originator of the all-terrain-vehicle tours on Kaua'i. Their $99 three-hour jaunt takes you through a private sugar plantation and historic cane-haul tunnel. The $145 four-hour tour visits secluded waterfalls and includes a picnic lunch. The more popular longer excursion includes a hike through a bamboo forest and a swim in a freshwater pool at the base of the falls—to rinse off all that mud. You must be 16 or older to operate your own ATV, but Kaua'i ATV also offers its four-passenger and two-passenger "Mud Bugs" to accommodate families with kids age five and older. ⊠ *5330 Kōloa Rd., Kōloa* ☎ *808/742–2734 or 877/707–7088* ⊕ *www.kauaiatv.com.*

Biking

Kaua'i is a labyrinth of cane-haul roads, which are fun for exploring on two wheels. The challenge is to find the roads where biking is allowed and then to not get lost in the maze. Maybe that explains why Kaua'i is not a hub for the sport . . . yet. Still, there are some epic rides for those who are interested—both the adrenaline-rushing and the mellower beach cruiser kinds. If you want to grind out some mileage, the main highway that skirts the coastal areas is perfectly safe, though there are only a few designated bike lanes. It's hilly, but you'll find that keeping your eyes on the road and not the scenery is the biggest challenge. You can rent bikes (with helmets) from the activities desks of certain hotels, but these are not the best quality. You're better off renting from either Kaua'i Cycle in Kapa'a, or Outfitters Kaua'i in Po'ipū. ■ TIP→ **If you're headed for the dirt tracks, be sure your bike is in top condition, take plenty of water and energy bars, and let someone know when and where you're going. If you're venturing into the unknown, explain what you've got in mind to someone who knows the area and heed any advice offered. And be sure to get explicit directions; don't expect signage.**

Best Spots

For the cruiser, **Keālia Coastal Road** (⊠ Trailhead: 1 mi north of Kapa'a; park at north end of Keālia Beach), a dirt-haul cane road, is easy to follow along the coastline to Donkey Beach. From here, the trail splinters into numerous, narrower trails through fallow sugarcane fields where dirt bikers now roam, especially on weekends. It's easy to get lost here, but eventually all trails lead to Anahola Beach Park, some 4 mi from Keālia. If you're not sure you'll find your way back the way you came, follow Anahola Road inland to Route 56 and return to Keālia via the highway.

For those wanting a road workout, climb **Waimea Canyon Road** (⊠ Road turns *mauka* off Rte. 50 just after grocery store in downtown Waimea), also known as Route 550. After a 3,000-foot climb, the road tops out at mile 12 adjacent to Waimea Canyon, which will pop in and out of view on your right as you ascend. From here it continues several miles (mostly level) past the Kōke'e Museum and ends at the Kalalau Lookout. It's paved the entire way, uphill 100%, and curvy. ■ TIP➔ **There's not much of a shoulder—sometimes none–so be extra cautious.** The road gets busier as the day wears on, so you might consider a sunrise ride.

For the novice mountain biker, the **Wailua Forest Management Road** is an easy ride and is easy to find. From Route 56 in Wailua, turn *mauka* on Kuamo'o Road and continue 6 mi to the picnic area, known as Keāhua Arboretum; park here. The potholed 4WD road includes some stream crossings—stay away during heavy rains as the streams flood—and continues for 2 mi to a T-stop, where you should turn right. Stay on the road for about 3 mi until you reach a gate; this is the spot where the gates to the movie Jurassic Park were filmed, though it looks nothing like the movie. Go around the gate and down the road for another mile to a confluence of streams at the base of Mt. Wai'ale'ale. Be sure to bring your camera.

Advanced riders should try **Powerline Trail.** The trail is actually a service road for the electric company that splits the island. It's 13 mi in length; the first 5 mi goes from 620 feet in elevation to almost 2,000. The remaining 8 mi is a gradual descent over a variety of terrain, some technical. Some sections will require carrying your bike. The views will stay with you forever. Trailhead is *mauka* just past stream crossing at Keāhua Arboretum (⇨ *see directions for* Wailua Forest Management Road *above*).

Bike Rentals & Guided Trips

Kaua'i Adventure Trek. This 4½-hour bike, hike, and beach adventure follows an old cane road through Grove Farm Plantation, stops for a tour of the island's first sugar mill, then heads for Māhā'ulepū Beach for a short hike to a hidden beach. The tour includes a picnic lunch on the beach. Trips are geared to novice and intermediate-level bikers and cost $96. ⊠ *Check in at Kilohana Plantation on Rte. 50, Puhi* ☎ *808/245–6400 or 808/635–8735* ⊕ *www.alohakauaitours.com/adventuretrek.*

Kaua'i Cycle. This reliable, full-service bike shop rents, sells, and repairs bikes. Mountain bikes and road bikes are available for $15 to $40 per day and $75 to $125 per week with directions to trails. ⊠ *Across from Beezers Old Fashioned Ice Cream, 1379 Kūhiō Hwy., Kapa'a* ☎ *808/ 821–2115* ⊕ *www.bikehawaii.com/kauaicycle.*

Outfitters Kaua'i. Beach cruisers and mountain bikes are available at this Po'ipū shop. You can ride out the door to tour Po'ipū, or get information on how to do a self-guided tour of Kōke'e State Park and Waimea Canyon. The company leads sunrise coasting tours (under the name **Bicycle Downhill**) from Waimea Canyon (downhill for 12 mi) to the island's West Side beaches. Rentals cost $20 to $45 per day. Tours cost $94. ⊠ *2827-A Po'ipū Rd., Po'ipū, Follow Po'ipū Rd. south from Kōloa town; shop is on right just before turnoff to Spouting Horn* ☎ *808/742–9667 or 888/742–9887* ⊕ *www.outfitterskauai.com.*

Pedal 'n' Paddle. This company rents beach cruisers and hybrid bicycles for $10 to $20 per day; $40 to $80 per week. ⊠ *Ching Young Village, Rte. 560, Hanalei* ☎ *808/826–9069* ⊕ *www.pedalnpaddle.com.*

Golf

For golfers, the Garden Isle might as well be known as the Robert Trent Jones Jr. Isle. Four of the island's nine courses, including Po'ipū Bay—home of the PGA Grand Slam of Golf—are the work of Jones, who maintains a home at Princeville. Combine these four courses with those from Jack Nicklaus, Robin Nelson, and local legend Toyo Shirai, and you'll see that golf sets Kaua'i apart from the other Islands as much as the Pacific Ocean does.

Fodor'sChoice ★ **Kaua'i Lagoons Golf Club.** When Jack Nicklaus opened the Kiele (pronounced kee-EL-ay) Course here in 1989, it was immediately compared to Mauna Kea, Robert Trent Jones Sr.'s Big Island masterpiece. Depending on the rater, Kiele continues to be considered among the top three or four courses in the state. Nicklaus's design is like a symphony, starting nice and easy, and finishing with a rousing par-4 that plays deceptively uphill—into the trade winds—to an island green. The adjacent Mokihana Course (Nicklaus, 1990) is flatter and doesn't have Kiele's oceanfront. According to handicap ratings it's supposed to play easier, but Nicklaus makes par a challenge with creative mounding, large waste areas, and false fronts for greens. The boomerang-shape par-5 18th is among the state's finest finales. ⊠ *3351 Ho'olaulea Way, Līhu'e* ☎ *808/241–6000* ⊕ *www.golfbc.com* ⚑ *Kiele Course: 18 holes. 6674 yds. Par 72. Green Fee: $195. Mokihana Course: 18 holes. 6578 yds. Par 72. Green Fee: $120* ⌕ *Facilities: Driving range, putting green, golf carts, rental clubs, lessons, restaurant, bar.*

Kiahuna Plantation Golf Course. A meandering creek, lava outcrops, and thickets of trees give Kiahuna its character. Robert Trent Jones Jr. (1983) was given a smallish piece of land just inland at Po'ipū, and defends par with smaller targets, awkward stances, and optical illusions. In 2003 a group of homeowners bought the club and brought Jones back to renovate the course, adding tees and revamping bunkers. ⊠ *2545 Kiahuna Plantation Dr., Kōloa* ☎ *808/742–9595* ⊕ *www.kiahunagolf.com* ⚑ *18 holes. 6183 yds. Par 70. Green Fee: $90* ⌕ *Facilities: Driving range, putting green, rental clubs, lessons, pro shop, restaurant, bar.*

Kukuiolono Golf Course. Local legend Toyo Shirai designed this fun, funky 9-holer where holes play across rolling, forested hills that afford views of the distant Pacific. Though Shirai has an eye for a good golf hole, Kukuiolono is out of the way and a bit rough, and probably not for everyone. But at $8 for the day, it's a deal. ⊠ *854 Pu'u Rd., Kalāheo* ☎ *808/332–9151* ⅃ *9 holes. 3173 yds. Par 36. Green Fee: $8* ☞ *Facilities: Driving range, putting green, golf carts, pull carts, rental clubs.*

Fodor's**Choice** **Po'ipū Bay Golf Course.** Po'ipū Bay ★ has been called the Pebble Beach of Hawai'i, and comparisons are apt. Like Pebble Beach, Po'ipū is a links course built on headlands, not true links land. And as at Monterey Bay, there's wildlife galore. It's not unusual for golfers to see monk seals sunning on the beach below, sea turtles bobbing outside the shore break, and humpback whales leaping offshore. ⊠ *2250 Ainako St., Kōloa* ☎ *808/742–8711* ⊕ *www.poipubay.com* ⅃ *18 holes. 6612 yds. Par 72. Green Fee: $145* ☞ *Facilities: Driving range, putting green, rental clubs, golf carts, golf academy/lessons, restaurant, bar.*

Fodor's**Choice** **Princeville Resort.** Robert Trent Jones Jr. built two memorable courses ★ overlooking Hanalei Bay, the 27-hole Princeville Makai Course (1971) and the Prince Course (1990). The three Makai nines—Woods, Lake, Ocean—offering varying degrees of each element, plus lush mountain views above. Three quick snapshots: the par-3 seventh on the Ocean nine drops 100 feet from tee to green, with blue Hanalei Bay just beyond. The Ocean's par-3 eighth plays across a small bay where dolphins often leap. On the Woods' par-3 eighth, two large lava rocks in Jones's infamous Zen Bunker really are quite blissful, until you plant a tee shot behind one of them. The Prince is often rated Hawai'i's best course. It's certifiably rated Hawai'i's second toughest (behind O'ahu's Ko'olau). This is jungle golf with holes running through dense forest and over tangled ravines, out onto headlands for breathtaking ocean views, then back into the jungle. **Makai Golf Course:** ⊠ *4080 Lei O Papa Rd., Princeville* ☎ *808/826–3580* ⊕ *www.princeville.com* ⅃ *27 holes. 6886 yds. Par 72. Green Fee: $125* ☞ *Facilities: Driving range, putting green, rental clubs, golf carts, pro shop, golf academy/lessons, snack bar.* **Prince Golf Course:** ⊠ *5-3900 Kūhiō Hwy., Princeville* ☎ *808/826–5001* ⊕ *www. princeville.com* ⅃ *18 holes. 6960 yds. Par 72. Green Fee: $175* ☞ *Facilities: Driving range, putting green, rental clubs, golf carts, pro shop, golf academy/lessons, restaurant, bar.*

Hiking

The best way to experience the *'āina* (the land) on Kaua'i is to step off the beach and into the interior. And the best way to do that is by hiking. The rewards are waterfalls so tall you'll strain your neck, pools of crystal cool water for swimming, tropical forests teeming with plant life, and ocean vistas that will make you wish you could stay forever.

LEPTOSPIROSIS

The sparkling waters of those babbling brooks trickling around the island can be potentially life-threatening, and we're not talking about the dangers of drowning, although they, too, exist. Leptospirosis is a bacterial disease that is transmitted from animals to humans. It can survive for long periods of time in fresh water and mud contaminated by the urine of infected animals, such as mice, rats, and goats. The bacteria enter the body through the eyes, ears, nose, mouth, and broken skin. To avoid infection, do not drink untreated water from the island's streams; do not wade in waters above the chest or submerge skin with cuts and abrasions in island streams or rivers. Symptoms are often mild and resemble the flu—fever, diarrhea, chills, nausea, headache, vomiting, body pains. Symptoms may occur two to 20 days after exposure. If you think you have these symptoms, see a doctor right away.

■ TIP→ For your safety wear sturdy shoes—preferably water-resistant ones for the many stream crossings you will most likely encouter—bring plenty of water, never hike alone, stay on the trail, and avoid hiking when it's wet and slippery. All hiking trails on Kaua'i are free, so far. There's a rumor that the Waimea Cayon and Kōke'e state parks will some day charge an admission fee. Whatever it may be, it will be worth it.

Hiking the Kalalau Trail See Page 443

Best Spots

Waimea Canyon and Kōke'e State Parks. The parks contain a 50-mi network of hiking trails of varying difficulty that take you through acres of native forests, across the highest-elevation swamp in the world, to the river at the base of the canyon, and onto pinnacles of land sticking out over Nā Pali Coast. All hikers should register at Kōke'e Natural History Museum, where you'll find trail maps, current trail information, and specific directions. All mileage mentioned here is one way.

The **Kukui Trail** descends 2½ mi and 2,200 feet into Waimea Canyon to the edge of the Waimea River—it's a steep climb. The **Awa'awapuhi Trail**, with 1,600 feet of elevation gains and losses over 3¼ mi, feels more gentle than the Kukui Trail; but it offers its own huffing-and-puffing sections in its descent along a spiny ridge to a perch overlooking the ocean.

The 3½-mi **Alaka'i Swamp Trail** is accessed via the **Pihea Trail** or a 4WD road. There's one strenuous valley section, otherwise it's a pretty level trail—once you access it. This trail is a birder's delight and includes a painterly view of Wainiha and Hanalei valleys at the trail's end. The trail traverses the purported highest-elevation swamp in the world on a boardwalk so as not to disturb the fragile plant- and wildlife.

The **Canyon Trail** offers much in its short 2 mi trek: spectacular vistas of the canyon and the only dependable waterfall in Waimea Canyon. The easy, 2-mi hike can be cut in half if you have a 4WD vehicle. Outfitted with a head lamp, this would be a great hike at sunset as the sun's light sets the canyon walls awash in color. ⊠ *Kōke'e Natural History Museum: Kōke'e Rd., Rte. 550* ☎ *808/335–9975 for trail conditions.*

Sleeping Giant Trail. An easy and easily accessible trail practically in the heart of Kapa'a, the Sleeping Giant Trail—or simply "Sleeping Giant"—gains 1,000 feet over 2 mi. We prefer an early-morning—say, sunrise—hike, with sparkling blue-water vistas, up the east-side trailhead. At the top you can see a grassy grove with a picnic table; don't stop here. Continue carefully along the narrow trail toward the Giant's nose and chin. From here there are 360-degree views of the island. ⊠ *In Wailua, turn mauka off Rte. 56 onto Haleilio Rd.; proceed 1 mi to small parking area on right.*

Horseback Riding

Most of the horseback riding tours on Kaua'i are primarily walking tours with very little trotting and no cantering or galloping, so there's no experience required. Zip. Zilch. Nada. If you're interested, most of the stables offer private lessons. The most popular tours are the ones including a picnic lunch by the water. Your only dilemma may be deciding what kind of water you want—waterfalls or ocean. You may want to make your decision based on where you're staying. The waterfall picnic tours are on the wetter North Shore, and the beach picnic tours take place on the South Side.

CJM Country Stables. Just past the Hyatt in Po'ipū, CJM Stables offers breakfast and lunch rides with noshing on the beach. Shorter rides are available. The landscapes here are rugged and beautiful, featuring sand dunes and limestone bluffs. Guides are real *paniolo*. CJM sponsors seasonal rodeo events that are free and open to the public. Prices range from $90 to $115. ⊠ *1.6 mi from Hyatt Regency Kaua'i off Po'ipū Rd., Kōloa* ☎ *808/742–6096* ⊕ *www.cjmstables.com.*

Esprit de Corps. If you ride, this is the company for you. Esprit de Corps has two- to eight-hour rides and allows some trotting and cantering based on the rider's experience and comfort with the horse. There are also pony parties and half-day horse camps for kids (usually summers). Weddings on horseback can be arranged, and custom rides for less-experienced and younger riders (as young as 2) are available, as well as private lessons. Rates range from $120 to $350. ⊠ *End of Kualapa Pl., Kapa'a* ☎ *808/822–4688* ⊕ *www.kauaihorses.com.*

★ **Princeville Ranch Stables.** A longtime *kama'āina* (resident) family operates Princeville Ranch. They originated the waterfall picnic tours, which run three or four hours and include a short but steep hike down to Kalihi Wai Falls, a dramatic three-tier waterfall, for swimming and picnick-

Continued on page 448

HIKING THE KALALAU TRAIL

Kalalau Lookout (above).
Nā Pali Coast (below).

There are few places left on earth where only your feet can take you. But even a small horse would not fit on some stretches of Kaua'i's prized hike, the Kalalau Trail. This ancient path, blazed by early inhabitants, winds through one of the most beautiful stretches of coastline in all Hawai'i, if not the entire world, the famed Nā Pali Coast.

TRAIL OPTIONS

Moderate	1 mi round-trip to half-mile mark for dramatic coastal views
Moderate	4 mi round-trip to Hanakāpī'ai Beach
Moderate/Advanced	8 mi round-trip to Hanakāpī'ai Falls
Advanced	22 mi round-trip, with camping at Kalalau Beach

The Kalalau Trail begins at the western end of Route 56 and proceeds 11 mi to Kalalau Beach. Folding sea cliffs thousands of feet high, sliced by deep valleys of tropical vegetation, tower over the narrow footpath. There are sea caves, arches, secluded beaches, waterfalls, and after it rains, rainbows. (Don't think a little rain spoils the views here.) And did we mention green? Every possible shade of green is revealed by the myriad plants growing along the coast.

Nā Pali Coast

Feral goats and wild pigs share the trails, while large marine and tiny forest birds soar on the wind currents above. Once, large settlements of Hawaiians lived in the valleys and terraced the land for taro cultivation. Many of the valleys still contain rock walls, housing platforms, and other remains of their communities.

In winter months the big surf is dramatic as seen—and heard—from the coastal trail, although heavy rains can cause flash floods at stream crossings and trail erosion in some places. Summers, the trail is dryer and, frankly, safer. It's also busier.

With hairpin turns and constant ups and downs, this hike is a true test of endurance and isn't tackled round-trip in one day, even by the fittest of the fit. Many people don't even make the 11 mi to Kalalau Beach in one day; actually, most don't event attempt it. Instead, most people hike the first 2 mi to Hanakāpī'ai Beach, a rewarding hike in itself.

There are small quarter-mile markers all along the trail (although some are missing). At the half-mile point, the wrinkles of Nā Pali Coast unfold before you. Even if you go no further, make every attempt to reach this point, and after you look down the coastline, look back. You'll see a dramatic view of the beach you came from.

TO HANAKĀPĪ'AI BEACH

The trailhead is easy to find just before Kē'ē Beach. It starts at sea level and doesn't waste any time gaining in

HIKING TIPS

■ The trail is rocky and frequently muddy, so wear comfortable shoes and recognize that they may never be clean again. We suggest *amphibious* shoes versus waterproof mountaineering boots. With the various stream crossings and mud, a self-bailing sort of shoe is perfect.

■ Even if you plan to complete only the first 2 mi of the 11-mi trek, start early and bring mosquito repellent, lots of drinking water, and a hat, as it gets hot on the hike back. No concessions or drinking water are available past Haena.

■ If you need any last-minute camping gear, try Wal-Mart in Līhu'e, Island Hardware in Princeville, or Kayak Kaua'i or Pedal 'N Paddle, both in Hanalei.

elevation. Take heart. The uphill *only* lasts about a mile and tops out at about 400 feet; then it's downhill all the way to Hanakāpī'ai Beach.

This two-mile portion of the trail will take about 1½ hours one way, possibly longer, depending on how often you stop to gawk at the scenic beauty of Nā Pali Coast along the way.

To reach Hanakāpī'ai Beach, you'll have to boulder-hop across a stream. During heavy rains or even just after, the stream can flood, stranding hikers on the wrong side. Don't cross unless the boulders are visibly exposed and easily hopped. The cats you'll most likely encounter here are feral, although quite friendly. With all the hikers tossing them crumbs, they tend to thrive.

Hanakāpī'ai Beach is a great spot for a picnic, but don't plan on cooling off with a refreshing swim. The waters here are what locals like to call "confused." The radical change in water depth and the sheer cliff walls create wicked rip currents, rogue waves, backwash, undertow, and cross waves. This is not water you want to mess with.

PERMITS:

Permits: Campers and anyone hiking past Hanakāpī'ai must obtain permits from the State Department of Land and Natural Resources in Līhu'e; there's a five-night limit in Nā Pali State Park and rangers do check permits. Campsites are numbered, and requests are recommended up to a year in advance, especially for summer months.

Department of Land and Natural Resources
3060 Eiwa St., Līhu'e 96766
808/274-3444
www.kauai-hawaii.com

TO HANAKĀPĪ'AI FALLS

If you're prepared with water and food, continue another 2 mi *inland*, criss-crossing the rough, slippery stream trail numerous times (read: easy to lose) and scrambling over boulders in some places, to the 300-foot Hanakāpī'ai Falls. The water here can be cool—okay, cold—because it originates up in

4

HIKING THE KALALAU TRAIL

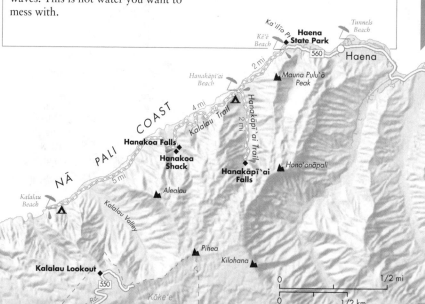

the mountains, but how many times will you have an opportunity to swim under a waterfall? (Just be careful, especially after a heavy rain, rocks and tree limbs do tumble over the falls.)

Keep in mind, round-trip to the waterfall is 8 mi; start early if you don't want to risk getting lost in the dark on your return trip.

TO HANAKOA VALLEY

Backpackers and serious hikers with the proper state permits can continue on another 4 mi to Hanakoa Valley.

Climb the steep switchback trail out of Hanakāpī'ai and follow the narrow, winding trail through numerous lush and humid valleys. A primitive camp shelter on the trail and lovely falls ⅓ mi inland distinguish Hanakoa, which is well above sea level and offers no access to the ocean. Once camping was permitted at Hanakoa, and you may still see some campers here; but it is now illegal and we don't recommend it. We do recommend mosquito repellent—for this valley in particular and all other inland areas that are heavily foliaged.

TO KALALAU BEACH

The last 5 mi of the hike tend to be the most treacherous, as the trail is often eroded, and the crumbly, loose soil can make hiking quite dangerous. The terrain is more open here, offering sweeping coastal views as it slowly drops down to sea level.

This is the magnificent Kalalau Valley, anchored on one end by a year-round stream and on the other by a refreshing and spectacular waterfall—which makes for a perfect shower. In summer the beach is broad, and you can walk right into a dry sea cave beyond the waterfalls. A number of campsites are tucked behind the beach and protected by trees.

In the summer you'll certainly not lack for company, including some free spirits who have shed their clothes and are (illegally) on extended stays in nature. Winter is not as populated. Throughout the year there's a friendly, sharing atmosphere among campers of all sorts, with group campfires and even potluck dinners.

ISLAND TREES

While the vistas are indeed magnificent, and in winter the possibility of spotting whales will tempt your gaze, don't overlook the flora. Some fascinating indigenous plants grow along Nā Pali Coast. The zany-looking trees you'll see all along the trail with aerial roots and long, skinny, serrated leaves are known as hala. Early Hawaiians plaited their leaves to make mats, baskets, and canoe sails. The red blossoms of the 'ōhi'a tree—which blankets the slope before the half-mile point—are known as Pele's (the volcano goddess's) favorite flower; they bloom in spring.

ōhi'a trees

HEALTH AND SAFETY TIPS

■ If you are planning to hike all the way to Kalalau, train. Arrive fit and ready for such an adventure. The only legal camping is 2 mi in at Hanakāpī'ai and at the end of the 11-mi trail at Kalalau.

■ Note that swimming is extremely dangerous due to strong currents and surf conditions at all the beaches along Nā Pali, although you can cool off in the many streams that bisect the trail.

■ To find a parking space, arrive early and do not leave any valuables in the car. While overnight parking is allowed, rental cars are easy prey for vandals.

OTHER WAYS TO SEE NĀ PALI

Nā Pali Coast kayakers

If you don't have the time or inclination to hike the Kalalau Trail, there are other ways to experience the majesty of Nā Pali Coast.

■ For a truly up-close view, try **a Zodiac boat ride**. These inflatable rubber rafts are wet and wild. In summer months, many will dip into sea caves. Some tour operators have special permits to land at Nualolo Kai for a tour of the remains of an ancient fishing village. ⇨ *See* Boat Tours *earlier in this chapter.*

■ If you prefer enjoying a refreshing beverage—say, a mai tai—as you gaze upon the majesty of Nā Pali Coast, then the usually smooth, **leisurely sailing catamarans** are just the ticket. In calm waters, these boats are even known to back into a waterfall for a dip. ⇨ *See* Boat Tours *earlier in this chapter.*

■ For a once-in-a-lifetime adventure, consider **kayaking** Nā Pali Coast—summer months only. These day-long tours are definitely physical, but you don't need to train like Lance Armstrong to paddle out. ⇨ *See* Kayaking *earlier in this chapter.*

■ Somehow, only **a helicopter tour** gives a true perspective of the sheer enormity of the cliffs. Plus, there's nothing like zipping over a knife-edge cliff to truly understand how these cliffs are cut. ⇨ *See* Aerial Tours *earlier in this chapter.*

■ **Sunset at the Kalalau Lookout,** at the paved road's end in Kōke'e State Park, is the perfect end to a day in paradise. You'll take in views of the glorious Kalalau Valley with the sands of Kalalau Beach glimmering in the fading light. ⇨ *See* Exploring the West Side *earlier in this chapter.*

ing. Princeville also has shorter, straight riding tours, private rides, and if they're moving cattle while you're visiting, you can sign up for a cattle drive. Prices range from $80 to $185. ⊠ *Just west of Princeville Airport* mauka *between mile markers 27 and 28, Princeville* ☎ *808/826–6777* ⊕ *www.princevilleranch.com.*

Mountain Tubing Tours

Kaua'i Backcountry Adventures. Very popular with all ages, this laid-back adventure can book up two weeks in advance in busy summer months. Here's how it works: you recline in an inner tube and float down fern-lined irrigation ditches that were built more than a century ago—the engineering is impressive—to divert water from Mt. Wai'ale'ale to sugar and pineapple fields around the island. Simple as that. They'll even give you a headlamp so you can see as you float through a couple stretches of covered tunnels. The scenery from the island's interior at the base of Mt. Wai'ale'ale on Līhu'e Plantation land is superb. Ages five and up are welcome. The tour takes about three hours and includes a picnic lunch and a swim in a swimming hole. ■ TIP➔ In winter or after the rain, the water can be chilly; some people wear a surfer's rash guard over their swimsuit. You'll definitely want to pack water-friendly shoes (or rent some from the outfitter), sunscreen, a hat, bug repellent, and a beach towel. Tours cost $92 per person and are offered morning and afternoon, daily. ⊠ *3–4131 Kūhiō Hwy., across from gas station, Hanamā'ulu* ☎ *808/245–2506 or 888/270–0555* ⊕ *www.kauaibackcountry.com.*

Tennis

If you're interested in booking some court time on Kaua'i, there are public tennis courts in Waimea, Kekaha, Kōloa, Kalaheo, Līhu'e, Wailua Homesteads, Wailua Houselots, and Kapa'a New Park. For specific directions or more information, call the **County of Kaua'i Parks and Recreation Office** (☎808/241–4463). Many hotels and resorts have tennis courts on property; even if you're not staying there, you can still rent court time. Rates range from $10 to $30 per person per hour. On the South Side, try the **Hyatt Regency Kaua'i Resort and Spa** (☎ 808/742–1234) and **Kiahuna Swim and Tennis Club** (☎ 808/742–9533). On the North Shore try the **Princeville Tennis Center** (☎ 808/826–1230).

Zipline Tours

The latest adventure on Kaua'i is "zipping" or "zip lining." It's so new that the vernacular is still catching up with it, but regardless of what you call it, chances are you'll scream like a rock-star fan while trying it. Strap on a harness, clip onto a cable running from one side of a river or valley to the other and zip across. The step off is the scariest part. ■ TIP➔ Pack knee-length shorts or pants, athletic shoes, and courage for this adventure.

Outfitters Kaua'i. This company offers a half-day adventure of multiple zips, along with rope-swinging off a cliff adjacent to Kīpū Falls. There's only one zipline involved, so you'll be making the same crossing several times, but it's a Swiss Family Robinson–like setting with a tree-house launching pad and a swinging bridge. Plus, you'll trek over to Kīpū Falls to enjoy the rope swing. Price is $99. Outfitters Kaua'i also has a zi-pline stream crossing as part of their Kipu Safari tour (⇨ see Kayaking *earlier in this chapter*). ✉ *2827-A Po'ipū Rd., Po'ipū* 🕾 *808/742–9667 or 888/742–9887* ⊕ *www.outfitterskauai.com.*

Princeville Ranch Adventures. The North Shore's answer to ziplining is an eight-zipline course with a bit of hiking, waterfall crossing, and swimming thrown in for a half-day adventure. This is as close as it gets to flying; just watch out for the albatross. Prices start at $125. ✉ *Just west of Princeville Airport on Rte. 56., between mile markers 27 and 28, Princeville* 🕾 *808/826–7669* ⊕ *www.adventureskauai.com.*

SHOPPING

Along with one major shopping mall, a few shopping centers, and a grow-ing number of big-box retailers, Kaua'i has some delightful mom-and-pop shops and specialty boutiques with lots of character.

The Garden Isle also has a large and talented community of artisans and fine artists, with galleries all around the island showcasing their creations. You can find many unique island-made arts and crafts in the small shops, and it's worthwhile to stop in at craft fairs and outdoor markets to look for bargains and mingle with island residents.

If you're looking for a special memento of your trip that is unique to Kaua'i County, check out the distinctive Ni'ihau shell leis. The tiny shells are collected from beaches on Kaua'i and Ni'ihau, pierced, and strung into beautiful necklaces, chokers, and earrings. It's a time-consuming and exacting craft, and these items are much in demand, so don't be surprised by the high price tags. Those made by Ni'ihau residents will have certificates of authenticity and are worth collecting. You often can find cheaper versions made by non-Hawaiians at craft fairs.

Stores are typically open daily from 9 or 10 AM to 5 PM, although some stay open until 9 PM, especially those near resorts. Don't be surprised if the posted hours don't match the actual hours of operation at smaller shops, where owners may be fairly casual about keeping to a schedule.

The North Shore

Shopping Centers

Ching Young Village. This popular shopping center looks a bit worn, de-spite a recent face-lift, but that doesn't deter business. The town's only grocery store, **Big Save,** is here along with a number of other shops use-ful to locals and visitors. These include **Aloha Juice Bar,** with its sup-ply of fresh organic produce; **Hanalei Music and Video,** where you can buy Hawaiian sheet music, compact discs, and handmade instruments; **Village Variety,** which has a bit of everything; **Village Snack & Bakery;** and several restaurants. A few steps away is **Evolve Love Artists Gallery,** a good place to find quality work by local artisans; and **On The Road to Hanalei,** a neat boutique with gifts, clothing, jewelry, housewares, and collectibles from Indonesia. ✉ *In Hanalei, makai, after mile marker 2, 5-1590 Kūhiō Hwy., Hanalei* 🕾 *808/826–7222.*

Hanalei Center. Listed on the National Register of Historic Places, the old Hanalei school has been refurbished and rented out to boutiques and restaurants. You can dig through '40s and '50s vintage memorabilia in the **Yellow Fish Trading Company,** search for that unusual gift at **Sand People,** or buy beach gear at the classic **Hanalei Surf Company.** You can even catch a class at the **Hanalei Yoga studio** in the two-story modern addition to the center. ⊠ *In Hanalei,* mauka, *after mile marker 2, 5-5161 Kūhiō Hwy., Hanalei* 🕾 *808/826–7677.*

Princeville Shopping Center. Foodland, a full-service grocery store, and **Island Ace Hardware** are the big draws at this small center. This is the last stop for gas and banking on the North Shore. You'll also find two restaurants, a mail service center, post office, ice-cream shop, toy and hobby shop, and clothing stores. ⊠ Makai, *mile marker 28, 5-4280 Kūhiō Hwy., Princeville* 🕾 *808/826–7513.*

Shops & Stores

Kong Lung Co. Sometimes called the Gump's of Kaua'i, this gift store sells elegant clothing, exotic glassware, ethnic books, gifts, and artwork— all very lovely and expensive. The shop is housed in a beautiful 1892 stone structure right in the heart of Kīlauea. It's the showpiece of the pretty little Kong Lung Center, with shops featuring distinctive jewelry, handmade soaps and candles, hammocks, plants, excellent pizza and baked goods, art work, and consignment clothing. Next door is the Farmers' Market, a good place to buy natural and gourmet foods, wines, and sandwiches. ⊠ *2490 Keneke St., Kīlauea* 🕾 *808/828–1822.*

Village Variety Store. How about a fun beach towel for the folks back home? That's just one of the gifts you can find here, along with shell leis, Kaua'i T-shirts, macadamia nuts, and other great souvenirs at low prices. The store also has many small, useful items like envelopes, housewares, and toiletries. ⊠ *Ching Young Village, Kūhiō Hwy., Hanalei* 🕾 *808/826–6077.*

The East Side: Kapa'a & Wailua

Shopping Centers

Coconut Marketplace. This visitor-oriented complex is on the busy Coconut Coast near resort hotels and condominiums. Sixty shops sell everything from snacks and slippers (as locals call flip-flop sandals) to scrimshaw. There are also two movie theaters with first-run features, restaurants open from breakfast to evening, and a free Wednesday evening Polynesian show at 5 PM. ⊠ *4-484 Kūhiō Hwy., Kapa'a* 🕾 *808/822–3641.*

Kaua'i Village Shopping Center. The buildings of this Kapa'a shopping village are in the style of a 19th-century plantation town. **ABC Discount Store** sells sundries; **Safeway** carries groceries and alcoholic beverages; **Long's Drugs** has a pharmacy, health and beauty products, and a good selection of Hawaiian merchandise; **Papaya's** has health foods; and other shops sell jewelry, gift items, children's clothes and toys, and art. For children, there's the **Kaua'i Children's Discovery Museum,** which, in addition to interactive exhibits, offers children's day-camp programs. ⊠ *4-831 Kūhiō Hwy., Po'ipū Beach* 🕾 *808/822–3900.*

Kinipopo Shopping Village. Kinipopo is a tiny little center on Kūhiō Highway in Wailua. **Korean Barbeque** fronts the highway, as does **Goldsmith's Gallery,** which sells handcrafted Hawaiian-style gold jewelry. Worth a stop is **Tin Can Mailman,** with its eclectic collection of used books, stamps and coins, rare prints, vintage maps, and collectibles. ✉ *4-356 Kūhiō Hwy., Kapa'a* 🕾 *No phone.*

Waipouli Town Center. **Foodland** is the focus of this small retail plaza, one of three shopping centers anchored by a grocery store in Kapa'a. You can also find a **Blockbuster** video outlet, **McDonald's, Pizza Hut,** and **Fun Factory** video arcade, along with a local-style restaurant and a bar. ✉ *4-901 Kūhiō Hwy., Kapa'a* 🕾 *808/524–2023.*

Shops & Galleries

★ **Bambulei.** Two 1930s-style plantation homes have been transformed into this unique boutique featuring vintage and contemporary clothing, antiques, jewelry, and accessories. ✉ *4-369 Kūhiō Hwy., Wailua* 🕾 *808/823–8641.*

Jim Saylor Jewelers. Jim Saylor has been designing beautiful keepsakes for more than 20 years on Kaua'i. Gems from around the world appear in his unique settings, including black pearls and diamonds. ✉ *1318 Kūhiō Hwy., Kapa'a* 🕾 *808/822–3591.*

Kahn Galleries. You can purchase the works of many local artists—including seascapes by George Sumner and Roy Tabora—at this gallery's many locations. ✉ *Coconut Marketplace, 4-484 Kūhiō Hwy., Kapa'a* 🕾 *808/822–3636* ✉ *Kōloa Rd., Old Kōloa Town* 🕾 *808/742–2277* ✉ *Hanalei Center, 5-5161 Kūhiō Hwy., Hanalei* 🕾 *808/826–6677* ✉ *Po'ipū Shopping Village, 2360 Kiahuna Plantation Dr., Po'ipū* 🕾 *808/742–5004.*

Kaua'i Gold. A wonderful selection of rare Ni'ihau shell lei ranges in price from $20 to $200. Ask about how these remarkable necklaces are made to appreciate the craftsmanship, understand the sometimes high prices, and learn to care for and preserve them. The store also sells a selection of 14-karat gold jewelry. ✉ *Coconut Marketplace, 4-484 Kūhiō Hwy., Kapa'a* 🕾 *808/822–9361.*

Kaua'i Products Fair. Open weekends, this outdoor market features fresh produce, tropical plants and flowers, aloha wear, and collectibles along with craftspeople, artisans, and wellness practitioners who will give you a massage right on the spot. ✉ *Outside on north side of Kapa'a, next to Shack restaurant* 🕾 *808/246–0988.*

Tin Can Mailman Books and Antiques. Both new and used books can be found here, along with an extensive collection of Hawaiian and South Pacific literature. The shop also sells maps, tapa cloth from Fiji, and specialty gift items. ✉ *Kinipopo Shopping Village, 4-356 Kūhiō Hwy., Kapa'a* 🕾 *808/822–3009.*

The East Side: Līhu'e

Shopping Centers

Kilohana Plantation. This 16,000-square-foot Tudor-style mansion contains art galleries, a jewelry store, and Gaylord's restaurant. The restored outbuildings house a craft shop and a Hawaiian-style clothing shop. The house itself is filled with antiques from its original owner and is worth a look. Horse-drawn carriage rides are available, with knowledgeable guides reciting the history of sugar on Kaua'i. ⊠ *3-2087 Kaumuali'i Hwy., 1 mi west of Līhu'e* ☎ *808/245–5608.*

Kukui Grove Center. This is Kaua'i's only true mall. Besides **Sears Roebuck** and **Kmart,** anchor tenants are **Longs Drugs, Macy's,** and **Star Market,** a local grocery store. **Borders Books & Music,** and its coffee shop, is one of the island's most popular stores. **Starbucks** recently opened its first outlet on Kaua'i here. The mall's stores offer women's clothing, surf wear, art, toys, athletic shoes, jewelry, and locally made crafts. Restaurants range from fast food and sandwiches to Mexican and Chinese. The center stage often has entertainment. ⊠ *3-2600 Kaumuali'i Hwy., west of Līhu'e* ☎ *808/245–7784.*

Shops & Galleries

Hilo Hattie Fashion Factory. This is the big name in aloha wear for tourists throughout the Islands. You can visit the only store on Kaua'i, a mile from Līhu'e Airport, to pick up cool, comfortable aloha shirts and mu'umu'u in bright floral prints, as well as other souvenirs. While there, check out the line of Hawaiian-inspired home furnishings. ⊠ *3252 Kūhiō Hwy., Līhu'e* ☎ *808/245–3404.*

Fodor'sChoice **Kapaia Stitchery.** Hawaiian quilts made by hand and machine, a beautiful selection of fabrics, quilting kits, and fabric arts fill this cute little red plantation-style structure. The staff is friendly and helpful, even though a steady stream of customers keeps them busy. ⊠ *Kūhiō Hwy., ½ mi north of Līhu'e* ☎ *808/245–2281.*

Kaua'i Fruit and Flower Company. At this shop near Līhu'e you can buy fresh sugarloaf pineapple, sugarcane, ginger, coconuts, local jams, jellies, and honey, plus Kaua'i-grown papayas, bananas, and mangos in season. Stop by on your way to the airport (although it's hard to make a left turn back onto Kūhiō Highway) to buy fruit that's been inspected and approved for shipment to the mainland. ⊠ *3-4684 Kūhiō Hwy., Kapa'a* ☎ *808/245–1814 or 800/943–3108.*

★ **Kaua'i Museum.** The gift shop at the museum sells some fascinating books, maps, and prints, as well as lovely feather lei hatbands, Ni'ihau shell jewelry, handwoven *lau hala* hats, and other quality local crafts at reasonable prices. ⊠ *4428 Rice St., Līhu'e* ☎ *808/245–6931.*

Kaua'i Products Store. Every seed lei, every finely crafted koa-wood box, every pair of tropical-flower earrings; indeed, every item in this boutique is handcrafted on Kaua'i. Other gift options include koa oil lamps, pottery, hand-painted silk clothing, sculpture, and homemade fudge. Although some of the merchandise isn't all that appealing, it's nice to support local talent when you can. ⊠ *Kukui Grove Center, 3-2600 Kaumuali'i Hwy., Līhu'e* ☎ *808/246–6753.*

Kilohana Clothing Company. This store in the guest cottage by Gaylord's restaurant offers vintage Hawaiian clothing as well as contemporary styles using traditional Hawaiian designs. The store also features a wide selection of home products in vintage fabrics. ⊠ *Kilohana Plantation, 3-2087 Kaumuali'i Hwy., Līhu'e* ☎ *808/246–6911.*

★ **Piece of Paradise Gallery.** Fine art, koa-wood clocks and sushi platters, handblown glass, sculptures, and unique jewelry—all designed by talented Kaua'i-based artisans—are available here. ⊠ *Kaua'i Beach Resort, 4331 Kaua'i Beach Dr., Līhu'e* ☎ *808/246–2834.*

The South & West Side

Shopping Centers

'Ele'ele Shopping Center. Kaua'i's West Side has a scattering of stores, including those at this no-frills strip-mall shopping center. It's a good place to rub elbows with local folk or to grab a quick bite to eat at the casual **Grinds Cafe** or **McDonald's.** ⊠ *Rte. 50 near Hanapēpē, 'Ele'ele* ☎ *808/246–0634.*

Po'ipū Shopping Village. Convenient to nearby hotels and condos on the South Side, the two-dozen shops here sell resort wear, gifts, souvenirs, and art. The upscale **Black Pearl Kaua'i** and **Na Hoku** shops are particularly appealing jewelry stores. There's a couple of art galleries and several fun clothing stores, including **Making Waves** and **Blue Ginger.** Restaurants include **Keoki's Pardise, Roy's, Po'ipū Tropical Burgers,** and **Pattaya Asian Cafe.** A Tahitian dance troupe performs in the open-air courtyard Tuesday and Thursday at 5 PM. ⊠ *2360 Kiahuna Plantation Dr., Po'ipū Beach* ☎ *808/742–2831.*

Waimea Canyon Plaza. As Kekaha's retail hub and the last stop for supplies before heading up to Waimea Canyon, this tiny, tidy complex of shops is surprisingly busy. Look for local foods, souvenirs, and island-made gifts for all ages. ⊠ *Kōke'e Rd. at Rte. 50, Kekaha* ☎ *No phone.*

Shops & Galleries

Kaua'i Coffee Visitor Center and Museum. Kaua'i produces more coffee than any other island in the state. The local product can be purchased from grocery stores or here at the source, where a sampling of the nearly one dozen coffees is available. Be sure to try some of the estate-roasted varieties. ⊠ *870 Halawili Rd., off Rte. 50, west of Kalāheo* ☎ *808/335–0813 or 800/545–8605.*

Kaua'i Tropicals. You can have this company ship heliconia, anthuriums, ginger, and other tropicals in 5-foot-long boxes directly from its flower farm in Kalaheo. Phone-in orders only. ⊠ *Kalāheo* ☎ *808/742–9989 or 800/303–4385.*

Fodor's Choice ★ **Kebanu Gallery.** A stunning collection of original wood sculptures, whimsical ceramics, beaded jewelry, colorful glassware, and other creations—many of them by Hawai'i artists—makes this contemporary shop a pleasure to visit. ⊠ *Old Kōloa Town, 3440 Po'ipū Rd., Ko'loā* ☎ *808/742–2727.*

Paradise Sportswear. This is the retail outlet of the folks who invented Kaua'i's popular "red dirt" shirts, which are dyed and printed with the characteristic local soil. Ask the salesperson to tell you the charming story behind these shirts. Sizes from infants up to 5X are available. ✉ *4350 Waialo Rd., Port Allen* ☎ *808/335–5670.*

SPAS

Kaua'i is often touted as the healing island, and local spas try hard to fill that role. With the exception of the Hyatt's Anara Spa, the facilities aren't as posh as some might want. But it's in the human element that Kaua'i excels. Island residents are known for their warmth, kindness, and humility, and you can find all these attributes in the massage therapists and technicians who work long hours at the resort spas. These professionals take their therapeutic mission seriously; they genuinely want you to experience the island's relaxing, restorative qualities. Private massage services abound on the island—your spa therapist may offer the same services at a much lower price outside the resort—but if you're looking for a variety of health-and-beauty treatments, an exercise workout, or a full-day of pampering, a spa will prove most convenient. Though most spas on Kaua'i are associated with resorts, none are restricted to guests only.

Alexander Day Spa at the Kaua'i Marriott. This sister spa of Alexander Simson's Beverly Hills spa focuses on body care rather than exercise, so don't expect any fitness equipment or exercise classes. Tucked away in the back corner of the Marriott, the spa has the same ambience of stilted formality as the rest of the resort, but is otherwise a sunny, pleasant facility. Massages in treatment rooms are more enjoyable than those offered beachside, where it's often windy and the calm is disrupted by the roar of jets using nearby Līhu'e Airport. Wedding-day and custom spa packages can be arranged. ✉ *Kaua'i Marriott Resort & Beach Club, 3610 Rice St., Līhu'e* ☎ *808/246–4918* ⊕ *www.alexanderspa.com* ⚲ *$50–$185 massage. Services: Body treatments, facials, hair styling, manicures, massages, pedicures.*

Fodor's Choice **Anara Spa.** This luxurious facility is far and away the best on Kaua'i, ★ setting a standard that no other spa has been able to meet. It has all the equipment and services you expect from a top resort spa, along with a pleasant, professional staff. Best of all, it has indoor and outdoor areas that capitalize on its tropical locale and balmy weather, further distinguishing it from the Marriott and Princeville spas. It's also big, covering 25,000 square feet of space, including a landscaped courtyard where you can relax or enjoy a healthful breakfast, lunch, or smoothie from adjacent Kupono Café. Relax and unwind with a single treatment or full day of luxurious pampering. Local ingredients are featured in some of the treatments, such as a coconut-mango facial and a body brush scrub that polishes your skin with a mix of ground coffee, orange peel, and vanilla bean. The open-air lava-rock showers are wonderful, introducing many guests to the delightful island practice of showering outdoors. The spa adjoins the Hyatt's legendary swimming pool. ✉ *Hyatt Regency Kaua'i Resort and Spa, 1571 Po'ipū Rd., Po'ipū* ☎ *808/240–6440* ⊕ *www.anaraspa.com* ⚲ *$145–$215 massage. Gym with: cardiovascular machines, free weights, weight-training equipment. Services: Body* *scrubs and wraps, facials, manicures, massage, pedicures. Classes and programs: aerobics, aquaerobics, body sculpting, fitness analysis, flexibility training, personal training, Pilates, step aerobics, weight training, yoga.*

★ **Hart-Felt Massage & Day Spa.** This is the only full-service day spa on the laid-back West Side. It's in one of the restored plantation cottages that comprise the guest quarters at Waimea Plantation Cottages, creating a distinctive setting you won't find elsewhere. The overall feel is relaxed, casual, and friendly, as you'd expect in this quiet country town. The staff is informal, yet thoroughly professional. ✉ *Waimea Plantation Cottages, 9400 Kaumuali'i Hwy., Waimea* 🕿 *808/338–2240* ⊕ *www.waimeaplantation.com* ☞ *$46–$132 massage. Services: acupuncture, body scrubs and wraps, facials, hydrotherapy, massage.*

Princeville Health Club & Spa. Inspiring views of mountains, sea, and sky provide a lovely distraction in the gym area of this spa, which is well equipped, but small and often overly air-conditioned. The treatment area is functional, but lacks charm and personality. Luckily the gorgeous setting helps to make up for it. This is the only facility of this kind on the North Shore, so it's well used, and has a generally well-heeled clientele that pays attention to gym attire. It's in the Princeville Clubhouse, at the Prince Golf Course, several miles from the Princeville Hotel. A room in the hotel or round of golf at a Princeville course entitles you to reduced admission to the spa, otherwise it's $20 for a day pass. ✉ *Princeville Resort, 53-900 Kūhiō Hwy., Princeville* 🕿 *808/826–5030* ⊕ *www.princeville.com* ☞ *$97–$130 massage. Gym with: cardiovascular machines, free weights, weight-training equipment. Services: body scrubs and wraps, facials, massage. Classes and programs: aerobics, aquaerobics, personal training, Pilates, step aerobics, tai chi, yoga.*

ENTERTAINMENT & NIGHTLIFE

Kaua'i has never been known for its nightlife. It's a rural island, where folks tend to retire early, and the streets are dark and deserted well before midnight. The island does have its nightspots, though, and the after-dark entertainment scene is expanding, especially in areas frequented by tourists.

Most of the island's dinner and lū'au shows are held at hotels and resorts. Hotel lounges are a good source of live music, often with no cover charge, as are a few bars and restaurants around the island.

Check the local newspaper, *The Garden Island,* for listings of weekly happenings, or tune in to community radio station KKCR—found at 90.9 and 91.9 on the FM dial—at 5:30 PM for the arts and entertainment calendar. Free publications such as *Kaua'i Gold, This Week on Kaua'i,* and *Kaua'i Beach Press* also list entertainment events. You can pick them up at Līhu'e Airport near the baggage-claim area, as well as at numerous retail areas on the island.

Kaua'i: Undercover Movie Star

CLOSE UP

THOUGH KAUA'I HAS PLAYED ITSELF IN THE MOVIES (you may remember Nicolas Cage frantically shouting "Is it Kapa'a or Kapa'a-a?" into a pay phone in *Honeymoon in Vegas* [1992]), most of its screen time has been as a stunt double for a number of tropical paradises. The island's remote valleys and waterfalls portrayed Venezuelan jungle in Kevin Costner's *Dragonfly* (2002) and a Costa Rican dinosaur preserve in Steven Spielberg's *Jurassic Park* (1993). Spielberg was no stranger to Kaua'i, having filmed Harrison Ford's escape via seaplane from Menehune Fishpond in *Raiders of the Lost Ark* (1981). The fluted cliffs and gorges of Kaua'i's rugged Nā Pali Coast play the misunderstood beast's island home in the original *King Kong* (1976), and a jungle dweller of another sort, in *George of the Jungle* (1997), frolicked on Kaua'i. Harrison Ford returned to the island for 10 weeks during the filming of *Six Days, Seven Nights* (1998), a romantic adventure set in French Polynesia.

But these are all relatively recent movies. What's truly remarkable is that Hollywood discovered Kaua'i in 1933 with the making of *White Heat*, which was set on a sugar plantation and—like another more memorable movie filmed on Kaua'i—dealt with interracial love stories. In 1950, Esther Williams and Rita Moreno arrived to film *Pagan Love Song*, a forgettable musical. Then, it was off to the races, as Kaua'i saw no fewer than a dozen movies filmed on island in the 1950s, not all of them Oscar contenders. Rita Hayworth starred in *Miss Sadie Thompson* (1953) and no one you'd recognize starred in the tantalizing *She Gods of Shark Reef* (1956).

The movie that is still immortalized on the island in the names of restaurants, real estate offices, a hotel, and even a sushi item is *South Pacific* (1957). (You guessed it, right?) That mythical place called Bali Hai is never far away on Kaua'i. There's even an off-off-off-Broadway musical version of the movie performed today—some 50 years later—at the Kaua'i Beach Resort in Līhu'e.

In the 1960s Elvis Presley filmed *Blue Hawaii* (1961) and *Girls! Girls! Girls!* (1962) on the island. A local movie tour likes to point out the stain on a hotel carpet where Elvis's jelly doughnut fell.

Kaua'i has welcomed a long list of Hollywood's A-List: John Wayne in *Donovan's Reef* (1963); Jack Lemmon in *The Wackiest Ship in the Army* (1961); Richard Chamberlain in *The Thorn Birds* (1983); Gene Hackman in *Uncommon Valor* (1983); Danny DeVito and Billy Crystal in *Throw Momma From the Train* (1987); and Dustin Hoffman, Morgan Freeman, Renee Russo, and Cuba Gooding Jr. in *Outbreak* (1995).

Yet the movie scene isn't the only screen on which Kaua'i has starred. A long list of TV shows, TV pilots, and made-for-TV movies make the list as well, including *Gilligan's Island*, *Fantasy Island*, *Starsky & Hutch*, *Baywatch-Hawai'i*—even reality TV shows *The Bachelor* and *The Amazing Race 3*.

For the record, just because a movie was filmed here, doesn't mean the entire movie was filmed on Kaua'i. Take *Honeymoon in Vegas*—just one scene.

Entertainment

Lūʻau

Although the commercial lūʻau experience is a far cry from the backyard lūʻau thrown by local residents to celebrate a wedding, graduation, or baby's first birthday, they're nonetheless entertaining and a good introduction to the Hawaiian food that isn't widely sold in restaurants. Besides the feast, there's often an exciting dinner show with Polynesian-style music and dancing. It all makes for a fun evening that's suitable for couples, families, and groups, and the informal setting is conducive to meeting other people. Every lūʻau is different, reflecting the cuisine and tenor of the host facility, so compare prices, menus, and entertainment before making your reservation. Most lūʻau on Kauaʻi are offered only on a limited number of nights each week, so plan ahead to get the lūʻau you want. We tend to prefer those *not* held on resort properties, because they feel a bit more authentic. The lūʻau shows listed below are our favorites.

Lūʻau Kilohana. This lūʻau—on a former sugar plantation manager's estate—has a twist: all guests arrive by horse-drawn carriage (reservations are staggered to prevent lines). Families especially seem to enjoy the food and fun. Even though sugar plantations are a decidedly Western affair, it feels more authentic than those on a portable stage on resort grounds. The evening's theme is the history of sugar on the Islands. ✉ *3-2087 Kaumualiʻi St., Līhuʻe* ☎ *808/245–9593* 🍽 *$65* 🕙 *Tues. and Thurs. wagon rides begin at 5, dinner at 6, show at 7.*

Paʻina o Hanalei. A conch shell is blown in the traditional way to signal the start of this gourmet lūʻau feast held on the shore of Hanalei Bay. It's lavish, as one might expect from the Princeville Hotel, with a buffet line that's heavy on upscale, Pacific Rim cuisine and light on traditional lūʻau fare. The event includes entertainment that celebrates the songs and dances of the South Pacific. ✉ *Princeville Resort, 5520 Ka Haku Rd.* ☎ *808/826–2788* 🍽 *$69* 🕙 *Mon. and Thurs. at 6.*

Fodor'sChoice ★ **Smith's Tropical Paradise Lūʻau.** A 30-acre tropical garden provides the lovely setting for this popular lūʻau, which begins with the traditional blowing of the conch shell and *imu* ceremony, followed by cocktails, an island feast, and an international show in the amphitheater overlooking a torch-lighted lagoon. It's fairly authentic and a better deal than the pricier resort events. ✉ *174 Wailua Rd., Kapaʻa* ☎ *808/821–6895* 🍽 *$58* 🕙 *Mon., Wed., and Fri. 5–9:15.*

Film & Theater

The **Kauaʻi Community Players** (✉ Līhuʻe Parish Hall, 4340 Nāwiliwili Rd., Līhuʻe ☎ 808/245–7700) is a talented local group that presents plays throughout the year.

Music

Check the local papers for outdoor reggae and Hawaiian-music shows, or one of the numbers listed below for more formal performances.

Hanalei Slack Key Concerts (✉ Turn *mauka* on dirt road before soccer fields, Hanalei ☎ 808/826–1469) are held every Friday evening at 4 and Sunday at 3 at the Hanalei Community Center. Tickets are $10.

Kaua'i Community College Performing Arts Center (✉ 3-1901 Kaumuali'i Hwy., Līhu'e ☎ 808/245–8270) is the main venue for island entertainment, hosting a concert music series, visiting musicians, dramatic productions, and special events such as the International Film Festival.

Kaua'i Concert Association (✉ 3-1901 Kaumuali'i Hwy., Līhu'e ☎ 808/ 245–7464) offers a seasonal program at the arts center.

Bars & Clubs

Nightclubs that stay open to the wee hours are rare on Kaua'i, and the bar scene is pretty limited. The major resorts generally host their own live entertainment and happy hours. All bars and clubs that serve alcohol must close at 2 AM, except those with a cabaret license, which allows them to close at 4 AM.

The North Shore

★ **Happy Talk Lounge.** Hawaiian entertainment takes center stage Monday through Friday evenings (6:30–9:30) in this lounge at the Hanalei Bay Resort. Come Saturday (6:30–9:30) and Sunday (4–7), this joint is swinging to the sounds of jazz in jam sessions. Tuesday evenings at 7, there's a hula show. ✉ *5380 Honoiki Rd., Princeville* ☎ *808/826–6522.*

Tahiti Nui. This venerable and decidedly funky institution in sleepy Hanalei no longer offers its famous lū'au, ever since owner and founder Auntie Louise Marston died. Its fun-loving new owner, a Kiwi from New Zealand, is doing his best to keep the place hopping with nightly entertainment. Hawaiian music Tuesday, Thursday, and Friday; karaoke on Monday and Thursday; and rock-and-roll Sunday, Wednesday, and Saturday. ✉ *Kūhiō Hwy., Hanalei* ☎ *808/826–6277.*

The East Side

Duke's Barefoot Bar. This is one of the liveliest bars on Kalapakī Beach. Contemporary Hawaiian music is performed in the beachside bar on Friday, and upstairs a traditional Hawaiian trio plays nightly for diners. The bar closes at 11 most nights. ✉ *Kalapakī Beach, Līhu'e* ☎ *808/ 246–9599.*

Rob's Good Times Grill. Let loose at this sports bar, which also houses Kaua'i's hottest DJs spinning Thursday through Saturday from 9 PM to 2 AM. Wednesday you can kick up your heels with country line dancing from 7:30 PM to 11. Sunday, Monday, and Tuesday evenings are open mike for karaoke enthusiasts. ✉ *4303 Rice St., Līhu'e* ☎ *808/ 246–0311.*

The Shack. The combination of live music and DJs offered several nights a week draws a crowd to this sports bar and burger joint on the north end of Kapa'a. It stays open until 2 AM if there's a crowd. ✉ *4-139 Kūhiō Hwy., Kapa'a* ☎ *808/823–0200.*

The South Shore & West Side

Keoki's Paradise. A young, energetic crowd makes this a lively spot on Thursday, Friday, and Saturday nights, with live music from 7 PM to 9 PM. After 9 PM, when the dining room clears out, there's a bit of a bar scene for singles. The bar closes at midnight. ⊠ *2360 Kiahuna Plantation Dr., Po'ipū* ☎ *808/742–7354.*

The Point at Sheraton Kaua'i. This is the place to be on the South Shore to celebrate sunset with a drink; the ocean view is unsurpassed. Starting at 8 PM on Friday, Saturday, and Monday, there's live entertainment until 12:30 AM, with a live band on Friday, salsa dancing and a DJ on Saturday, and swing dancing on Monday. ⊠ *2440 Ho'onani Rd., Po'ipū* ☎ *808/742–1661.*

WHERE TO EAT

Food is a big part of local culture, playing a prominent role at parties, celebrations, events, and even casual gatherings. The best grinds (food) are homemade, so if you're lucky enough to win an invitation to a potluck, baby lū'au, or beach party, accept. Folks are urged to eat until they're full, then rest, eat some more, and make a plate to take home, too. Small, neighborhood eateries are a good place to try local-style food, which bears little resemblance to the fancy Pacific Rim cuisine served in upscale restaurants. Expect plenty of meat—usually deep-fried or marinated in a teriyaki sauce and grilled *pulehu*-style over an open fire—and starches. Rice is ubiquitous, even for breakfast, and often served alongside potato-macaroni salad, another island specialty. Another local favorite is *poke*, made from chunks of raw tuna or octopus seasoned with sesame oil, soy sauce, onions, and pickled seaweed. It's a great *pūpū* (appetizer) when paired with a cold beer.

Kaua'i's cultural diversity is apparent in its restaurants, which offer authentic Vietnamese, Chinese, Korean, Japanese, Thai, Filipino, Mexican, Italian, and Hawaiian specialties. Less specialized restaurants cater to the tourist crowd, serving standard American fare—burgers, pizza, sandwiches, surf-and-turf combos, and so on. Kapa'a offers the best selection of restaurants, with options for a variety of tastes and budgets; most fast-food joints are in Lihū'e.

Parents will be relieved to encounter a tolerant attitude toward children, even if they're noisy. Men can leave their jackets and ties at home; attire tends toward informal, but if you want to dress up, you can. Reservations are accepted in most places, and required at some of the top restaurants. ■ TIP→ **One cautionary note: most restaurants stop serving dinner at 8 or 9 PM, so plan to eat early.**

WHAT IT COSTS				
$$$$	**$$$**	**$$**	**$**	**¢**
RESTAURANTS over $35	$27–$35	$18–$26	$10–$17	under $10

Prices are for one main course at dinner.

The North Shore

American–Casual

¢–$$$ ✕ **Kīlauea Bakery and Pau Hana Pizza.** This bakery has garnered tons of well-deserved good press for its Hawaiian sourdough loaf made with guava starter, and its specialty pizzas topped with such yummy ingredients as smoked ono, Gorgonzola-rosemary sauce, barbecued chicken, goat cheese, or roasted onions. Open from 6:30 AM, the bakery serves coffee drinks, delicious fresh pastries, bagels, and breads in the morning. Late-risers beware: breads and pastries sell out quickly on weekends. Pizza, soup, and salads can be ordered for lunch or dinner. If you want to hang out or do the coffee shop bit in Kīlauea, this is the place. A pretty courtyard with covered tables is a pleasant place to linger. ⊠ *Kong Lung Center, 2490 Keneke St., Kīlauea* ☎ *808/828–2020* ▭ *MC, V. $6–$30.*

¢–$$ ✕ **Hanalei Gourmet.** In Hanalei's restored old school house, this North Shore spot offers diners dolphin-free tuna, low-sodium meats, fresh-baked breads, and homemade desserts as well as a casual atmosphere where both families and the sports-watching crowds can feel equally comfortable. Early birds can order coffee and toast or a hearty breakfast. Lunch and dinner menus feature sandwiches, burgers, filling salads, and nightly specials of fresh local fish. They also will prepare a picnic and give it to you in an insulated backpack. A full bar and frequent live entertainment keep things hopping even after the kitchen closes. ⊠ *5-5161 Kūhiō Hwy., Hanalei* ☎ *808/826–2524* ▭ *D, DC, MC, V. $7–$26.*

Contemporary

★ **$$–$$$** ✕ **Café Hanalei and Terrace.** You're in for a very romantic evening here: the view from the Princeville Resort overlooking Hanalei Bay is mesmerizing, and the food and service are superb. In all but the rainiest weather you'll want to be seated outside on the terrace. The Sunday brunch ($42 or $46 with champagne) and daily breakfast buffet are enormous feasts, as is the Friday night seafood buffet ($50). The Japanese specialties, fresh-fish specials, and Kaua'i coffee rack of lamb are excellent choices for dinner. If you're on a budget, come for lunch when you can enjoy the fabulous views and a leisurely, relaxing meal—try the Cobb salad—for less than you'd spend at dinner. The pastry chef deserves praise for delicious, innovative desserts. Save room for the decadent "Tower of Passion," a chocolate tower filled with passion-fruit mousse. ⊠ *Princeville Resort, 5520 Ka Haku Rd., Princeville* ☎ *808/826–2760* ▭ *AE, D, DC, MC, V. $21–$35.*

★ **$$** ✕ **Postcards Café.** With its postcard artwork, beamed ceilings, and light interiors, this plantation-cottage restaurant has a menu consisting mostly of organic, additive-free vegetarian foods. But don't get the wrong idea—this isn't simple cooking: specials might include carrot-ginger soup, taro fritters, or fresh fish served with peppered pineapple-sage sauce. Desserts are made without refined sugar. Try the chocolate silk pie made with barley malt chocolate, pure vanilla, and creamy tofu with a crust of graham crackers, sun-dried cherries and crushed cashews. This is probably your best bet for dinner in Hanalei town. ⊠ *5-5075A Kūhiō Hwy., Hanalei* ☎ *808/826–1191* ▭ *AE, MC, V* ☺ *No lunch. $18–$24.*

Eclectic

$-$$ ✕ **Zelo's Beach House.** When you're traveling with a family or group and everyone wants to eat something different, a restaurant like Zelo's comes in handy. The menu is extensive and eclectic, borrowing from Hawaiian, American, Thai, and Mexican cuisines. The portions are huge and the prices moderate. The tropical decor, relaxed family atmosphere, and outdoor seating add to its appeal, as does its prime location on Hanalei's main drag. The one drawback is the inconsistent quality of the food. As is often the case in restaurants with such wide-ranging menus, the food is not always as tasty as it sounds. ⊠ *5-5156 Kūhiō Hwy., Hanalei* ☎ *808/826–9700* ▭ *MC, V. $14–$24.*

Italian

★ $$–$$$$ ✕ **La Cascata.** Terra-cotta floors, hand-painted murals, and trompe-l'oeil paintings give La Cascata a Tuscan-villa flair that makes it ideal for cozy, romantic dining. Picture windows offer dazzling views of Hanalei Bay, though you'll have to come before sunset to enjoy them. Local ingredients figure prominently on a fairly standard menu of pasta, fresh seafood, beef, and lamb prepared with competence and creativity. Savor *Brodetto di Pesce* (Kaua'i prawns, snapper, scallops, and clams with *Arrabbiata* sauce served over linguine), or seared 'ahi with roasted garlic mashed potatoes and a Kaffir lime lobster sauce. The service is professional and efficient. This is one of two excellent—though pricey—restaurants at the luxurious Princeville Resort. ⊠ *Princeville Resort, 5520 Ka Haku Rd., Princeville* ☎ *808/826–2761* ⌲ *Reservations essential* ▭ *AE, D, DC, MC, V* ☽ *No lunch. $24–$38.*

Steak & Seafood

$$–$$$$ ✕ **Bali Hai.** Sweeping views of Hanalei Bay and Nā Pali Coast are the highlight at this open-air restaurant—though it can be a bit too exposed to winter winds and rain (bring a jacket). When it comes to surf and turf, this restaurant's selection is hard to beat: Black Angus tenderloin, pork loin, New York strip, shrimp, scallops, lobster, and even fish served five ways—we prefer the Pele Goddess of Fire selection—fresh catch blackened and glazed with a peppered pineapple-mango chutney. If you can't decide, try the Chef's Trio with filet mignon, lobster tail, and jumbo prawns. Breakfast includes poi pancakes, fried taro, and eggs; lunch is a mix of salads and sandwiches. The menu descriptions sound good, but the food lacks refinement, making it hard to justify prices that are among the highest on the island. If you arrive before sunset, however, the view makes it worth it. (Or come for a drink and *pūpū*—we suggest the sashimi.) ⊠ *Hanalei Bay Resort, 5380 Honoiki Rd., Princeville* ☎ *808/826–6522* ▭ *AE, D, DC, MC, V. $22–46.*

The East Side: Kapaʻa & Wailua

American–Casual

¢–$ ✕ **The Eggbert's.** If you're big on breakfasts, try Eggbert's, in the Coconut Marketplace, which serves breakfast items until 3 PM daily. This family-friendly restaurant, with a sunny soft-yellow interior, lots of windows, and lānai seating, is a great spot for omelets, banana pancakes, and eggs Benedict in five styles. Lunch selections include club sandwiches,

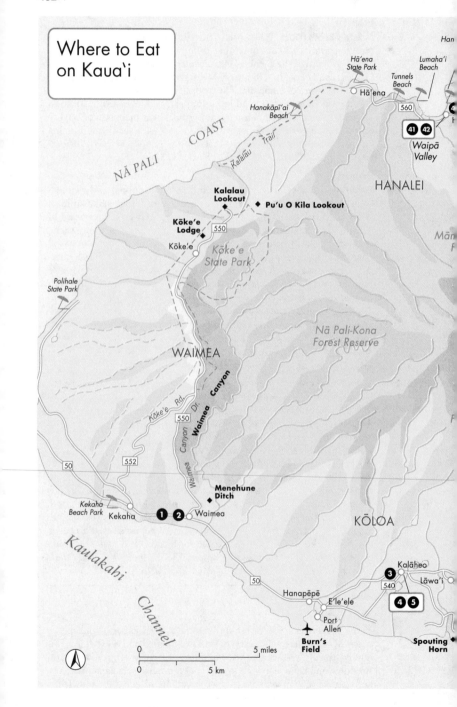

Where to Eat on Kaua'i

Han

Hā'ena State Park

Lumaha'i Beach

Tunnels Beach

Hā'ena

560

41 42

4

Waipā Valley

Hanakāpī'ai Beach

NĀ PALI COAST

Kalalau Trail

HANALEI

Mān P

Kalalau Lookout

♦ Pu'u O Kila Lookout

Kōke'e Lodge ♦

550

Kōke'e ○

Kōke'e State Park

Polihale State Park

Nā Pali-Kona Forest Reserve

WAIMEA

Waimea Canyon

Kōke'e Rd.

Canyon Dr.

550

Waimea Canyon

50

552

Kekaha Beach Park

Kekaha ○

1 2 ○ Waimea

Menehune Ditch ♦

KŌLOA

Kaulakahi

50

Kalāheo ○

3

540

Lāwa'i ○

4 5

Hanapēpē ○

E'le'ele

Channel

Port Allen

Burn's Field ✈

Spouting Horn ♦

N

0 —————— 5 miles

0 —————— 5 km

stir-fry, and fresh fish. Take-out orders are also available. They are not open for dinner. ⊠ *Coconut Marketplace, 4-484 Kūhiō Hwy., Kapa'a* ☎ *808/822–3787* ☰ *MC, V* ☺ *No dinner. $6–$14.*

Cafés

¢–$ ✕ **Mermaids Café.** Pretty much a sidewalk café, this restaurant will entice you with its pan-searing aromas wafting out the chef's tiny kitchen. All seating is outdoors—right on the main drag in Kapa'a—and quite limited, so we suggest a take-out order and a picnic table at the beach around the corner. Although there are chicken options, the specialty here is fish and tofu wraps. Try the 'ahi nori wrap—a 12-inch green tortilla wrapped around huge chunks of seared 'ahi, rice, cucumber, nori, wasabi cream sauce, pickled ginger, and soy sauce. It's an island favorite. In addition to wraps, there are organic salads, a black bean burrito, and a focaccia veggie sandwich. All items are made fresh with local fruit and vegetables and are organic whenever possible. Be sure to try the hibiscus iced tea or lemonade—the perfect refreshing drink. ⊠ *1384 Kūhiō Hwy., Kapa'a* ☎ *808/821–2026* ☰ *MC, V. $9–$11.*

Contemporary

$–$$ ✕ **Caffé Coco.** A restored plantation cottage set back off the highway and surrounded by tropical foliage is the setting for this island café. You'll know it by its bright lime-green storefront. An attached black-light art gallery and a vintage apparel shop called Bambulei make this a fun stop for any meal. Outdoor seating in the vine-covered garden is pleasant during nice weather, although on calm nights, it can get buggy. Acoustic music is offered regularly, attracting a laid-back local crowd. Pot stickers filled with tofu and chutney, 'ahi wraps, Greek and organic salads, fresh fish and soups, and a daily list of specials are complemented by a full espresso bar and wonderful desserts. Allow plenty of time, because the tiny kitchen can't turn out meals quickly. ⊠ *4-369 Kūhiō Hwy., Wailua* ☎ *808/822–7990* ☰ *MC, V* ☺ *Closed Mon. $12–$20.*

Eclectic

¢–$ ✕ **Wailua Family Restaurant.** Catering to families, seniors, and folks on a budget, this restaurant offers basic food in a basic setting. Hearty eaters will appreciate the self-serve, all-you-can-eat, hot-and-cold salad bar; tostada, taco, and pasta bar; sushi bar; and dessert bar. Steaks, chops, and seafood fill out the menu. Breakfast buffets on weekend mornings include eggs Benedict, a mahimahi and eggs combo, fresh tropical fruit, and cornbread muffins. It gets crowded after church on Sunday mornings. This is a good way to sample some local foods. ⊠ *4-361 Kūhiō Hwy., Kapa'a* ☎ *808/822–3325* ☰ *AE, D, MC, V. $5–$16.*

¢ ✕ **Ono Family Restaurant.** It's not always easy to grab a table at Ono, especially on weekend mornings. Dependable food and efficient service account for its popularity with locals and tourists alike. The decor is country diner, with wooden booths and tables, local antiques, and old-fashioned fixtures. The menu has a touch of Hawaiian style, with local favorites like kim chee, banana macadamia-nut pancakes, breakfast burritos, Portuguese sausage, and fried rice offered alongside such all-American choices as eggs Canterbury (poached eggs, ham, turkey, jack cheese, tomato, hollandaise sauce, and mushrooms on an English muffin). Lunch is less interesting, with the usual burgers, sandwiches, salads, and soups. You have a choice of indoor or outdoor seating in this downtown Kapaʻa eatery. ⊠ *4-1292 Kūhiō Hwy., Kapaʻa* ☎ *808/822–1710* ▤ *AE, D, DC, MC, V* ☺ *No dinner. $5–$9.*

Italian

¢–$$ ✕ **Kauaʻi Pasta.** If you want affordable, no-frills atmosphere with five-star food, this is the place. The husband in this husband-and-wife team left his executive chef position at Roy's to open a catering business and leased a kitchen that happened to have a small dining area. Rather than let it go to waste, they open for dinner every evening except Monday. We recommend the specials—written on the white-erase board at the entrace–which are always scrumptuous. The locals have this place figured out; they show up in droves. The food's fabulous and the price is right. Bring your own bottle of wine, the restaurant does not have a liquor license; they will provide a corkscrew and wine glasses for a $5 corkage fee. ⊠ *4-939B Kūhiō Hwy., Kapaʻa* ☎ *808/822–7447* ▤ *MC, V* ☺ *Closed Mon. $8–$20.*

Japanese

$–$$$$ ✕ **Restaurant Kintaro.** If you want to eat someplace that's a favorite with locals, visit Kintaro's. But be prepared to wait, because the dining room and sushi bar are always busy. Try the Bali Hai, a roll of eel and smoked salmon, baked and topped with wasabi mayonnaise. For an "all-in-one-dish" meal, consider the *Nabemono,* a single pot filled with a healthy variety of seafood and vegetables. We like the teppanyaki dinners, with meat, seafood, and vegetables flash-cooked on tabletop grills in an entertaining display. Tatami-mat seating is available behind shoji screens that provide privacy for groups. The restaurant was expanded in 2004, making the dining room feel less cramped and hectic than it did in the past. ⊠ *4-370 Kūhiō Hwy., Wailua* ☎ *808/822–3341* ▤ *AE, D, DC, MC, V* ☺ *Closed Sun. No lunch. $14–$42.*

Steak & Seafood

$–$$$$ ✕ **Bull Shed.** The A-frame exterior of this popular restaurant imparts a distinctly rustic feel. Inside, light-color walls and a full wall of glass highlight an ocean view that is one of the best on Kauaʻi. Ask for a window seat, where you can watch surf crashing on the rocks while you study the menu. The food is simple and basic—think white bread and iceberg lettuce—but they know how to do surf and turf. You can try both in one of several combo dinner platters, or order fresh island fish and thick steaks individually. The restaurant is best known for its prime rib and Australian rack of lamb. Longtime visitors love this place, which hasn't changed much in 20 years. Arrive by 5:30 for early-bird specials and your best shot at a window seat. ⊠ *796 Kūhiō Hwy., Kapaʻa* ☎ *808/822–3791 or 808/822–1655* ▤ *AE, D, DC, MC, V* ☺ *No lunch. $12–$38.*

$–$$$ ✕ **Wailua Marina Restaurant.** Offering the island's only river view, this marina restaurant—an island fixture for almost 40 years—is a good spot to stop after a boat ride up the Wailua River to the Fern Grotto. With more than 40 selections, the menu is a mix of comfort food and more sophisticated dishes; portions are gigantic. The chef is fond of stuffing: you'll find stuffed baked pork chops, stuffed chicken baked in plum sauce, and 'ahi stuffed with crab. The steamed mullet is a classic island dish. ⊠ *Wailua River State Park, Wailua Rd., Wailua* ☎ *808/822–4311* ⊟ *AE, D, DC, MC, V* ⊙ *Closed Mon. $10–$28.*

Thai

¢–$$ ✕ **Mema Thai Chinese Cuisine.** Refined and intimate, Mema Thai serves its dishes on crisp white linens accented by tabletop orchid sprays. Menu items such as broccoli with oyster sauce and cashew chicken reveal Chinese origins, but the emphasis is on Thai dishes. A host of curries—red, green, yellow, and house—made with coconut milk and Kaffir lime leaves run from mild to mouth-searing. The traditional green-papaya salad adds a cool touch for the palate. ⊠ *Wailua Shopping Plaza, 369 Kūhiō Hwy., Kapa'a* ☎ *808/823–0899* ⊟ *AE, D, DC, MC, V* ⊙ *No lunch weekends. $7–$19.*

Vegetarian

¢–$$ ✕ **Blossoming Lotus.** There are other vegetarian restaurants on the island, but there are no other *vegan* restaurants. Blossoming Lotus has been known to convert die-hard meat lovers. The restaurant bills its fare as "Vegan World Fusion Cuisine" and its menu lives up to the claim: curry, tacos, mung dahl, baba ghanoush, and spring rolls—all made fresh, with loving attention. Try the enchilada casserole made from marinated and baked tempeh, beans, rice, chili sauce, and cashew cheeze layered between sprouted wheat tortillas and topped with carob mole, salsa, and nondairy sour cream. ⊠ *4504 Kukui Street, Kapa'a* ☎ *808/822–7678* ⊟ *AE, D, DC, MC, V. $9–$18.*

¢ ✕ **Papaya's.** Kaua'i's largest natural foods market recently remodeled its café, converting it to a buffet. The good food and low prices make it a popular place. Food items change daily, however, there's usually a breakfast burrito and oftentimes spinach lasagna, stuffed peppers, and fish tacos for lunch and dinner. The soup and salad bar is a fixture with fresh organic lettuce and vegetables—most grown nearby on the island. You can order takeout, or eat at a covered table in the courtyard. ⊠ *Kaua'i Village Shopping Center, 4-831 Kūhiō Hwy., Kapa'a* ☎ *808/823–0190* ⊟ *AE, D, MC, V* ⊙ *Closed Sun. $6.50 per pound.*

The East Side: Līhu'e

American–Casual

$–$$$ ✕ **JJ's Broiler.** This spacious, low-key restaurant is almost like two eateries in one. Hearty American fare, including burgers and 2-pound buckets of steamer clams bathed in white wine, garlic, and herbs, is served in the bar and dining room downstairs. On sunny afternoons, ask for a table on the lānai overlooking Kalapakī Bay and try one of the generous salads. Upstairs you can feast on fancier Pacific Rim dishes, including sugarcane shrimp and Peking chicken tacos in a garlic oyster sauce. The house specialty is Slavonic steak, a broiled sliced tenderloin dipped in a buttery wine sauce. ■ TIP➔ **Although the restaurant is open until 11 PM, making it one of the few places on Kaua'i where you can eat late,** we prefer it for lunch for two reasons: the view, and dinner options are hit-or-miss. ⊠ *Anchor Cove, 3146 Rice St., Nāwiliwili* ☎ *808/246–4422* ▭ *D, MC, V. $10–$30.*

$–$$ ✗ **Līhu'e Barbecue Inn.** Few Kaua'i restaurants are more beloved than this family-owned eatery, a mainstay of island dining since 1940. The menu runs from traditional American fare to Asian. Try the baby back ribs, macadamia nut chicken, or Cajun seafood medley with king crab. Or choose a full Japanese dinner from the other side of the menu. If you can't make up your mind, the Inn's tri-sampler is a good compromise. Choose the fruit cup—fresh, not canned—instead of the soup or salad, and save room for a hefty slice of homemade cream pie, available in all your favorite flavors. ⊠ *2982 Kress St., Līhu'e* ☎ *808/245–2921* ▭ *MC, V. $10–$25.*

Eclectic

$$–$$$$ ✗ **Gaylord's.** Located in what was at one time Kaua'i's most expensive plantation estate, Gaylord's pays tribute to the elegant dining rooms of 1930s high society. Tables with candlelight sit on a cobblestone patio surrounding a fountain and overlooking a wide lawn. The innovative menu features classic American cooking with an island twist. Try won-ton-wrapped prawns with a wasabi plum sauce, New Zealand venison, blackened prime rib, or fresh-fish specials. Lunches are a mix of salads, sandwiches, and pasta, enjoyed in a leisurely fashion. The lavish Sunday brunch may include such specialties as sweet-potato hash and Cajun 'ahi in addition to the standard omelets and pancakes. Before or after dining you can wander around the estate grounds or take a horse-drawn carriage ride. ⊠ *Kilohana Plantation, 3-2087 Kaumuali'i Rd., Līhu'e* ☎ *808/245–9593* ▭ *AE, D, DC, MC, V. $24–$50.*

Hawaiian

¢ ✗ **Dani's Restaurant.** Kaua'i residents frequent this big, sparsely furnished eatery near the Līhu'e Fire Station for hearty, local-style food at breakfast and lunch. Dani's is a good place to try lū'au food without commercial lū'au prices. You can order Hawaiian-style *laulau* (pork and taro leaves wrapped in ti leaves and steamed) or *kālua* pig, slow-roasted in an underground oven. Other island-style dishes include Japanese-prepared *tonkatsu* (pork cutlet) and teriyaki beef, and there's always the all-American New York steak. Omelets are whipped up with fish cake, *kālua* pig, or seafood; everything is served with rice. ⊠ *4201 Rice St., Līhu'e* ☎ *808/245–4991* ▭ *MC, V* ⊙ *Closed Sun. No dinner. $6–$9.*

★ ¢ ✗ **Hamura Saimin.** Folks just love this funky old plantation-style diner. Locals and tourists stream in and out all day long, and neighbor islanders stop in on their way to the airport to pick up take-out orders for friends and family back home. *Saimen* is the big draw, and each day the Hiraoka family dishes up about 1,000 bowls of steaming broth and homemade noodles, topped with a variety of garnishes. We love the barbecued chicken and meat sticks, which adopt a smoky flavor during grilling. The landmark eatery is also famous for its *liliko'i* (passion fruit) chiffon pie. ■ TIP➡ **As one of the few island eateries open until 11 PM on week nights and midnight on Friday and Saturday, it's favored by night owls.** ⊠ *2956 Kress St., Līhu'e* ☎ *808/245–3271* ▭ *No credit cards. $4–$7.*

Italian

$–$$$ ✗ **Café Portofino.** The menu at this authentic northern Italian restaurant is as inspired as the view of Kalapakī Bay and Hā'upu range. Owner Giuseppe Avocadi's flawless dishes have garnered a host of culinary awards and raves from dining critics. The fresh 'ahi carpaccio is a signature dish, while pasta, scampi, and veal are enhanced by sauces that soar like Avocadi's imagination. Excellent service and a soothing, dignified ambience complete the delightful dining experience. ✉ *Kaua'i Marriott & Beach Club, 3610 Rice St., Līhu'e* ☎ *808/245–2121* 🖃 *AE, D, DC, MC, V* ⊘ *No lunch. $17–$30.*

Japanese

¢–$ ✗ **Hanamā'ulu Restaurant, Tea House, Sushi Bar, and Robatayaki.** Business is brisk at this landmark Kaua'i eatery. The food is a mix of Japanese, Chinese, and local-style cooking, served up in hearty portions. The ginger chicken and fried shrimp are wildly popular, as are the fresh sashimi and sushi. Other choices include tempura, chicken *katsu*, beef broccoli, and *robatayaki* (grilled seafood and meat). The main dining room is rather unattractive, but the private rooms in back look out on the Japanese garden and fish ponds and feature traditional seating on tatami mats at low tables. These tearooms can be reserved, and are favored for family events and celebrations. ✉ *1-4291 Kūhiō Hwy., Rte. 56, Hanamā'ulu* ☎ *808/245–2511* 🖃 *MC, V* ⊘ *Closed Mon. $8–$16.*

Seafood

$–$$$$ ✗ **Duke's Canoe Club.** Surf legend Duke Kahanamoku is immortalized at this casual bi-level restaurant set on Kalapakī Bay. Guests can admire surfboards, photos, and other memorabilia marking his long tenure as a waterman. It's an interesting collection, and an indoor garden and waterfall add to the pleasing ambience. Downstairs you can find simple fare ranging from fish tacos and stir-fried cashew chicken to hamburgers, served 11 AM to 11 PM. At dinner, upstairs, when prices increase, fresh fish prepared in a variety of styles is the best choice. Duke's claims to have the biggest salad bar on the island, though given the lack of competition that isn't saying much. A happy-hour drink and appetizer is a less expensive way to enjoy the moonrises and ocean views here—though it can get pretty crowded. The Barefoot Bar is a hot spot for after-dinner drinks, too. ✉ *Kaua'i Marriott & Beach Club, Līhu'e* ☎ *808/246–9599* 🖃 *AE, D, DC, MC, V. $13–$45.*

BUDGET-FRIENDLY EATS: EAST SIDE

At these small, local-style eateries, two people can generally eat dinner for under $20.

- **Garden Island BBQ and Chinese Restaurant.** ✉ 4252-A Rice St., Līhu'e ☎ 808/245-8868.
- **Hamura's Saimin.** ✉ 2956 Kress St., Līhu'e ☎ 808/245-3271.
- **Korean BBQ.** ✉ 4-356 Kūhiō Hwy., Wailua ☎ 808/823-6744.
- **Papaya's.** ✉ 4-831 Kūhiō Hwy., Kapa'a ☎ 808/823-0190.
- **Waipouli Restaurant.** ✉ Waipouli Town Centre, Kūhiō Hwy., Wailua ☎ 808/822-9311.

The South Shore & West Side

American–Casual

¢–$$ ✕ **Camp House Grill.** A plantation-style camp house with squeaky wooden floors has become a simple, down-home restaurant. The food is equally basic: hamburgers, chicken, pork ribs, and fresh fish aimed for families who aren't choosy and don't mind cranky service. Large breakfasts are available, and pies are baked fresh daily; you can eat a slice on the premises or take home an entire pie for a late-night craving. As you enter Kalāheo heading west toward Waimea Canyon, look for the blue building on the right. The food and setting at the Kalāheo branch are superior to the Kapaʻa eatery. ☒ *Kaumualiʻi Hwy., Rte. 50, Kalāheo* ☎ *808/ 332–9755* ☒ *Kauaʻi Village, Kūhiō Hwy., Kapaʻa* ☎ *808/822–2442* ▭ *AE, D, MC, V. $6–$19.*

Contemporary

$$–$$$
Fodor's Choice
★

✕ **The Beach House.** This restaurant is one of our favorites, with a dreamy ocean view and impressive cuisine. Few Kauaʻi experiences are more delightful than sitting at one of the outside tables and savoring a delectable meal while the sun sinks into the glassy blue Pacific. It's the epitome of tropical dining, and no other restaurant on Kauaʻi can offer anything quite like it. The menu changes often, but the food is consistently creative and delicious. A few trademark dishes appear regularly, such as fire-roasted ʻahi and lemongrass and Kaffir lime sea scallops. Seared macadamia nut–crusted mahimahi, a dish ubiquitous on island menus, gets a refreshing new twist when served with a citrus *aki* miso sauce. Save room for the signature molten chocolate desire, a decadent finale at this pleasing and deservedly popular restaurant. ☒ *5022 Lāwaʻi Rd., Kōloa* ☎ *808/742–1424* ⌲ *Reservations essential* ▭ *AE, DC, MC, V* ☽ *No lunch. $19–$32.*

¢–$$$ ✕ **Waimea Brewing Company.** Housed within the Waimea Plantation Cottages, this brewpub-restaurant is spacious, with hardwood floors and open-air decks. Dine indoors amid rattan furnishings or at a bar decorated with petroglyphs and colored with Kauaʻi red dirt. Kalua pork enchiladas, hamburgers, *kal-bi* beef short ribs, and fresh fish are highlights. Entrées come in two sizes (small and big!) and are reasonably priced. It's a good place for a snack or appetizer while traveling to or from Waimea Canyon, but you can find better choices for dinner if you push on to Kalāheo or Poʻipū. ☒ *9400 Kaumualiʻi Hwy., Waimea* ☎ *808/338–9733* ▭ *AE, D, MC, V. $8–$30.*

¢–$$ ✕ **Tomkats Grille.** Tropical ponds, a waterfall, a large bar area, and a porch overlooking an inner courtyard give this grill a casual island ambience. Try the blackened "katch of the day" with tropical salsa, or the homemade chili and burger. Wash it down with a glass of wine or one of 35 ales, stouts, ports, and lagers. Plenty of Tomkats' Nibblers—such as buffalo wings and sautéed shrimp—enliven happy hour from 3 to 6 PM. ☒ *Old Kōloa Town, 5402 Kōloa Rd., Kōloa* ☎ *808/742–8887* ▭ *MC, V. $7–$26.*

Eclectic

$–$$$$ ✕ **Roy's Poʻipū Bar & Grill.** Hawaiʻi's culinary superstar Roy Yamaguchi is fond of sharing his signature "Hawaiian Fusion" cuisine by opening clones of the successful Honolulu restaurant where he got his start. One of these copycat eateries can be found on Kaua'i's South Side, in a shopping-center locale that feels too small and ordinary for the exotic food. The menu changes daily, with the hardworking kitchen staff dreaming up 15 to 20 (or more) new specials each night—an impressive feat. The food reflects the imaginative pairings and quality ingredients that characterized the original Roy's, and the presentation is spectacular, but the atmosphere is a little different. As with most restaurant branches, it just doesn't have the same kind of heart and soul as the original. The visitors who fill this celebrity restaurant each night don't seem to mind, but those looking for authenticity may prefer the Beach House, just a little way down the road. ⊠ *Po'ipū Shopping Village, 2360 Kiahuna Plantation Dr., Po'ipū Beach* ☎ *808/742–5000* ▭ *AE, D, DC, MC, V* ⊗ *No lunch. $15–$42.*

Italian

$$–$$$$ ✕ **Dondero's.** The inlaid marble floors, ornate tile work, and Italianate
Fodor$Choice murals that comprise the elegant decor at this restaurant compete with
★ a stunning ocean view. And in addition to the beautiful setting, Dondero's offers outstanding food, a remarkable wine list, and impeccable service, making this Kaua'i's best restaurant. Chef Vincent Pecoraro combines old-world techniques with new energy to create menu selections as enticing as the surroundings. Pistachio-crusted rack of lamb with a root vegetable fritter and pancetta mashed sweet potatoes, and lobster piccata on a bed of fettuccine with sun-dried tomatoes and a truffle cream sauce thrill the palate and delight the eye. Order a light, traditional tiramisu or chocolate crème brûlée with fresh raspberries so you can linger over coffee. The waitstaff deserves special praise for its thoughtful, discrete service. ⊠ *Hyatt Regency Kaua'i Resort and Spa, 1571 Po'ipū Rd., Po'ipū Beach* ☎ *808/742–1234* ▭ *AE, D, DC, MC, V* ⊗ *No lunch. $26–$42.*

$–$$$ ✕ **Casa di Amici.** Tucked away in a quiet neighborhood above Po'ipū Beach, this "House of Friends" has live classical piano music on weekends and an outside deck open to sweeping ocean views. Entrées from the internationally eclectic menu include a saffron-vanilla paella risotto made with black tiger prawns, fresh fish, chicken breast, and homemade Italian sausage. For dessert, take the plunge with a baked Hawai'i: a chocolate-macadamia nut brownie topped with coconut and passionfruit sorbet and flambéed Italian meringue. The food and setting are pleasant, but service can be maddeningly slow, especially when you're really hungry. ⊠ *2301 Nalo Rd., Po'ipū* ☎ *808/742–1555* ▭ *AE, D, DC, MC, V* ⊗ *No lunch. $16–$27.*

★ **$$** ✕ **Plantation Gardens.** A historic plantation manager's home has been converted to a restaurant that serves Italian food in a Polynesian atmosphere—an interesting mix with good results. You'll walk through a tropical setting of torch-lighted orchid gardens and lotus-studded koi ponds to a cozy, European-feeling dining room with cherrywood floors and veranda dining. The menu is based on fresh, local foods: fish right off the boat, herbs and produce picked from the plantation's gardens, fruit delivered by neighborhood farmers. The result is Italian cuisine with an island flair—seafood *laulau* (seafood wrapped in ti leaves and steamed) served with mango chutney—served alongside traditional classics like rosemary-skewered pork tenderloin and pan-roasted scallops. New chefs and a new menu make this a good choice, even for a second visit. ⊠ *Kiahuna Plantation, 2253 Po'ipū Rd., Kōloa* ☎ *808/742–2216* ▤ *AE, DC, MC, V* ⊘ *No lunch. $19–$26.*

$–$$ ✕ **Pomodoro Ristorante Italiano.** Begin with prosciutto and melon, then proceed directly to the multilayer meat lasagna, a favorite of the chefs—two Italian-born brothers. Other highlights include eggplant or veal parmigiana, chicken saltimbocca, and scampi in a garlic, caper, and white wine sauce. Two walls of windows brighten this intimate second-story restaurant in the heart of Kalāheo, where you'll find good food at reasonable prices. ⊠ *Upstairs at Rainbow Plaza, Kaumuali'i Hwy., Rte. 50, Kalāheo* ☎ *808/332–5945* ▤ *MC, V* ⊘ *Closed Sun. No lunch. $14–$24.*

Steak & Seafood

★ $$$–$$$$ ✕ **Tidepools.** The Hyatt Regency Kaua'i is notable for its excellent restaurants, which differ widely in their settings and cuisine. This one is definitely the most tropical and campy, sure to appeal to folks seeking a bit of island-style romance and adventure. You'll dine in your own private grass-thatch hut, which seems to float on a koi-filled pond beneath starry skies while torches flicker in the lushly landscaped grounds nearby. The food is equally distinctive, with an island flavor that comes from the chef's advocacy of Hawai'i regional cuisine and extensive use of Kaua'i-grown products. You won't go wrong ordering the fresh-fish specials or one of the signature dishes, such as wok-seared soy, sake and ginger marinated 'ahi, grilled mahimahi or pan-seared beef tenderloin. Start with Tidepools' *pūpū* platter for two—with a lobster cake, peppered beef filet and 'ahi sashimi—to wake up your taste buds, and if you're still hungry at the end of the meal, the ginger crème brûlée is sure to satisfy. ⊠ *Hyatt Regency Kaua'i Resort and Spa, 1571 Po'ipū Rd., Po'ipū Beach* ☎ *808/742–1234 Ext. 4260* ▤ *AE, D, DC, MC, V* ⊘ *No lunch. $29–$36.*

$$–$$$$ ✕ **Brennecke's Beach Broiler.** Brennecke's is decidedly casual and fun, with a busy bar, windows overlooking the beach, and a cheery blue-and-white interior. It specializes in big portions in a wide range of offerings. If you can't find something you like here, that means you just ate. Although rumor has it the menu might be refreshed by the time you read this, you're pretty much assured New York steaks, lobster, crab legs, shrimp, and the fresh catch of the day. Can't decide? They'll let you create your own combination meals. We especially like this place for happy hour (3 PM to 5 PM)–the drink and *pūpū* menus are tomes, as well. There's a take-out deli downstairs. ⊠ *2100 Ho'one Rd., Po'ipū* ☎ *808/742–7588* ▤ *AE, D, DC, MC, V. $20–$40.*

$–$$$$ ✕ **Keoki's Paradise.** Built to resemble a dockside boathouse, this is an active, boisterous place that fills up quickly on weekend nights because of live music. Seafood appetizers span the tide from sashimi to Thai shrimp sticks, crab cakes, and scallops crusted in panko (Japanese-style breadcrumbs). The day's fresh catch is available in half a dozen styles and sauces. And there's a sampling of beef, chicken, and pork-rib entrées for the committed carnivore. A lighter menu is available at the bar for lunch and dinner. ⊠ *Po'ipū Shopping Village, 2360 Kiahuna Plantation Dr., Po'ipū Beach* ☎ *808/742–7534* ▤ *AE, D, DC, MC, V. $16–$46.*

$–$$$$ ✕ **Wrangler's Steakhouse.** Denim-cover seating, decorative saddles, and a stagecoach in a loft helped to transform the historic Ako General Store in Waimea into a West Side steak house. You can eat under the stars on the deck out back or inside the old-fashioned, wood-panel dining room. The 16-ounce New York steak comes sizzling and the rib eye is served with capers. Those with smaller appetites might consider the vegetable tempura or the 'ahi served on penne pasta. Local folks love the special lunch: soup, rice, beef teriyaki, and shrimp tempura served in a three-tier *kaukau* tin, or lunch pail, just like the ones sugar-plantation workers once carried. A gift shop has local crafts (and sometimes a craftsperson doing demonstrations). ✉ 9852 *Kaumuali'i Hwy., Waimea* ☎ 808/338–1218 ☰ AE, MC, V ☉ *Closed Sun. $17–$38.*

> **BUDGET-FRIENDLY EATS: SOUTH SHORE & WEST SIDE**
>
> ▪ **Grind's Cafe and Espresso.** ✉ *Rte. 50, 'Ele'ele* ☎ 808/335–6027.
> ▪ **Taqueria Nortenos.** ✉ *2827-A Po'ipū Rd., Kōloa* ☎ 808/742–7222.
> ▪ **Wong's Chinese Restaurant.** ✉ *Kaumuali'i Hwy., Hanapēpē* ☎ 808/335–5066.

$$–$$$ ✕ **Shells Steak and Seafood.** Chandeliers made from shells light the dining room and give this restaurant its name. The menu is upscale surf and turf, with prime cuts of steak and fresh fish enhanced by tropical spices and sauces. Shells is one of three signature restaurants in the Sheraton's Oceanfront Galleria. Each of these restaurants has been designed to embrace the view of the Pacific Ocean from sunrise to starlight. ✉ *Sheraton Kaua'i Resort, 2440 Ho'onani Rd., Po'ipū Beach, Kōloa* ☎ 808/742–1661 ☰ AE, D, DC, MC, V ☉ *No lunch. $26–$33.*

$–$$ ✕ **Kalāheo Steak House.** Prime rib, tender top sirloin, Cornish game hen in citrus marinade, Kalāheo shrimp, Alaskan king crab legs, and Portuguese bean soup are competently prepared and served up in hearty portions at this cozy, country-ranch-house style restaurant. Weathered wood furnishings and artifacts pay tribute to Hawai'i's *paniolo* (cowboys), who can still be found in these parts. Fresh-baked rum cake comes with Lappert's ice cream (made at a factory up the road). Wines range from $8 to $25 a bottle. ✉ *4444 Pāpālina Rd., Kalāheo* ☎ 808/332–9780 ☰ AE, D, MC, V ⚄ *Reservations not accepted* ☉ *No lunch. $17–$26.*

WHERE TO STAY

The Garden Isle has lodgings for every taste, from swanky resorts to rustic cabins, and from family-friendly condos to romantic B&Bs. When choosing a place to stay, location is an important consideration—Kaua'i may look small, but it takes more time than you might think to get around. If at all possible, stay close to your desired activities. ▪ TIP➔ **Prices are highest near the ocean and in resort communities like Princeville and Po'ipū.**

As a rule, resorts offer a full roster of amenities and large, well-appointed rooms. They are all oceanfront properties that lean toward the luxurious. If you want to golf, play tennis, or hang at a spa, stay at a resort.

The island's hotels tend to be smaller and older, with fewer on-site amenities.

Individual condominium units are equipped with all the comforts of home, but each property offers different services, so inquire if you want tennis courts, golf, and on-site restaurants. They're ideal for families, couples traveling together, and longer stays.

Vacation rentals run the gamut from fabulous luxury estates to scruffy little dives. It's buyer-beware in this unregulated sector of the visitor industry, so choose carefully. Many homes are in rural areas far from beaches, or in crowded neighborhoods that may be a bit too local-style for some tastes. ■ TIP→ **Condos and vacation rentals typically require a minimum stay of three nights to a week, along with a cleaning fee.**

The island's bed-and-breakfasts allow you to meet local residents and more directly experience the aloha spirit. They tend to be among the more expensive types of lodging, though, and don't assume you get a lavish breakfast unless it's a featured attraction. You'll usually get a very comfortable room in a private house along with a morning meal; some properties have stand-alone units on-site.

If you need help choosing a property, **Bed and Breakfast Kaua'i** (☎ 800/822–1176 🖨 503/826–0087 ⊕ www.bnbkauai.com) may prove helpful. Liz Hay, a longtime island resident, maintains a network of more than three-dozen cottages, condos, and B&Bs that consider all lifestyles and budgets. Most large real estate companies also maintain a roster of vacation rentals.

WHAT IT COSTS				
$$$$	**$$$**	**$$**	**$**	**¢**
HOTELS over $340	$261–$340	$181–$260	$100–$180	under $100

Hotel prices are for two people in a standard double room in high season. Condo price categories reflect studio and one-bedroom rates.

The North Shore

The North Shore is mountainous and wet, which accounts for its rugged, lush landscape. Posh resorts and condominiums await you at Princeville, a community with dreamy views, excellent golf courses, and lovely sunsets. If you want to visit other parts of the island, be prepared for a long drive—that's very dark at night.

Hotels & Resorts

★ **$$$$** 🏨 **Princeville Resort.** Built into the cliffs above Hanalei Bay, this sprawling resort offers expansive views of the mountains and sea. You'll surely recognize Makana, a landmark peak that Hollywood immortalized as mysterious "Bali Hai" island in the film South Pacific. Guest rooms are spacious and designed in primary colors to match those of Kaua'i's abundant yellow hibiscus, red 'ōhi'a flower, and dark green mokihana berry. Little details make a difference, like lighted closets, dimmer switches on all lamps, original artwork, and door chimes. Bathrooms feature height-adjustable showerheads and a privacy window—flip a switch and it goes from clear to opaque so you can see the sights without becoming an attraction yourself. Two restaurants serve excellent food in dining rooms that capitalize on the views, and the poolside lū'au is lavish. The Living Room is a swanky bar with nightly entertainment and big windows that showcase gorgeous sunsets. There's shuttle service to the resort's two top-ranked golf courses, spa, and tennis center, none of which are on the hotel grounds. ⊠ *5520 Ka Haku Rd., Princeville 96722* 📞 *808/826–9644 or 888/488–3535* 📠 *808/826–1166* ⊕ *www.starwood.com/hawaii* 🛏 *201 rooms, 51 suites* ♨ *4 restaurants, room service, A/C, minibars, 2 18-hole golf courses, 8 tennis courts, pool, gym, health club, massage, spa, beach, 2 bars, children's programs (ages 5–12), dry cleaning, laundry service, business services, travel services* ▤ *AE, D, DC, MC, V.* *$500–$735.*

Condos

$$–$$$$ 🏨 **Hanalei Bay Resort.** This condominium resort has a lovely location overlooking Hanalei Bay and Nā Pali Coast. Three-story buildings angle down the cliffs, making for some steep walking paths. Units are extremely spacious, with high, sloping ceilings and large private lānai. Rattan furniture and island art add a casual feeling to rooms. Studios have small kitchenettes not meant for serious cooking, the larger units have full kitchens. The resort's upper-level pool is one of the nicest on the island, with authentic lava-rock waterfalls, an open-air hot tub, and a kid-friendly sand "beach." The restaurant is expensive, but the food and views are worth the price. The friendly tropical bar offers live music. The tennis courts are on-site, and guests have golf privileges at Princeville Resort. More than half the units on this property are now dedicated to vacation ownership rentals. ⊠ *5380 Honoiki Rd., Princeville 96722* 📞 *808/826–6522 or 800/827–4427* 📠 *808/826–6680* ⊕ *www.hanaleibayresort.com* 🛏 *134 units* ♨ *Restaurant, A/C, in-room safes, kitchenettes, refrigerators, cable TV, golf privileges, 8 tennis courts, 2 pools, hot tub, massage, beach, shop, babysitting, children's programs (ages 5–12), laundry facilities* ▤ *AE, D, DC, MC, V. Studios $240, 1-bedroom $360–$400.*

> ### CONDO COMFORTS
>
> Foodland, in the Princeville Shopping Center, has the best selection of groceries, sundries, and other items needed to supply the kitchen. It's open daily from 7 AM to 11 PM. Be sure to ask for a Maka'i discount card, as the prices may give you sticker shock.

B&Bs & Vacation Rentals

$$$$ 🏨 **Kīlauea Lakeside Estate.** The world revolves around you at this private island retreat, where the amenities and activities are custom-designed to create your dream vacation. The proprietors can arrange for personal chefs, windsurfing lessons, lakeside spa treatments, and on-site weddings. A private 20-acre freshwater lake teeming with bass and catfish awaits your fishing pole. You can also have your own par-3 golf hole and putting green and 3 acres of botanical gardens to stroll through. The modern three-bedroom house includes a romantic master suite and bath.

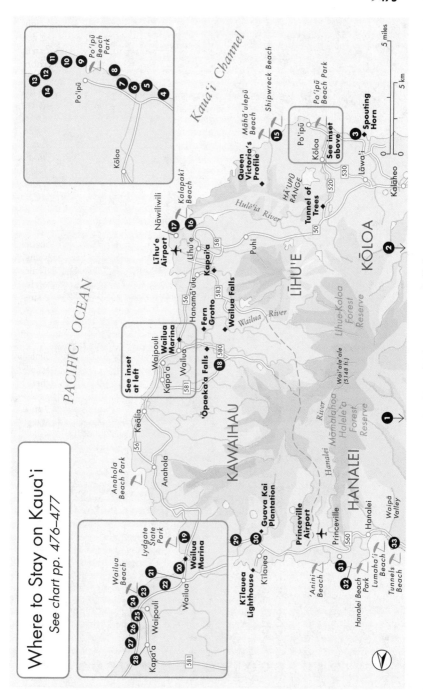

Where to Stay on Kaua'i
See chart pp. 476–477

WHERE TO STAY ON KAUA'I

HOTEL NAME	Worth Noting	Cost $	Pools	Beach	Golf Course	Tennis Courts	Gym	Spa	Children's Programs	Rooms	Restaurants	Other	Location
THE NORTH SHORE													
Hotels & Resorts													
★ ③ Princeville Resort	Lavish poolside lū'au	500–735	1	yes	yes	8	yes	yes	5–12	252	4		Princeville
Condos													
㉜ Hanalei Bay Resort	Great views	240–400	2	yes	priv.	8	yes	yes	5–12	134	1	kitchen	Princeville
B&Bs & Vacation Rentals													
㉝ Hanalei Colony Resort	Go-barefoot kind of place	185–300	1	yes						48		no A/C	Hā'ena
㉚ Kilauea Lakeside Estate	Private lake	595–850								1		no A/C	Kīlauea
★ ㉙ North Country Farms	Popular with families	130								2		no A/C	Kīlauea
THE EAST SIDE													
Hotels & Resorts													
⑲ Aloha Kaua'i Beach Resort	Beach cottages available	219–359	2	yes		2	yes			216	1		Kapa'a
㉖ Courtyard Kaua'i	Popular nightly lū'au	239–409	1	yes		3				311	1		Kapa'a
㉘ Hotel Coral Reef	Good location, low price	99–149		yes						26		no A/C	Kapa'a
㉒ Kaua'i Sands	Hawaiian-owned & operated	125–160	2	yes		1	yes			200		kitchen	Kapa'a
㉓ ResortQuest Islander	Plantation-style design	195–295	1	yes						198			Kapa'a
Condos													
㉕ Best West. Plantation Hale	Beach across the street	185–205	3							110		kitchens	Kapa'a
⑳ Kapa'a Sands	Ocean views	110–135	1	yes						20		no A/C	Kapa'a
㉔ Kaua'i Coast Resort	Uncrowded beach	265–305	2	yes		1	yes	yes		108	1	kitchen	Kapa'a
㉑ Outrigger at Lae Nani	Cultural programs	250–310	1	yes		1				84		no A/C	Kapa'a
B&Bs and Vacation Rentals													
★ ㉗ Aloha Cottages	Oceanfront	110–300		yes						2		no A/C	Kapa'a
⑱ Rosewood Bed & Breakfast	Located on a plantation	45–135								7		no A/C	Kapa'a

		Price											Location
LIHU'E													
Hotels & Resorts													
16 Garden Island Inn	Beach across the street	90–135	1							24		kitchen	Kalapaki Beach
17 Kaua'i Marriott Resort	26,000-sq-ft pool	354–469		yes	yes	7	yes	yes	5–12	599	2		Lihu'e
THE SOUTH SIDE													
Hotels & Resorts													
★ 15 Hyatt Regency Kaua'i	5 acres of swimming lagoons	485–705	1	yes	yes	4	yes	yes	5–12	602	6	shops	Kōloa
10 Sheraton Kaua'i Resort	Ocean wing right on water	355–655	2	yes	yes	3	yes		5–12	413	4		Kōloa
Condos													
13 Makahuena at Po'ipū	Close to center of Po'ipū	260	1			1				78		no A/C	Po'ipū
8 Outrigger Kiahuna Plantation	Popular with families	245–479	1	yes	yes	6				333	1	no A/C	Kōloa
7 Po'ipū Kapili	Deluxe PH suites available	255–285	1			2				60		no A/C	Kōloa
12 Po'ipū Shores	Excellent whale-watching	300	1							39		no A/C	Kōloa
9 Suite Paradise Po'ipū Kai	Short walk to beach	133–370	6			9				130	1	kitchen	Kōloa
5 Whalers Cove	Rocky beach	355–485	1	yes						30		no A/C	Kōloa
B&Bs & Vacation Rentals													
4 Garden Isle Cottages	Beautiful ocean view	169–190								4		no A/C	Kōloa
3 Gloria's Spouting Horn B&B	Romantic	325	1	yes						3		no A/C	Po'ipū
14 Hideaway Cove	Quiet	125–160											Po'ipū
6 Kaua'i Cove Cottages	Excellent snorkeling	105–145								3		no A/C	Po'ipū
11 Po'ipū Plantation Resort	Cottages available	120–190								12		kitchen	Kōloa
THE WEST SIDE													
Hotels & Resorts													
★ 2 Waimea Plantation Cottages	Good for large groups	175–350	1	yes				yes		48	1	no A/C	Waimea
Vacation Rentals													
1 Kōke'e Lodge	Rustic wilderness cabins	45								12	1	no A/C	Kōke'e

✉ *4613 Waiakalua Rd., Kīlauea 96754* ☎ *310/379–7842* 🖶 *310/379–0034* ⊕ *www.kauaihoneymoon.com* 🛏 *1 house* ⚒ *BBQs, fans, kitchen, cable TV, in-room VCRs, beach, fishing, laundry facilities; no A/C* ▭ *AE, D, MC, V. $595–$850.*

$$–$$$ 🏨 **Hanalei Colony Resort.** This 5-acre property is a laid-back, go-bare-foot kind of place sandwiched between towering mountains and the sea. The only true beachfront resort on Kaua'i's North Shore, its charm is in its simplicity. There are no phones, TVs, or stereos in the rooms. Each of the two-bedroom units can sleep a family of four. The units are well maintained, with Hawaiian-style furnishings, full kitchens, and lānai. Amenities, like cocktail receptions and cultural activities, vary from season to season. There's an art gallery with coffee bar on-site. ✉ *5-7130 Kūhiō Hwy., Hā'ena 96714* ☎ *808/826–6235 or 800/628–3004* 🖶 *808/826–9893* ⊕ *www.hcr.com* 🛏 *48 units* ⚒ *BBQs, fans, kitchens, pool, hot tub, beach, shop, laundry facilities; no A/C, no room phones, no room TVs* ▭ *AE, MC, V. $185–$300.*

★ $ 🏨 **North Country Farms.** These comfortable lodgings are tucked away on a 4-acre organic fruit, flower, and vegetable farm just east of Kīlauea. Although simple, they're clean and provide everything a couple or family might need, including kitchenettes. Owner Lee Roversi and her children are warm, friendly, and creative. You'll enjoy the thoughtful selection of videos, puzzles, and reading material. The setting is rural and quiet, with lush tropical landscaping around the two units. Guests are welcome to pick fresh produce. Several nice beaches are just a few minutes' drive away. ✉ *Kahili Makai, Box 723, Kīlauea 96754* ☎ *808/828–1513* 🖶 *808/828–0899* ⊕ *www.northcountryfarms.com* 🛏 *2 cottages* ⚒ *Kitchenettes, cable TV, in-room VCRs; no A/C. $130.*

The East Side: Kapa'a & Wailua

The East Side, or Coconut Coast, is a good centralized home base if you want to see and do it all. It has a number of smaller, older properties that are modestly priced, but still comfortable. This region also has a wider choice of inexpensive restaurants and shops than the resort areas. The beaches here are so-so for swimming but nice for sunbathing, walking, and watching the sun and moon rise.

Hotels & Resorts

$$–$$$$ 🏨 **Aloha Kaua'i Beach Resort.** Nestled between Wailua Bay and the Wailua River, this low-key, low-rise resort is an easy, convenient place to stay. Families will enjoy being within walking distance of Lydgate Beach Park. It's also close to shops and low-cost restaurants. Rooms are in two wings and have beach, mountain, or ocean views. The resort also offers one-bedroom beach cottages with kitchenettes. ✉ *3-5920 Kūhiō Hwy., Kapa'a 96746* ☎ *808/823–6000 or 888/823–5111* 🖶 *808/823–6666* ⊕ *www.abrkauai.com* 🛏 *216 rooms, 10 suites, 24 beach cottages* ⚒ *Restaurant, A/C, in-room data ports, in-room safes, tennis court, 2 pools, gym, hot tub, shuffleboard* ▭ *AE, D, DC, MC, V. $219–$359.*

$$–$$$$ 🏨 **Courtyard Kaua'i at Waipouli Beach.** Formerly known as the Kaua'i Coconut Beach Resort, this popular oceanfront hotel was bought and refurbished by Courtyard by Marriott in 2005 and at press time was under contract with Resort Quest. The bright, spacious rooms face the ocean or pool and have been outfitted with modern amenities, including free wireless high-speed Internet access. Each oceanfront room has a large lānai. The 11-acre site has always been desirable, nestled as it is among ancient coconut groves and close to a coastal bike and walking path, shops, restaurants, and the airport. The new owners wisely kept the best of the old resort, including its sunset torch-lighting ceremony. ⊠ *4-484 Kūhiō Hwy., Kapaʻa 96746* ☎ *808/822–3455 or 800/760–8555* 📠 *808/822–1830* ⊕ *www.marriott.com* ➯ *311 rooms* ⚐ *Restaurant, A/C, Wi-Fi, in-room safes, 3 tennis courts, pool, hot tub, beach, shuffleboard, no-smoking rooms* ▭ *AE, D, DC, MC, V. $239–$409.*

$$–$$$ 🏨 **ResortQuest Islander on the Beach.** A Hawaiʻi plantation-style design gives this 6-acre beachfront property a pleasant, low-key feeling. Rooms are spread over eight three-story buildings, with lānai that look out on lovely green lawns. Rooms have showers but not tubs. A free-form pool sits next to a golden-sand beach, and you can take the lounge chairs to the ocean's edge. ⊠ *4-484 Kūhiō Hwy., Kapaʻa 96746* ☎ *808/822–7417 or 877/977–6667* 📠 *808/822–1947* ➯ *198 rooms, 2 suites* ⚐ *In-room safes, cable TV, pool, hot tub, beach, bar, laundry facilities* ▭ *AE, D, DC, MC, V. $195–$295.*

$ 🏨 **Kauaʻi Sands.** Hawaiian-owned and operated, this oceanfront inn is an example of what island accommodations were like before the arrival of the megaresorts. This is basic, no-frills lodging. Furnishings are spare, simple, and clean. It's so retro it's unintentionally hip. A big grassy courtyard opens to the beach and there's plenty of dining and shopping at the Coconut Marketplace. ⊠ *420 Papaloa Rd., Kapaʻa 96746* ☎ *808/822–4951 or 800/560–5553* 📠 *808/822–0978* ⊕ *www.kauaisandshotel.com* ➯ *200 rooms, 2 suites* ⚐ *A/C, some kitchenettes, cable TV, 2 pools, gym, beach, laundry facilities, no-smoking rooms* ▭ *AE, D, DC, MC, V. $125–$160.*

¢–$ 🏨 **Hotel Coral Reef.** Coral Reef has been in business since the 1960s and is something of a beachfront landmark. The location is better than the hotel, which is perfectly adequate and not much more, although a major renovation is expected to begin in 2006. The two two-room units are good for families. ⊠ *1516 Kūhiō Hwy., Kapaʻa 96746* ☎ *808/822–4481 or 800/843–4659* 📠 *808/822–7705* ⊕ *www.hotelcoralreefresort.com* ➯ *24 rooms, 2 suites* ⚐ *In-room safes, some refrigerators, cable TV, gym, beach, laundry facilities; no A/C, no room phones* ▭ *MC, V. $99–$149.*

Condos

Location, location, location. The Coconut Coast is the only resort area on Kauaʻi where you can actually walk to the beach, restaurants, and stores from your condo. It's not only convenient, but comparatively cheap. You pay less for lodging, meals, services, merchandise, and gas here—all because the reefy coastline isn't as ideal as the sandy-bottomed bays that front the fancy resorts found elsewhere. We think the shoreline is just fine. There are pockets in the reef to swim in, and the coast is very scenic and uncrowded.

$$$ 🏨 **Kauaʻi Coast Resort at the Beachboy.** Fronting an uncrowded stretch of beach, this three-story primarily time-share resort is convenient, and a bit more upscale than nearby properties. The fully furnished one- and two-bedroom condo units, each with a private lānai and well-equipped kitchen, are housed in three buildings. They are decorated in rich woods, tropical prints, and Hawaiian-quilt designs. The 8-acre property looks out on the ocean and offers a heated pool with waterscapes, a day spa, a children's pool, a good restaurant, and an ocean-side hot tub. ⊠ *520 Aleka Loop, Kapa'a 96746* ☎ *808/822–3441 or 877/977–4355* 🖷 *808/ 822–0843* ⊕ *www.shellhospitality.com* ➲ *108 units* △ *Restaurant, A/ C, in-room data ports, in-room safes, kitchens, microwaves, refrigerators, tennis court, pool, gym, hot tub, spa, beach* ▤ *AE, D, DC, MC, V. 1-bedroom $265–$305, 2-bedroom $340–$385.*

$$–$$$ 🏨 **Outrigger at Lae Nani.** Ruling Hawaiian chiefs once returned from ocean voyages to this spot, now host to condominiums comfortable enough for minor royalty. Hotel-sponsored Hawaiiana programs and a booklet for self-guided historical tours are nice extras. Units are all uniquely decorated, with bright, full kitchens and expansive lānai. Your view of landscaped grounds is interrupted only by a large pool before ending at a sandy, swimmable beach. You can find plenty of dining and shopping at the nearby Coconut Marketplace. ⊠ *410 Papaloa Rd., Kapa'a 96746* ☎ *808/822–4938 or 800/688–7444* 🖷 *808/822–1022* ⊕ *www. outriggerlaenani.com* ➲ *84 condominiums* △ *BBQs, fans, in-room safes, kitchens, microwaves, cable TV, tennis court, pool, beach, laundry facilities; no A/C* ▤ *AE, D, DC, MC, V. 1-bedroom $250–$310, 2-bedroom $270–$370.*

$$ 🏨 **Best Western Plantation Hale Suites.** These attractive plantation-style one-bedroom units have well-equipped kitchenettes and garden lānai. Rooms are clean and pretty, with white-rattan furnishings and pastel colors. You couldn't ask for a more convenient location for dining, shopping, and sightseeing: it's across from Waipouli Beach and near Coconut Marketplace. Request a unit on the *makai* side, away from noisy Kūhiō Highway. ⊠ *484 Kūhiō Hwy., Kapa'a 96746* ☎ *808/822–4941 or 800/ 775–4253* 🖷 *808/822–5599* ⊕ *www.plantation-hale.com* ➲ *110 units* △ *BBQs, A/C, in-room safes, kitchenettes, microwaves, cable TV with movies and video games, 3 pools, hot tub, shuffleboard, laundry facilities* ▤ *AE, D, DC, MC, V. 1-bedroom $185–$205.*

$ 🏨 **Kapa'a Sands.** An old rock etched with *kanji*, Japanese characters, reminds you that the site of this condominium gem was formerly occupied by a Shinto temple. Two-bedroom rentals—equipped with full kitchens and private lānai—are a fair deal. Studios feature pull-down Murphy beds to create more daytime space. Ask for an oceanfront room to get the breeze. ⊠ *380 Papaloa Rd., Kapa'a 96746* ☎ *808/822–4901 or 800/222–4901* 🖷 *808/822–1556* ⊕ *www.kapaasands.com* ➲ *20 units* △ *Fans, kitchens, microwaves, cable TV, in-room VCRs, pool, beach; no A/C* ▤ *MC, V. Studios $110–$135, 2-bedroom $155–$175.*

B&Bs and Vacation Rentals

★ **$–$$$** 🏨 **Aloha Cottages.** Owners Charlie and Susan Hoerner restored this three-bedroom plantation home located on Baby Beach in Kapa'a—with plank flooring, gingerbread, and stained glass, to reflect the charm of yesteryear with the conveniences of today. Think Wolf stove, Boshe dishwasher, granite countertops. The orientation is due east; you won't have to leave your bed—or living room, or lānai—to watch the sun rise, the whales breach or the full moon rise. In addition to the main house, there's a cozy bungalow in back that's perfect for honeymooners and couples on good speaking terms. Rent both to sleep a total of eight. Weekly rentals only. The location, the view, and the home doesn't get much better than this. Credit cards accepted via PayPal only. ⊠ *1041 Moana Kai Rd., Kapa'a 96746* ☎ *808/823–0933 or 877/915–1015* ⊕ *www. alohacottages.com* ⇥ *2 cottages* ♿ *BBQs, fans, kitchen, cable TV; no A/C* ⊟ *MC, V. $110–$300.*

¢–$ ⊞ **Rosewood Bed and Breakfast.** This charming B&B on a macadamia nut plantation estate offers four separate styles of accommodations, including a two-bedroom Victorian cottage, a little one-bedroom grass-thatch cottage, a bunkhouse with three rooms and a shared bath, and the traditional main plantation home with two rooms, each with private bath. The bunkhouse and thatched cottage feature outside hot–cold private shower areas hidden from view by a riot of tropically scented foliage. ⊠ *872 Kamalu Rd., Kapa'a 96746* ☎ *808/822–5216* 🖷 *808/ 822–5478* ⊕ *www.rosewoodkauai.com* ⇥ *2 cottages, 3 rooms in bunkhouse, 2 rooms in main house* ♿ *Kitchens, some cable TV; no A/ C, no room phones, no smoking* ⊟ *No credit cards. $45–$135.*

The East Side: Līhu'e

Hotels & Resorts

$$$$ ⊞ **Kaua'i Marriott Resort & Beach Club.** An elaborate tropical garden, waterfalls right off the lobby, Greek statues and columns, and an enormous 26,000-square-foot swimming pool characterize the grand—and grandiose—scale of this resort on Kalapakī Bay, which looks out at the dramatic Hā'upu mountains. This resort has it all—fine dining, shopping, a spa, golf, tennis, and water activities of all kinds. Rooms have tropical decor, and most have expansive ocean views. It's comfortable and convenient, though the airport noise can be a turnoff. ⊠ *3610 Rice St., Kalapakī Beach, Līhu'e 96766* ☎ *808/245–5050 or 800/220–2925* 🖷 *808/245–5148* ⊕ *www.marriotthotels.com* ⇥ *356 rooms, 11 suites, 232 time-share units* ♿ *2 restaurants, room service, A/C, minibars, 2 18-hole golf courses, 7 tennis courts, pool, health club, outdoor hot tub, spa, beach, boating, children's programs (ages 5–12), airport shuttle* ⊟ *AE, D, DC, MC, V. $354–$469.*

¢–$ ⊞ **Garden Island Inn.** Bargain hunters will love this three-story inn near Kalapakī Bay and Anchor Cove shopping center. You can walk across the street and enjoy the majesty of Kalapakī Beach or check out the facilities and restaurants of the Marriott. It's clean and simple, and the innkeepers are friendly, sharing fruit and beach gear. ⊠ *3445 Wilcox Rd., Kalapakī Beach 96766* ☎ *808/245–7227 or 800/648–0154* 🖷 *808/ 245–7603* ⊕ *www.gardenislandinn.com* ⇥ *21 rooms, 2 suites, 1 condo* ♿ *A/C in some rooms, fans, some kitchens, microwaves, refrigerators, cable TV; no smoking* ⊟ *AE, DC, MC, V. $90–$135.*

The South Shore

Sunseekers usually head south to the condo-studded shores of Po'ipū, where three- and four-story complexes line the coast and the surf is ideal for swimming. Po'ipū has more condos than hotels, with prices in the moderate to expensive range. ■ TIP→ **The area's beaches are the best on the island for families.**

Hotels & Resorts

$$$$ ⌂ **Hyatt Regency Kaua'i Resort and Spa.** Dramatically handsome, this clas-
Fodor's Choice sic Hawaiian low-rise is built into the cliffs overlooking an unspoiled
★ coastline. It's open, elegant, and very island-style, making it our favorite
of the megaresorts. It has three very good restaurants, including Don-
dero's, the best on Kaua'i. Spacious rooms, two-thirds with ocean views,
have a plantation theme with bamboo and wicker furnishings and is-
land art. Five acres of meandering fresh- and saltwater-swimming la-
goons—a big hit with kids—are beautifully set amid landscaped grounds.
While adults enjoy treatments at the first-rate Anara Spa, kids can check
out Camp Hyatt. ⊠ *1571 Po'ipū Rd., Kōloa 96756* ☎ *808/742–1234
or 800/633–7313* 🖷 *808/742–1557* ⊕ *www.kauai.hyatt.com* 🛏 *565
rooms, 37 suites* ⚏ *6 restaurants, room service, A/C, in-room data
ports, in-room safes, minibars, refrigerators, cable TV with movies, 18-
hole golf course, 4 tennis courts, pool, health club, hot tub, massage,
spa, beach, 4 bars, nightclub, shops, babysitting, children's programs
(ages 5–12)* 🖃 *AE, D, DC, MC, V. $485–$705.*

$$$$ ⌂ **Sheraton Kaua'i Resort.** The ocean wing accommodations here are so
close to the water you can practically feel the spray of the surf as it hits
the rocks below. Beachfront rooms have muted sand and eggshell col-
ors, which complement the soothing atmosphere of this quiet, calm re-
sort. Brighter palettes enliven the garden rooms. Dining rooms, king beds,
and balconies differentiate the suites. Hawaiian artisans stage crafts
demonstrations under a banyan tree in the central courtyard. The din-
ing Galleria was designed so that all restaurants take advantage of the
endless ocean horizon. At press time a $24 million renovation project
was in the works. ⊠ *2440 Ho'onani Rd., Po'ipū Beach, Kōloa 96756*
☎ *808/742–1661 or 888/488–3535* 🖷 *808/742–9777* ⊕ *www.starwood.
com/hawaii* 🛏 *399 rooms, 14 suites* ⚏ *4 restaurants, room service, A/
C, Wi-Fi, in-room safes, some minibars, refrigerators, cable TV, 3 ten-
nis courts, 2 pools, gym, massage, beach, bar, babysitting, children's pro-
grams (ages 5–12), laundry facilities* 🖃 *AE, D, DC, MC, V. $355–$655.*

Condos

$$$$ ⌂ **Whalers Cove.** Perched about as close to the water's edge as they can
get, these two-bedroom condos are the most luxurious on the south side.
The rocky beach is good for snorkeling, and a short drive or brisk walk
will get you to a sandy stretch. A handsome koa-bedecked reception area
offers services for the plush units. Two barbecue areas, big picture win-
dows, spacious living rooms, lānai, and modern kitchens with washer-dry-
ers make this a home away from home. ⊠*2640 Pu'uholo Rd., Kōloa 96756*
☎ *808/742–7400 or 800/367–8020* 🖷 *808/742–9121* ⊕ *www.suite-
paradise.com* 🛏 *30 units* ⚏ *Fans, in-room data ports, some kitchens, mi-
crowaves, cable TV with movies, in-room VCRs, pool, hot tub, beach,
laundry facilities; no A/C* 🖃 *AE, MC, V. 2-bedroom $355–$485.*

$$–$$$$ ⌂ **Outrigger Kiahuna Plantation.** Kaua'i's largest condo project is lackluster, though the location is excellent. Forty-two plantation-style, low-
rise buildings arc around a large, grassy field leading to the beach. The
individually decorated one- and two-bedroom units vary in style, but

all are clean, have lānai, and get lots of ocean breezes. This is a popular destination for families who take advantage of the swimmable beach and lawn for picnics and games. Great sunset and ocean views are bonuses in some units. ⊠ *2253 Poʻipū Rd., Kōloa 96756* ☎ *808/742–6411 or 800/688–7444* 🖷 *808/742–1698* ⊕ *www.outrigger.com* ⇆ *333 units* ⚘ *Restaurant, fans, in-room broadband, kitchens, cable TV, in-room VCRs, 18-hole golf course, 6 tennis courts, pool, beach; no A/C* ▭ *AE, DC, MC, V. 1-bedroom $245–$479, 2-bedroom $385–$525.*

$–$$$$ 🏨 **Suite Paradise Poʻipū Kaī.** Condominiums, many with cathedral ceilings and all with big windows overlooking the lawns, give this property the feeling of a spacious, quiet retreat inside and out. Large furnished lānai have views to the ocean and across the 110-acre grounds. All the condos are furnished with modern kitchens. Some units are two-level; some have sleeping lofts. Three-, four-, and five-bedroom units are also available. A two-night minimum stay is required. Walking paths connect to both Brennecke and Shipwreck beaches. ⊠ *1941 Poʻipū Rd., Kōloa 96756* ☎ *808/742–6464 or 800/367–8020* 🖷 *808/742–9121* ⊕ *www.suite-paradise.com* ⇆ *130 units* ⚘ *Restaurant, A/C in some rooms, fans, in-room data ports, in-room safes, kitchens, cable TV, in-room VCRs, 9 tennis courts, 6 pools, hot tub* ▭ *AE, D, DC, MC, V. 1-bedroom $133–$370, 2-bedroom $205–$416, 3-bedroom $275–$319, 4-bedroom $428.*

$$$ 🏨 **Poʻipū Shores.** Sitting on a rocky point above pounding surf, this is a perfect spot for whale- or turtle-watching. Weddings are staged on a little lawn beside the ocean, and a sandy swimming beach is a 10-minute walk away. There are three low-rise buildings, with a pool in front of the middle one. Condo units are individually owned and decorated. All have large windows and many of them have bedrooms on the ocean side; each unit either shares a sundeck or has a lānai. ⊠ *1775 Peʻe Rd., Kōloa 96756* ☎ *808/742–7700 or 800/367–5004* 🖷 *808/742–9720* ⊕ *www.castleresorts.com/PSC* ⇆ *39 units* ⚘ *Fans, kitchens, microwaves, cable TV, pool, laundry facilities; no A/C* ▭ *AE, MC, V. 1-bedroom $300, 2-bedroom $395, 3-bedroom $495.*

$$–$$$ 🏨 **Poʻipū Kapili.** Spacious one- and two-bedroom condo units are minutes from Poʻipū's restaurants and beaches. White-frame exteriors and double-pitched roofs complement the tropical landscaping. Interiors include full kitchens and entertainment centers. There are garden and across-the-street ocean views to choose from. Three deluxe 2,600-square-foot penthouse suites have enormous lānai, private elevators, and cathedral ceilings. You can mingle at a weekly coffee hour held beside the ocean-view pool, or grab a good read from the resort library. Fresh seasonings are ready to be picked from the herb garden, and there's a barbecue located poolside. In winter you can whale-watch as you cook. ⊠ *2221 Kapili Rd., Kōloa 96756* ☎ *808/742–6449 or 800/443–7714* 🖷 *808/742–9162* ⊕ *www.poipukapili.com* ⇆ *60 units* ⚘ *Fans, in-room broadband, kitchens, microwaves, cable TV, in-room VCRs, 2 tennis courts, pool, library; no A/C* ▭ *MC, V. 1-bedroom $255–$285, 2-bedroom $335–$560.*

$$ 🏨 **Makahuena at Poʻipū.** Situated close to the center of Poʻipū, on a rocky point over the ocean, the Makahuena is near Shipwreck and Poʻipū beaches. It's a better deal for the price than some of the nearby properties. Large, tastefully decorated one-, two- and three-bedroom suites with white-tile and sand-color carpets are housed in white-wood buildings on well-kept lawns. Each unit has a kitchen and washer and dryer; there's also a small pool and shared barbecue area on the property. ⊠ *1661 Pe'e Rd., Po'ipū 96756* ☎ *808/742–2482 or 800/367–5004* 🖷 *808/742–2379* ⊕ *www.castleresorts.com/MKH* ⟿ *78 units* ⚇ *BBQs, fans, kitchenettes, in-room VCRs, tennis court, pool, hot tub; no A/C* 🖿 *AE, MC, V. 1-bedroom $260, 2-bedroom $265–$475, 3-bedroom $340–$410.*

B&Bs & Vacation Rentals

$$$ 🏨 **Gloria's Spouting Horn Bed & Breakfast.** The most elegant oceanfront B&B on Kaua'i, this cedar home was built specifically for guests. The common room has a soaring A-frame ceiling and deck. Waves dash the black rocks below, while just above the ocean's edge a tiny beach invites sunbathers. All three bedrooms have four-poster beds with canopies created from koa, willow, or bamboo woods, ocean-side lānai, and bathrooms with deep soaking tubs and separate showers. You'll be treated to a full breakfast each morning, and in late afternoon there's an open bar with *pūpū*, timed to the setting of the sun. Book well in advance. ⊠ *4464 Lāwa'i Rd., Po'ipū* ☎ *808/742–6995* ⊕ *www. gloriasbedandbreakfast.com* ⟿ *3 rooms* ⚇ *Fans, refrigerators, cable TV, in-room VCRs, pool, beach; no A/C* 🖿 *No credit cards. $325.*

$–$$ 🏨 **Garden Isle Cottages.** Tropical fruit trees and flower gardens surround these spacious ocean-side cottages. Contemporary Hawaiian furnishings include some rattan; amenities include kitchens with microwaves, ceiling fans, and washers and dryers. The restaurants of nearby Po'ipū are a five-minute walk away. The best part of staying here is the ocean view. ⊠ *2660 Pu'uholo Rd., Kōloa 96756* ☎ *808/742–6717 or 800/ 742–6711* ⊕ *www.oceancottages.com* ⟿ *4 cottages* ⚇ *Fans, kitchens, microwaves, laundry facilities; no A/C* 🖿 *No credit cards. $169–$190.*

$–$$ 🏨 **Po'ipū Plantation Resort.** Plumeria, ti, and other tropical foliage create a lush landscape for this resort, which has one B&B-style plantation home and nine one- and two-bedroom cottage apartments. All cottage units have wood floors and full kitchens and are decorated in light, airy shades. The 1930s plantation home has two rooms with private baths and two suites. A full complimentary breakfast is served daily for those staying in the main house. A minimum three-night stay is required, but rates decrease with the length of stay. ⊠ *1792 Pe'e Rd., Po'ipū 96756* ☎ *808/742–6757 or 800/634–0263* 🖷 *808/742–8681* ⊕ *www. poipubeach.com* ⟿ *3 rooms, 9 cottages* ⚇ *BBQs, A/C, fans, kitchens, in-room VCRs, hair salon, hot tub, laundry facilities* 🖿 *D, MC, V. $120–$190, 3-night minimum.*

$ 🏨 **Hideaway Cove.** On a residential street ending in a cul-de-sac, Hideaway Cove is very quiet, even though it's one block from the ocean's edge in the heart of Po'ipū. What was once two homes has been converted to seven complete vacation homes. Owner Herb Lee appointed each with resort-quality furniture and furnishings—even original artwork. The two-bedroom Seabreeze villa comes with a hot tub on the lānai. The three-bedroom Oceanview villa connects via an internal staircase with the two-bedroom Aloha villa to provide a large five-bedroom home with two complete living areas—perfect for two families traveling together. Rates drop with a seven-night stay, effectively making the seventh night free. ✉ *2307 Nalo Rd., Po'ipū 96756* ☎ *808/635–8785 or 866/849–2426* 🌐 *www.hideawaycove.com* *7 units* *BBQs, A/C, fans, kitchens, cable TV, in-room DVD/VCR players, laundry facilities* ▭ *AE, D, MC, V. Studio $125–$140, 1-bedroom $160, 2-bedroom $210–$235, 3-bedroom $320.*

$ **Kaua'i Cove Cottages.** Three modern studio cottages sit side by side at the mouth of Waikomo Stream, beside an ocean cove that offers super snorkeling. The studios have airy tropical decor under cathedral ceilings; each has a complete kitchen. Private patios on the ocean side have gas barbecue grills. There's a $25 cleaning fee for stays of fewer than three nights. VCRs are available on request. ✉ *2672 Pu'uholo Rd., Po'ipū 96756* ☎ *808/651–0279 or 800/624–9945* 🌐 *www.kauaicove.com* *3 cottages* *BBQs, fans, kitchens, cable TV, snorkeling; no A/C* ▭ *D, MC, V. $105–$145.*

4

The West Side

If you want to do a lot of hiking or immerse yourself in the island's history, find a room in Waimea. A few very spartan cabins are rented in Kōke'e State Park.

Hotels & Resorts

$–$$$$ Fodor'sChoice ★ **Waimea Plantation Cottages.** History buffs will adore these reconstructed sugar-plantation cottages, which offer a vacation experience unique in all Hawai'i. The one- to five-bedroom cottages are tucked among coconut trees along a lovely stretch of coastline on the sunny West Side. (Note that swimming waters here are sometimes murky, depending on weather conditions.) ■ TIP→ **It's a great property for family reunions or other large gatherings.** These cozy little homes, replete with porches, feature plantation-era furnishings, modern kitchens, and cable TV. BBQs, hammocks, porch swings, a gift shop, a spa, and a museum are on the property. Complimentary wireless Internet access is available in the main building; in-room data ports are available if requested in advance. ✉ *9400 Kaumuali'i Hwy., Box 367, Waimea 96796* ☎ *808/338–1625 or 800/992–4632* 🖷 *808/338–2338* 🌐 *www.waimeaplantation.com* *48 cottages* *Restaurant, fans, some kitchens, cable TV, pool, spa, beach, horseshoes, bar, Internet room; no A/C* ▭ *AE, D, DC, MC, V. Studio $175, 1-bedroom $260–$350, 2-bedroom $330–$405, 3-bedroom $390–$455, 4-bedroom $505, 5-bedroom $775.*

KIDS RULE

Islanders love kids, and kids love the Islands. Kids are welcome most everywhere, but some places make a special effort to enhance their stay. The **Hyatt** has a great camp for kids, if you can pry them away from its swimming pool—the largest on the island and replete with cool stuff like a waterslide and tunnels. The **Aloha Kaua'i Beach Resort** is next door to a fabulous playground designed by kids, and a beach with a protected swimming lagoon perfect for small fry. At **North Country Farms** in Kīlauea, they'll feel right at home with the books, toys, videos, and games carefully selected for their entertainment.

Vacation Rentals

¢ ⊡ **Kōke'e Lodge.** If you're an outdoor enthusiast, you can appreciate Kaua'i's mountain wilderness from the 12 rustic cabins that comprise this lodge. They are austere, to say the least, but more comfortable than a tent, and the mountain setting is grand. Wood-burning stoves ward off the chill and dampness (wood is a few dollars extra). If you aren't partial to dormitory-style sleeping, request the cabins with two bedrooms; both styles sleep six and have kitchenettes. The lodge restaurant serves a light breakfast and lunch between 9 and 3:30 daily. ✉ *3600 Kōke'e Rd., at mile marker 15, Kekaha* ☏ *Box 819, Waimea 96796* ☎ *808/335–6061* ⤴ *12 cabins* ⛄ *Restaurant, hiking, shops; no A/C, no room phones, no room TVs* ⊟ *D, DC, MC, V. $45.*

KAUA'I ESSENTIALS

Transportation

BY AIR

Regular air service from Honolulu, and a few direct flights from Maui, the Big Island, and select West Coast cities make for convenient, if not quick, travel to the Garden Island.

CARRIERS   Two Hawaii-based carriers, Aloha Airlines and Hawaiian Airlines, offer daily round-trip flights from Honolulu and Neighbor Islands to Līhu'e Airport. Rates vary widely from $63 to $170 one-way. It's generally a 20- to 40-minute flight, depending on where you start. Aloha and Hawaiian airlines also provide a few direct flights from select West Coast cities, as do United Airlines and American Airlines. ⇨ *See* Smart Travel Tips *at the front of this book for airline contact information.*

AIRPORTS   The Līhu'e Airport is 3 mi east of the town of Līhu'e. All commercial and cargo flights use this modern airport. It has just two baggage-claim areas, each with a visitor information center. There's a heliport that serves tour helicopters nearby.

Used only by a tour helicopter company and a few private planes, the Princeville Airport is a tiny strip on the North Shore, set within rolling ranches and sugarcane fields. It's a five-minute drive from the Princeville Resort and condo development, and a 10-minute drive from the shops and accommodations of Hanalei.

🛈 **Līhu'e Airport** ☎ 888/697–7813 visitor information center. **Princeville Airport** ☎ 808/826–3040.

TO & FROM THE   Līhu'e Airport is a five-minute drive from Līhu'e. If you're staying in Wailua AIRPORT   or Kapa'a, your driving time from Līhu'e is 15 to 25 minutes; to Princeville and Hanalei it's about 45 to 60 minutes.

To the south, it's a 30- or 40-minute drive from Līhu'e to Po'ipū, the major resort area. To Waimea, the drive takes a little more than an hour; to the mountains of Kōke'e, allow a good two hours driving time from Līhu'e.

Check with your hotel or condo to see if there's free shuttle service from the airport.

Taxi fares around the island are $2.50 at the meter drop plus $2.50 per mile. That means a taxicab from Līhu'e Airport to Līhu'e town runs $8–$10 and to Po'ipū about $40, excluding tip. Akiko's Taxi offers its services from the east side of the island. Po'ipū Taxi will take you to Līhu'e and Po'ipū. Scotty Taxi provides quick service around the airport and Līhu'e.
Akiko's Taxi ☎ 808/822-7588. **Po'ipū Taxi** ☎ 808/639-2042 or 808/639-2044. **Scotty Taxi** ☎ 808/245-7888 or 808/639-9807.

BY CAR

CAR RENTAL Unless you plan to stay strictly at a resort or do all of your sightseeing as part of guided tours, you'll need a rental car. You can take the bus, but it's a slow mode of travel that don't take you everywhere you might want to go. You can easily walk to the rental-car counters, directly across the street from the baggage claim at Līhu'e Airport. They'll shuttle you to their nearby lot to pick up your car. All the major companies have offices at the Līhu'e Airport. Several companies operate small reservation desks at major hotels, but spur-of-the-moment rentals will cost you more than prearranged ones.

CAR TRAVEL Although Kaua'i is relatively small, its sights stretch across the island and its narrow, often busy roads are not especially conducive to walking or bicycling. You may be able to walk to beaches, stores, and restaurants in your resort area, but major attractions are not usually within walking distance.

It's easy to get around on Kaua'i, but be prepared for slow travel and high gas prices. A two-lane highway that widens to three lanes in several places nearly encircles the island. It's essentially one road, called Kūhiō Highway on its northwest course and Kaumuali'i Highway when it turns to the southwest. Līhu'e serves as the juncture point. Your rental-car company will supply you with a decent map, and others can be found in the free tourist magazines.

Traffic is a major source of irritation for residents, who encounter it at unpredictable times and the usual rush-hour periods. It's thickest between Līhu'e and the South Side, and all around Kapa'a. Residents know the tight spots, so don't worry, they'll let you into the line of traffic or stop so you can make your left turn. Be sure to acknowledge them with a wave and repeat the kindness when you can. Aggressive driving is not appreciated. And if you're gawking at the sights and holding up traffic, pull over and let cars go by.

■ TIP→ Although Kaua'i looks like paradise, it does have crime. Lock your car whenever you park and never leave valuables in your rental car, even for a short time. Pay attention to parking signs and speed limits. And be sure to buckle up, as seat-belt citations carry hefty fines.

BY TAXI

Cabs are costly on Kaua'i and must be called for service. Each mile is $2.50, after a $2.50 meter drop; from Līhu'e to Po'ipū the price is $40; from Līhu'e to Princeville it's $70, excluding tip. It's best to use a cab for short distances only (to a restaurant, for instance).

Akiko's Taxi operates from Kapa'a and has minivans in its fleet. City Cab is a reliable taxi company with islandwide services; it uses Līhu'e as a home base. North Shore Cab Company, based in Princeville, caters to the north and east sections of the island.

🚖 **Akiko's Taxi** ☎ 808/822-7588 or 808/634-6018. **City Cab** ☎ 808/245-3227 or 808/639-7932. **North Shore Cab Company** ☎ 808/826-4118 or 808/639-7829.

Contacts & Resources

EMERGENCIES

To reach the police, ambulance, or fire department in case of any emergency, dial **911**.

Kaua'i's Wilcox Memorial Hospital in Līhu'e has X-ray facilities, physical therapy, a pharmacy, and an emergency room. It's linked to Kaua'i Medical Clinic (KMC), with physicians trained in many different specialties, and clinics all around the island. Major emergency cases are airlifted to O'ahu. West Kaua'i Medical Center serves the area from Po'ipū to Kekaha.

Most pharmacies close around 5 PM, though Longs Drugs, Safeway, and Wal-Mart stay open a few hours later.

🏥 Doctors **Kaua'i Medical Clinic** ✉ 3420-B Kūhiō Hwy., Līhu'e ☎ 808/245-1500, 808/245-2471 pharmacy, 808/245-1831 24-hr on-call physicians, 808/338-9431 after-hours emergencies ✉ North Shore Clinic, Kīlauea and Oka Rds., Kīlauea ☎ 808/828-1418 ✉ 4392 Waialo Rd., 'Ele'ele ☎ 808/335-0499 ✉ 5371 Kōloa Rd., Kōloa ☎ 808/742-1621 ✉ 4-1105 Kūhiō Hwy., Kapa'a ☎ 808/822-3431.

🏥 Hospitals **West Kaua'i Medical Center** ✉ 4643 Waimea Canyon Dr., Waimea ☎ 808/338-9431. **Wilcox Memorial Hospital** ✉ 3420 Kūhiō Hwy., Līhu'e ☎ 808/245-1010.

🏥 Pharmacies **Longs Drugs** ✉ Kukui Grove Center, Rte. 50, Līhu'e ☎ 808/245-8871. **Safeway Food and Drug** ✉ Kaua'i Village Shopping Center, 4-831 Kūhiō Hwy., Kapa'a ☎ 808/822-2191. **Shoreview Pharmacy** ✉ 4-1177 Kūhiō Hwy., Suite 113, Kapa'a ☎ 808/822-1447. **Westside Pharmacy** ✉ 1-3845 Kaumuali'i Hwy., Hanapēpē ☎ 808/335-5342.

VISITOR INFORMATION

The Kaua'i Visitors Bureau has an office at 4334 Rice Street, Līhu'e's main thoroughfare, near the Kaua'i Museum.

You'll find plenty of kiosk-type activity centers that can help you book tours, schedule activities, and rent recreational gear, convertibles, mopeds, and motorcycles all over the island. Beware, some of them are linked to time-share projects, and you may have to sit through a sales pitch to get those great deals.

Po'ipū Beach Resort Association is the central source of information about the South Side. You can make online reservations, find out about activities and attractions, and request maps and brochures.

The many free visitor magazines are also helpful, offering maps, descriptions of activities, discount coupons, sightseeing and shopping tips, and other tidbits of advice and information.

🗺 **Kaua'i Visitors Bureau** ✉ 4334 Rice St., Suite 101, Līhu'e 96766 ☎ 808/245-3971 or 800/262-1400 🖨 808/246-9235 ⊕ www.kauaidiscovery.com.

Po'ipū Beach Resort Association ✉ Box 730, Kōloa 96756 ☎ 808/742-7444 or 888/744-0888 🖨 808/742-7887 ⊕ www.poipu-beach.org.

Moloka'i

WORD OF MOUTH

"It was a beautiful experience and we really didn't do anything. Beautifully boring. We walked to the beach twice a day . . . read our books a lot, walked a lot, played golf once, looked for whales, talked to a few people . . . and just hung out. I'd go again in a heartbeat."

—pdx

WELCOME TO MOLOKA'I

TOP 5
Reasons to Go

1 Kalaupapa Peninsula: Hike or take a mule ride down the world's tallest sea cliffs to a fascinating, historic community.

2 Biking Single-Track Trails at Moloka'i Ranch: A complex network of trails offers some of the best mountain-bike experiences in the world.

3 Deep-Sea Fishing: Big sport fish are plentiful in these waters, as are gorgeous views of several islands.

4 Nature: Deep valleys, sheer cliffs, and the untamed ocean are the main attractions on Moloka'i.

5 Pāpōhaku Beach: This 3-mile stretch of sand is one of the most sensational beaches in all of Hawai'i.

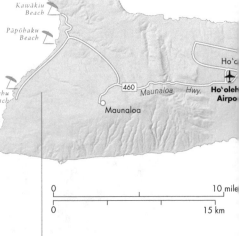

Kawākiu Beach

Pāpōhaku Beach

Kapukahehu Beach

460 Maunaloa Hwy.

Maunaloa

Ho'o

Ho'oleh Airpo

0 — 10 mile
0 — 15 km

■ TIP→ **Directions on the island are often given as** *mauka* **(toward the mountains) and** *makai* **(toward the ocean).**

The most arid part of the island, the West End has two inhabited areas: the coastal stretch includes a few condos and luxury homes, and the largest beaches on the island. Nearby, the hilltop hamlet of Maunaloa boasts the finest accommodation on the island, the Lodge at Moloka'i Ranch.

Getting Oriented

Shaped like a long bone, Moloka'i is only about 10 mi wide on average, and four times that long. The North Shore thrusts up from the sea to form the tallest sea cliffs on Earth, while the South Shore slides almost flat into the water, then fans out to form the largest shallow-water reef system in the United States. Surprisingly, the highest point on Moloka'i rises only to about 4,000 feet.

The island's only true town, Kaunakakai, with its mile-long wharf, lies in Central Moloka'i. Nearly all the island's eateries and stores are in or close to Kaunakakai. Highway 470 crosses the center of the island, rising to the top of the sea cliffs and the Kalaupapa overlook.

The scenic drive around the East End passes through the green pastures of Pu'u O Hoku Ranch and climaxes with a descent into Hālawa Valley. The farther east you go, the lusher the island gets.

MOLOKA'I PLANNER

What You Won't Find on Moloka'i

Moloka'i is a great place to be outdoors. And that's a good thing, because with only about 7,000 residents Moloka'i has very little of what you would call "indoors." There are no tall buildings, no traffic lights, no street lights, no stores bearing the names of national chains, and almost nothing at all like a resort. Among the Hawaiian Islands, Moloka'i has distinguished itself as the one least interested in attracting tourists. At night the whole island grows dark, creating a velvety blackness and a wonderful, rare thing called silence.

Where to Stay

Moloka'i appeals most to travelers who appreciate genuine Hawaiian hospitality rather than swanky digs. Aside from the upscale Lodge at Moloka'i Ranch, most hotel and condominium properties range from adequate to funky. Visitors who want to lollygag on the beach should choose one of the condos or home rentals at the West End. Locals tend to choose Hotel Moloka'i, located seaside just 2 mi from Kaunakakai, with its on-site restaurant, bar, and live music. Travelers who want to immerse themselves in the spirit of the island should seek out a bed-and-breakfast or cottage, the closer to the East End the better.

Additional planning details are listed in Moloka'i Essentials at the end of this chapter.

Timing is Everything

If you're keen to explore Moloka'i's beaches, coral beds, or fishponds, summer is your best bet for non-stop calm seas and sunny skies. For a real taste of Hawaiian culture, plan your visit around a festival. In January, islanders and visitors compete in ancient Hawaiian games at the Ka Moloka'i Makahiki Festival. The Moloka'i Ka Hula Piko, an annual daylong event in May, draws the state's premiere hula troupes, musicians, and storytellers to perform. The Festival of Lights includes an Electric Light Parade down the main street of Kaunakakai in December. While never crowded, the island is busier during these events—book accommodations and transportation six months in advance.

Will it Rain?

Moloka'i's weather mimics that of the other islands: mid to low 80s year-round, slightly rainier during winter. Because the island's accommodations are clustered at low elevation or along the leeward coast, warm weather is a dependable constant for visitors (only 15 to 20 inches of rain fall each year on the coastal plain). As you travel up the mountainside, the weather changes with bursts of forest-building downpours.

Cell Phones and the Internet

Communication with the outside world is a real challenge on Moloka'i. Most of the island lies outside the range of cell-phone service. Even regular telephone service, at Hotel Moloka'i for example, can be unreliable. Travelers who absolutely need to stay in touch with home or the office should get a room at the Lodge at Moloka'i Ranch.

By Paul Wood

Updated by
Joana Varawa

NICKNAMED THE FRIENDLY ISLAND, Moloka'i is generally thought of as the last bit of "real" Hawai'i. Tourism has been held at bay by the island's unique history (Moloka'i was once occupied solely by a leper's colony), despite the fact that the longest white sand beach in Hawai'i can be found along its western shore. With working ranches and sandy beaches to the west, sheer sea cliffs to the north, and a rainy, lush eastern coast, Moloka'i offers a bit of everything, including a peek at what the islands were like 50 years ago. The sign at the airport says it all, "Slow down, you're in Moloka'i."

Only 38 mi long and 10 mi wide at its widest point, Moloka'i is the fifth-largest island in the Hawaiian archipelago. Eight thousand residents call Moloka'i home, nearly 40% of whom are Hawaiian. Supplies are delivered once a year to the store and hospital at Kaunakakai, by barge from Honolulu.

Geology

Roughly 1.5 million years ago two large volcanoes—Kamakou in the east and Maunaloa in the west—broke the surface of the Pacific Ocean and created the island of Moloka'i. Shortly thereafter a third and much smaller caldera, Kauhako, popped up to form the Makanalua peninsula on the north side. After hundreds of thousands of years of rain, surf and wind, an enormous landslide on the north end sent much of the mountain into the sea, leaving behind the sheer sea cliffs that make Moloka'i's North Shore so spectacularly beautiful.

History

In 1886, Moloka'i's Makanalua Peninsula, surrounded on three sides by the Pacific and accessible only by a steep, switchback trail, seemed the ideal place to exile people cursed with leprosy. The first patients were thrown into the waters and left for 7 years with no facilities, shelter or supplies. In 1893 a missionary named Father Damien arrived and created Moloka'i's famous leper's colony. Though the disease is no longer contagious, many patients chose to stay in their long-time home, and the colony still has roughly 100 residents. Visitors are welcome, but must pay $40 for a tour operated by Damien Tours of Kalaupapa.

The Birthplace of Hula

Legend has it that Laka, goddess of the hula, gave birth to the dance on Moloka'i, at a sacred place in Ka'ana. The island recognizes the birth of this sacred dance with a celebration called Ka Hula Piko every year during the third weekend in May. When Laka died, it is believed that her remains were secretly hidden somewhere beneath the hill Pu'u Nana. The hula was finally established, the work of Laka was complete, and the dance has flourished ever since throughout Hawai'i.

EXPLORING MOLOKA'I

The first thing to do on Moloka'i is to drive everywhere. It's a feat you can accomplish in less than a day. Basically you have one 40-mi west-to-east highway (two lanes, no stop lights) with three side trips: the little west end town of Maunaloa; the Highway 470 drive (just a few miles) to the top of the North Shore and the overlook of Kalaupapa Peninsula; and the short stretch of shops in Kaunakakai town. After you learn the general lay of the land, you can return for in-depth experiences on foot.

West Moloka'i

The region is largely made up of the 53,000-acre Moloka'i Ranch. The rolling pastures and farmlands are presided over by Maunaloa, a sleepy little plantation town with a dormant volcano of the same name. West Moloka'i has another claim to fame: Pāpōhaku, the island's best beach.

What to See

❶ Kaluako'i Hotel and Golf Club. This late-1960s resort passed through several owners, and the hotel itself is now closed, awaiting its next incarnation. Some very nice condos are still operating here, however. Stroll the grounds—an impressive 6,700 acres of beachfront property, including the newly revived golf course and 5 mi of coastline. ⊠ *Kaluako'i Rd., Maunaloa* ☎ *808/552–2555 or 888/552–2550.*

★ **❸ Maunaloa.** This sleepy town was developed in 1923 to support the island's pineapple plantation. Although the fields of golden fruit have gone fallow, some of the workers' dwellings still stand, anchoring the west end of Moloka'i. Colorful local characters run the half-dozen businesses (including a kite shop and an eclectic old market) along the town's short main street. This is also the headquarters for Moloka'i Ranch. ⊠ *Western end of Maunaloa Hwy., Rte. 460.*

❷ Pāpōhaku Beach. The most splendid stretch of white sand on Moloka'i, Pāpōhaku is also the island's largest beach—it stretches 3 mi along the western shore. Even on busier days you're likely to see only a handful of other people. If the waves are up, swimming is dangerous. ⊠ *Kaluako'i Rd.; 2 mi beyond Kaluako'i Hotel and Golf Club.*

Central Moloka'i

Most residents live central, near the island's one and only true town, Kaunakakai. It's just about the only place on the island to get food and supplies. It *is* Moloka'i. Go into the shops along and around Ala Mālama Street. Buy stuff. Talk with people. You'll learn the difference between being a tourist and being a visitor. ■ TIP➔ **Don't forget that Central Moloka'i (except for a few restaurants) closes at sunset and all day Sunday.**

A Tale of Tragedy & Triumph See Page 497

What to See

❾ Church Row. Standing together along the highway are several houses of worship with primarily native Hawaiian congregations. Notice the unadorned, boxlike style of architecture so similar to missionary homes. ⊠ Mauka *(toward the mountains) side of Rte. 460, 5½ mi southwest of airport.*

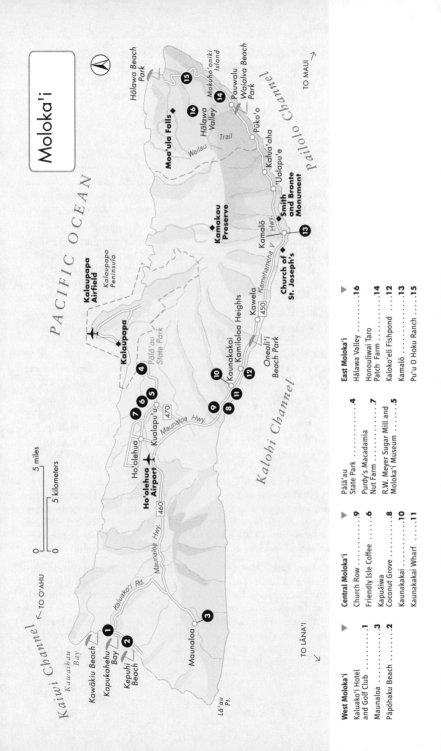

Moloka'i

PACIFIC OCEAN

Kaiwi Channel

←TO OAHU

Kawaihau Bay

Kawākiu Beach

Kapukahehu Bay

Kepuhi Beach

Lā'au Pt.

TO LĀNA'I ↙

Maunaloa

Maunaloa Hwy.

Kaluako'i Rd.

Ho'olehua

Ho'olehua Airport

Kualapu'u

Maunaloa Hwy.

Kalaupapa Airfield

Kalaupapa Peninsula

Kalaupapa

Pālā'au State Park

Kaunakakai

Kamiloloa Heights

Kawela

Kamalō

Kamehameha V Hwy.

Kamakou Preserve

Church of St. Joseph's

Kaunakakai

Oneali'i Beach Park

Kalobi Channel

Smith and Bronte Monument

'Ualapu'e

Kalua'aha

Pūko'o

Pōhaku

Mapulehu

Wailau Trail

Moa'ula Falls

Hālawa Valley

Hālawa Beach Park

Mokuho'oniki Island

Pauwalu

Waialva Beach Park

Pailolo Channel

→TO MAUI

Hālawa Beach Park

5 miles

5 kilometers

West Moloka'i ▶
Kaluako'i Hotel and Golf Club 1
Maunaloa 3
Pāpōhaku Beach 2

Central Moloka'i ▶
Church Row 9
Friendly Isle Coffee 6
Kapuāiwa Coconut Grove 8
Kaunakakai 10
Kaunakakai Wharf 11

Pālā'au State Park 4
Purdy's Macadamia Nut Farm 7
R.W. Meyer Sugar Mill and Moloka'i Museum 5

East Moloka'i ▶
Hālawa Valley 16
Honouliwai Taro Patch Farm 14
Kaloko'eli Fishpond ...12
Kamalō 13
Pu'u O Hoku Ranch 15

➏ Friendly Isle Coffee. Visit the headquarters of a 500-acre plantation of Moloka'i coffee. The espresso bar serves java in artful ways, sandwiches, and *liliko'i* (passion fruit) cheesecake. The gift shop offers a wide range of Moloka'i handicrafts and memorabilia, and, of course, coffee. ⊠ *Farrington Hwy., off Rte. 470, Kualapu'u* ☎ *800/709–2326 or 808/567–9023* ⊕ *www.molokaicoffee.com.*

➑ Kapuāiwa Coconut Grove. At first glance this looks like a sea of coconut trees. Close-up you can see that the tall, stately palms are planted in long rows leading down to the sea. This is one of the last surviving royal groves planted by Prince Lot, who ruled Hawai'i as King Kamehameha V from 1863 until his death in 1872. Watch for falling coconuts; protect your head and your car. ⊠ Makai *side of Rte. 460, 5½ mi south of airport.*

★ ➓ Kaunakakai. Kaunakakai looks like an Old West movie set. Along the one-block main drag is a cultural grab bag of restaurants and shops. People are friendly and willing to supply directions. The preferred dress is shorts and a tank top, and no one wears anything fancier than a *mu'umu'u* or aloha shirt. ⊠ *Rte. 460, about 3 blocks north of Kaunakakai Wharf.*

⓫ Kaunakakai Wharf. Docks, once bustling with watercraft exporting pineapples, now host boats shipping out potatoes, tomatoes, baby corn, herbs, and other produce. The wharf is also the starting point for excursions, including deep-sea fishing, sailing, snorkeling, whale-watching, and scuba diving. ⊠ *Rte. 450 and Ala Mālama St.; drive* makai *on Kaunakakai Pl., which dead-ends at wharf.*

Fodor'sChoice
★ **Moloka'i Mule Ride.** Mount a friendly mule and wind along a 3-mi, 26-switchback trail to reach the town of Kalaupapa. The path was built in 1886 as a supply route for the settlement below. Once in Kalaupapa, you can take a guided tour of the town and have a picnic lunch. The trail is very steep, down some of the highest sea cliffs in the world. Only those in good shape should attempt the ride, as two hours each way on a mule can take its toll. The entire event takes seven hours. It's wise to make reservations ahead of time, as spots are limited. The same outfit can also arrange for you to hike down or fly in, or some combination of a hike in and fly out. *See* A Tale of Tragedy & Triumph p. 497 *for more information.* ⊠ *100 Kala'e Hwy., Rte. 470, Kualapu'u* ☎ *808/567–6088* ⊕ *www.muleride.com* ⊠ *$165* ☉ *Mon.–Sat. 8–3:30.*

★ ➍ Pālā'au State Park. One of the island's few formal recreation areas, this retreat covers 233 acres at a 1,000-foot elevation. A short path through a pine forest leads to **Kalaupapa Lookout,** a magnificent overlook with views of the town of Kalaupapa and the 1,664-foot-high sea cliffs protecting it. Informative plaques have facts about leprosy, Father Damien, and the colony. The park is also the site of **Phallic Rock,** known as Kauleonānāhoa to the ancient Hawaiians. It's said that if women sit by this rock formation they will become more fertile. The park is well main-

Continued on page 501

Father Damien's Church, St. Philomena

A TALE OF TRAGEDY & TRIUMPH

For those who crave drama, there is no better destination than Mokoka'i's Kalaupapa Peninsula—but it wasn't always so. For 100 years this remote strip of land was "the loneliest place on earth," a feared place of exile for those suffering from leprosy (now known as Hansen's Disease).

The world's tallest sea cliffs, rain-chiseled valleys, and tiny islets dropped like exclamation points along the coast emphasize the passionate history of the Kalaupapa Peninsula. Today, it's impossible to visit this stunning national historic park and view the evidence of human ignorance and heroism without responding. You'll be tugged by emotions—awe and disbelief for starters. But you'll also glimpse humorous facets of every day life in a small town. Whatever your experience here may be, chances are you'll return home feeling that the journey to present-day Kalaupapa is one you'll never forget.

THE SETTLEMENT'S EARLY DAYS

Father Damien with patients outside St. Philomena church

IN 1865, PRESSURED BY FOREIGN RESIDENTS, the Hawaiian Kingdom passed "An Act to Prevent the Spread of Leprosy." Anyone showing symptoms of the disease was to be permanently exiled to Kalawao, the north end of Kalaupapa Peninsula—a spot walled in on three sides by nearly impassable cliffs. The peninsula had been home to a fishing community for 900 years, but those inhabitants were evicted and the entire peninsula declared settlement land.

The first twelve patients were arrested and sent to Kalawao in 1866. People of all ages and many nationalities followed, taken from their homes and unceremoniously dumped on the isolated shore. Officials thought the patients could become self-sufficient, fishing and farming sweet potatoes in the stream-fed valleys. That was not the case. Settlement conditions were deplorable.

Father Damien, a Belgian missionary, was one of four priests who volunteered to serve the leprosy settlement at Kalawao on a rotating basis. His turn came first; when it was up, he refused to leave. He is cred-ited with turning the settlement from a merciless exile to a place where hope could be heard in the voices of his recruited choir. He organized the building of the St. Philomena church, nearly 300 houses, and a home for boys. A vocal advocate for his adopted community, he pestered the church for supplies, administered medicine, and oversaw the nearly daily funerals. Sixteen years after his arrival, in 1889, he died from the effects of leprosy, having contracted the disease during his service. Known around the world for his sacrifice, Father Damien was beatified by the Catholic Church in 1995, achieving the first step towards sainthood.

Mother Marianne heard of the mission while working at a hospital in Syracuse, New York. Along with six other Franciscan Sisters, she volunteered to work with those with leprosy in the Islands. They sailed to the desolate Kalaupapa Peninsula in November of 1888. Like the Father, the Sisters were considered saints for their tireless work. Mother Marianne stayed at Kalaupapa until her death in 1918; she was beatified by the Catholic Church in 2005.

VISITING KALAUPAPA TODAY

Kalaupapa Peninsula

FROZEN IN TIME, Kalaupapa's one-horse town has unbeatable charm. Signs posted here and there remind residents when the bank will be open (once monthly), where to pick up lost sunglasses, and what's happening at the tiny town bar. The town has the nostalgic, almost naive ambience expected from a place almost wholly segregated from modern life.

About 30 former patients remain at Kalaupapa (by choice, as the disease is controlled by drugs and the patients are no longer carriers), but many travel frequently to other parts of the world and all are over the age of 60. Richard Marks, the town sheriff and owner of Damien Tours, will likely retire soon, as will the elderly postmistress. They haven't, however, lost their chutzpah. Having survived a lifetime of prejudice and misunderstanding, Kalaupapa's residents aren't willing to be pushed around any longer—several recently made the journey to Honolulu to ask for the removal of a "rude and insensitive" superintendent.

To get a feel for what their lives were like, look up the National Park Service website (www.nps.gov/kala/docs/start.htm) or buy one of several heartbreaking memoirs at the park's library-turned-bookstore.

THE TRUTH ABOUT HANSEN'S DISEASE

■ A cure for leprosy has been available since 1941. Multidrug therapy, a rapid cure, has been available since 1981.

■ With treatment, none of the disabilities traditionally associated with leprosy need occur.

■ Most people have a natural immunity to leprosy. Only 5% of the world's population is even susceptible to the disease.

■ There are still about 500,000 new cases of leprosy each year; at least two-thirds are in India.

■ All new cases of leprosy are treated on an outpatient basis.

■ The term "leper" is offensive and should not be used. It is appropriate to say a person is "affected by leprosy" or " by Hansen's Disease."

GETTING HERE

The Kalaupapa Trail and Peninsula are all part of Kalaupapa National Historic Park (☎ 808/567–6802; ⊕ www.nps.gov/kala/), which is open every day but Sunday. Keep in mind, there are no public facilities (except an occasional restroom) anywhere in the park. Pack your own food and water, as well as light rain gear, sunscreen, and bug repellent.

Hiking: Hiking allows you to travel at your own pace and stop frequently for photos—not an option on the mule ride. The hike takes about 1 hour down and 1½ hours up. You'll want to hit the trail by 8 AM to avoid a trail hazard—fresh mule poop.

Mule-Skinning: You'll be amazed as your mule trots up to the edge of the switchback, swivels on two legs, and com-

Kalaupapa Beach & Peninsula

THE KALAUPAPA TRAIL

Unless you fly, the only way into Kalaupapa National Historic Park is on a dizzying switchback trail. The switchbacks are numbered—26 in all—and descend 1,700 feet to sea level in just under 3 miles. The steep trail is really more of a staircase, and most of the trail is shaded. Keep in mind, however, footing is uneven and little exists to keep you from pitching over the side. If you don't mind heights, you can stare straight down to the ocean for most of the way. *Access Kalaupapa Trail off Hwy. 470 near the Kalaupapa Overlook. There is ample parking near end of Hwy. 470.*

TO HIKE OR TO RIDE?

There are two ways to get down the Kalaupapa Trail: in your hiking boots, or on a mule.

pletes a sharp-angled turn—26 times. The guides tell you the mules can do this in their sleep, but that doesn't take the fear out of the first few switchbacks. Make reservations well in advance. *Moloka'i Mule Ride,* ☎*808/567-6088* ⊕ *www.muleride.com*

IMPORTANT PERMIT INFORMATION

The only way to visit Kalaupapa settlement is on a tour. Book through Damien Tours (☎808/567–6171) if you're hiking or flying in; Moloka'i Mule Ride (808/567–6088) if you're riding. Daily tours are offered Monday through Saturday. Be sure to reserve in advance. Visitors ages 16 and under are not allowed at Kalaupapa, and photographing patients without their explicit permission is forbidden.

tained, with camping facilities, restrooms, and picnic tables. ✉ *Take Rte. 460 west from Kaunakakai and then head* mauka *on Rte. 470, which ends at park* ☎ *No phone* ✆ *Free* ☉ *Daily dawn–dusk.*

❼ Purdy's Macadamia Nut Farm. Moloka'i's only working macadamia nut farm is open for educational tours hosted by the knowledgeable and entertaining owner. A family business on Hawaiian homestead land in Ho'olehua, the farm takes up 1½ acres with a flourishing grove of some 50 trees more than 70 years old. Taste a delicious nut right out of its shell, or fresh macadamia-blossom honey; then buy some at the shop on the way out. Look for Purdy's sign behind Moloka'i High School. ✉ *Lihipali Ave., Ho'olehua* ☎ *808/567–6601* ✆ *Free* ☉ *Weekdays 9:30–3:30, Sat. 10–2.*

❺ R. W. Meyer Sugar Mill and Moloka'i Museum. Built in 1877, this old mill has been reconstructed as a testament to Moloka'i's agricultural history. The equipment is still in working order, including a mule-driven cane crusher, redwood evaporating pans, some copper clarifiers, and a steam engine. A museum with changing exhibits on the island's early history and a gift shop are on-site as well. The facility serves as a campus for Elderhostel programs. ✉ *Rte. 470, 2 mi southwest of Pālā'au State Park, Kala'e* ☎ *808/567–6436* ✆ *$2.50* ☉ *Mon.–Sat. 10–2.*

East Moloka'i

On the beautifully undeveloped East End of Moloka'i, you can find ancient fishponds, a magnificent coastline, splendid ocean views, and a gaping valley that's been inhabited for centuries. The east is flanked by Mt. Kamakou, the island's highest point at 4,961 feet, and home to The Nature Conservancy's Kamakou Preserve. Mist hangs over waterfall-filled valleys, and ancient lava cliffs jut out from the sea.

What to See

⓰ Hālawa Valley. As far back as AD 650 a busy community lived in this valley, one of the oldest recorded habitations in Hawai'i. Hawaiians lived in a perfectly sustainable relationship with the valley's resources, growing taro and fishing, until the 1960s, when pressures of the modern economy forced the old-timers to abandon their traditional lifestyle. Now a new generation of Hawaiians has returned to the valley and begun the challenging work of clearing trees and restoring the taro fields. Much of this work involves rerouting stream water to flow through carefully engineered level ponds called *lo'i.* The taro plants with their big dancing leaves grow in the submerged mud of the *lo'i,* where the water is always cool and flowing. The Hālawa Valley Cooperative gives tours of this restoration project and leads hikes through the valley, which is home to many historic sites and the 3-mi trail to Moa'ula Falls, a 250-foot cascade. The $75 fee ($45 for children) goes to support the restoration work. ✉ *Eastern end of Rte. 450* ☎ *800/274–9303 or 808/553–9803* ⊕ *www.gomolokai.com.*

⓮ Honouliwai Taro Patch Farm. Although they are not reviving an entire valley and lifestyle, like the folks in Hālawa, Jim and Lee Callahan are reviving taro cultivation on their small East End farm watered by a year-round spring. The owners provide 1½-hour educational tours so visitors can experience all phases of taro farming, from planting to eating. Lee was born and raised in Thailand, so she uses a traditional Southeast Asian farm device—a docile, plow-pulling water buffalo named Bigfoot. Tours are available every day, but you must call for an appointment. ⊠ *East of mile marker 20*, mauka *side, where sign says "Honouliwai Is a Beautiful Place to Be"* ☎ 808/558–8922 ⊕ *www. angelfire.com/film/chiangmai/index.html* 🖼 *$20*.

★ ⑫ **Kaloko'eli Fishpond.** With its narrow rock walls connecting two points of the shore, Kaloko'eli is typical of the numerous fishponds that define southern Moloka'i. Many of them were built around the 13th century. This early type of aquaculture, particular to Hawai'i, exemplifies the ingenuity of precontact Hawaiians. One or more openings were left in the wall, where gates called *makaha* were installed. These gates allowed seawater and tiny fish to enter the enclosed pond but kept larger predators out. The tiny fish would then grow too big to get out. At one time there were 62 fishponds around Moloka'i's coast. ⊠ *Rte. 450, about 6 mi east of Kaunakakai*.

OFF THE
BEATEN
PATH

KAMAKOU PRESERVE – Tucked away on the slopes of Mt. Kamakou, Moloka'i's highest peak, the 2,774-acre preserve is a dazzling wonderland full of wet *'ōhi'a* (hardwood trees of the myrtle family, with red blossoms called *lehua* flowers) forests, rare bogs, and native trees and wildlife. Guided hikes, limited to eight people, are held on the first Saturday of each month. Reservations are required well in advance. You can visit the park without a tour, but you need a good four-wheel-drive vehicle, and the Nature Conservancy requests that you sign in at the office and get directions first. ⊠ *The Nature Conservancy, 23 Pueo Pl., Kualapu'u* ☎ 808/553–5236 ⊕ *www.nature.org* 🖼 *Free; donation suggested for guided hike, $10 members, $25 nonmembers, includes 1-yr membership*.

⑬ **Kamalō.** A natural harbor used by small cargo ships during the 19th century, this is also the site of the **Church of St. Joseph's,** a tiny white church built by Father Damien in the 1880s. The door is always unlocked. Slip inside and sign the guestbook. The congregation keeps this church in beautiful condition. ⊠ *Rte. 450, about 11 mi east of Kaunakakai, on* makai *side*.

NEED A
BREAK?

The best place to grab a snack or stock up on picnic supplies is the Neighborhood Store 'N Counter (⊠ Rte. 450, 16 mi east of Kaunakakai, Puko'o ☎ 808/ 558–8498). It's the only place on the East End where you can find essentials such as ice and bread, and not-so-essentials such as burgers and shakes.

GUIDED TOURS

Moloka'i Off-Road Tours and Taxi. Visit Hālawa Valley, Kalaupapa Lookout, Maunaloa town, and other points of interest in the comfort of an air-conditioned van on four- or six-hour tours. Pat and Alex Pua'a, your personal guides, will even help you mail a coconut back home. Tours start at $85 per person and usually begin at 9 AM. Charters are also available. ☎ 808/553–3369.

⓯ Puʻu O Hoku Ranch. A 14,000-acre private spread in the highlands of East Molokaʻi, Puʻu O Hoku was developed in the '30s by wealthy industrialist Paul Fagan. Route 450 cuts right through this rural gem with its green pastures and grazing horses and cattle. As you drive along, enjoy the splendid views of Maui and Lānaʻi. The small island off the coast is Mokuhoʻoniki, a humpback whale nursery where the military practiced bombing techniques during World War II. The ranch offers horseback trail rides, two large guest cottages, and a retreat facility for groups. ⊠ *Rte. 450 about 20 mi east of Kaunakakai* ☎ *808/558–8109* ⊕ *www.puuohoku.com.*

BEACHES

Molokaʻi's strange geography gives the island plenty of drama and spectacle along the shorelines but not so many places for seaside basking and bathing. The long North Shore consists mostly of towering cliffs that plunge directly into the sea. Much of the South Shore is enclosed by a huge reef that stands as far as a mile offshore and blunts the action of the waves. Within this reef you will find a thin strip of sand, but the water here is flat, shallow, and clouded with silt. This reef area is best suited to kayaking or learning how to windsurf.

The big, fat, sandy beaches lie along the West End. The largest of these—one of the largest in the Islands—is Pāpōhaku Beach, which adjoins a grassy park shaded by a grove of *kiawe* (mesquite) trees. These stretches of West End sand are generally unpopulated. ■ TIP→ **The solitude can be a delight, but it should also be a caution; the sea here can be treacherous.** At the East End, where the road hugs the sinuous shoreline, you encounter a number of pocket-size beaches in rocky coves, good for snorkeling. The road ends at Hālawa Valley with its unique double bay.

If you need beach gear, head to Molokaʻi Fish & Dive at the west end of Kaunakakai's one commercial strip. You can rent equipment (snorkels, boogie boards, kayaks) from Molokaʻi Outdoors, in the lobby of Hotel Molokaʻi.

All of Hawaiʻi's beaches are free and open to the public. None of the beaches on Molokaʻi have telephones or lifeguards and they're all under the jurisdiction of the **Department of Parks, Land and Natural Resources** (⊕ Box 153, Kaunakakai 96746 ☎ 808/553–1745).

West Molokaʻi

Molokaʻi's West End looks across a channel to the island of Oʻahu. Crescent-shaped, this cup of coastline holds the island's best sandy beaches as well as the most arid and sunny weather. Developers have envisioned resorts here and a few signs of this development dream mark the coast—good-looking condos, the Kaluakoʻi Resort (now closed), and some expensive ocean-view homes. Remember: all beaches are public property, even those that front these developments. Beaches below are listed from north to south.

Kawākiu Beach. Seclusion is the reason to come to this remote beach, accessible only by four-wheel drive or a 45-minute walk. ■ TIP→ **The**

white-sand beach is beautiful, but rocks and undertow can make swimming extremely dangerous at times, so use caution. ⊠ *Past Ke Nani Kai condos on Kaluako'i Rd., look for dirt road off to right. Park here and hike in or, with 4WD, drive along dirt road to beach* ☞ *No facilities.*

Kepuhi Beach. Kaluako'i Hotel is closed but nine holes of its golf course are open, and so is this half-mile of ivory white sand. The beach shines beautifully against the turquoise sea, black outcroppings of lava, and magenta bougainvillea flowers of the resort's landscaping. When the water is perfectly calm, lava ridges in the water make good snorkeling spots. With any surf at all, however, the water around these rocky places churns and foams, wiping out visibility and making it difficult to avoid being slammed into the jagged rocks. ⊠ *Kaluako'i Hotel and Golf Club, Kaluako'i Rd.* ☞ *Toilets, showers.*

Fodor'sChoice
★ **Pāpōhaku Beach.** One of the most sensational beaches in Hawai'i, Pāpōhaku is a 3-mi-long strip of light golden sand, the longest of its kind on the island. ■ TIP➔ Some places are too rocky for swimming, so look carefully before entering the water and go in only when the waves are small (generally in summer). There's so much sand here that Honolulu once purchased barge-loads in order to replenish Waikiki Beach. Moloka'i people laugh about the fact that gradually, year by year, the sea is returning all that sand to the place it's meant to be. A shady beach park just inland is the site of the Ka Hula Piko Festival of Hawaiian Music and Dance, held each year in May. The park is also a great sunset-facing spot for a rustic afternoon barbecue. ⊠ *Kaluako'i Rd.; 2 mi south of Kaluako'i Hotel and Golf Club* ☞ *Toilets, showers, picnic tables, grills/firepits.*

Kapukahehu Bay. Locals like to surf just out from this bay in a break called Dixie's or Dixie Maru. The sandy protected cove is usually completely deserted during the weekdays but can fill up when the surf is up. The water in the cove is clear and shallow with plenty of well-worn rocky areas. These conditions make for excellent snorkeling, swimming, and boogie boarding on calm days. ⊠ *Drive about 3½ mi south of Pāpōhaku Beach to end of Kaluako'i Rd.; beach-access sign points to parking lot* ☞ *No facilities.*

Central Moloka'i

The South Shore is mostly a huge, reef-walled pool of flat saltwater edged with a thin strip of gritty sand and stones, mangrove swamps, and the amazing system of fishponds constructed by the residents of ancient Moloka'i. From this shore you can look out across glassy water to see people standing on top of the sea—actually, way out on top of the reef—casting fishing lines into the distant waves. This is not a great area for beaches, but is interesting in its own right.

One Ali'i Beach Park. Clear, close views of Maui and Lāna'i across the Pailolo Channel dominate One Ali'i Beach Park (*One* is pronounced *o-nay*, not *won*), the only decent beach park on the island's south-central shore. Moloka'i folks gather here for family reunions and community celebrations; the park's tightly trimmed expanse of lawn could accommodate the entire island population. Swimming within the reef is perfectly safe, but don't expect to catch any waves. ✉ *Rte. 450, east of Hotel Molokaʻi* ☞ *Toilets, showers, picnic tables.*

East Molokaʻi

The East End unfolds as a coastal drive with turnouts for tiny cove beaches—good places for snorkeling, shore fishing, or scuba exploring. Rocky little Mokuhoʻoniki Island marks the eastern point of the island and serves as a nursery for humpback whales in the winter. The road loops around the East End, then descends and ends at Hālawa Valley.

> **KEEP IN MIND**
>
> Unlike protected shorelines such as Kāʻanapali on Maui, the coasts of Molokaʻi are exposed to rough sea channels and dangerous rip currents. The ocean tends to be calmer in the morning and in summer. No matter what the time, however, always study the sea before entering. Unless the water is placid and the wave action minimal, it's best to simply stay on shore or keep within touch of solid ground. And don't forget to protect yourself with sunblock. Cool breezes make it easy to underestimate the power of the sun.

Waialua Beach Park. This arched strip of golden sand, a roadside pull-off near mile marker 20, also goes by the name Twenty Mile Beach. The water here, protected by the flanks of the little bay, is often so clear and shallow (sometimes too shallow) that even from land you can watch fish swimming among the coral heads. ■ TIP➔ This is the most popular snorkeling spot on the island, a pleasant place to stop on the drive around the East End. ✉ *Drive east on Rte. 450 to mile marker 20* ☞ *No facilities.*

Hālawa Beach Park. The vigorous water that gouged the steep, spectacular Hālawa Valley, also carved out two bays side by side. Coarse sand and river rock has built up against the sea along the wide valley mouth, creating some protected pool areas that are good for wading or floating around. Most people come here just to hang out and absorb the beauty of this remote valley. Sometimes you'll see people surfing, but it's not wise to entrust your safety to the turbulent open sea along this coast, except on the calmest summer days. ✉ *Drive east on Rte. 450 to dead end* ☞ *Toilets.*

WATER ACTIVITIES & TOURS

Molokaʻi's unique shoreline topography limits opportunities for water sports. The North Shore is all sea cliffs; the South Shore is largely encased by a huge, taming reef. ■ TIP➔ Open-sea access at West End and East End beaches should be used with caution because seas are rough, especially in winter. Generally speaking, there's no one around—certainly not lifeguards—if you get into trouble. For this reason alone, guided excursions are recommended. At least be sure to ask for advice from outfitters or residents. Two kinds of water activities predominate: kayaking within the reef area, and open-sea excursions on charter boats, most of which tie up at Kaunakakai Wharf.

Boogie Boarding, Bodysurfing & Surfing

You rarely see people boogie boarding or bodysurfing on Moloka'i and the only sufing is for advanced wave riders only. One outfitter, **Moloka'i Outdoors** (⌧ Hotel Moloka'i Lobby ☎ 808/553–4227) rents boogie boards for $5 a day, $20 a week. The best spots for boogie boarding, when conditions are safe (occasional summer mornings), are the West End beaches, especially Kepuhi Beach at the old Kaluako'i Hotel. Or seek out waves at the East End around mile marker 20.

Two companies offer good surf–snorkel excursions—for advanced surfers only—with guides. One is **Moloka'i Fish and Dive** (⌧ Hotel Moloka'i Activities Desk ☎ 808/553–5926), the island's main resource for all outdoor activities. The other is **Fun Hogs Hawai'i** (⌧ Kaunakakai Wharf ☎ 808/567–6789), which takes people to good wave action on its charter boat *Ahi*.

Fishing

For Moloka'i people, as in days of yore, the ocean is more of a larder than a playground. It's common most any day to see residents fishing along the shoreline or atop the South Shore reef, using poles or lines. If you'd like to try your hand at this form of local industry, go to **Moloka'i Fish and Dive** (⌧ Hotel Moloka'i Activities Desk ☎ 808/553–5926) for gear and advice. You can also rent poles from **Moloka'i Outdoors** (⌧ Hotel Moloka'i Lobby ☎ 808/553–4227) for $5 a day.

Deep-sea fishing by charter boat is a great Moloka'i adventure. The sea channels here, though often rough and windy, provide gorgeous views of several islands. The big sport fish are plentiful in these waters, especially mahimahi, small marlin, and various kinds of tuna. Generally speaking, boat captains will customize the outing to your interests, share a lot of information about the island, and let you keep some or all of your catch. That's Moloka'i style—personal and friendly.

Boats & Charters

Alyce C. The six-passenger, 31-foot cruiser runs excellent sportfishing excursions. The cost is $400 for a nine-hour trip, $300 for five to six hours. Shared charters are available. Gear is provided. In the fish-rich waters of Moloka'i, it's a rare day when you don't snag at least one mahimahi. ⌧ *Kaunakakai Wharf* ☎ *808/558–8377* ⊕ *www.alycecsportfishing.com.*

Fun Hogs Hawai'i. Trim and speedy, the 27-foot flybridge sport-fishing boat named *Ahi* takes people out for half-day ($400), six-hour ($500), and full-day ($600) sportfishing excursions. Skipper Mike Holmes also provides one-way or round-trip journeys to Lāna'i, as well as (in winter only) sunset cruises. ⌧ *Kaunakakai Wharf* ☎ 808/567–6789.

Moloka'i Action Adventures. Walter Naki's Moloka'i roots go back forever, and he knows the island intimately. What's more, he has traveled (and fished) all over the globe, and he's a great talker. He will create customized fishing and hunting expeditions and gladly share his wealth of experience. His 21-foot Boston Whaler is usually to be seen at the mouth of Hālawa Valley, in the East End. ☎ *808/558–8184.*

Kayaking

Moloka'i's South Shore is enclosed and tamed by the largest reef system in the United States—an area of shallow, protected sea that stretches over 30 mi. This reef gives inexperienced kayakers an unusually safe, calm environment for shoreline exploring. ■ TIP➔ **Outside the reef, Moloka'i waters are often rough and treacherous. Kayakers out here should be strong, experienced, and cautious.**

Best Spots

The **South Shore Reef** area is superb for flat-water kayaking any day of the year. It's best to rent a kayak at Hotel Moloka'i and slide into the water right there, though another easy entry spot is Kaunakakai Wharf, either side. Get out in the morning before the wind picks up and paddle east, exploring the ancient Hawaiian fishponds. When you turn around to return, you'll usually get a push home by the wind, which blows strong and westerly along this shore in the afternoon.

Independent kayakers who are confident about testing their skills in rougher seas can launch at the West End of the island from **Hale O Lono Harbor** (at the end of a long dirt road from Maunaloa town). At the East End of the island, enter the water near mile marker 20 or beyond and explore in the direction of Mokuho'oniki Island. ■ TIP➔ **Kayaking anywhere outside the South Shore Reef is only safe on calm days in summer.**

Lessons & Equipment Rentals

Moloka'i Fish and Dive. At the west end of Kaunakakai's commercial strip, this all-around outfitter provides guided kayak excursions inside the South Shore Reef. One excursion paddles through a dense mangrove forest and explores a huge, hidden ancient fishpond. One bonus of going with guides: if the wind starts blowing hard, they can tow you back with their boat. The fee is $85 for the half-day trip. Check at the store (on Ala Mālama Street) for numerous other outdoor activities. ✉ *61 Ala Mālama St., Kaunakakai* ☎ *808/553–5926.*

Moloka'i Outdoors. This is the place—right on the shoreline in Central Moloka'i, 2 mi east of Kaunakai—to rent a kayak for exploring on your own. Kayaks rent for $12 to $15 an hour. Car racks and extra paddles are also available. ✉ *Hotel Moloka'i lobby* ☎ *808/553–4477.*

Sailing

Moloka'i is a place of strong predictable winds that make for good and sometimes rowdy sailing. The island views in every direction are stunning. Kaunakakai Wharf is the home base for all of the island's charter sailboats.

Moloka'i Charters. The 42-foot Cascade sloop *Satan's Doll* is your craft with Moloka'i Charters. The company arranges two-hour sails for $40 per person. Half-day sailing trips cost $50 per person, including soft drinks and snacks. One commendable trip is the sail to Lāna'i with stops for snorkeling. A minimum of four people is required, but shared charters can be arranged. ✉ *Kaunakakai Wharf* ☎ 808/553–5852.

Gypsy Sailing Adventures. The 33-plus-foot ocean-going catamaran *Star Gypsy* has a large salon, three staterooms, and a fully equipped galley. They do any kind of sailing you want—"any kind of adventure that's prudent and safe"—from two-hour explorations of Moloka'i's huge reef (stopping at otherwise inaccessible coves and beaches) to interisland cruising (Maui and Lāna'i). In summer, this company does two-day trips that explore the island's North Shore. Full days cost $500 to $750, depending on the amount of catering involved. Half days are $300. ✉ *Kaunakakai Wharf* ☎ 808/553–5852.

Scuba Diving

Moloka'i Fish and Dive is the only PADI-certified purveyor of scuba gear, training, and dive trips on Moloka'i. Shoreline access for divers is extremely limited, even nonexistent in winter. Boat diving is the way to go. Without guidance, visiting divers can easily find themselves in risky situations with wicked currents. Proper guidance, though, opens an undersea world rarely seen.

Moloka'i Fish and Dive. Tim and Susan Forsberg, owners, can fill you in on how to find dive sites, rent you the gear, or hook you up with one of their PADI-certified dive guides to take you to the island's best underwater spots. (They work with Fun Hogs Hawai'i's 27-foot power boat called *Ahi*.) They know the island's best blue holes and underwater cave systems, and they can take you swimming with hammerhead sharks. ✉ *61 Ala Mālama St., Kaunakakai* ☎ 808/553–5926.

Snorkeling

During the times when swimming is safe—mainly in summer—just about every beach on Moloka'i offers good snorkeling along the lava outcroppings in the island's clean and pristine waters.

Best Spots

Kepuhi Beach. In winter, the sea here is deadly. But in summer, this half-mile-long beach offers plenty of rocky nooks that swirl with sea life. The presence of outdoor showers is a bonus. Take Kaluako'i Road all the way to the West End. Park at Kaluako'i Resort (it's presently closed) and walk through the lobby area to the beach.

Waialua Beach Park. A thin curve of sand rims a sheltered little bay loaded with coral heads and aquatic life. The water here is shallow—sometimes so shallow that you bump into the underwater landscape—and it's crystal clear. To find this spot, head to the East End on Route 450, and pull off near mile marker 20. When the sea is calm, you'll find several other good snorkeling spots along this stretch of road.

Dive Tours & Equipment Rental

Rent snorkel sets from either of the two outfitters previously mentioned—Moloka'i Outdoors in the lobby of Hotel Moloka'i, or Moloka'i Fish and Dive in Kaunakakai. Rental fees are nominal—$6 a day. All the charter boats carry snorkel gear and include dive stops as part of the expedition.

Fun Hogs Hawai'i. Mike Holmes, captain of the 27-foot power boat *Ahi*, knows the island waters intimately, likes to have fun, and is willing to arrange any type of excursion—for example, one dedicated entirely to snorkeling. His 2½-hour snorkel trips leave early in the morning and explore rarely seen fish and turtle posts outside the reef west of the wharf. Bring your own food and drinks; the trips cost $65 per person. ⊠ *Kaunakakai Wharf* ☎ *808/567–6789.*

Moloka'i Charters. The 42-foot sloop *Satan's Doll* harnesses the power of wind to seek the island's best snorkel spots. The full-day snorkeling excursion to the island of Lāna'i costs $100 per person. Four passengers are the minimum they will carry. Soft drinks and a picnic lunch are included. ■ TIP➔ **You can generally count on rough seas for the afternoon return channel crossing.** ⊠ *Kaunakakai Wharf* ☎ *808/658–0559.*

Whale-Watching

Maui gets all the credit for the local wintering humpback whale population. Most people don't realize that the beautiful big cetaceans also come to Moloka'i. Mokuho'oniki Island at the East End serves as a whale nursery and playground, and the whales pass back and forth along the South Shore. This being Moloka'i, whale-watching here will never involve floating amid a group of boats all ogling the same whale.

Alyce C. Although this six-passenger sportfishing boat is usually busy hooking mahimahi and marlin, the captain gladly takes three-hour excursions to admire the humpback whales. The price is about $65 per person, depending on the number of passengers in the group. ⊠ *Kaunakakai Wharf* ☎ *808/558–8377* ⊕ *www.alycecsportfishing.com.*

Fun Hogs Hawai'i. The *Ahi*, a flybridge sportfishing boat, takes 2½-hour whale-watching trips in the morning from December to April. The cost is $65 per person. Bring your own snacks and drinks. ⊠ *Kaunakakai Wharf* ☎ *808/567–6789.*

Gypsy Sailing Adventures. Being a catamaran, the *Star Gypsy* can drift silently under sail and follow the whales without disturbing them. Captain Richard Messina and crew share a lot of knowledge about the whales and pride themselves on being ecologically-minded. The 2½-hour trip costs $75 and includes soft drinks and water. ⊠ *Kaunakakai Wharf* ☎ *808/658–0559.*

GOLF, HIKING & OTHER ADVENTURES

Biking

★ **Single-Track Trails at Moloka'i Ranch.** Moloka'i Ranch, headquartered in the small town of Maunaloa, has developed some of the best mountain-bike experiences in the world, compared favorably by enthusiasts to Moab and Hood River. Moloka'i Fish and Dive runs the activity desk at the Ranch, and has a well-stocked rental shop for mountain bikes and related two-wheel gear. With or without guides, you can head out from here to a complex network of trails that are rated like ski slopes according to their difficulty. Excursions can be super-challenging or as easy as a mild gravity ride over miles of twisty terrain down to the coast, with van transport back. ✉ *61 Ala Mālama St., Kaunakakai* ☎ *808/553–5926.*

Na'iwa Mountain Trails. Guides from Moloka'i Fish and Dive take biking extremists on a gorgeous but challenging adventure in Na'iwa—the remote central mountains—for convoluted forest courses, daredevil verticals (if you want), and exhilarating miles at the brink of the world's tallest sea cliffs. ✉ *61 Ala Mālama St., Kaunakakai* ☎ *808/553–5926.*

East End Trails. Moloka'i Bicycle will take mountain-bikers out to two-wheel the expansive East End spread of Pu'u O Hoku Ranch. You might ride along an eastern ridge rimming Hālawa Valley to four waterfalls and a remote pool for swimming, or pedal on sea cliffs to a secluded beach. ☎ *808/553–3931 Moloka'i Bicycle.*

Street biking on this island is a dream for peddlers who like to eat up the miles. Moloka'i's few roads are long, straight, and extremely rural. You can really stretch out and go for it—no traffic lights and most of the time no traffic.

If you don't happen to be one of those athletes who always travels with your own customized cycling tool, you can rent something from **Moloka'i Bicycle** (☎ 808/553–3931) in Kaunakakai. Another place to rent bikes is **Moloka'i Outdoors** (☎808/553–4227), based in the lobby of Hotel Moloka'i.

Golf

While the golf is good on Moloka'i, there isn't much of it—just two courses and a total of 27 holes.

Ironwood Hills Golf Course. Like the other 9-hole plantation era courses with which it shares lineage, Ironwood Hills is not for everyone. It helps if you like a bit of rugged history with your golf, and can handle the occasionally rugged conditions. On the plus side, most holes here offer lovely views of the ocean and the island of Lāna'i. Fairways are *kukuya* grass and run through pine, ironwood, and eucalyptus trees. Carts are rented, but there's not always someone there to rent you a cart—in which case, there's a wooden box for your green fee (honor system), and happy walking. ✉ *Kala'e Hwy., Kualapu'u* 🏌 *9 holes. 3088 yds. Par 35. Green Fee: $20* ☞ *Facilities: Putting green, golf carts, pull carts.*

★ **Kaluakoi Golf Course.** Kaluakoi Golf Course, associated with the Lodge at Moloka'i Ranch, has more ocean frontage than any other Hawai'i course. Ted Robinson (1976) was given a fantastic site and created some excellent holes, starting with the par-5 first, with the beach on the right from tee to green. The course, closed by former owners for financial reasons, reopened in 2002 after substantial refurbishing. The front nine is generally flat, never running far from the sea, and providing dramatic views of the island of O'ahu. The back nine winds through rolling hills and dense forest. ✉ *Moloka'i Ranch, Maunaloa* ☎ *808/552–0255*

⊕ *www.molokairanch.com* 🏌 *18 holes. 6200 yds. Par 72. Green Fee: $70* ☞ *Facilities: Driving range, putting green, golf carts, rental clubs.*

Hiking

Rural and rugged, Moloka'i is an excellent place for hiking. Roads and developments are few, so the outdoors is always beckoning. The island is steep, so hikes often combine spectacular views with hearty physical exertion. Because the island is small, you can traverse quite a bit of it on foot and come away with the feeling of really knowing the place. And you won't see many other people around. Most of the time, it's just you and the *'aina* (the land).

Kalaupapa Trail. You can make a day of hiking down to Kalaupapa Peninsula and back by means of a 3-mi, 26-switchback trail. The trail is nearly vertical, traversing the face of some of the highest sea cliffs in the world. *See* A Tale of Tragedy & Triumph *on pp. 497–500 for more information.*

Kamakou Preserve. Four-wheel drive is essential for this half-day (minimum) journey into the Moloka'i highlands. The Nature Conservancy of Hawai'i manages the 2,774-acre Kamakou Preserve, one of the last stands of Hawai'i's native plants and birds. A long, rough dirt road, that begins not far from Kaunakakai town, leads to the preserve. The road is not marked, so you must check in with the **Nature Conservancy's Moloka'i office** (✉ At Moloka'i Industrial Park about 3 mi west of Kaunkakai, 23 Pueo Pl. ☎ 808/553–5236 ⊕ www.nature.org), for directions. Let them know that you plan to visit the preserve, and pick up the informative 24-page brochure with trail maps.

On your way up to the preserve, be sure to stop at Waikolu Overlook, which gives a head-spinning view into a precipitous North Shore canyon. Once inside the preserve, various trails are clearly marked. The trail of choice—and you can drive right to it—is the 1½-mi boardwalk trail through Pēpē'ōpae Bog, an ecological treasure trove. Organic deposits here date back at least 10,000 years, and the plants are undisturbed natives. This is the true landscape of prediscovery Hawai'i. It's a mean trek; you have to be tough, nimble, and reverential all at the same time. ■ TIP→ Wear long pants and bring rain gear. Your shoes ought to provide good traction on a slippery, narrow boardwalk.

Kawela Cul-de-Sacs. Just east of Kaunakakai, three streets—Kawela One, Two, and Three—jut up the mountainside from the Kamehameha V Highway. These roads end in cul-de-sacs that are also informal trailheads. Rough dirt roads work their way from here to the top of the mountain. The lower slopes are dry, rocky, steep, and austere. (It's good to start in the cool of the early morning.) A hiker in good condition can get all the way up into the high forest in two or three hours. There's no park ranger and no water fountain—these are not for the casual stroller. But if you're prepared for the challenge, you will be well rewarded.

Guided Hikes

Historical Hikes of West Moloka'i. This company has six guided hikes, ranging from two to six hours. The outings focus on Moloka'i's cultural past taking you to sites such as an ancient quarry, an early fishing village, or high sea cliffs where Hawaiian chiefs played games during the traditional *Makahiki* (harvest festival) season. Backpacks are provided, as is lunch on intermediate and advanced hikes. Guides Lawrence and Catherine Aki also run A Hawaiian Getaway vacation rental. ✉ *The Lodge at Moloka'i Ranch Activity Desk, Maunaloa Hwy., Maunaloa* ☎ *808/552–2797, 808/553–9803, or 800/274–9303* ⊕ *www.gomolokai.com* ✉ *$45–$125.*

Hālawa Valley Cultural Waterfall Hike. Hālawa is a gorgeous, steep-walled valley carved by two rivers and rich in history. Site of what could be the earliest Polynesian settlement in Hawai'i, Hālawa sustained island culture with its ingeniously designed *lo'i*, or taro fields. In the 1960s the valley became derelict and increasingly mysterious. Now Hawaiian families are restoring the *lo'i* and walking people through the valley, which includes two-thirds of Moloka'i's *luakini heiau* (sacred temples). Half-day visits, morning or afternoon, cost $75 (less for children) and support the work of restoration. Call ahead to visit any day at 9:30 AM or 2 PM. Bring water, food, and insect repellent. ☎ *808/553–9803 or 808/274–9303* ⊕ *www.gomolokai.com* ✉ *$75.*

Horseback Riding

Pu'u O Hoku Ranch. Set on the prow of the island's Maui-facing East End, this ranch keeps a stable of magnificent, amiable horses that are available for trail rides starting at $55 an hour. The peak experience is a four-hour beach ride ($120) that culminates at a secluded cove where the horses are happy to swim, rider and all. Bring your own lunch. This is a good experience for people with little or no horse skills. They match skill levels with appropriate steeds. ✉ *Rte. 450, 20 mi east of Kaunakakai* ☎ *808/558–8109* ⊕ *www.puuohoku.com.*

SHOPPING

Moloka'i has one main commercial area: Ala Mālama Street in Kaunakakai. There are no department stores or shopping malls, and the clothing available is typical island wear. A handful of family-run businesses line the main drag of Maunaloa, a rural plantation town.

Most stores in Kaunakakai are open Monday through Saturday between 9 and 6. In Maunaloa most shops close by 4 in the afternoon and all day Sunday.

Arts & Crafts

The **Big Wind Kite Factory and Plantation Gallery** (✉ 120 Maunaloa Hwy., Maunaloa ☎ 808/552–2364) has custom-made appliquéd kites you can fly or display. Designs range from hula girls to tropical fish. Also in stock are kite-making kits, paper kites, minikites, and wind socks. Ask to go on the factory tour, or take a free kite-flying lesson. The gallery is intermingled with the kite shop and carries everything from locally made crafts to Hawaiian books and CDs, sunglasses, and incense.

Kamakana Fine Arts Gallery (✉ 110 Ala Mālama St., Kaunakakai ☎ 808/553–8520) only represents artists who live on the island, including world-class talent in photography, wood carving, ceramics, and Hawaiian musical instruments. This business actively supports the local community by showcasing talents that might otherwise go undiscovered. It's above American Savings Bank.

Clothing

Casual, knockabout island wear is sold at **Imports Gift Shop** (✉ 82 Ala Mālama St., Kaunakakai ☎ 808/553–5734), across from Kanemitsu Bakery. **Moloka'i Island Creations** (✉ 62 Ala Mālama St., Kaunakakai ☎ 808/553–5926) carries exclusive swimwear, beach cover-ups, sun hats, and tank tops. **Moloka'i Surf** (✉ 130 Kamehameha V Hwy., Kaunakakai ☎ 808/553–5093) is known for its wide selection of Moloka'i T-shirts, swimwear, and sports clothing.

Grocery Stores

Friendly Market Center (✉ 90 Ala Mālama St., Kaunakakai ☎ 808/553–5595) is the best-stocked supermarket on the island. Its slogan—"Your family store on Moloka'i"—is truly credible: hats, T-shirts, and sun-and-surf essentials keep company with fresh produce, meat, groceries, liquor, and sundries. Locals say the food is fresher here than at the other major supermarket in town. It's open weekdays 8:30–8:30 and Saturday 8:30–6:30.

Victuals and travel essentials are available at the **Maunaloa General Store** (✉ 200 Maunaloa Hwy., Maunaloa ☎ 808/552–2346). Open Monday–Saturday 8 to 6, it's convenient for guests staying at the nearby condos of the Kaluako'i Resort area. The store sells meat, produce, dry goods, drinks, and all the little things you find in a general store.

Misaki's Inc. (✉ 78 Ala Mālama St., Kaunakakai ☎ 808/553–5505) is a grocery with authentic island allure. It has been in business since 1922. Pick up housewares and beverages here, as well as your food staples, Monday through Saturday 8:30 to 8:30, and Sunday 9 to noon.

Don't let the name **Moloka'i Wines 'n' Spirits** (✉ 77 Ala Mālama St., Kaunakakai ☎ 808/553–5009) fool you. Along with a surprisingly good selection of fine wines and liquors, the store also carries gourmet cheeses and snacks. It's open Sunday through Thursday 9 AM to 10 PM, Friday and Saturday until 10:30.

Jewelry

Imports Gift Shop (✉ 82 Ala Mālama St., Kaunakakai ☎ 808/553–5734) sells a decent collection of 14-karat-gold chains, rings, earrings, and bracelets, plus a jumble of Hawaiian quilts, pillows, books, and postcards. It also carries Hawaiian heirloom jewelry, a unique style of jewelry, inspired by popular Victorian pieces, that has been crafted in Hawai'i since the late 1800s. These stunning gold pieces are made to order with your Hawaiian name inscribed on them.

Moloka'i Island Creations (✉ 62 Ala Mālama St., Kaunakakai ☎ 808/553–5926) carries its own unique line of jewelry, including sea opal, coral, and sterling silver, as well as other gifts and resort wear.

Sporting Goods

Moloka'i Bicycle (✉ 80 Mohala St., Kaunakakai ☎ 808/553–3931 or 800/709–2453 ⊕ www.bikehawaii.com/molokaibicycle) rents and sells mountain and road bikes as well as jogging strollers, kids' trailers, helmets, and racks. It supplies maps and information on biking and hiking and will drop off and pick up equipment for a fee nearly anywhere on the island. Call or stop by after 4 PM to arrange what you need.

Moloka'i Fish and Dive (✉ 61 Ala Mālama St., Kaunakakai ☎ 808/553–5926) is *the* source for sporting needs, from snorkel rentals to free and friendly advice. These folks handle all activities for the Lodge at Moloka'i Ranch. This is also a good place to pick up original-design Moloka'i T-shirts and gifts.

ENTERTAINMENT & NIGHTLIFE

Local nightlife consists mainly of gathering with friends and family, sipping a few cold ones, strumming 'ukuleles and guitars, singing old songs, and talking story. Still, there are a few ways to kick up your heels for a festive night out. Pick up a copy of the weekly *Moloka'i Dispatch* and see if there's a church supper or square dance. The bar at the Hotel Moloka'i is always a good place to drink by the tiki torches. Most nights they have some kind of live music by island performers. The "Aloha Friday" weekly gathering here, 4 to 6 PM, always attracts a couple dozen old-timers with guitars and 'ukuleles. This impromptu, feel-good event is a peak experience for any Moloka'i trip. The Paddler's Inn in Kaunakakai has live music every night. The bar stays open until 2 AM on the weekends.

Movie fans can head to **Maunaloa Town Cinemas** (✉ Maunaloa Hwy., Maunaloa ☎ 808/552–2707). Folks from all around Moloka'i come here nightly for current blockbusters.

WHERE TO EAT

During a week's stay, you might easily hit all the dining spots worth a visit, then return to your favorites for a second round. The dining scene is fun because it's a microcosm of Hawai'i's diverse cultures. You can find locally grown vegetarian foods, spicy Filipino cuisine, and Hawaiian fish with a Japanese influence—such as 'ahi or *aku* (types of tuna), mullet, and moonfish grilled, sautéed, or mixed with seaweed and eaten raw as *poke* (marinated raw fish). Most eating establishments are on Ala Mālama Street in Kaunakakai, with pizza, pasta, and ribs only a block away. What's more, the price is right.

WHAT IT COSTS				
$$$$	**$$$**	**$$**	**$**	**¢**
RESTAURANTS over $35	$27–$35	$18–$26	$10–$17	under $10

Prices are for a main course at dinner.

West Moloka'i

★ **$-$$$**   ✗ **Maunaloa Room.** Order haute cuisine appetizers such as coconut-crusted shrimp, Moloka'i 'opihi (a crunchy limpet), or *lumpia* (egg roll) stuffed with *kālua* duck (roasted in an underground oven). Entrées follow a steak-and-seafood theme, and the catch of the day can be prepared with *alae* (a pale-orange salt found in Moloka'i and Kaua'i). Inside, wagon-wheel chandeliers with electric candles typify the hotel restaurant's ranch fixtures. A dinner on the outside deck can't be beat. ✉ *The Lodge at Moloka'i Ranch, 8 Maunaloa Hwy., Maunaloa* ☎ *808/ 660–2725* ▭ *AE, MC, V. $14–$31.*

Central Moloka'i

$–$$ ✕ **Oceanfront Dining Room.** This is *the* place to hang out on Moloka'i. Locals relax at the bar listening to live music on weekends, or they come in for theme-night dinners (posters around town tell you what's in store for the week). Prime-rib specials on Friday and Saturday nights draw a crowd. Try the broiled baby back ribs smothered in barbecue sauce. Every Friday from 4 to 6 PM Moloka'i's *kūpuna* (old-timers) bring their instruments here for a lively Hawaiian jam session, a wonderful experience of grassroots aloha spirit. ✉ *Hotel Moloka'i, Kamehameha V Hwy., Kaunakakai* ☎ *808/553–5347* ▭ *AE, DC, MC, V. $12–$18.*

¢–$$ ✕ **Kamuela's Cookhouse.** Kamuela's is the only eatery in rural Kualapu'u. From the outside, this laid-back diner looks like a little plantation house; inside, paintings of hula dancers and island scenes enhance the green-and-white furnishings. Typical fare is a plate of chicken or pork *katsu* served with rice. They shut down the grill by 2 PM, so unless you order takeout ahead of time, this is not a dinner option. It's across the street from the Kualapu'u Market. ✉ *Farrington Hwy., 1 block west of Rte. 470, Kulapūu* ☎ *808/567–9655* ▭ *No credit cards* ☉ *Closed Mon. No dinner. $8–$20.*

¢–$$ ✕ **Moloka'i Pizza Cafe.** A cheerful, busy restaurant, Moloka'i Pizza is a popular gathering spot for families. Pizza, sandwiches, salads, pasta, fresh fish, and homemade pies are simply prepared and tasty. Kids keep busy on a few little coin-operated rides. ✉ *Kaunakakai Pl. on Wharf Rd., Kaunakakai* ☎ *808/553–3288* ▭ *No credit cards. $8–$19.*

¢–$ ✕ **Paddler's Inn.** A roomy, comfortable restaurant with an extensive menu, Paddler's Inn is right in Kaunakakai town but on the ocean side of Kamehameha V Highway. There are three eating areas—standard restaurant seating, a shady cool bar, and an open-air courtyard where you can sit at a counter eating raw fish and drinking beer while getting cooled with spray from an overhead misting system. The food is a blend of island-style and standard American fare (fresh *poke* every day; a prime-rib special every Friday night). There's live entertainment every night. ✉ *10 Mohala St., Kaunakakai* ☎ *808/553–5256* ▭ *AE, DC, MC, V. $5–$14.*

¢ ✕ **Kanemitsu Bakery and Restaurant.** Come here for a taste of *lavosh,* a

Fodor'sChoice flatbread flavored with sesame, taro, Maui onion, Parmesan cheese, or ★ jalapeño. Or try the round Moloka'i bread—a sweet, pan-style white loaf that makes excellent cinnamon toast. ✉ *79 Ala Mālama St., Kaunakakai* ☎ *808/553–5855* ▭ *No credit cards* ☉ *Closed Tues. $4–$8.*

¢ ✕ **Moloka'i Drive Inn.** Fast food Moloka'i-style is served at a walk-up counter. Hot dogs, fries, and sundaes are on the menu, but residents usually choose the foods they grew up on, such as *saimin,* plate lunches, shave ice (snow cone), and the beloved *loco moco* (rice topped with a hamburger and a fried egg, covered in gravy). ✉ *857 Ala Mālama St., Kaunakakai* ☎ *808/553–5655* ☰ *No credit cards. $3–$9.*

¢ ✕ **Outpost Natural Foods.** A well-stocked store, Outpost is the heart of Moloka'i's health-food community. At the counter you can get fresh juices and delicious sandwiches geared toward the vegetarian palate. It's a great place to pick up local produce and all the ingredients you need for a picnic lunch. ✉ *70 Makaena St., Kaunakakai* ☎ *808/553–3377* ☰ *AE, MC, V* ☾ *Closed Sat. No dinner. $3–$5.*

¢ ✕ **Oviedo's.** This modest lunch counter specializes in *adobos* (stews) with traditional Filipino spices and sauces. Try the tripe, pork, or beef adobo for a real taste of tradition. The locals say that Oviedo's makes the best roast pork in the state. You can eat in or take out. ✉ *145 Ala Mālama St., Kaunakakai* ☎ *808/553–5014* ☰ *No credit cards* ☾ *No dinner. $8–$9.*

¢ ✕ **Sundown Deli.** This clean little rose-color deli focuses on freshly made takeout food. Sandwiches come on half a dozen types of bread, and the Portuguese bean soup and chowders are rich and filling. Specials, such as vegetarian quiche, change daily. ✉ *145 Ala Mālama St., Kaunakakai* ☎ *808/553–3713* ☰ *No credit cards* ☾ *Closed Sun. No dinner. $4–$8.*

WHERE TO STAY

The coastline along the West End has ocean-view condominium units and luxury homes available as vacation rentals. In the hills above, little Maunaloa town offers the superb Lodge at Moloka'i Ranch and the oddly luxurious seaside tents at Kaupoa Beach Village. Central Moloka'i has B&Bs with extremely helpful owners, two seaside condominiums, and the icon of the island—Hotel Moloka'i. The only lodgings on the East End are some guest cottages in magical settings.

	WHAT IT COSTS				
	$$$$	**$$$**	**$$**	**$**	**¢**
HOTELS	over $340	$261–$340	$181–$260	$100–$180	under $100

Hotel prices are for two people in a standard double room in high season. Condo price categories reflect studio and one-bedroom rates.

West Moloka'i

Hotels & Resorts

$$$$ 🏠 **The Lodge at Moloka'i Ranch.** Moloka'i's plushest accommodation is Fodor'sChoice this Old West–style lodge. Ranching memorabilia and local artwork ★ adorn guest-room walls, with each of the 22 suites individually decorated. All rooms have private lānai and some have skylights. An impressive stone fireplace warms up the central Great Room, and there's a games room for pleasant socializing during cool Moloka'i evenings. Pathways and a greenhouse delineate the grounds. Spa facilities include massage rooms, a juice bar, and men's and women's saunas. ✉ *Maunaloa Hwy., Box 259, Maunaloa 96770* ☎ *888/627–8082* ⊕ *www. molokairanch.com* ⇆ *22 rooms* ⚒ *Restaurant, in-room safes, refrig-*

erators, in-room data ports, pool, gym, sauna, spa, beach, boating, fishing, mountain bikes, billiards, hiking, horseback riding, horseshoes, bar, lounge, library, recreation room, children's programs (ages 5–12) ☞ *AE, D, MC, V. $418–$508.*

★ **$$$–$$$$** ⊡ **Kaupoa Beach Village.** This dream-come-true campground consists of two-bedroom canvas bungalows, mounted on wooden platforms. Don't let the presence of ecotravelers fool you—the rooms are unexpectedly luxurious, with queen-size beds, self-composting flush toilets, and private outdoor showers. Breakfast, lunch, and dinner are served family-style in an open-air pavilion (price not included in room rate). Extensive activities, including snorkeling, kayaking, clay shooting, and mountain biking, are available. ✉ *Maunaloa Hwy., Box 259, Maunaloa 96770* ☎ *888/627–8082* ⊕ *www.molokairanch.com* ⊃ *40 tents* ⚇ *Restaurant, fans, beach, snorkeling, boating, mountain bikes, hiking, horseback riding, airport shuttle; no A/C, no room phones, no room TVs* ☞ *AE, D, MC, V. $280–$370.*

Condos & Vacation Rentals

$$–$$$$ ⊡ **Hale Aloha.** This spacious four-bedroom, three-bath vacation rental is on 12 secluded acres, has ocean views, and is surrounded by woodlands and an orchard. Wood floors stretch the length of the house, connecting the two kitchens. A wraparound porch leads to a gazebo-covered hot tub. Rooms are open and simple, with wood-beam ceilings. The managers of this property, 1-800-Molokai, also handle a number of other West End condos for as little as $100 a night. ✉ *Kaluako'i Rd., Box 20, Maunaloa 96770* ☎ *800/665–6524 or 808/552–2222* ⊕ *www.1-800-molokai.com* ⊃ *1 house* ⚇ *Fans, kitchen, cable TV, in-room VCRs, pool, hot tub; no A/C* ☞ *AE, MC, V. $214–$500.*

★ **¢–$$$** ⊡ **Paniolo Hale.** Perched high on a ledge overlooking the beach, Paniolo Hale is one of Moloka'i's best condominium properties. Some units have spectacular ocean views. Studios and one- or two-bedroom units all have beautiful screened lānai and well-equipped kitchens. Rooms are tidy and simple. The property is adjacent to the Kaluako'i Golf Course and a stone's throw from the Kaluako'i Hotel and Golf Club. ✉ *Lio Pl., Box 1979, Kaunakai 96748* ☎ *808/553–8334 or 800/367–2984* ⊟ *808/553–3783* ⊕ *www.molokai-vacation-rental.com* ⊃ *77 condos* ⚇ *Kitchens, microwaves, 18-hole golf course, golf privileges, pool, paddle tennis* ☞ *AE, MC, V. $95–$275.*

¢–$$ ⊡ **Kaluako'i Villas.** Studios and one-bedroom ocean-view suites are decorated in blue and mauve, with island-style art, rattan furnishings, and private lānai. Units are spread out in 21 two-story buildings covering 29 acres, adjacent to the now defunct Kaluako'i Resort. The view to-

> **SPAS**
>
> **Moloka'i Lomi Massage.** Allana Noury has been studying natural medicine for more than 30 years and is a licensed massage therapist, herbalist, and naturopathic physician. Ask for a traditional Hawaiian *lomi lomi* treatment. A 30-minute massage is $35; one hour is $55. It's just across the street from the Friendly Market in Kaunakakai. ✉ *107 Ala Mālama, Kaunakakai* ☎ *808/553–8034.*

ward the ocean looks across the newly revived golf course. The seclusion and sunsets make this a great find. ✉ *1131 Kaluako'i Rd., Box 200, Maunaloa 96770* ☎ *808/552–2721 or 800/367–5004* 🖷 *808/552–2201* ⊕ *www.castleresorts.com* 🛏 *47 units, 2 cottages* ♻ *Fans, kitchens, in-room VCRs, 18-hole golf course, pool, beach, shops; no A/C* ▤ *AE, MC, V.* $75–$200.

¢–$ 🏨 **Ke Nani Kai.** These pleasant one- and two-bedroom condo units have ocean views and use of the facilities at the former Kaluako'i Hotel and Golf Club. Furnished lānai have flower-laden trellises, and the spacious interiors are decorated with rattans and pastels. Each unit has a washer-dryer unit and a fully equipped kitchen. The beach is a five-minute walk away. ✉ *Kaluako'i Rd., Box 289, Maunaloa 96770* ☎ *808/553–8334 or 800/367–2984* 🖷 *808/553–3784* ⊕ *www.molokai-vacation-rental. com* 🛏 *120 units (22 rentals)* ♻ *Fans, kitchens, cable TV, 18-hole golf course, 2 tennis courts, pool, laundry facilities; no A/C* ▤ *AE, D, DC, MC, V.* $95–$150.

Central Moloka'i

Hotels & Resorts

$ 🏨 **Hotel Moloka'i.** Friendly staff members here embody the aloha spirit.

FodorsChoice Low-slung Polynesian-style buildings with wood roof shingles are set

★ waterside. Simple, tropical furnishings with white rattan accents fill the rooms, and a basket swing awaits on the lānai. The Oceanfront Dining Room serves breakfast, lunch, dinner, and libations—with entertainment on weekend nights. Ask about deals in conjunction with airlines and rental-car companies when you make your reservation. ✉ *Kamehameha V Hwy., Box 1020, Kaunakakai 96748* ☎ *808/553–5347* 🖷 *808/553–5047* ⊕ *www.hotelmolokai.com* 🛏 *45 rooms* ♻ *Restaurant, fans, some kitchenettes, cable TV, pool, lounge, laundry facilities; no A/C* ▤*AE, D, DC, MC, V.* $100–$160.

Condos & B&Bs

$ 🏨**Moloka'i Shores.** Every room in this oceanfront, three-story condominium complex has a view of the water. One-bedroom, one-bath units or two-bedroom, two-bath units all have full kitchens and furnished lānai, which look out on 4 acres of manicured lawns with picnic tables. There's a great view of Lāna'i in the distance. ✉ *1000 Kamehameha V Hwy., Box 1887, Kaunakakai 96748* ☎ *808/553–5954 or 800/535–0085* 🖷*800/633–5085* ⊕ *www.marcresorts.com* 🛏 *100 units* ♻ *Fans, kitchens, cable TV, pool, shuffleboard; no A/C* ▤*AE, D, MC, V.* $129.

¢–$ 🏨 **Wavecrest.** This oceanfront condominium complex is convenient if you want to explore the east side of the island—it's 3 mi east of Kaunakakai. Individually decorated one- and two-

---

CONDO COMFORTS

Friendly Market Center (✉ 93 Ala Mālama St., Kaunakakai ☎ 808/553–5595) is the best-stocked supermarket on the island. **Misaki's Inc.** (✉ 78 Ala Mālama St., Kaunakakai ☎ 808/553–5505) is a good spot for housewares, beverages, and food staples. **Moloka'i Wines 'n' Spirits** (✉ 77 Ala Mālama St., Kaunakakai ☎ 808/553–5009) carries a good selection of fine wines and liquors, as well as gourmet cheese and snacks.

bedroom units have full kitchens. Each has a furnished lānai, some with views of Maui and Lāna'i. Be sure to ask for an updated unit when you make your reservation. The shallow water here is bad for swimming but good for fishing. ⊠ *Rte. 450 near mile marker 13* ⌂ *Friendly Isle Realty, 75 Ala Mālama, Kaunakakai 96748* ☎ *808/553–3666 or 800/600– 4158* 📠 *808/553–3867* ⊕ *www.molokairesorts.com* ↪ *126 units* ⚒ *Fans, kitchens, 2 tennis courts, pool, beach, shuffleboard; no A/C* ▤ *V. $85–$125.*

East Moloka'i

B&Bs & Vacation Rentals

$ ⛺ **Dunbar Beachfront Cottages.** These two spotlessly clean two-bedroom, one-bath cottages with complete kitchens—each with its own secluded beach—are set about ¼ mi apart. The beach is good for swimming and snorkeling during the summer months and great for whale-watching in winter. Covered lānai have panoramic vistas of Maui, Lāna'i, and Kaho'olawe across the ocean. ⊠ *King Kamehameha V Hwy., mile marker 18, HC01, Box 901, Kauanakakai 96748* ☎ *808/558–8153 or 800/673–0520* 📠 *808/558–8153* ⊕ *www.molokai-beachfront-cottages. com* ↪ *2 cottages* ⚒ *BBQ, fans, kitchens, in-room VCRs, beach; no A/C, no smoking* ▤ *No credit cards. $170, 3-night min.*

$ ⛺ **Pu'u O Hoku Ranch.** At the east end of Moloka'i, near mile marker 25, lie these three ocean-view accommodations, on 14,000 isolated acres of pastures and forest. One country cottage has two bedrooms, basic wicker furnishings, and *lau hala* (natural fiber) woven matting on the floors. An airy four-bedroom cottage has a small deck and a somewhat Balinese air. For large groups—family reunions, for example—the Ranch has a lodge with 11 rooms, nine bathrooms, and a large kitchen. The full lodge goes for $1,250 nightly (rooms are not available on an individual basis). Inquire about horseback riding on the property. ⊠ *Rte. 450, Box 1889, Kaunakakai 96748* ☎ *808/558–8109* 📠 *808/558– 8100* ⊕ *www.puuohoku.com* ↪ *1 2-bedroom cottage, 1 4-bedroom cottage, 11 rooms in lodge* ⚒ *Kitchens, pool, hiking, horseback riding; no A/C* ▤ *MC, V. $140.*

¢–$ ⛺ **Kamalō Plantation Cottage and Moanui Beach House.** Both of these Polynesian-style cottages have a fully equipped kitchen, living room, dining room, and deck. Kamalō is at the base of a mountain and sleeps two. Moanui sleeps four and has a TV and VCR. It's on a good snorkeling beach and has great views from its huge deck. Homegrown fruit and fresh-baked bread are provided for breakfast at both cottages. ⊠ *East of Kaunakakai off Rte. 450* ⌂ *HC 01, Box 300, Kaunakakai 96748* ☎ *808/558–8236* ⊕ *www.molokai.com/kamalo* ↪ *2 cottages* ⚒ *Fans, kitchens; no A/C* ▤ *No credit cards. $95–$150.*

¢ ⛺ **Honomuni House.** This cottage sits on an acre of tropical gardens that are complemented by waterfalls and a freshwater stream. The rental can sleep up to four and includes one bedroom, one bath, a large living-dining room with pullout couch, and a kitchen. An outdoor shower with hot water is an added bonus. It's 17 mi east of Kaunakakai on Route 450. ⊠ *Rte. 450, HC 1, Box 700, Kaunakakai 96748* ☎ *808/558–8383* ↪ *1 house* ⚒ *Kitchen; no A/C, no room TVs* ▤ *No credit cards. $85 per night; $550 per week.*

MOLOKA'I ESSENTIALS

Transportation

BY AIR

If you're flying in from the mainland United States, you must first make a stop in Honolulu. From there, it's a 25-minute trip to the Friendly Isle.

CARRIERS Island Air, the puddle-jumper arm of Aloha Airlines, provides daily flights between Moloka'i and O'ahu or Maui on its 37-passenger de Haviland Dash-8 aircrafts. Pacific Wings operates chartered flights of its nine-passenger Cessna between O'ahu and Moloka'i.

If you fly into the airstrip at Kalaupapa, your arrival should coincide with one of the authorized ground tours of the area. Otherwise you'll be asked to leave. Pacific Wings and Moloka'i Air Shuttle fly from Honolulu to Kalaupapa. Paragon Air runs charter flights from Maui to Kalaupapa.

Island Air ☎ 800/323-3345 ⊕ www.islandair.com. **Moloka'i Air Shuttle** ☎ 808/567-6847 in Honolulu. **Pacific Wings** ☎ 808/873-0877 or 888/575-4546 ⊕ www.pacificwings.com.

AIRPORTS Moloka'i's transportation hub is Ho'olehua Airport, a tiny airstrip 8 mi west of Kaunakakai and about 18 mi east of Maunaloa. An even smaller airstrip serves the little community of Kalaupapa on the North Shore.

Ho'olehua Airport ☎ 808/567-6140. **Kalaupapa Airfield** ☎ 808/567-6331.

TO & FROM THE AIRPORT From Ho'olehua Airport, it takes about 10 minutes to reach Kaunakakai and 25 minutes to reach the West End of the island by car. Since there's no rush hour, traffic won't be a problem. There's no public bus.

Shuttle service for two passengers costs about $18 from Ho'olehua Airport to Kaunakakai. A trip to Moloka'i Ranch costs $28, divided by the number of passengers. For shuttle service, call Moloka'i Off-Road Tours and Taxi or Molokai Outdoors.

Moloka'i Off-Road Tours and Taxi ☎ 808/553-3369. **Moloka'i Outdoors** ☎ 808/553-4227 ⊕ www.molokai-outdoors.com.

BY CAR

If you want to explore Moloka'i from one end to the other, it's best to rent a car. With just a few main roads to choose from, it's a snap to drive around here.

The gas stations are in Kaunakakai and Maunaloa. When you park your car, be sure to lock it—thefts do occur. Drivers must wear seat belts or risk a $75 fine. Children under three must ride in a federally approved child passenger restraint device, easily leased at the rental agency. Ask your rental agent for a free *Moloka'i Drive Guide.*

CAR RENTAL Budget maintains a counter near the baggage-claim area at the airport. Dollar also has offices at Ho'olehua Airport, and your rental car can be picked up in the parking lot. Expect to pay $40–$50 per day for a standard compact and $50–$70 for a midsize car. Rates are seasonal and may run higher during the peak winter months. It's best to make arrangements in advance. If you're flying on Island Air or Hawaiian Airlines, see whether fly-drive package deals are available—you might luck out on a less-expensive rate. Hotels and outfitters might also offer packages.

Locally owned Island Kine Rent-a-Car offers airport or hotel pickup and sticks to one rate year-round for vehicles in a broad spectrum from two- and four-wheel drives to 15-passenger vans. The same is true for Moloka'i Rentacar, located right on the main street in Kaunakakai.

🚗 Major Agencies **Budget** ☎ 808/451-3600 or 800/527-7000 ⊕ www.budget.com. **Dollar** ☎ 808/567-6156 or 800/367-7006 ⊕ www.dollar.com.

🚗 Local Agencies **Island Kine Rent-a-Car** ☎ 808/553-5242 ⊕ www.molokai-car-rental.com. **Moloka'i Rentacar** ✉ 82 Ala Mālama, Kaunakakai ☎ 808/553-3929 🖨 808/553-9808.

BY FERRY

The Moloka'i Ferry crosses the channel every day between Lahaina (Maui) and Kaunakakai, making it easy for West Maui visitors to put Moloka'i on their itineraries. The 1½-hour trip takes passengers but not cars, so arrange ahead of time for a car rental or tour at the arrival point. The easiest way to do this is to contact Moloka'i Outdoors, who will arrange your transportation and lodgings. Tack this trek onto the end of a vacation in West Maui.

🚢 **Moloka'i Ferry** ☎ 808/667-2585 ⊕ www.molokaiferry.com.

Contacts & Resources

EMERGENCIES

Round-the-clock medical attention is available at Moloka'i General Hospital. Severe cases or emergencies are often airlifted to Honolulu.

🚨 Emergency Services **Ambulance and general emergencies** ☎ 911. **Coast Guard** ☎ 808/552-6458 on O'ahu. **Fire** ☎ 808/553-5601 in Kaunakakai, 808/567-6525 at Ho'olehua Airport. **Police** ☎ 808/553-5355.

🏥 Hospital **Moloka'i General Hospital** ✉ 280A Puali St., Kaunakakai ☎ 808/553-5331.

VISITOR INFORMATION

There's tourist information available in kiosks and stands at the airport in Ho'olehua or at the Moloka'i Visitors Association. The Maui Visitors Bureau has travel information for Maui County, of which Moloka'i is a part.

Molokaievents.com, Inc., has information on island events and can help you plan your own events on the island.

Car-rental agencies distribute the free *Moloka'i Drive Guide* along with maps and other up-to-date information.

ℹ️ **Maui Visitors Bureau** 🏠 On Maui: Box 580, Wailuku 96793 ☎ 808/244-3530 ⊕ www.visitmaui.com. **Molokaievents.com, Inc.** ☎ 808/567-6789 ⊕ www.molokaievents.com. **Moloka'i Visitors Association** ✉ 10 Kamehameha V Hwy., Box 960, Kaunakakai ☎ 808/553-5221 or 800/800-6367 ⊕ molokai-hawaii.com.

Lāna`i

Polihua Beach

WORD OF MOUTH

"If you are going for golf or tennis or lazing around in the sun, it is wonderful. Other than that, it is very, very low key with minimal shopping and no evening activities other than hotel restaurants and bar."

—breckgal

"The day we went [to Polihua Beach] it was only us and three locals who were fishing. The sand is so soft and the water is crystal clear."

—alex

WELCOME TO LĀNA'I

Polihua Beach

TOP 5
Reasons to Go

1. **Seclusion & Serenity:** Lāna'i is small: local motion is slow motion. Go home rested instead of exhausted.

2. **Garden of the Gods:** Walk amid the eerie red rock spires that ancient Hawaiians believed to be the home of the spirits.

3. **A Dive at Cathedrals:** Explore underwater pinnacle formations and mysterious caverns lit by shimmering rays of light.

4. **Dole Square:** Hang out in the shade of the Cook pines and talk story with the locals.

5. **Lāna'i Pine Sporting Clays & Archery Range:** Play a Pacific William Tell, aiming your arrow at a pineapple.

◆ **Ka'ena Pt.**

◆ **Garden of the Gods**

Kaumala...

440

Kaumalapau Harbor

✈ **Lāna'i Airport**

■ TIP→ Directions on the island are often given as *mauka* (toward the mountains) and *makai* (toward the ocean).

Hulopo'e Beach

Garden of the Gods

Getting Oriented

Unlike the other Hawaiian islands with their tropical splendors, Lāna'i looks like a desert; *kiawe* trees right out of Africa, red dirt roads that glow molten at sunset, and a deep blue sea that literally leads to Tahiti. Lāna'ihale (house of Lāna'i), the mountain that bisects the island, is carved into deep canyons by rain and wind on the windward side, and the dryer leeward side slopes gently to the sea, where waves pound against surf-carved cliffs.

Spinner Dolphins

Windward Lāna'i is the long white sand beach at the base of Lāna'ihale. Now uninhabited, it was once occupied by thriving Hawaiian fishing villages and a sugarcane plantation.

WINDWARD LĀNA'I

Hwy.

Keomuku

Lāna'i City

Lodge at Kō'ele

Mānele Rd.

UPCOUNTRY

▲ Mt. Lāna'ihale
3,370ft

440

Mānele Bay Hotel ◆

Mānele Bay

Lāna'i City is really a tiny plantation village. Locals hold conversations in front of Dole Park shops and from their pickups on the road, and kids ride bikes in colorful impromptu parades while cars wait for them.

Cool and serene, **Upcountry** is graced by Lāna'i City, towering Cook Pine trees, and misty mountain vistas.

The more developed beach side of the island, **Mānele Bay** and harbor are where it's happening: swimming, picnicking, off-island excursions, and boating are all concentrated in this very accessible area.

Lāna'i Pine Archery

LĀNAʻI PLANNER

Sunsets and Moonrises

One of the best ways to tap into Lānaʻi's Pacific Island pace is to take the time not just to watch the sun set but also to watch the moon rise. The best sunset-viewing spots are the veranda at The Lodge, the grassy field past the Lodge's tennis courts, Hulopoʻe Beach, and the Challenge at Mānele clubhouse. For full moons, nothing beats the trail that leads to Puʻu Pehe or the many stopping places along Keōmoku Road.

Navigating Without Signs

Lānaʻi has no traffic, no traffic lights, and only three paved roads. Bring along a good topographical map, study it, and keep in mind your directions. Stop from time to time and re-find landmarks and gauge your progress. Distance is better measured in the condition of the road than in miles. Watch out for other jeep drivers who also don't know where they are. Never drive to the edge of lava cliffs, as rock can give way under you.

Timing Is Everything

Whales are seen off Lānaʻi's shores from December through April. A Pineapple Festival on the 4th of July Saturday in Dole Park features local food, Hawaiian entertainment, a pineapple-eating and cooking contest and fireworks. Buddhists hold their annual outdoor Obon Festival honoring departed ancestors with joyous dancing, food booths, and *taiko* drumming in early July. Lānaʻi celebrates the state-wide Aloha Festivals in mid-October with a hometown parade, car contests, more food, and more music. Beware hunting season weekends—from mid-February through mid-May, and mid-July through mid-October. Most of the private lodging properties are booked way in advance.

A Special Island

Castle & Cooke Resorts, LLC, which is owned by David H. Murdock, owns 98% of the land on Lānaʻi—resorts, luxury developments, commercial properties, and stores. The exceptions are private residences, the school, the police station, the airport, and county highways. As Castle & Cooke allows the public to use its land without compensation, the company has no liability or legal responsibility under Hawaiian law for your safety. So be careful.

Will It Rain?

As higher mountains on Maui capture the trade-wind clouds, Lānaʻi receives little rainfall and has a desert ecology. It's always warmer at the beach and can get cool or even cold (by Hawaiian standards) Upcountry. Consider the wind direction when planning your day. If it's blowing a gale on the windward beaches, head for the lee at Hulopoʻe or check out Garden of the Gods. Overcast days, when the wind stops or comes lightly from the southwest, are common in whale season. Try a whale-watching trip or the windward beaches.

By Joana
Varawa

WITH NO TRAFFIC OR TRAFFIC LIGHTS and miles of open space, Lāna'i seems lost in time. The tiny plantation town is really a village; where locals hold conversations in front of shops around Dole Park, and from their pickups on the road, and kids ride bikes in colorful impromptu parades. Both resorts on the island are now run by the Four Seasons. If you yearn for a beach with amenities, a luxury resort and golf course at Mānele beckons from the shoreline. Upcountry, "Lāna''i City" and the luxurious Lodge at Kō'ele provide cooler pleasures. This leaves the rest of the 100,000 acre island open to explore.

Small (141 square miles) and sparsely populated, Lāna'i is the smallest inhabited Hawaiian Island. The only city on Lāna'i, Lāna'i City, boasts just 3,000 residents, and no one lives elsewhere on the island. Though it may seem a world away, Lāna'i is separated from Maui and Moloka'i by two narrow channels, and easily accessed by boat from either island.

Flora & Fauna
Lāna'i bucks the "tropical" trend of the other Hawaiian Islands with African Keawe trees, Cook Pines, and Eucalyptus in place of palm trees, fiery red dirt instead of black lava rock, and deep blue sea where you might expect shallow turquoise bays. Abandoned pineapple fields are overgrown with drought-resistant grasses, Christmas berry and lantana; native plants, *a'ali'i* and *'ilima*, are found in uncultivated areas. Axis deer from India dominate the ridges, and flocks of wild turkeys lumber around the resorts. Whales can be seen December through April and a family of resident spinner dolphins drops in regularly at Hulopo'e Bay.

On Lāna'i Today
Despite its fancy resorts, Lāna'i still has that sleepy old Hawai'i feel. Residents are a mix of just about everything—Hawaiian/Chinese/German/Portuguese/Filipino/Japanese/French/Puerto Rican/English/Norwegian, you name it. The plantation was divided into ethnic camps which helped retain cultural cuisines. Pot-luck dinners feature sashimi, Portuguese bean soup, *laulau,* potato salad, teriyaki steak, chicken *hekka* (a gingery Japanese chicken stir-fry), and Jello. The local language is pidgin, a mix of words as complicated and rich as the food. In recent years, David Murdock's plan to pay for the resorts by selling expensive homes next to them has met with opposition from locals who don't want their limited water supply being used to fill someone's hot tub.

The Ghosts of Lāna'i
Lāna'i has a reputation for being haunted (at one time by "cannibal spirits") and evidence abounds: a mysterious purple *lehua* at Keahialoa; the crying of a ghost chicken at Kamoa; Pohaku O, a rock that calls at twilight; and remote spots where cars mysteriously stall, strange sounds are heard, and lights are seen at night. Tradition has it that Pu'upehe (an offshore sea stack) was a child who spoke from the womb, demanding *awa* root. A later story claims it is the grave of a woman drowned in a cave at the nearby cliffs. Hawaiians believe that places have *mana* (spiritual power), and Lāna'i is far from an exception.

6

EXPLORING LĀNA'I

Most of Lāna'i's sights are out of the way—rent a four-wheel-drive vehicle, ask for a road map, be sure you have a full tank, and bring a snack and plenty of water. Ask your hotel's concierge about road conditions and driving directions before you set out.

Lāna'i has an ideal climate year-round, hot and sunny at the sea and a few delicious degrees cooler Upcountry. In Lāna'i City, the nights and mornings can be almost chilly when a mystic fog or harsh trade winds settle in.

The main road in Lāna'i, Route 440, refers to both Kaumalapau Highway and Mānele Road. On the Islands, the directions *mauka* (toward the mountains) and *makai* (toward the ocean) are often used.

Lāna'i City & Mānele Bay

Pineapples once blanketed the Pālāwai, the great basin south of Lāna'i City. Before that it was a vast dryland forest; now most of it is fenced-in pasture or a game bird reserve, and can only be viewed from the Mānele Road. Although it looks like a volcanic crater, it isn't. Some say that the name Pālāwai is descriptive of the mist that sometimes fills the basin at dawn and looks like a huge shining lake.

What to See

Halulu Heiau. The well-preserved remains of an impressive *heiau* at Kaunolu village, which was actively used by Lāna'i's earliest residents, attest to this spot's sacred history. As late as 1810, this hilltop temple was considered a place of refuge, where those who had broken *kapu* (taboos) were forgiven and where women and children could find safety in times of war. If you explore the area, be very respectful, take nothing with you and leave nothing behind. This place is hard to find so get someone to mark a map for you. The road down has recently been graded, but is quite sandy and soft at the bottom. ⊠ *From Lāna'i City follow Hwy. 440 west toward Kaumalapau Harbor. Pass airport, then look for carved boulder on hill on your left. Turn left on dirt road, follow it to another carved boulder, then head downhill.*

❷ **Ka Lokahi o Ka Mālamalama Church.** This picturesque church was built in 1938 to provide services for Lāna'i's growing population—for many people, the only other Hawaiian church, in coastal Keōmuku, was too far away. A classic structure of preplantation days, the church had to be moved from its original Lāna'i Ranch location when the Lodge at Kō'ele was built. Sunday services are still held, in Hawaiian and English; visitors are welcome, but are requested to attend quietly. ⊠ *Left of entrance to Lodge at Kō'ele.*

❻ **Kaumalapau Harbor.** Built in 1926 by the Hawaiian Pineapple Company, which later became Dole, this is Lāna'i's principal seaport. The cliffs that flank the western shore are as much as 1,000 feet tall. Water activities aren't allowed here, but it's a dramatic sunset spot. The harbor is closed

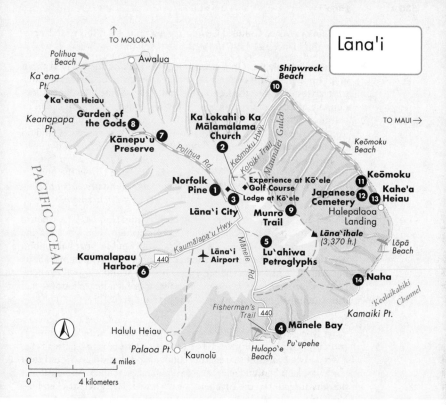

Lāna'i

↑ TO MOLOKA'I

Polihua Beach
Awalua
Ka'ena Pt.
Shipwreck Beach 10
Ka'ena Heiau
Garden of the Gods 8
Keanapapa Pt.
Kānepu'u Preserve 7
TO MAUI →
Ka Lokahi o Ka Mālamalama Church 2
Keōmoku Beach
Kō'ele Gulch
Polihua Rd.
Kololki Trail
Keōmoku Hwy.
Maunalei Gulch
Norfolk Pine 1
Experience at Kō'ele Golf Course ◆
Keōmoku 11
Lodge at Kō'ele 3
Japanese Cemetery 12 **Kahe'a Heiau** 13
Lāna'i City
Munro Trail 9
Halepalaoa Landing
Kaumālapa'u Hwy.
Lu'ahiwa Petroglyphs 5
▲ **Lāna'ihale** (3,370 ft.)
Lōpā Beach
Mānele Rd.
Kaumalapau Harbor 6
440
✈ **Lāna'i Airport**
Naha 14
'Kealaikahiki Channel
Fisherman's Trail 440
Kamaiki Pt.
Halulu Heiau
Palaoa Pt. Kaunolū
Mānele Bay 4
Hulopo'e Beach
Pu'upehe

PACIFIC OCEAN

0 ——— 4 miles
0 ——— 4 kilometers

to visitors on barge days: Wednesday, Thursday, and Friday. ⊠ *From Lāna'i City follow Hwy. 440 (Kaumalapau Hwy.) west as far as it goes.*

Kaunolū. Close to the island's highest cliffs, Kaunolū was once a prosperous fishing village. This important archaeological site includes a major *heiau,* terraces, stone floors, and house platforms. The impressive 90-foot drop to the ocean through a gap in the lava rock is called **Kahekili's Leap.** Warriors would make the dangerous jump into the shallow 12 feet of water below to show their courage. Hawai'i's King Kamehameha I is said to have visited the village to collect taxes and enjoy the excellent fishing found in the offshore waters. A newly graded road gets soft and sandy at the bottom. Get a marked map before you set out. ⊠ *From Lāna'i City follow Hwy. 440 (Kaumalapau Hwy.) west; at carved boulder on hill, turn left onto dirt road; go until you reach the second carved boulder and then head* makai.

❸ **Lāna'i City.** This tidy plantation town, built in 1924 by Jim Dole, is home to old-time residents and recently arrived resort workers, and is slowly changing from a quiet rural village to a busy little town. A simple grid of roads here is lined with stately Cook pines, and all the basic services a person might need. The pace is slow and the people are friendly. Visit the **Lāna'i Arts & Cultural Center** to get a glimpse of this island's creative abundance. ⊠ *339 7th Ave.*

❺ **Lu'ahiwa Petroglyphs.** On a steep slope overlooking the Pālāwai Basin are 34 boulders with carvings. Drawn in a mixture of ancient and historic styles dating to the late 1700s and early 1800s, the simple stick-figures depict animals, people, and mythic beings. A nearby *heiau*, or temple, no longer visible, was used to summon the rains and was dedicated to the god Kāne. Do not draw on or deface the carvings, and do not add to the collection. ⊠ *From Lāna'i City turn left on Hwy. 440 (Mānele Rd.) and continue to first dirt road on your left, marked by large carved boulder and sign. Follow road the road marked by the boulder through fields; do not go left uphill but continue going straight and when you see boulders on hillside, park and walk up to petroglyphs.*

❹ **Mānele Bay.** The site of a Hawaiian village dating from AD 900, Mānele Bay is flanked by lava cliffs hundreds of feet high. Though a Marine Life Conservation District, it's the island's only public boat harbor and was the location of most post-contact shipping until Kaumalapau Harbor was built in 1926. The ferry to and from Maui also pulls in here. Public restrooms, water, and picnic tables make it a nice pit-stop—you can watch the boating activity as you rest and refuel.

Just offshore you can catch a glimpse of **Pu'upehe.** Often called Sweetheart Rock, the isolated 80-foot-high islet carries a sad Hawaiian legend that is probably not true. The rock is said to be named after Pehe, a woman so beautiful that her husband, afraid that others would steal her away, kept her hidden in a sea cave. One day, while Pehe was alone, the surf surged into the cave and she drowned. Her grief-stricken husband buried her on the summit of this rock and then jumped to his own death. A more authentic, if less romantic, story is that the enclosure on the summit is a shrine to birds, built by bird-catchers. Archaeological investigation has revealed that the enclosure was not a burial place. ⊠ *From Lāna'i City follow Hwy. 440 (Mānele Rd.) south to bottom of hill and look for harbor on your left.*

❶ **Norfolk Pine.** More than 100 feet high, this majestic pine tree was planted here, at the former site of the manager's house, in 1875. Almost 30 years later, George Munro, then the ranch manager, would observe how, in foggy weather, water collected on its foliage, forming a natural rain. This fog drip led Munro to supervise the planting of Cook pines along the ridge of Lāna'ihale and throughout the town in order to add to the island's water supply. ⊠ *Entrance of Lodge at Kō'ele.*

Garden of the Gods & Windward Lāna'i

The north and east sections of Lāna'i are wild and untouched. An inaccessible *heiau* is the only trace of human habitation, with the exception of stacks of rocks marking old shrines, and trails. Four-wheel drive is a must to explore this side of the isle, and be prepared for hot, rough conditions. Pack a picnic lunch and bring plenty of drinking water.

What to See

❽ Garden of the Gods. This preternatural plateau is scattered with boulders of different sizes, shapes, and colors, the products of a million years of wind erosion. Time your visit for sunset, when the rocks begin to glow—from rich red to purple—and the fiery globe sinks to the horizon. Magnificent views of the Pacific Ocean, Moloka'i, and, on clear days, O'ahu provide the perfect backdrop for photographs.

Fodor'sChoice ★

The ancient Hawaiians shunned Lāna'i for hundreds of years, believing the island was the inviolable home of spirits. Standing beside the oxide-red rock spires of this strange, raw landscape, you might be tempted to believe the same. This lunar savannah still has a decidedly eerie edge; but the shadows disappearing on the horizon are those of mouflon sheep and axis deer, not the fearsome spirits of lore. According to tradition, the spirits were vanquished by Kā'ulula'au, a chief's son from Maui who was exiled here for destroying his father's prized breadfruit groves. The clever boy outwitted and exhausted the spirits, and announced their banishment with a giant bonfire. ⊠ *From Stables at Kō'ele, follow dirt road through pasture, turn right at crossroad marked by carved boulder, head through abandoned fields and ironwood forest to open red-dirt area marked by a carved boulder.*

⓬ Japanese Cemetery. In 1899 sugar came to this side of Lāna'i. A plantation took up about 2,400 acres and seemed a profitable proposition, but that same year, disease wiped out the labor force. This authentic Buddhist shrine commemorates the Japanese workers who died. ⊠ *6½ mi southeast from where Keōmoku Hwy. dead-ends at Shipwreck Beach, on dirt road running along north shore.*

⓭ Kahe'a Heiau. What was once an important place of worship for the people of Lāna'i may be hard to find through the *kiawe* overgrowth. The wharf at **Halepaloa Landing** has been rebuilt however. The wharf was used by the Maunalei Sugar Company (1899) to ship cane, and some say the company failed because the sacred stones of the *heiau* were used for the construction of the cane railroad. Angry gods turned the drinking water salty, forcing the sugar company to close in 1901. There's good public beach access here and clear shallow water for swimming, but no other facilities. ⊠ *6½ mi southeast from where Keōmuku Hwy. dead-ends at Shipwreck Beach, on dirt road running along north shore.*

❼ Kānepu'u Preserve. The 590 acres of this native dryland forest were under the stewardship of the Nature Conservancy of Hawai'i until recently

> ### MYTHOLOGICAL MYTHS
>
> When tour boats travel the coast, their captains give out the "fafa" about places they are passing. Some of the fafa gets pretty fanciful and departs wildly not only from the truth, but from myth as well. The more outlandish or romantic the better, but the real stories suffer in the telling. This is how a bird shrine on the top of Pu'upehe has become the grave of an imprisoned princess. Place names shift around with the whim of the storyteller. So, since there's plenty of salt in the sea, take your stories with a grain or two.

6

and are now managed by Castle & Cooke Resorts. Kānepu'u contains the largest remnant of this rare indigenous forest type. More than 45 native species of plants, including the endangered Hawaiian gardenia, grow in the shade of such rare trees as Hawaiian sandalwood, olive, and ebony. A short self-guided loop trail, with eight signs illustrated by local artist Wendell Kaho'ohalahala, reveals this ecosystem's beauty and the challenges it faces. ⊠ *Polihua Rd., 6 mi north of Lāna'i City.*

⓫ Keōmoku. There's an eerie beauty about Keōmoku, with its faded memories and forgotten homesteads. During the late 19th century, this busy Lāna'i community of some 900 to 2,000 residents served as the headquarters of Maunalei Sugar Company. After the company failed, the land was used for ranching, but by 1954 the area lay abandoned. Its church, **Ka Lanakila O Ka Mālamalama,** was built in 1903. It has been partially restored by volunteers, and visitors often leave some small token, a shell or faded lei, as an offering. Among the overgrown *keawe* trees you may find the remnants of a Portuguese beehive-shape communal bread oven, or the weathered boards of what was the last windmill. ⊠ *5 mi along unpaved road southeast of Shipwreck Beach.*

★ ⓷ Munro Trail. This 9-mi jeep trail along a fern- and pine-clad narrow ridge was named after George Munro, manager of the Lāna'i Ranch Co., who began a reforestation program in the 1950s to restore the island's much-needed watershed. The trail climbs **Lāna'ihale** (House of Lāna'i), which, at 3,370 feet, is the island's highest point; on clear days you'll be treated to a panorama of canyons and almost all of the Hawaiian Islands. ■ TIP→ The one-way road gets very muddy, and trade winds can be strong. A sheer drop-off in some sections requires an attentive driver. Keep an eye out for hikers along the way. You can also hike the Munro Trail (⇨ *See* Hiking *later in this chapter*), though it's a difficult trek: it's steep, the ground is uneven, and there's no water. ⊠ *From Lodge at Kō'ele head north on Keōmoku Hwy. for 1¼ mi, then turn right onto dirt road; trailhead is ½ mi past cemetery on right.*

⓮ Naha. An ancient rock-walled fishpond—visible at low tide—lies here, where the sandy shorelines end and the cliffs begin their rise along the island's shores. The beach is a frequent resource for local fisherfolk. ■ TIP→ Treacherous currents make this a dangerous place for swimming. ⊠ *East side of Lāna'i, at end of dirt road that runs from end of Keōmoku Hwy. along eastern shore.*

★ ⓾ Shipwreck Beach. The rusting World War II tanker may be a clue that the waters off this 8-mi stretch of sand aren't friendly. Strong trade winds have propelled innocent vessels onto the reef since at least 1824, when the first shipwreck was recorded. Some believe that the unknown oiler you see stranded today, however, was merely abandoned. ■ TIP→ The water is unsafe for swimming; stick to beachcombing. ⊠ *End of Keōmoku Hwy. heading north.*

BEACHES

Lāna'i offers miles of secluded white-sand beaches on its windward side, and the moderately developed Hulopo'e Beach, which is adjacent to the Mānele Bay Hotel. Hulopo'e is accessible by car or hotel shuttle bus; to reach the windward beaches you'll need a four-wheel-drive vehicle. An offshore reef, rocks, and coral make swimming on the windward side problematic, but it's fun to splash around in the shallow water. Driving on the beach itself is illegal and can be dangerous. Beaches are listed alphabetically.

Road conditions can change overnight and become impassable due to rain in the Uplands. Car-rental agencies should be able to give you updates before you hit the road. Many of the spur roads leading to the windward beaches from the coastal dirt road cross private property and are closed off by chains. Look for open spur roads with recent tire marks (a fairly good sign that they are safe to drive on). It's best to park on firm ground and walk in to avoid getting your car mired in the sand.

Hulopo'e Beach. A short stroll from the Mānele Bay Hotel, Hulopo'e is considered one of the best beaches in all of Hawai'i. The sparkling crescent of this Marine Life Conservation District beckons with calm waters safe for swimming almost year-round, great snorkeling reefs, tide pools, and, sometimes, spinner dolphins. A shady, grassy beach park is perfect for picnics. If the shore break is pounding, or if you see surfers riding big waves, stay out of the water. ☒ *From Lāna'i City follow Hwy. 440 (Mānele Rd.) south to bottom of hill; turn right, road dead-ends at beach's parking lot* ⚲ *Toilets, showers, picnic tables, grills, parking lot.*

Lōpā Beach. A popular surfing spot for locals, Lōpā is also an ancient fishpond. With majestic views of West Maui and Kaho'olawe, this remote, white-sand beach is a great place for a picnic. ■ TIP➔ **Don't let the sight of surfers fool you: the channel's currents are too strong for swimming.** ☒ *East side of Lāna'i, 7 mi south down a dirt road that runs from end of Keōmuku Hwy. along eastern shore* ⚲ *No facilities.*

Polihua Beach. This often-deserted beach should get a star for beauty with its long, wide stretch of white sand and the clear views of Moloka'i. The dirt road to get here can be bad with deep, sandy places (when it rains it's impassable), however, and frequent high winds whip up sand and waves. ■ TIP➔ **Strong currents and a sudden drop in the ocean floor make swimming extremely dangerous.** On the northern end, the beach ends at a rocky lava cliff with some interesting tide pools. Polihua is named after the sea turtles that lay their eggs in the sand. Do not drive on the beach and endanger their nests. Curiously, wild bees sometimes gather around your car for water at this beach. To get rid of them, put out water some place away from the car and wait a bit. ☒ *Windward Lāna'i, 11 mi from Lāna'i City, past Garden of the Gods* ⚲ *No facilities.*

Shipwreck Beach. Beachcombers come to this fairly accessible beach for shells and washed-up treasures; photographers for great shots of Moloka'i, just across the 9-mi wide Kalohi Channel; and walkers for the long stretch of sand. It may still be possible to find glass ball fishing floats but more common is waterborne debris from the Moloka'i channel. Kaiolohia, its Hawaiian name, is a favorite local diving spot. ■ TIP→ **An offshore reef and rocks in the water mean that it's not for swimmers, though you can play in the shallow water on the shoreline.** ⊠ *North shore, 10 mi north of Lāna'i City at end of Keōmuku Hwy.* ☞ *No facilities.*

WATER ACTIVITIES & TOURS

Boat Tours & Charters

Trilogy Oceansports Lāna'i. If you're staying in Lāna'i and want to play on the ocean, Trilogy is your outfitter.

A 2½-hour blue-water snorkeling and adventure rafting trip includes lessons, equipment, and a hot barbecue lunch at the Trilogy Pavilion when you return to Mānele harbor. Tours are offered Monday, Tuesday, Thursday, and Friday; costs are $91 for adults and $46 for kids 15 and under.

On Wednesday you can opt for a snorkel and sail aboard one of their large catamarans, departing at 11:15 AM. This trip is perfect if you want to sleep in or spend your early morning over a leisurely breakfast. The three-hour sail includes the barbecue lunch and a cruise up the coast to a remote snorkel site. The tour costs $134 for adults, $67 for children.

Serious divers should go for Trilogy's two-tank dive; location depends on the weather. You must be certified, so don't forget your documentation. The $149 fee includes a light breakfast of cinnamon rolls and coffee. Beginners (minimum age 12) can try a one-tank introductory dive for $80. You'll wade into Hulopo'e Bay with an instructor at your side; actual dive time is 20 to 30 minutes. Certified divers can choose a 35- to 40-minute wade-in dive at Hulopo'e for $70.

If that's not enough, sign up for a blue-water dolphin watch, whale-watching sail, or a sunset cruise. You can book trips through your hotel concierge, but try online first, where discounts are often available. ☎ *888/628–4800* ⊕ *www.sailtrilogy.com.*

Deep-Sea Fishing

Some of the best sportfishing grounds in Maui County are off the southwest shoreline of Lāna'i. Pry your eyes open and go deep-sea fishing in the early morning, with departures at 6 or 6:30 AM from Mānele Harbor. Prime seasons are spring and summer, although good catches have been landed year-round. Mahimahi, ono, 'ahi, and marlin are prized catches, with mahi and ono (which means delicious in Hawaiian) preferred eating.

Kila Kila. Jeff Menze, with 30 years' experience in Hawaiian waters, captains this elegant 53-foot Merritt, which has world records to its credit. If there are fish to find, Menze can find them. The sleek *Kila Kila* has a fly bridge, spacious cockpit, air-conditioned salon, showers, and two toilets. Menze and his crew clean your catch, cut fillets, and send them up to the Mānele chefs to be cooked to order. Or you can take the fillets for a picnic barbecue or dinner elsewhere. A four-hour trip with up to six passengers costs $825; a full-day run is $1,200. Pastries and soft drinks are provided. A sunset sail or sightseeing along the coast are other options, but they do not allow snorkeling. Book with the concierge at the resort. ☎ 808/565–2387 or 808/565–4555.

Fish-N-Chips. This 32-foot Hatteras Sport Fisher with tuna tower will get you to the fishing grounds in comfort, and Captain Jason will do everything except reel in the big one for you. Plan on trolling along the south coast for ono and around the point at Kaunolu for mahi or marlin. A trip to the offshore buoy often yields skipjack tuna or big ahi, and the captain and crew are always open to a bit of bottom fishing for fun and relaxation. Fishing gear, sodas, and water are included. Let them know if you would also like breakfast or lunch for an additional charge. A four-hour charter (six-passenger maximum) will set you back $625; each additional hour costs $110. You can keep up to one-third of all fish caught. Shared charters on Sunday and Wednesday are $130 per person. Book with the concierge at your resort or give them a call directly. ☎ 808/565–7676.

Kayaking

Lāna'i's southeast coast offers leisurely paddling inside the windward reef. Curious sea turtles and friendly manta rays may tag along. There are miles of scenic coastline with deserted beaches on the inside reef to haul up on for an informal picnic. When the wind comes from the southwest, the windward coast is tranquil. Kayaking along the leeward cliffs is more demanding with rougher seas and strong currents. No kayaking is permitted in the Marine Conservation District at Hulopo'e Bay.

Early mornings tend to be calmer. The wind picks up as the day advances. ■ TIP→ **Expect strong currents along all of the coasts.** Experience on the water is advised, and knowing how to swim is essential.

■ TIP→ **There's one major drawback to kayaking on Lāna'i: you'll have to travel with your own kayak or arrange for a Maui vendor to meet you on the island, as there are no kayak rentals or guides on Lāna'i.**

Scuba Diving

When you have a dive site such as Cathedrals—with eerie pinnacle formations and luminous caverns—it's no wonder that scuba-diving buffs consider exploring the waters off Lāna'i akin to having a religious experience.

Just outside of Hulopo'e Bay, the boat dive site **Cathedrals** was named the best cavern dive site in the Pacific by *Skin Diver* magazine. Shimmering light makes the many openings in the caves look like the stained-glass windows. A current

THE COUSTEAU FALLACY

Never turn your back on the ocean seems easy to remember, but many forget it. Much to the amusement of water-smart locals, hundreds of visitors get smashed trying to wade in backwards through breaking waves, wearing fins, mask and snorkel. Wading in facing the waves is equally dangerous, so always swim in past the breakers, and in the comparative calm put on your fins, then mask and snorkel. It will save you, at the least, getting laughed at, or at the worst, getting seriously injured.

generally keeps the water crystal clear, even if it's turbid outside. In these unearthly chambers, large ulua and small reef shark add to the adventure. **Sergeant Major Reef,** off Kamaiki Point, is named for big schools of yellow- and black-striped manini (sergeant major fish) that turn the rocks silvery as they feed. The site is made up of three parallel lava ridges, a cave, and an archway, with rippled sand valleys between the ridges. Depths range 15–50 feet.

Trilogy (⇨ *See* Boat Tours & Charters, *above*) is the only company running boat dives from Lāna'i.

Snorkeling

Snorkeling is the easiest ocean sport available on the island, requiring nothing but a snorkel, mask, fins, and good sense. Purchase equipment in Lāna'i City if you don't bring your own. The basic rules of snorkeling are: never turn your back on the ocean; wait to enter the water until you are sure no big sets are coming; and observe the activity of locals on the beach. If little kids are playing in the shore break, it's usually safe to enter (although little local kids are expert wave riders). Put your mask and fins on once you have passed the shore break, rather than trying to wade in with fins through the waves.

Hulopo'e Beach is an outstanding snorkeling destination. The bay is a State of Hawai'i Marine Conservation District and no spearfishing or diving is allowed. Schools of manini feeding on the coral coat the rocks with flashing silver, and you can view kala, uhu, and papio in all their rainbow colors. Wade in from the sandy beach, the best snorkeling is toward the left. Beware of rocks and surging waves. When the resident spinner dolphins are in the bay, it's courteous to watch them from the shore. If swimmers and snorkelers go out, the dolphins may leave and be deprived of their necessary resting place. Another wade-in snorkel spot is just beyond the break wall at **Mānele Small Boat Harbor.** Enter over the rocks just past the boat ramp. ■ TIP➔ **It's dangerous to enter if waves are breaking.**

Book with Trilogy (⇨ *See* Boat Tours & Charters, *above*) for snorkel sails.

GOLF, HIKING & OTHER ADVENTURES

Biking

Many of the same red-dirt roads that invite hikers are excellent for biking, offering easy flat terrain and long clear views. There's only one hitch: you may have to bring your own bike, as there are no rentals or tours for nonresort guests available.

A favorite biking route is along the fairly flat red-dirt road northward from Lāna'i City through the old pineapple fields to Garden of the Gods. Start your trip on Keōmuku Highway in town. Take a left just before the Lodge's tennis courts, and then a right where the road ends at the fenced pasture, and continue on to the north end and the start of Polihua and Awalua dirt roads. If you're really hardy you could bike down to Polihua Beach and back, but it would be a serious all-day trip. In wet weather these roads turn to slurry and are not advisable. Go in the early morning or late afternoon because the sun gets hot in the middle of the day. Take plenty of water, spare parts, and snacks.

For the exceptionally fit, it's possible to bike from town down the Keōmuku Highway to the windward beaches and back or to bike the Munro Trail (⇨ *See* Hiking, *below*). Experienced bikers also bike up and down the Mānele Highway from Mānele Bay to town.

Camping

Camping isn't encouraged outside Lāna'i's one official campground at Hulopo'e: the island is privately owned; islanders are keen on privacy; and, unless you know about local conditions, camping on the beach can be hazardous.

Castle & Cooke Resorts Campground. The inviting, grassy campground at Hulopo'e Beach has shade trees, clean restrooms, grills, and beach-side showers. Buy charcoal in Lāna'i City, as well as basic camping supplies and food. Cutting fire wood is not allowed and camping on the beach itself is reserved for residents only. Call in advance; it's $20 for a permit, plus a $5 fee per person per night (three-night limit). ☎ *808/565–2970 for permits and advance reservations.*

Golf

Lāna'i has just three courses and a total of 45 holes (not counting an 18-hole putting course), but all three are good and offer very different environments and challenges. The two resort courses, especially, are so different, it's hard to believe that they're on the same island, let alone just 20 minutes apart by resort shuttle.

Cavendish Golf Course. At this unique 9-holer, there's no phone, no clubhouse, no starter, just a slotted wooden box on the first tee requesting a monetary donation—go ahead, be generous!—to help with maintenance costs. This is a legacy of the plantation era, designed in 1947 by E. B. Cavendish, superintendent of factory guards, and is used by locals for Sunday tournaments and popular skins games. Holes run through chutes of stately Norfolk pines, and most greens are elevated. ✉ *Call Lodge at Kō'ele for directions* ⛳ *9 holes. 3071 yds. Par 36. Green Fee: Donation* ☞ *No facilities.*

The Challenge at Mānele. Designed by Jack Nicklaus (1993), this course sits right over the water of Hulopo'e Bay. Built on lava outcroppings, the course features three holes on cliffs that use the Pacific Ocean as a water hazard. The five-tee concept challenges the best golfers—tee shots over natural gorges and ravines must be precise. This dramatic, unspoiled natural terrain is a stunning backdrop, and every hole offers majestic ocean views. ✉ *1 Challenge Dr., Lāna'i City* ☎ *808/565–2222* ⊕ *www.go-lanai.com* ⛳ *18 holes. 6310 yds. Par 72. Green Fee: $225* ☞ *Facilities: Driving range, putting green, golf carts, rental clubs, pro shop, lessons, restaurant, bar.*

The Experience at Ko'ele. The Experience at Ko'ele is a challenging Greg Norman (1991) layout that begins at an elevation of 2,000 feet. The front nine moves dramatically through ravines wooded with pine, koa, and eucalyptus trees; seven lakes and streams with cascading waterfalls dot the course. No other course offers a more incredible combination of highland terrain, inspired landscape architecture, and range of play challenges. Quite different from the sea-level Challenge at Mānele, it's hard to believe that these two courses are separated by only a 20-minute resort shuttle ride on the same island. ⊠ *Kaimuko Dr., Lāna'i City* ☎ *808/565-4653* ⊕ *www.go-lanai.com* ⚐ *18 holes. 6310 yds. Par 72. Green Fee: $225* ☞ *Facilities: Driving range, putting green, golf carts, rental clubs, pro shop, lessons, restaurant, bar.*

Hiking

Only 30 mi of Lāna'i's roads are paved. But red-dirt roads and trails, ideal for hiking, will take you to sweeping overlooks, isolated beaches, and shady forests. Don't be afraid to leave the road to follow deer trails, but make sure to keep your landmarks in clear sight so you can always retrace your steps, if necessary. Or take a self-guided walk through Kāne Pu'u, Hawai'i's largest native dryland forest. You can explore the Munro Trail over Lāna'ihale with views of plunging canyons, or hike along an old, coastal fisherman trail or across Koloiki Ridge. Wear hiking shoes, a hat, and sunscreen, and carry plenty of water.

BEST TRAILS **Koloiki Ridge**, a marked, moderate trail that starts behind the Lodge at Kō'ele, takes you along the cool and shady Munro Trail to overlook the windward side, with impressive views of Maui, Moloka'i, Maunalei Valley, and Naio Gulch. The average time for the 5-mi round-trip is three hours. Bring snacks and water, and take your time.

Local fishermen still use the **Lāna'i Fisherman Trail** to get to their favorite fishing spots. The trail takes about 1½ hours to hike and follows the rocky shoreline below the Mānele Bay Hotel, along cliffs bordering the golf course. Caves and tide pools beckon beneath you, but be careful climbing down. The marked trail entrance begins at the west end of Hulopo'e Beach. Keep your eyes open for spinner dolphins cavorting off-shore and the silvery flash of fish feeding in the pools below you. The condition of the trail varies with weather and frequency of maintenance.

Pu'upehe Trail begins to the left (facing the ocean) of Hulop'i Beach, travels a short distance around the coastline, and then climbs up a sharp, rocky rise. At the top, you're level with the offshore stack of Pu'upehe and can overlook miles of coastline in both directions. The trail is not difficult, but it's hot and steep. ■ TIP➔ Never go next to the edge, as the cliff can easily give way. The hiking is best in the early morning or late afternoon, and it's a perfect place to look for whales in season (December–April). Wear shoes, this is not a hike for sandals or slip-ons.

The **Munro Trail** is the real thing: a strenuous 9-mi trek that begins behind the Lodge and follows the ridge of Lāna'ihale through the rain forest. The island's most demanding hike, it has an elevation gain of 1,400 feet and leads to a lookout at the island's highest point, Lāna'ihale. It's also a narrow dirt road so watch out for careening jeeps that are as unfamiliar with the terrain as you are. The trail is named after George Munro, who supervised the planting of Cook pine trees and eucalyptus wind breaks. Mules used to wend their way up the mountain carrying the pine seedlings. Unless you arrange for someone to pick you up at the trail's end, you have a long boring hike back through the Palawai Basin to return to your starting point. The top is often cloud-shrouded and can be windy and muddy, so check conditions before you start.

Horseback Riding

Stables at Kō'ele. The subtle beauty of the high country slowly reveals itself to horseback riders. Sunset rides, private saunters, and two-hour adventures traverse leafy trails with scenic overlooks. There's a fancy horse-drawn carriage for romantic couples and well-trained horses for riders of all ages and skill levels. Prices start at $85 for one hour and climb to $150 for a two-hour private ride. Book rides at The Lodge at Kō'ele. ☎ *808/565–4555.*

Sporting Clays & Archery

★ **Lāna'i Pine Sporting Clays and Archery Range.** Outstanding rustic terrain, challenging targets, and a well-stocked pro shop make this sporting-clays course top-flight in the expert's eyes. Sharpshooters can complete the meandering 14-station course, with the help of a golf cart, in 1½ hours. There are group tournaments, and even kids can enjoy skilled instruction at the archery range and compressed air rifle gallery. The $45 archery introduction includes an amusing "pineapple challenge"—contestants are given five arrows with which to hit a pineapple target. The winner takes home a crystal pineapple as a nostalgic souvenir of the old Dole Plantation days. Guns and ammunition are provided with the lessons. ⊠ *Just past Cemetery Rd. on windward side of island, first left off Keōmuku Hwy.* ☎ *808/559–4600.*

SHOPPING

Shopping at Dole Park

A miniforest of Cookpine trees in the center of Lāna'i City surrounded by small shops and restaurants, Dole Park is the closest thing to a mall on Lāna'i. Except for the high-end resort boutiques and pro shops, it provides the island's only shopping. A morning or afternoon stroll around the park offers an eclectic selection of gifts and clothing, plus a chance to chat with residents. Friendly general stores are straight out of the '20s, and new galleries and a boutique have original art and fashions for men, women, and children. The shops close on Sunday and after 5 PM, except for the general stores, which are open a bit later.

General Stores

International Food and Clothing Center. You may not find everything the name implies, but this old-fashioned emporium does stock items for your everyday needs, from fishing gear to beer. It's a good place for last-minute camping supplies. ⊠ *833 'Ilima Ave., Lāna'i City* ☎ *808/565–6433.*

Lāna'i City Service. In addition to being a gas station, auto parts store, and car-rental operation, this outfit sells Hawaiian gift items, sundries, T-shirts, beer, sodas, and bottled water in the **Plantation Store.** Open 7 to 7 daily for gas and sundries; auto parts store open weekdays 7–4. ⊠ *1036 Lāna'i Ave., Lāna'i City* ☎ *808/565–7227.*

Pine Isle Market. This is one of Lāna'i City's two supermarkets, stocking everything from cosmetics to canned vegetables. It's a great place to buy fresh fish. Take a look at the photographs of famous local fish and fishermen over the beer case. ⊠ *356 8th St., Lāna'i City* ☎ *808/565–6488.*

Richard's Shopping Center. Richard Tamashiro founded this store in 1946, and the Tamashiro clan continues to run the place. Along with groceries, the store has a fun selection of Lāna'i T-shirts. Richard's has a good selection of what they call "almost" fine wines, and a few gourmet food items. ⊠ *434 8th St., Lāna'i City* ☎ *808/565–6047.*

Sergio's Oriental Store. Sergio's, the closest thing to a Costco on Lāna'i, has Filipino sweets and pastries, case loads of sodas, water, juices, family-size containers of condiments and frozen fish and meat. Open 8 to 8 daily. ⊠ *831-D Houston St., Lāna'i City* ☎ *808/565–6900.*

Specialty Stores

Dis 'n Dat. This tiny, jungle-green shop packs in thousands of art, gift and jewelry items in a miniscule space enlivened by a glittering crystal ceiling. Fanciful garden ornaments, serene Buddhas, and Asian antiques add to the charm. Owners Barry and Suzie Osman are visitor-friendly and will help with almost anything you need. ⊠ *418 8th St., Lāna'i City* ☎ *808/565–9170.*

Gifts with Aloha. Casual resort wear is sold alongside a great collection of Hawaiiana books and the work of local artists, including ceramic ware, raku (Japanese-style lead-glazed pottery), fine handblown glass, and watercolor prints. Look for a complete selection of Hawaiian music CDs and Lāna'i-designed Stone Shack shirts. ⊠ *811-B Houston St., Lāna'i City* ☎ *808/565–6589.*

Heart of Lāna'i. The bright yellow house behind the Hotel Lāna'i shows watercolors by Denise Hennig, oil paintings by Macario Pascual, and bowls and 'ukulele by Cyrus Keanini. Afternoon tea is served at the gallery Tuesday through Saturday from 2:30 to 4:30. ⊠ *758 Queens St., Lāna'i City* ☎ *808/565–7815.*

Lāna'i Arts and Cultural Center. Local artists practice and display their crafts at this dynamic center. Workshops in the pottery, photography, woodworking, and painting studios welcome visitors, and individual instruction may be arranged. The center's gift shop sells original art and unique Lāna'i handicrafts. ⊠ *337 7th Ave., Lāna'i City* ☎ *808/565–7503.*

Local Gentry. This tiny, classy store has clothing for every need, from casual men's and women's beachwear to evening resort wear, shoes, jewelry, and hats. A small selection of fashionable children's apparel is also available. Proprietor Jenna Gentry will mail your purchases for the cost of the postage. ⊠ *363 7th St., Lāna'i City* ☎ *808/565–9130.*

Mike Carrol Gallery. The dreamy, soft-focus oil paintings of resident painter Mike Carroll are showcased along with wood bowls and koa 'ukulele by Warren Osako and fish-print paper tapestries by Joana Varawa. Local photographer Ron Gingerich, island artists Cheryl McElfresh, and jeweler Susan Hunter are also featured. ⊠ *443 7th St., Lāna'i City* ☎ *808/565–7122.*

SPAS

If you're looking for rejuvenation, the whole island could be considered a spa, though the only spa facilities are at the Four Seasons Resort Lāna'i at Mānele Bay or the Health Center at the Lodge at Ko'ele. For a quick polish in town, try Neda at **Island Images** (☎ 808/565–7870) for haircuts, waxing, and eyebrow shaping with threads (an ancient technique); Kathy at **Highlights** (☎ 808/565–7207) for hair, nails, and makeup; or Nita at **Nita's In Style** (☎ 808/565–8082) for hair care.

Lodge at Kō'ele's Healing Arts Center. Adjacent to the Lodge's pool and Jacuzzis, this bright, modest center provides cardiovascular equipment and free weights. Pump iron and watch yourself in the floor-to-ceiling mirrors or look out at the formal gardens and majestic trees. A single massage room offers specialty treatments and massages. ⊠ *Lodge at Kō'ele* ☎ *808/565–7300* ⊕ *www.fourseasons.com* ☞ *$105–$145 50-minute massage. Gym with: cardiovascular machines, free weights. Services: aromatherapy, body wraps, hot rock massage, facials, chemical peel, lash and brow tinting, herbal therapy consulting. Classes and programs: yoga.*

The Spa at Mānele. State-of-the-art pampering enlists a panoply of oils and unguents that would have pleased Cleopatra. The Spa After Hours Experience drenches you in private service including pineapple tea, neck and shoulder massage, and 50-minute treatment of your choice. Then melt down in the sauna or steam room, finish off with a scalp massage and light pūpū, and ooze out to your room. The *Ali'i* banana coconut scrub and pineapple citrus polish treatments have inspired their own cosmetic line. Massages in private *hale* (houses) in the courtyard gardens are available for singles or couples. A tropical fantasy mural, granite stone floors, eucalyptus steam rooms, and private cabanas overlooking the sea set the scene for indulgence. ⊠ *Four Seasons Resort Lāna'i at Mānele Bay* ☎ *808/565–2000* ⊕ *www.fourseasons.com* ☞ *$135–$145 50-minute massage; $320 per person 2-hr Spa After Hours Experience (2-person minimum), $20 extra for use of facilities with a 50-minute massage. Hair salon, sauna, steam room. Gym with: cardiovascular equipment, free weights. Services: aromatherapy, reflexology, body wraps, facials, pedicures, hair care, nails, waxing. Classes and programs: yoga, tai chi, aquaerobics, hula classes, guided hikes, personal training.*

6

ENTERTAINMENT & NIGHTLIFE

Lāna'i is certainly not known for its nightlife. Fewer than a handful of places stay open past 9 PM. At the resorts, excellent piano music or light live entertainment makes for a quiet, romantic evening. Another romantic alternative is star-watching from the beaches or watching the full moon rise in all its glory.

Hotel Lāna'i. A trip to the small, lively bar here is an opportunity to visit with locals. Last call is at 9. ☎ *808/565–7211.*

Lāna'i Theater and Playhouse. This 153-seat, '30s landmark presents first-run movies Friday through Tuesday, with showings at 6:30 and 8:30.

This is also the venue that shows films from the Hawai'i Film Festival. ⊠ *465 7th Ave., Lāna'i City* ☎ *808/565–7500.*

Lodge at Kō'ele. The cozy cocktail bar stays open until 11 PM. The Lodge also features quiet piano music in its Great Hall every evening from 7 to 10, as well as special performances by well-known Hawaiian entertainers and local hula dancers. The Saturday afternoon keiki hula show is at 12:30. ☎ *808/565–7300.*

Four Seasons Resort Lāna'i at Mānele Bay. Hale Aheahe (House of Gentle Breezes), the classy open-air lounge, with upscale pūpū and complete bar, offers musical entertainment Tuesday through Saturday evenings from 5:30 to 9:30. There's a Saturday keiki hula show in the grand lobby at 2:30. ☎ *808/565–7700.*

WHERE TO EAT

Lāna'i's own version of Hawai'i regional cuisine draws on the fresh bounty provided by local hunters and fishermen, combined with the skills of well-trained chefs. The upscale menus at the Lodge at Kō'ele and Mānele Bay Hotel encompass European-inspired cuisine and innovative preparations of quail, 'ahi, wild deer, and boar. Lāna'i City's eclectic ethnic fare runs from construction-worker-size local plate lunches to Cajun ribs and pesto pasta.

WHAT IT COSTS				
$$$$	**$$$**	**$$**	**$**	**¢**
RESTAURANTS over$35	$27–$35	$18–$26	$10–$17	under $10

Prices are for one main course at dinner.

Mānele Bay

★ **$$–$$$$** ✕ **'Ihilani.** The Four Seasons Mānele Bay Hotel's fine dining room shimmers with crystal chandeliers and gleaming silver in a serene setting illuminated by floor-to-ceiling etched-glass doors. Executive chef Oliver Beckert offers an upscale version of Italian comfort food designed around fresh local fish. Puna goat cheese ravioli with pine nuts and baby vegetables, and *onaga* (red snapper) served alla Puttanesca, with artichoke puree, and a spicy tomato and caper sauce, are good choices. Service is nonintrusive but attentive. ⊠ *Four Seasons Mānele Bay Resort Lāna'i at* ☎ *808/565–2296* ⚱ *Reservations essential* 🖃 *AE, DC, MC, V* ☉ *No lunch. $20–$44.*

$–$$$$ ✕ **The Challenge At Mānele Clubhouse.** This terraced restaurant has a stunning view of the legendary Pu'upehe offshore island, which only enhances its imaginative fare. Tuck into a Hulopo'e Bay prawn BLT at lunch. At night, under a gorgeous full moon, enjoy cocktails or a glass of chilled wine with pan-seared opakapaka or pad Thai noodles with shrimp and crab in a macadamia nut curry sauce. Specialty drinks add to the informal fun. ⊠ *Four Seasons Resort Lāna'i at Mānele Bay* ☎ *808/565–2290* 🖃 *AE, DC, MC, V* ☉ *No dinner Tues. and Wed. $14–$36.*

$–$$$$ ✕ **The Ocean Grill Bar & Restaurant.** Poolside at the Four Seasons Resort Lānaʻi at Mānele Bay, the Ocean Grill offers informal lunch and dinner in a splendid setting. The big yellow-and-white umbrellas are cool and cheerful, and bamboo-inspired upholstered chairs in yellow and green are deliciously comfortable. Favorite lunch items include the *kālua* (pit-roasted) pork and cheese quesadilla, or the rare ʻahi salade niçoise with fresh island greens. The dinner menu includes seasonal fresh island fish—*onaga* (red snapper), *opakapaka* (white snapper), and *hapuʻupuʻu* (sea bass), or an herb-crusted rack of lamb. The view of Hulopoʻe Bay is stunning, the service is Four Season's brand of cool aloha, and the decor is impeccable. ⊠ *Four Seasons Resort Lānaʻi at Mānele Bay* ☎ 808/565–2000 ▭ *AE, DC, MC, V. $12–$40.*

$$–$$$ ✕ **Four Seasons Hulopoʻe Court.** The Hulopoʻe overlooks the wide sweep of the bay and offers an extensive breakfast buffet, lunch, and dinner in airy comfort. Choose between indoor or outdoor tables, with comfortable chairs upholstered in beige and burgundy. Cream-colored walls provide a restful backdrop indoors, and pale pink umbrellas shade the terrace dining. Fresh baked pastries and made-to-order omelets ensure your day will start well. For lunch the ʻahi or mahimahi tacos are good choices; at dinner the daily fish special, the baked Pacific prawns stuffed with Dungeness crab, or Kurobuta pork chops marinated in hoisin sauce with Lānaʻi pineapple relish are all local favorites. Their chocolate cake is perfect. ⊠ *Four Seasons Resort Lānaʻi at Mānele Bay* ☎ 808/565–2290 ⚭ *Reservations essential* ▭ *AE, DC, MC, V. $19–$34.*

Upcountry & Lānaʻi City

$$$$ ✕ **Formal Dining Room.** Reflecting the Lodge's country-manor elegance,
★ this romantic octagonal restaurant is one of the best in the state. Intimate tables are clustered close to a roaring fireplace with room between for private conversation. Expanding Hawaiʻi regional cuisine, the changing menu includes the signature crispy seared moi (a fish once reserved for Hawaiian chiefs). Start with tiny roasted quail on baby greens and finish with a warm pear soufflé (ordered in advance). Expect visiting chefs as well as a master sommelier who provides exclusive wine pairings. ⊠ *Lodge at Kōʻele* ☎ 808/565–7300 ⚭ *Reservations essential* 🍴 *Jacket required* ▭ *AE, DC, MC, V* ⊘ *No lunch. $42–$46.*

$–$$$ ✕ **Henry Clay's Rotisserie.** With the only bar and comparatively fine dining in Lānaʻi City, this is a lively spot, right at the Hotel Lānaʻi. Louisiana-style ribs, Cajun-style shrimp, and gumbo add up to what chef Henry Clay Richardson calls "American country," but he brings it back home with island venison and locally caught fish. A fireplace and paintings by local artists add to the Upcountry feel. Large parties can be accommodated and are sometimes quite noisy. ⊠ *Hotel Lānaʻi, 828 Lānaʻi Ave., Lānaʻi City* ☎ 808/565–7211 ▭ *MC, V. $17–$35.*

$–$$$ ✕ **The Terrace.** Floor-to-ceiling glass doors open onto formal gardens and lovely vistas of the mist-clad mountains. Breakfast, lunch, and dinner are served in an informal atmosphere with attentive service. Try poached eggs on crab cakes to start the day and a free-range strip loin with pesto mashed potatoes to finish it. A complete wine list and the soothing sounds of the grand piano in the Great Hall in the evening complete the ambience. ☒ *Lodge at Kō'ele* ☎ *808/565–7300* 🖃 *AE, DC, MC, V. $12–$35.*

$–$$ ✕ **Pele's Other Garden.** Mark and Barbara Zigmond's colorful little eatery is a deli and bistro all in one. For lunch, deli sandwiches or daily hot specials reward an arduous hike. At night the restaurant turns into an intimate tablecloth-dining bistro, complete with soft jazz music. A nice wine list enhances an Italian-inspired menu. Start with bruschetta, then choose from a selection of pasta dishes or pizzas. ☒ *811 Houston St., Lāna'i City* ☎ *808/565–9628 or 888/764–3354* 🖃 *AE, DC, MC, V. $16–$22.*

¢–$$ ✕ **565 Café.** Named after the only telephone prefix on Lāna'i, this is a convenient stop for anything from pizza to a Palawai chicken breast sandwich on fresh-baked focaccia. Make a quick stop for plate lunches or try a picnic *pūpū* platter of chicken *katsu* to take along for the ride. If you need a helium balloon for a party, you can find that here, too. The patio and outdoor tables are kid-friendly, and an outdoor Saturday afternoon flea market adds to the quirkiness. ☒ *408 8th St., Lāna'i City* ☎ *808/565–6622* 🖃 *No credit cards. $7–$20.*

> ## FOOD WITH A VIEW
>
> Don't miss a meal at the Challenge at Mānele clubhouse, overlooking Hulopo'e Bay. Day or night, the view is spectacular. Palm trees frame a vista of the curving white-sand beach with the rocky headland of Pu'upehe (Sweetheart Rock), punctuating the luminous sky. In the distance is Kaho'olawe, recently rescued as a bombing target from the U.S. Navy, and in the foreground, the Challenge golf course with its scurrying golf carts adds visual interest. At night, with the full moon scattering sequins on the sea, it's enough to get you singing the whole score of *South Pacific*.

¢–$ ✕ **Blue Ginger Café.** This cheery eatery is a Lāna'i City institution. Owners Joe and Georgia Abilay have made this place into one of the town's most popular hangouts with consistent, albeit simple, food. Locally inspired paintings and photos line the walls inside, while the town passes the outdoor tables in parade. For breakfast, try the Portuguese sausage omelet with rice or fresh pastries. Lunchtime selections range from burgers and pizza to Hawaiian staples such as *saimin* and *musubi* (fried Spam wrapped in rice and seaweed). Try a shrimp stir-fry for dinner. ☒ *409 7th Ave., Lāna'i City* ☎ *808/565–6363* 🖃 *No credit cards. $7–$14.*

¢–$ ✕ **The Experience at Ko'ele Clubhouse.** The clubhouse overlooks the emerald greens of the golf course. Sit inside and watch sports on the TV or on the terrace to enjoy the antics of lumbering wild turkey families. A grilled fresh-catch sandwich is accompanied by fries, or try their succulent hamburgers, the best on the island. Salads and sandwiches, beer and wine, soft drinks, and some not very inspiring desserts complete the menu. ☒ *Lodge at Kō'ele* ☎ *808/565–4605* 🖃 *AE, DC, MC, V* ⊘ *No dinner. $8–$15.*

¢ ✕ **Lāna'i Coffee.** A block off Dole Park, you can sit outside on the large deck, sip cappuccinos, and watch the slow-pace life of the town slip by. Bagels with lox, deli sandwiches, and pastries add to the caloric content, while blended espresso shakes and gourmet ice cream complete the old-world illusion. Caffeine-inspired specialty items make good gifts and souvenirs. ☒ *604 'Ilima St., Lāna'i City* ☎ *808/565–6962* ⊘ *Closed Sun. $4–$7.*

WHERE TO STAY

Though Lāna'i has few properties, it does have a range of price options. The Four Seasons properties—Lodge at Kō'ele and Lāna'i at Mānele Bay—form a single luxury resort with beachside and Upcountry locations. Although the room rates are different, guests can partake all the resort amenities at both properties. If you're on a budget, seek out a friendly bed-and-breakfast or consider the Hotel Lāna'i. Vacation house rentals, a great option for families, give you a feel for everyday life on the island. In hunting seasons, from mid-February through mid-May, and from mid-July through mid-October, most of the private properties are booked way in advance.

	WHAT IT COSTS				
	$$$$	**$$$**	**$$**	**$**	**¢**
HOTELS	over $340	$261–$340	$181–$260	$100–$180	under$100

Prices are for two people in a standard double room in high season. Condo price categories reflect studio and one-bedroom rates.

Hotels & Resorts

★ **$$$$** **Four Seasons Resort Lāna'i at Mānele Bay.** Reached by a sweeping circular driveway lined with redrose bushes, this refurbished and refurnished ornate property overlooking Hulopo'e Bay has spectacular views of Lāna'i's coastline and beyond. Courtyard gardens, breezeways, and bridges connect two-story guest-room buildings. The architecture combines Mediterranean and Asian elements; elaborate life-size paintings of Chinese court officials, gold-brocade warrior robes, and antique vases, sculpture, and artifacts, decorate the open-air lobbies. Hulopo'e Beach's white-sand crescent, with facilities for resort guests, is just below the pool terrace, and a *keiki* (children's) program focuses on the island's cultural and environmental heritage, with petroglyph walks, crab hunting, 'ukulele playing, and more. A state-of-the-art fitness center overlooks the sea, and an adjacent movement studio offers yoga, tai chi, and personal training. *Box 631380, Lāna'i City 96763* ☎ *808/565–2000 or 800/321–4666* 📠 *808/565–2483* ⊕ *www.fourseasons.com* 🛏 *215 rooms, 21 suites* △ *3 restaurants, room service, in-room broadband, in-room safes, minibars, cable TV with movies and video games, in-room DVD players, 18-hole golf course, 3 tennis courts, pool, health club, spa, billiards, 2 bars, recreation room, library, babysitting, children's programs (ages 5–13), laundry service, Internet room, no-smoking rooms* ⊟ *AE, DC, MC, V. $400–$900.*

$$$$ **Lodge at Kō'ele.** In the highlands edging Lāna'i City, this grand coun-
Fodor'sChoice try estate, managed by Four Seasons, exudes luxury and quiet romance.
★ Secluded by old pines, 1½ mi of paths meander through formal gardens with a huge reflecting pond, a wedding gazebo and an orchid greenhouse. Afternoon tea is served in front of the immense stone fireplaces beneath the high-beamed ceilings of the magnificent Great Hall. The music room

lounge is a relaxing haven after a day on the Lodge's golf course or sporting clays range. A long veranda, furnished with wicker lounge chairs, looks out over rolling green pastures toward spectacular sunsets. 🛏 *Box 360310, Lāna'i City 96763* 🕿 *808/565–7300 or 800/321–4666* 🖷 *808/565–3868* 🌐 *www.lodgeatkoele.com* 🛏 *84 rooms, 12 suites* ⌂ *2 restaurants, room service, fans, in-room safes, minibars, cable TV with movies and video games, 18-hole golf course, shop, tennis courts, pool, gym, hot tub, massage, bicycles, archery, croquet, hiking, horseback riding, lawn bowling, bar, library, children's programs (ages 5–12), laundry service, no-smoking rooms, Internet room* 🖴 *AE, DC, MC, V. $400–$575.*

$ 🏠 **Hotel Lāna'i.** Built in 1923 to house visiting pineapple executives, this 10-room inn was once the only accommodation on the island. The recently refurbished plantation-inspired rooms, with country quilts, light pine woods, and local art, make it seem like you're staying in someone's home. Rooms with porches overlooking the pine trees and Lāna'i City are especially nice. The restaurant has a small bar. A self-serve Continental breakfast with fresh-baked breads is served on the veranda and is included in the rate. ✉ *828 Lāna'i Ave., Lāna'i City 96763* 🕿 *808/565–7211 or 800/795–7211* 🖷 *808/565–6450* 🌐 *www.hotellanai.com* 🛏 *10 rooms, 1 cottage* ⌂ *Restaurant; no a/c, no room TVs, no smoking* 🖴 *AE, MC, V. $115–$175.*

B&Bs & Vacation Rentals

All vacation rentals are in Lāna'i City, where altitude and prevailing trade winds replace air-conditioning. During hunting seasons, rentals are booked months—possibly years—in advance.

$ 🏠 **Sheila Black.** A log cabin cottage next to the Black's residence on "Haole Hill" is available as a vacation rental. This simply furnished, family-friendly, two-bedroom–two-bath cottage offers a fully equipped kitchen with all appliances, linens, pine trees, and country peace. It can accommodate up to seven, with extra beds in the living room ($15 extra per night per additional person over four). ✉ *656 Pu'ulani Pl., 96763* 🕿 *808/565–6867* 🖷 *808/565–7695* ✉ *adblack@aloha.net* 🛏 *2-bedroom cottage* ⌂ *Kitchen, cable TV; no A/C, no smoking* 🖴 *No credit cards. 2-bedroom cottage $150.*

¢ 🏠 **Dreams Come True.** Michael and Susan Hunter rent out a four-bedroom, four-bathroom plantation home in the heart of Lāna'i City, available in its entirety or as individual guest rooms. Antiques gleaned from many trips through South Asia add to the atmosphere. Some rooms have canopy beds, and each has its own marble bath with whirlpool tub. The living room has a TV and VCR, and the kitchen is available for guest use. There's also a veranda and garden. Enjoy the Hunters' company and gather information about the island each morning, when a home-cooked full breakfast becomes a special occasion. They will arrange vehicle rental and book activities, too. ✉ *1168 Lāna'i St., Lāna'i City 96763* 🕿 *808/565–6961 or 800/566–6961* 🖷 *808/565–7056* 🌐 *www.circumvista.com/dreamscometrue.html* 🛏 *3 rooms* ⌂ *Laundry facilities; no A/C, no room phones, no room TVs, no smoking* 🖴 *AE, D, MC, V. $112.*

¢ 🏠 **Hale Moe.** Momi Suzuki has turned her elegant esthetic into a peaceful Japanese-inspired retreat. This serenely furnished bed-and-breakfast has a well-tended garden with expansive views of the distant ocean. There's TV in the living room and a kitchen available for guest use. Help yourself to coffee and Continental breakfast on the sunny deck. Momi will advise you on where to go and what to do on the island. Sometimes her jeep is available for rent as well. You can also rent the three-bedroom, three-bath house for $300 a night with a limit of six people. ✆ *Box 630196, 96763* ☎ *808/565–9520* ⊕ *staylanai.com* ⇆ *3 rooms* ⚓ *No A/C, no phones in some rooms, no TV in some rooms, no smoking* ▭ *No credit cards. $80–$90.*

¢ 🖼 **McOmber Enterprises.** Five different houses in Lānaʻi City are available as short-term economy vacation rentals. They can accommodate from two to eight persons. Kitchens are fully furnished and equipped, and linens are supplied. ✆ *Box 630646, 96763* ☎ *808/565–6071* ✉ *mcomber@aloha.net* ⇆ *5 houses* ⚓ *Kitchen, laundry facilities; no A/C, no room phones, no TV in some rooms, no smoking* ▭ *No credit cards. $35 per person per night.*

LĀNAʻI ESSENTIALS

Transportation

6

BY AIR

You can reach Lānaʻi from Oʻahu's Honolulu International Airport via Island Air. Island Air offers several flights daily on 18-passenger Dash-6s and 37-seat Dash-8s; round-trip tickets start at $150 depending on the season. Royal Hawaiian Air Service has two daily flights to and from Honolulu. Traveling from other islands requires a stop in Honolulu and a transfer to Island Air and is booked through Aloha Airlines.

AIRPORT The airport has a federal agricultural inspection station so that guests departing to the mainland can check luggage directly.
🚩 **Lānaʻi Airport** ☎ 808/565–6757.

TO AND FROM Lānaʻi Airport is a 10-minute drive from Lānaʻi City. If you're staying at
THE AIRPORT the Hotel Lānaʻi, the Lodge at Kōʻele, or the Four Seasons Resort Lānaʻi at Mānele Bay, you'll be met by a shuttle for a $25 fee, which includes all transportation for the length of your stay. Day rates are $5 round-trip to town, and $10 round-trip to Mānele. See the resort receptionist at the airport. Dollar will pick you up if you're renting a car or jeep. Call from the red courtesy phone at the airport. See the resort shuttle driver.

BY CAR

There are only 30 mi of paved road on the island. Keōmuku Highway starts just past the Lodge at Kōʻele and runs north to Shipwreck Beach. Mānele Road (Highway 440) runs south down to Mānele Bay and Hulopoʻe Beach. Kaumalapau Highway (also Highway 440) heads west to Kaumalapau Harbor. The rest of your driving takes place on bumpy, muddy, secondary roads, which generally aren't marked.

You'll never find yourself in a traffic jam, but it's easy to get lost on the unmarked dirt roads. Before heading out, ask for a map at your hotel desk and verify that you're headed in the right direction. Always remember *mauka* (toward the mountain) and *makai* (toward the sea) for basic directions. If you're traveling on dirt roads take water. People still drive slowly here, wave, and pull over to give each other lots of room. The only gas station on the island is in Lāna'i City, at Lāna'i City Service (open 7–7 daily).

CAR RENTAL Renting a four-wheel-drive vehicle is expensive but almost essential. Make reservations far in advance of your trip, because Lāna'i's fleet of vehicles is limited. Lāna'i City Service, a subsidiary of Dollar Rent A Car, is open daily 7–7. Jeep Wranglers and minivans go for $139 a day, full-size cars are $80, and compact cars are about $60.

🚗 **Lāna'i City Service** ⊠ Lāna'i Ave. at 11th St. ☎ 808/565-7227 or 800/533-7808.

BY FERRY

Expeditions ferries cross the channel five times daily, departing from Lahaina on Maui and Mānele Bay Harbor on Lāna'i. The crossing takes 45 minutes and costs $25 each way.

🚗 **Expeditions** ☎ 808/661-3756 or 800/695-2624 ⊕ www.go-lanai.com.

TO & FROM THE Lāna'i City Service will shuttle you from the harbor to downtown for
HARBOR $10 one way. However, the service is only available if they're already making the trip. The resort shuttle will bring you from the harbor to the Four Seasons Resort Lāna'i at Mānele Bay for a day fee of $5 round-trip or to town for a day-fee of $10 round-trip. See the shuttle driver.

🚗 **Lāna'i City Service** ⊠ Lāna'i Ave. at 11th St. ☎ 808/565-7227 or 800/533-7808.

BY SHUTTLE

A shuttle transports hotel guests among the Hotel Lāna'i, the Lodge at Kō'ele, the Four Seasons Resort Lāna'i at Mānele Bay, and the airport. A $25 fee covers all transportation during the length of stay.

Contacts & Resources

EMERGENCIES

In an emergency, dial **911** to reach an ambulance, the police, or the fire department.

The Lāna'i Family Clinic, part of the Straub Clinic & Hospital, is the island's health-care center. It's open daily from 8 to 5 and closed on weekends. There's a limited pharmacy. In emergencies, call 911 or go to the emergency room of the hospital next door.

🚗 **Straub Clinic & Hospital** ⊠ 628 7th St., Lāna'i City ☎ 808/565-6423 clinic, 808/565-6411 hospital.

VISITOR INFORMATION

Lāna'i Visitor's Bureau is your best bet for general information and maps. Feel free to stop in between 8 AM and 4 PM. The Maui Visitors Bureau also has some information on the island.

🚗 **Lāna'i Visitor's Bureau** ⊠ 431 7th St., Suite A, Lāna'i City 96763 ☎ 808/565-7600.
Maui Visitors Bureau ☎ 808/244-3530 ⊕ www.visitlanai.com.

UNDERSTANDING HAWAI'I

HAWAI'I AT A GLANCE

Fast Facts

Nickname: Aloha State
Capital: Honolulu
State song: "Hawai'i Pono'i"
State bird: The nēnē, an endangered land bird and variety of goose
State flower: Yellow Hibiscus Brackenridgii
State tree: Kukui (or candlenut), a Polynesian-introduced tree
Administrative divisions: There are four counties with mayors and councils: City and County of Honolulu (island of O'ahu), Hawai'i County (Hawai'i Island), Maui County (islands of Maui, Moloka'i, Lāna'i and Kahoolawe), and Kaua'i County (islands of Kaua'i and Ni'ihau)
Entered the Union: August 21, 1959, as the 50th state
Population: 1,334,023
Life expectancy: Female 82, male 76

Literacy: 81%
Ethnic groups: Hawaiian/part Hawaiian 22.1% Caucasian 20.5% Japanese 18.3% Filipino 12.3% Chinese 4.1%
Religion: Roman Catholic 22%; Buddhist, Shinto and other East Asian religions 15%; Mormon 10%; Church of Christ 8%; Assembly of God and Baptist 6% each; Episcopal, Jehovah's Witness and Methodist 5% each
Language: English is the first language of the majority of residents; Hawaiian is the native language of the indigenous Hawaiian people and an official language of the state; other languages spoken include Samoan, Chinese, Japanese, Korean, Spanish, Portuguese, Filipino, and Vietnamese

The loveliest fleet of islands that lies anchored in any ocean.
Mark Twain

Geography & Environment

Land area: An archipelago of 137 islands encompassing a land area of 6,422.6 square mi in the north-central Pacific Ocean (about 2,400 mi from the West Coast of the continental U.S.).
Coastline: 750 mi
Terrain: Volcanic mountains, tropical rain forests, verdant valleys, sea cliffs, canyons, deserts, coral reefs, sand dunes, sandy beaches
Natural resources: Dimension limestone, crushed stone, sand and gravel, gemstones
Natural hazards: Hurricanes, earthquakes, tsunamis
Flora: More than 2,500 species of native and introduced plants throughout the islands.
Fauna: Native mammals include the hoary bat, Hawaiian monk seal, and Polynesian rat. The humpback whale migrates to Hawaiian waters every winter to mate and calve. More than 650 fish and 40 different species of shark live in Hawaiian waters. Freshwater streams are home to hundreds of native and alien species. The humuhumunukunukuāpua'a (Hawaiian triggerfish) is the unofficial state fish.
Environmental issues: Plant and animal species threatened and endangered due to hunting, overfishing, overgrazing by wild and introduced animals, and invasive alien plants

Hawai'i is not a state of mind, but a state of grace.
Paul Theroux

Economy

Tourism and federal defense spending continue to drive the state's economy. Efforts to diversify in the areas of science and technology, film and television production, sports, ocean research and development, health and education, tourism, agriculture, and floral and specialty food products are ongoing.

GSP: $40.1 billion
Per capita income: $30,000
Inflation: 1%
Unemployment: 4.3%
Work force: 595,450
Debt: $7.3 billion
Major industries: Tourism, federal government (defense and other agencies)
Agricultural products: Sugar, pineapple, papayas, guavas, flower and nursery products, asparagus, alfalfa hay, macadamia nuts, coffee, milk, cattle, eggs, shellfish, algae
Exports: $616 million
Major export products: Aircraft and parts, naphthas, medical equipment and supplies, fruit, steel scrap, electronic components, unleaded gasoline, artwork, cocoa, coffee, flowers, macadamia nuts
Imports: $2.6 billion
Major import products: Crude oil, electronic and digital equipment, coal, passenger motor vehicles

In what other land save this one is the commonest form of greeting not "Good day," or How d'ye do," but "Love?" That greeting is "Aloha"–love, I love, my love to you . . .It is a positive affirmation of the warmth of one's own heart, giving.

Jack London

Debate has waxed and waned for more than a century over how and when to return to native Hawaiians more than 1 million acres of land and other assets seized when American business interests overthrew the island monarchy in 1893. Certain native factions still advocate a return to independent nationhood. Sovereignty gained new momentum in the 1990s with the passage of a federal law formally apologizing for the overthrow and urging reconciliation. Momentum has since fizzled. Hawaiʻi's current governor has renewed efforts to have Congress recognize Hawaiians as an indigenous people, much like Native Americans and Alaskans. The governor also has pledged to support continued funding of health care, language, and other cultural programs, and to achieve state and federal obligations to distribute homestead lands to qualified Hawaiians.

Did You Know?

- Hawaiʻi is home to the world's most active volcano: Kīlauea, on the Big Island.

- ʻIolani Palace had electricity and telephones installed several years before the White House, and is the only palace on U.S. soil.

- Hawaiʻi has about 12% of all endangered plants and animals in the United States; 75% of the country's extinct plants and birds were Hawaiian.

- The Royal Hawaiian Band is the only intact organization from the time of Hawaiian monarchy that is fully functional and still preserves Hawaiʻi's musical history.

THESE VOLCANIC ISLES

DAWN AT THE CRATER ON HORSEBACK. It's cold at 10,023 feet above the warm Pacific—maybe 45°F. The horses' breath condenses into smoky clouds, and the riders cling to their saddles. It's eerily quiet except for the creak of straining leather and the crunch of volcanic cinders underfoot, sounds that are absurdly magnified in the vast empty space that yawns below.

This is Haleakalā, the "house of the sun." It's the crown of East Maui and the largest dormant volcanic depression in the world. The park encompasses 28,665 acres, and the valley itself is 21 mi in circumference and 19 square mi in area. At its deepest, it measures 3,000 feet from the summit, and could accommodate all of Manhattan. What you see here isn't actually a crater at all but something called a caldera, formed by the collapsing of the main cone, the result of eons of wind and rain wearing down what was once a small dip at the original summit peak. The small hills within the valley are volcanic cinder cones, each the site of an eruption.

Every year thousands of visitors drive the world's steepest auto route to the summit of Haleakalā National Park. Sunrise is extraordinary here. Mark Twain called it "the sublimest spectacle" he had ever witnessed.

But sunrise is only the beginning.

Hiking Haleakalā is like walking on the moon, with 32 mi of trails weaving around volcanic rubble, crater cones, frozen lava flows, vents, and tubes. The colors are muted yet dramatic—black, yellow, russet, orange, lavender, brown, even a pinkish blue—and change throughout the day.

This ecosystem sustains the surefooted mountain goat; the rare *nēnē* goose (no webbing between its toes, the better to negotiate this rugged terrain); and the strange, delicate silversword. A spiny, metallic-leaf plant, the silversword once grew abundantly on Haleakalā's slopes. Today it survives in small numbers at Haleakalā and at high elevations on the Big Island of Hawai'i. The plants live up to 40 years, bloom only once, scatter their seeds, and die.

It's not difficult to see this place as a bubbling, sulfurous cauldron, a direct connection to the core of the earth. Haleakalā's last—and probably final—eruption occurred in 1790, a few years after a Frenchman named Jean-François de Galaup, Comte de La Pérouse, became the first European to set foot on Maui. The rocky area on the southwest side of East Maui known as La Pérouse Bay is the result of that flow.

Large and small, awake or sleeping, volcanoes are Hawai'i's history and heritage. Behind their beauty is the story of the flames that created this ethereal island chain. The islands in the Hawaiian archipelago are actually the upper bodies of immense mountains rising from the bottom of the sea. Formed by molten rock known as magma, the islands have slowly grown from the earth's volatile mantle, lava forced through a "hot spot" in the thin crust of the ocean floor. The first ancient eruptions cooled and formed pools on the Pacific bottom. Then as magma spilled from the vents over millions of years, the pools became ridges and grew into crests. The latter built upon themselves over the eons, until finally they towered above the surface of the sea. This type of volcano, with its slowly formed, gently sloping sides, is known as a shield volcano. All of the Hawaiian Islands were created this way.

As the Islands cooled in the Pacific waters, the lava slopes slowly bloomed, over centuries, with colorful flora. About once every 35,000 years a seed, spore, bird, or insect arrived here on the winds or waves. They found a fertile, sun-and-rain–drenched home, free of predators. Over time, these migrants developed into highly specialized organisms. A land with no predatory species breeds a population of plants and animals devoid of biological protections, making them especially fragile and vulnerable to foreign species and human development. Today Hawai'i suffers from one of the world's highest species extinction rates; eighty percent of native Hawaiian birds are now gone.

But for all the talk of geology, Hawaiian myth casts a different history of the islands. Pele, the beautiful and tempestuous daughter of Haumea, the Earth Mother, and Wakea, the Sky Father, is the Hawaiian goddess of fire, the maker of mountains, melter of rock, eater of forests—a creator and a destroyer. Legend has it that Pele came to the Islands long ago to flee from her cruel older sister, Na Maka o Kahai, goddess of the sea. Pele ran first to the small island of Ni'ihau, making a crater home there with her digging stick. But Na Maka found her and destroyed her hideaway, so Pele again had to flee. On Kaua'i she delved deeper, but Na Maka chased her from that home as well. Pele ran on—from O'ahu to Moloka'i, Lāna'i to Kaho'olawe, Molokini to Maui—but always Na Maka pursued her.

Pele came at last to *Halema'uma'u,* the vast fire-pit crater of Kīlauea, and there, on the Big Island, she dug deepest of all. There she is said to remain, all-powerful, quick to rage, and often unpredictable; the mountain is her impenetrable fortress and domain—a safe refuge, at least for a time, from Na Maka o Kahai.

The chronology of the old tales of Pele's flight from isle to isle closely matches the reckonings of modern volcanologists regarding the ages of the various craters. Today, the Big Island's Kīlauea and Mauna Loa retain the closest links with the earth's superheated core and are active and volatile. The other volcanoes have been

carried beyond their magma supply by the movement of the Pacific Plate. Those on Kaua'i, O'ahu, and Moloka'i are completely extinct. Those at the southeasterly end of the island chain—Haleakalā, Mauna Ke'a, and Hualālai—are dormant and slipping away, so that the implacable process of volcanic death has begun. As erosion continues, the islands will someday melt back into the sea.

The largest island of the archipelago, the Big Island of Hawai'i rises some 13,796 feet above sea level at the summit of Mauna Ke'a. Mauna Loa is nearly as high at 13,667 feet. Geologists believe it required more than 3 million years of steady volcanic activity to raise these peaks up above the waters of the Pacific. From their bases on the ocean floor, these shield volcanoes are the largest mountain masses on the planet.

Mauna Loa's little sister, Kīlauea, at about 4,077 feet, is the most active volcano in the world. Between the two volcanoes, they have covered nearly 200,000 acres of land with their red-hot lava flows over the past 200 years. In the process, they have ravished trees, fields, meadows, villages, and more than a few unlucky humans. For generations, Kīlauea, in a continually eruptive state, has pushed molten lava up from the earth's magma at 1,800°F and more. But as active as she and Mauna Loa are, their eruptions are comparatively safe and gentle, producing continuous small flows rather than large bursts of fire and ash. The exceptions were two explosive displays during recorded history—one in 1790, the other in 1924. During these eruptions, Pele came close to destroying the Big Island's largest city, Hilo.

It is around these major volcanoes that the island's Hawai'i Volcanoes National Park was created. A sprawling natural preserve, the park attracts visitors from around the world for the unparalleled opportunity to view lava up-close and personal. Geology experts and volcanologists have been coming for a century or more to study and to improve methods for predicting the times and sites of eruptions.

Thomas Augustus Jaggar, preeminent volcanologist and student of Kīlauea, built his home on stilts wedged into cracks in the volcanic rock of the crater rim. Harvard-trained and universally respected, he was the driving force behind the establishment of the Hawaiian Volcano Observatory at Kīlauea in 1912. When he couldn't raise research funds from donations, public and private, he raised pigs to keep the scientific work going. After Jaggar's death, his wife scattered his ashes over the great fiery abyss.

The park is on the Big Island's southeastern flank, about 30 minutes out of Hilo on the aptly named Volcano Highway. Wear sturdy walking shoes and carry a warm sweater. It can be a long hike across the lava flats to see Pele in action, and at 4,000 feet above sea level temperatures can be brisk, however hot the volcanic activity. So much can be seen at close range along the road circling the crater that Kīlauea has been dubbed the "drive-in volcano."

At the park's visitor center sits a large display case. It contains dozens of lava-rock "souvenirs"—removed from Pele's grasp and then returned, accompanied by letters of apology. They are sent back by visitors who say they regret having broken the *kapu* (taboo) against removing even the smallest grain of native volcanic rock from Hawai`i. A typical letter might say: "I never thought Pele would miss just one little rock, but she did, and now I've wrecked two cars . . . I lost my job, my health is poor, and I know it's because I took this stone." The letters can be humorous, or poignant and remorseful, requesting Pele's forgiveness.

It is surprisingly safe at the crater's lip. Unlike Japan's Mount Fuji or Washington State's Mount St. Helens, Hawai`i's shield volcanoes spew their lava downhill, along the sides of the mountain. Still, the clouds of sulfur gas and fumes produced during volcanic eruptions are noxious and heady and can make breathing unpleasant, if not difficult. It has been pointed out that the chemistry of volcanoes—sulfur, hydrogen, oxygen, carbon dioxide—closely resembles the chemistry of the egg.

It's an 11-mi drive around the Kīlauea crater via the Crater Rim Road, and the trip takes about an hour. But it's better to walk a bit. There are at least eight major trails in the park, ranging from short 15-minute strolls to the three-day, 18-mi (one way) Mauna Loa Trail. An easy, comfortable walk is Sulfur Banks, with its many steaming vents creating halos of clouds around the rim of Kīlauea. The route passes through a forest of sandalwood, flowers, and ferns.

Just ahead is the main attraction: the center of Pele's power, Halema`uma`u. This yawning pit of flame and burning rock measures some 3,000 feet wide and is a breathtaking sight. When Pele is in full fury, visitors come in droves, on foot and by helicopter, to see her crimson expulsions coloring the dark earth and smoky sky. Kīlauea's most recent violent activity has occurred at mountainside vents instead of at the summit crater. Known as rift zones, they are lateral conduits that often open in shield volcanoes.

Kīlauea has two rift zones, one extending from the summit crater toward the southwest, through Kau, the other to the eastnortheast through Puna, past Cape Kumakahi, into the sea. In the last two decades, repeated eruptions in the east rift zone have blocked off 12 mi of coastal road—some under more than 300 feet of rock—and have covered a total of 10,000 acres with lava. Where the flows entered the ocean, roughly 200 acres have been added to the Big Island.

Farther along the Crater Rim Road is the Thurston Lava Tube, an example of a strangely beautiful volcanic phenomenon common on the Islands. Lava tubes form when lava flows rapidly downhill. The sides and top of this river of molten rock cool, while the fluid center flows on. Most formations are short and shallow, but some measure 30 to 50 feet high and hundreds of yards long. Lava tubes were often used to store remains of the ancient Hawaiian royalty—the *ali'i*. The Thurston Lava Tube sits in a beautiful prehistoric fern forest.

Throughout the park, new lava formations are continually being created. These volcanic deposits exhibit the different types of lava produced by Hawai'i's volcanoes: *'a'ā*, the dark, rough lava that solidifies as cinders of rock; and the more common *pāhoehoe*, the smooth, satiny lava that forms the vast plains of black rock in ropy swirls known as lava flats, which in some areas go on for miles. Other terms that help identify what may be seen in the park include *caldera*, which are the open, bowl-like lips of a volcano summit; *ejecta*, the cinders and ash that float through the air around an eruption; and *olivine*, the semiprecious chrysolite (greenish in color) found in volcanic ash.

But this volcanic landscape isn't all fire and flash, cinders, and devastation. Hawai'i Volcanoes National Park is also the home of some of the most beautiful of the state's black-sand beaches; forest glens full of lacy butterflies and colorful birds such as the dainty flycatcher, called the *'elepaio*; and exquisite grottoes sparked with bright wild orchid sprays and crashing waterfalls. Even as the lava cools, still bearing a golden, glassy skin, lush, green native ferns—*ama'uma'u, kupukupu,* and *'ōkupukupu*—spring up in the midst of Pele's fallout, as if defying her destructiveness or simply confirming the fact that after fire she brings life.

Some 12 centuries ago, in fact, Pele brought humans to her verdant islands: the fiery explosions that lit Kīlauea and Mauna Loa probably guided the first explorers to Pele's side from the Marquesas Islands, some 2,400 mi away across the ocean.

Once settled, they worshiped her from a distance. Great numbers of religious *heiau* (outdoor stone platforms) dot the landscapes near the many older and extinct craters scattered throughout Hawai'i, demonstrating the reverence the native islanders have always held for Pele and her creations. But the ruins of only two *heiau* are to be found near the very active crater at Halema'uma'u. There, at the center of the capricious Pele's power, native Hawaiians caution one even today to "step lightly, for you are on holy ground."

In future ages, when mighty Kīlauea is no more, this area will still be a volcanic isle. Beneath the blue Pacific waters, fiery magma flows and new mountains form and grow. Off the south coast of the Big Island, a new island is forming. Still ½ mi below the water's surface, it won't be making an appearance any time soon, but already has a name: Lōihi.

— Gary Diedrichs

HAWAIIAN VOCABULARY

Although an understanding of Hawaiian is by no means required on a trip to the Aloha State, a *malihini*, or newcomer, will find plenty of opportunities to pick up a few of the local words and phrases. Traditional names and expressions are widely used in the Islands, thanks in part to legislation enacted in the early '90s to encourage the use of the Hawaiian language. You're likely to read or hear at least a few words each day of your stay. Such exposure enriches a trip to Hawai'i.

With a basic understanding and some uninhibited practice, anyone can have enough command of the local tongue to ask for directions and to order from a restaurant menu. One visitor announced she would not leave until she could pronounce the name of the state fish, the *humuhumunukunukuāpua'a*. Luckily, she had scheduled a nine-day stay.

Simplifying the learning process is the fact that Hawaiian contains only eight consonants—*H, K, L, M, N, P, W,* and the silent *'okina*, or glottal stop, written '—plus one or more of the five vowels. All syllables end in a vowel. Each vowel, except a few diphthongized double vowels such as *au* (pronounced "ow") or *ai* (pronounced "eye"), is pronounced separately. Thus *'Iolani* is four syllables (ee-oh-la-nee), not three (yo-la-nee). Although some Hawaiian words have only vowels, most also contain some consonants, which are never doubled.

Pronunciation is simple. Pronounce *A* "ah" as father; *E* "ay" as in weigh; *I* "ee" as in marine; *O* "oh" as in no; *U* "oo" as in true.

Consonants mirror their English equivalents, with the exception of *W*. When the letter begins any syllable other than the first one in a word, it is usually pronounced as a *V*. *'Awa*, the Polynesian drink, is pronounced "ava," *'ewa* is pronounced "eva."

Nearly all long Hawaiian words are combinations of shorter words; they are not difficult to pronounce if you segment them into shorter words. *Kalaniana'ole,* the highway running east from Honolulu, is easily understood as *Kalani ana 'ole.* Apply the standard pronunciation rules—the stress falls on the next-to-last syllable of most two- or three-syllable Hawaiian words—and Kalaniana'ole Highway is as easy to say as Main Street.

Now about that fish. Try *humu-humu nuku-nuku āpu a'a.*

The other unusual element in Hawaiian language is the *kahakō*, or macron, written as a short line ‾ placed over a vowel. Like the accent ´ in Spanish, the kahakō puts emphasis on a syllable that would normally not be stressed. The most familiar example is probably *Waikīkī.* With no macrons, the stress would fall on the middle syllable; with only one macron, on the last syllable, the stress would fall on the first and last syllables. Some words become plural with the addition of a macron, often on a syllable that would have been stressed anyway. No Hawaiian word becomes plural with the addition of an *S,* since that letter does not exist in the *'ōlelo Hawai'i* (which is Hawaiian for "Hawaiian language").

What follows is a glossary of some of the most commonly used Hawaiian words. Don't be afraid to give them a try. Hawaiian residents appreciate visitors who at least try to pick up the local language.

'a'ā: rough, crumbling lava, contrasting with *pāhoehoe,* which is smooth.
'ae: yes.
aikane: friend.
āina: land.
akamai: smart, clever, possessing savoir faire.
akua: god.
ala: a road, path, or trail.
ali'i: a Hawaiian chief, a member of the chiefly class.
aloha: love, kindness; also a salutation meaning greetings and farewell.

'ānuenue: rainbow.

'a'ole: no.

'apōpō: tomorrow.

'auwai: a ditch.

auwē: alas, woe is me!

'ehu: a red-haired Hawaiian.

'ewa: in the direction of 'Ewa plantation, west of Honolulu.

hala: the pandanus tree, whose leaves (*lau hala*) are used to make baskets and mats.

hālau: school.

hale: a house.

hale pule: church, house of worship.

ha mea iki or ha mea 'ole: you're welcome.

hana: to work.

haole: ghost. Since the first foreigners were Caucasian, *haole* now means a Caucasian person.

hapa: a part, sometimes a half; often used as a short form of *hapa haole,* to mean a person who is part-Caucasian; thus, the name of a popular local band, whose members represent a variety of ethnicities.

hau'oli: to rejoice. *Hau'oli Makahiki Hou* means Happy New Year. *Hau'oli lā hānau* means Happy Birthday.

heiau: an outdoor stone platform; an ancient Hawaiian place of worship.

holo: to run.

holoholo: to go for a walk, ride, or sail.

holokū: a long Hawaiian dress, somewhat fitted, with a yoke and a train. Influenced by European fashion, it was worn at court, and at least one local translates the word as "expensive mu'umu'u."

holomū: a post–World War II cross between a *holokū* and a mu'umu'u, less fitted than the former but less voluminous than the latter, and having no train.

honi: to kiss; a kiss. A phrase that some tourists may find useful, quoted from a popular hula, is *Honi Ka'ua Wikiwiki:* Kiss me quick!

honu: turtle.

ho'omalimali: flattery, a deceptive "line," bunk, baloney, hooey.

huhū: angry.

hui: a group, club, or assembly. A church may refer to its congregation as a *hui* and a social club may be called a *hui.*

hukilau: a seine; a communal fishing party in which everyone helps to drive the fish into a huge net, pull it in, and divide the catch.

hula: the dance of Hawai'i.

iki: little.

ipo: sweetheart.

ka: the. This is the definite article for most singular words; for plural nouns, the definite article is usually *nā.* Since there is no S in Hawaiian, the article may be your only clue that a noun is plural.

kahuna: a priest, doctor, or other trained person of old Hawai'i, endowed with special skills that often included the gift of prophecy or other supernatural powers; the plural is *kāhuna.*

kai: the sea, saltwater.

kalo: the taro plant from whose root poi is made.

kama'āina: literally, a child of the soil; it refers to people who were born in the Islands or have lived there for a long time.

kanaka: originally a man or humanity in general, it's now used to denote a male Hawaiian or part-Hawaiian, but is occasionally taken as a slur when used by non-Hawaiians. *Kanaka maoli,* originally a full-blooded Hawaiian person, is used by some native Hawaiian rights activists to embrace part-Hawaiians.

kāne: a man, a husband. If you see this word on a door, it's the men's room. If you see *kane* on a door, it's probably a misspelling; that is the Hawaiian name for the skin fungus tinea.

kapa: also called by its Tahitian name, *tapa,* a cloth made of beaten bark, usually dyed and stamped with a repeat design.

kapakahi: crooked, cockeyed, uneven. You've got your hat on *kapakahi.*

kapu: keep out, prohibited. This is the Hawaiian version of the more widely known Tongan word *tabu* (taboo).

kapuna: grandparent; elder.

kēia lā: today.

keiki: a child; *keikikāne* is a boy, *keikiwahine* a girl.

kona: the leeward side of the Islands, the direction (south) from which the *kona* wind and *kona* rain come.

kula: upland.

kuleana: a homestead or small plot of ground on which a family has been installed for some generations without necessarily owning it. By extension, *kuleana* is used to denote any area or department in which one has a special interest or prerogative. You'll hear it used this way: If you want to hire a surfboard, see Moki; that's his *kuleana*. And conversely: I can't help you with that; that's not my *kuleana*.

lā: sun.

lamalama: to fish with a torch.

lānai: a porch, a balcony, an outdoor living room. Almost every house in Hawai'i has one. Don't confuse this two-syllable word with the three-syllable name of the island, Lāna'i.

lani: heaven, the sky.

lau hala: the leaf of the *hala,* or pandanus tree, widely used in Hawaiian handicrafts.

lei: a garland of flowers.

limu: sun.

lolo: stupid.

luna: a plantation overseer or foreman.

mahalo: thank you.

makai: toward the ocean.

malihini: a newcomer to the Islands.

mana: the spiritual power that Hawaiians believe inhabits all things and creatures.

manō: shark.

manuwahi: free, gratis.

mauka: toward the mountains.

mauna: mountain.

mele: a Hawaiian song or chant, often of epic proportions.

Mele Kalikimaka: Merry Christmas (a transliteration from the English phrase).

Menehune: a Hawaiian pixie. The *Menehune* were a legendary race of little people who accomplished prodigious work, such as building fishponds and temples in the course of a single night.

moana: the ocean.

mu'umu'u: the voluminous dress in which missionaries enveloped Hawaiian women. Now made in bright printed cottons and silks, it is an indispensable garment in a Hawaiian woman's wardrobe. Culturally sensitive locals have embraced the Hawaiian spelling but often shorten the spoken word to "mu'u." Most English dictionaries include the spelling "muumuu."

nani: beautiful.

nui: big.

ohana: family.

'ono: delicious.

pāhoehoe: smooth, unbroken, satiny lava.

Pākē: Chinese. This *Pākē* carver makes beautiful things.

palapala: document, printed matter.

pali: a cliff, precipice.

pānini: prickly pear cactus.

paniolo: a Hawaiian cowboy, a rough transliteration of *español,* the language of the Islands' earliest cowboys.

pau: finished, done.

pilikia: trouble. The Hawaiian word is much more widely used here than its English equivalent.

puka: a hole.

pupule: crazy, like the celebrated Princess Pupule. This word has replaced its English equivalent in local usage.

pu'u: volcanic cinder cone.

waha: mouth.

wahine: a female, a woman, a wife, and a sign on the ladies' room door; the plural form is *wāhine.*

wai: freshwater, as opposed to saltwater, which is *kai.*

wailele: waterfall.

wikiwiki: to hurry, hurry up (since this is a reduplication of *wiki,* quick, neither W is pronounced as a V).

Note: Pidgin is the unofficial language of Hawai'i. It is a Creole language, with its own grammar, evolved from English, Hawaiian, Japanese, Portuguese, and other languages spoken in 19th-century Hawai'i. You'll hear it everywhere: on ranches, in warehouses, on beaches, and in the hallowed halls of the University of Hawai'i.

SMART TRAVEL TIPS

Finding out about your destination before you leave home means you won't spend time organizing everyday minutiae once you've arrived. You'll be more streetwise when you hit the ground as well, better prepared to explore the aspects of Hawai'i that drew you here in the first place. The organizations in this section can provide information to supplement this guide; contact them for up-to-the-minute details, and consult the A to Z sections that end each chapter for facts on the various topics as they relate to the state's many regions. Happy landings!

AIR TRAVEL

Hawai'i is a major destination link for flights traveling to and from the U.S. mainland, Asia, Australia, New Zealand, and the South Pacific. Some of the major airline carriers serving Hawai'i fly direct to the islands of Maui, Kaua'i, and the Big Island, allowing you to bypass connecting flights out of Honolulu. For the more spontaneous traveler, island-hopping is easy, with flights departing every 20 to 30 minutes daily until mid-evening. International travelers also have options: O'ahu and the Big Island are gateways to the United States.

BOOKING

When you book, look for nonstop flights and remember that "direct" flights stop at least once. Try to avoid connecting flights, which require a change of plane. Two airlines may operate a connecting flight jointly, so ask whether your airline operates every segment of the trip; you may find that the carrier you prefer flies you only part of the way. To find more booking tips and to check prices and make online flight reservations, log on to www.fodors.com.

CARRIERS

ATA, Continental, and Northwest fly into O'ahu (Honolulu). ATA also has a new non-stop from Oackland, CA to Hilo on the Big Island. From the U.S. mainland, Delta serves O'ahu (Honolulu), Maui, and the Big Island. From the West Coast of the United States, American and United fly to Honolulu, Maui, the Big Island, and

Kaua'i. United also flies from Chicago and Denver to Honolulu and the Big Island.

Aloha Airlines flies from California (Oakland, Sacramento, San Diego, and Orange County) and Nevada (Las Vegas and Reno). Hawaiian Airlines flies from Arizona (Phoenix), California (Los Angeles, Sacramento, San Diego, San Francisco, San Jose), Nevada (Las Vegas), Oregon (Portland), and Washington (Seattle). Hawaiian also services Australia, American Samoa, and Tahiti.

Aloha and Hawaiian offer regular service between the islands. Island Air and Pacific Wings provide interisland service to the smaller airports on Maui, Moloka'i and Lāna'i. Paragon Airlines offers private charter service to all the Islands.

🛪 Major Airlines ATA ☎ 800/435-9282 ⊕ www. ata.com. **Aloha Airlines** ☎ 800/367-5250 ⊕ www. alohaairlines.com. **America West** ☎ 800/327-7810 ⊕ www.americawest.com. **American** ☎ 800/433-7300 ⊕ www.aa.com. **Continental** ☎ 800/523-3273 ⊕ www.continental.com. **Delta** ☎ 800/221-1212 ⊕ www.delta.com. **Hawaiian Airlines** ☎ 800/367-5320 ⊕ www.hawaiianair.com. **Northwest** ☎ 800/225-2525 ⊕ www.nwa.com. **United** ☎ 800/241-6522 ⊕ www.united.com.

🛪 Direct Flights from the U.K. to Honolulu American ☎ 0208/572-5555 ⊕ www.aa.com. **Continental** ☎ 0800/776-464 ⊕ www.continental.com. **Delta** ☎ 0800/414-767 ⊕ www.delta.com. **United** ☎ 0845/844-4777 ⊕ www.united.com.

🛪 Interisland Flights **Aloha Airlines** ☎ 800/367-5250 ⊕ www.alohaairlines.com. **Hawaiian Airlines** ☎ 800/367-5320 ⊕ www.hawaiianair.com. **Island Air** ☎ 800/323-3345 ⊕ www.islandair.com. **Pacific Wings** ☎ 888/575-4546 ⊕ www. pacificislandtravel.com. **Paragon Airlines** ☎ 808/244-3356 ⊕ www.paragon-air.com.

CHECK-IN & BOARDING

Although the Neighbor Island airports are smaller and more casual than Honolulu International, during peak times they can also be quite busy. Allot extra travel time to all airports during morning and afternoon rush-hour traffic periods.

Always **find out your carrier's check-in policy.** Plan to arrive at the airport about two hours before your scheduled departure time for domestic flights and 2½ to 3 hours before international flights. You may need to arrive earlier if you're flying from one of the busier airports or during peak air-traffic times. Plan to **arrive at the airport 45 to 60 minutes before departure for interisland flights.**

To avoid delays at airport-security checkpoints, try not to wear any metal. Jewelry, belt and other buckles, steel-toe shoes, barrettes, and underwire bras are among the items that can set off detectors.

Assuming that not everyone with a ticket will show up, airlines routinely overbook planes. When everyone does, airlines ask for volunteers to give up their seats. In return, these volunteers usually get a several-hundred-dollar flight voucher, which can be used toward the purchase of another ticket, and are rebooked on the next available flight out. If there are not enough volunteers, the airline must choose who will be denied boarding. The first to get bumped are passengers who checked in late and those flying on discounted tickets, so get to the gate and check in as early as possible, especially during peak periods.

Always **bring a government-issued photo ID** to the airport; even when it's not required, a passport is best.

AGRICULTURAL INSPECTION

Plants and plant products are subject to regulation by the Department of Agriculture, both on entering and leaving Hawai'i. Upon leaving the Islands, you'll have to have your bags X-rayed and tagged at one of the airport's agricultural inspection stations before you proceed to check-in. Pineapples and coconuts with the packer's agricultural inspection stamp pass freely; papayas must be treated, inspected, and stamped. All other fruits are banned for export to the U.S. mainland. Flowers pass except for gardenia, rose leaves, jade vine, and mauna loa. Also banned are insects, snails, soil, cotton, cacti, sugarcane, and all berry plants.

You'll have to **leave dogs and other pets at home.** A 120-day quarantine is imposed to keep out rabies, which is nonexistent in Hawai'i. If specific pre- and post-arrival requirements are met, animals may qualify for a 30-day or 5-day-or-less quarantine.

🔸 **U.S. Customs and Border Protection** ✉ For inquiries and equipment registration, 1300 Pennsylvania Ave. NW, Washington, DC 20229 ⊕ www.cbp. gov ☎ 877/227–5511 or 202/354–1000 ✉ For complaints, Customer Satisfaction Unit, 1300 Pennsylvania Ave. NW, Room 5.2C, Washington, DC 20229.

CUTTING COSTS

Check local and community newspapers when you're on the Islands for deals and coupons on interisland flights. Both Hawaiian Airlines and Aloha Airlines have stopped offering the once-popular multi-island air passes, but there are other ways to save money on interisland fares. Sign up for either airlines' free frequent-flyer programs, and you'll be eligible for excellent online specials that aren't available by phone or elsewhere.

The least expensive airfares to Hawai'i are often priced for round-trip travel and must usually be purchased in advance. Airlines generally allow you to change your return date for a fee; most low-fare tickets, however, are nonrefundable. It's smart to call a number of airlines and check the Internet; when you are quoted a good price, book it on the spot—the same fare may not be available the next day, or even the next hour. Always check different routings and look into using alternate airports. Also, price off-peak flights and red-eye, which may be significantly less expensive than others. Travel agents, especially low-fare specialists (⇨ Discounts & Deals), are helpful.

Consolidators are another good source. They buy tickets for scheduled flights at reduced rates from the airlines, then sell them at prices that beat the best fare available directly from the airlines. Sometimes you can even get your money back if you need to return the ticket. Carefully read the fine print detailing penalties for changes and cancellations, purchase the ticket with a credit card, and confirm your consolidator reservation with the airline.

When you fly as a courier, you trade your checked-luggage space for a ticket deeply subsidized by a courier service. There are restrictions on when you can book and

how long you can stay. Some courier companies list with membership organizations, such as the Air Courier Association and the International Association of Air Travel Couriers; these require you to become a member before you can book a flight.

Trailfinders can arrange bargain flights from the United Kingdom.

🔸 **Courier Resources Air Courier Association/ Cheaptrips.com** ☎ 800/461–8856 ⊕ www. aircourier.org or www.cheaptrips.com; $39 annual membership. **Courier Travel** ☎ 303/570–7586 ⊕ www.couriertravel.org; $40 one-time membership fee. **International Association of Air Travel Couriers** ☎ 308/632–3273 ⊕ www.courier.org; $45 annual membership.

🔸 **Online Consolidators AirlineConsolidator.com** ⊕ www.airlineconsolidator.com; for international tickets. **Best Fares** ☎ 800/880–1234 ⊕ www. bestfares.com; $59.90 annual membership. **Cheap Tickets** ⊕ www.cheaptickets.com. **Expedia** ⊕ www. expedia.com. **Hotwire** ⊕ www.hotwire.com. **lastminute.com** ⊕ www.lastminute.com specializes in last-minute travel; the main site is for the U.K., but it has a link to a U.S. site. **Luxury Link** ⊕ www. luxurylink.com has auctions (surprisingly good deals) as well as offers at the high-end side of travel. **Onetravel.com** ⊕ www.onetravel.com. **Orbitz** ⊕ www.orbitz.com. **Priceline.com** ⊕ www. priceline.com. **Travelocity** ⊕ www.travelocity.com.

🔸 **Direct Flights from the U.K. Trailfinders** ✉ 194 Kensington High St., London W8 7RG ☎ 0845/058–5858 ⊕ www.trailfinders.com.

ENJOYING THE FLIGHT

State your seat preference when purchasing your ticket, and then repeat it when you confirm and when you check in. For more legroom, you can request one of the few emergency-aisle seats at check-in, if you're capable of moving obstacles comparable in weight to an airplane exit door (usually between 35 pounds and 60 pounds)—a Federal Aviation Administration requirement of passengers in these seats. Seats behind a bulkhead also offer more legroom, but they don't have underseat storage. Don't sit in the row in front of the emergency aisle or in front of a bulkhead, where seats may not recline. SeatGuru.com has more information about specific seat configurations, which vary by aircraft.

Ask the airline whether a snack or meal is served on the flight. If you have dietary concerns, request special meals when booking. These can be vegetarian, low-cholesterol, or kosher, for example. It's a good idea to pack some healthful snacks and a small (plastic) bottle of water in your carry-on bag. On long flights, try to maintain a normal routine, to help fight jet lag. At night, get some sleep. By day, eat light meals, drink water (not alcohol), and move around the cabin to stretch your legs. For additional jet-lag tips consult *Fodor's FYI: Travel Fit & Healthy* (available at bookstores everywhere).

Smoking policies vary from carrier to carrier. Most airlines prohibit smoking on all of their flights; others allow smoking only on certain routes or certain departures. Ask your carrier about its policy.

FLYING TIMES

Flying time is about 10 hours from New York, 8 hours from Chicago, 5 hours from Los Angeles, and 15 hours from London, not including layovers.

HOW TO COMPLAIN

If your baggage goes astray or your flight goes awry, complain right away. Most carriers require that you **file a claim immediately.** The Aviation Consumer Protection Division of the Department of Transportation publishes *Fly-Rights*, which discusses airlines and consumer issues and is available online. You can also find articles and information on mytravelrights.com, the Web site of the nonprofit Consumer Travel Rights Center.

▪ Airline Complaints **Aviation Consumer Protection Division** ✉ U.S. Department of Transportation, Office of Aviation Enforcement and Proceedings, C-75, Room 4107, 400 7th St. SW, Washington, DC 20590 ☎ 202/366-2220 ⊕ airconsumer.ost.dot.gov. **Federal Aviation Administration Consumer Hotline** ✉ For inquiries: FAA, 800 Independence Ave. SW, Washington, DC 20591 ☎ 866/835-5322 ⊕ www.faa.gov.

RECONFIRMING

Check the status of your flight before you leave for the airport. You can do this on your carrier's Web site, by linking to a flight-status checker (many Web booking services offer these), or by calling your carrier or travel agent.

AIRPORTS

All of Hawai'i's major islands have their own airports, but Honolulu's International Airport is the main stopover for most domestic and international flights. From Honolulu, there are departing flights to the Neighbor Islands leaving almost every half-hour from early morning until evening. In addition, some carriers now offer nonstop service directly from the Mainland to Maui and the Big Island on a limited basis. No matter the island, all of Hawai'i's airports are open-air, meaning you can enjoy those trade-wind breezes up until the moment you step on the plane.

HONOLULU/O'AHU AIRPORT

Hawai'i's major airport is Honolulu International, on O'ahu, 20 minutes (9 mi) west of Waikīkī. To travel interisland from Honolulu, you can depart from either the interisland terminal or the commuter-airline terminal, located in two structures adjacent to the main overseas terminal building. A free bus service, the Wiki Wiki Shuttle, operates between terminals.

▪ **Honolulu International Airport (HNL)** ☎ 808/836-6413.

MAUI AIRPORTS

Maui has two major airports. Kahului Airport handles major airlines and interisland flights; it's the only airport on Maui that has direct service from the mainland. Kapalua–West Maui Airport is served by Aloha Airlines and Pacific Wings. If you're staying in West Maui and you're flying in from another island, you can avoid an hour's drive from the Kahului Airport by flying into Kapalua–West Maui Airport. The tiny town of Hāna in East Maui also has an airstrip, served by commuter planes from Honolulu and charter flights from Kahului and Kapalua. Fly here if you want to avoid the long drive to Hāna from one of the other airports.

▪ **Kahului Airport (OGG)** ☎ 808/872-3893. **Kapalua–West Maui Airport (JHM)** ☎ 808/669-0623. **Hāna Airport (HNM)** ☎ 808/248-8208.

BIG ISLAND AIRPORTS

Those flying to the Big Island of Hawai'i regularly land at one of two fields. Kona International Airport at Keāhole, on the west side, best serves Kailua-Kona, Keauhou, and the Kohala Coast. Hilo International Airport is more appropriate for those going to the east side. Waimea-Kohala Airport, called Kamuela Airport by residents, is used primarily for commuting among the Islands.

Ⅰ Hilo International Airport (ITO) ☎ 808/934-5838. **Kona International Airport at Keāhole (KOA)** ☎ 808/329-3423. **Waimea-Kohala Airport (MUE)** ☎ 808/887-8126.

KAUA'I, MOLOKA'I & LĀNA'I

On Kaua'i, visitors fly into Līhu'e Airport, on the east side of the island.

Moloka'i's Ho'olehua Airport is small and centrally located, as is Lāna'i Airport. Both airports handle a limited number of flights per day. Visitors coming from the mainland must stop in O'ahu (Honolulu) and change to an interisland flight.

Ⅰ Kaua'i: Līhu'e Airport (LIH) ☎ 808/246-1448. **Lāna'i: Lāna'i Airport (LNY)** ☎ 808/565-6757. **Moloka'i: Ho'olehua Airport (MKK)** ☎ 808/567-6361.

BOAT & FERRY TRAVEL

Moloka'i Ferry offers twice-daily ferry service between Lahaina, Maui, and Kaunakakai, Moloka'i. Travel time is about 90 minutes each way, and the round-trip fare is $80 per person. There's daily ferry service between Lahaina, Maui, and Mānele Bay, Lāna'i, with Expeditions Lāna'i Ferry. The 9-mi crossing costs $50 cash ($52 if you pay with a credit card) round-trip per person and takes about 45 minutes, depending on ocean conditions. Reservations are recommended for both ferries.

At this writing, a high-speed ferry service that will run among O'ahu (Honolulu), Maui, the Big Island, and Kaua'i, is scheduled to begin sometime in 2006.

Ⅰ Boat & Ferry Information Expeditions Lāna'i Ferry ☎ 800/695-2624 ⊕ www.go-lanai.com. **Moloka'i Ferry** ☎ 866/307-6524 ⊕ www.molokaiferry.com.

BUS TRAVEL

Getting around by bus is a wonderfully inexpensive option on O'ahu, especially in urban Honolulu and Waikīkī. On the Neighbor Islands, bus services are limited and car rental is recommended.

THEBUS IN HONOLULU–O'AHU

O'ahu's transportation system, known just as TheBus, is one of the island's best bargains. Fares per ride are $2, and with more than 90 bus routes you can even do an O'ahu circle-island tour. Taking TheBus in the Waikīkī and downtown Honolulu areas is especially convenient, with buses making stops in Waikīkī every 15 minutes to take passengers to nearby shopping areas, such as Ala Moana Center.

Ⅰ TheBus ☎ 808/848-5555 on O'ahu ⊕ www.thebus.org.

BUS TRAVEL ON MAUI

Maui Public Transit, operated by Roberts Hawai'i, offers seven routes in and between various central, south, and west Maui communities from Monday through Saturday. There's no service on Sunday. Passengers can travel between Wailuku, Kā'anapali, Kahului, Kapalua, Kīhei, Wailea, Mā'alaea, and Lahaina. Inexpensive one-way, round-trip, and all-day passes are available.

Ⅰ Roberts Hawai'i ☎ 808/871-4838 ⊕ www.co.maui.hi.us/bus.

BUS TRAVEL ON THE BIG ISLAND

The Hele-On bus, operated by the Hawai'i County Mass Transit Agency, travels around the island, with fares varying depending on the route. Visitors staying in Hilo can take advantage of the Transit Agency's Shared Ride Taxi program which provides door-to-door transportation in the area. A one-way fare is $2 and a book of 15 coupons can be purchased for $30.

Ⅰ Hele-On Bus ☎ 808/961-8744 ⊕ www.co.hawaii.hi.us/mass_transit/transit_main.htm.

BUS TRAVEL ON KAUA'I

On Kaua'i, the County Transportation Agency operates the Kaua'i Bus, which provides service between Hanalei and Kekaha. It also provides service to the airport and limited service to Kōloa and Po'ipū. The fare is $1.50 for adults and

frequent-rider passes are available.
⛰ **Kaua'i Bus** ☎ 808/241-6410 ⊕ www.kauai.gov/
OCA/Transportation.

CAMERAS & PHOTOGRAPHY

Today's underwater disposable cameras
can provide terrific photos for those once-
in-a-lifetime underwater experiences. Film
developing is available on all of the Islands. The *Kodak Guide to Shooting
Great Travel Pictures* (available at bookstores everywhere) is loaded with tips.
⛰ **Photo Help Kodak Information Center** ☎ 800/
242-2424 ⊕ www.kodak.com.

EQUIPMENT PRECAUTIONS

**Don't pack film or equipment in checked
luggage,** where it is much more susceptible to damage. X-ray machines used to
view checked luggage are extremely powerful and therefore are likely to ruin your
film. Try to ask for hand inspection of
film, which becomes clouded after repeated exposure to airport X-ray machines, and keep videotapes and computer
disks away from metal detectors. Always
keep film, tape, and computer disks out of
the sun. Carry an extra supply of batteries,
and be prepared to turn on your camera,
camcorder, or laptop to prove to airport
security personnel that the device is real.

CAR RENTAL

While in the Islands, you can rent anything
from an econobox to a Ferrari. It's wise to
make reservations in advance, especially if
visiting during peak seasons or for major
conventions or sporting events.

Rates begin at $25 to $35 a day for an
economy car with air-conditioning, automatic transmission, and unlimited mileage.
This does not include vehicle registration
fee and weight tax, insurance, sales tax,
and a $3-per-day Hawai'i state surcharge.
⛰ **Major Agencies Alamo** ☎ 800/327-9633
⊕ www.alamo.com. **Avis** ☎ 800/331-1212, 800/
879-2847 or 800/272-5871 in Canada, 0870/606-
0100 in U.K., 02/9353-9000 in Australia, 09/526-
2847 in New Zealand ⊕ www.avis.com. **Budget**
☎ 800/527-0700 ⊕ www.budget.com. **Dollar**
☎ 800/800-4000, 0800/085-4578 in U.K. ⊕ www.
dollar.com. **Hertz** ☎ 800/654-3131, 800/263-0600
in Canada, 0870/844-8844 in U.K., 02/9669-2444 in
Australia, 09/256-8690 in New Zealand ⊕ www.

hertz.com. **National Car Rental** ☎ 800/227-7368
⊕ www.nationalcar.com.

CUTTING COSTS

Many rental companies in Hawai'i offer
coupons for discounts at attractions.

For a good deal, book through a travel
agent who will shop around. Also, price
local car-rental companies—whose prices
may be lower still, although their service
and maintenance may not be as good as
those of major rental agencies—and research rates on the Internet. Consolidators
that specialize in air travel can offer good
rates on cars as well (⇨ Air Travel). Remember to ask about required deposits,
cancellation penalties, and drop-off
charges if you're planning to pick up the
car in one city and leave it in another. If
you're traveling during a holiday period,
also make sure that a confirmed reservation guarantees you a car.
⛰ **Local Agencies AA Aloha Cars-R-Us** ☎ 800/
655-7989 ⊕ www.hawaiicarrental.com. **Aloha Rent
A Car (Maui)** ☎ 877/452-5642 ⊕ www.
aloharentacar.com. **Discount Hawaii Car Rentals**
☎ 888/292-3307 ⊕ www.discounthawaiicarrental.
com. **Harper Car and Truck Rental (Big Island)**
☎ 800/852-9993 ⊕ www.harpershawaii.com. **JN
Car and Truck Rentals (O'ahu)** ☎ 800/475-7522
⊕ www.jnautomotive.com.

INSURANCE

When driving a rented car you are generally responsible for any damage to or loss
of the vehicle. You also may be liable for
any property damage or personal injury
that you may cause while driving. Before
you rent, see what coverage you already
have under the terms of your personal
auto-insurance policy and credit cards.

For about $9 to $25 a day, rental companies sell protection, known as a collision- or
loss-damage waiver (CDW or LDW), that
eliminates your liability for damage to the
car; it's always optional and should never
be automatically added to your bill. In most
states you don't need a CDW if you have
personal auto insurance or other liability insurance. However, **make sure you have
enough coverage to pay for the car.** If you
do not have auto insurance or an umbrella
policy that covers damage to third parties,

purchasing liability insurance and a CDW or LDW is highly recommended.

REQUIREMENTS & RESTRICTIONS

In Hawai'i you must be 21 years of age to rent a car and you must have a valid driver's license and a major credit card. Those under 25 will pay a daily surcharge of $15–$25.

In Hawai'i your unexpired mainland driver's license is valid for rental for up to 90 days.

SURCHARGES

Before you pick up a car in one city and leave it in another, ask about drop-off charges or one-way service fees, which can be substantial. Also inquire about early-return policies; some rental agencies charge extra if you return the car before the time specified in your contract while others give you a refund for the days not used. Most agencies note the tank's fuel level on your contract; to avoid a hefty refueling fee, return the car with the same tank level. If the tank was full, refill it just before you turn in the car, but be aware that gas stations near the rental outlet may overcharge. It's almost never a deal to buy a tank of gas with the car when you rent it; the understanding is that you'll return it empty, but some fuel usually remains. Surcharges may apply if you're under 25 or if you take the car outside the area approved by the rental agency. You'll pay extra for child seats (about $8 a day), which are compulsory for children under five, and usually for additional drivers (up to $25 a day, depending on location).

CAR TRAVEL

Technically, the Big Island of Hawai'i is the only island you can completely circle by car, but each island offers plenty of sightseeing from its miles of roadways. O'ahu can be circled except for the roadless west-shore area around Ka'ena Point. Elsewhere, major highways follow the shoreline and traverse the island at two points. Rush-hour traffic (6:30 to 8:30 AM and 3:30 to 6 PM) can be frustrating around Honolulu and the outlying areas, as many thoroughfares don't allow left turns due to contra-flow lanes. Traffic on

Maui can be very bad branching out from Kahului to and from Pā'ia, Kīhei and Lahaina. Drive here during peak hours and you'll know why local residents are calling for restrictions on development. Parking along many streets is curtailed during these times, and towing is strictly practiced. Read curbside parking signs before leaving your vehicle, even at a meter.

Asking for directions will almost always produce a helpful explanation from the locals, but you should be prepared for an island term or two. Instead of using compass directions, remember that Hawai'i residents refer to places as being either *mauka* (toward the mountains) or *makai* (toward the ocean) from one another. Other directions depend on your location: in Honolulu, for example, people say to "go Diamond Head," which means toward that famous landmark, or to "go *'ewa*," meaning in the opposite direction. A shop on the *mauka*–Diamond Head corner of a street is on the mountain side of the street on the corner closest to Diamond Head. It all makes perfect sense once you get the lay of the land.

GASOLINE

Regardless of today's fluctuating gas prices, you can pretty much count on having to pay more at the pump for gasoline on the Islands than on the U.S. mainland.

ROAD CONDITIONS

It's difficult to get lost in most of Hawai'i. Roads and streets, although they may challenge the visitor's tongue, are well marked; just watch out for the many one-way streets in Waikīkī. **Keep an eye open for the Hawai'i Visitors and Convention Bureau's red-caped King Kamehameha signs,** which mark major attractions and scenic spots. Ask for a map at the car-rental counter. Free publications containing good-quality road maps can be found on all Islands.

O'ahu and the Big Island have well-maintained roads, which can be easily negotiated and do not require a four-wheel-drive vehicle. Maui has its share of impenetrable areas, although four-wheel-drive vehicles rarely run into problems on the island.

Kaua'i has a well-maintained highway running south from Līhu'e to Barking Sands Beach; a spur at Waimea takes you along Waimea Canyon to Kōke'e State Park. A northern route also winds its way from Līhu'e to end at Hā'ena, the beginning of the rugged and roadless Nā Pali Coast. Although Moloka'i and Lāna'i have fewer roadways, car rental is still worthwhile and will allow plenty of interesting sightseeing. **Opt for a four-wheel-drive vehicle** if dirt-road exploration holds any appeal.

RULES OF THE ROAD

Be sure to **buckle up.** Hawai'i has a strictly enforced seat-belt law for front-seat passengers. Always strap children under age five into approved child-safety seats. Children 18 and under, riding in the backseat, are also required by state law to use seat belts. The highway speed limit is usually 55 mph. In-town traffic moves from 25 to 40 mph. Jaywalking is very common, so be particularly watchful for pedestrians, especially in congested areas such as Waikīkī. Unauthorized use of a parking space reserved for persons with disabilities can net you a $150 fine.

CHILDREN IN HAWAI'I

Sunny beaches and many family-oriented cultural sites, activities, and attractions make Hawai'i a very *keiki-* (child-) friendly place. Here kids can swim with a dolphin, surf with a boogie board, check out an active volcano, or ride a sugarcane train. Parents should **use caution on beaches and during water sports.** Even waters that appear calm can harbor powerful rip currents. Be sure to **read any beach-warning guides your hotel may provide.** Ask around for kid-friendly beaches that might have shallow tide pools or are protected by reefs. And remember that the sun's rays are in operation full-force year-round here. Sunblock is essential.

Most major resort chains in Hawai'i offer children's activity programs for kids ages 5 to 12. These kid clubs provide opportunities to learn about local culture, make friends with children from around the world, and experience age-appropriate activities while giving moms and dads a time-out. Upon arrival, check out the daily

local newspapers for children's events. The *Honolulu Advertiser's* TGIF section each Friday includes a section on *keiki* activities with a local flavor.

If you rent a car, don't forget to arrange for a car seat when you reserve. For advice about traveling with children, consult *Fodor's FYI: Travel with Your Baby* (available in bookstores everywhere).

FLYING

If your children are two or older, ask about children's airfares. As a general rule, infants under two not occupying a seat fly at greatly reduced fares or even for free. But if you want to guarantee a seat for an infant, you have to pay full fare. Consider flying during off-peak days and times; most airlines will grant an infant a seat without a ticket if there are available seats.

Experts agree that it's a good idea to use safety seats aloft for children weighing less than 40 pounds. Airlines set their own policies: if you use a safety seat, U.S. carriers usually require that the child be ticketed, even if he or she is young enough to ride free, because the seats must be strapped into regular seats. And even if you pay the full adult fare for the seat, it may be worth it, especially on longer trips. Do **check your airline's policy about using safety seats during takeoff and landing.** Safety seats are not allowed everywhere in the plane, so get your seat assignments as early as possible.

When reserving, request children's meals or a freestanding bassinet (not available at all airlines) if you need them. But note that bulkhead seats, where you must sit to use the bassinet, may lack an overhead bin or storage space on the floor.

LODGING

Families can't go wrong choosing resort locations that are part of larger hotel chains such as Hilton, Sheraton, Outrigger, and Westin. Many of these resorts are on the best beaches, have activities created for children, and are centrally located. Outrigger's Ohana brand hotels are off the beachfront but provide great value at good prices. Many condominium resorts now also offer children's activities and amenities during holiday periods.

Most hotels in Hawai'i allow children under a certain age to stay in their parents' room at no extra charge, but others charge for them as extra adults; be sure to find out the cutoff age for children's discounts. Also **check for special seasonal programs,** such as kids eat free promotions.

⚡ Best Choices Embassy Suites Hotels ☎ 800/362-2779 ⊕ embassysuites.hilton.com. **The Fairmont Orchid, Hawaii (Big Island)** ☎ 800/257-7544 ⊕ www.fairmont.com/orchid. **Four Seasons Hotels and Resorts** ☎ 800/819-5053 ⊕ www.fourseasons.com. **Hilton** ☎ 800/445-8667 ⊕ www.hilton.com. **Hyatt Hotels & Resorts** ☎ 888/591-1234 ⊕ www.hyatt.com. **Kona Village (Big Island)** ☎ 800/367-5290 ⊕ www.konavillage.com. **Marriott** ☎ 888/236-2427 ⊕ www.marriott.com. **Mauna Lani Bay Hotel&Bungalows (Big Island)** ☎ 866/877-6982 ⊕ www.maunalani.com. **Molokai Ranch** ☎ 888/627-8082 ⊕ www.molokairanch.com. **Outrigger Hotels & Resorts** ☎ 800/688-7444 ⊕ www.outrigger.com. **Prince Resorts Hawaii** ☎ 866/774-6236 ⊕ www.princeresortshawaii.com. **ResortQuest Hawaii** ☎ 877/997-6667 ⊕ www.resortquesthawaii.com. **The Ritz-Carlton Hotels and Resorts (Maui)** ☎ 800/241-3333 ⊕ www.ritzcarlton.com. **Starwood Hotels and Resorts** ☎ 888/625-5144 for Westin and Sheraton, 800/325-3589 for Luxury Collection, 877/946-8357 for W Hotels ⊕ www.starwood.com. **Turtle Bay Resort (O'ahu)** ☎ 800/203-3650 ⊕ www.turtlebayresort.com.

SIGHTS & ATTRACTIONS

Places that are especially appealing to children are indicated by a rubber-duckie icon (🐤) in the margin.

On O'ahu, favorites include surfing lessons at Waikīkī Beach, hiking Diamond Head, snorkeling Hanauma Bay, learning about marine life at Sea Life Park, splashing about the 29-acre Hawaiian Waters Adventure Park, and touring through South Pacific cultures at the Polynesian Cultural Center. On Maui, kid favorites include the Sugarcane Train that runs between Lahaina and Kā'anapali, snorkeling to Molokini Island, and whale-watching after a visit to the Maui Ocean Center. Visiting Hawai'i Volcanoes National Park, stargazing atop Mauna Kea, touring the Mauna Loa Macadamia Factory near Hilo, swimming with dolphins at the Hilton Waikoloa, and horseback riding at Parker Ranch are fun things to do on the Big Island.

Kaua'i is where kids go to explore film locations such as Peter Pan's *Never-Never Land* and *Jurassic Park*. They can learn to water-ski on the Wailua River, visit Kōke'e National Park, or just spend the day swimming Po'ipū's sunny south shores. Lāna'i and Moloka'i are great islands for adventurous youngsters. At Moloka'i Ranch, families can sleep in canvas bungalows and enjoy everything from stargazing and spear fishing to horseback riding with a paniolo (Hawaiian cowboy). On Lāna'i, four-wheel-drive off-road adventure tours take families to destinations such as Shipwreck Beach and Mānele Bay, where the dolphins sometimes come to play.

CONSUMER PROTECTION

Whether you're shopping for gifts or purchasing travel services, **pay with a major credit card** whenever possible, so you can cancel payment or get reimbursed if there's a problem (and you can provide documentation). If you're doing business with a particular company for the first time, contact your local Better Business Bureau and the attorney general's offices in your state and (for U.S. businesses) the company's home state as well. Have any complaints been filed? Finally, if you're buying a package or tour, always consider travel insurance that includes default coverage (⇨ Insurance).

⚡ BBBs Council of Better Business Bureaus ✉ 4200 Wilson Blvd., Suite 800, Arlington, VA 22203 ☎ 703/276-0100 🖷 703/525-8277 ⊕ www.bbb.org.

CRUISE TRAVEL

When Pan Am's amphibious *Hawai'i Clipper* touched down on Pearl Harbor's waters in 1936, it marked the beginning of the end of regular passenger-ship travel to the Islands. From that point on, the predominant means of transporting visitors would be by air, not by sea. Today, however, cruising to Hawai'i is making a comeback.

Norwegian Cruise Lines is the only major operator to offer interisland cruises in Hawai'i. Three of their ships—*Pride of Aloha, Pride of Hawai'i,* and *Pride of America*—offer seven-day itineraries within the islands.

Carnival, Celebrity, Holland America, Norwegian, Princess, and Royal Caribbean cruise lines circle Hawai'i in a number of itineraries that typically begin and end on the U.S. West Coast. Most of these itineraries include a ports of call on O'ahu, Maui, Kaua'i and the Big Island.

To get the best deal, **consult a cruise-only travel agency.** For more information, *see* Cruising the Hawaiian Islands, above.

Even if you choose, as most travelers do, to travel by air to the Islands, you can get the flavor of what the luxury-cruise era in Hawai'i was like by checking out Aloha Tower Marketplace's Boat Day Celebrations in Honolulu. Vessels stopping here are met upon arrival by hula dancers and the kind of entertainment and floral festivities that once greeted travelers almost a century ago. Contact Aloha Tower Marketplace for a schedule upon arrival.

🚢 **Cruise Lines Carnival** ☎ 888/227-6482 ⊕ www.carnival.com. **Celebrity** ☎ 800/647-2251 ⊕ www.celebritycruises.com. **Holland America** ☎ 877/724-5400 ⊕ www.hollandamerica.com. **Norwegian Cruise Lines** ☎ 800/327-7030 ⊕ www.norwegiancruiselines.com. **Princess** ☎ 800/774-6237 ⊕ www.princess.com. **Royal Caribbean Cruise Line** ☎ 866/562-7625 ⊕ www.royalcaribbean.com.

🚢 **Aloha Tower Marketplace** ⊠ 1 Aloha Tower Dr., at Piers 8, 9, and 10, Honolulu ☎ 808/528-5700 ⊕ www.alohatower.com.

CUSTOMS & DUTIES

IN AUSTRALIA

Australian residents who are 18 or older may bring home A$900 worth of souvenirs and gifts (including jewelry), 250 cigarettes or 250 grams of cigars or other tobacco products, and 2.25 liters of alcohol (including wine, beer, and spirits). Residents under 18 may bring back A$450 worth of goods. If any of these individual allowances are exceeded, you must pay duty for the entire amount (of the group of products in which the allowance was exceeded). Members of the same family traveling together may pool their allowances. Prohibited items include meat products. Seeds, plants, and fruits need to be declared upon arrival.

🚢 **Australian Customs Service** ⊘ Customs House, 10 Cooks River Dr., Sydney International Airport, Sydney, NSW 2020 ☎ 02/6275-6666 or 1300/363263, 02/8334-7444 or 1800/020-504 quarantine-inquiry line ⊟ 02/8339-6714 ⊕ www.customs.gov.au.

IN CANADA

Canadian residents who have been out of Canada for at least seven days may bring in C$750 worth of goods duty-free. If you've been away fewer than seven days but more than 48 hours, the duty-free allowance drops to C$200. If your trip lasts 24 to 48 hours, the allowance is C$50; if the goods are worth more than C$50, you must pay full duty on all of the goods. You may not pool allowances with family members. Goods claimed under the C$750 exemption may follow you by mail; those claimed under the lesser exemptions must accompany you. Alcohol and tobacco products may be included in the seven-day and 48-hour exemptions but not in the 24-hour exemption. If you meet the age requirements of the province or territory through which you reenter Canada, you may bring in, duty-free, 1.5 liters of wine *or* 1.14 liters (40 imperial ounces) of liquor *or* 24 12-ounce cans or bottles of beer or ale. Also, if you meet the local age requirement for tobacco products, you may bring in, duty-free, 200 cigarettes, 50 cigars or cigarillos, and 200 grams of tobacco. You may have to pay a minimum duty on tobacco products, regardless of whether or not you exceed your personal exemption. Check ahead of time with the Canada Border Services Agency or the Department of Agriculture for policies regarding meat products, seeds, plants, and fruits.

You may send an unlimited number of gifts (only one gift per recipient, however) worth up to C$60 each duty-free to Canada. Label the package UNSOLICITED GIFT—VALUE UNDER $60. Alcohol and tobacco are excluded.

🚢 **Canada Border Services Agency** ⊠ Customs Information Services, 191 Laurier Ave. W, 15th fl., Ottawa, Ontario K1A 0L5 ☎ 800/461-9999 in Canada, 204/983-3500, 506/636-5064 ⊕ www.cbsa.gc.ca.

IN NEW ZEALAND

All homeward-bound residents may bring back NZ$700 worth of souvenirs and gifts; passengers may not pool their allowances, and children can claim only the concession on goods intended for their own use. For those 17 or older, the duty-free allowance also includes 4.5 liters of wine or beer; one 1,125-ml bottle of spirits; and either 200 cigarettes, 250 grams of tobacco, 50 cigars, *or* a combination of the three up to 250 grams. Meat products, seeds, plants, and fruits must be declared upon arrival to the Agricultural Services Department.

New Zealand Customs ✉ Head office: The Customhouse, 17–21 Whitmore St., Box 2218, Wellington ☎ 04/473–6099 or 0800/428–786 ⊕ www.customs.govt.nz.

IN THE U.K.

From countries outside the European Union, including the United States, you may bring home, duty-free, 200 cigarettes, 50 cigars, 100 cigarillos, or 250 grams of tobacco; 1 liter of spirits or 2 liters of fortified or sparkling wine or liqueurs; 2 liters of still table wine; 60 ml of perfume; 250 ml of toilet water; plus £145 worth of other goods, including gifts and souvenirs. Prohibited items include meat and dairy products, seeds, plants, and fruits.

HM Customs and Excise ✉ Portcullis House, 21 Cowbridge Rd. E, Cardiff CF11 9SS ☎ 0845/010–9000 or 0208/929–0152 advice service, 0208/929–6731 or 0208/910–3602 complaints ⊕ www.hmce.gov.uk.

DISABILITIES & ACCESSIBILITY

The Society for the Advancement of Travel for the Handicapped has named Hawai'i the most accessible vacation spot for people with disabilities. Ramped visitor areas and specially equipped lodgings are relatively common. Travelers with vision impairments who use a guide dog don't have to worry about quarantine restrictions. Do bring documentation that the animal is a trained guide dog and has a current inoculation record for rabies. Access Aloha Travel is the state's only travel planner specializing in the needs of Hawai'i-bound travelers with disabilities. The company can arrange accessible accommodations, sightseeing, dining, activities, transportation, personal care attendants, and rentals of medical equipment.

Local Resources Access Aloha Travel ✉ 414 Kuwili St., Suite 101, Honolulu 96817 ☎ 800/480–1143 or 808/545–1143 🖷 808/545–7657 ⊕ www.accessalohatravel.com. **Disability and Communication Access Board** ✉ 919 Ala Moana Blvd., Room 101, Honolulu 96814 ☎ 808/586–8121 ⊕ www.hawaii.gov/health/dcab/.

LODGING

Despite the Americans with Disabilities Act, the definition of accessibility seems to differ from hotel to hotel. Some properties may be accessible by ADA standards for people with mobility problems but not for people with hearing or vision impairments, for example.

If you have mobility problems, ask for the lowest floor on which accessible services are offered. If you have a hearing impairment, check whether the hotel has devices to alert you visually to the ring of the telephone, a knock at the door, and a fire/emergency alarm. Some hotels provide these devices without charge. Discuss your needs with hotel personnel if this equipment isn't available, so that a staff member can personally alert you in the event of an emergency.

If you're bringing a guide dog, get authorization ahead of time and write down the name of the person with whom you spoke.

RESERVATIONS

When discussing accessibility with an operator or reservations agent, ask hard questions. Are there any stairs, inside *or* out? Are there grab bars next to the toilet *and* in the shower/tub? How wide is the doorway to the room? To the bathroom? For the most extensive facilities meeting the latest legal specifications, opt for newer accommodations. If you reserve through a toll-free number, consider also calling the hotel's local number to confirm the information from the central reservations office. Get confirmation in writing when you can.

SIGHTS & ATTRACTIONS

Many of Hawai'i's sights and attractions are accessible to travelers with disabilities.

The Honolulu Department of Parks and Recreation provides "all-terrain" wheelchairs and beach mats at several beach parks on O'ahu.

🔌 **Honolulu Department of Parks and Recreation**
☎ 808/692–5461 Therapeutic Recreation Unit
⊕ www.co.honolulu.hi.us/parks/programs/beach.

TRANSPORTATION

O'ahu: Paratransit Services (TheHandi-Van) will take you to a specific destination on O'ahu—not on sightseeing outings—in shared-ride vans with lifts and lock-downs. With TheHandi-Van Pass, one-way trips cost $2. Passes are free and can be obtained from the Honolulu Department of Transportation Services, which is open weekdays 7:45–4:30; you'll need a doctor's written confirmation of your disability or a Paratransit ID card. Application forms can be obtained in advance by calling the Department of Transportation Services or going online. Handi-Cabs of the Pacific is a private company that provides a wheelchair-accessible taxi and tour service. Fares are $9 plus $2 per mile for curbside service and $19 plus $2 per mile for door-to-door service. Reservations at least 24 hours in advance are required by both companies, so plan ahead.

Maui: Kapalua Executive Transportation & Super Shuttle provides an accessible taxi and tour service on the island.

Big Island: The County of Hawai'i provides accessible transportation for the general public using the Hele-On Bus. Discounted ticket prices for the Hele-On Bus are available for persons with disabilities from the County of Hawai'i Mass Transit Authority.

Kaua'i: The Kaua'i County Transportation Agency (CTA) operates a fixed-route system using wheelchair-accessible buses. The system operates weekdays (except holidays) from approximately 5:30 AM to 7 PM, depending on the route. The CTA also operates a paratransit service for persons who meet the CTA's requirements for service eligibility. Visitors who bring with them valid ADA Paratransit Eligibility identification cards may use the CTA paratransit. The Kaua'i Center for Independent

Living offers limited lift-van transportation and guided tours, arranged on an individual basis. Five working days advance notice is requested.

Accessible Vans of Hawai'i rent wheelchairs and scooter vans on O'ahu, Maui, Kaua'i, and the Big Island.

Those who prefer to do their own driving may rent hand-controlled cars from Alamo, Avis, Budget, Dollar, Hertz and National. You can use the windshield card from your own state to park in spaces reserved for people with disabilities. All require at least 48 hours notice.

The U.S. Department of Transportation Aviation Consumer Protection Division's online publication *New Horizons: Information for the Air Traveler with a Disability* offers advice for travelers with a disability, and outlines basic rights. Visit DisabilityInfo.gov for general information.

🔌 **Buses & Vans Accessible Vans of Hawai'i**
☎ 800/303–3750 ⊕ www.accessiblevanshawaii.com. **Department of Transportation Services**
✉ 711 Kapiolani Blvd., Suite 250, Honolulu 96813
☎ 808/523–4083 ⊕ www.co.honolulu.hi.us/dts/.
Handi-Cabs of the Pacific ☎ 808/524–3866.
Hawai'i County Mass Transit Hele-On Bus
☎ 808/961–8744. **Kapalua Executive Transportation & Super Shuttle** ☎ 800/833–2303 ⊕ www.mauishuttle.com. **Kaua'i Center for Independent Living** ☎ 808/245–4034. **Kaua'i County Transportation Agency (CTA)** ☎ 808/241–6410. **Paratransit Services (TheHandi-Van)** ☎ 808/456–5555.

🔌 **Information and Complaints Aviation Consumer Protection Division** (⇨ Air Travel) for airline-related problems; ⊕ airconsumer.ost.dot.gov/publications/horizons.htm for airline travel advice and rights. **Departmental Office of Civil Rights**
✉ For general inquiries, U.S. Department of Transportation, S-30, 400 7th St. SW, Room 10215, Washington, DC 20590 ☎ 202/366–4648, 202/366–8538 TTY 📠 202/366–9371 ⊕ www.dotcr.ost.dot.gov. **Disability Rights Section** ✉ NYAV, U.S. Department of Justice, Civil Rights Division, 950 Pennsylvania Ave. NW, Washington, DC 20530 📠 ADA information line 202/514–0301, 800/514–0301, 202/514–0383 TTY, 800/514–0383 TTY ⊕ www.ada.gov. **U.S. Department of Transportation Hotline** 📠 For disability-related air-travel problems, 800/778–4838 or 800/455–9880 TTY.

TRAVEL AGENCIES

In the United States, the Americans with Disabilities Act requires that travel firms serve the needs of all travelers. Some agencies specialize in working with people with disabilities.

📳 Travelers with Mobility Problems **Access Adventures/B. Roberts Travel** ✉ 1876 East Ave., Rochester, NY 14610 ☎ 800/444-6540 ⊕ www.brobertstravel.com, run by a former physical-rehabilitation counselor. **Access Aloha Travel** ✉ 414 Kuwili St., Suite 101, Honolulu, HI 96817 ☎ 800/480-1143 🖨 808/545-7657 ⊕ www.accessalohatravel.com. **Accessible Vans of Hawaii** ✉ 355 Hukulike St., Suite 121A, Kahului, HI 96732 ☎ 808/871-7785 or 800/303-3750 🖨 808/871-7536 ⊕ www.accessiblevanshawaii.com. **Flying Wheels Travel** ✉ 143 W. Bridge St., Box 382, Owatonna, MN 55060 ☎ 507/451-5005 🖨 507/451-1685 ⊕ www.flyingwheelstravel.com.

📳 Travelers with Developmental Disabilities **New Directions** ✉ 5276 Hollister Ave., Suite 207, Santa Barbara, CA 93111 ☎ 805/967-2841 or 888/967-2841 🖨 805/964-7344 ⊕ www.newdirectionstravel.com. **Sprout** ✉ 893 Amsterdam Ave., New York, NY 10025 ☎ 212/222-9575 or 888/222-9575 🖨 212/222-9768 ⊕ www.gosprout.org.

DISCOUNTS & DEALS

Be a smart shopper and compare all your options before making decisions. A plane ticket bought with a promotional coupon from travel clubs, coupon books, and direct-mail offers or purchased on the Internet may not be cheaper than the least expensive fare from a discount ticket agency. And always keep in mind that what you get is just as important as what you save.

DISCOUNT RESERVATIONS

To save money, look into discount reservations services with Web sites and toll-free numbers, which use their buying power to get a better price on hotels, airline tickets, even car rentals. When booking a room, always **call the hotel's local toll-free number** (if one is available) rather than the central reservations number—you'll often get a better price. Always ask about special packages or corporate rates.

📳 Hotel Rooms **Accommodations Express** ☎ 800/444-7666 or 800/277-1064. **Hotels.com** ☎ 800/219-4606 or 800/364-0291 ⊕ www.hotels.com. **Quik-** book ☎ 800/789-9887 ⊕ www.quikbook.com. **Steigenberger Reservation Service** ☎ 800/223-5652 ⊕ www.srs-worldhotels.com. **Turbotrip.com** ☎ 800/473-7829 ⊕ w3.turbotrip.com.

PACKAGE DEALS

Don't confuse packages and guided tours. When you buy a package, you travel on your own, just as though you had planned the trip yourself. Fly/drive packages, which combine airfare and car rental, are often a good deal. In cities, ask the local visitor's bureau about hotel and local transportation packages that include tickets to major museum exhibits or other special events.

EATING & DRINKING

Food in Hawai'i is a reflection of the state's diverse cultural makeup and tropical location. Fresh seafood is the hallmark of Hawai'i regional cuisine, and its preparations are drawn from across the Pacific Rim, including Japan, the Philippines, Korea, and Thailand. But Hawaiian food is a cuisine in its own right.

The restaurants we list are the cream of the crop in each price category. Properties indicated by an ✕⌂ are lodging establishments whose restaurant warrants a special trip. Unless otherwise noted, the restaurants listed in this guide are open daily for lunch and dinner.

CATEGORY	COST
$$$$	over $35
$$$	$27–$35
$$	$18–$26
$	$10–$17
¢	under $10

Prices are for one main course at dinner.

RESERVATIONS & DRESS

Reservations are always a good idea; we mention them only when they're essential or not accepted. Book as far ahead as you can, and reconfirm as soon as you arrive. (Large parties should always call ahead to check the reservations policy.)

Hawai'i is decidedly casual. Aloha shirts and shorts or long pants for men and island-style dresses or casual resort wear for women are standard attire for evenings in most hotel restaurants and local eateries.

T-shirts and shorts will do the trick for breakfast and lunch.

We mention dress only when men are required to wear a jacket or a jacket and tie.

SPECIALTIES

Fish, fruit, and fresh island-grown produce are the base of Hawai'i regional cuisine. The "plate lunch" is the heart of most Hawaiians' days and usually consists of grilled teriyaki chicken, beef, or fish, served with two scoops of white rice and two side salads. *Poke,* marinated raw tuna, is a local hallmark.

WINE, BEER & SPIRITS

Hawai'i has a new generation of microbreweries, including on-site microbreweries at many restaurants. The drinking age in Hawai'i is 21 years of age, and a photo ID must be presented to purchase alcoholic beverages. Bars are open until 2 AM; venues with a cabaret license can stay open until 4 AM. No matter what you might see in the local parks, drinking alcohol in public parks or on the beaches is illegal. It's also illegal to have open containers of alcohol in motor vehicles.

ECOTOURISM

Hawai'i's connection to its environment is spiritual, cultural, and essential to its survival. You'll find a rainbow of natural attractions to explore, from the ribbons of beaches to volcanic peaks, where lava shows after dark are spectacular. There are 13 climatic regions in the world, and Maui and the Big Island offer ecotravelers a glimpse of 11 of them. Maui has the exhilaration of a rain-forest hike in Hāna, the cool Upcountry climes of Kula, and the awe-inspiring Haleakalā Crater. Much of Kaua'i's natural beauty can be seen only on foot. Its Nā Pali Coast/Waimea Canyon/Kōke'e trail network includes 28 trails totaling some 45 mi rich in endemic species of flora and fauna. Moloka'i and Lāna'i, two of the least-developed islands, hold adventures best experienced on foot and by four-wheel-drive vehicle.

Ecotouring in Hawai'i gives you the opportunity to learn from local guides who are familiar with the *āina* (land) and Hawai'i's unique cultural heritage. Many

of these tours take clients to locations less traveled, so it helps to be in good physical shape. The views at the ends of these roads are an exceedingly rich reward.

Nature and all its ornaments are sacred to Hawaiians, so before taking pieces of lava rock home for souvenirs, listen to what residents (and some vacationers) will tell you: don't touch! Hapless travelers who take souvenir rocks speak of bad luck consequences in the form of stalled cars, travel delays, and bouts of illness. Park rangers spin tales about lava rocks mailed from around the world with attached tales of woe and pleas for the rocks to be put back. If nothing else, with millions of visitors a year, there aren't enough cool rocks to go around.

During the winter months, be sure to watch the beachfronts for endangered sea turtles, or recently laid nests. If you spot one, notify local authorities—they'll be thankful for your help in tracking these elusive creatures.

The Hawai'i State Division of Land and Natural Resources has an online brochure, "Hiking Safely in Hawai'i," as well as a 31-page online guide to Hawai'i's state parks. There are dozens of organizations that offer programs to explore Hawai'i's breathtaking environment, as well volunteer opportunities to help preserve the fragile ecosystem.

🎏 **Alternative-Hawai'i** 🕾 808/695-5113 ⊕ www. alternative-hawaii.com. **Hawai'i Department of Land and Natural Resources, Division of State Parks** 🕾 808/587-0400 ⊕ www.hawaii.gov/dlnr/dsp/ index.html. **Hawai'i Ecotourism Association** 🕾 877/ 300-7058 ⊕ www.hawaiiecotourism.org. **Hawai'i Forest & Trail** 🕾 800/464-1993 ⊕ www.hawaii-forest.com. **Hawai'i Nature Center** 🕾 888/955-0104 ⊕ www.hawaiinaturecenter.org. **Nā Ala Hele Trail & Access Program** 🕾 808/973-9782 ⊕ www. hawaiitrails.org. **The Nature Conservancy** 🕾 808/ 537-4508 ⊕ www.nature.org/hawaii. **Sierra Club** 🕾 808/538-6616 ⊕ www.hawaii.sierraclub.org.

ETIQUETTE & BEHAVIOR

Hawai'i was admitted to the Union in 1959, so residents can be sensitive when visitors refer to their own hometowns as "back in the States." Remember, when in

Hawai'i, refer to the contiguous 48 states as "the mainland" and not as the United States. When you do, you won't appear to be such a *malihini* (newcomer).

GAY & LESBIAN TRAVEL

A few small hotels and some bed-and-breakfasts in Hawai'i are favored by gay and lesbian visitors; Purple Roofs is a listing agent for gay-friendly accommodations in Hawai'i. Pacific Ocean Holidays specializes in prearranging package tours for independent gay travelers. The organization also offers an online directory of gay-owned and gay-friendly businesses and community resources on O'ahu, Maui, Kaua'i, and the Big Island.

For details about the gay and lesbian scene, consult *Fodor's Gay Guide to the USA* (available in bookstores everywhere). 🚩 Local Resources **Pacific Ocean Holidays** ✆ Box 88245, Honolulu 96830 ☎ 808/923-2400 or 800/735-6600 ⊕ www.gayHawaiivacations.com and www.gayHawaii.com. **Purple Roofs** ⊕ www.purpleroofs.com.

🚩 Gay- & Lesbian-Friendly Travel Agencies **Different Roads Travel** ✉ 155 Palm Colony Palm Springs, CA 92264 ☎ 310/289-6000 or 800/429-8747 📠 310/855-0323 ✉ lgernert@tzell.com. **Skylink Travel and Tour/Flying Dutchmen Travel** ✉ 1455 N. Dutton Ave., Suite A, Santa Rosa, CA 95401 ☎ 707/546-9888 or 800/225-5759 📠 707/636-0951; serving lesbian travelers.

HEALTH

Hawai'i is known as the Health State. The life expectancy here is 79 years, the longest in the nation. Balmy weather makes it easy to remain active year-round, and the low-stress aloha attitude certainly contributes to general well-being. When visiting the Islands, however, there are a few health issues to keep in mind.

The Hawai'i State Department of Health recommends that you drink 16 ounces of water per hour to avoid dehydration when hiking or spending time in the sun. **Use sunblock, wear UV-reflective sunglasses, and protect your head with a visor or hat for shade.** If you're not acclimated to warm, humid weather you should allow plenty of time for rest stops and refreshments. When visiting freshwater streams,

be aware of the tropical disease leptospirosis, which is spread by animal urine and carried into streams and mud. Symptoms include fever, headache, nausea, and red eyes. If left untreated it can cause liver and kidney damage, respiratory failure, internal bleeding, and even death. To avoid this, don't swim or wade in freshwater streams or ponds if you have open sores and **don't drink from any freshwater streams or ponds.**

On the Islands, fog is a rare occurrence, but there can often be "vog," an airborne haze of gases released from volcanic vents on the Big Island. During certain weather conditions such as "Kona Winds," the vog can settle over the Islands and wreak havoc with respiratory and other health conditions, especially asthma or emphysema. If susceptible, stay indoors and get emergency assistance if needed.

PESTS & OTHER HAZARDS

The Islands have their share of bugs and insects that enjoy the tropical climate as much as visitors do. Most are harmless but annoying. When planning to spend time outdoors in hiking areas, **wear long-sleeve clothing and pants** and **use mosquito repellent containing deet.** In very damp places you may encounter the dreaded local centipede. On the Islands they usually come in two colors, brown and blue, and they range from the size of a worm to an 8-inch cigar. Their sting is very painful, and the reaction is similar to bee- and wasp-sting reactions. When camping, **shake out your sleeping bag before climbing in, and check your shoes in the morning,** as the centipedes like cozy places. If planning on hiking or traveling in remote areas, always carry a first-aid kit and appropriate medications for sting reactions.

INSURANCE

The most useful travel-insurance plan is a comprehensive policy that includes coverage for trip cancellation and interruption, default, trip delay, and medical expenses (with a waiver for preexisting conditions).

Without insurance you'll lose all or most of your money if you cancel your trip, regardless of the reason. Default insurance covers you if your tour operator, airline, or cruise line goes out of business—the chances of which have been increasing. Trip-delay covers expenses that arise because of bad weather or mechanical delays. Study the fine print when comparing policies.

U.K. residents can buy a travel-insurance policy valid for most vacations taken during the year in which it's purchased (but check preexisting-condition coverage).

Always **buy travel policies directly from the insurance company**; if you buy them from a cruise line, airline, or tour operator that goes out of business you probably won't be covered for the agency or operator's default, a major risk. Before making any purchase, review your existing health and home-owner's policies to find what they cover away from home.

🚩 Travel Insurers In the U.S.: **Access America** ✉ 2805 N. Parham Rd., Richmond, VA 23294 ☎ 800/729-6021 🖷 804/673-1469 or 800/346-9265 ⊕ www.accessamerica.com. **Travel Guard International** ✉ 1145 Clark St., Stevens Point, WI 54481 ☎ 715/345-1041 or 800/826-4919 🖷 800/955-8785 or 715/345-1990 ⊕ www.travelguard.com.

FOR INTERNATIONAL TRAVELERS

For information on customs restrictions, *see* Customs & Duties.

CAR RENTAL

When picking up a rental car, non-U.S. residents need a reservation voucher for any prepaid reservations that were made in the traveler's home country, a passport, a driver's license, and a travel policy that covers each driver.

Your driver's license may not be recognized outside your home country. International driving permits (IDPs) are available from the American and Canadian automobile associations and, in the United Kingdom, from the Automobile Association and Royal Automobile Club. These international permits, valid only in conjunction with your regular driver's license, are universally recognized; having one may save you a problem with local authorities.

CAR TRAVEL

Gas costs range from $2.50 to $3.50 a gallon. Stations are plentiful. Most stay open late (24 hours along large highways and in big cities), except in rural areas, where Sunday hours are limited and where you may drive long stretches without a refueling opportunity. Highways are well paved. Tolls may be levied on limited-access highways. So-called U.S. highways and state highways are not necessarily limited-access but may have several lanes.

State police and tow trucks patrol major highways and lend assistance. If your car breaks down, pull onto the shoulder and wait for help, or have your passengers wait while you walk to an emergency phone (available in most states). If you carry a cell phone, dial 911, noting your location on the small green roadside mileage markers.

Driving in the United States is on the right. Do obey speed limits posted along roads and highways. Watch for lower limits in small towns and on back roads. On weekdays between 6 and 10 AM and again between 4 and 7 PM expect heavy traffic.

Bookstores, gas stations, convenience stores, and rest stops sell maps (about $3) and multiregion road atlases (about $10).

CONSULATES & EMBASSIES

🚩 Australia **Australian Consulate** ✉ 1000 Bishop St., Honolulu 96813 ☎ 808/524-5050.
🚩 Canada **Canadian Consulate** ✉ 1000 Bishop St., Honolulu 96813 ☎ 808/524-5050.
🚩 New Zealand **New Zealand Consulate** ✉ 900 Richards St., Room 414, Honolulu 96813 ☎ 808/543-7900.
🚩 United Kingdom **British Consulate** ✉ 1000 Bishop St., Honolulu 96813 ☎ 808/524-5050.

CURRENCY

The dollar is the basic unit of U.S. currency. It has 100 cents. Coins are the copper penny (1¢); the silvery nickel (5¢), dime (10¢), quarter (25¢), and half-dollar (50¢); and the golden $1 coin, replacing a now-rare silver dollar. Bills are denominated $1, $5, $10, $20, $50, and $100, all mostly green and identical in size; designs and background tints vary. In addition, you may come across a $2 bill, but the chances are slim. The exchange rate at this writing is US$1.73 per British pound, 85¢ per Canadian dollar, 74¢ per Australian dollar, and 70¢ per New Zealand dollar.

ELECTRICITY
The U.S. standard is AC, 110 volts/60 cycles. Plugs have two parallel flat pins.

EMERGENCIES
For police, fire, or ambulance, **dial 911** (0 in rural areas).

INSURANCE
Britons and Australians need extra medical coverage when traveling overseas.
🔢 Insurance Information In the U.K.: **Association of British Insurers** ✉ 51 Gresham St., London EC2V 7HQ ☎ 020/7600-3333 🖷 020/7696-8999 ⊕ www. abi.org.uk. In Australia: **Insurance Council of Australia** ✉ Level 3, 56 Pitt St., Sydney, NSW 2000 ☎ 02/9253-5100 🖷 02/9253-5111 ⊕ www.ica.com. au. In Canada: **RBC Insurance** ✉ 6880 Financial Dr., Mississauga, Ontario L5N 7Y5 ☎ 800/387-4357 or 905/816-2559 🖷 888/298-6458 ⊕ www. rbcinsurance.com. In New Zealand: **Insurance Council of New Zealand** ✉ Level 7, 111-115 Customhouse Quay, Box 474, Wellington ☎ 04/472-5230 🖷 04/473-3011 ⊕ www.icnz.org.nz.

MAIL & SHIPPING
You can buy stamps and aerograms and send letters and parcels in post offices. Stamp-dispensing machines can occasionally be found in airports, bus and train stations, office buildings, drugstores, and the like. You can also deposit mail in the stout, dark blue, steel bins at strategic locations everywhere and in the mail chutes of large buildings; pickup schedules are posted. You can deposit packages at public collection boxes as long as the parcels are affixed with proper postage and weigh less than one pound. Packages weighing one or more pounds must be taken to a post office or handed to a postal carrier.

For mail sent within the United States, you need a 39¢ stamp for first-class letters weighing up to 1 ounce (24¢ for each additional ounce) and 24¢ for postcards. You pay 84¢ for 1-ounce airmail letters and 75¢ for airmail postcards to most other countries; to Canada and Mexico, it costs 63¢ for a 1-ounce letter and 55¢ for

a postcard. An aerogram—a single sheet of lightweight blue paper that folds into its own envelope, stamped for overseas airmail—costs 75¢.

To receive mail on the road, have it sent c/o General Delivery at your destination's main post office (use the correct five-digit ZIP code). You must pick up mail in person within 30 days and show a driver's license or passport.

PASSPORTS & VISAS
When traveling internationally, carry your passport even if you don't need one (it's always the best form of ID) and **make two photocopies of the data page** (one for someone at home and another for you, carried separately from your passport). If you lose your passport, call the nearest embassy or consulate and the local police.

Visitor visas aren't necessary for Canadian or European Union citizens, or for citizens of Australia who are staying fewer than 90 days.
🔢 Australian Citizens **Passports Australia** ☎ 131-232 ⊕ www.passports.gov.au. **United States Consulate General** ✉ MLC Centre, Level 59, 19-29 Martin Pl., Sydney, NSW 2000 ☎ 02/9373-9200, 1902/941-641 fee-based visa-inquiry line ⊕ usembassy-australia.state.gov/sydney.
🔢 Canadian Citizens **Passport Office** ✉ to mail in applications: Foreign Affairs Canada, Gatineau, Québec K1A 0G3 ☎ 800/567-6868 ⊕ www.ppt.gc.ca.
🔢 New Zealand Citizens **New Zealand Passports Office** ✉ For applications and information, Level 3, Boulcott House, 47 Boulcott St., Wellington ☎ 0800/ 22-5050 or 04/474-8100 ⊕ www.passports.govt.nz. **Embassy of the United States** ✉ 29 Fitzherbert Terr., Thorndon, Wellington ☎ 04/462-6000 ⊕ usembassy.org.nz. **U.S. Consulate General** ✉ Citibank Bldg., 3rd fl., 23 Customs St. E, Auckland ☎ 09/303-2724 ⊕ usembassy.org.nz.
🔢 U.K. Citizens **U.K. Passport Service** ☎ 0870/ 521-0410 ⊕ www.passport.gov.uk. **American Consulate General** ✉ Danesfort House, 223 Stranmillis Rd., Belfast, Northern Ireland BT9 5GR ☎ 028/ 9038-6100 🖷 028/9068-1301 ⊕ www.usembassy. org.uk. **American Embassy** ✉ For visa and immigration information or to submit a visa application via mail (enclose an SASE), Consular Information Unit, 24 Grosvenor Sq., London W1A 2LQ ☎ 090/ 5544-4546 or 090/6820-0290 for visa information

(per-minute charges), 0207/499–9000 main switch-board ⊕ www.usembassy.org.uk.

TELEPHONES

All U.S. telephone numbers consist of a three-digit area code and a seven-digit local number. Within many local calling areas, you dial only the seven-digit number. Within some area codes, you must dial "1" first for calls outside the local area. To call between area-code regions, dial "1" then all 10 digits; the same goes for calls to numbers prefixed by "800," "888," "866," and "877"—all toll-free. For calls to numbers preceded by "900" you must pay—usually dearly.

For international calls, dial "011" followed by the country code and the local number. For help, dial "0" and ask for an overseas operator. The country code is 61 for Australia, 64 for New Zealand, 44 for the United Kingdom. Calling Canada is the same as calling within the United States, although you might not be able to get through on some toll-free numbers. Most local phone books list country codes and U.S. area codes. The country code for the United States is 1.

For operator assistance, dial "0." To obtain someone's phone number, call directory assistance at 555–1212 or occasionally 411 (free at many public phones). To have the person you're calling foot the bill, phone collect; dial "0" instead of "1" before the 10-digit number.

At pay phones, instructions often are posted. Usually you insert coins in a slot (25¢–50¢ for local calls) and wait for a steady tone before dialing. When you call long-distance, the operator tells you how much to insert; prepaid phone cards, widely available in various denominations, are easier. Call the number on the back, punch in the card's personal identification number, then dial your number.

If you're taking your cell phone on vacation with you, make sure roaming is included, otherwise, your minutes and bill will quickly add up. Prepaid phone cards are convenient and cost-effective.

LANGUAGE

English is the primary language on the Islands. Making the effort to learn some Hawaiian words can be rewarding, however. Despite the length of many Hawaiian words, the Hawaiian alphabet is actually one of the world's shortest, with only 12 letters: the five vowels, *a, e, i, o, u,* and seven consonants, *h, k, l, m, n, p, w.* Hawaiian words you're most likely to encounter during your visit to the Islands are *aloha, mahalo* (thank you), *keiki* (child), *haole* (Caucasian or foreigner), *mauka* (toward the mountains), *makai* (toward the ocean), and *pau* (finished, all done). Hawaiian history includes waves of immigrants, each bringing their own languages. To communicate with each other, they developed a sort of slang known as "pidgin." If you listen closely, you'll know what is being said by the inflections and by the extensive use of body language. For example, when you know what you want to say but don't know how to say it, just say "you know, da kine." For an informative and somewhat-hilarious view of things Hawaiian, check out Jerry Hopkins's series of books titled *Pidgin to the Max* and *Fax to the Max,* available at most local bookstores in the Hawaiiana sections.

LEI GREETINGS

When you walk off a long flight, perhaps a bit groggy and stiff, nothing quite compares with a Hawaiian lei greeting. The casual ceremony ranks as one of the fastest ways to make the transition from the worries of home to the joys of your vacation. Though the tradition has created an expectation that everyone receives this floral garland when they step off the plane, the state of Hawai'i cannot greet each of its nearly 7 million annual visitors.

Still, it's easy to **arrange for a lei ceremony before you arrive.** Contact Kama'āina Leis, Flowers & Greeters if you have not signed up with a tour company that provides it. If you really want to be wowed by the experience, request a lei of plumeria, some of the most divine-smelling blossoms on the planet. Kama'āina requires two days' notice and charges

$13.30 for a standard lei greeting at the gate upon arrival into Honolulu.

Kamaʻāina Leis, Flowers & Greeters 808/836-3246 or 800/367-5183 808/836-1814.

LODGING

The lodgings we list are the cream of the crop in each price category. Properties marked ✕▥ are lodging establishments whose restaurants warrant a special trip.

We always list the facilities that are available, but we don't specify whether they cost extra; when pricing accommodations, always ask what's included and what costs extra.

Properties are assigned price categories based on the range between their least and most expensive standard double rooms at high season (excluding holidays) for two people. Condo price categories reflect studio and one-bedroom rates.

CATEGORY	COST
$$$$	over $340
$$$	$261–$340
$$	$181–$260
$	$100–$180
¢	under $100

Prices are for two people in a standard double room in high season. Condo price categories reflect studio and one-bedroom rates.

APARTMENT & HOUSE RENTALS

If you want a home base that's roomy enough for a family and comes with cooking facilities, consider a furnished rental. These can save you money, especially if you're traveling with a group. Home-exchange directories sometimes list rentals as well as exchanges.

International Agents Hideaways International ✉ 767 Islington St., Portsmouth, NH 03801 603/430-4433 or 800/843-4433 603/430-4444 ⊕ www.hideaways.com, annual membership $185. **Vacation Home Rentals Worldwide** ✉ 235 Kensington Ave., Norwood, NJ 07648 201/767-9393 or 800/633-3284 201/767-5510 ⊕ www.vhrww.com.

HOME EXCHANGES

If you would like to exchange your home for someone else's, join a home-exchange organization, which will send you its updated listings of available exchanges for a year and will include your own listing in at least one of them. It's up to you to make specific arrangements.

Exchange Clubs HomeLink USA ✉ 2937 NW 9th Terrace, Fort Lauderdale, FL 33311 954/566-2687 or 800/638-3841 954/566-2783 ⊕ www.homelink.org; $75 yearly for a listing and online access; $45 additional to receive directories. **Intervac U.S.** ✉ 30 Corte San Fernando, Tiburon, CA 94920 800/756-4663 415/435-7440 ⊕ www.intervacus.com; $140 yearly for a listing, online access, and a catalog; $95 without catalog.

HOSTELS

No matter what your age, you can save on lodging costs by staying at hostels. Most Hawaiʻi hostels cater to a lively international crowd of backpackers, hikers, surfers, and windsurfers; those seeking intimacy or privacy should seek out a B&B.

In some 4,500 locations in more than 70 countries around the world, Hostelling International (HI), the umbrella group for a number of national youth-hostel associations, offers single-sex, dorm-style beds and, at many hostels, rooms for couples and family accommodations. Membership in any HI national hostel association, open to travelers of all ages, allows you to stay in HI-affiliated hostels at member rates; one-year membership is about $28 for adults in the United States (C$35 for a two-year minimum membership in Canada, £15.50 in the U.K., A$52 in Australia, and NZ$40 in New Zealand); hostels charge about $10–$30 per night. Members have priority if the hostel is full; they're also eligible for discounts around the world, even on rail and bus travel in some countries.

Hostels.com has on online listing of several other hostels on Oʻahu, as well as on Maui, Kauaʻi and the Big Island.

Organizations Hostelling International–USA ✉ 8401 Colesville Rd., Suite 600, Silver Spring, MD 20910 301/495-1240 301/495-6697 ⊕ www.hiusa.org. **Hostelling International–Canada** ✉ 205 Catherine St., Suite 500, Ottawa, Ontario K2P 1C3 613/237-7884 or 800/663-5777 613/237-7868 ⊕ www.hihostels.ca. **YHA England and Wales** ✉ Trevelyan House, Dimple Rd., Matlock, Derbyshire DE4 3YH, U.K. 0870/870-8808, 0870/770-8868, 01629/592-600 0870/770-6127

⊕ www.yha.org.uk. **YHA Australia** ✉ 422 Kent St., Sydney, NSW 2001 ☎ 02/9261-1111 🖷 02/9261-1969 ⊕ www.yha.com.au. **YHA New Zealand** ✉ Level 1, Moorhouse City, 166 Moorhouse Ave., Box 436, Christchurch ☎ 03/379-9970 or 0800/278-299 🖷 03/365-4476 ⊕ www.yha.org.nz.

HOTELS

All hotels listed have private bath unless otherwise noted.

🔒 **Toll-Free Numbers Best Western** ☎ 800/780-7234 ⊕ www.bestwestern.com. **Castle Resorts** ☎ 800/367-5004 ⊕ www.castleresorts.com. **Choice** ☎ 877/424-6423 ⊕ www.choicehotels.com. **Comfort Inn** ☎ 800/424-6423 ⊕ www.choicehotels.com. **Days Inn** ☎ 800/325-2525 ⊕ www.daysinn.com. **Destination Resorts Hawaii** ☎ 800/367-5246 ⊕ www.drhmaui.com. **Double-tree Hotels** ☎ 800/222-8733 ⊕ www.doubletree.com. **Embassy Suites** ☎ 800/362-2779 ⊕ www.embassysuites.com. **Fairfield Inn** ☎ 800/228-2800 ⊕ www.marriott.com. **Fairmont Hotels & Resorts** ☎ 800/257-7544 ⊕ www.fairmonthotels.com. **Four Seasons** ☎ 800/332-3442 ⊕ www.fourseasons.com. **Hilton** ☎ 800/445-8667 ⊕ www.hilton.com. **Holiday Inn** ☎ 800/465-4329 ⊕ www.ichotelsgroup.com. **Hyatt Hotels & Resorts** ☎ 800/233-1234 ⊕ www.hyatt.com. **La Quinta** ☎ 800/531-5900 ⊕ www.lq.com. **Marc Resorts Hawaii** ☎ 800/535-0085 ⊕ www.marcresorts.com. **Marriott** ☎ 800/236-2427 ⊕ www.marriott.com. **Ohana Hotels** ☎ 800/462-6262 ⊕ www.ohanahotels.com. **Outrigger Hotels & Resorts** ☎ 800/688-7444 ⊕ www.outrigger.com. **Prince Resorts Hawaii** ☎ 866/774-6236 ⊕ www.princeresortshawaii.com. **Quality Inn** ☎ 800/424-6423 ⊕ www.choicehotels.com. **Radisson** ☎ 800/333-3333 ⊕ www.radisson.com. **Ramada** ☎ 800/333-3333 ⊕ www.ramada.com or www.ramadahotels.com. **Renaissance Hotels & Resorts** ☎ 800/468-3571 ⊕ www.marriott.com. **Re-sortQuest Hawaii** ☎ 877/997-6667 ⊕ www.resortquesthawaii.com. **Ritz-Carlton** ☎ 800/241-3333 ⊕ www.ritzcarlton.com. **Sheraton** ☎ 800/325-3535 ⊕ www.starwood.com/sheraton. **Sleep Inn** ☎ 800/424-6423 ⊕ www.choicehotels.com. **Starwood Hotels and Resorts** ☎ 888/625-5144 for Sheraton and Westin Hotels, 800/325-3589 for Luxury Collection Hotels, 877/946-8357 for W Hotels ⊕ www.starwood.com. **Westin Hotels & Resorts** ☎ 800/228-3000 ⊕ www.starwood.com/westin.

MEDIA

NEWSPAPERS & MAGAZINES

Each of the Islands has its own daily newspaper, available through many hotel bell desks; in sundry stores, restaurants, and cafés; and at newsstands. Many hotels will deliver one to your room upon request. The *Honolulu Advertiser* is O'ahu's morning and Sunday paper; the *Honolulu Star-Bulletin* is O'ahu's evening paper and also prints on Sundays. *West Hawai'i Today* is the Big Island's Kona Coast newspaper, and the *Hawai'i Tribune-Herald* serves the Hilo side of the island. On Maui, it's the *Maui News*. On Moloka'i, it's the *Moloka'i Island Times* and *The Dispatch*. On Kaua'i, it's the *Garden Island* and *Kaua'i Times*. The *Honolulu Weekly* is a great guide for arts and alternative events, and the *Pacific Business News* provides the latest in business news. The monthly *Honolulu Magazine* focuses on O'ahu issues and happenings. Check out local bookstores for Neighbor Island magazines, some of which publish on a quarterly schedule.

RADIO & TELEVISION

Radio airwaves on the Islands are affected by natural terrain, so don't expect to hear one radio station islandwide. For Hawaiian music, tune your FM radio dial to 98.5 KDNN (O'ahu), 100.3 KCCN (O'ahu), 99.5 KHUI (O'ahu), 105.1 KINE (O'ahu), 100.3 KAPA (East Hawai'i), 99.1 KAGB (West Hawai'i), 93.5 KPOA (Maui), and 95.9 KSRF (Kaua'i). News junkies can get their fill of news and talk by tuning to the AM radio dial and the following island stations: 830 KHVH (O'ahu), 870 KHNR (O'ahu), 990 KHBZ (O'ahu), 1080 KWAI (O'ahu), 670 KPUA (East Hawai'i), 1110 KAOI (Maui), 570 KQNG (Kaua'i). National Public Radio enthusiasts can tune to the FM dial for NPR programming on 88.1 KHPR (O'ahu), 89.3 KIPO (O'ahu), 91.1 KANO (West Hawai'i) and 90.7 KKUA (Maui). On Kaua'i check out the only commercial-free public radio station on the Islands, KKCR, at 90.9 and 91.9 FM. It broadcasts Hawaiian music, jazz, blues, rock, and reggae, as well as talk shows on local issues.

On Oʻahu, many residents wake up with Perry & Price on KSSK AM 59 or FM 92. The lively duo provides news, traffic updates, and weather reports between easy-listening music and phone calls from listeners from 5 to 10 AM.

Television channels on the Islands are plentiful between network and cable channels. Channel allocation varies by island and location. On Oʻahu, you can find the following network programming with its channel and local affiliate call sign: FOX (2) KHON, ABC (4) KITV, UPN/WB (5) KHVE, CBS (9) KGMB, PBS (10) KHET, and NBC (13) KHNL.

MONEY MATTERS

Prices throughout this guide are given for adults. Substantially reduced fees are almost always available for children, students, and senior citizens. For information on taxes, *see* Taxes.

ATMS

Automatic teller machines for easy access to cash are everywhere on the Islands. ATMs can be found in shopping centers, small convenience and grocery stores, inside hotels and resorts, as well as outside most bank branches. For a directory of locations, call 800/424–7787 for the Master-Card/Cirrus/Maestro network or 800/843–7587 for the Visa/Plus network.

CREDIT CARDS

Throughout this guide, the following abbreviations are used: **AE**, American Express; **D**, Discover; **DC**, Diners Club; **MC**, MasterCard; and **V**, Visa.

🔢 Reporting Lost Cards **American Express** ☎ 800/992–3404. **Diners Club** ☎ 800/234–6377. **Discover** ☎ 800/347–2683. **MasterCard** ☎ 800/622–7747. **Visa** ☎ 800/ 847–2911.

NATIONAL PARKS & STATE PARKS

Hawaiʻi has seven national parks. On the island of Oʻahu, the USS *Arizona* Memorial at Pearl Harbor is a national shrine to those who lost their lives when Japan bombed Pearl Harbor on December 7, 1941. Maui boasts one of the most spectacular national parks in the country. Stretching for nearly 30,000 acres from the summit at Haleakalā crater to the lush, verdant valleys of Kīpahulu, Haleakalā National Park affords dozens of opportunities for exploration.

The Big Island, Hawaiʻi's largest island, has four national parks. Hawaiʻi Volcanoes National Park is the state's number-one attraction, where vents have been spewing lava for more than 20 years. The other three are Puʻuhonua O Hōnaunau National Historical Park, Puʻukoholā Heiau National Historical Park, and Kaloko-Honokōhau National Historical Park, all of which give a glimpse into Hawaiʻi's rich cultural history.

Molokaʻi's Kalaupapa National Historical Park was once a leper colony where victims of Hansen's disease were sent into exile in the late 1800s and cared for by Father Damien, a Belgian missionary.

Hawaiʻi's 52 state parks encompass more than 25,000 acres on five islands and include many of its most beautiful beaches and coastal areas. The State Parks Division of the Hawaiʻi State Department of Land and Natural Resources can provide information on state parks and historic areas.

Look into discount passes to save money on park entrance fees. For $50, the National Parks Pass admits you (and any passengers in your private vehicle) to all national parks, monuments, and recreation areas, as well as other sites run by the National Park Service, for a year. (In parks that charge per person, the pass admits you, your spouse and children, and your parents, when you arrive together.) Camping and parking are extra. The $15 Golden Eagle Pass, a hologram you affix to your National Parks Pass, functions as an upgrade, granting entry to all sites run by the NPS, the U.S. Fish and Wildlife Service, the U.S. Forest Service, and the Bureau of Land Management. The upgrade, which expires with the parks pass, is sold by most national-park, Fish-and-Wildlife, and BLM fee stations. A major percentage of the proceeds from pass sales funds National Parks projects.

Both the Golden Age Passport ($10), for U.S. citizens or permanent residents who are 62 and older, and the Golden Access

Passport (free), for persons with disabilities, entitle holders (and any passengers in their private vehicles) to lifetime free entry to all national parks, plus 50% off fees for the use of many park facilities and services. (The discount doesn't always apply to companions.) To obtain them, you must show proof of age and of U.S. citizenship or permanent residency—such as a U.S. passport, driver's license, or birth certificate—and, if requesting Golden Access, proof of disability. The Golden Age and Golden Access passes are available only at NPS-run sites that charge an entrance fee. The National Parks Pass is also available by mail and phone and via the Internet.

📷 **National Park Foundation** ⊠ 11 Dupont Circle NW, Suite 600, Washington, DC 20036 ☎ 202/238-4200 ⊕ www.nationalparks.org. **National Park Service** ⊠ National Park Service/Department of Interior, 1849 C St. NW, Washington, DC 20240 ☎ 202/208-6843 ⊕ www.nps.gov. **National Parks Conservation Association** ⊠ 1300 19th St. NW, Suite 300, Washington, DC 20036 ☎ 202/223-6722 or 800/628-7275 ⊕ www.npca.org.

📷 Passes by Mail & Online **National Park Foundation** ⊕ www.nationalparks.org. **National Parks Pass** National Park Foundation ⊄ Box 34108, Washington, DC 20043 ☎ 888/467-2757 ⊕ www.nationalparks.org; include a check or money order payable to the National Park Service, plus $3.95 for shipping and handling (allow 8 to 13 business days from date of receipt for pass delivery), or call for passes.

📷 State Parks **State Parks Division, Hawai'i State Department of Land and Natural Resources** ⊠ 1151 Punchbowl St., Room 310, Honolulu 96813 ☎ 808/587-0300 ⊕ www.hawaii.gov/dlnr/dsp/index.html.

PACKING

Hawai'i is casual: sandals, bathing suits, and comfortable, informal clothing are the norm. In summer synthetic slacks and shirts, although easy to care for, can be uncomfortably warm.

Probably the most important thing to tuck into your suitcase is sunscreen. This is the tropics, and the ultraviolet rays are powerful, even on overcast days. Doctors advise putting on sunscreen when you get up in the morning, whether it's cloudy or sunny. Don't forget to **reapply sunscreen periodically during the day,** since perspiration can wash it away. Consider using sunscreens with a sun protection factor (SPF) of 30 or higher. There are many tanning oils on the market in Hawai'i, including coconut and *kukui* (the nut from a local tree) oils, but they can cause severe burns. Too many Hawaiian vacations have been spoiled by sunburn and even sun poisoning. Hats and sunglasses offer important sun protection, too. Both are easy to find in island shops, but if you already have a favorite packable hat or sun visor, bring it with you, and don't forget to wear it. All major hotels in Hawai'i provide beach towels.

As for clothing, there's a saying that when a man wears a suit during the day, he's either going for a loan or he's a lawyer trying a case. Only a few upscale restaurants require a jacket for dinner. The aloha shirt is accepted dress in Hawai'i for business and most social occasions. Shorts are acceptable daytime attire, along with a T-shirt or polo shirt. There's no need to buy expensive sandals on the mainland—here you can get flip-flops for a couple of dollars and off-brand sandals for $20. Golfers should remember that many courses have dress codes requiring a collared shirt; call courses you're interested in for details. If you're not prepared, you can pick up appropriate clothing at resort pro shops. If you're visiting in winter or planning to visit a high-altitude area, **bring a sweater or light- to medium-weight jacket.** A polar fleece pullover is ideal, and makes a great impromptu pillow.

In your carry-on luggage, pack an extra pair of eyeglasses or contact lenses and enough of any medication you take to last a few days longer than the entire trip. You may also ask your doctor to write a spare prescription using the drug's generic name, as brand names may vary from country to country. In luggage to be checked, **never pack prescription drugs, valuables, or undeveloped film.** And don't forget to carry with you the addresses of offices that handle refunds of lost traveler's checks.

To avoid customs and security delays, carry medications in their original packaging. Don't pack any sharp objects in your carry-on luggage, including knives of any size or material, scissors, nail clippers, and corkscrews, or anything else that might arouse suspicion.

To avoid having your checked luggage chosen for hand inspection, don't cram bags full. The U.S. Transportation Security Administration suggests packing shoes on top and placing personal items you don't want touched in clear plastic bags.

CHECKING LUGGAGE

You're allowed to carry aboard one bag and one personal article, such as a purse or a laptop computer. Make sure what you carry on fits under your seat or in the overhead bin. Get to the gate early, so you can board as soon as possible, before the overhead bins fill up.

Baggage allowances vary by carrier, destination, and ticket class. On international flights from the U.S., as of September 2005, you're allowed to check two bags weighing up to 50 pounds (23 kilograms) each, although a few airlines allow checked bags of up to 88 pounds (40 kilograms) in first class. Some international carriers don't allow more than 66 pounds (30 kilograms) per bag in business class and 44 pounds (20 kilograms) in economy. If you're flying to or through the United Kingdom, your luggage cannot exceed 70 pounds (32 kilograms) per bag. On domestic flights, the limit is usually 50 to 70 pounds (23 to 32 kilograms) per bag. In general, carry-on bags shouldn't exceed 40 pounds (18 kilograms). Most airlines won't accept bags that weigh more than 100 pounds (45 kilograms) on domestic or international flights. Expect to pay a fee for baggage that exceeds weight limits. Check baggage restrictions with your carrier before you pack.

Airline liability for baggage is limited to $2,500 per person on flights within the United States. On international flights it amounts to $9.07 per pound or $20 per kilogram for checked baggage (roughly $540 per 50-pound bag), with a maximum of $634.90 per piece, and $400 per passenger for unchecked baggage. You can buy additional coverage at check-in for about $10 per $1,000 of coverage, but it often excludes a rather extensive list of items, shown on your airline ticket.

Before departure, itemize your bags' contents and their worth, and label the bags with your name, address, and phone number. (If you use your home address, cover it so potential thieves can't see it readily.) Include a label inside each bag and **pack a copy of your itinerary.** At check-in, make sure each bag is correctly tagged with the destination airport's three-letter code. Because some checked bags will be opened for hand inspection, the U.S. Transportation Security Administration recommends that you leave luggage unlocked or use the plastic locks offered at check-in. TSA screeners place an inspection notice inside searched bags, which are re-sealed with a special lock.

If your bag has been searched and contents are missing or damaged, file a claim with the TSA Consumer Response Center as soon as possible. If your bags arrive damaged or fail to arrive at all, file a written report with the airline before leaving the airport.

🔂 Complaints **U.S. Transportation Security Administration Contact Center** ☎ 866/289–9673 ⊕ www.tsa.gov.

SAFETY

Hawai'i is generally a safe tourist destination, but it's still wise to follow the same common sense safety precautions you would normally follow in your own hometown. Hotel and visitor-center staff can provide information should you decide to head out on your own to more remote areas. **Rental cars are magnets for break-ins, so don't leave any valuables in the car, not even in a locked trunk.** Avoid poorly lighted areas, beach parks, and isolated areas after dark as a precaution. When hiking, **stay on marked trails,** no matter how alluring the temptation might be to stray. Weather conditions can cause landscapes to become muddy, slippery, and tenuous, so staying on marked trails will lessen the possibility of a fall or getting lost. Ocean safety is of the utmost importance when visiting an island destination. **Don't swim alone, and follow the international signage posted at beaches** that alerts swimmers to strong currents, man-of-war jellyfish, sharp coral, high surf, sharks, and dangerous shore breaks. At coastal lookouts along cliff tops, heed the signs indicating that waves can climb over the ledges. Check with lifeguards at each beach for current conditions, and **if the red flags are up, indicating swimming and surfing are not allowed, don't go in.** Waters that look calm on the surface can harbor strong currents and undertows, and not a few people who were just wading have been dragged out to sea.

LOCAL SCAMS

Be wary of those hawking too-good-to-be-true prices on everything from car rentals to attractions. Many of these offers are just a lure to get you in the door for time-share presentations. When handed a flyer, read the fine print before you make your decision to participate.

WOMEN IN HAWAI'I

Women traveling alone are generally safe on the Islands, but always follow the safety precautions you would use in any major destination. When booking hotels, **request rooms closest to the elevator,** and always keep your hotel-room door and balcony doors locked. Stay away from isolated areas after dark; camping and hiking solo are not advised. If you stay out late visiting nightclubs and bars, **use caution when exiting night spots** and returning to your lodging.

SENIOR-CITIZEN TRAVEL

Hawai'i is steeped in a tradition that gives great respect to elders, or *kapuna,* and considers them "keepers of the wisdom." Visitors may not be so esteemed, but senior citizens traveling in Hawai'i will find discounts, special senior citizen–oriented activities, and buildings with easy access. Many lodging facilities have discounts for members of the American Association of Retired Persons (AARP).

To qualify for age-related discounts, mention your senior-citizen status up front when booking hotel reservations (not when checking out) and before you're seated in restaurants (not when paying the bill). Be sure to have identification on hand. When renting a car, ask about promotional car-rental discounts, which can be cheaper than senior-citizen rates.

⚑ Educational Programs Elderhostel ✉ 11 Ave. de Lafayette, Boston, MA 02111 ☎ 877/426-8056, 978/323-4141 international callers, 877/426-2167 TTY 🖷 877/426-2166 ⊕ www.elderhostel.org. **Interhostel** ✉ University of New Hampshire, 6 Garrison Ave., Durham, NH 03824 ☎ 603/862-1147 or 800/733-9753 🖷 603/862-1113 ⊕ www.learn.unh.edu.

SHOPPING

SMART SOUVENIRS

Aloha shirts and resort wear, Hawaiian-music recordings, shell leis, coral jewelry, traditional quilts, island foods, Kona coffee, and koa-wood products are just a few of the gifts that visitors to Hawai'i treasure. For the more elegant gift items, check out the Hawaiian boutiques in major island shopping centers. Island crafts fairs and swap meets offer a bargain bazaar of standard items such as T-shirts and tiki statues as well as the original works of local artisans.

WATCH OUT

Souvenirs made from coral or tortoise shell may not have been harvested legally, so in the interest of preserving Hawai'i's environment, it's best to avoid these.

SPORTS & OUTDOORS

If you like to swim, hike, fish, bike, scuba dive, kayak, or play golf, Hawai'i is your kind of place. Alternative Hawai'i's Web site provides detailed information on hiking, diving, camping, kayaking, and outfitters on each island. The environment is particularly fragile here, so whatever you do outdoors, don't forget to tread lightly.
⚑ Alternative Hawai'i ☎ 808/695-5113 ⊕ www.alternative-hawaii.com.

BEACHES

Hawai'i's beaches are the stuff of legend, with white sand wedged between palm trees and turquoise water, or even colorful black-and-green stretches of sand. All beaches are free and open to the public unless otherwise noted—even the most luxurious hotels have to share their beachfronts. Note that riptides and strong undertows can challenge even the strongest swimmers, so if you see a beach where no one is swimming, ask a local about its safety before diving in. **Use care when diving into lagoons** as well, as they often are not as deep as they appear. Alcohol is not permitted on most beaches.

HIKING & CAMPING

Hiking is a wonderful way to explore the Islands, but **don't stray off trails,** and be sure to **wear sturdy hiking shoes,** especially if you're doing lava hikes. It's also prudent to bring along a cellular phone, and it's especially helpful if it has GPS tracking. When camping, **be prepared for radical weather shifts,** especially at high altitudes. Haleakalā National Park, for example, can reach 85°F by day and drop to 35°F by night. Fog, wind, and rain can and do blow in with little or no warning. Ask local outdoor shops which areas are best for you based on your fitness level and camping experience. Note that Hawai'i doesn't have drive-to camping sites; most locations require a hike in or a night on the beach.

KAYAKING

Kayaking is an excellent low-impact way to enjoy the scenery. Kayak rentals are available on each island, and you can arrange guided trips. **Remain close to shore** if you don't want to be whooshed out to sea. Check with the kayak rental shop for weather advisories.

SCUBA DIVING & SNORKELING

Underwater Hawai'i is breathtaking, but diving tends to be pricey. You can arrange trips with countless outfitters, or rent equipment on your own. Whether snorkeling or diving, remember **never go alone,** and be sure to **ask at the dive shop about rip currents and places to avoid.** Undersea life is extremely fragile, so **don't touch (or take) the coral,** and **watch that your fins don't hit the reefs** behind you.

STUDENTS IN HAWAI'I

Hawai'i is a popular destination for exchange students from around the world, who mainly attend the University of Hawai'i in Honolulu. Contact your hometown university about study and intern-

ship possibilities. To check out the student scene on the Islands, stop by any of the University of Hawai'i campuses or community college campuses, and read the *Honolulu Weekly* upon arrival for club and event information. Be sure to ask about discounts for students at all museums and major attractions and be prepared to show ID to qualify.

IDs & Services STA Travel ⊠ 10 Downing St., New York, NY 10014 ☎ 212/627-3111, 800/781-4040 24-hr service center in the U.S. ⊕ www.sta.com. **Travel Cuts** ⊠ 187 College St., Toronto, Ontario M5T 1P7, Canada ☎ 800/592-2887 in the U.S., 416/979-2406, 888/359-2887 and 888/359-2887 in Canada ⊕ www.travelcuts.com.

TAXES

SALES TAX

There's a 4.16% state sales tax on all purchases, including food. A hotel room tax of 7.25%, combined with the sales tax of 4%, equals an 11.41% rate added onto your hotel bill. A $3-per-day road tax is also assessed on each rental vehicle.

TIME

Hawai'i is on Hawaiian Standard Time, 5 hours behind New York, 2 hours behind Los Angeles, and 10 hours behind London.

When the U.S. mainland is on daylight saving time, Hawai'i is not, so add an extra hour of time difference between the Islands and U.S. mainland destinations. You may also find that things generally move more slowly here. That has nothing to do with your watch—it's just the laid-back way called Hawaiian time.

TIPPING

Tip cab drivers 15% of the fare. Standard tips for restaurants and bar tabs run from 15% to 20% of the bill, depending on the standard of service. Bellhops at hotels usually receive $1 per bag, more if you have bulky items such as bicycles and surfboards. Tip the hotel room maid $1 per night, paid daily. Tip doormen $1 for assistance with taxis; tips for concierge vary depending on the service. For example, tip more for hard-to-get event tickets or dining reservations.

TOURS & PACKAGES
Because everything is prearranged on a prepackaged tour or independent vacation, you spend less time planning—and often get it all at a good price.

BOOKING WITH AN AGENT
Travel agents are excellent resources. But it's a good idea to collect brochures from several agencies, as some agents' suggestions may be influenced by relationships with tour and package firms that reward them for volume sales. If you have a special interest, find an agent with expertise in that area. The American Society of Travel Agents (ASTA) has a database of specialists worldwide; you can log on to the group's Web site to find one near you.

Make sure your travel agent knows the accommodations and other services of the place being recommended. Ask about the hotel's location, room size, beds, and whether it has a pool, room service, or programs for children, if you care about these. Has your agent been there in person or sent others whom you can contact? Local tourism boards can provide information about lesser-known and small-niche operators, some of which may sell only direct.

BUYER BEWARE
Each year consumers are stranded or lose their money when tour operators—even large ones with excellent reputations—go out of business. So check out the operator. Ask several travel agents about its reputation, and try to **book with a company that has a consumer-protection program.** (Look for information in the company's brochure.) In the United States, members of the United States Tour Operators Association are required to set aside funds (up to $1 million) to help eligible customers cover payments and travel arrangements in the event that the company defaults. It's also a good idea to choose a company that participates in the American Society of Travel Agents' Tour Operator Program; ASTA will act as mediator in any disputes between you and your tour operator.

Remember that the more your package or tour includes, the better you can predict the ultimate cost of your vacation. Make sure you know exactly what is covered, and beware of hidden costs. Are taxes, tips, and transfers included? Entertainment and excursions? These can add up.

🚩 Tour-Operator Recommendations **American Society of Travel Agents** (⇨ Travel Agencies). **CrossSphere-The Global Association for Packaged Travel** ⊠ 546 E. Main St., Lexington, KY 40508 ☎ 859/226-4444 or 800/682-8886 🖷 859/226-4414 ⊕ www.CrossSphere.com. **United States Tour Operators Association** (USTOA) ⊠ 275 Madison Ave., Suite 2014, New York, NY 10016 ☎ 212/599-6599 🖷 212/599-6744 ⊕ www.ustoa.com.

TRANSPORTATION AROUND HAWAI'I
Renting a car is definitely recommended for those who plan to move beyond their hotel lounge chair. With the exception of O'ahu, public transportation is extremely limited, and even if you are staying in Honolulu or Waikīkī you may want a car if you plan to explore or if you're short on time. **Reserve your vehicle in advance,** particularly during peak travel times and on the smaller islands, where car-rental fleets are limited. Most major companies have airport counters and complimentary transportation for pickup/drop-off at the airport upon departure.

Taxis can be found at island airports, through your hotel doorman, in the more popular resort areas, or by contacting local taxi companies by telephone. Flag-down fees are $2, and each additional mile is $1.70. Most companies will also provide a car and driver for half-day or daylong island tours if you don't want to rent a car, and a number of companies also offer personal guides. Remember, however, that rates are quite steep for these services, ranging from $100 to $200 or more per day.

TRAVEL AGENCIES
A good travel agent puts your needs first. Look for an agency that has been in business at least five years, emphasizes customer service, and has someone on staff who specializes in your destination. In addition, **make sure the agency belongs to a professional trade organization.** The

American Society of Travel Agents (ASTA) has more than 10,000 members in some 140 countries, enforces a strict code of ethics, and will step in to mediate agent-client disputes involving ASTA members. ASTA also maintains a directory of agents on its Web site; ASTA's TravelSense.org, a trip planning and travel advice site, can also help to locate a travel agent who caters to your needs. (If a travel agency is also acting as your tour operator, *see* Buyer Beware *in* Tours & Packages.)

Local Agent Referrals American Society of Travel Agents (ASTA) ✉ 1101 King St., Suite 200, Alexandria, VA 22314 ☎ 703/739-2782 or 800/965-2782 24-hr hotline 🖷 703/684-8319 ⊕ www. astanet.com and www.travelsense.org. **Association of British Travel Agents** ✉ 68-71 Newman St., London W1T 3AH ☎ 0901/201-5050 ⊕ www.abta. com. **Association of Canadian Travel Agencies** ✉ 350 Sparks St., Suite 510, Ottawa, Ontario K1R 7S8 ☎ 613/237-3657 🖷 613/237-7052 ⊕ www.acta. ca. **Australian Federation of Travel Agents** ✉ Level 3, 309 Pitt St., Sydney, NSW 2000 ☎ 02/9264-3299 or 1300/363-416 🖷 02/9264-1085 ⊕ www.afta.com.au. **Travel Agents' Association of New Zealand** ✉ Level 5, Tourism and Travel House, 79 Boulcott St., Box 1888, Wellington 6001 ☎ 04/499-0104 🖷 04/499-0786 ⊕ www.taanz.org.nz.

VISITOR INFORMATION

Before you go, contact the Hawai'i Visitors & Convention Bureau (HVCB) for general information on each island, including a free visitors guide, "Islands of Aloha" with information on accommodations, transportation, sports and activities, dining, arts and entertainment and culture. Take a virtual visit to Hawai'i on the Web, which can be most helpful in planning many aspects of your vacation. The HVCB site has a calendar section that allows you to see what local events are in place during the time of your stay.

Tourist Information Hawai'i Visitors & Convention Bureau ✉ 2270 Kalakaua Ave., Suite 801, Honolulu 96817 ☎ 808/923-1811, 800/464-2924 for brochures ⊕ www.gohawaii.com. In the U.K. contact the **Hawai'i Visitors & Convention Bureau**

⚓ 36 Southwark Bridge Rd., London, SE1 9EU ☎ 020/7202-6384 🖷 020/7928-0722.

Government Advisories Consular Affairs Bureau of Canada ☎ 800/267-6788 or 613/944-6788 from overseas ⊕ www.voyage.gc.ca. **U.K. Foreign and Commonwealth Office** ✉ Travel Advice Unit, Consular Directorate, Old Admiralty Building, London SW1A 2PA ☎ 0845/850-2829 or 020/7008-1500 ⊕ www.fco.gov.uk/travel. **Australian Department of Foreign Affairs and Trade** ☎ 300/139-281 travel advisories, 02/6261-3305 Consular Travel Advice ⊕ www.smartraveller.gov.au. **New Zealand Ministry of Foreign Affairs and Trade** ☎ 04/439-8000 ⊕ www.mft.govt.nz.

WEB SITES

Do check out the World Wide Web when planning your trip. You'll find everything from weather forecasts to virtual tours of famous cities. Be sure to visit Fodors.com (⊕ www.fodors.com), a complete travel-planning site. You can research prices and book plane tickets, hotel rooms, rental cars, vacation packages, and more. In addition, you can post your pressing questions in the Travel Talk section. Other planning tools include a currency converter and weather reports, and there are loads of links to travel resources.

For more information on Hawai'i, visit ⊕ www.gohawaii.com, the official Web site of the Hawai'i Visitors & Convention Bureau.

Other sites to check out include ⊕ www.bigisland.org (Big Island Visitors Bureau); ⊕ www.visitmaui.com (Maui County Visitors Bureau); ⊕ www.visit-oahu.com (O'ahu Visitors Bureau); ⊕ www.kauaidiscovery.com (Kaua'i Visitors Bureau); and ⊕ www.molokai-hawaii.com (Moloka'i Visitors Association).

Visit ⊕ www.bestplaceshawaii.com for the Hawai'i State Vacation Planner; ⊕ www.honoluluweekly.com for a weekly guide to the arts, entertainment, and dining in Honolulu; and ⊕ www.hawaii.gov, the state's official Web site, for all information on the destination, including camping.

INDEX

PHOTO CREDITS

Introduction: 8, Walter Bibikow/www.viestiphoto.com. 9 *(left)*, Corbis. 9 *(right)*, Walter Bibikow/www. viestiphoto.com. 12, Molokai Ranch. 13, Douglas Peebles/age fotostock. 14, SuperStock/age fotostock. 15 *(left)*, Walter Bibikow/www.viestiphoto.com. 15 *(right)*, J. Luke/PhotoLink/Photodisc/Getty Images. 18, Oahu Visitors Bureau. **Chapter 1: Oahu:** 21, Polynesian Cultural Center. 22 *(top)*, Ken Ross/www.viestiphoto. com. 22 *(bottom left)*, Michael S. Nolan/age fotostock. 22 *(bottom right)*, SuperStock/age fotostock. 23 *(top)*, Oahu Visitors Bureau. 23 *(bottom left)*, Corbis. 23 *(bottom right)*, Oahu Visitors Bureau. 24, SuperStock/age fotostock. 25, Oahu Visitors Bureau. 26, Andre Seale/age fotostock. 31, J.D. Heaton/ Picture Finders/age fotostock. 32, Oahu Visitors Bureau. 33 *(left and center)*, Walter Bibikow/viestiphoto.com. 33 *(right)*, Douglas Peebles/age fotostock. 34, Stuart Westmorland/age fotostock. 35 *(left)*, The Royal Hawaiian. 35 *(center)*, Atlantide S.N.C./age fotostock. 35 *(right)*, Liane Cary/age fotostock. 45, U.S. National Archives. 47 *(top)*, Corbis. 47 *(bottom)*, NPS/USS Arizona Memorial Photo Collection. 48, Army Signal Corps Collection in the U.S. National Archives. 48 *(inset)*, USS Missouri Memorial Association. 49, USS Bowfin Submarine Museum & Park. 59, ASP Tostee. 60, ASP Tostee. 61, ASP Tostee. 62, Carol Cunningham/cunninghamphotos.com. **Chapter 2: Maui:** 147, Michael S. Nolan/age fotostock. 148 *(top)*, S. Alden/PhotoLink/Photodisc/Getty Images. 148 *(bottom left)*, Douglas Peebles/age fotostock. 148 *(bottom right)*, Walter Bibikow/www.viestiphoto.com. 149 *(top)*, Ron Dahlquist/Maui Visitors Bureau. 149 *(bottom left)*, Walter Bibikow/www.viestiphoto.com. 149 *(bottom right)*, Chris Hammond/www.viestiphoto. com. 157, Maui Visitors Bureau. 165, National Park Service. 168, Maui Visitors Bureau. 169, Karl Weatherly/Photodisc/Getty Images. 170, Maui Visitors Bureau. 177, Chris Hammond/www.viestiphoto.com. 179, Ron Dahlquist/Maui Visitors Bureau. 180, Chris Hammond/www.viestiphoto.com. 183, Richard Genova/www.viestiphoto.com. 184, SuperStock/age fotostock. 185, Chris Hammond/www.viestiphoto.com. **Chapter 3: The Big Island of Hawaii:** 271, Walter Bibikow/www.viestiphoto.com. 272 *(top)*, Big Island Visitors Bureau. 272 *(bottom left)*, Big Island Visitors Bureau. 272 *(bottom right)*, S. Alden/PhotoLink/Photodisc/ Getty Images. 273 *(top)*, Big Island Visitors Bureau. 273 *(bottom left)*, Big Island Visitors Bureau. 273 *(bottom right)*, Big Island Visitors Bureau. 275, Big Island Visitors Bureau. 276, Big Island Visitors Bureau. 295, Big Island Visitors Bureau. 297, Russ Bishop/age fotostock. 299 *(left)*, R. Hoblitt/U.S. Department of Interior, U.S. Geological Survey. 299 *(right)*, G. Brad Lewis/age fotostock. 301, R. Hoblitt/U.S. Department of Interior, U.S. Geological Survey. 302, J. Kauahikaua/U.S. Department of Interior, U.S. Geological Survey. 328, Ron Dahlquist/HVCB. **Chapter 4: Kauai:** 393, Karl Weatherly/age fotostock. 394 *(top)*, Kauai Visitors Bureau. 394 *(bottom left)*, Kauai Visitors Bureau. 394 *(bottom right)*, Kauai Visitors Bureau. 395 *(top)*, Kauai Visitors Bureau. 395 *(center)*, Kauai Visitors Bureau. 395 *(bottom)*, Kauai Visitors Bureau. 397 *(left)*, Corbis. 397 *(right)*, SuperStock/age fotostock. 406, Luca Tettoni/viestiphoto.com. 407, Jack Jeffrey. 443 *(top)*, Kauai Visitors Bureau. 443 *(bottom)*, SuperStock/age fotostock. 444, Andre Seale/age fotostock. 446, Karen Shigematsu/Lyon Arboretum. 447, Kauai Visitors Bureau. **Chapter 5: Molokai:** 489, Molokai Visitors Association. 490 *(top)*, Walter Bibikow/www.viestiphoto.com. 490 *(bottom left)*, Molokai Visitors Association. 490 *(bottom right)*, Molokai Visitors Association. 491 *(top)*, Molokai Ranch. 491 *(center)*, Walter Bibikow/www.viestiphoto.com. 491 *(bottom left)*, Douglas Peebles/ age fotostock. 491 *(bottom right)*, Walter Bibikow/www.viestiphoto.com. 497, Walter Bibikow/ viestiphoto.com. 498, IDEA. 499, Walter Bibikow/viestiphoto.com. 500, Walter Bibikow/viestiphoto.com. **Chapter 6: Lanai:** 523, Lanai Image Library. 524 *(top)*, Walter Bibikow/www.viestiphoto.com. 524 *(bottom left)*, Lanai Visitors Bureau. 524 *(bottom right)*, Walter Bibikow/www.viestiphoto.com. 525 *(top)*, Michael S. Nolan/age fotostock. 525 *(bottom left)*, Lanai Image Library. 525 *(bottom right)*, Lanai Image Library. 526, Lanai Image Library. **Color Section:** Surfers walking along Waikiki Beach, Oahu: *Allan Seiden/Oahu Visitors Bureau.* Catching a wave: *SuperStock/age fotostock.* Garden of the Gods, Lanai: *Walter Bibikow/ www.viestiphoto.com.* Fire eater: *SuperStock/age fotostock.* Children with haku (head) lei: *SuperStock/age fotostock.* Waikiki, Oahu: *J.D.Heaton/Picture Finders/age fotostock.* Hula dancers: *Hawaii Visitors & Convention Bureau.* Hawaii Volcanoes National Park, Big Island: *G. Brad Lewis/age fotostock.* Waianapanapa State Park, Maui: *SuperStock/age fotostock.* Surfers, North Shore, Oahu: *Ken Ross/www.viestiphoto.com.* Lava flow, Hawaii Volcanoes National Park, Big Island: *Larry Carver/www.viestiphoto.com.* Golf Course at Mauna Lani Resort, Kohala Coast: *Big Island Visitors Bureau.* Haleakala National Park, Maui: *Maui Visitors Bureau.* Na Pali Coast, Kauai: *Scott West/www.viestiphoto.com.* Coffee picking contest, Kona, Big Island: *Joe Viesti/www.viestiphoto.com.* Cyclists overlooking Kalaupapa peninsula, Molokai: *Molokai Visitors Association.* Green Sea Turtles: *HVCB/Na Pali Explorer.*

NOTES

NOTES

NOTES

NOTES

NOTES

NOTES

NOTES

NOTES

NOTES

NOTES

NOTES

ABOUT OUR WRITERS

Wanda A. Adams was born and raised on Maui and now makes her home on Oʻahu. She has been a newspaper reporter for more than 25 years, specializing in food, dining, and travel. Wanda worked on the Exploring and Where to Eat sections of the Oʻahu chapter.

Don Chapman is the editor of the award-winning *MidWeek,* Hawaiʻi's largest-circulated newspaper. The golf writer for this guide, Don has played 88 golf courses in Hawaiʻi and writes about golf for a variety of national publications. He is also the author of four books.

Elaine Gast is a freelance writer and communications consultant for foundations, nonprofits, businesses, and individuals. A published author of six books, Elaine writes out of her home in Kula, Maui. She worked on Beaches, Entertainment and Nightlife, and the sports sections of the Maui chapter.

Katherine Nichols is a writer in the Features department of the *Honolulu Star-Bulletin.* She has won four awards from the Society of Professional Journalists and has written for numerous publications, including *Town & Country, Runner's World, Shape,* and the Associated Press. She covered Oʻahu's shops and spas.

Chad Pata covers the beaches and sports of Hawaiʻi for *MidWeek* and *The Honolulu Advertiser.* Originally from Atlanta, Georgia, he moved to Oʻahu in 1993, married a local girl, and now lives for his two kids, Honu and Calogero. Chad worked on the beaches and sports sections of the Oʻahu chapter.

Cathy Sharpe, who handled Smart Travel Tips, was born and reared on Oʻahu. For 13 years, she worked at a Honolulu public relations agency representing major travel industry clients. Now living in Maryland, she is a marketing consultant. Cathy returns home once a year to visit family and friends, relax at her favorite beaches, and enjoy island cuisine.

Kim Steutermann Rogers, our Kauaʻi updater, is a freelance journalist living on Kauaʻi, where she hikes the mountains in her backyard and paddles the ocean's waters in her front yard. She writes about her adventures for regional and national travel and outdoor magazines, as well as editing www.kauaibackstory.com.

Joana Varawa has lived on Lānaʻi for 30 years and is editor of *The Lānaʻi Times.* She writes for Hawaiian and Aloha airlines' magazines, has authored three books, and—along with her beloved dog—could lead you around "her" island blindfolded. She updated the Molokaʻi and Lānaʻi chapters.

Amy Westervelt was lucky enough to spend summers growing up on the Big Island, and now divides her time between Kona and San Francisco. She writes about travel and all things wedding-related for publications including *Travel + Leisure, Modern Bride,* and the *San Francisco Chronicle.* Amy updated the Big Island chapter, wrote all the island introductions, and created the Island Finder chart.

Shannon Wianecki was raised on Maui and loves divulging its secrets. She is the food editor for *Maui nō ka ʻoi* magazine and the outreach coordinator for a high-school science curriculum based on the ecosystems of Haleakalā. She worked on the Exploring, Shopping, Spas, and the Where to Eat and Stay sections of the Maui chapter.

Maggie Wunsch, who worked for 20 years as a Hawaiʻi hotel executive, now covers Hawaiʻi for a variety of radio, print, and broadcast media. She is an unabashed fan of room service and the delicious scents of her state—from pīkake jasmine to teriyaki barbecue. Maggie updated the Where to Stay in Oʻahu section.

Katie Young works as a writer, columnist, and editor for *MidWeek,* covering everything from entertainment to island living. Her work has also appeared in *Makai* magazine and the *Honolulu Star-Bulletin.* Katie updated Oʻahu's Entertainment and Nightlife.